RUNNING
A PERFECT
WEB SITE,
SECOND EDITION

RUNNING A PERFECT WEB SITE,

SECOND EDITION

Written by Stephen Wynkoop with

John Burke • Davis Chapman • Yvonne DeGraw • Nelson Howell
Richard Irving • Lori Leonardo • Juan Molinari
James R. O'Donnell Jr.

Running a Perfect Web Site, Second Edition

Screen reproductions in this book were created using Collage Plus from Inner Media, Inc., Hollis, NH.

Credits

PRESIDENT
Roland Elgey

PUBLISHER
Joseph B. Wikert

PUBLISHING MANAGER
Fred Slone

SENIOR TITLE MANAGER
Bryan Gambrel

EDITORIAL SERVICES DIRECTOR
Elizabeth Keaffaber

MANAGING EDITOR
Sandy Doell

ACQUISITIONS EDITOR
Kelly Marshall

PRODUCT DEVELOPMENT SPECIALIST
Rob Tidrow

SENIOR EDITOR
Mike La Bonne

EDITORS
Cynthia Felando, Jean Jamison, Bonnie
Lawler, Susan Ross Moore, Mary Anne
Sharbaugh, Faithe Wempen

TECHNICAL EDITORS
Richard Irving, Jeff Bankston

DIRECTOR OF MARKETING
Lynn E. Zingraf

STRATEGIC MARKETING MANAGER
Barry Pruett

PRODUCT MARKETING MANAGER
Kristine Ankney

ASSISTANT PRODUCT MARKETING MANAGERS
Christy M. Miller, Karen Hagen

TECHNICAL SUPPORT SPECIALIST
Nadeem Muhammed

ACQUISITIONS COORDINATOR
Carmen Krikorian

EDITORIAL ASSISTANTS
Andrea Duvall, Jennifer Condon,
Chantal Mees Koch

BOOK DESIGNER
Ruth Harvey

COVER DESIGNER
Dan Armstrong

PRODUCTION TEAM
Michael Beaty
Jenny Earhart
Jessica Ford
Steph Mineart

INDEXER
Brad Herriman

Composed in *Century Old Style* and *ITC Franklin Gothic* by Que Corporation.

To my best friend and wife, Julie.

About the Authors

Stephen Wynkoop is an author and lecturer working extensively with Microsoft-based products and technologies, with emphasis on Internet and client/server technologies. Stephen has been developing applications and consulting in the computer industry for more than 14 years. He is a coauthor of *Special Edition Using Microsoft SQL Server 6.5*, and *Special Edition Using Windows NT Server 4.0*. He has also contributed to other Que titles about the Internet. Stephen is a regular speaker at Microsoft's technical conferences and has written books on Microsoft Access and Microsoft Office 95 integration. Stephen is also a Microsoft Certified Professional (MCP) for both Windows for Workgroups and Windows NT technologies. Reach Stephen via the Internet at **swynk@pobox.com**, or visit his Web site at **http://www.pobox.com/~swynk**.

John Burke is the owner of Santa Cruz Consulting, a California-based company offering database and Internet business system solutions/seminar training to corporations and people in Internet- and Windows-based business software. He has helped develop corporate database information systems at Intel Corporation, the Santa Cruz Operation, United Technologies Chemical Systems, Tymshare, the Santa Clara Unified Water System, and is currently working as part of the Innovation Network Intranet development team at Varian Corporation of Palo Alto.

Davis Chapman first began programming computers while working on his master's degree in music composition. While writing applications for computer music, he discovered that he enjoyed designing and developing computer software. It wasn't long before he knew that he stood a much better chance of eating if he stuck with his new found skill and demoted his hard-earned status as a "starving artist" to a part-time hobby. Since that time, Davis has striven to perfect the art of software design and development, with a strong emphasis on the practical application of client/server technology. For the past six years, he has been with the Dallas, Texas-based consulting firm of B.R. Blackmarr & Associates. Davis can be reached at **davischa@onramp.net**.

Yvonne DeGraw is a freelance technical writer and Web site designer. She specializes in creating books and Web sites for Internet-related products and other software. She also has expertise in relational database design and user-interface design. She founded the Santa Barbara chapter of the Society for Technical Communication and has contributed numerous articles to the society's international publications. Her Web address is **http://www.silcom.com/~yvonne** and her e-mail address is **yvonne@silcom.com**.

Nelson Howell is a veteran of the computer industry. Starting with IBM mainframes in 1967, he has survived the changes from mainframes to minis to microcomputers. In addition to writing, he provides support to users of software for Icon Technology Solutions. Now at home in Tucson, Arizona, he is surrounded by his family of four sons and a very tolerant wife.

Richard Irving is the product support supervisor and assistant Webmaster at Icon Technology Solutions. His areas of expertise are Web site design and the Internet in general. Currently, he is working on obtaining his master's degree in computer science. You can contact him via e-mail at **ricci@azstarnet.com** or you can stop by his personal Web site at **http://www.azstarnet.com/~ricci**. (And for those who wonder, ricci stands for Ricc I., not Ricky.)

Lori Leonardo is owner of L. Leonardo Consulting, a computer services company that provides Internet consulting and training. She is also an instructor at Brown University Learning Community where she teaches "Personal Finance: How to Capitilize on the Web," and "For KIDS" Web Ventures—Cyber Out on the Web." You can reach Lori at e-mail: **lorileo@aol.com**.

Juan Molinari will admit to understanding his work and little else. He wrote his first programs on a Timer Sinclair 1000 doorstop and, by the age of 11, taught himself machine code on a Commodore 64. His formal studies have taken him to Hampshire College, the Rochester Institute of Technology, and the Internet Services group of Walcoff & Associates, where the trade winds have labeled him a systems consultant.

James R. O'Donnell Jr., Ph.D., was born Oct. 17, 1963, (you may forward birthday greetings to **odonnj@rpi.edu**), in Pittsburgh, Penn. After a number of unproductive years, he began his studies in electrical engineering at Rensselaer Polytechnic Institute. He liked college so much that he spent 11 years there getting three degrees, graduating for the third (and final) time in the summer of 1992. He can now be found plying his trade at the NASA Goddard Space Flight Center. He's not a rocket scientist, but he's close.

Jim's first experience with a "personal" computer was in high school with a Southwest Technical Products computer using a paper tape storage device, quickly graduating up to a TRS-80 Model II. His fate as a computer geek was sealed when Rensselaer gave him an Atari 800 as part of a scholarship. After a long struggle, Jim finally chucked his Atari (sniff) and joined the Windows world. When he isn't writing or researching for Que or talking on IRC (Nick: JOD), Jim likes to run, row, play hockey, collect comic books and PEZ dispensers, and play the best board game ever, Cosmic Encounter.

Acknowledgments

A lot of work, a lot of people, and a lot of understanding goes in to writing any book, and this one is no different. At the absolute top of this list of contributing efforts is certainly my family. To Julie, Brennan, and Caitlin, thank you for putting up with my groggy and sometimes not-so-nice spells of late nights and early mornings. It's an easy thing to say that without your help, understanding, and constant push to keep chasing the edge, this would be a far different, far more difficult process.

To Seth Morris—thanks for being patient with my questions and introducing me to the 'Net what seems like so long ago. This all started with your overwhelming passion for using the technology and I certainly appreciate being an apprentice!

At Que, Kelly Marshall—this may be the first, but certainly won't be the last! Thanks for shooting straight and putting up with the tirades. I appreciate working with you, Mike La Bonne, Rob Tidrow, all of the editorial folks, and Carmen Krikorian; what can I say but "Thanks!" It's a pleasure to work with all of you and this book is certainly a testament to working with some of the best talent in the industry. I appreciate the opportunity to work with you all.

We'd Like to Hear from You!

As part of our continuing effort to produce books of the highest possible quality, Que would like to hear your comments. To stay competitive, we *really* want you, as a computer book reader and user, to let us know what you like or dislike most about this book or other Que products.

You can mail comments, ideas, or suggestions for improving future editions to the address below, or send us a fax at (317) 581-4663. For the online inclined, Macmillan Computer Publishing has a forum on CompuServe (type **GO QUEBOOKS** at any prompt) through which our staff and authors are available for questions and comments. The address of our Internet site is **http://www.mcp.com** (World Wide Web).

In addition to exploring our forum, please feel free to contact me personally to discuss your opinions of this book: I'm **104470,324** on CompuServe, and I'm at **klmarshall@que.mcp.com** on the Internet.

Thanks in advance—your comments will help us to continue publishing the best books available on computer topics in today's market.

Kelly Marshall
Acquisitions Editor
Que Corporation
201 W. 103rd Street
Indianapolis, Indiana 46290
USA

Contents at a Glance

Appendixes

Table of Contents

II   Setting Up Your Web Site

5   Setting Up and Configuring a Web Server   95

6   Setting Up an FTP Site   125

III | Enhancing Your Web Site

Appendixes

Introduction

Running a Perfect Web Site, Second Edition, is a unique book in that it helps bring together the different components of an Internet or Intranet site and in doing so, it shows how you can create a powerful information network for your company and customers.

This book is written by a senior systems professional who uses the different technologies covered in this book every day. Integra Technology International (**http:// www.integra.net**), a Microsoft Solution Provider and senior technology partner with Microsoft, is the home of the author, where he manages the content and access for the company's Intranet and Internet presence.

From UNIX-based technologies to database-enabling your site to understanding the different scripting alternatives available, this book shows how to pull all of the different pieces together. This book also focuses on the reality of these technologies, giving many hints, suggestions, and information about lessons learned so you can leverage your time toward providing the best possible service level for your user base.

This Running series book is just that—a book about the real process of running your Internet or Intranet to provide these services. As such, this book provides information ranging from the basic understanding and installation details for these technologies, to content management and troubleshooting.

With new operating system versions, new server software releases and more already introduced and more on the way, understanding these technologies is extremely important to the success of your Web site. The information provided here is done so with all the latest releases of these products, saving you time and effort in bringing the products online.

Of course, at the heart of your Intranet is your Web server and its ability to provide content for your site. There are several powerful, standards-driven systems that provide Web, FTP, and in some cases, Gopher-based access, to the information on your site.

You can also extend many of these environments, allowing everything from custom-developed applications, to database-centric applications, to extensions to the server environment itself in the form of gateways and firewalls to be added to the system. This flexibility means that, after you have your arms around the system and its capabilities, you'll be able to have a well-rounded site.

Microsoft has stepped into the Internet arena with a vengeance by providing the tools necessary to control content, the server engine, and additional functionality only now coming into Beta testing. This functionality ranges from gateway and proxy services to site-wide search engines. This book brings these different tools into perspective and shows how you can implement them, allowing your users to develop their own content, and at the same time control access to your system. This book also shows what other tools are available, how they interact with your site, and more. ■

Who Should Use this Book

This book is aimed at *system administrators* and *Webmasters* for networks developed largely for internal use by their company. In addition, the book applies to *information system managers* faced with understanding planning issues presented when providing this level of access to information, and *software developers* who develop applications and interfaces used with Internet products.

The readers of this book will learn how to install, configure, use, and understand different versions and platforms that support Web servers and the Internet and Intranet environments in general. These tools include Internet Assistants for the Microsoft Office product line and understanding the manner in which these servers interact with your site. This book provides excellent advice for administrators tasked with implementing the Web site and other integrated components.

This book also provides good advice for managers on how to use and understand the technologies to improve their business footing and leverage their automated information systems to maximize return on investment. Not only will managers learn what to do with their site, but also how to do it, and most important of all, why they should do it.

With the variety of information presented in this book, coupled with the high quality of content, up-to-date material, level of detail, and easy-to-follow "how-to" format guides, this book will be the all-encompassing book you will quickly come to depend upon to supply answers to your Web server installation and administration questions.

How this Book Is Organized

This book is organized in a logical sequence starting with Part I, "Planning for Your Web Site." This part provides an in-depth discussion that shows you how to install the key components of the server environment and includes different topics that will influence the planning for your site.

Part II, "Setting Up Your Web Site," shows you how to install your site, establish your server, set up security, and provides other topics that will arise when you bring your site online. These topics include information that will help ensure your site is a success and, at the same time, help you manage the growth of your site with the different tools and techniques covered in this section.

After your site is online, you'll want to consider different ways you can increase your service offering. Part III, "Enhancing Your Web Site," provides several helpful examples. From data encryption to conducting transactions on the Internet, this section of the book covers it all, showing how you can add this functionality to your system.

Part IV, "Understanding the Content Possibilities for Your Site," shows you how the different technologies work that have appeared in the recent past. These include VBScripting, Java, and more.

Reality Check Site

This book employs one additional approach that you'll not find with any other publisher. The Que Reality Check Site is an example, true-life production site that employs many of the different techniques and approaches covered in each chapter. At the end of every major chapter, you'll find a Reality Check section. This section tells how the techniques worked out as applied to the site and what it meant to the users of the site.

Many of the techniques are used at Integra Technology's site, one of the sites managed by the author. Integra can be found on the World Wide Web at **http://www.integra.net** and can be contacted at:

Integra Technology International, Inc.
3561 E. Sunrise Drive, Suite 235
Tucson, Arizona 85718

E-mail: webmaster@integra.net
Phone: (520) 577-2661

IntelliCenter, a professional development and training company located in Tucson, Arizona, was a major focus of the Reality Checks done throughout the book. In addition to the information provided here, you can also visit the IntelliCenter Reality Check site on the Internet to see how they have implemented the different approaches in this book. They can be found at **http://www.intellicenter.com**. For additional information about IntelliCenter, please contact them at:

IntelliCenter, Inc.
2700 N. Campbell Ave, Ste 200
Tucson, Arizona 85719

E-mail: Greg Keseric at gregk@intellicenter.com
Phone: (520) 318-9908

After you've implemented some or all of the techniques in this book, you can become a Reality
Check site as well. See the "Becoming a Reality Check Site" appendix for more information.
You'll be able to display the Reality Check logo on your page and you'll be privy to additional
information on new products, new titles, and more, all available to the Reality Check network of
sites.

Part I

Part I, "Planning for Your Web Site," provides information on installation and setup of the different component parts of your installation.

Chapter 1, "Understanding Web Sites and Web Servers," lays the groundwork for understanding DNS, IP addresses, and overall Internet and Intranet fundamentals. This chapter covers the
basic technologies present on the Web from Archie to Veronica.

Chapter 2, "Choosing a Web Server and Service Provider," explains the details regarding getting established with your service provider to gain access to the Internet. Information about
line speeds, hardware requirements, registering your domain name with Internic, and understanding the UNIX versus Windows NT debate is provided.

Chapter 3, "Planning an Intranet Site," covers what an Intranet is and how you can use it to
distribute information within your company. Information on different helper applications and
viewers is provided, and you can find out about how you apply UNIX permissions to your installation.

Chapter 4, "Implementing an Intranet Site," shows different ways to leverage your server in an
Intranet environment. Techniques for optimizing your Intranet site to understanding example
database queries are all provided in the chapter.

Part II

Part II, "Setting Up Your Web Site," provides you with the information you'll need to set up and
maintain, on a day-to-day basis, your Web server.

Chapter 5, "Setting Up and Configuring a Web Server," goes into detail about how you install a
server, regardless of whether it's for a UNIX or Windows NT environment.

In Chapter 6, "Setting Up an FTP Site," you'll find out about different FTP service monitoring
techniques, and how to work with an FTP site from your Web pages to working with basic log
files.

Chapter 7, "Running an Internet Site," shows how you can provide access to your Internet site
to your users, allowing them to interact with the site. Find out about FTP sites, Virtual servers,
and home pages.

Chapter 8, "Running an Intranet Site," gives you the information you need to leverage your Intranet site by showing you how to combine native applications with objects posted on the server. In addition, you'll find out about how you can share your server between an Internet and Intranet site.

Chapter 9, "Firewalls and Proxy Servers," gives detailed information about how firewalls work and what you can look for if you decide you need to implement one. You'll also find out about tools like proxy servers that you can use to bring Internet connectivity to the desktop for your users.

Chapter 10, "Maintenance Utilities," details how the different tools work that you can use to make managing your site a bit easier. Microsoft's FrontPage product is used as an example to show how these types of tools can provide a very big benefit to you and your user community.

Chapter 11, "Usage Statistics," shows what you can gain from closely monitoring the log files and statistics generated from your site. There are a number of utilities available, and this chapter will help weed out what types of things you'll want to consider as you look into a package for your site.

Chapter 12, "Search Engines," gives information about setting up a search engine on your site. One of the key features on any Internet or Intranet site, a search engine makes your site much more accessible to your users because they'll be able to quickly locate the information they need.

Chapter 13, "Forms and Surveys," goes into detail on how you use forms on your site, be it on a local server under your control or a site managed by your Service Provider.

Part III
Part III, "Enhancing Your Web Site," gives you information on the finishing touches that you can add to your site. From marketing your site to deciding on a browser, this portion of the book answers your questions on how to take your site to the next level of functionality and presentation.

Chapter 14, "Marketing Your Web Sites," gives you the inside scoop on how you can work with search engines, co-marketing opportunities, and more, all bringing more traffic to your site. Learn how to increase exposure to your site and find out what makes your site one of the ones that gets noticed.

Chapter 15, "Data Encryption and Digital Signatures," shows how you can use secure technologies on your site, including how to digitally sign applications you may be distributing on your site.

Chapter 16, "Conducting Transactions on the Internet," provides key information about how you can implement the secure sockets layer for transactions and pages on your site. It will also give you information about emerging standards from industry leaders that affect the future of secure communications on the Internet.

Part IV

Part IV, "Understanding the Content Possibilities for Your Site," takes a look at some of the advanced technologies available for your site. This section helps you start implementing scripting technologies and more.

Chapter 17, "Browsers and Your Web Server," includes information comparing and contrasting different Web browsers and how they work. It also talks about what to do in the VBScript versus Java battles that are currently occurring in the market.

Chapter 18, "Basic HTML Techniques," gives you a quick start into the world of HTML coding for your pages. This chapter starts at ground zero and takes you through all the basics of HTML coding.

Chapter 19, "Advanced HTML," adds to Chapter 18 and provides information on advanced techniques, including style sheets, tables, and frames.

Chapter 20, "ActiveX and the Internet," provides information about how you can implement ActiveX controls, the basics of scripting, an overview of the ActiveX control pad, and more.

Chapter 21, "Java Applets and the Internet," is a primer to the technology of Java and how it will enhance your Web sites. Find out about how the environment works, what types of things you can do with it, and see lots of example source code explaining all the details.

Chapter 22, "Database Access and Integrity," gives you an inside look at how you integrate database access into your pages, proving dynamic content to those accessing your site. Find out about the Internet Database Connector and Cold Fusion and how they work with databases you've set up.

Chapter 23, "Network/Video Conferencing, Internet Phone, and Real Audio," shows you what it takes to bring these technologies to your Internet or Intranet site. You'll find out how to implement some of the most advanced technologies available on your site.

Chapter 24, "JavaScript," teaches you about Internet Explorer's support for Netscape's JavaScript Web browser programming language. You also learn how JavaScript can be used to interact with Web page elements and users, and how to use different JavaScript language elements to add functionality to your Web pages.

Chapter 25, "Visual Basic Script," teaches you about Visual Basic Script, Microsoft's own scripting language for adding interactivity to Internet Explorer and other applications. You also learn how VBScript is related to the Microsoft's Visual Basic for Applications and Visual Basic programming environments.

Chapter 26, "CGI Scripts and Server-Side Includes," teaches you to configure the Netscape server to activate CGIs and SSIs, gather form data on the server side, design and install a CGI program by using various programming languages that will fully preprocess and parse the given data, produce a response page for the client from the CGI program, write simple and useful programs by using CGI, such as e-mail gateways and password checkers, and learn some of the security issues involving CGI and SSI on the Web server.

Appendixes

Appendix A, "What's on the CD?" shows you the source pages and reference materials referred to throughout the book that are on the CD-ROM. The CD-ROM also contains a huge array of software, including add-ins, viewers, utilities, and other software packages.

Appendix B is "About the Que WebReference Site." Que has set up a Web site to be used to share ideas, download software, and receive updates to certain content as new information becomes available. The site includes areas that enable you to post and review messages, see new, related information that may be helpful, and gives you a place to post your page addresses.

Appendix C, "Becoming a Reality Check Site," provides a checkpoint of sorts on the techniques and technologies presented in a given chapter so you can see how it works where the rubber meets the road. The other aspect of the Reality Check is to provide additional feedback on any bumps in the road that may be encountered along the way when you implement the different techniques in a given chapter

Conventions Used in this Book

This book assumes you are already familiar with the graphical user interface used in Windows-based applications. As such, no attempt has been made to describe "how" to select or choose various options in the dialog boxes discussed throughout this book. Instead, we have generically used the terms click, select, choose, highlight, activate, disable, and turn on/off to describe the process of positioning the cursor over a dialog box element (radio button, check box, command button, drop-down list arrow, and so on) and clicking a mouse button. Users familiar with using the keyboard to select various dialog box options may relate this selection process to keystrokes instead of mouse clicks. Either method is acceptable.

Tips, notes, cautions, warnings, and troubleshooting annotations, which are used generously throughout the book, appear in specially formatted boxes to make this important information easier to locate. References to figures, chapter numbers, or paragraph headings that have appeared previously in the book, or that will follow later in the book, will generally be annotated as cross references and will appear next to the text to which they pertain.

At times you may be required to depress keyboard keys in selected combinations to activate a command or cause a selected display window to appear. When these situations occur, you will see the key combinations described in a couple different ways. When two or more keys need to be depressed simultaneously, a plus sign (+) will be used to combine the keys. For example, when the Alt and Tab keys need to be depressed simultaneously, you will see the annotation Alt+Tab. Likewise, when the Ctrl and Y keys need to be depressed simultaneously, it will be annotated Ctrl+Y. When keys need to be depressed in a certain sequence with no intervening actions, a comma (,) will be used as a separator.

Some lines of code will be too long to fit on a single line of the book. When this occurs, you'll see the special code continuation character (➡) at the beginning of the line that should really be part of the previous line. If you're typing in the code and see this character, just disregard the character and continue typing on the same line.

Contacting the Author

I welcome your comments and feedback and will certainly do my best to clarify any points presented in this book. Please understand that it's not possible to answer specific questions or provide code examples, but I will do my best to make sure you are able to get started in the right direction.

In addition, I would really like to hear how you apply these technologies to your site. Feel free to drop me a note at **swynk@pobox.com** any time.

It's difficult to cover every conceivable angle to a given option; it seems that there is always another angle just around the corner! If you have ideas to be included "next time," I'd be more than happy to hear them. ●

Planning for Your Web Site

## CHAPTER 1

Understanding Web Sites and Web Servers

If ever there were a catch all term for an industry that's nearly impossible to explain, it's almost certainly the Internet. If you ask people what they understand the Internet to be, you'd probably have a different answer from each person with whom you talk. The Internet is ActiveX, JAVA, VBScript, Web Browsers, Netscape, Microsoft, Mosaic, RealAudio, Streaming Video, FTP, and more. This is not to say that the Internet is made up of a number of acronyms and strange terms, but it does mean that it defies a single sentence description. The key is that the Internet is none of these terms and technologies, but is the foundation for all of them and more. ∎

Understanding the Internet

The Internet is a large wide area network of computers running a common protocol, but divergent operating systems and environments.

Knowing the differences between a Web site and a Web server

An effective Web site administrator needs to understand the differences between these terms.

Determining your return on investment

Creating a presence on the Internet gives instant access to your material to about 30 million people—a big benefit of moving content online.

Understanding the Internet

The Internet is, by its loosest definition, the backbone that connects the computers around the world. This backbone started out supporting educational and government institutions. The original intent was to support information sharing on research projects and other endeavors to optimize communications and learning cycles.

The Internet has become so important to computer technologies because of the enhanced capabilities of local and wide area networking. Since LANs and WANs have become so popular, and the next obvious evolutionary step is to begin connecting these systems, the Internet is a natural step.

This comes from the fact that this informational backbone exists that can connect systems, and the LANs and WANs have the systems to connect. A natural "marriage" of technologies and a few brilliant minds later, you've gained a tool that can help in many different ways to provide access to information and other resources that, taken separately, are truly less than the sum of their parts.

The Internet is so powerful because there is so much information. When you search a local database for information on intranets, for example, you may return an article or two from within your organization. A search of the Internet, however, at the time this book was written, yielded more than 80 different articles, ranging from electronic newsletters on the subject to service providers that will help set up your system.

ON THE WEB

An example of these articles resides at the Intranet Journal's Web site. The site, located at **http:// www.brill.com/intranet/**, provides a discussion section, articles, and product reviews. There is even a search engine that searches the site for products and services reviewed and discussed, for your reference. You can also find intranet information at the Microsoft site, **http://www.microsoft.com** and the Netscape site, located at **http://www.netscape.com**.

The Internet is truly a very large wide area network of computers running a common protocol, but divergent operating systems and environments. This commonality of protocols allows for the exchange and sharing of information literally around the world.

Understanding the Differences Between a Web Site and a Web Server

Since the World Wide Web and the Internet as a whole are such new frontiers, there tends to be some confusing terms for different technologies, features, and capabilities. One of these is the mixing of the terms *Web site* and *Web server*. To become an effective Web site administrator, you need to understand the differences between these terms. Indeed, they represent two different pieces of the puzzle that makes up your Internet presence.

A Web *site* is a location on the Internet, represented by a unique address. A Web site typically provides more than just World Wide Web services. As you'll see later in this chapter, there are a number of technologies that can be provided from a site, ranging from search capabilities to file downloads to real-time audio feeds. Of course, a Web site also provides the Web-based content so often associated with the Internet. For example, the Wynkoop Pages Web site is located at **http://www.pobox.com/~swynk**, but the site provides more than Web content. You can also see PowerPoint presentations and download files.

A Web *server* is the software component, or the hardware component that it runs on, that provides the services to the Internet. This server is the system that provides access to the technologies just mentioned. The server runs the software to provide information to the users browsing the site. Most people refer to the computer that runs their Internet services as the Web server, regardless of the services that run on it.

Determining Your Return on Investment

The Internet is many things to many people. The payback you can expect from having a Web site varies depending on the type of site you're running and the audience you want to attract. It's often said that the Internet makes everyone an instant publisher. The Internet makes it relatively easy to get information and content out to the public, especially compared to printing and distributing a document by more traditional means.

The Internet enables you to put information about your business, hobbies, or any other interest you may have in a medium available to the masses. It then enables you to let the world know about it, and give the world access to the information 24 hours a day, seven days a week. The big draw of the Internet is, quite simply, connectivity. You can provide information to anyone, anywhere in the world, at any time of the day or night. You can also send additional information through electronic mail, and you can make other items available, from catalogs to pictures, from your Web site.

The truly attractive part of all of this is the seemingly low cost of bringing this type of information to the masses. While this low cost is a big draw, it's also a big misconception. The cost of bringing up your Web site will likely be low, but the cost of keeping an active, well-trafficked Web site up, running, interesting and useful may be substantial. This book is about the tools and knowledge you need to leverage your site. Make no mistake, though—a good Web site takes ongoing maintenance and creative talent. If you plan for it now, you won't be sorry.

Creating a presence on the Internet gives instant access to your material to approximately 30 million people. For many companies, this is the big attraction to the Internet, and the big benefit of moving content online. You can effectively offer comprehensive services to more people with a carefully planned and managed site than you can with traditional marketing activities. The Internet helps you provide information on demand to the customers and prospective customers that most need it.

An intranet, on the other hand, gives you leverage of a different sort. Intranets are like closed, miniature versions of the Internet that operate within the logical confines of specific group of computer systems. Intranets provide a new level of communications between departments, users, and divisions. With an intranet, you can publish confidential company information, "lessons learned" databases, documents, spreadsheets, and more. Intranets also bring the ease of publishing on the Web to the corporate environment, providing content creation and management tools to the people who know the most about the topics and ideas to be presented. When the tools are in the experts' hands, you can manage the site while other people provide the content.

The next few sections provide information about just a few of the different things you can publish, what types of names have been assigned to them, and how they can benefit your company.

Providing Company and Product Information

One of the more common reasons for creating a Web site is to provide information about you and your company. This is probably the single most named reason people provide when asked why they are considering moving to the Web. The information you provide can range from overall company information and press releases to product-related information. See Figure 1.1 for an example of this type of site.

FIG. 1.1

The Adobe Web site features complete product information about their product offerings.

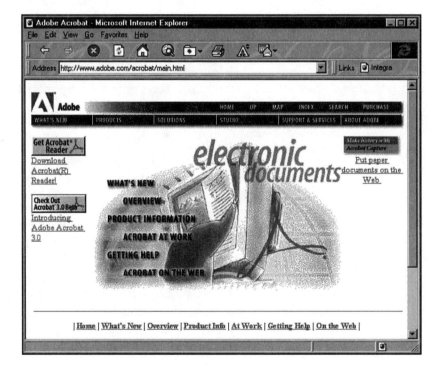

The Web provides a good forum for this type of information because people can obtain the information nearly any time they want, and they don't have to wait for the information to be sent to them by way of traditional mail. Another advantage the Web provides is the capability to get your information out to people that don't even necessarily know they want it. This sounds strange at first, but consider that you can control what search terms will be used to represent your pages in the large array of search engines used. By carefully controlling the key words provided to represent your page, you can entice people to your site when they are looking for similar products, regardless of whether they wanted your specific goods or not. A person can search the Internet for a term that describes your business generically and come up with your company as well as others that are at least loosely related.

A favorite trick with new users is to sit them down in front of one of the many different search engines and ask them what they want to know about. Of course the first thing they'll do is shrug and say "I don't know, what's available and how do I find it?" If you can convince them to type in even the most obscure topic, they'll be stunned by the many links they find. The vast amount of information out there, and the capability to search for it, is the power of the Internet. Your Web site can harness this power to help ensure your success.

N O T E One Webmaster loaded a copy of a dictionary listing into his Web page's keyword tags. It was done as an experiment just to see what would happen. The site soon received thousands of visits per day just based on the information that was turning up in search engines.

This site, now referred to as the Red Herring site, still gets many hits every day and continues to show what can be done with the correct use, or misuse, of keywords on your site. ■

▶ For more information about marketing your site, see Chapter 14, "Marketing Your Web Site."

Customer Purchases Over the Internet

You can also set up your site to allow the purchase of your products over the Internet. If you're selling software, you can provide the purchased product on the spot, allowing users to download their newly purchased software immediately after they have paid for it.

There are several applications that you can run on a Web site to accommodate this type of activity. This software ranges from shopping cart applications, which give you a virtual shopping bag in which to amass your purchases, to applications that interactively build a temporary database listing of the products a customer is interested in. See Figure 1.2 for an example, taken from the Que Publishing site at **http://www.mcp.com/que,** which is accessible from the Bookstore link on their pages.

When you're finished selecting your purchases, the software prompts you for payment and shipping information. In some cases, sites provide an encrypted and protected connection through which to provide your financial information. This protects credit card numbers and other critical information as it is transmitted across the Internet.

FIG. 1.2

Shopping bag applications enable a customer to select one or more products and then purchase them directly from a Web site.

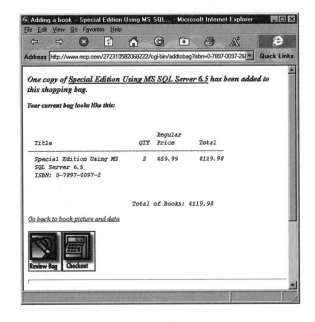

▶ For more information about secure transactions and encryption techniques, see Chapter 15, "Data Encryption and Digital Signatures" and Chapter 16, "Conducting Transactions on the Internet."

Figure 1.3 shows an example of the final checkout screen prompting for the shipping information for the order.

FIG. 1.3

The capability to complete a sale on the Web is very attractive, saving time for the customer and shortening the order cycle for your company.

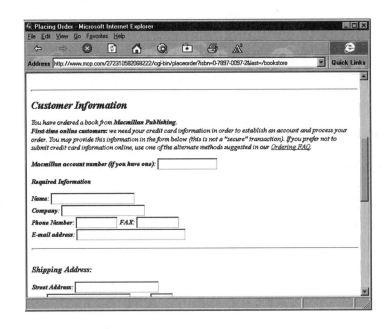

You can use the same sort of technique to provide information about your products for people. Instead of ordering products, the user requests literature. The literature can be downloaded, e-mailed, sent by standard mail, or any other means needed.

Providing the capability to order online fulfills one of the underlying themes of the Internet— immediately gratifying a user's request for products or information. If you can use people's desire for immediacy to your advantage, it will help draw people to your site, and it will help keep them coming back in the future.

Publish Online Reference Guides

The CD accompanying this book includes an online version of the book. You can review this book online and cut-and-paste examples from it into your applications, Web content, and other areas of your Web site. Just as Que Corporation has provided this service to you, you can provide a similar service to your users. You can provide manuals or other literature your company produces on your Web site for the ready access of your site visitors.

Some utilities exist that can help you take your content from existing documents. These utilities will generally plug into existing applications that you are running, such as Microsoft Office applications, and add new capabilities to your standard tools. There's a very good chance that the materials you have already created can create compelling content for your site.

Creating a Knowledge Base

Frequently Asked Questions, or FAQs, are supplements to documentation. They help answer questions that come up repeatedly about a product. Product support staff hear these same questions over and over, and the majority of their time is spent answering them for individual customers.

By posting FAQs and other supplemental information about products and services you offer, you can decrease the workload for your support staff. Visitors can access the information on your products and services whenever they need it, and the calls you get will likely be a bit more screened, as the customer has already had access to the answers for the most typical problems.

Knowledge base systems are generally broken down into two types. The first type is the FAQ discussed above. An FAQ typically answers several questions in a single report-like document.

In contrast, knowledge-base articles are typically more in-depth than an FAQ. Knowledge-base articles provide development or debugging details that can be used to troubleshoot or correct more complex problems. If you decide to provide troubleshooting information on your site, chances are good that you'll find uses for both types of troubleshooting documents. Keep in mind too, that you may already have much of the material you need to create these FAQs from different department's informal reference documents that may have been created.

Understanding What Makes the Web a Web: Hyperlinks

The term World Wide Web is an interesting one. It comes from the fact that pages on the Web are interrelated and linked to one another. As you've no doubt seen when researching a specific task on the Web, it's tempting to follow related links you encounter. If you give in to the temptation to "surf," you may find that in a couple of hours you've managed to travel all over the world.

This Web of sites is the foundation of the World Wide Web. The completely distributed nature of the Web provides an endless supply of links, related sites and more. The "distributed" description comes from the fact that Web pages do not physically exist on a single Web server, but are created, maintained, and accessed on their own servers. The fact that you have links to a site in Australia is not a problem, as it just shows off the flexibility of the Web. With a simple click on a graphic or bit of text, your browser takes you automatically to the remote location.

When you're viewing a page in your browser, links to other locations, or even links within the current Web site, are typically indicated by a change in the mouse pointer to a pointing hand and by an underlined phrase if the link is represented by text. See Figure 1.4 for an example of a page with both graphic and text-based links.

▶ For more information about formatting your Web documents, see Chapter 18, "Basic HTML Techniques" and Chapter 19, "Advanced HTML."

FIG. 1.4
Pages can have both text-based and graphically represented links to other information.

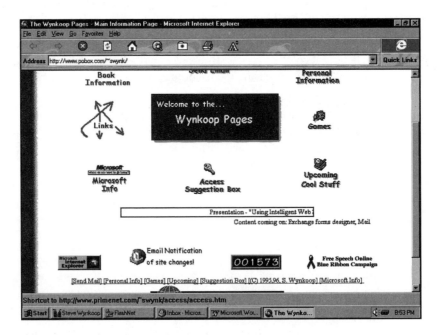

HyperText Markup Language HyperText Markup Language, or HTML, is the name for the language that creates the content on Web pages. HTML is the foundation for all presentation of materials when someone is viewing or working with your Web site. Even if your site employs

Java, ActiveX scripting, or other tools, HTML is still the basis on which these languages are provided to the user.

It's important to understand the limitations of HTML. Since it is a "markup" language, it enables you to emphasize and somewhat control the look and feel of content on a Web page, but you must create pages that are system-independent. Your pages must be able to be viewed on any of a very large, very diverse set of systems that are accessing the Web.

HTML attempts to provide a standard by which you can create content. This content is formatted behind the scenes and then interpreted and displayed by your Web browser when you access a page. Listing 1.1 shows a portion of the HTML that is used to create the page shown in Figure 1.4.

Listing 1.1 Sample HTML Page

```
<!DOCTYPE HTML PUBLIC "-//W3O/DTD HTML//EN">
<html>
<head>
<title>The Wynkoop Pages - Main Information Page</title>
<meta http-equiv="PICS-Label" content="(PICS-1.0 "
➥ http://www.rsac.org/ratingsv01.html" l gen true comment rsaci
➥ north america server" by swynk@pobox.com" for
➥ http://www.primenet.com/~swynk" on t08:15-0500" exp t08:15-0500" r n s v l>
<meta name="GENERATOR" content="Microsoft FrontPage 1.1">
<base href="http://www.primenet.com/~swynk/">
<meta name="FORMATTER" content="Microsoft FrontPage 1.1">
</head>
<body text="#00000B" >
<body background="white.jpg" bgproperties="fixed">

<!-- BEGIN INTERNET LINK EXCHANGE CODE -->
<p align="center">
<a href="http://ad.linkexchange.com/X964455/gotoad.map" target="_top">
<img src="http://ad.linkexchange.com/X964455/logoshowad?free"
➥ alt="Internet Link Exchange" align="bottom" border="1" width="440"
➥ height="40" ismap></a>
<br>
<a href="http://www.linkexchange.com/" target="_top">
<font size="1">
Member of the Internet Link Exchange</font></a><br>
<!--  END INTERNET LINK EXCHANGE CODE  -->
<p>
...


...
<p align="center"><a href="mailto:swynk@pobox.com ">[Send Mail] </a>
<a href="http://www.primenet.com/~swynk/personal/persinfo.htm">
➥ [Personal Info] </a><a
href="http://www.primenet.com/~swynk/games/games.htm">[Games] </a>
<a href="http://www.primenet.com/~swynk/upcoming/upcome.htm ">
➥ [Upcoming] </a>
<a href="http://www.primenet.com/~swynk/access/access.htm">
```

continues

Listing 1.1 Continued

```
➥ [Suggestion Box] </a>
<a href="http://www.primenet.com/~swynk/copyright/copyrite.htm">
➥ [(C)1995,96, S. Wynkoop] </a>
<a href="http://www.primenet.com/~swynk/msinfo/msinfo.htm">
➥ [Microsoft Info] </a>
<br>
<a href="http://www.synet.net/hwg"><img src="htmlgld.gif"
➥ align="bottom" border="0" width="266" height="56"></a>
</p>
<address>
Microsoft is a registered trademark and the Microsoft
➥ Internet Explorer Logo is a trademark of Microsoft.
</address>
</body>
</html>
```

You don't necessarily need to understand this listing right now. Note, however, that this plain text listing produced the graphically-oriented page shown in Figure 1.4. HTML provides you with the means of indicating links, graphics, and other elements in your pages. It also gives you special capabilities to add custom touches, like extensions specific to the browser of your choosing, if you should decide to do so.

The next few sections explain more about the capabilities of the HTML language.

Hyperlinks in Web Documents Hyperlinks in documents give you a way to take the user to another location, either on your site or elsewhere on the Web, by clicking on an item on your page. These links can be to any of the following:

- Other pages
- Other sites
- Bookmarks or other locations on the current page
- Bookmarks on other pages
- Files to be viewed or downloaded
- Other protocol-based locations (such as Gopher and News servers)

NOTE As mentioned in the final item above, links can also be included that point to other types of locations, from News servers to Gopher servers. More about these other technologies is included later in this and other chapters. ■

Hyperlinks are the reason for the Web's great convenience and ease of use, but ironically, they are also the reason why so many people lose so many hours to Web exploration. You will rarely visit a site at which you don't see links to other sites that contain related (or completely unrelated) information. By selecting these links, you're whisked off to see another site and another set of links.

ON THE WEB

A picture is worth a thousand words, and this also holds true for Web pages. A fabulous graphic, interactively used, can be a very powerful element on your Web page. Graphics can even be animated, providing motion on the Web page that certainly helps to draw the viewer's eye to a specific element of the page. Consider for a minute the Que Reality check logo, included on the CD with this book.

The real fun comes in when you link a graphic to another location. Just as with hyperlinks, you can create links that are represented by graphics or portions of graphics. You create a map of the image, and when the user clicks on a specific location of the graphic, the map is consulted and the user is taken to the alternate location.

You'll notice this behavior with the Que Reality Check logo; if you click on it, it takes you to a location on the Que Publishing site. Graphics can be subdivided so that different portions of the graphic take you to different locations on the Web, providing flexibility when you're setting up the graphics for your pages.

Graphics can also be a real problem on some sites. As with anything else in life, too much of a good thing is a problem. A site that is graphic-intensive can bog down users with slower connections and can render a site unusable to text browsers if a text-based link is not also provided. You'll find out more about these types of challenges to Web page design throughout this book.

Internet Technologies Overview

There are as many different technologies that support Internet activities as there are ways of using them. These range from sending mail to viewing Web pages, from downloading files to writing programmatic extensions to the different services. In the coming sections, you see the basics of what these technologies are all about.

Most Internet activities take place based on a Universal Resource Locator or URL. These addresses are unique to a given location or site and give you the means of indicating not only the address of the site, but also the protocol to be used when accessing the site. For example, in the address for the Microsoft site **http://www.microsoft.com**, the **http://** prefix on the address indicates that it's a Web site.

▶ For more information on how browsers work with your Web server, see Chapter 17, "Browsers and Your Web Server."

Understanding Electronic Mail Services

Electronic mail, known to the masses as e-mail, provides for what equates to electronic note-passing. While that's an oversimplification, you can think of e-mail as a way to get a message from one location to another electronically by passing the message through several electronic handlers points along the way.

The Internet lets computers that are not directly connected to each other communicate with one another. Messages do not pass directly from the sender to the recipient in most cases;

instead, systems are able to communicate by way of hops between systems that eventually lead to the system the message is intended for. For example, the Listing 1.2 shows the hops that will be completed going to the Netscape site, **netscape.com**, from an example account.

Listing 1.2 Sample Traceroute Listing

```
traceroute to www1.netscape.com (198.95.251.30), 30 hops max,
➥ 40 byte packets
1  phx-10-e1/4.primenet.net (198.68.32.1)  1 ms  4 ms  2 ms
 2  dca-1-atm1/0-t3.primenet.net (206.165.127.41)  66 ms  82 ms  69 ms
 3  mae-east-plusplus.washington.mci.net (192.41.177.181)  165 ms
➥ 222 ms  257 ms
4  204.70.1.213 (204.70.1.213)  86 ms  154 ms  70 ms
 5  core2.SanFrancisco.mci.net (204.70.4.201)  142 ms  142 ms  149 ms
 6  borderx2-fddi-1.SanFrancisco.mci.net (204.70.158.68)  142 ms
➥ 142 ms  143 ms
7  netscape-ds3.SanFrancisco.mci.net (204.70.158.122)  144 ms
➥ 146 ms  143 ms
8  www1.netscape.com (198.95.251.30)  142 ms  144 ms  141 ms
```

N O T E Traceroute is a UNIX application that checks the routing for packets from your system to the remote system, showing response times along the way. There are a number of applications available that allow you to check this information, and they are generally available for nearly any platform.

You can also run a similar application, tracert from the DOS or Windows environment; the output is identical. ■

To use electronic mail, you must first have an e-mail server that you typically log into with your e-mail client application. This server accepts your outgoing mail and provides you with your incoming mail. When you send a message, the server forwards your message to the remote post office service for delivery to the recipient.

Understanding World Wide Web Services

The World Wide Web is one of the most well known of the Internet technologies. This is because it's easy to use and most people can relate to a document-centric approach to presenting information. The Web is largely responsible for the explosive growth on the Internet and continues to fuel this flame by expanding to provide additional support for technologies that go beyond simple documents on the Internet to the complex objects that can be supported today, like spreadsheets and online presentations. As a term, "Web services" includes all of the different aspects of what makes up the Web page that the user sees. There are a number of factors, both executing on the server and possibly on the user's system, that make that Web page a reality. These include the following:

■ Server automation, including server-side applications, extensions to the server's capabilities, and so on.

- Database access.
- Client-side automation, including handling of forms, user-authentication with the server, and more.
- Scripting languages including Java, Javascript, and ActiveX scripting.

In any case, the Web service, running a protocol called HTTP, works with your browser to transfer, format, and display the information that makes up pages that you view on the Internet.

Web servers are accessed with Web browsers like Netscape Navigator or Microsoft's Internet Explorer. The server address is indicated in the URL with a prefix of http://.

N O T E   In many browsers, the HTTP protocol is assumed if no other is specified. Therefore, typing **http://www.microsoft.com** is the same as typing **www.microsoft.com** for an address. ■

File Transfer Protocol

File Transfer Protocol, commonly called FTP, is one way of downloading files over the Internet. FTP is generally a binary transfer mechanism and is used to download program updates, freeware and shareware, and other types of documents and objects not suitable or meant for viewing online.

Typically, when you access an FTP site, files are listed in a familiar file-by-file listing, often showing a file size and resembling the listing from Windows' File Manager or Explorer applications. See Figure 1.5.

FIG. 1.5
FTP software shows listings of both the files on the remote system and those on your system, allowing you to send or receive files easily.

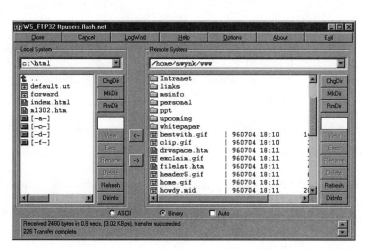

With a Web browser, the site is usually viewed within the browser and does not typically include information about files on your local system, as shown in Figure 1.6.

FIG. 1.6
When you view a site with a Web browser, the results are nearly the same, but you don't see files on your local system.

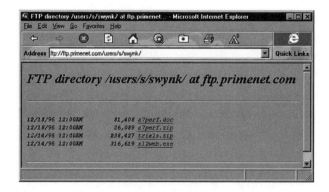

FTP can be hosted in a Web browser and indicated with a URL beginning with "ftp://..." In addition, an FTP location can be reached using a dedicated application that works for that protocol only, such as WS_FTP.

Network News Transfer Protocol

Network News, also referred to as Usenet, is a more informal way of communicating with other people with common interests. Usenet is divided into interest areas, or *newsgroups*. These newsgroups are named and often described to help determine what they represent and incorporate a naming convention that sets up a group hierarchy. You'll notice similar, very general categories make up the first part of the name, followed by more specific name segments as you move to the right. See Figure 1.7 for an example listing of these types of groups.

FIG. 1.7
Newsgroups cover nearly any topic you can imagine, and provide a central location for the exchange of lessons learned, viewpoints, and concepts.

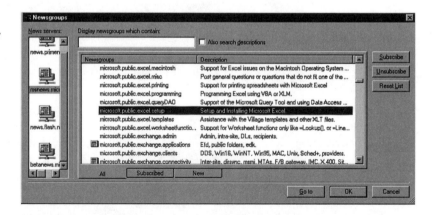

Newsgroups can be subscribed to with most news readers. This simply means that you register an interest in the group and that the news reader you use will keep track of which messages you've read. This is helpful because many newsgroups have hundreds of messages each day. Keeping track of those new messages alone can be quite a load, let alone managing older messages.

News servers are dispersed all over the globe and they host everything from the most bizarre topics to private information forums for corporations, software applications, and more.

There are both free, public news servers and private, closed servers. For example, at Microsoft, there is a server responsible for beta software support, to which you are granted access if you're enrolled in certain beta testing programs. The server is located at **news://betanews.microsoft.com**, but is closed unless you're in one of the beta programs. Microsoft also provides a free, open-access news server through which the general public can ask questions and exchange ideas about Microsoft products. The address for that server is **news://msnews.microsoft.com**.

You can use dedicated, single-function news readers to access news servers or you can use your Web browser if you're using a more current version of any of the popular browsers. In either case, you'll generally have an option to show messages in a threaded discussion listing, keeping questions and responses grouped together to more easily follow discussions. If you want to access news servers from your Web browser, you indicate the address with a prefix of news://.

Understanding Mailing Lists

Mailing lists are a combination of e-mail and newsgroups. Mailing lists, often referred to as Listservers, are mailing lists, usually maintained automatically by a special software package, that allow people to correspond with others who subscribe to the list. You typically sign up to a given list by sending mail to the server process supporting the list. The actual command you use to subscribe will vary depending on the server hosting the list. You can find a vast array of lists at **http://www.lsoft.com**, where there is also a search engine that will assist in finding a list that interests you.

Lists are very helpful for support and help issues. You can, for instance, send a piece of e-mail to the list whose Internet address is **msoffice-l@peach.ease.lsoft.com**, asking for help in developing with Microsoft Office. When you do, the message you send is forwarded to the list's members, which, in this case, is approximately 700 users.

The key advantage of listservers over newsgroups is that your correspondence with the group requires no unique software, only your e-mail reader. You can participate in discussions and see other discussions that are occurring directly from your e-mail client because each post to the group is forwarded to you either individually or as a digest of all messages for the day.

You can host listservers using software that runs on your server, or you can ask another network administrator to host your listserver for you. Mail volumes on active lists can soar, so keep this in mind when you decide to host a list. Remember, if a single user sends a single message to a list with 500 people on it, it's instantly the equivalent of sending 500 messages.

N O T E Microsoft's Exchange Server provides an intelligent mail system with client/server capabilities built in. The client/server approach means that much of the work of routing and managing your e-mail occurs at the host, rather than the workstation. This can be a big help in limiting the load on the workstation and moving the load to the server where the information can be put to good use as a reference for your company.

You can use public folders in Exchange to represent discussion groups and avoid the overhead of more typical mailing lists. Users can set up folders that mirror their favorites and use these to monitor the message flow in the system. ▓

To host a list, you'll need to install the software on your system and then publish the e-mail address and pertinent commands to subscribe and use the list to other lists or newsgroups that will be interested. Once completed, the list becomes reasonably self-maintaining, allowing users to sign on and off the list as needed without your intervention. The one thing that you will be required to do is handle bounced mail, those mail items that are unable to reach their destination for any of a number of reasons. In these cases, it's often possible to simply check that the user's system still exists on the network. If it does, you can ignore any bounced mail messages for that user until they happen again. In cases where users "disappear," you will need to do the maintenance on the list and remove them from the subscriber base.

Understanding Archie

Archie is an older technology that provides an interesting service. Archie is a utility that lets you search FTP sites for files based on names or descriptions. If a file is found, the utility returns the address of the file, pertinent dates, file sizes, and more. You can then use this information to download the file to your system as needed.

You can access Archie with DOS, Windows, or UNIX-based applications and tools, but rarely, if ever, via your Web browser, as the technology is older and not a frequently used technology for many progressive sites.

Understanding Veronica

Veronica is a search engine, much like Archie, but for the Gopher world of documents. With Veronica, you can search Gopher servers for information that you need. The results of the search will show the different links to sites and documents that match your criteria.

Also, as with Archie, Veronica is an older technology and not used in newer systems coming on line on a regular basis. You can access Veronica from DOS, Windows, or UNIX-based Gopher clients.

Understanding CGI, ISAPI, and NSAPI Technologies

The Common Gateway Interface (CGI), Internet Server Advanced Programming Interface (ISAPI), and the Netscape Server Advanced Programming Interface (NSAPI) are all different ways to extend server-based functionality. Though not the only ways to extend servers and their capabilities, these are the most common interfaces available as of this writing.

CGI is common across most mainstream servers. It lets you add programs, scripting languages, and other elements that execute on the server to your Web-based applications. These applications range from Web page counters to database interfaces.

ISAPI, a Microsoft evolving standard, is an extension for Microsoft's Internet Information Server. ISAPI extensions include those outlined for CGI, but they also enable you to use Visual Basic to write extensions. Additional examples include Microsoft's database connector and site search engines, both examples of ISAPI applications and server extensions.

NSAPI is Netscape's answer to Microsoft's offerings. NSAPI lets you write the same types of applications as ISAPI, but with a focus on the Netscape server offerings.

Many of these extensions are discussed at different locations throughout this book. Each warrants entire volumes on the details, characteristics, and how-to information for the protocol. Whenever possible, there will be additional reference information about where you can turn for added depth and detail on working with these protocols.

Understanding Network Infrastructure Basics

When you connect your server to the Internet, you typically install a high-speed modem and a router to handle the connection. In Chapter 2, you'll find out more about selecting an appropriate service provider, but your basic overall configuration will be like that shown in Figure 1.8.

The Channel Service Unit/Data Service Unit (CSU/DSU) you see mentioned in Figure 1.8 is similar in function to a modem. It translates the signal coming over the line into your establishment and makes it possible to send the signal to the router. The CSU/DSU terminates the service provider's signal at your location, and the router makes sure the incoming packets are able to get onto your network and are sent to the proper location. The CSU portion of the unit is responsible for negotiating the conversation with the incoming signal from the Internet. The DSU portion is used to communicate with the router in your establishment.

Typically, when you choose a provider to gain access to the Internet, you'll have a number of options available to you relating to how much hardware the service provider will furnish toward your installation. Your options range from the ISP providing full connectivity to your organization to the provider connecting the line to your establishment while you retain the responsibility for terminating to a CSU/DSU and installing and testing the router equipment. Of course the price you'll be charged for bringing your establishment online will depend on the package you select.

FIG. 1.8
With an Internet installation, you'll need to address how you'll get the network to your computer.

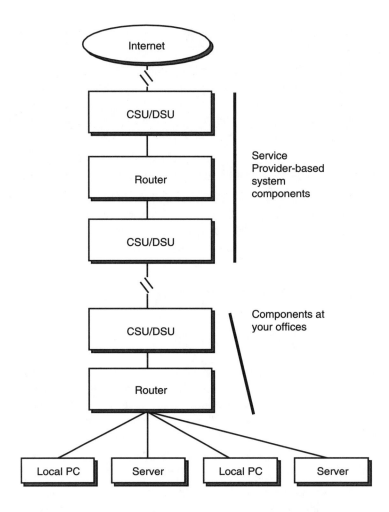

From Here...

This chapter introduced a number of terms and technologies. In doing so, it only scratched the surface, however. The Internet is becoming a network of tools and wide-open capabilities that make it possible for you to develop some interesting content. In the following chapters, specifics of many of these technologies and others are covered so you can understand what the options are and how they might best be used for your sites.

Throughout the rest of the book, detailed information about these opportunities is provided. In particular, the following areas may be of interest:

- Chapter 5, "Setting Up and Configuring a Web Server," provides excellent reference information about what you must do to get your World Wide Web server up and running.

- Chapter 8, "Running an Intranet Site," shows how you can set up your server for your internal network, and provides some great alternatives for getting information out to the users in your organization.

- Chapter 17, "Browsers and Your Web Server," begins a multi-chapter series on providing content on your site. Everything from HTML to ActiveX scripting is covered, giving you the information you'll need to decide which way to go in developing your site.

Choosing a Web Server and Service Provider

When you decide to conduct business on the Internet, you're making only the first of many decisions that are required to accomplish the feat. You'll be faced with all kinds of decisions, from selecting the software that you'll use to choosing the method of connecting to the Internet. In many cases, there are performance, design, or capability factors that will help you in this process.

This chapter focuses on explaining the technologies you'll encounter and helping you identify the points to keep in mind when you start the process of bringing up a Web server. ■

Find out about the different ways to connect to the Internet

One of the more important sets of decisions you'll make is how you want to connect to the Internet, including the speed and type of connection. Find out what type of connection makes sense for your needs.

See how to set up your "friendly" name on the Internet

You'll see how the Internet resolves names like www.microsoft.com and how it determines where to send people requesting access to that name. You'll also find out how to register your own domain name on the Internet for others to access.

Learn about key comparison points among server software choices

The range of capabilities for your server software can vary greatly. Find out what you really need to keep in mind to determine the platform you need.

Establishing Your Web Presence

One key ingredient to your selection of how you'll get on the Internet is the amount of content you'll provide. You'll need to know how much you plan to store on the system before you can begin to select line speeds, providers, and other features.

As mentioned in Chapter 1, your company's link to the Internet will be provided by an Internet Service Provider, usually referred to as an ISP. The decision about who will provide this service should not be taken lightly, as it affects not only the people within your company, but also those accessing your site from the outside—potential clients and customers.

Another concern when you select your provider is that there are additional costs that can come into play after you've selected the manner in which you're going to connect. For example, if you implement a 56K connection to your ISP, it's possible that you'll be required to purchase the equipment for both sides of the connection, placing one set at the ISP's place of business and the other set of equipment at your location. When combined, the costs for these types of connections can exceed $5,000–$10,000.

Choosing an Internet Service Provider

The number of ISPs offering Internet services is growing rapidly. It used to be that choosing an ISP was simple, as there were very few providers. As the popularity of the Internet has grown, so, too, has the number of businesses vying for your connectivity dollars. Some of the names will be familiar: MCI, Sprint, GTE, and so on. Your local phone system carrier may have joined the game as well. Other ISPs are literally run out of an enterprising person's basement.

Some of the important points to consider while choosing an ISP include the following:

- **Price.** Though becoming less of an issue through increasing competition, price will still be a top consideration when you select an ISP to partner with in your connectivity.

- **Type of connections offered.** Not all ISPs provide all of the services that you may need. Be sure you have a complete understanding of what you need, and use this as a critical determining factor in selecting the ISP you use.

- **Capacity.** Be sure to ask what capacity connection your ISP has to the Internet backbone. If they have a 56K connection and hundreds of users, response will likely not be acceptable during times of peak loads. Depending on their load, a reputable ISP should have a T1 connection to the Internet as a bare minimum.

- **Fault-tolerance.** High-end providers will have multiple connections to the Internet backbone. That way, if one circuit fails, another will continue to provide connectivity.

- **Service.** What kind of service agreement is standard for the ISP? Can they guarantee a minimum bandwidth or minimal downtime? Do they provide 24-hours-a-day, 7-days-per-week access to their support staff?

- **The company's reputation.** References are always desirable when entering into an agreement that your business will depend on. You can consider talking with businesses in your area, and you can research the ISP on the Internet in newsgroups and on mailing lists.

- **Stability of the company.** The person working from his or her basement may leave the business just as quickly as he or she entered it.
- **Other services.** An ISP should be able to provide domain name services, electronic mail, and UseNet news services if you need them. Your ISP should also be able to help you secure IP addresses for your internal network and register your domain name.

Understanding Connection Types

Just as important as whom you choose to provide your Internet connectivity is what technology you plan to use to make the connection. Table 2.1 shows the more common technologies and their capacities in raw bits-per-second, approximate number of users supported, approximate monthly cost, and interface type.

Table 2.1   Different Types of Connections to the Internet Are Available

Connection	Data Rate	Simultaneous Interface Users	Approximate Monthly Cost	Local Loop
Dial-up	28.8K	1-2	$15-50	2-wire twisted pair
56K	56K	10-20	$300-500	2- or 4-wire twisted pair
ISDN	14.4K	10-40	$50-250	2-wire twisted pair
Frame Relay	up to 1.544M	5-250	$200-2,000	2- or 4-wire twisted pair or fiber
T1	1.544M	50-250	$100-3,000	4-wire twisted pair or fiber
T3	44.736M	250-4,000	$50,000-150,000	Fiber or coaxial

N O T E   A "local loop" refers to the local wiring it will require to run from your place of business to the local provider's access points on their network or hub. ■

As you can see, there are many different ways that you can approach becoming connected to the Internet. Your decision will be based primarily upon anticipated traffic, which services are available from your ISP, and the ability of your local carrier to provide this service to your site. These prices are the combined monthly rates of what your ISP and local carrier will charge you. These prices do not include hook-up fees or the necessary equipment such as CSU/DSUs and routers. Of course, the pricing in your area may vary, but these should give you a good idea of what to expect.

Selecting a Dial-Up Access Method   The most familiar and popular way to gain access to the Internet is simply to use a modem and ordinary voice line to dial into an ISP. This is an inexpensive and relatively pain-free method for one or two users to gain access. Typically, each computer will have its own modem, and access will be available only to the user of that computer.

It is possible, however, using Windows NT Remote Access Server or hardware router, to use a standard telephone line for multi-user access. The performance of this type of connection will be acceptable only for a few users. More than two simultaneous users may slow response to unacceptable levels. While dial-up access may be acceptable for a few internal users surfing the Net, it is unlikely that external customers will want to spend a lot of time visiting your Web site if this is your primary means of connection. Of course, external customers would also be limited in their access to your site based on the time you were actually dialed in to your ISP.

The limiting factor of dial-up access is the standard analog telephone circuit, otherwise known as Plain Old Telephone Service or POTS. The analog circuit provided to your residence or business has changed little in decades. Because computers communicate digitally, the signal from your computer must be converted to an analog signal before being transmitted over the wire, and then converted back to digital format at the receiving end. The bottleneck of this approach is the analog bandwidth of a phone line. The typical bandwidth on an analog circuit is around 4kHz. The theoretical maximum digital bandwidth over an analog phone line is around 40K. Practical considerations usually make this limit considerably lower. While there are currently modems capable of 33.6K, the standard is 28.8K. Barring a radically different digital-to-analog encoding scheme, technology is quickly reaching the upper limits of digital communication over analog phone circuits.

NOTE   Most modem manufacturers talk about their compatibility with various compression technologies. One manufacturer claims an 8 to 1 compression ratio, turning its 28.8K modem into a 230.4K modem. While this is possible using certain types of textual data, don't count on throughput being anything near this using real-life information. Web site content in particular can be heavily graphical in nature. Graphic files are particularly difficult to compress, and, in the case of JPEG files, compression has already taken place and little or no additional compression is likely. ■

Selecting a 56K Connection   If you plan to host a Web server on your local premises, or if you have several users who need to access the Internet, 56K is probably where you should start your search for a connection. These circuits go by many names, and are carrier dependent. Your carrier may call it DDS, Digital Data Service, Dataphone Digital Service, or some other variation. The 56K digital circuits have been around for quite some time, and were the first commonly available high-speed technology to move information between remote sites. Although 56K communication doesn't seem all that fast by today's standards, it was blistering in the days when 1200-baud modems were all the rage.

In telecommunications vocabulary, a 56K circuit is known as a DS0 circuit. A DS0 is one of the basic building blocks used by telecommunication companies. Since a fully digital circuit is being used, there is no digital-to-analog conversion necessary, and accordingly, many problems inherent in analog circuits and modems are taken out of the equation since they are not part of the installation.

The additional bandwidth and reliability don't come free, however. The cost of a 56K circuit is often an order of magnitude higher than that of a voice circuit. You will also need more equipment to set up the link. A router and a Channel Service Unit/Data Service Unit, or CSU/DSU, will be required at each end of the circuit. Figure 2.1 shows the physical configuration of using a 56K circuit to connect your LAN to the Internet through an ISP.

FIG. 2.1
There are several important links that you install when you use a 56K connection to the Internet.

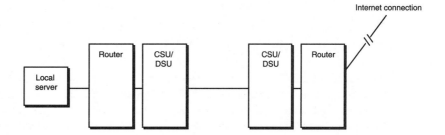

In addition to a router to direct the TCP/IP traffic, you will need a CSU/DSU (Channel Service Unit/Data Service Unit) to connect to your carriers' circuit. The CSU is used to terminate the digital circuit in a method acceptable to the phone company. The CSU will usually have LEDs on the front of the unit to indicate the status of the link, the loopback testing, and other conditions. The DSU is located between the CSU and your router. DSUs are responsible for converting the electrical signal from your router into a signal that the CSU can accept.

N O T E   The disadvantage of using 56K lines lies in their point-to-point operation. While this is obviously not a problem if you have a single site, the set-up and equipment expenses can become significant if you are connecting multiple sites. If you have several sites to connect, you should investigate frame-relay, discussed later in this chapter. ■

Selecting an ISDN Connection   While your telephone cable may struggle with a 28.8K analog modem connection, it is probably capable of carrying a 14.4K digital ISDN signal. ISDN, or Integrated Services Digital Network, has long been hailed as the ideal service for telecommuters and small businesses. But due to real and imagined political and technological problems, the ISDN promise has only recently become reality. If anything, ISDN's recent popularity has proven that consumers and telecommuters were starved for its advanced capabilities.

The integrated part of ISDN comes from its ability to handle voice and data simultaneously over the same twisted pair cable that currently provides your voice or modem service. ISDN is a point-to-point, connection-based system that is purely digital. If fact, its digital nature allows it to dial, handshake, and connect in only a second or two. The average modem can take nearly a minute to perform the same task.

The standard ISDN circuit is called BRI service. BRI stands for Basic Rate Interface. BRI consists of two 64K data channels and one 16K signal channel. The 64K channels are called *B* or *bearer* channels. The 16K channel is called the *D* or *data* channel and is used for circuit signaling and management. BRI service is also referred to as 2B + D service. The two 64K channels can be used for voice or data in parallel or combination. You can use one channel for data and the other for voice, or both channels for data or voice. You can't make direct use of the D channel.

Through a technique called *bonding*, both B channels can be combined to form a single 128K data connection channel. The most popular type of bonding is called *multi-link PPP* or *MLPPP*. Currently, no standards for bonding exist, though industry groups are working on one. You will most likely need the same brand of equipment on each end of the circuit to enable bonding.

The service termination point is called the TA or terminal adapter. The TA may be provided by you or your carrier, or may be built in to your ISDN equipment. The TA will terminate a single twisted-pair cable. The NT1 is the network terminator and is responsible for breaking the signal into its B and D channels. Typical ISDN equipment contains the TA and the NT1, and is often referred to as an ISDN adapter. An ISDN adapter is roughly analogous to a CSU/DSU. Your terminal equipment such as your PC or your router will connect to your ISDN adapter with an RS-232 (serial) connection. The ISDN adapter then appears to your PC or router as a very fast modem. Many routers support an ISDN interface, as does the Windows NT Remote Access Service.

Some ISDN routers support dial-on-demand. If the connection is idle for a preset period of time, the line will disconnect. When a packet needs to be forwarded over the ISDN link, the router reconnects and forwards the traffic. Since ISDN connects so quickly, the user notices little or no delay. The cost savings from using a dial-on-demand configuration can be significant if your carrier charges for connect time.

Cost and availability of ISDN vary considerably. In many areas of the country, ISDN's popularity has pushed its demand way beyond supply. You may have to wait several months for your carrier to provide you with service. In addition, you may have to wait to even have ISDN available in your area. Many smaller or rural municipalities don't have ISDN service at all. Carriers in other communities realized the benefits of ISDN years ago and have built substantial infrastructure to handle the demand. ISDN's cost is just as variable; prices range from $50 to $250 per month and may depend on usage.

Selecting Frame Relay Connectivity   Currently, frame relay is the rage of the wide-area networking industry. Frame relay is a switch-based technology developed by the local carriers. The local exchange carriers, or LECs, have developed a network of frame relay switches. Any point in the frame relay network can access any of the other frame relay switches. A company with multiple locations can communicate across the frame relay network ("cloud"), with each location having to maintain only a single WAN connection.

A frame relay connection point is called an *access link*. Access links are 56K or T1 interfaces. The maximum data rate at each access link is called the *port speed* and is equal to or less than the interface link. For example, you may have a 56K access link but only a 32K port speed. Customers with a T1 access link might have a 128K, 512K, or 1.544M port speed.

Routes across the frame relay network are determined by a permanent virtual circuit, or PVC. PVCs connect frame relay devices, and a single access link can support multiple virtual circuits.

Your guaranteed bandwidth across a frame relay network is called the *committed information rate (CIR)*. The CIR is always less than the port speed, and will be the biggest decision you make when ordering a frame relay circuit. One highly touted feature of frame relay is its capability to burst above the CIR. Bursting allows network traffic to take advantage of a period of lower activity in the frame relay network to grab some extra bandwidth. The bursting capacity is available up to the port speed. However, the total bandwidth available within the network is finite and each PVC is given a percentage based on its CIR.

As the popularity of frame relay has grown, many carriers are finding networks running at close to maximum throughput. Don't count on operating in burst mode very often. In fact, packets that go above the CIR are eligible to be discarded if the burst bandwidth is not available at that particular instant. Needless to say, the delays caused by packets being discarded and the protocol recovery mechanism operating can make for some long delays and unhappy users.

One scenario would be for you to have a T1 access link with a 512K port speed and a 256K CIR. Under this configuration, you would always have at least 256K of throughput. Under ideal conditions, the circuit would be able to temporarily burst up to 512K. If you find that you need a bigger pipe, both the port speed and CIR can be increased.

Selecting Connections at T1 Speeds and Above   T1 connections are a necessity for organizations that have large numbers of employees accessing the Internet, or that have large numbers of Internet users accessing their servers. T1 connections are very similar in concept and functionality to 56K lines. The obvious difference is a 24-fold increase in bandwidth. T1 circuits have a data rate of 1.544M. The point-to-point configuration remains.

A T1 circuit is another major building block for telecommunications networks. Also known as a DS1, a DS1 consists of 24 DS0s. Some carriers offer a variation on the T1 called Fractional T1. Fractional T1 (FT1) offers speeds from DS0 to DS1, usually in 2, 4, or 6 DS0 multiples. Fractional T1 is not always financially advantageous. For a slight increase in cost, you may be able to purchase a full T1 circuit. Check with your carrier and ISP for price differentials.

Those of you with truly huge bandwidth requirements (and very deep pockets) should investigate T3 service. This service provides a data rate of 44.736M. T3, also known as a DS3 circuit, is equivalent to 28 DS1s. If you are in the market for T1 and higher speed circuit, plan on spending some time with your local carriers and ISP to determine the best approach and work out the best pricing you can.

In addition to T3 circuits, SMDS, ATM, Sonet, and other technologies have come into being for truly high-speed access. You'll need to work with your ISP to determine the best of these types of access methods for your needs.

Name Resolution and the Domain Name System

Names on the Internet mean everything, and the system that ties all of the names together is Domain Name Services (DNS). DNS is a hierarchical naming system used for navigation around the Internet and within many organizations.

The Internet started as a simple network of a few systems. Each system was responsible for maintaining a *hosts* file that mapped every system's name to its IP address. The drawbacks of maintaining a static, textual database of system names becomes apparent when considering a network of more than a few dozen systems. DNS was developed to overcome these limitations and dynamically provide name services as the Internet grew and evolved. Even though the original designers of DNS had no idea the Internet would grow to millions of systems internationally, the system has, with a few enhancements along the way, scaled quite well.

DNS works in a totally distributed environment, which adds to its scalability. When you ask to be connected to a domain, InterNIC provides the DNS IP address to your software. This address is not the address of the system you are looking for; instead, it is an address to a system that will know where to look to find your site.

The DNS name space is a tree. Domain names are leaf-nodes and systems are leaves on the tree. A fully qualified domain name is constructed by concatenating the domain names to the system name from left to right as you climb the tree. Each component is separated by a dot. The root domain is omitted.

New to Windows NT 4.0 is a native DNS service. Previously, third-party DNS packages had to be purchased or, more likely, DNS services were provided by UNIX systems. You can install the Windows NT DNS service as you do other network services.

- From the Network applet within the Control Panel, choose the Services tab.
- Click the Add button to get a list of services available under Windows NT Server.
- Select Microsoft DNS Server and click OK.
- If the Windows NT Server CD-ROM is not available, type the path to the distribution files.

The setup program installs the DNS service and copies several files to the `%system root%\system32\dns\samples` directory. If you are building a DNS server from scratch, copy all of these files to the `%systemroot%\system32\etc` directory. You can modify the sample files to start creating your own DNS configuration.

If your DNS is currently maintained on a UNIX system, copy the appropriate files from the `/etc` directory on the UNIX system. The Windows NT main DNS configuration file is named BOOT. If you are migrating from another system, you may need to rename your current configuration file to BOOT. All of the other database files are referenced from within this file.

N O T E DNS and how it works is a very complex topic, warranting its own book. The now-classic DNS book is *DNS and Bind* by Paul Albitz and Cricket Liu from O'Reilly and Associates, Inc. If you are new to DNS, find a copy of the book and start with it. If you are experienced with DNS, you can probably copy the necessary files from your current DNS server and go from there.

You can also find DNS information references on the Yahoo! search engine at `http://msn.yahoo.com/msn/Computers_and_Internet/Software/Protocols/DNS/`. ■

The Windows NT DNS service can integrate with the Windows Internet Name Service, or WINS. You may already be using WINS in combination with DHCP to dynamically manage your IP addresses on your internal networks. In this case, DNS handles name resolution at the upper layers and passes the request to WINS for final resolution. This capability is particularly important for those shops that use DNS and Dynamic Host Configuration Protocol, or DHCP.

Naming Your Site and Registering Your Name

Part
I
Ch
2

To start the process of obtaining a unique name assigned for your site's IP address, you'll need to first determine whether the names you're interested in are already in use. A good way to do this is to point your browser at **http://rs.internic.net/cgi-bin/whois** and provide the domain name you're interested in. See Listing 2.1 for an example.

Listing 2.1 Sample Listing for an Existing Domain Name

```
Integra Technology International, Inc. (INTEGRA2-DOM)
    3561 East Sunrise Drive #235
    Tucson, AZ 85718
    USA

    Domain Name: INTEGRA.NET

    Administrative Contact, Technical Contact, Zone Contact:
        Bernstein, Mike  (MB1415)  MikeB@INTEGRA.NET
        520-577-2661
    Billing Contact:
        Canatsey, Brian  (BC800)  BrianC@MIDAK-INT.COM
        520-577-2661

    Record last updated on 22-Jan-96.
    Record created on 22-Jan-96.

    Domain servers in listed order:

    MIDAKDNS.MIDAK-INT.COM        199.181.82.75
    INTEGRADNS.MIDAK-INT.COM      199.181.82.76


The InterNIC Registration Services Host contains ONLY Internet
➥ Information (Networks, ASN's, Domains, and POC's).
Please use the whois server at nic.ddn.mil for MILNET Information.
```

The other item you'll need before registering your name with InterNIC is two different DNS servers that can be used to reference your system on the Internet. With the distributed nature of the Internet, these servers provide the "hand-off point" for your domain name and IP address resolution. Once you have a name that is not yet registered, and you have the DNS servers to refer to your systems, you're ready to register your name with InterNIC.

TIP Have all of your DNS configurations done when you submit your entry to InterNIC for processing. Since you have no indication of when they'll be setting up your domain, you don't want to have your domain registration waiting on the setup of the DNS servers. You can access your domain while the registration is in process by going directly to the IP address, such as `http://198.68.72.1`.

N O T E Even though your domain name does not show up on a search of the currently assigned domain names, it may still have been requested by other users. Try to keep in mind an alternative domain name if the registration process uncovers any previous requests. Given the huge volume of requests InterNIC works on at any given time, there may be requests pending that may conflict with your choice.

This also leads to the suggestion that, if you need to have a name in the future, register it now. You can reserve the name and have it assigned to you even if it's not actively used by your organization. If you believe you'll be using a given name in the future, the cost of registration is minimal, but the cost of the hassle if you should be unable to get it in the future can be quite substantial. ■

As mentioned earlier, in order to be able to reference your domain name on the Internet, you must register it with InterNIC. You can start the process of registering your domain name on the Internet at **http://www.internic.net**.

InterNIC is responsible for managing domain names on the Internet. By registering with them, you can be sure that no one else has your domain name, and that no one uses your domain name in the future. Remember, your domain name is not only your unique "friendly" name on the Internet, but is also tied to your fixed IP address assigned by your Service Provider.

You can use registration services to accomplish this for you, or you can go to the InterNIC site and register your own name. Keep in mind that it takes between 20 and 30 days for your domain name to activate on the Internet. InterNIC is currently processing thousands of registrations every day.

The cost to register your domain name is $50 per year, with the first two years payable with the initial registration. You'll be billed in single-year increments after the first two years. This cost can be impacted slightly if you use a registration service, as they typically charge for their services to set up your account, both with InterNIC and on their DNS servers. At this writing, registration fees typically range from $25 to $100 in addition to the $50 per year that InterNIC charges.

Understanding TCP/IP

TCP/IP is a series of standardized protocols used to communicate on the Internet—and optionally, on your Intranet. TCP/IP is a combination protocol. The Transmission Control Protocol (TCP) portion represents the protocol used for the physical transmission of information over the network. IP is the specification for what is termed *connectionless datagram services*. These services not only enable you to send a message to a remote system, but they have a way of knowing whether the system received the message without actually connecting to the remote system.

The IP portion of the methodology refers to the addressing scheme used to manage information flow over the network. There are several different points to understand about IP addresses. How addresses break out and how they are defined are covered in the next section.

In short, TCP/IP is a method of ensuring accurate transmission of information on the network.

N O T E As with DNS, TCP/IP warrants an entire book or series of books to explain all of the details about how it works. To that end, consider reviewing the online bookstore's search engine by going to **http://www.mcp.com/bookstore/do-searches.html** and entering TCP/IP in the search criteria. You'll receive several different titles available that will be helpful. This section is provided only as a primer to explain what you'll need to get started setting up your network. ■

What Is an IP Address?

IP addresses are unique numbers assigned to your connections to the Internet. By examining the IP address for a given message, you can route the message to the correct recipient's system. Today, typical IP addresses break down into four segments, such as in the following example:

`199.89.62.10`

Segments are most significant for routing purposes from left to right. This means that the first numerical set is the most important for routing the message. IP addresses divide into *classes*. Classes refer to the type or uniqueness for an address and are assigned according to the values in Table 2.2.

Table 2.2	Determining IP Classes		
IP Address	**Class**	**Subnet Mask**	**Notes**
1.0 to 127.0	A	255.0.0.0	This address range supports approximately 16 million unique addresses.
128.0 to 191.255.0	B	255.255.0.0	Supports 65,536 addresses
192.0 to 223.255.255	C	255.255.255.0	Support for 255 addresses

The example address of 199.89.62.10 is a class C address. The subnet mask in the table is the mask determining the significant portion of the address. The subnet masks shown are typical for the address classes. While the topic is out of scope for this book, you also can use subnet masks to divide the addresses in a range, providing you with logical subnets in your network.

ON THE WEB

http://www.internic.net You can also find out more about IP addressing and subnets on the World Wide Web. You can find links to Requests for Comment (RFC) technical documents as well as a search engine to find the information you need. Be sure to check their site for the latest in evolving standards.

If you set up an Intranet with no outside connectivity to the Web, you can assign IP addresses of any values you like. Keep in mind, though, that if you connect to the Web in the future, you need to reestablish your IP addresses in line with Internet standards.

To get an idea of how your system is configured, check your IP address and subnet mask from your Windows 95 client by selecting Start, Run and specify **WINIPCFG** as the program to run. As you can see in Figure 2.2, after you select the Mo re Info>> button, the utility shows you your IP address, subnet mask, and more.

FIG. 2.2

The WINIPCFG.EXE utility shows the current computer name and the IP information for each active adapter in your system.

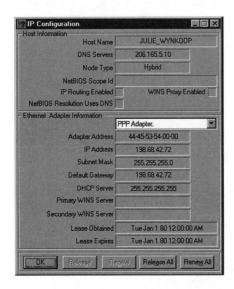

Your requirements will depend greatly on the server software you decide to use on your site. The operating system on which you base your site will largely dictate the type of computer. This can be anything from a 386 system with 8M of memory to a Pentium 200 or better with 64M of memory or more.

As an example, if you're going to be using Microsoft's IIS software, you need a system capable of running Windows NT Server version 3.51 or later. Although you can run the processes with as little as 16M of RAM, you should strongly consider a system with at least 32M of RAM, especially if you implement other services on the server or if you expect a heavily loaded system. Examples of loading factors include:

- Microsoft Exchange Server
- Microsoft SQL Server
- Heavy, constant usage of the Web, FTP, or Gopher engines
- Proxy Server Activity

> **N O T E** For a high-traffic site to use as an example, go to **http://www.microsoft.com**. They have 12 different systems with 128M of RAM each and four processors. Microsoft has moved FTP services to separate systems, leaving the main Web server free to serve requests for Web pages and shorter-length file transfers.
>
> As is the case with Microsoft's system, you may find after analyzing your usage patterns that it is necessary to break certain services apart so they reside on separate systems. Putting Exchange, SQL Server, the Proxy Server, and other server-based processes on the same system is a poor idea if you have more than moderate volume on any one of these services. ▪

Part
I
Ch
2

The required hard disk size will vary greatly from installation to installation. This is influenced by many factors, not the least of which is the size of your planned site. At a minimum, counting on a server with 1G of disk space is a good starting point, assuming that you have some or all of the services mentioned previously installed and running on your system. You also need to have a network card suitable for your connection to the network.

Other hardware may be necessary, depending on your configuration with the services, both Web server-related and otherwise. For example, if you establish this server as a wireless server, or if you use it for Remote Access Services (RAS) connections, you need to have an appropriate modem or modems installed at the server.

▶ For more information about installing, configuring, and maintaining your NT Server, refer to *Special Edition Using Microsoft NT Server* by Roger Jennings, published by Que Corporation.

Selecting the Right Operating System

Operating systems are very difficult to gauge and are littered with emotional attachments. The decision is further confused by vastly differing reviews of them. Keep in mind that the most important factor in your decision is probably not the operating system, but rather the server software that you choose. Once you select the server software, you may find that your operating system has been selected for you.

Understanding the Debate: Windows NT versus UNIX

This section will not make the decision any easier in your hunt for the perfect operating system. There are too many variables, and the items outlined here may muddy the waters even more. Perhaps, though, these will present some additional consideration items that you can combine with your own experiences to help determine the right course of action for you.

There are really two main options when it comes to operating systems for your Web server: UNIX and Windows NT. You can use other operating systems and computers, even Windows for Workgroups and Apple Macintosh systems. For performance-aware servers, however, the consensus among Web site administrators in general is strongly in favor of UNIX and Windows NT.

To be fair, both operating systems environments are extremely powerful and capable of hosting even the most trafficked of sites. It's difficult to go wrong with either choice, if you implement them correctly. Still, you will have to decide which is the best for you overall.

Selecting between these options relies on a number of variables. If the Web server software you're selecting supports both platforms, you'll need to consider other factors. Some of the key questions are:

- Are other systems using either of these platforms installed at your place of business?
- What are your technical resources expertise levels on these platforms?
- What other types of applications will you be running on these systems?
- What corporate directives do you have regarding the use of one or the other of these platforms?

It's easy to see that if you have previously installed servers using one of these platforms, you'll gain a certain amount of technical knowledge leverage in staying with the same environment. This relates strongly to the second item as well, that of preexisting technology resources that you may have access to. This is more than people, but also books you may have, contacts, employees, your own expertise, and so on. This is perhaps one of the strongest influences on the decision process. Be very careful on your weighting of this, however. While an option may be the most comfortable based on past experiences, it's probably possible to make a strong case in favor of either operating environment option.

A practical approach to determining the proper operating system is to examine the types of application support you want to provide on the system. If you'll be implementing applications such as the Microsoft BackOffice suite and other applications in that realm, Windows NT is the only choice. Windows NT also has a massive software development following, which means software will continue to be actively developed for it.

If, on the other hand, you need to support existing applications, such as powerful database engines and applications that run on specific operating systems, you'll need to go the UNIX route. There are other factors important to this decision, including stability, time on the market, and your own personal preferences for how you prefer the user interface, just to name a few.

Windows NT has been described as "UNIX with fine clothes." Windows NT implements many of the same functions as UNIX, but it adds the Graphical User Interface to these applications. This makes bringing up the server more intuitive. Everything from DNS services to setting up the server software is completed by answering interactive prompts and letting the system do the work for you. Many of the capabilities NT offers have been offered in UNIX for many years. The multi-user aspects of UNIX's operating system and security subsystem are excellent.

UNIX is a well-established operating system offering significant technical backing as well. This means you'll find easy access to technical resources such as books, developers and support personnel. With standardization of low-level development languages, the gap in development tools between UNIX and Windows NT has somewhat closed, allowing for better portability between environments for applications developers.

UNIX is largely text-based, and has well-established tools and utilities. Its power comes from the fact that it is a standardized environment that has been built from the ground up for multi-user, multitasking, secure operation. UNIX takes no more or less effort to learn than Windows NT, if you have to climb one learning curve or the other, and there is a large assortment of public domain, freeware, and commercially available applications to help with your Internet efforts.

UNIX's time on the market means a certain level of maturity in the additional utilities as well. Logging, analysis, and troubleshooting utilities are readily available, and the information gleaned from these services is generally low-level enough to point to a problem directly. This is not yet true for Windows NT, still in its relative infancy as an operating system. The utilities for Windows NT can be lacking in their analysis, and relying on the Event Log subsystem to tell exactly what's happening can be disappointing. With Windows NT, there are fewer public domain, freeware, and shareware utilities that offer "down and dirty" analysis of the system when problems do occur.

On the other hand, Windows NT is also a robust operating system featuring tight integration between the operating system and the Web services, at least in the case of the Internet Information Server from Microsoft. NT includes attributes such as integration of the users' desktop Office applications and the BackOffice applications suite. Windows NT presents somewhat of a paradigm shift in how it presents the network, the associated services, and solutions. Windows NT has not been traditionally considered a candidate for hosting Web services, but Microsoft has of late proven that the platform is not only viable, but can be a high-performance, stable, and secure environment for hosting Web sites and more.

Examining Major Server Software Players in the Internet Marketplace

When it comes to Internet server software, there are two major names in the market, accompanied by several additional, though lesser-known, alternatives. Of course, the big names are Netscape and Microsoft. Netscape, best known for their innovative browser Netscape Navigator, has a powerful suite of server software that includes e-mail, Gopher, and FTP services. They have several different offerings in this arena, and they support several different operating systems. To that end, Netscape is, as of this writing, a market-leader in the Internet server and browser market.

Microsoft's offerings provide a lesson in what can be done when extreme pressure and amazing amounts of talented resources are applied to a problem. The problem in this case was Microsoft's non-presence in the Internet marketplace in the recent past. After Microsoft saw the potential, and after Bill Gates decided to address the Internet and its potential, things rapidly changed. Microsoft is now one of the biggest, fastest-emerging technological, if not marketshare, leaders in the Internet playing field.

Microsoft's Internet Explorer and Netscape's browser are running in a leapfrog race for features, standards, and innovation. The result has been fabulous for the user community, which is now starting to benefit from scripting technology alternatives, database interaction, platform options, and more.

TIP If you have a favorite site, or if you're simply curious, there is an Internet service that will query a site and tell you what brand and version of server software they're running. The URL for the site is **http://www.netcraft.co.uk/Survey/whats**. Simply enter the full site address, for example **www.integra.net**, and the Web-based form will tell you want software is active. See Figure 2.3 for an example.

FIG. 2.3
By querying a site, you can quickly determine what server software is popular on the sites you frequent.

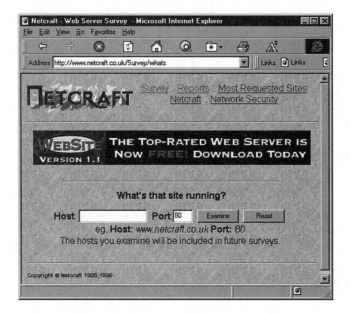

Understanding the Microsoft Server Software

Microsoft's Internet and Intranet strategy is now almost all-encompassing. Most Microsoft products on the near horizon incorporate Internet connections, from embedded hyperlinks to support for content retrieved from the Internet. This is one distinct difference between Microsoft and other vendors. Since Microsoft has so many different successful applications, by Internet-enabling their entire product line, the effect is that of suddenly bringing the Internet into play in many different areas of the average user. See Table 2.3 for examples of Microsoft's applications suite.

Table 2.3   Microsoft's Initiatives to Internet-Enable Software Are Company-Wide

Internet Information Server	IIS provides Web, FTP, and Gopher services to your users.
Exchange	Exchange is Microsoft's client/server mail system. Exchange provides access to public folders, connectivity to the Internet for electronic mail, and more.
Internet Software Development Kit (SDK)	If you do development work with IIS, you need the software development kit.
SQL Server	Microsoft's client/server database system is able to link not only with client/server applications, but Web-based applications as well.
SNA Server	The SNA server is a client/server system providing host access to your users.
Systems Management Server	SMS provides tools to manage your user base and their system configurations, and tools to satisfy your users' technical support needs.
Internet Explorer	The Internet Explorer provides the client-side Web browsing, FTP file transfer capabilities, and Gopher capabilities that are the core of your Internet and Intranet ventures.
FrontPage	An all-in-one Web site creation and management package that helps you design and manage a site through a graphical user interface.
Proxy Server	The Microsoft Proxy Server, code-named Catapult while in development, provides firewall security for your site. If you implement a system hosting a connection to both the Internet and your Intranet, carefully consider a proxy server.
Content Indexing and Searching	The indexing engine provides site search and retrieval capabilities.
Various	Other software, including Microsoft Office 95/97, the Office viewer add-ins, the Office Assistants for HTML content creation, and so on are all optional but helpful components.

As of this writing, you can also expect a new package from Microsoft, currently referred to as Normandy. This package provides additional capabilities and enhanced control over the Intranet and Internet environments. Among its features are a news server, mail server, and point-of-sale capability. Watch the Que Reality Check site at **http://www.mcp.com/que/ expert_developer/backokit/index.html** for more information on this technology as it is introduced.

Understanding the Netscape Server Software

Netscape has been working hard to increase its offerings in the Internet marketplace to keep up with the incredible demand. To answer the requests for bigger, more powerful servers and more comprehensive server software offerings, Netscape has introduced several server software suites, most of which include some or all of the components of the Netscape SuiteSpot Server. See Table 2.4 for a summary of the Netscape offerings.

Table 2.4 Netscape's Server Software Offerings	
Enterprise Server	The server provides Web services to your users.
Mail Server	The mail server is Netscape's SMTP messaging system that enables e-mail for your user base.
News Server	Providing access to more than 15,000 newsgroups, the news server enables you to bring up your own news server, a great tool for collaborative discussions.
Catalog Server	The catalog server is a content search engine for your Intranet. Likened to a Yahoo! search engine for your internal Web.
Proxy Server	A proxy server provides firewall security for your site. If you implement a system hosting a connection to both the Internet and your Intranet, carefully consider a proxy server.
Directory Server	The Directory Server provides tools to combine disparate directory systems to make looking up people and resources easier.
Certificate Server	The certificate server lets you set up your own certificate authorities and manage your certificates for secure transmissions.
Netscape Navigator	The Navigator provides the Web browsing, FTP file transfer capabilities, and Gopher capabilities that are the core of your Internet and Intranet ventures. In addition, Navigator Gold features a content development system that allows you to author pages for the Internet.
LiveWire, LiveWire Pro	The LiveWire system lets you work with HTML and site management issues.

Netscape offers much of their software on a variety of platforms, including Windows NT and various versions of UNIX.

Understanding the NCSA Apache Server Software Options

The NCSA HTTPD server for UNIX provides Web services by making HTTP documents available to Web browsers. NCSA started out with the original, very popular Mosaic software, a Web browser application that was the foundation for Netscape's browser.

Reality Check

The Reality Check with this chapter is that no single option will solve all of your needs. To help understand this, consider the Integra site at **http://www.integra.net**. The problem we faced at this site was that of providing economical, high-performance access to the site. Of course, the inherent conflict between high-performance and economy produced quite a quandary when it came to selecting an Internet Service Provider.

The site has several goals, one of which is to provide the capability to download software products. The software ZIP files available to be downloaded are in excess of 6M in size, so the time on the line between the downloading party and the site is bound to be substantial. In addition, as you'll soon find out, determining what to expect for loading is a mixed science. The line speed of the initial Web site into Integra wouldn't support a number of people downloading the software simultaneously. At the same time, increasing the bandwidth on the line didn't seem to make sense.

The solution was to purchase disk space on an ISP's system. We shopped the ISP options, found out what types of connections each ISP had to the Internet, and, of course, found out what the costs were. We learned that some ISPs charge for download volumes from your site, while others don't. If you expect any significant amounts of traffic at all, be sure you query your potential ISP to find out what they charge.

The ISP we selected has multiple T1 access to the Internet and does not charge for download volumes. Integra placed the different data files on their server and provided protected links from our system to those files. The result is that the user accesses the Integra site, registers for the downloads, and is then transparently shifted to the T1 servicing the ISP. This means faster download times for the user, and at the same time optimum use of the Integra connection to the Internet. Integra also retains control of the user, to make sure the user's information is gathered before the download takes place.

 If you don't want to advertise for the ISP you select, try pinging their domain name to obtain the IP address they use. In your URL specifications from your site, give the IP address in place of the domain name. For example, if you're using an ISP at the **http://www.integra.net/files/public/wireless** URL, and the **www.integra.net** URL responds to the IP address of 199.181.82.78, you can provide an URL of **http://199.181.82.78/files/public/wireless** instead. This way, it's less apparent to the users that they are, in fact, downloading information from an alternate site.

From Here...

You've seen quite a lot of foundation-type information for your Web site in this chapter. From here, you'll start to see how you can apply this information, install and implement your Web site, and make it a success, whether it be for an Internet or Intranet installation. The following chapters will be of special interest as you start on your installation ventures:

- Chapter 5, "Setting Up and Configuring a Web Server," shows the specifics of installing several different Web servers.

- Chapter 6, "Setting Up an FTP Site," goes into detail about how you can set up your FTP server to provide the best possible level of service for your users.

- Chapter 9, "Firewalls and Proxy Servers," explains how the proxy servers work and outlines the considerations you'll want to think about when selecting a proxy server and firewall.

## CHAPTER 3

Planning an Intranet Site

Intranets are predicted to be the biggest Internet-related marketplace in the coming years, and for good reason. Many companies already have a wealth of information assembled that employees could benefit from. Intranets offer new ways of accessing this information, both with and without the use of the native applications in which the objects were originally created.

One key feature of the Intranet is that it's secure. You have complete control over who accesses your system and what they'll be accessing it with in terms of client-side software. This is in contrast to the Internet where you are faced with the requirement to address the security of your system since it's so much more open to the general public.

With Internet access for the masses only recently becoming a reality, many in upper management don't understand the access controls even when they are implemented. The action too many managers take is to effectively ban access to the Internet until they understand more about the connection. Add to this the fact that corporate confidential information simply has no business being on the Internet, and you can start to see why Intranets are sure to become extremely important to the corporate world. ■

Find out how to plan the installation of your server to support your Intranet

Using content on your Intranet may require special considerations when setting up the server. Find out what these are and how to implement them.

See how to use viewers and provide them to your users to get the most from your Intranet

When you enable users to see and work with content in its native format, they are able to get more done, faster. Find out how the viewers work and how to make them available to your user community.

Find out about the differences between some security models

UNIX, Linux, and Windows NT have different security models. Find out how they're implemented and how they affect your site.

▶ For more information on security, firewalls, and other techniques for protecting your site, see Chapter 9, "Firewalls and Proxy Servers." In addition, be sure to check out the installation information for the server you are using, as it may contain additional information about server-level access controls that you can implement. For more on the servers and their installation, see Chapter 5, "Setting up and Configuring a Web Server."

Understanding Intranets

An Intranet is that part of a network residing either behind a firewall or completely removed from the Internet. Typically, Intranets are corporate-wide information systems protected from outside users and containing proprietary information databases.

Intranets offer some unique new capabilities not feasible on a typical Internet-based system. Because you know the configuration and system requirements for the systems within your company, you can implement some features that require certain hardware or software that you could not depend on every Internet user to have. In fact, in many cases, evolved standards are implemented to ensure the systems run the selected software for your company.

Reasons for using an Intranet within a company range from providing online assistance for a product support group to workgroup collaboration on documents, databases, and other shared environments. By installing an Intranet, you can create shared environment by allowing more people access to the information they need to succeed at their jobs. In the product support example, you can implement systems that mimic applications that are supported without actually installing those applications. By showing diagrams, screen shots, and other information, and then mapping that information to a knowledge base database, the Intranet quickly becomes a key player in supporting the technicians that support your customers.

Intranets offer some advantages regarding configuration as well. Since you know the configuration of the systems on your internal networks, you can begin to use some specific tools to provide information to your user base. For example, on the World Wide Web, it's not very feasible to offer information in a solely Microsoft Word format without also providing that information in other formats. Because you are unfamiliar with the tools available to someone browsing your Web pages, you need to make sure your content is available to the lowest common denominator. This often forces you to present in HTML format, raw ASCII text files, and usually in many different formats as well.

Using an Intranet, you're free to distribute information by using those tools most likely to reside on a user's desktop system. This means if the source document is in Microsoft Word format, you can post the Word document as is, without converting it to HTML or text format.

On your local network, you can ensure that users have access to Word or the Word viewer applications to see the work as you intend it, without the need to plan for multiple, disparate platforms.

ON THE WEB

http://www.microsoft.com   Microsoft's Web site includes the latest versions of its different content viewers, including Word, Excel, and PowerPoint. You should check this site occasionally to ensure that you're offering the most recent release of the viewers you incorporate.

Understanding How Viewers Work

Setting up an Intranet is typically less demanding in the planning area than an Internet site because you won't need to worry about providing content and connectivity to outside users. Setting up the Intranet server requires only installation of the server software on the operating system you select. The hardware requirements are not much more than those of the platform you select as a bare minimum. Once you've started your Intranet, you'll be able to gauge performance and utilization and determine what types of resources would most benefit your system. To start your setup, you can use a basic server with minimal memory and hard disk space available. The actual requirements will vary with the operating system you use, so be sure to check into these requirements before you decide on the system to use as your initial server.

In many cases, disk space is a quickly emerging problem area because, as you allow more users to have access and contribute materials to the Intranet, quite a lot of material can be gathered quickly. The other area you can manage that will have a substantial impact not only on cost, but on the performance of your server is memory. Especially with a Windows NT-based system, you'll find that RAM is one of the items you can add to your server to increase performance on the whole.

Retrieving Documents on an Intranet

This section provides a quick overview of how you can access resources on an Intranet. You'll find additional information about specific topics in the chapters that relate more closely to those topics.

When you access a site, the directory and file name are provided as part of the URL. This is true whether the URL references an HTTP-based site or a site that you gain information from by using the FILE protocol. For example, if you want to review the SPEC.DOC file located on the server NETSERVER1 in the directory MyDOCS, the following URLs provide you with a copy of this file, assuming you have rights to the directory and files:

```
http://netserver1/mydocs/spec.doc
file:///netserver1/mydocs/spec.doc
```

N O T E   In some older browsers, some of the newer URL types are not supported. The "File:" URL is an example of this as it's not supported in Netscape's Navigator until its version 3.0 product. ■

In either case, notice that the extension of the file, in this case DOC, is specified, just as you would specify it if you were opening the file locally on your system. When your browser begins receiving the file, it examines the extension. As with other applications and data files on your system, if an application is associated with the extension, the application loads automatically. This may be anything from an in place OLE server to a viewer such as the Word and Excel viewers discussed in the "Making Viewers Available" sections.

Keeping this in mind, as long as extensions and content remain tied together, for the browser's sake at least, there are nearly unending possibilities for the client-side functionality offered by the Web.

In the next portion of this chapter, you'll see how to install and use just a few of the many add-ins that are currently available for your network. The listings are not provided as any type of comprehensive list, but only to show the types of things available. It's no exaggeration to say that more of these types of functional extensions are coming on the market every day and they're getting better and better.

Connecting to Your Internal Network (Intranet)

Once you have set up your server (see Chapter 5), the next step is to set up the server to be accessible to other network users. This chapter references the Microsoft server in examples, but they are valid with other servers as well.

The key to setting up for the Internet Information Server (IIS) software is the Transmission Control Protocol/Internet Protocol (TCP/IP). You set up this option by installing the appropriate driver stack in the Control Panel. This is a requirement if your users access the system from either the internal or external sites.

Your system probably connects by using an Ethernet adapter over a 10baseT line, similar to a phone line in appearance. When your system is connected to the central hub that connects your other systems to the network, your server can start providing content to your users.

For your Intranet name, use the computer name that was established for your system. The most recent versions of web browsers recognize computer names as residing on the local network when you specify them as a Universal Resource Locator (URL). It is not necessary to preface the address with **http://**.

N O T E Most e-mail applications now highlight a URL if it's found in a mail message by underlining it. By using this feature, your users can exchange addresses for information on your Intranet by simply placing them in their mail messages to other users. By including the hyperlink in the format **http://server/filename**, the recipient of the mail message can simply click the link and be taken directly to the file. See Figure 3.1 for an example of this. ▓

FIG. 3.1
Adding hyperlinks to mail messages helps to point the way directly to the object you're referring to for the message's recipients.

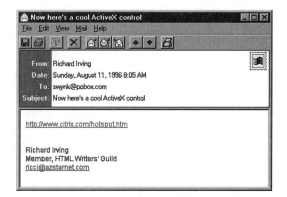

Configuring Your Server's Content Capabilities

There isn't too much to be done on the server side to support these add-in tools, aside from making sure you map them to the correct type of information transfer. The server is config-ured to send files and content using different formats that a typical browser will understand. Non-text information is sent by using MIME (Multipurpose Internet Mail Extension) protocol.

Configuring IIS's MIME Types

On IIS, you configure MIME types with the same type mapping as when you set up the Gopher server and its related content. You must set up the content type, the extension that it relates to, and the Gopher information type. Using this information, IIS can work more closely with the browser.

If you have a file that does not map directly to a MIME type, it is sent to the browser with the asterisk (*) type designation. Typically, the browser responds by prompting the user to save the file to disk, unless the browser has the capability to recognize the file type locally and re-spond with the appropriate viewer.

With the Microsoft Internet Explorer, if you transfer a DOC file, for example, Internet Explorer automatically loads the appropriate application. This may be the viewer, Microsoft Word, or another application associated with that extension, and it loads when the file is finished trans-ferring.

N O T E Remember, you don't typically have to update these keys to enable the browser to correctly use the appropriate viewer. The only time you should modify these values is if you're implementing non-standard content extensions. ■

On the server, if you want to add mappings to the Registry, you need to do so with the Registry Editor. The keys are located in the following Registry key:

```
HKEY_LOCAL_MACHINE\SYSTEM\CurrentControlSet\Services\InetInfo\
➥ Parameters\MimeMap
```

The items in this key are the different MIME mappings. Each item has the same format, as noted in the preceding listing, indicating the Gopher type corresponding to the data type to be associated with the information being transferred.

The format of the entry is:

`description,extension,reserved,gopher type`

The entry, when you add the new value to the Registry Key, is of type string. To add a new value, first move to the correct location in the tree. You should have MimeMap highlighted in the left pane. Click any value in the right pane and select Edit, Add Value from the menus. Figure 3.2 shows the dialog box that prompts you for the key information.

FIG. 3.2

File transfer formats help the browser determine how to display retrieved information.

NOTE You must enter all of the key value in the first prompt for Value Name. You also must choose a Data Type of REG_SZ, indicating a string. Once you select OK, the Registry Editor prompts you for a string value. You can leave this item blank, as it is not interpreted when the key is retrieved. ■

In Table 3.1, you can see some of the more frequently used MIME types and how they map in the Registry for IIS. The type of file transfer used determines how the browser displays the content. For the items in the table that have an asterisk, for example, the browser examines the extension of the incoming object and compares it against the local copy of the Registry. If it finds a file association, the helper application loads to display the item.

Table 3.1   Gopher MIME Transfer Types

Type	Meaning0 Text file
1	Gopher directory listing
4	Binary/Hex Macintosh file
5	MS-DOS Binary file
6	UUencoded file
9	Binary file
g	Graphic Interchange File graphic (GIF) (displays as a picture in most graphical browsers)
h	HTML World Wide Web hypertext page

Type	Meaning0 Text file
:	Bitmap image
;	Movie
<	Sound file

Items that don't directly match the multitude of predefined mappings on the server transfer with a type of 5, indicating a DOS binary file. This enables the browser to step in and handle the items.

Configuring Servers Other Than IIS

If you're not using IIS, but are using HTTPD, your server likely stores the file in the `c:\httpd\conf\mime.typ` subdirectory. If you're using HTTPD for Windows, or in the UNIX environment, you can find the file in `/usr/local/etc/httpd/conf/mime.types`. For other servers, you need to check the documentation index for reference to establishing the MIME mapping properties for the server. The files used to determine the server configuration are shown there, along with information pertaining to how you can add or remove types, make changes to existing types, and other system administration duties.

Some typical MIME type mappings are shown in Table 3.2.

Part

I

Ch

3

Table 3.2 Typical MIME Extension Mappings

MIME Type	File Extension
application/mac-binhex40	hqx
application/octet-stream	bin
application/oda	oda
application/pdf	pdf
application/postscript	ai eps ps
application/rtf	rtf
application/x-mif	mif
application/x-csh	csh
application/x-dvi	dvi
application/x-hdf	hdf
application/x-latex	latex
application/x-netcdf	nc cdf
application/x-sh	sh

continues

Table 3.2   Continued

MIME Type	File Extension
application/x-tcl	tcl
application/x-tex	tex
application/x-texinfo	texinfo texi
application/x-troff	t tr roff
application/x-troff-man	man
application/x-troff-me	me
application/x-troff-ms	ms
application/x-wais-source	src
application/zip	zip
application/x-bcpio	bcpio
application/x-cpio	cpio
application/x-gtar	gtar
application/x-shar	shar
application/x-sv4cpio	sv4cpio
application/x-sv4crc	sv4crc
application/x-tar	tar
application/x-ustar	ustar
audio/basic	au snd
audio/x-aiff	aif aiff aifc
audio/x-wav	wav
image/gif	gif
image/ief	ief
image/jpeg	jpeg jpg jpe
image/tiff	tiff tif
image/x-cmu-raster	ras
image/x-portable-anymap	pnm
image/x-portable-bitmap	pbm
image/x-portable-graymap	pgm
image/x-portable-pixmap	ppm

MIME Type	File Extension
image/x-rgb	rgb
image/x-xbitmap	xbm
image/x-xpixmap	xpm
image/x-xwindowdump	xwd
text/html	html htm htl
text/plain	txt c cc h
text/richtext	rtx
text/tab-separated-values	tsv
text/x-setext	etx
video/mpeg	mpeg mpg mpe
video/quicktime	qt mov moov
video/x-msvideo	avi
video/x-sgi-movie	movie

Providing Access to Information

Intranets remove some of the boundaries typically found with an Internet server. This is especially true when it comes to the size of objects presented on the Intranet. Because connection speeds are much faster than access times found when coming in over the Internet, you can skip at least some of the cautions about file size, image sizes, and so on.

The connection speed increase on Intranets also lends itself to using Internet content in its native format, rather than converting it to HTML for translation. Because this is true, you can post files rather than Web pages. For example, if you have a document that you've created that contains information on a worksheet, you can post the worksheet itself rather than posting an HTML table version of it. When users review the document, they can do so with either a viewer or the native application, depending on what is installed on their local machine.

The promise of your Intranet, and indeed the Internet, goes beyond just browsing content and referencing standard HTML pages. The real power behind this type of connectivity is the ability to view rich content or living documents. These are great buzzwords, and they represent some good technological capabilities. Internet and Intranet capabilities are starting to come of age in how they recognize the vast number of users and their expectations of the Internet. More sophisticated Web users and their software expect things like video, audio, animation, and more.

It would be an amazing feat to have to address these capabilities—and those that will be introduced tomorrow, and the next day —in any given fixed function browser. In fact, it would be nearly impossible. Browsers are released in increments that cannot begin to keep up with the changing specifications, capabilities, and increasing volume on a given network. To address the ever-increasing capabilities on the network, browsers are being created that enable you to extend their functionality with enhancement modules. Netscape refers to these add-on modules as *plug-ins*, which has quickly become the standard industry term for this capability, regardless of the browser.

In Figure 3.3 you can see that a PowerPoint presentation is loaded in the browser space in the Internet Explorer. While the presentation is indeed a PowerPoint ActiveX object, the PowerPoint Viewer makes it possible to view this document without launching a separate instance of PowerPoint.

FIG. 3.3
Viewers let you see the content you have downloaded from within the browser.

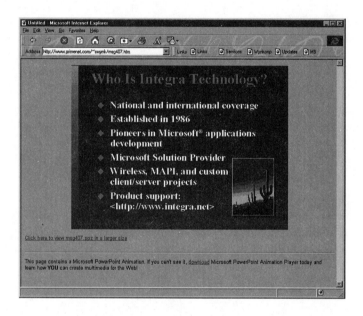

This capability is what keeps your time and energy investment in your browser from becoming invalid over time. Since users already know how to use the browser, all they need to do is to understand the specific add-in's capability and they can then understand how to work with the content.

Making the Viewers Available

If you are allowing your user base to access the Internet, as may be the case if you're using a proxy server or other gateway type of application, you should consider creating a page with links to appropriate viewers.

In cases where you have granted this type of external access, don't put the viewers on your site. If you do, you'll have out-of-date materials as soon as they are updated at their source. By linking to the original source of software, you are assured of the latest version.

Different Viewers and How to Use Them

Viewers range in function from letting you view content in its native form, as in the case of the Word viewer, to adding special functionality to your browser. These latter types of viewers can include support for development languages, 3-D virtual worlds, and more.

▶ Microsoft also publishes a number of Internet Assistants, also available at **http://www.microsoft.com/msdownload**, that give the Office applications the capability of generating the HTML code automatically. These applications take your existing content and translate it to a similar page created with HTML. For more information about these assistants, see Chapter 8, "Running an Intranet Site."

For a specific type of document or object, there may be several different ways to view it. In the case of a document, for example, you may want to use the Word viewer, or you may want to use the Adobe Acrobat reader to see the document if it's in a format more suitable for that viewer. One site located at **http://htext.com/HTMLCREA/htmlapps.html** contains 15 pages of add-ins, plug-ins, and helper applications that can be used by many of today's more popular browsers.

When you download and install a viewer, it's called up automatically when you load an object associated with the utility. Depending on the version of the utility, it may activate the content within your browser, or it may invoke an outside application to let you work with the content.

In some cases, the content is read-only, but you typically have the option of printing it and/or saving it locally. In the next few sections, you'll see how you can install the Microsoft viewers for several of the applications in the Microsoft Office suite.

ON THE WEB

http://www.microsoft.com/msdownload/   The Microsoft viewers are available from the Microsoft Web site's Free Downloads section located at. They are also included on the CD that comes with this book.

Installing and Using the Microsoft Word Viewer

One of viewers that is likely to gain wide usage and acceptance in your organization is the Microsoft Word viewer. This viewer lets you view documents from within the browser, keeping the rich formatting offered by Word in place in the document. The viewer presents the user with a read-only window to the document, but still allows for printing, saving, and opening other documents. When used with a Web browser, the viewer becomes the application that replaces the Web browser's role as presenter of the information in the document.

In some cases, depending on the version and brand of Web browser you're using, the viewer can even be activated in place. This means that it is activated in the actual Web browser window, and temporarily takes control of your Web browser, adding new menu and toolbar options. Figure 3.4 shows what the viewer looks like as you display a document.

Part

I

Ch

3

FIG. 3.4
The Word Viewer even allows you to print the document, fully formatted, without launching Word.

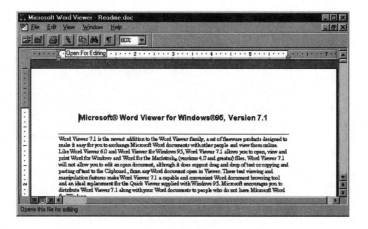

N O T E As with many of the viewers you can obtain, there is more than one version of the Word Viewer. There is a version for Word 6.x documents and a version for Office 95 (Word 7) documents. The differences between the two are subtle but important. In the Office 95 version, you can follow links to other documents or Web objects. Also, the user interface for the Office 95 version is slightly different, offering a toolbar and the capability to edit the object by simply calling it up in Word if Word is installed on your system. You can also view Word 6 documents with the newer viewer.

Be sure of two things when you obtain the viewer. First, make sure that it is the most recent version, and, second, make sure that you're getting the correct version for the objects you're trying to view. ■

Installation Considerations   When you install the Word viewer, what you see will vary a bit with the type and version of the viewer you're installing. With versions later than those supporting Word 6, the installation process will simply copy the files to your system and update the Registry. With the Word 6 version, if you have Word installed on your system, the objects you encounter automatically open in Word, not the viewer. In other words, if you have Word, installing the Word 6 Viewer will not provide any benefit to you unless you explicitly load the viewer and then load the document you want to review.

The Office 95 version asks whether you want to use the viewer as your default viewer for documents. Figure 3.5 shows the dialog that you can use to select the viewer as your primary means of reviewing these types of documents.

If you allow the viewer to be the default application for working with these types of objects, any time you open an object with an extension of DOC or DOT, they will open in the viewer. It's worth a minute or two of consideration about whether you want to make the viewer the default browser. There are quite a number of benefits, and the drawbacks are minimal.

Of key interest is the fact that the viewer is smaller, and therefore faster to load, than the full-blown Word application. If you find yourself waiting on your system while Word loads, starts up any initial processes, loads templates, and then loads your document, the viewer may be just the answer. By setting the viewer to be the default viewer for that file type, you save this time waiting for Word to load. You can still edit a document by selecting the Edit button, which loads Word as usual and passes the object to Word just as if you had called up Word originally.

FIG. 3.5
You should consider allowing the viewer to be the default mechanism for reviewing your documents, since it's faster to load and presents no roadblocks to editing an object that you're viewing.

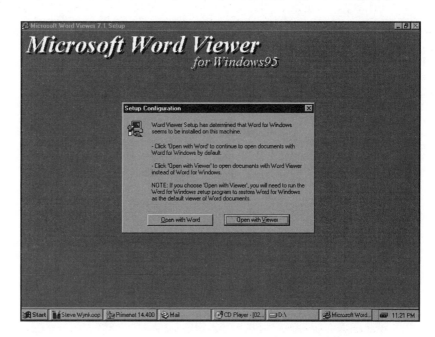

Using the Word Viewer   Using the viewer is easy and straightforward. When a document comes in over the network, if it has an appropriate name, it automatically opens in the correct viewer. You won't have to specifically load the viewer, as the Internet Explorer will load it for you.

Once in the viewer, you have several options, including how you want to review the document on-screen. You can use Page Layout, Normal, or Outline view. You can open additional documents, print the document, and format the page as you need it. The only thing missing is editing. You cannot make changes to the document. You can copy text to the Clipboard or to another document, however, and then make some modifications and save them in a separate document.

With more recent versions of viewers, you also can follow hyperlinks in the documents. If the author of the document inserted a hyperlink using the Internet Assistant for Word, you can simply click the link and the viewer loads the appropriate item for you.

If you set up the viewer as your default browser and you later determine that you want to use Word as your default browser instead, you can reinstall Office's default options by rerunning the setup program from the Office distribution set. When you do, run the setup program by using the /y parameter, indicating you want the settings in the installation refreshed. This removes the viewer from the content viewing options.

This also means that, if your browser encounters a DOC file, it loads Word instead of the viewer. You may have noticed that you can also set up file associations in the Internet Explorer that you can configure the Helper Applications and the applications they use. See Figure 3.6 for an example.

FIG. 3.6

You can control which applications your browser uses to view your content by setting up the file associations within Internet Explorer and other browsers.

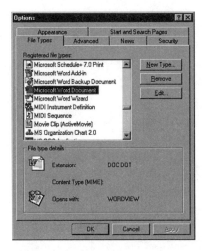

CAUTION

Be advised, though, that if you do this, you'll be changing settings system-wide, at least in the case of Internet Explorer. The application uses the system Registry to determine what items to load. If you make changes here in Internet Explorer, they will be reflected in other places if you load the same type of object. For example, if you indicate that files with an extension of .doc should be loaded with the snafu.exe application, this will hold true anytime you open a DOC file, whether it be from the Windows Explorer or from the Internet Explorer.

In some browsers, such as Netscape Navigator, this is less of an issue, as they maintain their own database of helper applications. In these cases, you may want to consider making the viewer your default for Internet content, and allow Word to be the viewer for other instances of these types of objects.

 One of the excellent side effects of the viewer applications is their inability to process macro commands from the incoming objects. This means that any virus or other problem materials that you may encounter are effectively neutralized, at least until they're opened in the native application.

The Microsoft Excel Viewer

As with the Word Viewer, the Excel Viewer makes viewing Excel worksheets from your browser convenient. Of course, the difference lies in the fact that with worksheets, you're working with columnar data, often consisting of formulas and dependencies.

As you can see in Figure 3.7, the Excel Viewer provides the same look and feel as Excel, while offering read-only access to the file.

FIG. 3.7

The Excel viewer brings with it the familiar look and feel of a worksheet.

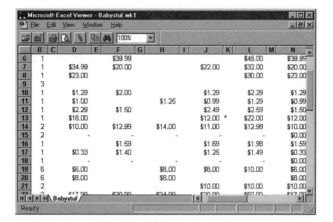

If you load a worksheet that contains modules, the tabs appear along the bottom of the display, but they are shown as standard worksheets with gridlines. As with the Word Viewer, Excel Viewer does not run code, so the modules are ignored. You are able to see any macro tabs you have, but as with modules, there is no mechanism for running them.

Another facet of the Excel viewer is that you cannot see the formulas. This can be a blessing and a curse, depending on what you distribute and what type of feedback you solicit. If you present only numbers, and the method of obtaining the numbers is not relevant to or needed by the person using the worksheet, this is a great way to protect your worksheet. If, on the other hand, you find you need to provide access to the formulas, the viewer may not be the answer for providing access to your worksheet. Keep in mind, though, that if you do have Excel loaded on your system, you can select File, Edit and load the native application to gain full access to the file.

Installation Considerations As you saw with the Word viewer, you have the option of making the Excel Viewer the default viewer for any object that you would normally open with Excel. Viewers load quickly and provide a good viewing medium for people who care about the results of your work rather than the behind-the-scenes information. Viewers are excellent tools for upper management when it comes to reviewing reports, budgets, and the like.

It's a good idea to select the default viewer to be the Excel Viewer. If, after an object loads, you find that it is something you want to work with, you can still do so by choosing to edit it. As with the other Office applications, if you do later decide to reverse this decision to use the viewer, you can do so by running the Office setup application with the /y switch on the command line.

Using the Excel Viewer   Using the Excel Viewer is simple. You have nearly all of the browsing options available that you have in Excel. You cannot make changes to the worksheets, but you can copy from them, taking the values and placing them into another application or worksheet.

Notice, too, that if you load a worksheet with outlining turned on and active, the viewer supports the display and manipulation of the outlined items. You also can use the data filtering with the AutoFilter option. It supports changing the panes and freezing them for viewing, as well as setting the column width and row height.

In short, it supports any manipulation of the look of the data, but not manipulation of the data itself.

The Microsoft PowerPoint Viewer

PowerPoint is a powerful tool for creating graphically-based materials. It's usually used to create materials for computer-based presentations, and if you've used PowerPoint 4 or later, you've no doubt used it for this purpose. One of the things PowerPoint does well is work with graphics. You can use PowerPoint's graphical capabilities in several ways to enhance your Web content, such as in the following ways:

- Create graphical images and then use the images in your HTML document.
- Create presentations with the PowerPoint Internet Assistant.
- Create ActiveX presentations with the Export functionality of the PowerPoint Assistant.
- Create native PowerPoint presentations and use the viewer to provide access to them on your site.

Both the viewer and the ActiveX approach enable you to view the presentations as standard PowerPoint presentations, rather than as pages created with the PowerPoint Assistant.

ON THE WEB

You can download the viewers from the Microsoft web site, located at **http://www.microsoft.com**.

In some cases, you may find that it's better to create HTML pages with the PowerPoint Assistant than it is to use the viewer to view native PowerPoint documents. If you create the pages with PowerPoint Assistant, they display in any Web browser, and your users don't need to have either the viewer or PowerPoint. HTML pages also load faster than a PowerPoint presentation does. The downside is that the images you see on an HTML page might not be as high-quality as those in the original PowerPoint presentation, and you won't be able to provide some of the more exotic features of PowerPoint like transitions and sounds.

Installing the PowerPoint Viewer   There are two ways to install the viewer—you can do it when you install PowerPoint on your system, or you can download it from **http:// www.microsoft.com/msdownload** or some other online service. You can provide a link to the software on your Internet site if it's required or helpful for reviewing the content on your site.

Installing the viewer is as easy as running the self-extracting file, PPTVW32.EXE. The program prompts you to accept the license agreement for the software, and then installs to either the existing PowerPoint subdirectory or to a directory you select during the standardized installation process.

Once the viewer is installed, your browser uses it automatically when needed.

> **N O T E**   With other viewers, it's possible to indicate which viewer you'd like to use as your default content browser. This can be either the complete application, like Microsoft Word for documents, or the newly installed viewer application. This is not the case with the PowerPoint viewer. If you have PowerPoint installed, the application will remain the default choice for browsing content. If you want to use the PowerPoint viewer, you need to manually open it to review the content online. ■

Using the PowerPoint Viewer   Using the PowerPoint viewer or PowerPoint is as simple as clicking the link to the document you want to view. There is not much to see except for the presentation when the show is running, as it runs full screen by default. There are a number of options that you can set, but to do so, you need to open the viewer manually. See Figure 3.8 for an example of the manual interface for the viewer.

FIG. 3.8
You can set the viewer options for future presentations by starting the viewer (PPVIEW32.EXE) manually and then modifying the options presented.

Perhaps one of the most interesting options for viewing content online in this manner is the Run in a Window feature. Using this option, you can still view and advance the presentation, but it executes in a window, providing you with continuing access to your other applications, including the Web browser.

T I P If you develop content that you want users who have the viewer to read, consider making the slides advance automatically. By doing so, you can make sure the user doesn't open the presentation and, being possibly unfamiliar with PowerPoint, get stuck on the first slide, not knowing how to advance the presentation.

As an alternative, consider placing a standard first slide in all online presentations you provide. This slide should show how to move about in a presentation and how to exit the presentation, and provide other tips for using the viewer.

One final point is to make sure you name your presentation with standardized extensions. While it's certainly possible to modify file extensions and behaviors on your system, you don't have this same level of control over the people that may be browsing your content online. Name your PowerPoint objects with the .ppt extension, your Excel worksheets with the .xls extension, and your Word documents with the standard .doc extension. This ensures the greatest compatibility on the various systems referencing your content.

Adobe Products

Adobe Systems Inc.'s claim to fame is in their handling of complex, often graphic-intensive documents. Adobe's Acrobat product is quickly becoming one of the most widely used viewers. The viewer is so popular because is retains the rich formatting of the underlying document, and at the same time presents the document in read-only fashion, protecting the document from being modified accidentally.

See Figure 3.9 for an example of using the Acrobat viewer to review content selected from the Web.

FIG. 3.9
The Adobe viewer lets you see the rich text formatting presented by PDF files.

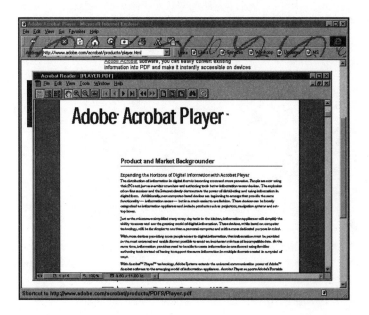

Adobe produces documents in Portable Document Format, or PDF, files. These files are built to be interchangeable between applications and environments, but are still in their relative infancy in accomplishing this goal. Even so, the documents can be used to present nicely for-matted, read-only information, complete with their fonts, font sizes, layout information, etc.

You install the Adobe Acrobat reader by downloading it from the Adobe site. See Figure 3.10 for an example of the Web site, located at **http://www.adobe.com**.

FIG. 3.10

Adobe has a number of software applications that help you create and present content.

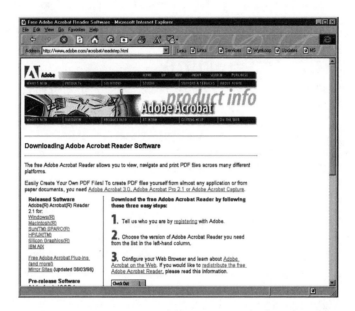

After you download Adobe Acrobat, run the executable acroread.exe. When you do, you're prompted for your user name and company and the destination of the utility. The reader will then install to your system and create the necessary associations that will make the browser aware of the reader. After installation, the only indication you'll have that the viewer is installed comes when you load a PDF object into your browser. When you do, the Adobe reader auto-matically starts to view the object.

Working Directly with Documents

If you have hyperlinks on your Intranet that point to files on your network, you may be able to edit the documents and save the changes back to the Intranet directly, just as if you open the file using the Windows Explorer. This happens when you link to files that do not necessarily exist on the Web server. In cases where you can link to the files directly, and those files are registered with a helper application that allows editing, you are able to make and save changes subject to your network security assignments.

If you click a hyperlink that points to a Word document, for example, and you don't have the Word Viewer installed, Word loads and the document appears.

You can use this to your advantage as a means of providing access to your company's documents, specifications, and the like. By providing this direct access to your users, they can contribute to the content in the documents and participate in the creation of the different objects at your business.

Of course, you still want to apply prudent security measures on your network if you have files that should not be edited. This is where a solid security system comes into play. You'll want to have the ability to grant user access to a specific directory, and possibly a particular file or set of files.

Planning Intranet Security

Security on an Intranet is typically a far smaller issue than when you're establishing an Internet presence. With an Intranet, you're typically figuring out how to allow everyone *except* specific individuals. On the other hand, with an Internet, you're trying to figure out how to *block* everyone, allowing only specific individuals. The allowed individuals include the anonymous Web user, anonymous FTP user, and so on, but you won't be allowing too many other individuals access to your site in an Internet situation.

Implementing Security with UNIX or Linux

With a UNIX system, the server components—the Web service and the FTP service—rely on their own security configuration files. For example, with a Linux server, this is the `access.conf` file. This file contains information that governs access to your site at a global level. This file is largely IP address-driven and you use the file to indicate what IP addresses are allowed on your site.

You create entries in the access.conf file that control the access to your server. See Listing 3.1 for an example of an access.conf that limits some aspects of access to your server.

Listing 3.1   Sample access.conf Entries

```
<Directory /usr/resources/www/que>
        AllowOverride None
        Options Indexes
        <Limit GET>
                order deny,allow
                deny from microsoft.com
        allow from intellicenter.com
        </Limit>
</Directory>
```

One background information item is that when a browser requests a page from a server, it issues a GET command, requesting that the server send the page to the browser. In the sample entries in Listing 3.1, you can see that you're setting up limitations on the GET command, indicating what domains can access the server and which domains are refused access.

Browsers use a PUT command to send information to a server. You can set up limitations on either or both of the GET and PUT functions.

In Listing 3.1, all requests from any user at microsoft.com will be denied. The user is not allowed access. On the other hand, any user from the intellicenter.com domain is allowed access. You also can specify IP addresses here, and you can indicate a range of addresses or a smaller or larger cross-section of the domain to consider.

For example, if you want to allow all users from **Intranet.microsoft.com**, but disallow those from **hackers.microsoft.com**, you can do so by using the following modified statements:

```
<Limit GET>
        order deny,allow
        deny from Intranet.microsoft.com
        allow from hackers.intellicenter.com
</Limit>
```

Recall from the start of this section on UNIX/Linux implementations that you can also control access at the directory level. To do so, you must modify the .htaccess file in each directory. Use the same file format as outlined in Listing 3.1, but all you need to do is add the <Limit> section to the .htaccess file since the directory is already inferred.

Keep in mind that these same approaches apply to the PUT command as well. Simply replace GET in the listing examples with PUT and you can apply the same level of control to PUT operations. PUT operations are often forms-related. If you're using forms on your server, be careful applying restrictions to the PUT command as people will not be able to post information to the server.

Of course, you must consult your operating system and server software documentation for a discussion of their specific implementation of security for the Web and FTP services.

Implementing Security with Windows NT

With Windows NT and IIS, the security model is completely integrated. There are no web-specific users on the system, only those that Windows NT has confirmed have accounts on the server. Since the Windows NT environment is so integral with the security system in IIS, the following few sections describe users and managing them in this environment.

If you are using Windows NT, consider creating a group for every set of user rights you'll be creating. Keep in mind as well that Windows NT operates on the domain model concept. This means shared rights and increased control over the maintenance requirements of the network.

Understanding Domains   *Domains* are the fundamental architecture that controls how your client systems access the server, if they are either on your local area network or on the Internet. Domains provide a means of logically grouping systems and users to facilitate administering the systems, accessing your server, and interacting with each other.

Windows for Workgroups introduced peer-to-peer networking for Microsoft platforms. Peer-level networking means that workstations share information stored on their local hard disks with other users on the network. While this is a great way to share small-to-medium amounts of information on a few workstations, a serious bottleneck arises as the number of workstations and the traffic they generate grows.

The bottleneck is the result of the requirement to manage access to the information and balance performance on a given user's system. This must be balanced against access to the information over the network. In systems where the number of workstations and the amount of shared information becomes a burden on the network, you should consider implementing a more "industrial strength" solution. That's where Windows NT comes in, and with it, domains become part of the network picture.

Figure 3.11 shows a sample domain configuration with a two-server domain and a single-server domain.

FIG. 3.11

Servers belong to only a single domain, while users and systems can use more than one domain.

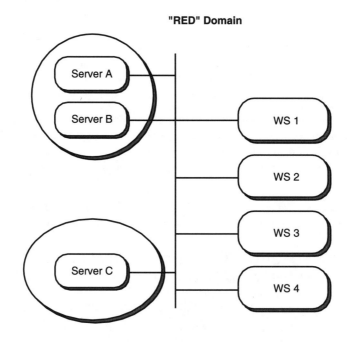

"RED" Domain

"Blue" Domain

At first, system administrators may argue with the drawing in Figure 3.11, because workstations belong in one domain or another. The point of the figure is that servers belong to one domain and one domain only. Workstations and users can sign into and out of different domains as needed, as long as they are authorized in another domain. The important thing is that once you enter, or log onto, a given domain, you must abide by the domain's accompanying rules and security parameters.

Be careful setting up user policies and rights on your network servers. When you install IIS, it creates a special user that it attempts to use for all accesses to the network. This may seem to simplify management of the server rights, but it actually has a tendency to complicate things.

Since you only have a single user account to work with in establishing rights, you need to be very careful about what you allow the account to access. Remember that all users accessing your server with the account will have access to the information. This means that you should carefully break out your user rights and security assignments and assign them individually where needed to provide the controlled access to resources.

You can protect information and force users to authenticate themselves on your server, but that requires that you establish user accounts for the secure materials. This is the correct way to approach managing the users. You should allow the broadest, most non-secure access to the default user, but disallow access to any protected information you might be concerned about.

Once you determine the information that you want to protect from the general public user, create users and assign them appropriate rights that allow them access to the materials. This way, when IIS attempts to access the information, it will prompt the users for their user names and passwords, and it will allow them to work with the protected materials only if they are authorized.

▶ For more information about using the Secure Transactions, see Chapter 16, "Conducting transactions on the Internet."

FTP is a different security concern because it allows the user to sign in directly to your system, specifying a user ID and password. Typically, users sign on as anonymous and they provide their e-mail address in the password field. However, those posing the biggest threat to your installation are seldom typical in their use of the system.

Set up and administer User Rights from the User Manager for Domains, located on the Administrative Tools menu in NT. The User Manager enables you to work with both users and groups. In addition, it enables you to assign all rights recognized by the system to those users. Once you create the necessary users and groups, apply rights to your system and control access to the files and directories on it. Figure 3.12 shows the User Manager for Domains.

 TIP You can work with more than one user at a time. If you manage existing users and want to set up the group associations, logon times, and many other attributes, first select the users from the list by shift- and control-clicking the names on the list, and then select User, Properties.

CAUTION

Be very wary of one particular user. Consider strongly whether to disable the account altogether. The GUEST account is dangerous, because any user that logs on to your system without a valid user name and assigned password is assigned to this account. Therefore, any privileges given that account are automatically provided to any user signing on to the system without otherwise defined access.

The built-in group EVERYONE is also in the system. Every user and group belongs to this group. In addition, its settings provide the default privileges to all resources when they are created, unless user access is explicitly revoked or modified. This means you can assign rights to limit access to your users, but unless you remove the rights for the group EVERYONE on the resource you set up, all users still have access to it.

FIG. 3.12

Users belong to groups, and you control access to resources either by these group assignments or the individual users.

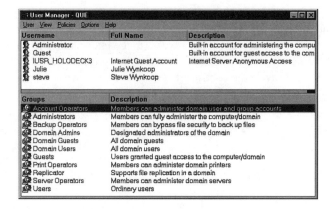

In almost all cases, your best option is granting group rights to resources rather than granting these rights to users. This is true even in those cases where you grant access to a resource to only a single user. You'll save time and effort later when the user is either replaced or gains an assistant that needs to have the same level of access. When that happens, you need only to modify the members of the group. You won't need to change access privileges on resources on your system. Consider the following steps in planning to implement your system's user database:

Decide whether you allow access to your system via the GUEST account. If not, disable the account. If you have a shared Internet and Intranet server, it is highly recommended that you never leave the GUEST account enabled.

Define the users required on your system.

Create the individual user accounts.

Define the security rights profiles you will apply to the system.

Create groups containing the users granted the rights you defined.

Apply the security to the resources. Use the groups as the means of indicating access— or lack of access—to the resource.

Apply the security to the resources based on individual users in those rare cases where it is warranted or required.

CAUTION

Windows NT assigns user rights based on a Least Restrictive model. This means that if you belong to two different profiles, and one profile indicates you have no access to a resource but the other indicates that you do have access, you can gain access to the resource. This is because the least restrictive of the two profiles indicates that you are allowed access.

Put simply, any user that you assign to the NOACCESS group, but that is not removed from other groups, may have more access rights than you planned. The effect of the NOACCESS group may be weakened because

---

the other groups allow overriding user rights, granting user rights to certain resources. When you revoke access to an individual, be sure to review the associated account and make sure it does not belong to other groups that may also influence effective rights.

Setting Up New Users The User Manager for Domains enables you to create new users a number of different ways. One of the ways offering you the most leverage for your time is the Copy command on the User menu to copy the rights of an existing user. As you can see in Figure 3.13, there are a number of items that you set up for those users who may access your system.

FIG. 3.13
When you copy an existing user, the copy inherits the groups and privileges of the original.

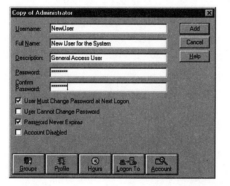

N O T E If you select the Must Change Password option, there is an additional step the first time a user logs onto the system. Each person must change his/her password. This may seem like a good idea at first, but be wary of the user's particular type of system. In some environments, specifically Windows 3.x systems, the system may not allow users to change their passwords. In these cases, you effectively lock the user out of the system, because NT bars them from the system until the password has been changed.

If you have a user blocked from signing onto the system, review the account and make sure this option is not checked. Also, make sure the Account Disabled option is not selected. This also prevents access to your system. ▄

When you set up IIS, you do not have to establish a user account for every person connecting to your server. You need to set up accounts only for the default IIS users you establish, and any specific privilege groups and/or accounts that you may need to set up. Specific privilege accounts are those accounts requiring different access rights above and beyond those afforded your typical user.

N O T E By default, if you're using IIS you need not set up the anonymous users for your Intranet server, at least on a general access basis. Installing IIS automatically creates the user associated with providing general access to your IIS controlled directories. ▄

The next sections briefly cover the different aspects of the user account.

Assigning Groups   The Groups button enables you to set up the groups to which the user belongs.

When you assign a user to a group, he gains the rights and privileges associated with that group. By double-clicking groups listed in the Member Of: and Not a Member Of: listboxes, you add and remove membership in groups. After the user is assigned to the appropriate groups, select OK to save the changes and return to the new user's Properties dialog box.

Controlling Access to Resources   After you create your users and groups, you must assign permissions. Assigning permissions is the final step toward securing your system at a general level. This section shows the basics of applying permissions to system resources.

The Windows Explorer is the key to applying security to various resources on your system. Select the directory resource you want to share, and right-click it. The shortcut menu that appears, shown in Figure 3.14, has an option to establish the sharing for the resource.

FIG. 3.14
Select Sharing from the menu to set up or maintain sharing options for the highlighted resource.

Selecting sharing not only sets up the share name and the number of users accessing the resource, but it also offers the option to set permissions on the resource by selecting the Permissions button. Figure 3.15 shows the dialog box setting these initial options.

FIG. 3.15
Setting up the initial share information is straightforward.

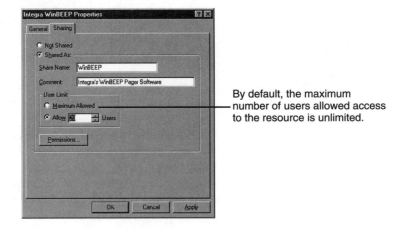

By default, the maximum number of users allowed access to the resource is unlimited.

N O T E The information presented here on securing share-level security on your system pertains to setting up shares on the server. With IIS, security is enforced by way of NTFS and directory level privileges. If you establish rights based on a share, they are not enforced unless the share is accessed. If you use the directory that the share relates to, without using the share, the rights will have no effect.

If you need to protect content on the site, you must use NTFS for the file system and you must set rights based on the permissions, outlined below, for the directory, not the share. ■

N O T E If you select a share name of more than the DOS-standard 8.3 format, some DOS workstations may not be able to access the resource. If you do select such a name, you are warned about this fact as you apply the share information for the resource. ■

If you select OK or Apply at this point, without setting Permissions, all users with access to the resource via a share, a parent directory, and so on will have open, Full Control access to the resource. Be sure to select the Permissions button.

The underlying file system dictates how permissions change. If the NTFS (the NT File System) is installed, you gain additional options. These enable you to apply specific permission subsets, rather than just generic permission categories. The following list shows the general access permission categories you can assign:

- No Access—Users are unable to access, read from, or write to it.
- Read—Read users and groups read the directory, load and execute files located in the directory, and so on. They cannot delete objects, nor can they add new objects to the resource.
- Change—Change users can read, modify, and execute existing objects, but cannot insert new objects nor delete objects.
- Full Control—Full Control users have all rights to the resource.

When you select Add, you have two options. First, you can select single or multiple users and groups. Second, as a set, you can assign rights applying to the set of users. When you select OK, the users are listed in the Permissions text box. This verifies that the permissions are properly applied. Selecting OK once again saves and applies the changes. Now the resource is available with your declared permissions.

Reality Check

At the Que Reality Check site, the server is implemented using Microsoft's IIS server. The server is configured to support both Intranet and Internet services, giving added access to Internal users. Problems arose in trying to lock down certain content as we forgot to remove the rights associated by default with the EVERYONE group. With the default rights assigned to this group, it was not possible to prevent the user, IUSR_Netserver1, from accessing certain sensitive materials. Once the group was updated and appropriate access rights assigned, however, the security worked correctly.

The decision to move to the Windows NT platform was one of convenience. Intellicenter teaches classes on Webmastering and client-side Internet access. With this in mind, and the preponderance of utilities, software, and browsers for Windows NT-based servers, Windows NT made the most sense.

From Here...

This chapter presented a whirlwind look at many different aspects associated with bringing up the Intranet server, regardless of the environment you select in which to do it. For more information, consider the following sources:

- *Special Edition Using Windows NT Server* by Roger Jennings, 1996, Que Corporation.
- Chapter 8, "Running an Intranet Site," provides additional information about security and additional tools you'll be using on your site.
- Chapter 9, "Firewalls and Proxy Servers," tells you what to consider when you provide both Internet and Intranet access to your users.

## CHAPTER 4

Implementing an Intranet Site

In the last chapter, you found out how to plan an Intranet site and make the content available to the different users from both a viewing standpoint and a contribution standpoint. An Intranet offers some unique opportunities in these areas as it's a relatively closed environment where you have more control over the users, what they can see, and how the content is presented.

In this chapter, you'll find out more about some of the differences in implementation details for an Intranet site. These range from a more open set of options for graphics and object types to considerations for what an Intranet may do to the bandwidth utilization at your organization. ■

Find out how you can put an Intranet to work in your organization

There are many things you can do with an Intranet in your company. Find out more about sample applications and approaches to this new information-sharing technology.

See how you can enhance the user experience on your site

By providing the user with consistent tools to work with your site, you can further enhance what they can get out of the site. Find out how these tools can really make a difference on your site.

Learn about judging the return on investment for your site

You'll find out about different ways you can determine what's working and what's not on your site. You'll also gain some insight into justification topics when it comes time to determine whether you want to move forward with the site.

Learn how to attract more traffic to your site

Find out the keys to success with your site. How can you get and keep users interested in using the Intranet?

Understanding the Difference Between an Intranet and an Internet Site

Intranet and Internet sites have a lot in common, but they have completely different audiences. These audiences are about as different as they can be. On the one hand, an Internet site is to provide your customer and prospective customers with somewhere to go to find out more about your company, your products and services, and how to transact business with you.

The Intranet site, on the other hand, is typically created to provide information about the internal running of your business, from personnel policy manuals to company-specific forms and software tools. Obviously this is information that, at the very least, is of little real interest to the public at large, and in many cases, should actually be protected as company confidential information.

In some cases, you'll want to identify the different sites within your Intranet to your browser software. This will allow the software to go directly to the internal site, rather than going out looking for it on the Internet. See Figure 4.1 for an example of establishing these settings with Internet Explorer. Though these are listed for the proxy settings, you can still increase performance by using these settings to call out the internal Web servers you have running.

FIG. 4.1
You can improve initial load times by bypassing Internet searches for Intranet Web sites.

Between the two types of implementations, there are some key differences in the circumstances controlling the site. Some of these are outlined in the next few sections.

Speed Differences

Even in those cases where you may have a high-speed connection to the Internet, your site will still have slower access to it than in the case of an Intranet site. Keep in mind that your users' experience at your site is limited by the following five different things:

- The speed of their system and their connection to the Internet.
- The speed and quality of the connection between their system and your server: for example, the telephone line.
- The speed of your connection to the Internet.
- The speed of your server, software, and related equipment.
- The load on each of these points at the time the user accesses your system.

Most users are constrained by the first and last items on the list. The number of actual CPU cycles on your server required to fulfill a request is surprisingly low. Even in times of moderate loading, the CPU rarely becomes the limiting factor. It's far more likely that the bandwidth between you and your users will be the issue.

N O T E You can see an excellent example of this if you consider Microsoft's recent release of Internet Explorer 3.0. Their server backbone consists of some 12 different servers with four processors and 128M of RAM in each server. With this horsepower behind the site, you'd expect that they'd be able to keep up with most levels of demand.

When the new browser became available, however, it was quickly evident that bandwidth to and from **microsoft.com** was a limiting factor. Even though they can support tens of thousands of users, they still had problems handling the sudden increase in demand for bandwidth.

You can understand how this might happen when you consider that the browser in its most limited form is over 5M in size, and over one million people downloaded it in the first week. That's a lot of information to be sending out over the Internet, and a lot of separate, somewhat long term connections to their site to facilitate the download. ■

With an Intranet, you don't have these concerns. You're constrained a bit by the speed of the network you're running internally, but the concerns about overall loading of the Internet is not an issue. You also are not dealing with modems, but rather workstations that are directly connected to the Internet. See Figure 4.2 for an example of an image more suited for an Intranet than an Internet, if only due to its color mix. This example file, provided on the CD, is 204K in size, far too large for use over the Internet, but probably not a problem for an Intranet installation.

What this means to your Intranet site is that you can create a much more bandwidth-intensive site with more graphics, more use of native objects, and so on. You can provide information in its optimum format, not just the most efficient and standardized format.

All of the same options are available for use on your Intranet. You can still use Java, ActiveX controls, ActiveX scripting, and the other technologies that are available. You just won't have to worry as much about how long it will take a page to load.

FIG. 4.2
Image file size is less of
a concern in an Intranet
situation.

You may also be able to take more advantage of automatic page refreshing. You can place a directive in a page's HTML coding that will automatically reload the page after a certain period of time. This can be a good way to create a dashboard-type application that shows the details of a continuing process, perhaps the call volume at the Help Desk or a manufacturing floor process or flow. This indicator, located in the <HEAD> section of the page, has the following syntax:

```
<html>
<head>
<META HTTP-EQUIV="Refresh" CONTENT="120; URL=/mywebpage.htm ">
</head>
</body>
</html>
```

In this example, the "Refresh" directive makes the page reload every 120 seconds, making for a good view of incrementally changing information for someone who wants to pull up the screen and know what's happening right now. In the ultimate solution for this audience, the reloaded page would contain a graphical image depicting the information desired.

▶ For more detailed information about HTML tips and techniques, see Chapters 18, "Basic HTML Techniques," and 19, "Advanced HTML."

Network Traffic

Since your Intranet functions within your internal network cabling system, you won't be relying on the Internet to provide passage for your information requests. Contention to fulfill requests will be lower than on the Internet at large, so you won't have to worry as much about the traffic facet of the access time equation.

There's a lot of concern when you bring up an Intranet about what it will do to the overall performance of your internal networks. It shouldn't have much impact at all in terms of network traffic unless your network is already at its upper bounds in terms of utilization.

The fact is that HTML is largely text, which is generally very fast to transmit and rarely requires solid blocks of transmission bandwidth. When you start adding custom objects and graphical images, this begins to change, but it's the nature of the Web environment that transactions are small and fulfilled quickly. Remember, the Web was designed for the Internet, where there *are* concerns about bandwidth. Therefore, you reap some of the rewards of this optimization work on your internal network when you bring up your Intranet.

You may begin to see a traffic impact if you or your users publish large numbers of complex objects, like the Microsoft PowerPoint slides, large word processing documents, etc. As network administrator, the number of people accessing this type of information on your network is an important piece of information to monitor. If you find a large number of objects being consistently accessed and causing traffic, you may want to consider placing different Intranet servers around your company and placing the information needed by users on segments of your LAN that are physically connected to the segments used by those users needing the information.

Controlling the User Environment

You can gain a significant advantage if you can somewhat control the user environment, and specify the tools people will use to view and access the content on your site. With the Internet site, this is an unrealistic goal, as there are just too many people that may be accessing your site. With an Intranet, however, you may be able to somewhat mandate what browsers, object viewers, and other tools your company will use.

It's likely that you'll have the renegade employee, the person that insists on using their father's, friend's, or cousin's favorite browser that no one has ever heard of. But in general, you'll have some control over what browser people use. You can enforce your choice a bit by making it known that your internal pages will be optimized for the browser you select, and you can also help this along by making the browser readily accessible.

Another consideration you'll need to keep in mind is that of display resolution settings. Both Windows 3.1 and Windows 95 let users operate at their choice of resolutions, such as 640 × 480, 800 × 600, or 768 × 1024. You can create the greatest 800 × 600 graphic in the world for navigating your site, but if most of your users run at 640 × 480, the graphic won't fit in their display area, and it defeats the purpose of having the image mapped in the first place.

One interesting test you can do is to send out a quick e-mail to the users in your organization asking what resolution they're using. You may be a bit surprised at the results. It appears that most systems, even high-end systems with outstanding monitors, are set to a 800 × 600 × 256 resolution. There are a number of people who will be at higher resolutions, and others who swear they'll never go to anything smaller, but you'll need to address the most common resolution found in your user base.

N O T E   You may find that many of your users don't know how to determine the display settings for
their systems. Be sure to include basic instructions for determining the settings in your
request e-mail. You may also want to consider discussing this with your system administration if you
have one that is different from the Intranet implementation team. ■

One consideration in the realm of resolution determination for your site is that people with
their systems set to higher resolutions can still see an image optimized for 800×600, but the
opposite is not true. Therefore, if you have a large number of 800×600 systems, even if it's not
the majority, you'll want to strongly consider designing for this resolution. You'll probably find
that this is the most common resolution developed for on the Internet today.

A real leverage point for your content comes from standardizing on the tools that are used to
create the content on your site. These tools include word processors, database applications,
and worksheet applications. By using a common application in these and other core areas, you
can present information in its native format.

▶ More information on using native tools to create content is provided in Chapter 3, "Planning an
Intranet Site."

Examining Types of Content for Intranets

There are a number of application-based ways that Intranets can benefit your company. These
are in addition to the posting of information and sharing of documents that you might typically
expect from an internal Web site. For example, with some search engines, you can index content from word processing documents, including Object Linking and Embedding, or OLE,
properties, and make them available for searching on your site. By making past project documents available, your users may be able to save time on new proposals, new ideas, and documents in general.

▶ For more information on search engines, see Chapter 12, "Search Engines."

Entire applications can also have their home on your Intranet. These applications have some
added benefit if used from your Intranet and accessed both from the Intranet and the Internet.
Just think, for the examples provided here, and for the systems you'll no doubt create on your
own, if you make them available to both the Internet and Intranet, you'll be able to access them
from anywhere in the world.

In the next two sections, you'll find out more about some possible applications that may be
suited to your Intranet environment. These are provided as examples. Your applications will
undoubtedly have different requirements and will need careful consideration and planning
prior to implementation.

> **CAUTION**
>
> If you do open your applications up to the Internet on a shared server basis, you will want to make sure you have very tight security implemented. The last thing you want to do is open up your customer management system, for example, and later find out that your competition has been quietly reading through your customer list in their attempts to gain greater market share.
>
> More information about security measures is provided in several areas, particularly in Chapters 5, "Setting Up and Configuring a Web Server," and 6, "Setting up an FTP site." Make sure you fully test any implementation that includes cross-access between your Intranet and Internet site.

Product Support

Most software development companies have a product support department. This type of department presents some unique challenges. Information about the customer base and how the support organization is interacting with customers must be cataloged and made available for easy retrieval by support staff, salespeople, and others.

Customers often call back their salesperson in an attempt to gain added attention, right a perceived wrong, or return a product. The customer may or may not be justified in seeking out the assistance of the salesperson, but the salesperson typically has no way of determining what's happening with the customer without picking up the phone and calling the support desk to find out what's up. Having support information available via the Intranet would enable salespeople to look up the needed information without bothering the support staff.

Another area often overlooked by organizations is the value of the support desk data in planning future product improvements. The calls that come in to the support desk often present the most realistic view of how a given product is doing. You can tell quite quickly how well a product is selling and whether it's fulfilling the needs of the customer by the number of bug reports that are received and by the overall call volume in general. The calls that are received by the support staff are extremely valuable as they contain information about not only what may truly be "broken" in a product, but also what the customer expects the product to do, a key indicator about where future development efforts should be focused.

This knowledge base is a wealth of information for other users, both internal and external to your company. See Figure 4.3 for an example of a query screen that can open this database to your customers, be they internal or external to your company.

By creating a customer support system that works with an Open Database Connectivity, or ODBC, data source, it's a simple matter to create an Internet Database Connector, or IDC file, that queries that data source and returns information from the knowledge base. It simply takes the information passed in by the form and sends it off to be parsed by the database engine. See Listing 4.1 for an example of the IDC file used in this query.

Part

I

Ch

4

FIG. 4.3

An example product support inquiry form, which is accessible only from the Intranet at the Integra Reality Check Site.

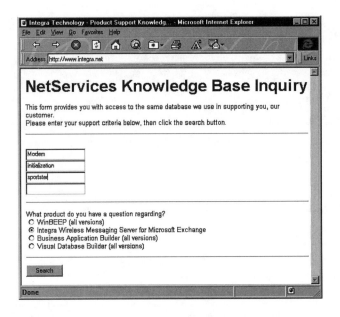

Listing 4.1   Knowledge Base Inquiry Form

```
datasource: kb_A7inetsupport
username: kbsa
template: supptest.htx
SQLStatement:
+ select * from incident where
+ (
+   (
+   (in_problem like '%%%search1%%%')  and (in_problem like '%%%search2%%%')
+   and (in_problem like '%%%search3%%%')  and (in_problem like '%%%search4%%%')
+   ) OR
+
+   (
+   (in_solution like '%%%search1%%%') and (in_solution like '%%%search2%%%')
+   and (in_solution like '%%%search3%%%') and (in_solution like
'%%%search4%%%')
+   )) AND
+
+   (in_type = '%product%')
```

The results, displayed by the code outlined in Listing 4.2, show all possible hits based on the query passed to the IDC. The result is a comprehensive listing of the public incidents that have been logged with the symptoms identified by the user.

Listing 4.2   Sample HTX File Used to Display the Search Results

```
<HTML>
<HEAD>
<TITLE>Search Results Page</TITLE>
</HEAD>
<BODY>
<body bgcolor="#ffffff">
<div align=Center><H1>Knowledge Base Search Results</h1></div>
<hr width=75% height=10 color=blue>

<%idc.product%>

<%begindetail%>
   <h2><font color="RED">Question:</font></h2><%in_problem%><%in_type%><br>
   <h2><font color="BLUE">Answer:</font></h2><%in_solution%><br>
   <hr>
<%enddetail%>

<p><address> 1996, Integra Technology International, Inc. For assistance, e-mail
‡ <a href="mailto:webmaster@integra.net"> webmaster@integra.net</a>.</p>

</BODY>
</HTML>
```

▶ For more information about setting up an IDC-based system, see Chapter 22, "Database Access and Integrity."

By opening up your database to internal users, you give them access to the information that is most useful to them. If you extend this information to also provide account feedback, you can offer an even greater service to the sales and marketing segment of your business. You can provide them up-to-date information through Web-based access to the same databases you on which you base your customer support system.

Sales and Marketing

It's a constant push to keep the sales and marketing staff updated with new product brochures, new sales techniques, and so on. By putting this type of information on the Intranet, you make it much easier, and very cost effective, to get this information to the sales staff.

You'll save on printing costs, and at the same time you'll be getting the information out to your executives very quickly. In fact, if you take a slightly different approach, you can enhance the sales tools at the same time. Consider making the sales information for a given product more of an active brochure by providing the brochure information as an on-screen presentation in a program like PowerPoint.

You can publish the PowerPoint presentation on the Intranet, enabling your staff to review and use the presentation online, possibly even in front of customers. By referring to the online versions, they're assured of always having the most updated version of the product information.

Understanding Client Software Differences

An area that is interesting to understand is what happens to your client applications once they are in use on an Intranet. In most functions, they are identical to what you'd expect, whether they are used against an Internet site or your internal network. There are some differences, though, and they can be a lot of fun to work with.

One thing that changes immediately on an Intranet is how your browser is able to interact with the objects that it presents to the users. If the user has the rights to do so, he or she can review and update objects in place, regardless of the object type. For example, if the user wants to make a change to a Web page, he or she can do so by selecting View, Source (or the equivalent command).

Once the page's source information is displayed, the user can make the changes and save the file as usual. The file is updated on the server and made immediately available to other users. In a more traditional Internet setting, the file would have to be saved locally and then uploaded to the server using an FTP utility or other special software that is able to post to the Web site's directories.

This holds true for other types of content as well, depending on the browser that you'll be using to view it. If the browser allows updates, and other users have appropriate rights on the server, they'll be able to make changes directly.

An additional capability that you have that's easier to exploit in the Intranet environment is that you can embed hyperlinks within your documents. Figure 4.4 shows an example of this in Microsoft Word.

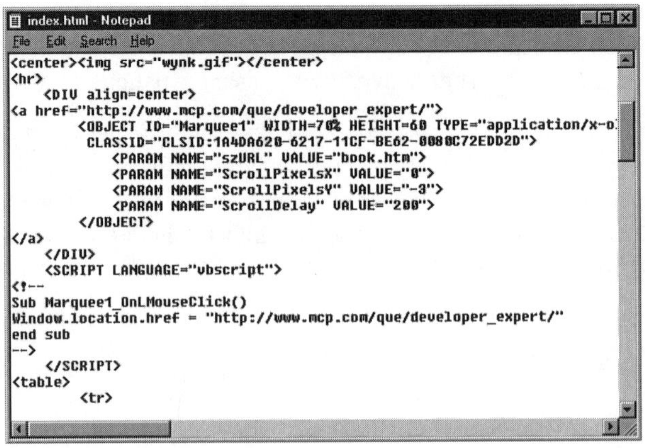

FIG. 4.4

Some applications enable you to embed hyperlinks to other documents within a file.

```
index.html - Notepad
File  Edit  Search  Help
<center><img src="wynk.gif"></center>
<hr>
      <DIV align=center>
<a href="http://www.mcp.com/que/developer_expert/">
         <OBJECT ID="Marquee1" WIDTH=70% HEIGHT=60 TYPE="application/x-o
            CLASSID="CLSID:1A4DA620-6217-11CF-BE62-0080C72EDD2D">
            <PARAM NAME="szURL" VALUE="book.htm">
            <PARAM NAME="ScrollPixelsX" VALUE="0">
            <PARAM NAME="ScrollPixelsY" VALUE="-3">
            <PARAM NAME="ScrollDelay" VALUE="200">
         </OBJECT>
</a>
      </DIV>
      <SCRIPT LANGUAGE="vbscript">
<!--
Sub Marquee1_OnLMouseClick()
Window.location.href = "http://www.mcp.com/que/developer_expert/"
end sub
-->
      </SCRIPT>
<table>
      <tr>
```

Though the hyperlink in Figure 4.4 is a link to another document, it could just as easily be a link to load an application. The following are some possibilities of the types of links you can have in your Intranet documents:

- Link to help files by creating hyperlinks to .HLP files. They'll load automatically into the Windows Help system.

- Link to worksheets to load automatically in your spreadsheet application by simply indicating the file in the hyperlink.

- Attach supporting documents to specifications. You can make the text hidden so it doesn't print for the end customer but it will be available if you ever need to research a proposal you've created.

- If you have access to the Internet, you can link to external sites. As with other links, you could just as easily create a link to another Web site external to your company.

If you can tell users the path to the file so they can retrieve it from your network, you can just as easily provide a URL to its location on your Intranet. One final note, you can also include a hyperlink to an object in an e-mail message. Most current versions of e-mail packages now support this, as shown in Figure 4.5. This lets you give readers of your mail message instant access to the resource you reference in your message.

FIG. 4.5
You can even send a hyperlink in an e-mail message.

Deciding Whether an Intranet Is Right for You

Intranets are a real fad right now. How do you determine if it's time for you to implement an Intranet for your company? What types of things can you do with the Intranet that you might not be able to do, or least not as easily, without the Intranet setting?

The next few sections cover some of these benefits and how you might be able to track the effectiveness of your site.

Part
I

Ch
4

Printing Costs

As covered earlier in this chapter, the Intranet offers some key advantages in several areas. Probably the first area in which you'll see a real benefit is in the printing, or lack of printing, of manuals, brochures, memorandums, and so forth. The costs saved by publishing the information on the Intranet are immediate and identifiable, and should be monitored closely.

In Chapter 11, "Usage Statistics," you will see how you can use any number of tools to analyze log files produced by your server. These log files are key to showing that people are aware of, using, and gaining benefit from your Intranet. By showing the number of times brochures are accessed, you can show real savings in printing, but also in providing other tools, as may be the case of brochures. It will be of interest to talk with your sales staff to see if they use the other tools mentioned earlier, such as animated presentations, and PowerPoint presentations, in their sales efforts. If so, you've added a level of service that is simply not available in print media.

Easier Access to Corporate Information

Web browsers are commonplace now and a huge number of users understand them. If you can provide access to your corporate information systems, from documents to spreadsheets to custom applications, all from within the common browser interface, you'll decrease training times and increase the amount of work that an employee can complete on your systems.

A key tool that you should consider is a comprehensive search and indexing engine. The engines now available include the ability to search non-HTML documents, provide links to external systems, and in some cases even provide some database search capabilities. A search server can make your Intranet the core of the internal networks and systems that support the employees at your company. If the search engine is configured accurately and is able to work with many of the stored documents on your system, you'll find that the Intranet can quickly become the starting point for many people when they use your network.

N O T E When you compare and contrast the engines available, be sure that you are looking for an engine that can run without a connection to the Internet if you'll be using it on your Intranet. ▮

▶ More information on search engines, both installing them and understanding how they work, is provided in Chapter 12, "Search Engines."

The uses for your Intranet are as varied as the applications your LAN hosts. Explaining these in detail is not within the scope of this book, but examples include:

- Workgroup computing
- Online training or orientation materials
- Personnel and policy manuals
- Intra-company communications between departments, divisions
- Online research tools

Reality Check

At the Integra Intranet site, we've published company-confidential information, including some of the following:

- Personnel policy manual
- Internet usage policy manual
- Expense report Excel templates
- Past sales proposals

Making these items more readily available to the users has made it much easier to distribute them. By placing them on the server, we were able to create a single page with links to the different areas of forms, documents, templates, and so on. Users can read them by simply selecting them from the Web page.

One challenge that we ran into at first was getting the documents and other items into an appropriate format. This included converting them to HTML, as we didn't have a grasp on what browsers were being used on the internal systems at that time. Over time, we've been able to migrate most employees to Netscape Navigator or Internet Explorer, enabling us to use more native objects. We now post two versions of an item if possible—the native format, such as a Word document or Excel worksheet, and an HTML version.

As we indexed the contents of past proposals and other information on the system, we were surprised how much disk space was required to get the level of indexing we felt was appropriate. In some cases, it took as much as 40 percent to 50 percent of the original file size in terms of overhead disk space requirements.

Making the search engine aware of the location for key information sources was the key to getting more use out of the Intranet at Integra. By putting online the Index Server from Microsoft, we were able to increase usage substantially.

Part

I

Ch

4

From Here...

In this chapter you've learned about some of the differences between an Internet and Intranet site, including the new level of control and content you can provide your user base. For more information on many of these topic, please consult the following chapters:

- Chapter 3, "Planning an Intranet Site," gives detailed information about the tools and techniques you can apply to your Intranet site when you bring it online.
- Chapter 8, "Running an Intranet Site," gives more information about things you can provide from your site, including the use of the Internet Assistants for content creation.
- Chapter 9, "Firewalls and Proxy Servers," details some of the considerations you'll want to keep in mind when you add Intranet access to an existing Internet site.

Setting Up Your Web Site

Setting Up and Configuring a Web Server

Setting up the Web server is one of the core components to bringing your Internet site online. In fact, with the increased support that the HTTPD protocol provides these days, the Web server is lately replacing many of the functions formerly provided by other services, such as FTP. This is most evident by the fact that you can download files using an **http://** URL at some sites, whereas in the past, it was necessary to use an **ftp://** URL to download.

See what things you need to consider before you install your server

You'll see what types of things will affect how you install your server software. These key items dictate your overall site configuration.

Find out how to configure your server for both general and secure access

Find out more about the configuration files and utilities that are used to control how your site provides and controls access to the content you provide.

Compare the graphical user interface of IIS to the configuration-file-based approach of UNIX server software

You'll be able to learn the concepts of setting up your server and how they are implemented in an NT-based, graphical environment, and a UNIX, configuration-file-centric environment.

N O T E Selecting which server to use can be a daunting task. There is a resource on the Web, located at **http://www.webcompare.com**, that shows important comparison information that may help in your decision. ▪

In this chapter you'll see how to install a Web server from a general standpoint. We'll look at the Microsoft Internet Information Server installation in detail, and compare the procedure to that for more traditional servers on the UNIX platform.

N O T E Installation of a Web server is quite constant in concept, if not implementation. Regardless of whether you plan to use IIS, Netscape's server, Apache, or NCSA, you should read through the IIS installation and understand what's being done, though the specifics of *how* it's being done may be different in the software you select. The knowledge of why certain options are established will benefit you greatly in your Web server installation. ▪

Understanding General Concepts and Planning Points

A primary concern with your Web site is where you're going to place the files that it will host. This is very important, regardless of platform, because it drives the security requirements, the disk space requirements, and more. You must answer several questions before you can sit down to install your Web server:

- Where will you start your site? Where will you locate your home page?
- Will you have protected or secure information on your site?
- Will you be doing secure transactions, such as those that require a credit card and SSL (Secure Sockets Layer) encryption, on your site?
- Will you be hosting only your own site, or will you be providing hosting services to other sites?
- Will you be hosting both an Intranet and Internet site?

You'll find that the answers to many of these questions will affect how you establish your directory structure. For example, with an installation that must support secure transactions, you'll typically have the SSL encryption enabled for only a portion of your site. To do this, you'll typically select a directory or series of directories on which to apply the SSL layer. This is true as well for the areas that you want to protect. This comes from the fact that you need to apply security up and down the directory tree in question.

In the best of cases, you'll be able to sit down and diagram the site, showing where everything will go and writing out the link relationships, security trusts, and general structure of your site. In reality, this is seldom feasible, and you may find that managing a Web site is among one of the more dynamic, challenging, and control-demanding tasks you will encounter in your career.

The dynamics of a Web site come largely from two factors. The first is the reputation of the Internet. People expect quality. Your audience expects your site to be operational, professionally managed, and containing exceptional content. This means that deadlines you set with the best of intentions for correctly planning out the system will be impacted by users expecting things to be installed and running yesterday. Yes, you can bring up a typical server quite quickly. No, it won't be long before it gets out of hand and you'll be forced to take a step back and redesign your site.

The second factor placing the pressure on you as a Web administrator is that the content on a Web site is what brings the visitors to your site, be they employees at your company (as in the case of an Intranet) or the public at large (in the case of an Internet site). Stale content will make people stop coming back, so you must constantly change the site. This means a constant flow of changes from contributing people, constant changes to layout and design, and more. It also follows that, as you get better at managing the site, you'll be interested in upgrading the underpinnings of the site to the latest and greatest tools.

As a Webmaster for your site, you need to take a step back and slow the process, even if it's only to implement scheduled updates and access control to the site. By instituting guidelines to control who can change content, and then putting schedules in place that indicate when a change will be seen on the system, you can take much of the heat off of yourself and your staff. One common approach that seems to work well is to appoint one person in charge of publishing information to the site. Then, for example, set up a weekly schedule so everyone knows that all information and updates received by Wednesday will be posted to the Web by the following Friday if at all possible.

N O T E Keep in mind that users on your network may see a really neat, new, currently-in-beta-test technology while cruising the Internet. When they request that you implement some of this technology on your site, you may not be in a position to do so. As much as it sounds like a dictatorship, you will want to keep someone in charge with the ultimate ability to say "no" to new content for whatever reason, be it for technological challenge or actual content restrictions.

It may also be the case that a request, while possible and desirable to implement, will require changes or other installed components on your system. You may want to grant the request, but it may take a bit longer than normal to implement. Don't get caught without a way of taking more time to do it right.

One exception to the gatekeeper approach to posting content may be the case of an Intranet. In an Intranet, it's usually a much looser situation in which users are able to post content directly to the server, saving you the trouble of filtering the content or reformatting it to look like the balance of the site. ■

Understanding HTTP and How It Works

Web sites are coming online at rates that are nothing less than astounding. Web servers provide content to Web browsers as documents. These documents contain special formatting called Hypertext Markup Language, or HTML. This HTML indicates to the browser exactly how a document should be displayed to the user.

Displaying a Web page requires a series of conversations between the Web browser and several components. When the user enters the address of the document to be displayed, the address he or she enters must be looked up. You may recall from Chapter 2, "Choosing a Web Server and Service Provider," that DNS and WINS services provide names to TCP/IP address resolutions on your Intranet. On the Internet, a network of DNS servers is responsible for the name resolution mapping to an IP address.

For example, when you decide you want to visit the Microsoft Web site, you simply enter **http://www.microsoft.com**. The "http" portion of the address indicates to the browser that the type of connection you're trying to make is to a Web server. The browser looks up the address on the Internet by referencing the DNS server specified by InterNIC for that domain. The address that is returned, (for example, 198.105.232.5) is then used to connect to the server.

> **N O T E** You'll be hearing more about URLs and the types of protocols later in this chapter in the "Understanding URLs" section. ▪

When your browser contacts the Web server, it requests a document, either by default or by specifically calling for a document. In cases where you don't specify any particular document name, as is the case in the previous paragraph, the default page is loaded automatically.

When the server "loads" the page, it sends the page to the Web browser for display and review. On the whole, Web pages are simple text files. As they are transmitted to the browser, formatting expressions, placement, and so on are implemented by the browser itself. Listing 5.1 shows a sample basic Web page.

Listing 5.1   A Simple HTML Document

```
<!doctype html public "-//IETF//DTD HTML//EN">
<HTML>
<HEAD>
<TITLE>HTML Sample pages</TITLE>
</HEAD>
<BODY BACKGROUND="../images/backgrnd.gif" BGCOLOR="FFFFFF">
<TABLE>
<TR>
<TD><IMG SRC="../images/SPACE.gif" ALIGN="top" ALT=" "></TD>
<TD><A HREF="/samples/IMAGES/mh_html.map">
➥ <IMG SRC="/SAMPLES/images/mh_html.gif" ismap BORDER=0
➥ ALIGN="top" ALT=" "></A></TD>
</TR>
<TR>
<TD><IMG SRC="../images/SPACE.gif" ALIGN="top" ALT=" "></TD>
<TD><HR> <font size=+3>HTML</font> <font size=+3>S</font>
➥ <font size=+2>tyle</font> <font size=+3>E</font>
➥ <font size=+2>xamples</font>
<P>
```

```
<font size=2>Below are links to several pages that demonstate styles that
are built in to the HTML language. While looking at these pages,
try using the View Source menu item in your browser to see the HTML
that defines each page. You can copy text from that view to use in
your own Web pages you are authoring.
</font>
</TD>
</TR>
<P>
<TR>
<TD><IMG SRC="../images/space.gif" ALIGN="center" ALT=" "></td>
<td>
<UL>
<IMG SRC="../images/bullet_H.gif" ALIGN="center" ALT=" ">
➡ <A HREF="/samples/htmlsamp/styles.htm">Very basic HTML styles</A>
<P><IMG SRC="../images/bullet_H.gif" ALIGN="center" ALT=" ">
➡ <A HREF="/samples/htmlsamp/styles2.htm">A few additional
➡ HTML styles</A>
<P><IMG SRC="../images/bullet_H.gif" ALIGN="center" ALT=" ">
➡ <A HREF="/samples/htmlsamp/tables.htm">Basic HTML tables</A>
</UL></font>
<P>
</td>
</tr>
</TABLE>
</BODY>
</HTML>
```

In addition to the plain text that you see in a typical HTML document, there are usually place-holders for graphics and other elements, including video clips, sound clips, and more. Even though these are binary files being called for, the notations in the HTML document that call them are text-based tags. You'll find out more about tags and how they work as this book explores different features and technologies.

When the browser encounters a tag that calls a binary file in an HTML document, it requests that file as a separate and distinct data stream. This allows the browser to control whether the object is transferred as well as when. You may notice that recently released versions of browsers display the text for a given page first. The graphics and other objects appear later, so the user can begin reading the text while the graphics load.

When the browser requests images and other binary files, they are sent, usually using the MIME (Multipurpose Internet Mail Extensions) protocol, to the requesting browser, which displays them according to the HTML page directions. With many browsers, including Microsoft's Internet Explorer shown in Figure 5.1, you can turn off images altogether, making pages load substantially faster. Select these options with the View, Options menu selection in Internet Explorer.

N O T E Image load time should be less of an issue with your Intranet since network speeds generally support good throughput. Users should usually leave the option to load pages/ view images selected to get the most out of the Web pages. ■

Part
II

Ch
5

FIG. 5.1

Turning off images can improve performance significantly, especially over slow connections to a server and those less than 28,800 baud.

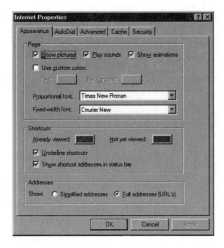

Installing Microsoft Internet Information Server (IIS)

When you install the Internet Information Server, make sure you have enough disk space to support the documents, objects, supporting graphics, and other items you plan to bring online. If you are not sure about the amount of content you are going to introduce, bring up your server now and segment the different sources of information onto other drives or servers as needed later.

Installation of the server and its components is pretty straightforward. From the distribution media, select the installation program, SETUP.EXE. You are first asked to confirm that you want to install the software on your system, and then asked to select the desired components for installation. See Figure 5.2 for an example.

FIG. 5.2

You can deselect components for your installation.

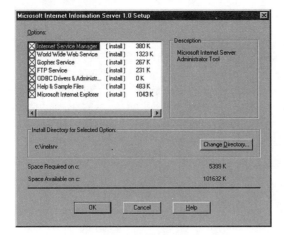

TIP Installation of ODBC components is recommended, because logging to ODBC data sources requires some items installed with these components.

You may find it curious that the IIS installs ODBC components. In addition to supporting logging capabilities that extend to ODBC databases, IIS also fully supports an integration of the IIS processes and ODBC databases. This means that your Web content is based on—or produced by—ODBC information. If you do not install this component, you cannot work with the databases later.

N O T E If you have previously installed some Microsoft Office 95/97 or other ODBC components on your system, you will notice that the disk space requirements for ODBC capabilities are 0. This is because the ODBC components are shared with the previously installed versions and require no additional application components.

It's a good idea to leave this item selected, even if it shows that the ODBC capabilities are already installed. By doing so, you allow the setup program to verify the ODBC installation and ensure that it's the most recent release. ■

▶ See how to implement database-intensive applications in Chapter 22, "Database Access and Integrity."

The next step is to indicate where you want to install the files for each of the three services (gopher, ftp and www). Be sure to note these directories because, by default, they are the starting point for each of the services. For example, consider the default directories specified in Figure 5.3. When users access your Web site, they access the **C:\INETSRV\WWWROOT** directory with these settings. This is where the Web service expects to find your initial starting pages.

FIG. 5.3
Default directories
where the Web service
expects to find your
initial starting pages.

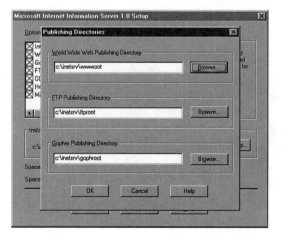

Part
II

Ch
5

You can change these directories to reflect any other directory, drive, or system you prefer. If you change them to point to a different server altogether, you introduce a new level of complexity that may be inadvisable on the initial installation. If the network connection is lost to the remote system, your service is effectively down, even though there may be nothing wrong with either the master server or the secondary server where the files reside.

Once you indicate where you want to base the services, the setup program installs each of the components and starts each of the services. You won't need to restart the server to begin using the services, they'll be ready to go immediately.

The IIS components run as NT services. After each service is installed and started, you can tell immediately if there are any potential problems with your installation. Just use the Internet Service Manager from the new Internet Services menu option. Services that start successfully are listed as running. If a service fails to start, it's listed as Stopped.

When prompted, you can select the ODBC drivers to install on your system. The drivers shipped with the server, and selected during your installation, list automatically. You can use other ODBC drivers later when you establish logging or database connectivity pages. Consequently, you do not install the driver(s) listed if they are not applicable to your installation.

The Advanced button enables you to indicate whether version checking should be done on your system during the installation. Version checking ensures that the most recent version of each of the drivers is installed by comparing the date of your system files with the date on the new, incoming files. This is generally helpful because version checking prevents your system files from being replaced if the incoming files are older. However, if you need to refresh the files, regardless of their current dates, as may be the case if you're doing extensive testing, you may want to select the Advanced option and deselect the version checking options, as shown in Figure 5.4.

FIG. 5.4
Turning off the version checking overwrites the files on your system regardless of whether they are newer than the incoming files.

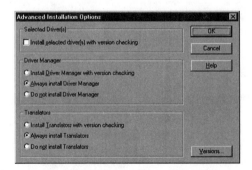

Once installed, the server installs the Internet Explorer browser and creates a new Start Menu program group.

At this point, if you review the running services in Control Panel, you see that the FTP Publishing Service, World Wide Web Publishing Service, and Gopher Publishing Services are running and ready to go.

Your server is up and running. As a quick test, start the newly installed browser. If everything is working, it displays the default home page automatically installed on your system. You should also try accessing your system by indicating **http://*machine name*** for the address. This accesses your server using the newly installed services.

Once the components are installed, configure them, making sure you maintain control in providing the best service possible to your users. In the next few sections, you'll see how to set the various options to enable logging, auditing, and other options for overseeing the activity on your system.

Setting Audit and Logging Options

While at first it may seem like an unnecessary step to begin logging accesses against your server, rest assured that logging, at least at a basic level, is more than a luxury. It's a necessity. While logging may seem like a security-only option, it is really much more. You need to know who is accessing the different components, content, and features of your server. User access information helps you to recognize the need for additional services, better ways to service users, and emerging trends in both usage and server loading.

You undoubtedly will find that some of your system components are not being used to their full potential. This is true at both the content level and at a wholesale level. In these areas, you might want to investigate updating or changing content, or removing the component completely.

Always enable logging. As you'll see, you can set up logging to maintain as much or as little history as you want. If you worry about history files piling up, consider setting options low to keep only five days of history. You can still begin to spot trends, and simultaneously use the logs to help in case of any problems that may arise.

All of the service options are managed from the Microsoft Internet Server menu option in the Internet Service Manager application group (see Figure 5.5).

FIG. 5.5

Each of the services on the server you are monitoring is shown in the Service Manager. You can make changes to configuration, logging and security from this application.

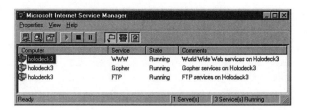

The WWW Server properties, shown in Figure 5.6, are broken into four distinct categories represented by tabs, Service, Directories, Logging, and Advanced.

FIG. 5.6

The Web Service Properties sheet provides a single point of maintenance for the options that control your World Wide Web service.

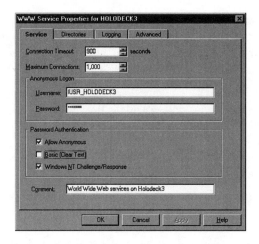

Configuring the Service Options   Two critical items on the Service Tab concern how users and their rights and privileges apply when using your system. The first, the Anonymous Logon section, specifies the default logon name and password for your system users. The second is the section that enables you to indicate the type of authentication to be used by the service.

Web browsing is typically an anonymous service, unless used in the realm of confidential information. You can lock down your entire site by removing the anonymous user feature. It is, however, more likely that you assign the anonymous user account while simultaneously securing different system areas for protected access.

When you installed your system, a new user was automatically added to your user database. The user, given a name of "IUSR_" plus the name of your system, HOLODECK3 in this case, is added with sufficient rights to access your server's services and browse your server's content. When this user is created, it is created with the same basic rights as a user that might be considered "average" without special considerations.

The user is created as a member of the DOMAIN USERS group and the GUEST group. Of course, the user also belongs to the EVERYONE group when allowed or disallowed access to a given resource. When the account is created, the initial password is blank.

An important facet about the IUSR_HOLODECK3 account is that it has been granted the right to Log on Locally, as shown in Figure 5.7.

A user must be able to log on locally because, when the user requests access, the request is made of the Web Server process. That process takes the name provided by the user and logs onto NT's standard security with it. By doing so, any security rights and permissions will also be assigned to the account, providing a solid security model, fully integrated with the NT domain model.

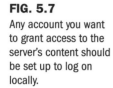

FIG. 5.7
Any account you want
to grant access to the
server's content should
be set up to log on
locally.

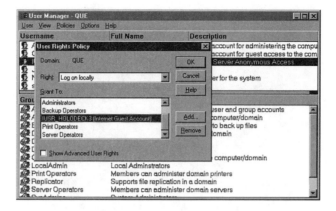

In situations in which you want every user to log into the server, deselect the Allow Anonymous checkbox. This will ensure that everyone provides a user name and password when accessing the server.

The good side effect of this is that your logging of resource usage will reflect the people who are really using the system, since it will log their user name and accesses. The downside is that you force the user to type a second login in addition to the network one. Users may consider this bothersome in today's industry push for fewer logons.

As mentioned earlier, the other important setup option is the type of authentication to be used. Two different types of authentication are used to secure all or part of your site. The mix of browsers employed on your Intranet dictates your decision of authentication type. As of this writing, the only browser supporting the Windows NT Challenge/Response option is the Microsoft Internet Explorer 2.0 or later. If you have a mixed browser community, for example if you have users using Netscape's browser, you'll be blocking them from access to your site if you select this option before Netscape has enabled it in their browser.

The NT Challenge/Response option works in this way: If a user requests a secured page and is not currently signed in with sufficient rights, the server fails the request and closes the connection to the browser. The browser knows what has happened by the server response. Since the attempt fails, the browser prompts the user for credentials, passing this information to the server along with another attempt to access the secured resources. The server uses the new credentials to log onto NT and attempts access to the resource. The renewed attempts generally occur up to three times, but are dependent on the browser used.

In addition, the user ID and password move across the link in encrypted format, protected from being stolen in transit by someone with less than noble intentions.

With the Basic (Clear Text) option, the user ID and password move across the link encoded, but still decipherable by prying eyes. The browser keeps a channel to the server open as it attempts to access the shared resource. In Figure 5.8 notice that, if you enable the Clear Text option, the Service Manager warns you that you are enabling a less secure method of user IDs and passwords. The Service Manager asks you to confirm your desire to do this.

Part
II

Ch
5

FIG. 5.8
The Service Manager warns you if you select the less secure option.

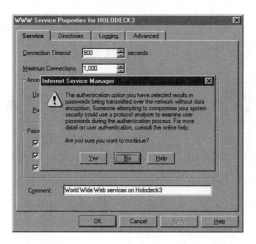

The bottom line is, if you have non-Microsoft browsers accessing secure material on your site, you must turn on the Clear Text option. If you know you do not have this concern, do not enable the Clear Text option. Simply use the NT Challenge/Response option.

> **N O T E** Most of the configuration options among the different IIS services are largely identical. Because of this, there is limited coverage in the FTP and Gopher section of this book for completing these basic options. The different configuration options are explained in the next few sections. The differences between the standard configuration with the Web server options and the FTP and Gopher services are covered later. ■

Configuring the Directories At first glance, the Directories tab may seem an unimportant feature. However, as time goes on and you provide more services to your users, you will find that the directory options are a central component of your system, especially helpful in both the Web and FTP services.

As you can see in Figure 5.9, you can establish any number of directory aliases. You can access each by an incoming Web browser request indicating the address of the alias in the URL. For example, look at the following URL:

> **http://www.intellicenter.com/users**

This URL loads the default document from the **C:\INETSRV\USERS** directory on your system.

FIG. 5.9

Setting up directories enables you to break up server content logically.

This dialog box indicates the default document option and name. Without indicating the default here, users must provide the directory name and file when accessing your Web server. If you specify a default page, the file indicated by the user's URL is provided, if the incoming URL request indicates a fully qualified document path. If it indicates only a root path, but no specific document, the default document is appended to the path. The preceding URL (**http://www.intellicenter.com/users**) actually loads the following document when the user enters the URL:

http://www.intellicenter.com/users/default.htm

You should disable this option only if you need to lock down the site and require the users accessing it to provide a fully-qualified URL to specific documents. If you deselect this option, users trying to access the site without indicating the document name receive an error message similar to the one shown in Figure 5.10.

FIG. 5.10

This message appears to the user who does not include a document name in the URL if you do not have the Default document option enabled.

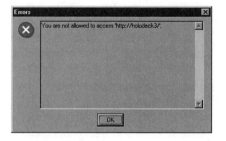

N O T E If you want to implement a system following the UNIX standard for default pages, change your default page from DEFAULT.HTM to INDEX.HTML. INDEX.HTML is the default starting page on a vast majority of Web servers, so setting the default to the standard makes it easier for an experienced Web user to maintain pages on the server. ■

One of the biggest reasons to use the Directories tab is to help manage and dissect the content you provide to the users of your system. By placing different content in different directory trees, you accomplish several things.

■ First, you place the information in physically different areas, potentially even on a different server.

■ Second, you limit the scope of any search engines incorporated at your site. You can generally limit the scope of the search engine to a particular directory structure. By separating content into different areas, you speed search time for your user base.

■ Third, you can move static content to a directory tree that may be backed up less frequently, perhaps only an a monthly basis. If you have other content that is more dynamic, perhaps pages such as those maintained by an online magazine or other constantly changing source, you can keep those types of pages in a directory tree that is backed up daily or at least more frequently than the other, more static information.

When you add a new directory, or when you update the Edit Properties for an existing directory you set up, you should establish the location of the directory and several other parameters for it. See Figure 5.11 for the dialog box that used to configure the directory aliasing.

FIG. 5.11
Use Home Directory to default to when the user fails to indicate another directory in the URL.

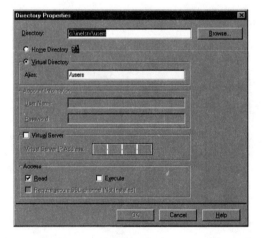

N O T E   If you depend on a Home directory to direct users to the beginning point at your site, be sure you select the Enable Default Document option for the Web Publishing Service. ■

The first item, Directory, is the physical directory location to make available to the Web service. Although this can be a Universal Naming Convention (UNC) path, plan carefully when placing content on a remote server. This is something that should be carefully planned out and is not to be taken lightly. If you provide a UNC name for the Directory entry, you must provide the User Name and Password shown in the Account Information section of the dialog box.

N O T E You can have only a single directory indicated to be the Home Directory per IIS system. If you select a new home directory, IIS prompts you to save the change to the new home location when you apply or accept the changes made. ▓

Placing content on a remote server is tricky because, when the remote server is accessed, it is accessed using the name and password you provide in all cases. If the user ID and password you provide do not have access to the resource, the user will not be able to access it. This is also true if the resource is protected and does not allow access to the user ID and password you indicate. This is true regardless of whether they should otherwise have access.

Consider the following scenario to help explain this approach. First, your main Web server is located on HOLODECK3. For your standard, default Intranet connections, users specify either **HOLODECK3** or **HTTP://HOLODECK3** to access your DEFAULT.HTM page, located in the WWWROOT directory. This works fine, because the user logs in to the system as your standard Internet Guest account, IUSR_HOLODECK3.

Now, suppose that you place some material on a system called TWINKIE. This server has a share, SECRET, that you want to connect to. Only one user, Julie, has access to \\TWINKIE\SECRET. In order to make the connection to the share, specify the full UNC path in the Directory text box and indicate both Julie's user ID and password.

The final step is to provide read access to the directory and call it SECRET. Once this is done, users will be able to access the share.

One item of caution with this scenario: Anyone accessing your server can access the new directory by simply indicating its URL. The URL is as follows:

http://holodeck3/secret

It also provides access to the DEFAULT.HTM file at that location. Remember, you initially set the directory for very limited access, only by the user named Julie. By providing the name and password in this manner in the Properties sheets for the directory mapping, you bypass the security on the directory entirely, making the information available to any user on your network. In essence, you hard-code the user name and password.

This apparent bypass of security happens because you provide NT's security layer with a valid user name and password. The remote machine does not provide the same level of security that you have if the user is attempting to access a secured directory or file physically located on the IIS server.

For this reason, carefully design your server to provide secure and non secure access to the information you want to make available. Never put information on a remote system if the information needs to be protected from some users and available to other users. Put public, widely available information on the remote server.

In cases where you have secure information, always put the information directly on the IIS server, allowing the NT security management to step in and protect the information.

Part

II

Ch

5

This same approach applies to virtual server configurations. When you indicate a virtual server, the provided username and password are used to connect to the remote system. If secure information resides at that remote location, move it to the local system and enable NT to manage the secure access to the information.

The final option in establishing a directory link is to indicate the access rights. To provide content, select Read access rights. To create a program directory to provide additional functionality to the user's Web browser experience, grant Execute rights.

Read access means read-only access. Users with those rights cannot make or save changes to the directory. *Execute access* is read-only as well, but without directory privileges—privileges that enable you to scan directory contents.

> **CAUTION**
>
> Never grant Read access to any of your established program or script subdirectories. If you do, users may not only browse the directory, looking for different programs that "look interesting," but they also can run these programs to see what they do. When you provide Execute rights, users can execute applications and scripts but cannot do blind directory listings or copy files from the location.

Configuring Logging Options   There should be no question in your mind regarding logging. You need to log accesses, and you need to monitor the resulting log files. Monitoring provides you with the needed feedback to manage the successful, and less-than-successful, content on your server. Monitoring also provides a good trace capability if your user experiences any troubles.

The log files created by the Internet Server contain the IP address for the incoming request, the type of request made, and information about the success or failure of the request. Note, too, that logs provide information about the actual accessed pages. In the case of your Web server, this information is very valuable in helping you determine what content to revise, keep, or remove from the system.

Set up logging on the Logging tab for the Web Publishing Service Properties sheet, seen in Figure 5.12.

Most logging options are self-explanatory, but there are a few items to note. Specifically, you probably want to select the Automatically open new log option and select Daily. When the service runs, the current log file is open, and you can't access it for review purposes. To provide information in a timely manner when first bringing up your Intranet, you'll want recent information as quickly as possible. By selecting the Daily option, you'll have to wait only until just after midnight to open the previous day's log.

Note that the Log file directory first points to a directory in the Windows NT directory structure. You may want to change this to a more accessible location, perhaps in the INETSRV directory structure. This is easier to manage if you use any logging or administrative utilities.

FIG. 5.12
Logging options include
logging to a text file or
to an ODBC data
source.

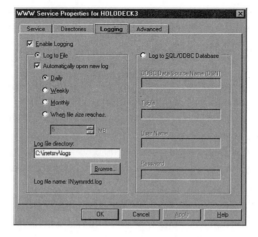

Use the Log to File option when you bring up your system, instead of setting up a database connection to log. This removes one more variable from your installation when tracking down any odd behavior seen in system startup. When your system is firmly in place, and if you are comfortable with it, implement the logging to the database.

Configuring Advanced Options   The Advanced options, common across IIS server processes, enable you to control computers whether or not they have access to your system. Figure 5.13 shows that you can indicate in which direction, either inbound or outbound, your rules govern your server. The default allows only those specifically called out to access the system.

FIG. 5.13
Setting controlling
parameters on the IP
addresses that are, or
are not, allowed access
is often a reactionary
measure to block
someone from
accessing your system.

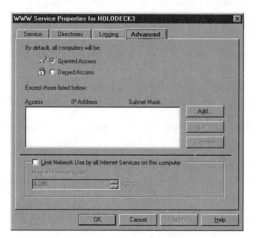

Part
II

Ch
5

The alternative is to indicate that everyone has access to the system except for those indicated on this tab. A very powerful tool, these options let you effectively lock either a person or a system out of your server. In cases where you have a confirmed attempt or attempts to compromise your system, you can remove the offending person's access rights and he'll no longer be able to bring problems to your support efforts.

Whether you're indicating who can or cannot access your system, you use the same dialog box, although it has a different title bar.

 TIP Remember, if the problem user uses DHCP, this does not necessarily prevent him or her from gaining access to the system because their address changes with each log in to the system.

When you enter the address, enter it with wild cards by selecting the Group of Computers option and providing the IP address only to the portion remaining constant for the systems addressed.

You also can specify an individual computer by indicating either the IP address, or by selecting the ellipses button and providing the computer name that should be granted or denied access.

The final option on the Advanced options tab controls the total throughput on your server. You may need to control your server's utilization. It may be too much of a hit on your company's Intranet access line. Further, you may need to maintain a certain level of performance on the server. In any event, you can control the volume of server-generated information by enabling the Limit Network Use check box. Usually, this is not a factor for an Intranet. The Limit Network Use check box is more useful for an Internet connection, to manage the flow of information through the connection to the Internet.

Installing the Apache Internet Server

Apache is a bit different from IIS in terms of how you install it and get it online. Of course, one of the biggest differences is that Apache and many other servers don't have a graphical user interface, and they're provided for the UNIX environment. As with many system-level applications for UNIX, Apache is often provided in source code format, requiring a compile of the program on your platform. This essentially builds a custom version of the application for your systems environment.

For information on building for your specific environment, see the distribution notes. Some key points to make sure you check on are:

- What optional modules do you want to install? If you want to change the modules that are used, you'll need to run the `configuration` script and indicate which ones you want to add, change, or delete.

- Will you be installing to a directory that is different from the default? The default directories, `/src` for the source code, etc., are called out in the link files. If you are changing these, you need to make sure you locate the new files in the configuration script.

- Update the `modules.c` file to include options you want to install.

There may be other options that you need to specify, depending on the installation parameters you select and the optional modules you install. Once you build the binary distribution set, you need to set up the run time configuration parameters. These are the important items that provide the key information about how your system will run, from multi-homing your server to providing support for directories, security, and more.

The core of these options is provided in the `httpd.conf`, `access.conf` and `srm.conf` files. The most basic of these is the `httpd.conf` file, which you'll need to rename from the distribution set. It's provided to you as `httpd.conf-dist`. Listing 5.2 shows the standard configuration file as provided with the distribution of Apache.

Listing 5.2   Listing of Default httpd.conf Configuration File

```
# This is the main server configuration file. See URL http://www.apache.org/
# for instructions.

# Do NOT simply read the instructions in here without understanding
# what they do, if you are unsure consult the online docs. You have been
# warned.

# Originally by Rob McCool

# ServerType is either inetd, or standalone.

ServerType standalone

# If you are running from inetd, go to "ServerAdmin".

# Port: The port the standalone listens to. For ports < 1023, you will
# need httpd to be run as root initially.

Port 80

# HostnameLookups: Log the names of clients or just their IP numbers
#   e.g.   www.apache.org (on) or 204.62.129.132 (off)
HostnameLookups on

# If you wish httpd to run as a different user or group, you must run
# httpd as root initially and it will switch.

# User/Group: The name (or #number) of the user/group to run httpd as.
#   On SCO (ODT 3) use User nouser and Group nogroup
User nobody
Group #-1

# ServerAdmin: Your address, where problems with the server should be
# e-mailed.

ServerAdmin you@your.address

# ServerRoot: The directory the server's config, error, and log files
# are kept in
```

Part

II

Ch

5

continues

Listing 5.2   Continued

```
ServerRoot /usr/local/etc/httpd

# BindAddress: You can support virtual hosts with this option. This option
# is used to tell the server which IP address to listen to. It can either
# contain "*", an IP address, or a fully qualified Internet domain name.
# See also the VirtualHost directive.

#BindAddress *

# ErrorLog: The location of the error log file. If this does not start
# with /, ServerRoot is prepended to it.

ErrorLog logs/error_log

# TransferLog: The location of the transfer log file. If this does not
# start with /, ServerRoot is prepended to it.

TransferLog logs/access_log

# PidFile: The file the server should log its pid to
PidFile logs/httpd.pid

# ScoreBoardFile: File used to store internal server process information
ScoreBoardFile logs/apache_status

# ServerName allows you to set a host name which is sent back to clients for
# your server if it's different than the one the program would get (i.e. use
# "www" instead of the host's real name).
#
# Note: You cannot just invent host names and hope they work. The name you
# define here must be a valid DNS name for your host. If you don't understand
# this, ask your network administrator.

#ServerName new.host.name

# CacheNegotiatedDocs: By default, Apache sends Pragma: no-cache with each
# document that was negotiated on the basis of content. This asks proxy
# servers not to cache the document. Uncommenting the following line disables
# this behavior, and proxies will be allowed to cache the documents.

#CacheNegotiatedDocs

# Timeout: The number of seconds before receives and sends time out
#   n.b. the compiled default is 1200 (20 minutes !)

Timeout 400

# KeepAlive: The number of Keep-Alive persistent requests to accept
# per connection. Set to 0 to deactivate Keep-Alive support

KeepAlive 5
```

```
# KeepAliveTimeout: Number of seconds to wait for the next request

KeepAliveTimeout 15

# Server-pool size regulation.  Rather than making you guess how many
# server processes you need, Apache dynamically adapts to the load it
# sees --- that is, it tries to maintain enough server processes to
# handle the current load, plus a few spare servers to handle transient
# load spikes (e.g., multiple simultaneous requests from a single
# Netscape browser).

# It does this by periodically checking how many servers are waiting
# for a request.  If there are fewer than MinSpareServers, it creates
# a new spare.  If there are more than MaxSpareServers, some of the
# spares die off.  These values are probably OK for most sites ---

MinSpareServers 5
MaxSpareServers 10

# Number of servers to start --- should be a reasonable ballpark figure.

StartServers 5

# Limit on total number of servers running, i.e., limit on the number
# of clients who can simultaneously connect --- if this limit is ever
# reached, clients will be LOCKED OUT, so it should NOT BE SET TOO LOW.
# It is intended mainly as a brake to keep a runaway server from taking
# Unix with it as it spirals down...

MaxClients 150

# MaxRequestsPerChild: the number of requests each child process is
#   allowed to process before the child dies.
#   The child will exit so as to avoid problems after prolonged use when
#   Apache (and maybe the libraries it uses) leak.  On most systems, this
#   isn't really needed, but a few (such as Solaris) do have notable leaks
#   in the libraries.

MaxRequestsPerChild 30

# Proxy Server directives. Uncomment the following line to
# enable the proxy server:

#ProxyRequests On

# To enable the cache as well, edit and uncomment the following lines:

#CacheRoot /usr/local/etc/httpd/proxy
#CacheSize 5
#CacheGcInterval 4
#CacheMaxExpire 24
#CacheLastModifiedFactor 0.1
#CacheDefaultExpire 1
#NoCache adomain.com anotherdomain.edu joes.garage.com
```

Part

II

Ch

5

continues

Listing 5.2 Continued

```
# Listen: Allows you to bind Apache to specific IP addresses and/or
# ports, in addition to the default. See also the VirtualHost command

#Listen 3000
#Listen 12.34.56.78:80

# VirtualHost: Allows the daemon to respond to requests for more than one
# server address, if your server machine is configured to accept IP packets
# for multiple addresses. This can be accomplished with the ifconfig
# alias flag, or through kernel patches like VIF.

# Any httpd.conf or srm.conf directive may go into a VirtualHost command.
# See alto the BindAddress entry.

#<VirtualHost host.foo.com>
#ServerAdmin webmaster@host.foo.com
#DocumentRoot /www/docs/host.foo.com
#ServerName host.foo.com
#ErrorLog logs/host.foo.com-error_log
#TransferLog logs/host.foo.com-access_log
#</VirtualHost>
```

The options presented in this configuration file are outlined at **http://www.apache.org/docs/core.html**, but there are some key items to keep an eye on in this file as they control some key aspects that you've been reading about. See Table 5.1 for several key configuration options you'll need to work with in your installation.

Table 5.1 Key Configuration Options

Option	Applies to
Port	What port the server will be listening to. A somewhat standard testing port is 8080. If you want to access a port other than the default 80, your browser will need to specify it as part of the URL. For example, **http://www.yoursite.com:8080**.
ServerRoot	This is where the directory structure for your files begins. In IIS, this equates to the HOME directory.
VirtualHost	Also known as multi-homing your server. This option sets up the other host names that will be supported by your server.

The access.conf file contains basic authentication information that will be used site-wide. Listing 5.3 shows the default file that contains this information. As with httpd.conf, you'll need to rename this file from the distribution set as it's provided as access.conf-dist.

Listing 5.3 The Default access.conf File

```
# access.conf: Global access configuration
# Online docs at http://www.apache.org/

# This file defines server settings which affect which types of services
# are allowed, and in what circumstances.

# Each directory to which Apache has access, can be configured with respect
# to which services and features are allowed and/or disabled in that
# directory (and its subdirectories).

# Originally by Rob McCool

# This should be changed to whatever you set DocumentRoot to.

<Directory /usr/local/etc/httpd/htdocs>

# This may also be "None", "All", or any combination of "Indexes",
# "Includes", "FollowSymLinks", "ExecCGI", or "MultiViews".

# Note that "MultiViews" must be named *explicitly* --- "Options All"
# doesn't give it to you (or at least, not yet).

Options Indexes FollowSymLinks

# This controls which options the .htaccess files in directories can
# override. Can also be "All", or any combination of "Options", "FileInfo",
# "AuthConfig", and "Limit"

AllowOverride None

# Controls who can get stuff from this server.

order allow,deny
allow from all

</Directory>

# /usr/local/etc/httpd/cgi-bin should be changed to whatever your ScriptAliased
# CGI directory exists, if you have that configured.

<Directory /usr/local/etc/httpd/cgi-bin>
AllowOverride None
Options None
</Directory>

# Allow server status reports, with the URL of http://servername/status
# Change the ".nowhere.com" to match your domain to enable.

#<Location /status>
#SetHandler server-status
```

Part

II

Ch

5

continues

Listing 5.3 Continued

```
#order deny,allow
#deny from all
#allow from .nowhere.com
#</Location>

# You may place any other directories or locations you wish to have
# access information for after this one.
```

The information in this file equates roughly to the Windows NT User Manager and how you apply security permissions in the earlier coverage of IIS. You can limit who has access, what resources they have access to, and what type of access they are allowed.

In addition, the final configuration file, srm.conf, provided as srm.conf-dist, gives you the ability to customize the users' experience on your site. "User experience" is what the user sees as different types of information presented. For example, consider the default file, shown in Listing 5.4. The icons that will be used when the site is accessed are each called out for the different types of content. You can add fancier icons, or you can leave them as their supplied defaults.

Listing 5.4 Listing of the Standard srm.conf File

```
# With this document, you define the name space that users see of your http
# server.  This file also defines server settings which affect how requests are
# serviced, and how results should be formatted.

# See the tutorials at http://www.apache.org/ for
# more information.

# Originally by Rob McCool; Adapted for Apache


# DocumentRoot: The directory out of which you will serve your
# documents. By default, all requests are taken from this directory, but
# symbolic links and aliases may be used to point to other locations.

DocumentRoot /usr/local/etc/httpd/htdocs

# UserDir: The name of the directory which is appended onto a user's home
# directory if a ~user request is recieved.

UserDir public_html

# DirectoryIndex: Name of the file or files to use as a pre-written HTML
# directory index.  Separate multiple entries with spaces.

DirectoryIndex index.html

# FancyIndexing is whether you want fancy directory indexing or standard
```

```
FancyIndexing on

# AddIcon tells the server which icon to show for different files or filename
# extensions

AddIconByEncoding (CMP,/icons/compressed.gif) x-compress x-gzip

AddIconByType (TXT,/icons/text.gif) text/*
AddIconByType (IMG,/icons/image2.gif) image/*
AddIconByType (SND,/icons/sound2.gif) audio/*
AddIconByType (VID,/icons/movie.gif) video/*

AddIcon /icons/binary.gif .bin .exe
AddIcon /icons/binhex.gif .hqx
AddIcon /icons/tar.gif .tar
AddIcon /icons/world2.gif .wrl .wrl.gz .vrml .vrm .iv
AddIcon /icons/compressed.gif .Z .z .tgz .gz .zip
AddIcon /icons/a.gif .ps .ai .eps
AddIcon /icons/layout.gif .html .shtml .htm .pdf
AddIcon /icons/text.gif .txt
AddIcon /icons/c.gif .c
AddIcon /icons/p.gif .pl .py
AddIcon /icons/f.gif .for
AddIcon /icons/dvi.gif .dvi
AddIcon /icons/uuencoded.gif .uu
AddIcon /icons/script.gif .conf .sh .shar .csh .ksh .tcl
AddIcon /icons/tex.gif .tex
AddIcon /icons/bomb.gif core

AddIcon /icons/back.gif ..
AddIcon /icons/hand.right.gif README
AddIcon /icons/folder.gif ^^DIRECTORY^^
AddIcon /icons/blank.gif ^^BLANKICON^^

# DefaultIcon is which icon to show for files which do not have an icon
# explicitly set.

DefaultIcon /icons/unknown.gif

# AddDescription allows you to place a short description after a file in
# server-generated indexes.
# Format: AddDescription "description" filename

# ReadmeName is the name of the README file the server will look for by
# default. Format: ReadmeName name
#
# The server will first look for name.html, include it if found, and it will
# then look for name and include it as plaintext if found.
#
# HeaderName is the name of a file which should be prepended to
# directory indexes.

ReadmeName README
HeaderName HEADER
```

Part

II

Ch

5

continues

Listing 5.4   Continued

```
# IndexIgnore is a set of filenames which directory indexing should ignore
# Format: IndexIgnore name1 name2...

IndexIgnore */.??* *~ *# */HEADER* */README* */RCS

# AccessFileName: The name of the file to look for in each directory
# for access control information.

AccessFileName .htaccess

# DefaultType is the default MIME type for documents which the server
# cannot find the type of from filename extensions.

DefaultType text/plain

# AddEncoding allows you to have certain browsers (Mosaic/X 2.1+) uncompress
# information on the fly. Note: Not all browsers support this.

AddEncoding x-compress Z
AddEncoding x-gzip gz

# AddLanguage allows you to specify the language of a document. You can
# then use content negotiation to give a browser a file in a language
# it can understand.  Note that the suffix does not have to be the same
# as the language keyword --- those with documents in Polish (whose
# net-standard language code is pl) may wish to use "AddLanguage pl .po"
# to avoid the ambiguity with the common suffix for perl scripts.

AddLanguage en .en
AddLanguage fr .fr
AddLanguage de .de
AddLanguage da .da
AddLanguage el .el
AddLanguage it .it

# LanguagePriority allows you to give precedence to some languages
# in case of a tie during content negotiation.
# Just list the languages in decreasing order of preference.

LanguagePriority en fr de

# Redirect allows you to tell clients about documents which used to exist in
# your server's namespace, but do not anymore. This allows you to tell the
# clients where to look for the relocated document.
# Format: Redirect fakename url


# Aliases: Add here as many aliases as you need (with no limit). The format is
# Alias fakename realname

#Alias /icons/ /usr/local/etc/httpd/icons/
```

```
# ScriptAlias: This controls which directories contain server scripts.
# Format: ScriptAlias fakename realname

#ScriptAlias /cgi-bin/ /usr/local/etc/httpd/cgi-bin/

# If you want to use server side includes, or CGI outside
# ScriptAliased directories, uncomment the following lines.

# AddType allows you to tweak mime.types without actually editing it, or to
# make certain files to be certain types.
# Format: AddType type/subtype ext1

# AddHandler allows you to map certain file extensions to "handlers",
# actions unrelated to filetype. These can be either built into the server
# or added with the Action command (see below)
# Format: AddHandler action-name ext1

# To use CGI scripts:
#AddHandler cgi-script .cgi

# To use server-parsed HTML files
#AddType text/html .shtml
#AddHandler server-parsed .shtml

# Uncomment the following line to enable Apache's send-asis HTTP file
# feature
#AddHandler send-as-is asis

# If you wish to use server-parsed imagemap files, use
#AddHandler imap-file map

# To enable type maps, you might want to use
#AddHandler type-map var

# Action lets you define media types that will execute a script whenever
# a matching file is called. This eliminates the need for repeated URL
# pathnames for oft-used CGI file processors.
# Format: Action media/type /cgi-script/location
# Format: Action handler-name /cgi-script/location

# For example to add a footer (footer.html in your document root) to
# files with extension .foot (e.g. foo.html.foot), you could use:
#AddHandler foot-action foot
#Action foot-action /cgi-bin/footer

# Or to do this for all HTML files, for example, use:
#Action text/html /cgi-bin/footer

# MetaDir: specifies the name of the directory in which Apache can find
# meta information files. These files contain additional HTTP headers
# to include when sending the document

#MetaDir .web
```

continues

Part

II

Ch

5

Listing 5.4 Continued

```
# MetaSuffix: specifies the file name suffix for the file containing the
# meta information.

#MetaSuffix .meta

# Customizable error response (Apache style)
#   these come in three flavors
#
#     1) plain text
#ErrorDocument 500 "The server made a boo boo.
#   n.b.  the (") marks it as text, it does not get output
#
#     2) local redirects
#ErrorDocument 404 /missing.html
#   to redirect to local url /missing.html
#ErrorDocument 404 /cgi-bin/missing_handler.pl
#   n.b. can redirect to a script or a document using server-side-includes.
#
#     3) external redirects
#ErrorDocument 402 http://other.server.com/subscription_info.html
#
```

The options in this example are self-explanatory, and generally well-commented. They lay out the different ways the server will respond to different types of requests. Of special note are the responses provided to error conditions. By changing the response files, you can add more information to be sent to the user when a problem is encountered. This lets you give, for example, a Webmaster mailto: address that can be used to report a problem encountered by the user.

You can see that the same basic options apply between servers. It's largely their implementation—and in some cases the terminology—that changes. To make it easier to manage your server implementation, learn the basics, and then base your knowledge of specific software on the changes from the "norm." In other words, if you learn and understand "multi-home" and how it works for Apache, to learn it for IIS you'd need only to understand the following:

■ It's called a *virtual server* in IIS.
■ It's implemented by indicating the different IP addresses in the Directories tab of the IIS Service Manager and then indicating the home directory for the virtual server.

Reality Check

At the Integra site, located at **http://www.integra.net**, we've had to implement many of the steps outlined in this chapter, especially as they relate to the control of the site. Initially, we brought the site up with many different people having direct access to the content. This was confusing, and presented content synchronization problems, since more than one person could be making changes to files on the system. Our site is based on the Microsoft IIS server and hosts several virtual servers.

We put into place some scheduling for updates and requests for changes. In the examples provided at the beginning of this chapter, it was mentioned that you may want to implement policies that provide timeframes for when you'll implement changes. We found this necessary, because several different offices were requesting changes and updates to content. By providing more concrete dates and timeframes for changes, it lessened the stress levels and let people know when to expect their changes to show up on the site.

One important note is you cannot always rely on fixed timeframes. Exceptions will inevitably arise. There will be times when you need to make quick changes, update pages, or remove information altogether. Keep flexible and be ready to judge specific requests on their immediacy to and impact on your site.

Integra has implemented an IIS-based site with other servers located within the company as experimental content providers. We've also implemented the system as a two-server system, placing Internet-related information on a primary server and Intranet information on a different server to help physically separate company-confidential information.

From Here...

In this chapter you've learned about the fundamentals that you need to consider when you install your server. From directories to security, there are several key areas to consider. For more information on these topics, you can refer to the following sources:

- Chapter 2, "Choosing a Web Server and Service Provider," gives you additional information about deciding which server is best for your needs.

- In Chapter 3, "Planning an Intranet Site," in the "Understanding Security" section you will find additional details about indicating specific access levels at the directory level.

- Chapter 10, "Maintenance Utilities," will help you determine what types of things to start looking for after you've brought your site online.

Part
II

Ch
5

Setting Up an FTP Site

In this chapter, you'll see how to set up an FTP (File Transfer Protocol) site that is both manageable and usable, both protected and accessible. These seem like divergent goals, but they will need to work together in your implementation.

When you bring up an FTP site, you're offering some pretty hard-core access to your server. You're also allowing people to upload and download files to and from your system. These are important capabilities, but they also bring with them some significant responsibilities and concerns about how you keep track of what's happening.

Before you start, be sure you have a profile of your different types of users. Users of your FTP site will probably fall into one or more of the following categories:

Practical application and use of the FTP service

You'll learn how to apply security and rights to your FTP site, including how to protect information on the site.

Advanced setup and monitoring of the FTP service

Continuing maintenance of your FTP service is a necessity if you're to keep it running and available to users. This means reviewing and understanding the logs and other analysis tools you use to judge the traffic on your server.

Making FTP information available from a Web browser

The vast majority of users on the Web, both internal and external to your organization, are probably using a Web browser. You'll see how you can create the pages that will reference your FTP site to provide documents on demand.

Sample site layout and implementation

In addition to working with the Reality Check site, you'll see how to set up a customer service site that allows controlled access to documents, program updates, and more.

■ General, public user—These types of users probably will fall under the Anonymous user heading, those that require no supervision on your system. There may actually be no users on your server that fall into this category. This may be the case when you're bringing up a highly secure server and do not have any need for uncontrolled access, even on a limited basis, to information on the system.

■ General, private user—These types of users are generally individually validated on the system, but have access to information that is available to a large class of users. For example, consider the case where you may be publishing information that pertains to your company that is not for general consumption. Employees of your company have access to the information just by being employees. For this type of user, you might create a login that is a group login or other general purpose login for users that belong to that group.

■ Member of unique private group—Unique, private groups are for those instances where you notice that a number of people are being granted a set of rights. You may recall from Chapter 2, "Choosing a Web Server and Service Provider," that it's recommended that you assign all rights based on a group, even in those cases where you're providing rights to only a single user. Granting rights based on groups allows for easier maintenance later down the road as you can add and delete group members and the rights will be applied automatically. Consider creating a "Public FTP" group and then one group for each controlled access area you are bringing online. For example, typical groups might include "Policy FTP" and "Authors FTP."

■ Unique private individual user—There will be those cases where you need to grant special, one-time access to a user. One example of this is where you need to allow the user only to quickly upload or download a specific file to fill an urgent need. In this case, it's recommended that you set up the account, let the user do what is needed, and then remove or disable the account. This will prevent access on the account later when you're not expecting it.

N O T E You'll find specific information about implementing each of these levels of security, along with any special precautions that may apply, in the sections that follow in this chapter. ■

You'll want to have a good idea of the different types of access you'd like to provide to these users. You won't have to know specifics for the examples in this chapter, but you will want to be able to apply the information as you go to your unique implementation. ■

Understanding FTP

File Transfer Protocol, or FTP, provides a way to transfer binary files over the network. In a situation such as an Intranet, this may seem like a moot issue, as you can simply share a network drive and then allow people to attach to it and get copies of their files in that manner.

While it's true that you can use the network sharing approach, there may be cases where you need to have a server providing only Intranet capabilities, not the ability to share directly to it.

This may be the case when you want to provide concurrent access to the information over the Internet and your internal network, or when you need to have someone administer a site who is not a network administrator.

If you're setting up an Intranet, you'll probably wonder why you'd implement an FTP server on an internal network. This is a good question, and there are several different reasons you may want to bring up this type of server, such as in the following situations:

- If you're using Windows NT, the FTP administrator does not have to be the domain administrator. Since control over which users access the site will reside with the security implemented at the server, the FTP administrator won't need to have access to overall network security.

- User access can be independent of direct access to the server. For example, when users access an FTP directory structure, there is no need to set up a separate network access point. The FTP virtual directories are separate and distinct from any network shares you may have implemented.

- HTTP protocol does not support walking down share directories, but you can create virtual directories with FTP and most browsers will allow you to interactively traverse the directories.

There are cases where, depending on how you implement links between objects on your site, you'll probably have both network shares and FTP virtual directories. Also, perhaps the biggest benefit is the one offered earlier, that of remote access to the information on your server. If you have an Internet/Intranet shared server, you can provide secure access to information to people who may be on the road or on a remote WAN connection.

In the coming sections, you'll see exactly how to set up these types of connections and what considerations you'll need to keep in mind as you do. You'll see several examples of how to implement scenarios that may be similar to what you're trying to do with your site. Keep in mind that these are examples only and that you'll likely begin taking pieces from each sample implementation to build the solution to your specific requirements.

Accessing Your FTP Site from Web Pages

When you design your site, you'll probably have software update pages or other occasions to allow downloads from your site. It's convenient to provide these capabilities from a Web page that allows access to the files by simply clicking the link. Figure 6.1 shows an example of this type of implementation.

There are several ways you can get to the location. Of course, you can always just specify the address at the DOS command line or URL Open: text box within your browser. To do so, you'll use the following format:

```
ftp://<site>.[<subdir>...].<file>
```

The following is an example:

```
ftp://ftp.intellicenter.com/classes/samples/iis.zip
```

FIG. 6.1

Providing links to file downloads from your FTP site is a convenient way to offer browser access to files.

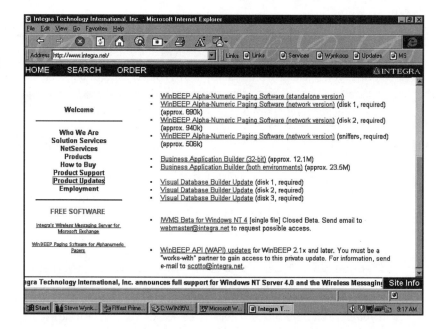

The preceding example indicates that you need to connect to the IntelliCenter FTP site and you want the IIS.ZIP file. It's located in the /classes/samples virtual directory. What happens when you indicate the file in this manner varies from browser to browser. In most cases, the file is downloaded and you have the option of opening it or just saving it to a disk.

The actual reaction will vary, however, because browsers are becoming more intelligent in how they work with files that are downloaded. For example, if you point your browser to a DOC file, and you have the Word Viewer installed, the document will automatically be opened for you in the Word Viewer. If you select a graphic with Internet Explorer, the graphic will be displayed in the browser if it's a compatible, known graphic format.

▶ For more information about using viewers, see Chapter 3, "Planning an Intranet Site."

Setting Up an FTP Site

As you've probably determined by now, installing the FTP service and getting it running is only the first step in making responsible FTP services available on your network. The term "responsible" may seem strange here, but it's important to understand that providing general read/write file access on your server is not the best solution for your users. If a system is too open, it lends itself to tampering, and once an altered file makes its way into your archives, you run the risk of users losing confidence in your site. Lost confidence means lost users, and if people aren't accessing your site, why have it in the first place? The responsibility that you have as site administrator is to take every reasonable precaution to provide reliable access to information for your users.

Installation on a LINUX System

After you've installed your LINUX system software, you need to enable and configure the FTP options. Under LINUX and UNIX installations, the FTP services spawned off by the inetd core process, the daemon process, are responsible for monitoring ports for activity. It handles each FTP connection individually. As requests arrive at the port, usually 21 in the case of FTP, an FTP process is launched to handle the session.

You have to tell the inetd process about your desire to run an FTP service, and you do so by setting up the inetd.config file, which should be located in your /etc directory. The following is an example configuration line you'll need to set up in the file:

```
ftp stream tcp nowait root /usr/etc/ftpd ftpd -l
```

N O T E This line may already exist in the configuration file and may be either fully functional or commented out. To uncomment the line, remove the comment character and save the file. You'll need to restart your server. ▇

The parameters to this line are shown in Table 6.1.

Table 6.1 FTP Configuration Parameters

Parameter	Description
ftp	The name of the service to configure. Must match the name of the service, including upper- and lowercase letters, as found in the /etc/services directory.
stream tcp	This indicates the type of connection to be expected. In this case, TCP will handle ordering and synchronizing the packets over the connection so that it appears to the application as if the packets were received in an ordered stream of information.
nowait	This indicates that a new request will be handled immediately, rather than sequentially as would be the case with this option set to wait.
root	The LINUX/UNIX user ID that will be used to run the service.
/usr/etc/ftpd	Indicates the name and path to the service.
ftpd -l	The command line to start the service, which, in this case, indicates that you want to have the logging option turned on.

Part
II

Ch
6

There are several options available on the command line when you start the ftpd process. These options are summarized in Table 6.2.

Table 6.2   Command Line Options for the ftpd Service

Option	Description
-l	Enables logging for the service.
-d	Enables debugging logging information. This information is written to the syslog.
-t *seconds*	Sets the timeout interval in seconds. This option defaults to 15 minutes, or 900 seconds. If no activity is occurring over an FTP session for 15 minutes, the connection will be terminated automatically. Notice the case of the option is lowercase compared with the next option.
-T *seconds*	In some cases, a client application can request a longer timeout value. This may be the case over known congested connections. This option allows you to specify what the maximum timeframe can be for the timeout value.

After you've restarted your server, the system will be actively monitoring port 21 for incoming requests. If a request arrives, the user will have to log in to the system and will be given access to the default directory structure as determined by the user's home directory on your system.

It's often the case, however, that you want to enable a user named *anonymous*. This user, the Internet standard for anonymous access to an FTP site, must be set up to be recognized by the FTP service on your system. To set up the user, you'll need to create a profile in the server's /etc/passwd file. When the FTP process starts, the first thing it checks is the passwd file to see what users are allowed. This file is for those users who are different from the standard users on your system. Users you have defined on your system will automatically have access to the server. You don't need to redefine them here.

You set up the anonymous user by making an entry in the passwd file as noted above. The entry calls out the user name and indicates what will be the root directory on the system.

```
ftp:*500:25:anonymous FTP user:/usr/anon:bin
```

The key item on this line is the /usr/anon specification for the root directory for the user. This indicates that, even in cases where the user changes to the root directory, if he or she is logged in as anonymous, the "root" directory will actually be in the /usr/anon directory on your system. This prevents the user from gaining access to other areas on your system.

Installation of IIS's FTP Service on a Windows NT System

When you install IIS, one of the default options is to install the FTP service. When you do, the default directory structure will include \FTPROOT, the starting point for the FTP services. By default, the <home> directory for IIS FTP services is the \FTPROOT directory, so you won't have to set up this directory and its associated access rights.

▶ For more information on installing IIS, see Chapter 5, "Setting Up and Configuring a Web Server."

IIS uses IUSR_*machinename* for the anonymous user for all accesses, whether they are from the Web services or the FTP services. When users log in as anonymous, they are automatically mapped to the IUSR_*machinename* user. The rights for that user are then applied to the FTP user's request to work with files and directories on your system.

Controlling Anonymous-Only Access with IIS   When you set up the FTP services, you must indicate the type of access that will be used to validate the users who want access to your site. This includes indicating the account that will be used when the user selects the special anonymous account when signing on to your site. As you can see in Figure 6.2, you have two options that indicate how secured access will be gained to your site. The Allow Anonymous Connections and Allow Only Anonymous Connections options control more than may first be apparent.

FIG. 6.2

If you want to secure your FTP materials, be sure to carefully consider how you'll indicate default user information in the FTP service property sheets.

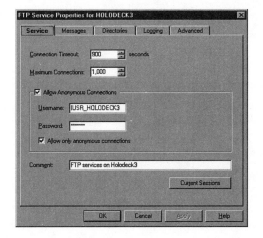

These options, while seemingly very similar, offer quite different results. The first, Allow Anonymous Connections, indicates whether a user will be able to sign on to your FTP service without first indicating a user name and password. Without this option, the name and password entered must be valid to Windows NT on the server that the user is attempting to sign in to. This means that if JohnSmith, with a password of BLAHBLAH, attempts to access your site, he must first have a valid account at the site. If not, he will not be able to access any content at the site. You'll notice that if you disable either of these options, you'll receive a dialog box indicating that you're selecting options that may be less secure. Figure 6.3 shows an example of this dialog box.

When you disable either or both of these options, you'll be requiring that the user be validated to the NT security system. This is true because there are no FTP clients that will encode or encrypt your user ID and password when signing on to the server. Therefore, the user ID and password must be sent without these precautions, leaving open the possibility that someone could be monitoring the lines on which your network runs.

Part
II

Ch

FIG. 6.3

If you turn off anonymous login, you're forcing the user to log in to the server, passing nonencrypted passwords over the Internet — IIS warns you of this fact if you disable either of the options.

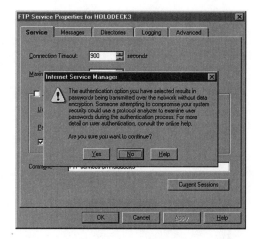

NOTE When you installed IIS, the user created to handle the FTP logins had the security options for it set automatically. One of the key items that is set up is the account right to "Log on locally" to the system. If you disable the A̲llow Only Anonymous Connections option, you must set this account right for every account you expect to log on to the system. If you do not, the users will be denied access when they try to access the system.

Use the following steps to create this type of account rights installation:

1. Create the new user account in User Manager for Domains.

2. Select the user account you want to work with. Note that this operation can be completed for groups of people as well. You can select multiple items by clicking the first user account you want to work with and then Ctrl-clicking all other accounts from the list for which you want to work with rights.

3. Select P̲olicies, U̲ser Rights. The dialog box you'll see should be similar to the one shown in Figure 6.4.

FIG. 6.4

Log on locally is a required right for all accesses against the server by outside users.

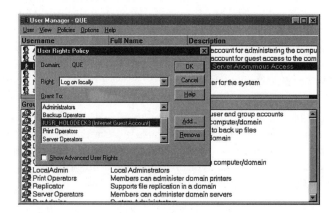

4. From the Right: drop-down list box, select the Log on locally privilege.

5. Verify that the user you're concerned with is listed in the Grant to: list box.

   If not, select Add: and then either select the group you want to grant access to, or select Show Users and find the specific user you want to have this right.

6. Select Add to give the right to the user.

7. Click OK. The user is added to the Grant to: list box in the User Rights Policy dialog box.

Once you've completed these steps, the user will be able to use his or her ID and password to gain access to your system. Standard security checking is still done at the NT domain level, and the user is logged into the different log files whenever he accesses the system. ▨

By turning on the requirement for valid user names, you may be causing problems for some users who are accessing your FTP site with their Web browsers. It may be that their browser of choice does not support accessing a secured FTP site. This is an important consideration if you'll be supporting many different user environments.

If at all possible, you should recommend to your user base that they use a "true" FTP client. Figure 6.5 shows what one of the more comprehensive and easy-to-use clients looks like today. Technology is constantly changing, so you can expect to see the user interface get simpler, allowing more secure access.

FIG. 6.5
WS_FTP32, a
shareware FTP client,
provides a solid
interface that allows
you to log on to a site
using a user name and
password.

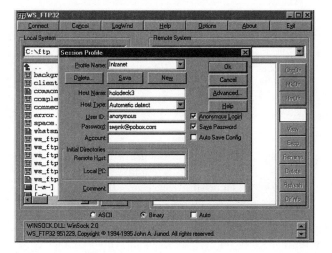

You can find the shareware version of ws_ftp32 on the CD that accompanies this book.

With this type of FTP utility, you can easily indicate the name and password you want to use to access the FTP site. If you turn off the ability to accept anonymous logon, you'll want to consider providing your users with a utility such as this.

Service-Level Read and Write Permissions with IIS   Another important consideration is the permissions associated with a given directory tree. Remember, the rights associated with a given login are a combination of rights first established at the service level and then modified at the operating system level. This means that, if your account has write privileges for a directory but the NT security system does not support the rights for your account, the rights will not be granted. Conversely, if you have NT-level rights to a directory that allow you to write to it, and the directory within IIS shows as read-only, the rights will be read-only.

You should think of rights that pertain to these users as applying the most restrictive case to their user rights. Figure 6.6 shows the Directory Properties dialog box that enables you to set these options.

FIG. 6.6

If you want to prevent the upload of files to your site, be sure you deselect the Write privileges associated with a virtual directory.

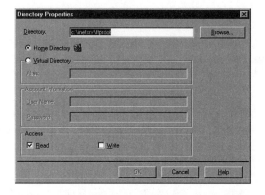

Remember, FTP is the most open protocol that allows access to your server. At its most permissive settings, you are basically granting the right to browse directories, upload and download files, create new directories, and more. FTP, and the rights you assign at the service and account levels, is worth the time to think about. Be sure you have the precautions in place that you need. In the next releases of browsers, users will even be able to upload files via their Web browser software. You can count on accessibility getting easier and easier for your user base.

Controlling IIS Access via IP Addresses A brute-force control method for your network, one that provides essentially bulletproof access control, is to limit access by IP address. When you set up your site, you can determine which IP addresses, or series of addresses, are allowed on your site. As you can see in Figure 6.7, you control IP access on an exception basis.

First, select the default access allowance. Will you generally allow all users to gain access, or will you generally *not* allow users on the system except in those cases where you've specifically granted access? Select the general rule you want, either Granted Access or Denied Access.

Whichever you select, you can then indicate which IP addresses, or IP address ranges, fall outside the rule you've indicated. In other words, if you say that most computers are granted access, the IP addresses you list will be denied access. If you indicate that the default is to provide denied access, the IP addresses you indicate *will* be provided access to the system.

By selecting the Add or Edit buttons, you can specify or update the IP addresses that are allowed on your system. Figure 6.8 shows the dialog box that is used to provide this information.

FIG. 6.7

Controlling access by IP address can be tedious, but it's a sure way to manage the people who can access your information.

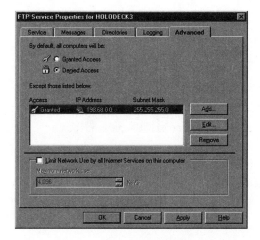

FIG. 6.8

When you indicate the IP address, you can select the ellipses ("...") button and provide a computer name to be looked up in DNS.

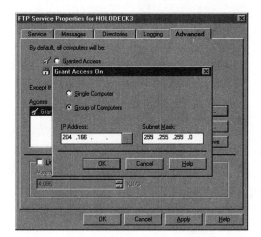

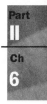

TIP Remember, you can specify a "wildcard" IP address range. For example, as you can see in Figure 6.8, only the first portion of the IP address, "204.166," is indicated. IIS will add the final portion of the address, but this address is combined with the Subnet Mask, and all computers that fall within that range are impacted by the setting.

This is especially helpful if you're running your Intranet over the Internet. If you're concerned about someone else coming into your system, and have an assigned range of values for your company's IP addresses, you can disable access by default and then grant access specifically to only those computers with IP addresses that are known to your system ahead of time.

You'll notice in Figure 6.8, the IP address is listed with trailing zeroes, indicating that all values in those portions of the address are acceptable.

Part

II

Ch

6

Understanding Logging Options

The first step in maintaining informational control over your site is to enable the logging options within the FTP service. Depending on your installation and operating system, the process will vary a bit. The next couple of sections provides information about setting up this option for a LINUX and Windows NT/IIS installation.

▶ For more information about log files, analyzing the information they contain, working with their different formats, and so on, see Chapter 11, "Usage Statistics."

Setting Logging Options for a LINUX System

When you set up the inetd.config file on your system, you'll be indicating one or more of several options, as outlined earlier in this chapter in the "Installation on a LINUX System" section. These options control whether logging will occur and at what level. An example of the syntax is:

```
ftp stream tcp nowait root /usr/etc/ftpd ftpd -l
```

In the example provided, the -l option is used to enable the logging. As with the Web services, it's highly recommended that you enable this option as it will not only help you to track down and debug problems but also to see trends in download patterns, how many people are accessing your system, and so on.

Setting Logging Options for an IIS-Based System

As shown in Figure 6.9, you have two options. These options are logging to a text file or logging to an ODBC data source.

FIG. 6.9
You should always enable logging for your FTP site for trouble-shooting both security and system problems.

When you log to a text file, the file contains a number of useful elements that will help you determine what information is being retrieved, what information is being uploaded to your server, and what problems are being encountered. FTP logging is a bit different from Web browser logging. Since FTP sessions are held open until the user logs off, you can follow a session and see exactly what was done from start to finish while the user was logged on, even if the user logged on anonymously.

When you enable logging, you'll be able to see the following information for each access to your server:

- Client's system IP address
- Client username - can be wwwuser@ for the Internet Explorer default user name, or Mozilla@ for a user using Netscape's browser
- Date of access
- Time of access
- Service used - can be W3SVC, MSFTPSVC or GopherSvc (these relate to the NT Services that are running)
- Server's computer name
- Server IP address—If you have a drive mapped to an alternate server for virtual directories, this will indicate that server's IP address
- Processing time in milliseconds
- Bytes received
- Bytes sent
- Status—Nearly always 200 or 0 indicating success.
- Windows NT status code
- Operation performed
- Target—The filename that was processed for the request
- Parameters

Any item that could not be determined or is not applicable will have a dash in the place of values for that column.

▶ See "Logging Internet Server Accesses to ODBC Databases" in Chapter 22, "Database Access and Integrity" for information about setting up and querying ODBC databases as logging sources.

For example, by connecting to the //HOLODECK3 site and reviewing several files on line, the log entries in Table 6.3 were created, showing the access and details of the session.

Part

II

Ch

6

Table 6.3 Example User Log for an FTP Session

Client IP	Client Name	Date	Time	Service	Svr Name	IP
198.68.42.72	anonymous	12/30/96	0:07:25	MSFTPSVC	HOLODECK3	-
198.68.42.72	WWWuser@	12/30/96	0:07:26	MSFTPSVC	HOLODECK3	-
198.68.42.72	WWWuser@	12/30/96	0:07:26	MSFTPSVC	HOLODECK3	-
198.68.42.72	WWWuser@	12/30/96	0:07:28	MSFTPSVC	HOLODECK3	-
198.68.42.72	WWWuser@	12/30/96	0:07:29	MSFTPSVC	HOLODECK3	-
198.68.42.72	WWWuser@	12/30/96	0:07:31	MSFTPSVC	HOLODECK3	-
198.68.42.72	WWWuser@	12/30/96	0:07:32	MSFTPSVC	HOLODECK3	-
198.68.42.72	WWWuser@	12/30/96	0:07:35	MSFTPSVC	HOLODECK3	-
198.68.42.72	WWWuser@	12/30/96	0:07:38	MSFTPSVC	HOLODECK3	-
198.68.42.72	WWWuser@	12/30/96	0:07:41	MSFTPSVC	HOLODECK3	-
198.68.42.72	WWWuser@	12/30/96	0:07:41	MSFTPSVC	HOLODECK3	-
198.68.42.72	WWWuser@	12/30/96	0:07:43	MSFTPSVC	HOLODECK3	-
198.68.42.72	joeuser	12/30/96	0:08:36	MSFTPSVC	HOLODECK3	-
198.68.42.72	-	12/30/96	0:08:36	MSFTPSVC	HOLODECK3	-
198.68.42.72	anonymous	12/30/96	0:08:55	MSFTPSVC	HOLODECK3	-
198.68.42.72	swynk@pobox.com	12/30/96	0:08:55	MSFTPSVC	HOLODECK3	-
198.68.42.72	swynk@pobox.com	12/30/96	0:09:04	MSFTPSVC	HOLODECK3	-
198.68.42.72	swynk@pobox.com	12/30/96	0:09:07	MSFTPSVC	HOLODECK3	-
198.68.42.72	swynk@pobox.com	12/30/96	0:09:11	MSFTPSVC	HOLODECK3	-
198.68.42.72	swynk@pobox.com	12/30/96	0:09:13	MSFTPSVC	HOLODECK3	-

Proc time	Rec	Sent	St	NT	Operation	Parameters/ Target
0	16	0	0	0	[1] USER	anonymous
731	15	0	0	0	[1] PASS	WWWuser@
10	22	0	0	2	[1] sent	/
10	42	0	0	2	[1] sent	/Private
10	58	0	0	2	[1] sent	/Private/iexplore
10	72	0	0	2	[1] sent	/Private/iexplore/docs
60	90	2443	0	0	[1] sent	/Private/iexplore/docs/backgrnd.gif
311	54	4086	0	0	[1] sent	/Private/iexplore/docs/client.gif
151	53	826	0	0	[1] sent	/Private/iexplore/docs/space.gif
50	52	1820	0	0	[1] sent	/Private/iexplore/docs/home.htm
10	56	2443	0	0	[1] sent	/Private/iexplore/docs/backgrnd.gif
1442	18	0	0	64	[1] closed	-
0	14	0	0	0	[2] USER	joeuser
0	15	0	0	1326	[2] PASS	-
0	16	0	0	0	[3] USER	anonymous
30	22	0	0	0	[3] PASS	swynk@pobox.com
50	234	2443	0	0	[3] sent	/Private/iexplore/docs/backgrnd.gif
191	41	4086	0	0	[3] sent	/Private/iexplore/docs/client.gif
210	41	826	0	0	[3] sent	/Private/iexplore/docs/space.gif
0	6	0	0	0	[3] QUIT	-

By Table 6.3 and recognizing the layout of it, you can quickly determine that this user accessed several files:

- backgrnd.gif
- client.gif
- space.gif
- home.htm

You can also see that the BACKGRND.GIF image was accessed twice in the session for some reason. If the client was using a Web browser, and if this image is truly a background image as its name suggests, several scenarios are possible. Perhaps the user accessed more than one page that used the image, or maybe the image was loaded independently of an HTML page. Perhaps the page was called for more than once in your HTML page.

Typical FTP convention calls for a user to use his or her e-mail address in the password field if he or she is accessing your site via anonymous FTP. This e-mail address is included in the log. You'll notice on the first two entries when the new session was established that the two tokens, USER and PASS, were shown, indicating that information about the user.

Note that session 3 indicates that the user was obtaining access by using a real FTP client. This means that he or she was not using a Web browser. You can tell this because the user logged in anonymous, but still specified a password, in this case "swynk@pobox.com." Also, in the log for session 2, you can see that the NT security subsystem has failed the user's logon attempt. A status of 1326 and a lack of any further activity on the session indicates this.

One way to read the log files is to use Microsoft Excel to view them. As you can see in Figure 6.10, this is a great way to quickly review your log files.

FIG. 6.10

Excel provides a good viewer for your server's log files.

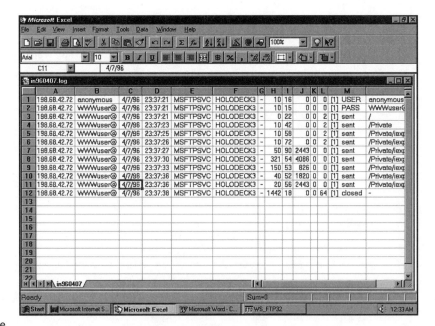

Follow these steps to take a quick look at the files:

1. Stop all services on your Intranet server.

2. In Excel, select <u>F</u>ile, <u>O</u>pen. Indicate that you want to see files of type "*.*" and choose the log file name that you want to open. Note that this defaults to INYYMMDD.LOG where Year, Month, and Day are provided for YY, MM, and DD. The IN and LOG are automatically provided by IIS.

3. You'll be prompted to select the original data type. Select <u>D</u>elimited, and then select Next.

4. In the Step 2 of 3 dialog box, in the Delimiters frame, select only the <u>C</u>omma check box, and then select <u>F</u>inish.

   Once your log file is imported into Excel, you're ready to reformat it as needed to get the information you want. A good tip is to click the corner square on the worksheet grid, and then double-click a column border to automatically resize columns to see all information within them.

Revisiting the Types of Users You'll Encounter

At the beginning of the chapter, four types of users were described:

- General, public user
- General, private user
- Member of a unique private group
- Unique private individual user

For the "General" users, you should create overall FTP rights groups. Typically, you'll want to create a group, "Public FTP," of which all FTP users are members. This group has access to all of the general access areas, including the root directory trees for the virtual directory structure. From there, you can grant specific access addenda that provide for access to closed, or private, areas.

General private users should first belong to the public groups, as this provides the overall access to the site. Next, you should create groups that all users of the specific category will fall into. Perhaps you're supporting a product on your site and you need to provide registered users of your product with updates to the software. Create a group, such as "MySoftware RegBase," that all of these users will be members of. Grant the rights to that group, allowing them access to the private areas only. Since they are also members of the Public FTP group, they'll have overall access to the site as well, along with the added access to the software updates they need.

The distinction between a unique private group and general public users/groups is that private groups will likely have more obscure rights assigned to them, perhaps an upload capability and access to additional directories. These are not implemented any differently than "normal" groups, but it may be easier to try to think of them as more exclusive, less public groups. For

Part
II

Ch
6

example, you could create a private group for use with Beta testers of your software. Private groups are often temporary and used to provide rights to a small subset of accounts for a short term. Again, don't be confused by the name. You don't do anything different setting these up, as the naming is only for clarification in this instance.

Of course, there are always exceptions. Unique users are just that, an exception. Let's say that JoeUser is a system administrator who absolutely must have access to the root directory of your system. Surely, this should be a very limited resource, and you may want to grant the right to JoeUser specifically.

Much of the task of assigning rights is brainwork and planning. Start by making lists and figuring out the types of access you'll have to accommodate. From there, you will see the groups fall out and almost create themselves. Taking the time now will save you from a splintered installation that later requires a significant amount of upkeep.

Building a Customer Support Site

In this section, you'll see how you can apply the permissions and setup techniques to your Web site. You'll see different techniques for user profiles, permissions groups, and directory structures, along with the specific steps to implement these techniques.

The goals for this site are as follows:

- Provide overview product information on offerings for the site.
- Provide product support materials, including Frequently Asked Questions (FAQs).
- Provide access to sample files, publicly available demonstration applications, and so on.
- Provide access to program updates, but only to authorized users.
- Provide a means to allow people to upload files to technical support for review.

These are typical goals for an Intranet or Internet presence for a customer support site. You need to provide your customers with access to the information they need to use your products. You also need to provide a mechanism for feedback, which is why the requirement to allow uploads is included.

In these example sites, except where it's not possible or feasible to do so, you'll be building the site for use with the Internet Explorer, as it provides a solid and easy interface. The user won't have to know how to use an FTP client unless he or she is going to be uploading files to a site.

In this site, you'll likely encounter many, if not all, of the types of users mentioned earlier. In the next few sections, you'll see how you can apply these groups and users to the FTP capabilities at your site.

Provide Overview Information and Product Support Materials

Providing information on products that are offered by your company is a perfect application of a Web site. You can provide access to the information 24 hours a day, 7 days a week, without additional staffing. Of all the things the Web can offer, leverage is one of its most powerful benefits. You gain leverage to publish information when and where it's needed by your customer base, while at the same time taking a significant load from your support staff. They can provide support, focusing on solving urgent issues instead of just responding to phone calls.

In this scenario, consider the directory tree shown below.

```
FTPRoot
    Product_Info
        Widgets
        ShoeShine_Kits
        CeilingFan_Cleaners
        Tire_Polish
        MySoftware
    Support_Info
        MySoftware
            Network
            StandAlone
        ThirdParty
```

You create the home FTP directory and point it at FTPROOT in the directory structure. You'll likely allow users to browse the directory structure, or you can create the HTML pages that will point the user to the correct directory to see its contents. Figure 6.11 shows how this might look to the user.

FIG. 6.11
You can provide the interface to the underlying FTP system with the use of FTP URLs that indicate the files that you want to provide.

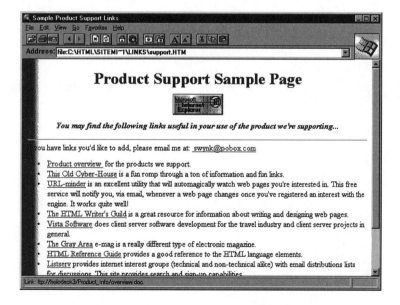

In this case, where you're providing general access, only the standard FTP setup is required. You'll notice that the links can be both HTTP addresses and FTP addresses. The first item on the list is an FTP address. If the user clicks on the link, the document will be loaded and the file will be displayed.

Since this file, a `.DOC` file, is known to your Web browser, the file is loaded and displayed automatically. This is shown in Figure 6.12. To the users, they simply opened a document and are now able to browse it, save it to their local hard disk, print a copy of it, and so on.

FIG. 6.12
Depending on the version of browser you have, the document may be loaded into the browser and displayed in place using either Microsoft Word or the Microsoft Word viewer if you have installed it.

The listing shown in Listing 6.1 is the HTML that is behind the document that provides these links and the access to the FTP document. Notice that the URL indicating the FTP link is different only in that it indicates the FTP protocol. The server and browser work together to make sure the display of the information is as seamless as possible.

Listing 6.1 Sample Links to an FTP Site from a Web Page (SUPPORT.HTM)

```
<HTML>
<HEAD>
<Title>Sample Product Support Links</title>
</HEAD>
<BODY>
<BODY BACKGROUND="../white.jpg" BGProperties=fixed LEFTMARGIN=50>
<center><h1>Product Support Sample Page</h1></center>
<body text=black>
<center><a href="http://www.microsoft.com"><img src="../bestwith.gif"
➥ ALT="Best Viewed with Internet Explorer" WIDTH=100 HEIGHT=42 border="0"></
center></a>
<p>
<B><i><center>
<MARQUEE BGCOLOR=White width=80%  Loop=-1 BEHAVIOR=Scroll>You may find the
➥ following links useful in your use of the product we're supporting...
➥ </MARQUEE></i></center>
</b>
<p>
<hr>
If you have links you'd like to add, please email me at:
➥   <A href="mailto:swynk@pobox.com"> swynk@pobox.com</A>
```

```
</b><p>
<p>
<ul>
<li><a href="ftp://holodeck3/Product_Info/overview.doc">Product overview </a>
➥ for the products we support. <li><a href="http://www.cyberhighway.net/
~clarkr/">This Old Cyber-House</a>
➥ is a fun romp through a ton of information and fun links.
<li><a href="http://www.netmind.com/URL-minder/URL-minder.html">
➥ URL-minder</a> is an excellent utility that will automagically
➥ watch web pages you're interested in. This free service will
➥ notify you, via email, whenever a web page changes once you've
➥ registered an interest with the engine. It works quite well!
<li><a href="http://www.synet.net/hwg/">The HTML Writer's Guild</a>
➥      is a great resource for information about writing and designing
➥ web pages.
...

...
<li><a href="http://www.cs.colostate.edu/~dreiling/smartform.html">
➥ Savvy Search</a>, <a href="http://www.infoseek.com">Infoseek</a>,
➥ <a href="http://www.yahoo.com">Yahoo!</a>, and <A
➥      HREF="http://www.stpt.com/"> Starting Point</A> are good search
➥ engines, and  <a href="http://www.mcp.com/
➥ 130672791559792/nrp/wwwyp/">the Internet Yellow Pages</a>
➥ provides a good resource for finding sites as well.
</ul>
</BODY>
</HTML>
```

Since this information is public and probably general marketing and sales information, access to it should not be restricted. Be sure that you set up two groups for access to the Web and FTP portions of this site as follows:

- Public FTP—Grants read-only access to all public directories in the FTP subdirectory structure.

- Public Web—Grants read-only access to all public directories in the Web subdirectory structure, grants execute privileges on the scripts subdirectory or subdirectories.

Make sure your anonymous users for the FTP and Web services are members of these groups. By doing so, you're creating the lowest common denominator type of approach to your site. In effect, you're saying that, at the very least, all users will have access to the information granted to these two groups.

Part

II

Ch

6

CAUTION

With Windows NT, when you apply rights to a directory or share, you have the option of applying the rights to all subdirectories within the target with NTFS. Chances are good that you should say yes to the question of applying the rights. But keep in mind that you're granting all the rights listed to all files and subdirectories within the current directory structure. This means that, if you've previously created a private subdirectory below one that you later declare public and apply rights against, your private subdirectory will suddenly be very public.

continues

continued

When you create a directory structure for which you're concerned about security for certain endpoints, create it from the top down, especially as it pertains to security levels. Apply the public security first, select the private directory, remove the public rights, and apply the more stringent rights. This will ensure that you have complete control over how the rights are applied.

Probably the best and most hassle-free approach to handling this situation is to set up different directory structures for the secure and nonsecure directories. You can create virtual directories that will point to these other locations from within your FTP service, and at the same time, you won't have to worry about overwriting the directories as you work with permissions.

Provide Access to Sample Files and Demos

As you could see with the earlier example, providing FTP access to the sample files and demonstrations you have on your system is straightforward. If you have a dynamic source of files, or if you simply have a large number of files, you can indicate in the URL that you simply want to provide a directory listing of the subdirectory containing the files. To do so, just leave off the portion of the URL that indicates the file to retrieve. So, using our example above, if you want to provide a file listing of everything in the PRODUCT_INFO subdirectory, the HTML line would read as follows:

```
<li><a href="ftp://holodeck3/Product_Info/">Product overviews </a>
➥ for the products we support.
```

The result, shown in Figure 6.13, is a listing of the available product information starting with the directory you indicate in the URL. The user can browse the directories at will and take a look at any items that look interesting.

FIG. 6.13

Listing a directory's contents can be a good way to provide up-to-date access to a dynamically changing source directory.

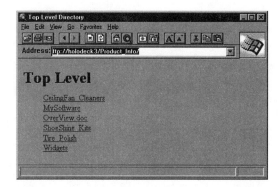

CAUTION

With Windows NT, security is applied to the items viewed only if you've implemented your security with NTFS. Share-level security does not apply to browsing the FTP directories. Of course, the FTP rights of read/write do still apply. If you need to protect an item, you need to physically move it, or be sure you implement NTFS and use the security offered by it.

Provide Access to Program Updates

Once you've applied security to a directory or file and the user requests it, he or she is prompted to enter his or her password if the user defined as the anonymous user is not allowed access to the object. Figure 6.14 shows the dialog box that prompts for the user name to access the resource.

FIG. 6.14

The user name and password provided by the user are used to log in to NT or UNIX to authenticate the account and its rights.

Once signed in, the user is treated as an authenticated user for further access. This allows the user to access the directories and objects that prompted the initial request for user name and password.

To allow access to program files, first create the directory that you need to place the files into. Map a virtual directory to that location, making them available to the service. Set the rights appropriately in the service, most likely to read privileges. Then remove the rights that were assigned to the directory when it was created. Be especially careful to remove the group EVERYONE and the user Guest if these are shown in the list of allowed accesses.

Add the group as having access to the directory, and apply the security to the directory, its subdirectories, and existing files. This locks down the content and provides it only to the people and groups indicated in the permissions list.

When users log into the system, depending on the capabilities of the browsers they use, they'll either be prompted by the Web browser for the login information or they'll be informed that they need to use a more typical FTP client package that allows access to restricted sites.

N O T E   If you find people are having difficulties accessing your protected information, have them try logging in with a dedicated FTP client. There are several Web browsers that may not be compatible with the security validation tests provided by the operating system. ■

If you want to make files available for several products, or several versions of the same product, you'll want to create a group specific to each version. This allows you to control very specifically who has access and who doesn't. Remember, a user can belong to more than one group at a time, so if you have the requirement to provide access to multiple areas, simply apply the rights based on the group, and then make the appropriate users part of those groups.

Downloading or accessing the updates or releases for retail software is likely to fall into the user-grouping described earlier, that of "Member of unique private group" or "Unique private individual user," as you'll be granting rather exclusive rights to these users.

One further caution with these accounts: You'll do yourself a favor if you implement a password change schedule or password expiration schedule for these accounts. This means that you'll have to modify the password assigned to the accounts on a regular basis. This keeps users from sharing passwords with friends, and it keeps access rights to the accounts more private and more elusive to any problematic users you may encounter. You set these rights from the User Manager for Domains. Double-click on the account and set the different properties using the buttons along the bottom of the display.

Allow File Uploads

File uploads are an interesting capability that you can offer. Whenever you are trying to solve a serious, inexplicable user problem, it can help to have the program, sample, or data uploaded to your site for review by your staff. This capability to upload files needs to be tempered so that other users cannot see the files uploaded and cannot download them from the upload directory.

The reason for this is twofold. First, you don't want to compromise any information provided to you from a customer,. If you're supporting a software product used to track job costing, for example, and a client just uploaded a sample, you don't want other clients getting that information.

The second reason is, once again, if you have people accessing your site with a malicious intent, they can upload a file containing harmful information, a virus, or some bad bit of code. If other users see this, you run the chance of being liable if they have problems with their systems. It was your system, after all, that provided the faulty item to them.

You'll want to make the FTP upload directory write permissible and read nonpermissible at the FTP service level. From the FTP service, select the Directories tab and then select the directory you want to use for uploads. Select Edit Properties and then set the privileges appropriately.

Before users upload files, you may want to warn them that they won't be able to see the uploaded files on your system.

Reality Check

At the IntelliCenter Reality Check site (**http://www.intellicenter.com**), there are a number of things implemented using the techniques here. There are three levels of employees, somewhat akin to the employees in the Customer Support sections earlier in this chapter. There are also unknown prospects, known prospects, and clients.

Basically prospects have been set up as anonymous users, to have only public rights. The following items are published for these users, all from a Web page interface:

- Course listing
- Instructor information and biographies
- Company information
- News releases
- Other publicly available sales information

If customers are interested in finding out more, they're directed to call IntelliCenter to gain access to more detailed information. This allows the company to garner more information about the contacts and make sure they get the information they need from the site. During the call, the potential customer receives a user ID and is assigned to the appropriate group that gives him additional access to the following types of information at your site:

- Course partial syllabus examples
- Sample course exam excerpts (where applicable)
- Detailed information about curriculum management offered by the company
- Schedule and fee information
- Sample access to discussion "BBSes" that have been set up

Finally, when a client has started a curriculum with the company, his account receives access to the protected student areas. The student areas include the following items:

- Course materials—demonstrations, documents, and so on.
- File upload and download area
- Location to upload a home page
- Access to their online curriculum, which is actually a combination of FTP and Web access to a SQL Server database

By providing different levels of access, it's possible to first spark some interest without giving away any unnecessary information. From there, if the client is interested in class information, he can find it online just by registering. By registering, IntelliCenter gets a new client contact and can track the contact to see how they can best help him.

One of the challenges was with the user access. Initially the NT Challenge/Response passwording was selected for Web access. Since this is incompatible with non-Microsoft browsers, this posed a limitation to the intent of the site. After disabling this option and allowing clear text authentication, it was possible to prompt for and receive the information required to authenticate the account.

The next issue was one of typical network browsers not allowing, at least easily, for the entry of user name and password when accessing the FTP site. In many cases, the client needs to use a true FTP client, as we mentioned earlier in the chapter, to access the protected information. By mentioning this fact on the Web page, we were able to help people gain access as needed.

From Here...

This chapter has been a series of practical applications and how-to's for your FTP site. From here, the best thing you can do is experiment with the permissions and different access methods. You'll need to choose your weapon of choice for accessing your site, even in cases where it means there will be exceptions, as is the case with protected FTP information and Web browsers.

You're safe in standardizing on Web browsers as the utility used to access your site, and you can assume that these browsers will only become more robust in the future.

Here are some additional resources that you may find helpful:

- Chapter 5, "Setting Up and Configuring a Web Server," has additional information about logging accesses on your site.
- Chapter 11, "Usage Statistics," gives some utilities and approaches to analyzing the log files created by your services.

Running an Internet Site

Now that you've most likely implemented the basic underpinnings of your site, you're probably ready to consider making it more open and accessible to the users of your networks. Once the site is installed, and any necessary security is applied, you may find that allowing your user base to contribute is one of the fastest ways to add content and gain user acceptance of the system.

By allowing users to create content to post to your system, you give the system a life of its own. As more and more information is posted, you'll find pockets of expertise that are available within your company. You'll find that, when combined with other key technology components like Exchange Server and SQL Server, your Internet server can provide for your organization and your customers a very nice finishing touch to sharing information effortlessly to the desktop.

In this chapter you'll see how to provide this access to your users and how you can begin to fulfill some of the more traditional benefits of a Web environment for your company. ■

Give users the ability to create their own Web pages

By allowing people to set up their own Web pages, you'll gain the confidence and interest of the different people accessing your site. Learn how you can provide Web sites to the people on your system.

See how to provide FTP access to your site

See how you can allow your users to move to the next level on your system, providing content and updating their own objects.

Learn about different things you can do to test your site

Beyond the basics of testing your pages for being accessible, you'll need to take into account many different variables when setting up your pages. Everything from database access to security concerns should be tested before you release your pages into production.

Learn how to set up virtual or multi-home servers and learn what this means to your site

Many servers support the use of a multi-home environment, letting you set up more than one domain name and IP address that is serviced by the server software. Learn why you might want to consider using this technology on your Intranet and Internet sites.

Becoming a Service Provider For Your Users

First of all, it's important to understand what the term *Service Provider* really means. Relative to the Internet, a Service Provider is typically a company that provides you with access to the Internet. The Service Provider, or SP or ISP (Internet Service Provider), has high-speed lines coming in to their business. They then split up these lines as appropriate for their user base. Typically, the user base for an established provider consists of a wide array of dial-up users. There may be a number of leased line or higher-speed connection customers, ranging in speed from 56k lines to T1 or greater.

▶ For more information about selecting a provider, understanding line speeds and technologies, see Chapter 2, "Choosing a Web Server and Service Provider."

In addition to simple access to the Internet, SPs typically also provide their customer base with a minimal amount of disk space that can be used for their Web sites and a few downloadable materials if needed. This Web site, and the maintenance of it, is the responsibility of the customer, but is provided for by the SP. The SP will issue the customer an address that can be used to access the customer's protected files. For example, the following URL indicates that, at least typically, a user named "SWYNK" has a Web site URL on the IntelliCenter server:

```
http://www.intellicenter.com/~swynk
```

The tilde "~" before the user name simply indicates, by convention, that the space is part of the user's allocated space. In some systems, there is no tilde. It corresponds largely to naming conventions imposed by the SP. This URL points the browser to the default document located in the directory indicated.

N O T E   Remember, if you have disabled default documents in your server software as defined in the properties for the WWW service, no document would be returned if the user indicated the address above. There would only be an error indicating that the requested object could not be found. Be sure to read Chapter 5, "Setting up and Configuring a Web Server," for more information.

You'll save yourself a lot of headaches by first instituting the default document and, second, informing your user of the name of the document and the fact that it's the required starting point.

Also note that if you have users familiar with a UNIX-based Web server environment, they may be used to starting their site with a file named INDEX.HTML. If so, that may be what they're expecting to be the starting document on your site. If you're using IIS, unless you change the default document name, you'll need to make sure that the users are aware of the difference.

Note, too, that you cannot change the default name for only a single user's access to the Web server;you can change it only for the system as a whole. If you do decide to change to a different default document, be sure to do it early in the process of bringing up your site; and be sure to notify your user community of the file name you select. Try not to change it after the fact because it will impact many different users' existing Web sites. ■

Becoming an SP generally means providing Web and FTP inbound access, as well as the typical download capabilities. It also means providing some security for the information that is maintained by a given user. In other words, you have some responsibility to prevent other users from changing any information besides that which they have provided directly. It would not be good to offer such open access only to find out that people are altering or altogether removing information made available by their peers.

> **CAUTION**
>
> A note of caution is in order with respect to allowing your internal user base to create and post pages. One of the all-time favorite bits of content to post on a personal Web page is a person's résumé. If not the résumé, certainly the person's name and credentials are sure to be a key topic on your site.
>
> At first this seems great! You'll increase communications between different people, between departments, and, in fact, between your company and your customers. Beware, though, that if you are offering simultaneous outside access and Intranet access, you're also providing a wonderful source for outside people to know some very juicy details about your company and the people that comprise it.
>
> At the very least, you're possibly exposing semi-sensitive information to outsiders. But perhaps one of the biggest concerns is that you're also posting a Who's Who of your company, providing job seekers and employee seekers alike a wonderful stomping ground for rummaging through your company's key individuals. It's happened many times where a company roster is published and an outside recruiter uses this information to find all the right people to talk with. This may seem borderline paranoid, but is worth the thought that goes into securing your site. At the very least, you'll want to educate your users about what types of information should not be posted.

Creating a Tree of Users and Their Pages

One of the first things you'll want to do is to give people a place to start their own pages and content. Perhaps the easiest way to do this is to start a new virtual directory to store these pages in. First, create a USERS directory. If this is an NT-based system, create the directory on an NTFS partitioned drive to be effective in controlling the access you are about to grant to users.

Next, assign permissions to the directory such that only the system administrators can change objects, but the general population has read-only access. This will be the starting security level for anyone accessing these pages. Figure 7.1 shows an example of setting this up with an NT environment. In UNIX, you'll have to set permissions based on the different access control files.

▶ This chapter focuses on Windows NT security as it applies to Internet users in the examples. This is because there are slightly different considerations when planning for an Internet site in the Windows NT environment. For information about user rights and how they relate to the World Wide Web service under UNIX, see Chapter 5, "Setting Up and Configuring a Web Server." For information about UNIX security rights and how they are implemented with FTP services, see Chapter 6, "Setting Up an FTP Site."

FIG. 7.1

Be sure to reset the group Everyone so that it has read-only access to the directory tree.

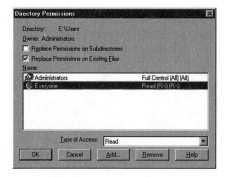

N O T E By applying the Windows NT permissions when you initially create the USERS subdirectory, you'll make it so that all of the different users' directories you create will automatically have these rights. This is because when you create a new directory, it inherits the rights from its parent directory.

If you apply the rights after the fact, be sure to check the Replace Permissions on Subdirectories and Replace Permissions on Existing Files options. This will make sure the security model you create is applied to all content in the directory structure. ■

The next step will need to correspond with creating users to whom you'll be granting this level of access. For each user, you must set up a User Account, and you must grant appropriate additional rights to his directory areas. Typically, for a user to whom you are giving this level of access, you'll be granting Full Control access, allowing the ability to make new directories under his home directory, add and delete files, etc. See Figure 7.2 for an example under Windows NT.

FIG. 7.2

Be sure to grant the user specific, complete rights to her directory. This will allow her to create and manage the content he will provide.

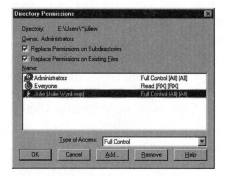

CAUTION

Be extra careful assigning the rights to the directories. Specifically, make sure you assign the open access only to the user's directory tree. Otherwise, you may end up authorizing the user access to any directory in the user's directory tree.

Remember that with UNIX you can assign individual access rights based on the .htaccess files. These allow you to indicate specific users and their rights on a given directory. Also, remember that if someone signs on to the FTP site with his standard UNIX sign on, he'll receive his standard rights and directory assignments.

Once you've assigned these rights, you'll have provided a way for people to put their own content on the server, while at the same time preventing other users from accessing it. When the user needs to upload items to the site, he needs to use a dedicated FTP client. When he does, he can log on to the site, indicate a user ID and password, and send and receive files in this directory. The user will also be able to browse other people's directories, but will not be able to make any changes or additions to any site but his own.

N O T E As of this writing, you'll need to be using a dedicated FTP client to access these protected sites for uploading. This is because there is not yet a convenient way to provide authentication information, such as user ID, password, and other data when you access a site with the FTP protocol.

You should expect this to change very soon, perhaps even by the time this book is published. As Web browsers become more intelligent, they'll also be able to handle the authentication of users, will work better with network security, and will natively handle uploads to a site. There are some instances already where partial support for uploading is provided, although the support offered is rudimentary at best, providing upload to generic, unprotected sites.

As integrated security becomes more and more prevalent, browsers will need to integrate with the network security on an overall basis, allowing the browser to use network login information to authenticate the user. This is already the case with a majority of other applications on the market, a fact that means you don't have to log in multiple times to different applications. ■

Windows 95 and all versions of Windows NT Workstation and Windows NT Server include command line FTP clients. These work great for testing your setup; they are extremely simple and provide a no-frills access to the site. Type FTP at the command line to start the application. There are a few key commands that you can use to quickly gain access to the site, shown in Table 7.1.

Table 7.1 Windows Command-Line FTP Command Basics

Open	Establishes a connection to the server. Syntax: Open <site> - - where <site> is full site name; e.g., "OPEN ftp.intellicenter.com" to open the Reality Check site. When you login, you'll be prompted for the UserID to use. You'll also be prompted for the password for the user, if one is required. To logon to a site anonymously, use a user name of ANONYMOUS. See Figure 7.3 for an example.
Close	Closes the current connection to the FTP site.
Get	Gets a file from the site, downloading it to your system.

Part
II

Ch
7

continues

Table 7.1   Continued

FIG. 7.3
The standard Windows
FTP software provides a
great no-frills testing
tool for your FTP site.

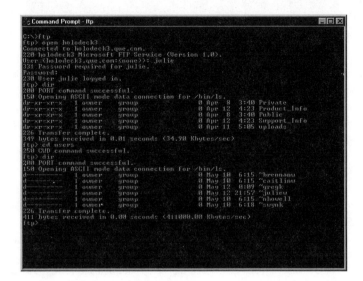

Put	Sends, or uploads, a file to the remote system. You must have sufficient rights to do this.
CD <dir>	Changes to a directory; as with DOS, <dir> can be any valid directory name relative to the current path. Note that backslashes in DOS, as in "C:\MYDIR," are represented as forward slashes, "/," on FTP on UNIX systems. Both the forward and backward slashes are supported with IIS's FTP Server. Also, remember that the FTP root directory, though specified as "/," really starts wherever the FTP home directory has been established.
Binary	Establishes your session to be a binary-mode session, providing better file download performance.
Bye	Exits the FTP client application.

You should test your setup extensively before making it public. Login as a user that you've established and try to upload a file to another user's directory. You should receive an Access Denied error message. If not, be sure you check the properties sheets for the directory and verify that the security has been set up appropriately. The biggest reason that you may experience problems with the security are the default security assignments.

With UNIX, make sure you've specified the security for the directory you're trying to protect and are not relying on overall security on the site. With Windows NT, make sure that you've disabled access for the group Everyone. Be sure the rights assigned to the group are appropriate, usually Read-Only.

Also with Windows NT, don't forget that you must have provided the "Log on locally" right for any account that will be accessing your site. If you don't, you'll receive an "Unable to logon" message, with not much more indication of what the problem is. Check the account's rights and make sure this right is enabled.

Examining Special FTP Options

If you want to take advantage of a built-in feature of the FTP service, you can allow it to assign default home directories. When a user logs in, the FTP Service will look in the default home directory for a directory with the user's login name. If found, the FTP service will make that directory the user's root directory.

You can put this to good use if you can make some assumptions about what people will be submitting by FTP. If it's largely HTML documents, you can map the directory to the USERS area. If you make the users' subdirectories with the same name as their login name, the effect will be of logging in to FTP and being taken directly and automatically to your respective subdirectory. You can then upload your content for use by others.

With UNIX, if users log in with their UNIX login name, they'll be automatically taken to the home directory you establish for their account. If they're logging in as users you've defined only at the FTP level, they'll be taken to the directory named the same as their account, relative to the root FTP directory.

The UNIX FTP service automatically does a `chroot()` and passes the user name to the operating system when it makes the call. This call will change the user's root directory to the directory indicated by user's name.

Windows NT, and IIS in particular, implements this feature in a less obvious manner. To implement this with Windows NT, follow these steps:

- Create a directory within the USERS directory that will contain the user's individual subdirectory.
- Assign appropriate rights to the directory, typically making it read-only for all users.
- Create the individual user's directories, assigning writable permissions to the directories for the users they are created for.
- In the FTP service, point the home directory to the USERS directory.
- In the Web service, create a virtual directory and point it to the USERS directory.

At this point, a couple of things are in place that bring some good usability to people using the system. First, when they sign in with FTP, they're automatically taken to their content area. They'll also not be able to move up and out of the directory area, thereby gaining a level of content security. An added benefit is that you're once again piggy-backing on the security already in place with NT Server. You know that the name the user signed in under will be the directory selected to work in.

Part
II

Ch
7

Second, the Web service can now provide access to all of the content in these areas with a simple and pretty logical URL. An example of this URL would be:

`http://www.intellicenter.com/users/swynk`

In the preceding example, swynk is the user name. Only the USERS directive in the URL has been introduced, which makes sense from the accessing users' points of view since they're requesting personal Web page information with the URL.

A key point to this technique is that it also works for the anonymous user. You'll recall that when FTP logs on the anonymous user through NT, it uses the user you set up in the FTP service properties. When the service looks for a directory using the techniques outlined here, it will simply look for a directory named ANONYMOUS. If it finds this directory, it will make it the user's root directory just as it would for other users. You can prevent directory browsing by implementing this because an anonymous user would not be able to see the other user directories on the system.

N O T E You will want to consider removing ALL Windows NT rights from the USER root directory. This way, if a user somehow logs on and does not have a home directory, he will not be able to wander around the available directories. The users would need to use one of the virtual directories you have established, or it would just appear to them that no files or directories were present. ▪

One caution of this approach with the FTP service is that you'll be locked into dropping the users into their FTP area. The only way to allow them to browse the site is by creating virtual directories and making them available to the users. Unfortunately, virtual directories don't show up if a simple directory is requested. You must know the directory name to access it successfully.

This drawback aside, by holding the user's hand a bit you can provide an increased perceived level of service by putting users in the right area for them to begin their work, all automatically.

Setting Up a Virtual, or Multi-Home Server

You'll recall from Chapter 5 that Multi-Homing your server is where you allow multiple IP addresses to access your server. In the case of an Internet, this can be a good solution to giving clients their own base URL to your server. For example, you may want to map several different domains to your server. While at first this may sound like an unlikely candidate for your Web site, it is key to providing a presence that is easily understood and that provides an added level of control for your users and clients alike.

Multi-Homing your server really entails two different things. First, you'll be setting up your server on a physical level, allowing more than one access point into the system. Second, you set up logical layers that handle the services and their appearance to the user.

In IIS terminology, Multi-Homing is referred to as a virtual server setup. You establish different settings in the IIS software that respond to incoming requests. In some cases, the handling of these requests differs between access points, while in others the same material may be available across server entry points.

Under UNIX, you'll establish the settings in the different configuration files that detail what domain names will be answered by your site.

▶ See Chapter 5 for specific settings that you'll need in your access.conf file for a multi-homed UNIX site.

In the next few sections, you'll see exactly what is entailed in setting up your server for this type of access.

Virtual Server Hardware and Operating System Requirements

The hardware-based portion of setting up a virtual server is quite simple. There is no *requirement* to add hardware, but you may find that your internal network structures require that you do so to address multiple LAN segments or access to the Internet.

Virtual servers rely on IP addresses to know how to work. You'll be associating one or more IP addresses with the network card(s) you're using. In the example shown in Figure 7.4, you can see that the addresses of 198.68.42.72 and 198.68.42.73 have been associated with the system.

FIG. 7.4

You can associate up to five different IP addresses with your server by default.

> **NOTE** Regardless of the server software you're using, if you're using Windows NT as the operating system, you'll need to set up the network settings as shown here. These are not specific to IIS. ▪

Of course for each IP address you want to assign, don't forget to create the DNS entry on your server so people can access the system by a more friendly name. A common naming convention is to stick by the root name for your site, perhaps QUE.COM, and preface it with a site-specific name for each unique IP you're setting up. In this type of scenario, you might have a server supporting the following different named access addresses:

Part
II

Ch
7

- sales.que.com

- support.que.com

- Intranet.que.com

- users.que.com

The Control Panel Network TCP/IP property sheet allows for only five different IP addresses for a given IIS installation. If you require additional Virtual Servers, you'll need to make a change to the system Registry, adding the IP addresses and Subnet Masks manually. The key that you will need to modify is:

```
HKEY_LOCAL_MACHINE\SYSTEM\CurrentControlSet\Services\
➥ <NIC><NIC#>\Parameters\Tcpip
```

As you can see in Figure 7.5, there are several parameters in this key that are important to the IP resolution for the services. Of special interest are the IPAddress and SubnetMask values.

FIG. 7.5

Setting up additional IP addresses to be supported by the Virtual Server options requires manipulation of the system Registry.

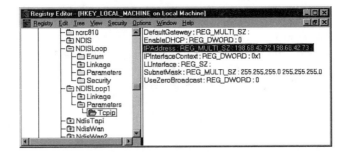

You can see that the display of the values lists each IP address you've assigned, separated by a space. If you double-click the IPAddress values, you'll be presented with the dialog box shown in Figure 7.6 that will allow you to enter more addresses to be used by the system. Press Enter after each address you enter.

FIG. 7.6

When you're entering the addresses manually in the Registry, there is no technical limitation to the number of addresses you can assign.

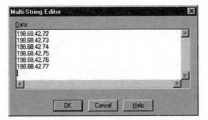

You need to follow the same procedure for the SubnetMask entries. Double-click the existing values and enter the values in the resulting dialog box. When you enter the values, they should be in the same order that they are to be applied to the IPAddresses you entered. When the addresses are resolved, they'll be done so in pairs. The first IPAddress will be paired with the first SubnetMask and so forth.

After you enter the addresses, you need to restart Windows NT to make the changes take effect. The final step to enabling this technique is to set up the IIS properties for the Web and FTP access. In the coming sections, you'll see exactly how this is done.

Virtual Server Internet Information Server Software Setup—Web Services

Once you've set up the server portion of your system to recognize the IP addresses you need, you will need to begin applying those addresses to your Web services. You can assign IP addresses to specific directories, even creating a home directory that is accessed based on the incoming IP address.

The first thing you'll need to do is to establish the home directory for each IP address you're setting up. This sets up the starting point for access to your server via the address you indicate.

N O T E A problem could occur if you are setting up virtual servers and establish only a single home directory with an IP address associated with it. If you leave the IP address blank on the original, you'll notice that the home address you set up with the IP address will become the home page that will be treated as the default. Be sure you establish an IP address for each home directory you set up, preventing this situation. ■

Establishing Virtual Server Home Pages   Setting up the Virtual Server's home page is the same as setting up the initial system home page, with the exception that you must designate the IP address for the Virtual Server. See Figure 7.7 for an example of setting up this type of system.

FIG. 7.7
Once you indicate the Virtual Server a directory will be associated with, only users accessing the system from that IP address will be able to see the content in the directory.

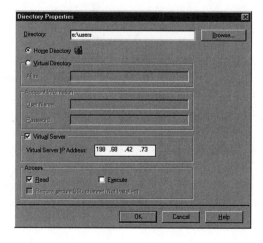

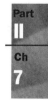

Part
II

Ch
7

Once you've indicated that the directory will be used for the new Home for this IP address, you need only indicate the IP address that it should be tied to for access. Select the Virtual Server option and provide the Virtual Server IP Address. You'll also need to set up the Read or Execute permissions for the directory.

Once you've set this up, any user accessing your server by way of that IP address will automatically be taken directly to that directory to start on the site.

 T I P   Virtual Servers are a great way to segregate content on your system when you're sharing your server for both an Intranet and an Internet presence. You can associate one set of content with the IP address associated with the Internet, and you can associate an entirely different set of content for those users accessing over your internal network.

By doing so, you can offer much of the same content across sites; but you'll be putting up a good wall between public users on the Internet and the employees of your company with the private, and perhaps confidential, information on the Intranet.

When you create the home directory, or any other directory associated with a Virtual Server, all directories under that directory will inherit the IP association you set up. In other words, if you set up a directory <home>, which refers to `c:\inetsrv\wwwroot\private`, all access to the `PRIVATE` subdirectory and its child directories will be available to the IP address you set up.

For this reason, if your intent is to provide a public and private access point to your server, you may wish to set up a `PUBLIC` root and a `PRIVATE` root, with links between the two as needed. You can always put links on your private pages into the `PUBLIC` area, providing access to that information as needed.

Keep in mind that once a user has accessed your site by an IP address that you've established in this manner, any time the user refers to the root, this will be referring to the home directory you're setting up. It won't be the root of the drive or the root of the default home page.

Once you've assigned an IP address to a home page, any access to your server over any different IP address will not be able to get to the location you indicate, unless of course you've created other virtual directories that point to the same directories.

Accessing Other Virtual Server Web Pages   As you create the virtual directories associated with your Virtual Servers, be sure you also create the fundamental directory pointers. You'll need one for your root, or home access. This was discussed in the previous section.

You'll also likely need to create a new directory to manage the scripts that you'll make available. The standard directory name is /SCRIPTS, so you'll want to adhere to this if possible. This brings up an interesting and key point about the virtual directories you create as they can have the same alias between Virtual Servers.

N O T E   Remember, in IIS, the scripts directory should not have the Read security assigned, but it must have the Execute permissions enabled in order to allow a user to run a script against the Virtual Server. ▪

What this means is that if you have three Virtual Servers, you can have three /SCRIPTS aliases set up. Each will be accessed only by the Virtual Server you associate each directory with. This is important for compatibility. If you have a site developed with directory-naming specifications, you can match the directory names between servers, keep the names of the directories the same, but still use the Virtual Directory features.

N O T E It may be easiest to test the IP addresses and Virtual Servers by using the IP address in the URL that you use to access the site. For example, instead of HTTP://HOLODECK3, indicate HTTP://198.68.42.72. You can change the IP address easily on the URL command line to make sure you're getting back the content you expect.

The next step is to try to access the site with the DNS names you've set up. Make sure they map to the correct IP addresses, and ensure that the server is picking up on the IP addresses. ■

Once you associate a page with an IP address, it's available only from that Virtual Server. If you have a directory that you want to be accessed by more than one Virtual Server, you will need to set up a Virtual Directory for each server that will access the resource. This applies only if you are excluding a Virtual Server from a directory. If you're granting access to a directory for all of your different Virtual Servers, you can do so by not supplying an IP address for the directory. If the IP address is blank, there will be no IP address restrictions of this type imposed on it.

Understanding the Advanced Management of Your Site

There are a number of different tools you have at your disposal that will help you manage your site, its performance, and the usefulness of the system to the users on it. Once you bring up your network, and after you begin offering open access to the system, you'll need to change into management mode for your system.

There are three different areas that you'll want to keep an eye on to start:

- Site accesses and page access counts
- Server impact, server loading, and overall utilization at your site
- Problems that arise, including failed access attempts and other error conditions

Each of these is covered in the next few sections of this chapter.

Site Accesses and Page Access Counts

The first of these areas of interest, monitoring specific page accesses, is covered extensively in Chapter 11, "Usage Statistics." As you'll see, you can run one of the scripts that was provided against your SQL server and see exactly what pages are accessed and how frequently. Listing 7.1 shows the output from one of these types of queries.

Part

II

Ch

7

Listing 7.1   Example of Site Activity from SQL Server

```
Total hits Last Access
---------- --------------------
90         May 13 1996  9:06PM
-

Hit summary Date
----------- -----------------
9           19960428
81          19960513
-

Time of day Hits
----------- ---------------------
22          9
23          81
-

Page                                        Hits
------------------------------------------- -----
/samples/gbook/register.htm                 4
/Default.htm                                3
/samples/dbsamp/dbsamp.htm                  2
/samples/sampsite/results.htm               2
/samples/sampsite/taste.htm                 2
/samples/dbsamp/dbsamp1.htm                 1
/samples/sampsite/about.htm                 1
/samples/sampsite/catalog.htm               1
/samples/sampsite/default.htm               1
/samples/sampsite/process.htm               1
/samples/sampsite/sampsite.htm              1
```

On the CD

The SQL scripts to query against the SQL server for this information are provided on the accompanying CD. You'll find them on the CD in the directory associated with Chapter 11 with filenames of WWW.SQL and FTP.SQL for Web and FTP inquiries, respectively.

▶ More information is provided about setting up ODBC data sources in Chapter 23, in the "Logging IIS Accesses to ODBC Databases" section.

By using and regularly reviewing the results of these scripts, you'll know what information can be removed and what information is most popular and may need to be expanded. Similar logging is available for both FTP and Gopher services.

One nice addition to the reports would be to break the report based on the user directory that was queried. If you can combine this with an IDC approach, giving the users an online resource about what information is accessed most often from their site, you provide a great tool for the users. Consider the following set of files that are found on the CD with this book.

First, the HTML file is listed that will prompt for the user name to query. This is shown in Listing 7.2.

Listing 7.2 SEEHITS.HTM Prompts for the User Name, Then Passes It to the IDC Layer to Query the Database

```html
<html>
<head>
<title>Sample Query to Review Site Statistics</title>
</head>
<h1>Please enter your user name below.</h1>
<form method="post" action="/scripts/access.idc">
<input name="user">
<input type="Submit" value="Run Query">
</form>
</body>
</html>
```

The HTML is simple and doesn't do much, beyond asking for information back from the user. The user will be shown a single text edit box and allowed to enter a value and submit the query. Once submitted, the ACCESS.IDC interface is called, passing in the named parameter, USER. Listing 7.3 shows the IDC file that is used to query the database in this case.

Listing 7.3 The IDC File Contains the SQL Query that Will Be Run Against the Database to Determine the Accesses that Have Occurred for the User's Pages

```
Datasource: Web SQL
Username: Logging
Password: Password
Template: Access.htx
SQLStatement:
+ SELECT "Page" = substring(target,1,40), "Hits" = count(target)
+ FROM logtable WHERE target like '%%user%%'
+ GROUP BY target
+ ORDER BY "Hits" desc
```

This is the same query that is used to query the database manually, with the exception that the new check on the user name is added. This allows the query to pull back only pages with the user name embedded in them, effectively limiting the display to only those pages pertinent to the signed in user. In Listing 7.4, you can see the HTX file, ACCESS.HTX, that is referenced in the IDC file. This file is used to display the results of the query as they are returned from the server.

Listing 7.4 The HTX File Is Responsible for Formatting and Display of the Results Set

```html
<html>
<head>
<title>Page hits for user <%idc.USER%></title>
```

continues

Listing 7.4 Continued

```
</head>
<h1>The following hits were recorded for your pages:</h1>
<p>

<%if currentrecord eq 0%>
 <h2>No hits were recorded, sorry!</h2>
<%else%>
   <table border>
   <%begindetail%>
     <tr>
     <th><%Page%></td><td><%Hits%></th>
     </tr>
   <%enddetail%>
<%endif%>

</table>
</body>
</html>
```

The result is a page showing the user the number of hits experienced on his personal materials, all presented to any remote workstation on the network and not necessarily only on the server. This proves to be valuable information to test the validity of advertising campaigns, customer assistance, and more. You can see, and start to profile, the types of users who are using your site.

Server Impact, Server Loading, and Overall Utilization at Your Site

There is a huge array of counters that are installed when you install IIS. Each of these is available from within the Performance Monitor of NT and can be used to profile your site. It's likely that you'll end up with more than one series of monitors running because it really makes sense to look at your server from several different angles. The counters that are installed are broken up into four different areas:

- FTP Server
- Gopher Server
- Internet Information Server
- Web (HTTP) Server

N O T E These sections are not meant to be a complete discussion of Windows NT logging. Since the user interface for Windows NT analysis is accomplished with tools you may already have onhand, the examples provided here outline these types of logging and analysis.

If you're using UNIX, there are a number of options you have available to you in the analysis and understanding of your logs. Please be sure to read through this information first, then refer to Chapter 11, "Usage Statistics." Chapter 11 goes into great detail regarding how you can work with the analysis tools, the log files, and more.

The information presented here is provided for ideas and concepts regarding running and monitoring the site. The approaches and considerations are valid for both Windows NT and UNIX environments, even in those cases where implementation varies between the two platforms. ■

In addition, there are third-party utilities, such as those from Media House, that will help in the administration of your site. These tools provide additional feedback on the site, including the number of current users, their associated IP address, the number of HTTP requests fulfilled and more.

On the CD

The CD accompanying this book includes the free versions of Media House's software. The software, implemented as ISAPI extensions to IIS, provides very valuable feedback on several different aspects of your server. Media House can also be found on the Internet at <**http:// www.mediahouse.com**>.

Table 7.2 shows some of the key counters and what they will tell you about the state of your server.

Table 7.2   Key IIS Counters

Counter	Description
ALL:Bytes Received/sec, Bytes Sent/Sec	Indicates the current activity level of the server. This is a good indicator of how hard your services are working to service requests.
ALL:Current Anonymous Users	This value lets you know how many non-specific users are currently using your services. For FTP services, these users are usually download-only users and represent someone that may be accessing a file from a link on a Web page, or has been directed to download a file directly using an FTP client. Note that if you reference this value in the display of the counters, you should also include the non-anonymous users (see the next item) to provide a complete picture of the system usage.
ALL:Current Non-Anonymous Users	These are validated, authenticated users that the system has allowed to log on. These are users who will typically have more rights on the system and are able to upload files, create directories, have access to secure areas on the site, etc. Note that if you reference this value in the display of the counters, you should also include the anonymous users (see the previous item) to provide a complete picture of the system usage.
ALL:Current Connections	All current connections to the given service. Note that this is the same as displaying both anonymous and non-anonymous users as noted above.

continues

Part

II

Ch

7

Table 7.2 Continued

Counter	Description
FTP:Files Sent, Received, Total	These will help you track how much incremental activity is occurring against your system. Of particular interest is the Files Received counter; it indicates that your disk space is being used by new objects on the system.
HTTP:POST requests	These requests typically indicate that a user is using a form type of HTML document. These can be helpful if you implement forms and need to know if people are really using them, and you can get a feel for when they are being used. Use this in conjunction with the WWW.SQL log analysis script and you'll be able to see any appropriate impact on your server if you have a heavily forms-based system.
HTTP:Bytes Sent/Sec	This number can help gauge the impact on the server a bit better than files sent, simply because it can be disconcerting to see how many files are included in a given Web page. Remember, each graphic is a separate image and file, increasing the file count. By monitoring trends in the Bytes Sent/Sec values, you'll be able to see the demand growing and you'll be able to quickly see busy times of the day for accessing the server.

N O T E There are a number of other counters, and each is outlined in the IIS help system. Search the system for the term "MIB Definitions" for a table of available counters. ■

Once you establish the performance monitor characteristics you want to use, you can set up the performance monitor so that you will be able to see at a glance what's happening on your server. There are also several predefined Performance Monitor profiles that are included with your server. In the tour directory under the samples that are installed when you install IIS, you'll find four files, all with a primary filename of MSIIS, and each has a different extension associated with the Performance Monitor. There are several different approaches provided, as can be see in the following list:

- ■ PMA—This configuration is in report alert mode. It looks for exceptions to occur on your system and then notifies you of a potential problem. The predefined set includes monitors on the overall system processor loading for the IIS system, and it watches the use of caching of information on the system.

- ■ PMC—The PMC settings provide for graphical monitoring of the overall processor load, the IIS processor load, caching information, and the current number of Web Server connections.

- PML—The Logging format is helpful for longer-term analysis. You can take a snapshot of your system on a regular basis, log the results to a file, and review the file on a periodic basis to make sure things are flowing smoothly. The PML configuration includes FTP, Gopher and HTTP server characteristics, overall performance summary information, and counters that relate to the Processes and system states on the server.

- PMR—The PMR configuration creates a constantly updating report version of this information. The information includes counters for the INETINFO process and the HTTP server. Several different aspects of each are included, providing for good feedback on the processes.

Once you have just the right settings showing the information you care to review, you will want to consider making this information a permanent fixture on the server because you'll want to know on a moment's notice the status of the server should someone ask or report a problem.

Troubleshooting Failed Access Attempts and Other Error Conditions

There are two different places to look when you experience a problem with your system. The first, which is probably rather apparent, is to review the Services in Windows NT, or the active processes in UNIX. Ensure that the different server processes are active and running with no apparent problem.

The second area to consider are the event and system Logs. These logs are where all notes of problems are stored, regardless of the system, application, or process that caused the problem. Figure 7.8 shows an example entry in the logs that indicates that there is a problem with an ODBC datasource in the Windows NT environment.

FIG. 7.8
When you reference the Event log, always be sure to review both the Application and System logs. Between these, you're likely to find the problem.

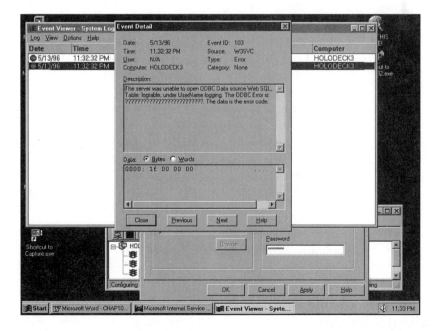

The two key areas of the event log in Windows NT are the Application and System areas. If you have a problem, chances are very good that it will be detailed within these two logs. By the same token, if you cannot find the problem in the logs, it's a good indication that you may have a problem at the client side of the picture, rather than the server side.

Unfortunately, there are nearly infinite combinations of messages you can receive with the event viewer, so outlining problems and solutions here would not be helpful. Just be sure to read the descriptive text of any problems you encounter and you should be able to correct the problem, or at least properly convey the situation to someone who can fix the problem.

Testing Your Site Configuration

One thing that you cannot do enough of with your Internet site is testing. Nothing turns people off at a site faster than a broken link, a passworded area that doesn't grant appropriate access, or completely off-standard implementation. Also, be sure to spellcheck, grammarcheck and proofread your site's content on a page-by-page basis. Nothing turns off a potential customer faster than the impression that you didn't take the time to proofread your pages.

In testing your site, especially in the case where you're setting up at least one Virtual Server, you'll need to test each service, each directory tree with each incoming IP address. Remember, security is applied differently depending not only on who you are to the system, but also based on the Virtual Server or multi-home server you're using and the access rights at the user level.

If you have a chance to, it's probably best to break the system and then figure out how to correct the problems you've created. If you have access to a different server, one other than the production system, it's probably a prime candidate for this type of testing. It sounds strange to break your system to test it, but it's the best way to learn and experience the things that can happen with a system.

Barring the availability of an alternate system, consider the following as you are testing:

- Be sure to log in as several different users. If you are the system administrator, the fact that you can access a specific portion of the system does not mean it's configured correctly as it relates to security. Remember, you have full access to the system as administrator. You should try accessing the system with a user whose rights are the absolute minimum and work up from there.

- Try logging in from different workstations. This helps test the IP limitations you may or may not have implemented. This also varies the user environment a bit, allowing you to see any obvious incompatibilities between the software you're using and the software on the users' systems.

- Try logging in from different LAN segments if you're sharing your Internet server with your Intranet. This will confirm that your DNS servers are working correctly to resolve names.

- If you're using Virtual Servers, try gaining access with their English name and their TCP/IP address. The results should be identical. Do *ALL* IP addresses work for accessing the system?

■ Remove the user that you're testing with from the system. Try to gain access again. Does it work? If so, you probably have a security problem.

■ Use as many different browsers as possible to access your site and attempt to gain access to protected areas. Are you able to access these areas, and are you properly prompted for your password? Does passing on your password work?

■ Can you upload files to someone else's FTP area?

■ Can you delete files from their FTP area?

■ Can you upload files to your FTP area?

■ Can you create new directories in your FTP area?

Once you've been through your site testing, do it again, but with someone else doing the driving. Teach him how to access the site. Watch what they do, how they expect to do it. This is perhaps one of the best learning tools available in designing access methods, how procedures work and, most importantly, how the user expects them to work.

Reality Check

It is a major goal of the IntelliCenter site to provide Internet and Intranet access to students and potential students. From the internal network, students are provided with the ability to create pages that are their own personal pages. To accomplish this, the user areas mentioned earlier in the FTP and Web sections have been implemented. Students have upload capability only to their directories on the server. They have read-only access to all remaining areas.

The tools to analyze site performance and page-hits are implemented and provide good feedback on the popularity, or lack thereof, of different features on the site.

The actual class time does not include Intranet time, unless of course the class was based on that technology. Instead, the site is available to students on breaks and before and after class. This seems to help break up classes by changing the technology focus entirely on these times.

Tending to trip up the flow of things is the fact that there is no mechanism for automatically creating user directories on the system when a user is created. If you forget to add the user directory to the system, rather than being placed into their directory automatically as needed, the user is presented with an empty directory and no way to upload files. This can be confusing to someone just learning to use the system. Several checklists have resulted, making sure several different things occur when students are first created on the system:

■ They are created as an NT user.

■ They are created as a SQL Server user, since integrated security is not implemented at this time, and given access to the TRANSCRIPTS database.

■ The user directory is created.

■ Directory rights are assigned.

Part

II

Ch

7

When the user is first created, the user account is created by copying a predefined "STU-DENT" user. This is to make sure the proper groups are assigned and that the user receives the required "Log on locally" user right, another common stumbling point in creating new users with access to the system.

After putting a process around creating student users, the system works well and provides the protection needed, giving the students a good resource to experiment with Internet techniques and approaches. Since the system is also published to the Internet, in cases where the corporate account has approved it, the students' personal Web pages may also be made available on the Internet as showcase pages.

From Here...

In this chapter you've seen how to manage some of the considerations in bringing up an Internet server. These include providing upload services, dynamic access to the system, and more. You've also seen some of the different tools you'll be using to manage your server. From here, you can check into the following materials for more information:

- Chapter 5, "Setting Up and Configuring a Web Server," helps with the process of installing and configuring your system.
- Chapter 6, "Setting Up an FTP Site," gives detailed information about setting up your FTP site.
- Chapter 11, "Usage Statistics," gives information about log files, tools to analyze them, and what types of information you can glean from them on your system.

Running an Intranet Site

Intranets introduce some astonishing capabilities for sharing company-related information with employees. At the same time, Intranets introduce some interesting questions to the staff responsible for providing and maintaining the network services. Some of these questions show how you can provide Intranet and Internet services on the same server, provide Intranet services over the Internet, let the users contribute the content with their native applications, and determine whether there are any special considerations that should be taken into account as far as outbound Internet access is concerned.

This chapter covers much of this information, showing you how you can both support the Intranet and at the same time cover the technology and security bases that must be addressed in this type of environment. ■

Find out how to host both an Intranet and an Internet site on the same server

You can organize your system to support both the internal and external access, providing some added security along the way.

Learn about the tools you can provide to your users

You'll find out about some of the different tools that you can provide to make content creation possible for users, rather than HTML programmers.

Share your Intranet over the Internet

You can access an Intranet site over the Internet from the Windows environment with a few simple tricks. Find out how.

Sharing Server Hardware Between Your Intranet and Internet Site

When you decide to bring up the Intranet, you'll need to decide whether you'll be simply allowing the same information to your internal users that matches that for outside Internet users, or whether there will be additional information available to the internal users. It's likely that the second option will be the case because it fulfills the real goal of the Intranet, which is easy access to information that is likely to be confidential to your company.

If you have a situation in which you want to bring up additional information for users within your company, you need to address the question of where the server software is to reside. You can bring up a new server to address these types of issues, or you can use the existing Internet server. If you use the Internet server, you'll need to implement security on the system to protect your confidential information from outside, prying eyes. There is a huge risk that must be addressed in sharing the system that hosts both your Intranet and Internet sites.

To lessen the security risk, with most server software, you can implement a new site on the same system. This is referred to by many different names, including the following:

- Virtual Server
- Virtual Host
- Multi-Home Server
- Shared Server

The list goes on, and often depends on the software you use. In essence, what happens in these types of installations is that the server software recognizes the IP address over which an access request is received. When the server receives the request, it points the request to the appropriate home directory.

You have probably seen this approach to presenting information, but were not aware of it to any great extent because it's transparent to the person accessing the site. If you visit a large ISP's site, for instance, notice they often offer web-hosting services. When you access their native site (for an ISP named ISP, for example) it might be **http://www.isp.com**. This takes you to the ISP's Web site, advertising their services, offering utilities for their users, and more.

As a user on their system, your home page is typically denoted by going to their site address and appending a tilde (~) and your user name. For example, to get to the Wynkoop Pages, the address is actually **http://www.pobox.com/~swynk**. This doesn't take you to the pobox Web site, but instead takes you to the Wynkoop pages specific to the swynk user.

The ISP maps this connection by simply paying attention to the user name. However, you don't access commercial sites by appending the commercial site name at the end of the URL. You typically reference the site by going directly to the site with the company's URL. To go to the Integra site, for example, you access the **http://www.integra.net** URL.

Chapter 2, "Choosing a Web Server and Service Provider," discussed how you register your domain name with Internic and then assign an IP address to it. That IP address is how people access your site. The ISP recognizes this IP address and redirects incoming requests to your Web site, giving the illusion of sorts that you have a server set up only for your domain. In actual practice, a server may host many different sites, especially in cases where the sites are lower volume in nature.

Providing Intranet Access from the Internet

Perhaps one of the more unusual tricks is to open your Intranet to the Internet as a means of sharing information between offices more than sharing information with clients or customers. To accomplish this, you need to place your system on the Internet, but you don't have to register a domain name for the server.

This may seem strange at first; but, since you're only expanding the scope of your Intranet, you have the option of doing so by using a little-used feature of Windows. Windows supports a workstation-based name resolution utility that references a file on the local hard drive to determine IP addresses. The file, LMHOSTS, resides in the Windows subdirectory for Windows 95 and in the windows\system32\drivers\etc directory for Windows NT.

The file is a simple text file that indicates a mapping between IP addresses and their friendly names, as shown in the following:

```
xxx.xxx.xxx.xxx   netserver1      #pre #DOM:intellicenter
xxx.xxx.xxx.xxx   system_1        #pre #DOM:intellicenter
```

The file supports many different options, including support for include files should you need to reference a common lookup file on the network. As you can see from the preceding short example, the file consists of an IP address and friendly name, along with other options. When you set up the mappings, you should keep the friendly name the same as the system you are accessing. While not required, it's much easier to maintain in the future.

N O T E Names can also be of the format www.intellicenter.com. Any valid computer name is allowed. ▪

If you distribute this file to the sites that need to access your Intranet server over the Internet, you can give them instant access to your system. In the case of the mappings shown earlier, an URL of **http://netserver1** would map to the server you indicate the IP address for. This makes it much easier for users to use your server.

Setting Up a Virtual Server with Microsoft's Internet Information Server (IIS)

In IIS, multi-homing is referred to as a virtual server setup. You establish different settings in the IIS software that respond to incoming requests. In some cases, the handling of these requests differs between access points, while in others the same material may be available across server entry points.

In the next few sections, you see what is entailed in setting up your server for this type of access.

Virtual Server Hardware and Operating System Requirements

The hardware-based portion of setting up a virtual server is quite simple. There is no *requirement* to add hardware, but you may find that your internal network structures require that you do so to address multiple LAN segments or access to the Internet.

Virtual servers rely on IP addresses to know how to work. You'll be associating one or more IP addresses with the network card(s) you're using. In the example shown in Figure 8.1, you can see that the addresses of 198.68.42.72 and 198.68.42.73 have been associated with the system.

FIG. 8.1

You can associate up to five different IP addresses with your server by default.

Of course, for each IP address you want to assign, don't forget to create the DNS entry on your server so people can access the system by a more friendly name. A common naming convention is to stick by the root name for your site, perhaps QUE.COM, and preface it with a site-specific name for each unique IP you set up. In this type of scenario, you might have a server supporting these different named access addresses, such as the following:

- sales.que.com
- support.que.com
- Intranet.que.com
- users.que.com

The Control Panel Network TCP/IP property sheet allows for only five different IP addresses for a given IIS installation. If you require additional virtual servers, you need to make a change to the system Registry, adding the IP addresses and Subnet Masks manually. The key you need to modify is the following:

```
HKEY_LOCAL_MACHINE\SYSTEM\CurrentControlSet\Services
➥\NICNIC#\Parameters\Tcpip
```

As you can see in Figure 8.2, there are several parameters in this key that are important to the IP resolution for the services. Of special interest are the IPAddress and Subnet Mask values.

FIG. 8.2

Setting up additional IP addresses to be supported by the virtual server options requires manipulation of the system Registry.

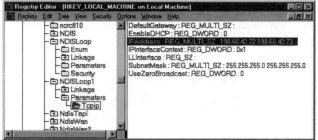

The display of the values lists each IP address you assign, separated by a space. If you double-click the IPAddress values, the dialog box shown in Figure 8.3 displays, which enables you to enter more addresses to be used by the system. Press Enter after each address you enter.

FIG. 8.3

When you're entering the addresses manually in the Registry, there is no technical limitation to the number of addresses you can assign.

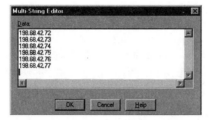

You need to follow the same procedure for the SubnetMask entries. Double-click the existing values and enter the values in the resulting dialog box. When you enter the values, they should be in the same order that they are to be applied to the IPAddresses you entered. When the addresses are resolved, they'll be done so in pairs. The first IPAddress is paired with the first SubnetMask and so forth.

After you enter the addresses, you need to restart Windows NT to make the changes take effect. The final step to enabling this technique is to set up the IIS properties for the Web and FTP access. The following sections show how this is done.

Creating Virtual Servers in IIS

Once you set up the server portion of your system to recognize the IP addresses you need, you must apply those addresses to your Web services. As shown in Figure 8.4, you can assign IP addresses to specific directories, even creating a home directory that is accessed based on the incoming IP address.

FIG. 8.4

Virtual servers come into use on your system by assigning them to directories that can be accessed.

The first thing to do is to establish the home directory for each IP address you set up. This sets up the starting point for access to your server via the address you indicate.

NOTE A problem could occur if you are setting up virtual servers and establish only a single home directory with an IP address associated with it. If you leave the IP address blank on the original, you'll notice that the home address you set up with the IP address will become the default home page. Be sure you establish an IP address for each home directory you set up, preventing this situation. ▪

Establishing Virtual Server Home Pages Setting up the virtual server's home page is the same as setting up the initial system home page, with the exception that you must designate the IP address for the virtual server. See Figure 8.5 for an example of setting up this type of system.

FIG. 8.5

Once you indicate the Virtual Server a directory will be associated with, only users accessing the system from that IP address will be able to see the content in the directory.

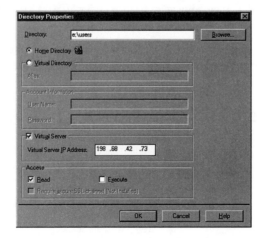

Once you indicate the directory that is used for the new Home for this IP address, you need only indicate the IP address that it should be tied to for access. Select the virtual server option and provide the virtual server IP address. You also need to set up the Read or Execute permissions for the directory.

Once you set up the permissions, any user accessing your server by way of that IP address will automatically be taken directly to that directory to start on the site.

When you create the home directory, or any other directory associated with a virtual server, all directories under that directory inherit the IP association you set up. If you set up a directory, for example, called <home> which refers to c:\inetsrv\wwwroot\private, all access to the PRIVATE subdirectory and its child directories will be available to the IP address you set up.

For this reason, if your intent is to provide a public and private access point to your server, you may wish to set up a PUBLIC root and a PRIVATE root with links between the two as needed. You can always put links on your private pages into the PUBLIC area, providing access to that information as needed.

Also, keep in mind that once a user has accessed your site by an IP address that you establish in this manner, any time the user, or the user's related HTML code, refers to the root, this refers to the home directory you're setting up, not the root of the drive or the root of the default home page.

Once you assign an IP address to a home page, any access to your server over any different IP address cannot access the location you indicate, unless of course you create other virtual directories that point to the same directories.

Accessing Other Virtual Server Web Pages

As you create the virtual directories associated with your virtual servers, be sure you also create the fundamental directory pointers. You need one for your root, or home, access, as described in the previous section.

You also may need to create a new directory to manage the scripts that you make available. The standard directory name is /SCRIPTS, so you want to adhere to this if possible. Virtual directories you create can have the same alias between virtual servers. What this means is that, if you have three virtual servers, you can have three /SCRIPT aliases set up. Each will be accessed only by the virtual server with which you associate each directory. This is important for compatibility. If you have a site developed with directory-naming specifications, you can match the directory names between servers, keep the names of the directories the same, but still use the Virtual Directory features.

N O T E In IIS the scripts directory should not have the Read security assigned. Instead, assign the Execute permissions to the directory to allow a user to run a script against the virtual server. ▨

N O T E It may be easiest to test the IP addresses and virtual servers by using the IP address in the URL that you use to access the site. For example, instead of **HTTP://HOLODECK3**,

continues

continued

indicate **HTTP://198.68.42.72**. You can change the IP address easily on the URL command line to make sure you're getting back the content you expect.

The next step is to try to access the site with the DNS names you have set up. Make sure they map to the correct IP addresses, and ensure that the server is picking up on the IP addresses. ■

Once you associate a page with an IP address, that page is available only from that virtual server. If you have a directory that you want to be accessed by more than one virtual server, you need to set up a virtual directory for each server that accesses the resource. This applies only if you are excluding a virtual server from a directory. If you grant access to a directory for all of your different virtual servers, you can do so by not supplying an IP address for the directory. If the IP address is blank, no IP address restrictions of this type are imposed on it.

Setting Up a VirtualHome with the Apache Server

With the Apache server, included on the CD-ROM with this book, you set up a configuration file that establishes the VirtualHome for incoming IP addresses. The hyttpd.conf file contains information about how to handle the request. See Listing 8.1 for an example.

Listing 8.1   Sample Entries Configuring a Multi-Home Server

```
<VirtualHost www.company.com>
ServerAdmin webmaster@yourserver.com
DocumentRoot /internet/root
ServerName www.company.com
ErrorLog /internet/logs/error.log
TransferLog /Internet/log/access.log
</VirtualHost>

<VirtualHost www.myserver.com>
ServerAdmin webmaster@myserver.com
DocumentRoot /intranet/root
ServerName www.myserver.com
ErrorLog /intranet/logs/error.log
TransferLog /Internet/log/access.log
</VirtualHost>
```

These entries set up two different access points on your server. The first could be used for general Internet access, while the second could be used for Intranet access.

Making User-Contributed Content Possible

Your Intranet has to become more than just publishing shares on your existing network. You need to make it possible to easily contribute content and you need to provide unique access to content that is either not otherwise available, or is easier to access with the Intranet. When you do take this approach, you're making a value-added service available to your users, and they'll use the Intranet more frequently.

One aspect of making the Intranet more dynamic and useful is making it possible to easily contribute content to it. By making some baseline utility software available to your users, they can begin creating the content independently, without the intervention of HTML coders to make the different informational items available. There are several tools currently available today; but even more are coming from many different sources, from CAD applications to database applications.

An example of these applications is the Adobe PageMill application. This application, currently going into Beta testing on the Windows platform, makes it possible to translate from nearly any source document to HTML, leaving the content's layout intact. The converter makes creating the HTML documents easy and enables the users to pay more attention to creating the content in their native applications, be it WordPerfect, Word, or other applications. You can receive more information about Adobe's products on the Web at **http://www.adobe.com**.

Another example is Lotus Notes approach of directly publishing the Lotus contents as Web content. Their Internotes application converts Notes information to Web content on a regular, scheduled basis, making sure your site is always up to date. If you use Lotus Notes, Internotes is a good way to publish your existing knowledge base to the Internet. Find out more about Lotus Internotes at **http://www.internotes.lotus.com/**.

Another company, Barnes and Associates, (on the Web at **http://www.baarns.com**) has an Excel worksheet converter that takes your existing Excel worksheet and makes the corresponding HTML tables for use on your Web site.

The current leader in the marketplace of Internet utilities, even if gauged only by number of available applications, is Microsoft. If you keep in mind that many Microsoft applications read most other applications' vendor file formats, the utility of the Microsoft suite becomes quickly significant. Even if your word processor environment of choice is WordPerfect, for example, you can use Word to read the file and then create the HTML version of the document for you automatically.

Using the Microsoft Office Assistants to Create Web Content

As you have seen throughout this book, content comes from a number of locations. There are interactive sources and static sources, as well as easier and more difficult ways to produce it. Microsoft has products that build the pieces of content you're likely to be using as spreadsheet, document processing, presentation, and database tools. You learn in Chapter 24 how you can connect your databases to your site.

The key to the Assistants, and where they provide you with the most benefit, is that time when you're either climbing the learning curve for HTML or you need to quickly bring up a page or series of pages. The Assistants shine as a learning tool. You can allow them to create the pages for you, then you can review the code created to understand how it was done.

T I P When you're creating and maintaining a Web site, you'll find that information, content, and layout are changing so fast and furiously that it may be difficult to keep up. One technique is to maintain a site mirror for your Web site. This site mirror should be located on a different system from the Web server.

One option you have is to create an \HTML subdirectory and then a \SITEMIRROR subdirectory under the HTML directory. The purpose of the SITEMIRROR directory is to mimic the root directory on your Web server.

Other directories off the HTML directory can include utilities, graphics, and so on. Directories off SITEMIRROR should match your production Web site. When you're developing code, you can place it in your SITEMIRROR first and run it to make sure it looks as you expected. When the code is ready, you can migrate it to the production site.

This approach offers a couple of benefits. First, you have an environment that allows you to test without impacting your production system. This is very valuable; one of the biggest benefits of these systems is their availability. You never know when someone will be looking to the system for information. This is good; but just in the time it can take you to put a page on your Web site and find out it isn't what you want, you can have people accessing it.

The second benefit is that this SITEMIRROR configuration provides an invaluable backup mechanism if your server should experience problems. In the worst case, if you have to take down the server and install new equipment and/or software, you can restore the SITEMIRROR directories into the WWWROOT area and you'll be all set and ready to go.

Using the Microsoft Word Internet Assistant

As you know, Word is an excellent tool for editing text-based content. Since much of the information on the Web is textbased, you can imagine that Word would be a nice environment for editing these pages. While it's possible to also edit and maintain pages using any text editor, you may find that Word's Internet Assistant gives you a quick leg up on the process. You can always come back and make further modifications to pages with your favorite text or HTML editor.

The concept behind the Assistants is that you are able to create documents in the tools you already know how to use. Then, using the Assistants you can automatically convert your documents to HTML for use on the Web, whether it be on an internal network or an Internet server.

Understanding How Word Assistant Works

The Word Assistant takes the styles and formatting you apply to your document and converts them to the corresponding HTML tags. In many cases, the translation is nearly transparent and the resulting HTML code mimics your original document very closely. You can apply the HTML formatting to an existing document, or you can create new documents in Word and save them as HTML documents.

In any event, when you save the file, you have the option to save it as an HTML file as shown in Figure 8.6.

FIG. 8.6

Web pages appear, along with applicable styles, and you can use these pages as templates to base your pages on, saving you time in the learning process.

 Included on the CD with this book are all of the Internet Assistants, including the Word Assistant.

On the CD

ON THE WEB

The Microsoft Word Assistant Site is located at the address **http://www.microsoft.com/msoffice/msword/internet/ia/**. You should occasionally check back with this site to determine the current version for the product.

In general, the Word Assistant helps turn your Microsoft Word word processing system into a Web browser and content creator. Since you're using the Word editor to create and manage content, as well as view it online, you can call up a page, change to the editing mode and make changes to the source. This can provide you with some real leverage because you can borrow code from other pages in the creation of your own Web content. As you can see in Figure 8.7, you don't leave Word to view the page, but can view and edit it without changing to a separate browser.

FIG. 8.7

You can review Web sites from within the Word Assistant.

N O T E Web content is usually copyrighted material to the author originally posting the material. When it's mentioned that you can *borrow code*, you should be looking to borrow the HTML approach or other techniques from the site, but not the content. If you like the content, create a link to the page and notify the author of the page. Perhaps that author will link to your site as well, creating a nice two-way exchange of the idea that caught your eye.

Never cut and paste content from another site and reuse it without asking the original author for permission. ■

In the coming sections, you see how to install the Word Assistant and what types of things you can do with it.

Installing the Word Assistant

The Word Assistant is installed from a single executable WRDIA20Z.EXE, which is a compressed file. When you run the installation procedure, it installs into your Word subdirectory structure and checks your system to see if you have a previous version of the Assistant installed. The process copies the files to your system and updates your system's Registry. You won't be selecting components to install, nor will you have optional portions of the system that you'll need to decide about installing or not installing on your system.

When the Assistant is installed, it creates a new file, FAVORITES.DOC, located in the Word directory. The Favorites file contains links to all of your different URLs that you save using the Favorites button in the Assistant. If there is an existing Favorites file, the setup process will prompt you to keep or replace the existing file.

N O T E If you save your previous version, it is saved as FAVORITES.BAK. You'll need to open Word and the favorites document and paste in your links from the backup file if you would like them to appear when you select the Favorites button. ■

After the Assistant has been installed, you'll be prompted about whether to use the Assistant as your default HTML editor. If you select Yes, your Registry will be updated to use Word any time you edit an HTML document. Note that Internet Explorer will still be your default Web page viewing tool. Word will be used only to modify HTML.

When finished, the setup program will prompt you about whether you want to go directly into Word or simply exit the setup routine. In either case, the file that is loaded on your system is WIAHTM32.WLL, a Word-based WLL that provides the Web-browsing capabilities. In addition, a new toolbar will be installed and a new standard button will appear in Word when you're working with standard documents (see Figure 8.8).

FIG. 8.8
The new browsing button allows you to switch between editing and browsing mode.

Understanding Word Assistant Menu Options

Once you have retrieved your Web document into Word, you can start using some of the different tools offered by the Assistant to work with the document. Some of the changes are provided in the toolbars, while others are available on the menus.

Understanding the File Menu Options   There are different options available depending on whether you are in Word editing mode or Browse mode. If you are in Word's editing mode, the following options are available on the File menu:

- Browse Web - this option is the same as selecting the "Switch to Web Browse View" icon from the Formatting toolbar.
- Open URL calls up the Open URL dialog box. This allows you to access any URL on the Intranet or Internet.
- Preview in Browser calls up your Web browser to show the document you're working on. Since it is sometimes difficult to test forms-based documents and other special-case documents from within Word, this option allows you to see exactly how the document will act on the Web.

When you are in Browse mode, the File Menu is modified with five additional options:

- Reload The reload option functions as the reload button does in standard browsers, causing Word to refresh its copy of the document. This will update your display with any changes that may have taken place since the document was last loaded.
- Open URL calls up the Open URL dialog box, as shown earlier in Figure 8.6. This enables you to access any URL on the Intranet or Internet.
- Close all Documents Since Word opens each page you review online in a separate document in Word, you may end up with several different files open at any given time. If you want to flush this "cache" of pages, you can select the Close all Documents option to do so.
- Preview in Browser will call up your Web browser to show the document you're working on. Since it is sometimes difficult to test forms-based documents and other special-case documents from within Word, this option enables you to see exactly how the document will act on the Web. This is the same function as that available from the File menu.
- HTML Document Info This option allows you to see general information about the currently loaded page, ranging from any META tags to the title of the page. The options available are shown in Figures 8.9, 8.10, and 8.11.

FIG. 8.9

You can review the Title assigned to the page with the <Title></Title> HTML tags when you initially select the HTML Document Info option.

If you write privileges to the file, as may be the case with your Intranet installation, you can make changes to the title directly in the dialog box. The changes will be saved to the HTML in the header of the document per HTML convention. If you don't have ready access to the file, as may be the case if the file is on a remote server, you may have to save the file to disk first, then upload the file to the site you want to host the document.

FIG. 8.10

By selecting Advanced from the initial dialog box, you can see the URL that is defined as the starting point for the current page. This is indicated by the <base></base> tags for the Web document.

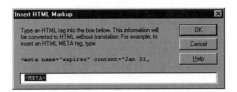

The Base URL is very important if you're using relative addressing at the site. Base URLs allow you to indicate where relative addressing should begin on your site for addresses referenced in the current page. Relative addressing allows you to indicate an URL for pages by specifying only the portion that changes. In other words, as in a DOS or Windows environment, if your base URL is //myserver/examples and you want to refer to a page in a subdirectory under "examples," you can do so by simply indicating /newdir/filename.html and the Web browser substitutes the fully qualified path for you automatically. The result is a fully qualified URL of //myserver/examples/newdir/filename.html.

The IsIndex option allows you to indicate that the file is a searchable page. This means that, when a browser is directed to the page, you can indicate the search parameter on the URL. If, in the example above, you were to make it a searchable page, you could call up the page by indicating:

http://myserver/examples/newdir/filename.html?findthis

where findthis is the reference on the page to which you want to directly move the user's browser.

N O T E The search capability is typically a server-side implementation. If you're developing an Internet site, and your site is to be hosted on an ISP's server, you may have to contact the service provider for an appropriate program that runs on their system and provides access to your pages in the way of a search engine. ■

The Meta option allows you to indicate any values you need represented in the <Meta> tag options for the document. The Meta tags provide additional information about your document to the browser. They are not displayed, but are used more to process the page and indicate other values that can control the refresh of the page, what editor was used to create the page, and so on.

▶ For more information about HTML tags, see Chapter 18, "Basic HTML Techniques," and Chapter 19, "Advanced HTML."

As you can see in Figure 8.11, the <u>M</u>eta option on the Advanced dialog box allows you to set up the Meta tags you want to implement.

FIG. 8.11

You can add META tags to your Web-based documents using the Insert HTML markup dialog box.

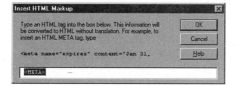

Using the <u>V</u>iew Menu Options   The view menu is modified with two new options as outlined below. These options are available regardless of whether you're browsing the Web or editing a document.

- Web Browse—the Web Browse option offers the same functionality as the Web Browse on the main menu, which is to provide you with the ability to use Word as your editor and page viewer on the Web.

- F<u>u</u>ll Screen—This can be a very interesting way to wander the Web. This removes from the screen the toolbars, rulers, Windows 95 task bar, and all other aspects of the Word environment. This leaves a way to review Web pages and provides the page with a bit more screen real estate to work with.

In addition, once you're browsing the Web, you'll have a new option, <u>H</u>TML Source. This option will open the page in Word and enable you to see and work with the HTML source directly. Figure 8.12 shows an example of how this is presented in Word.

FIG. 8.12

By reviewing the source of other people's Web pages, you can quickly understand how HTML is implemented and how it might be coded to work with your needs.

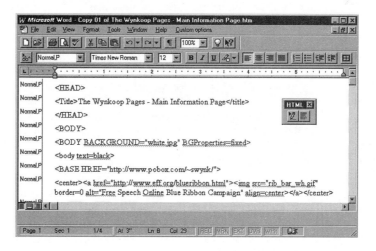

This can be helpful if you need to make small changes to HTML generated by the Assistant, or to implement features of HTML that the Assistant does not yet support.

 TIP You should check the Microsoft site at **http://www.microsoft.com** frequently to see if new versions of the Assistant are available. With the rapidly expanding offerings that are available on the Web, it's important to always use the most up-to-date tools available.

You may want to consider using a Web monitoring tool. Tools, such as the URL-Minder, allow you to indicate a Web page to watch. Periodically, the tool checks to see if the requested page has changed. If so, the tool will send you an e-mail message indicating that you should check back at the target site to see what has changed.

 ON THE WEB

You can find the URL-Minder at <**http://www.netmind.com/URL-minder**>. There you can register pages you have an interest in and allow the tool to monitor the page for you. The service is free and even includes information about how you can provide users of your site this service directly from your site.

 TIP The Internet and Intranet tools, policies, and capabilities are on the verge of exploding into something much larger than they are today. The possibilities are endless, and a number of people are working these markets very diligently. To that end, you can surely expect a flurry of enhancements, corrections, and the like to the software tools that you use to manage your sites, content, and presentation of the information on your network.

Insert Menu Options   There are a number of options that are added to the insert menu when you install the assistant. These options allow more control over your HTML that will be created for a given page. In Word document editing mode, there is only a single option added to the menu, Insert HyperLink. Whether you are working with a standard document or a document destined for your Intranet, you can insert a link to another file/location combination and insert it into your document. Figure 8.13 shows the HyperLink dialog box.

FIG. 8.13
Links to other content can be of any supported type, be it HTTP, file, or other protocols supported by your network connections.

When you insert the hyperlink in your document, it will be displayed in the document just as it would on a Web page. It's shown as underlined and in the color you've established for your Word environment. You can use these hyperlinks to connect to other documents, as might be the case where you want to create a master document and allow users to move around a "Web" of documents that, taken together, comprise a much larger book-type document.

N O T E It's good practice to simply make the hyperlink a part of the sentence rather than specifically directing the user to "click here." Consider the two following statements:

To get the latest copy of the Personnel Manual, click here. Be sure to review section...

The Personnel Manual has been updated. Be sure to review section...

The second statement follows emerging standards that indicate you use the hyperlink marking to indicate the link instead of calling it out specifically as in the first example. ■

When you are browsing pages, there are three different options available. These are:

- Horizontal Rule—In your documents, you should always be looking for ways to logically break up the information your users are viewing. By placing divider bars in your Web documents, you can break the page into logical units that may be easier for the user to become accustomed to.

   The Horizontal Rule option, shown in Figure 8.14, places a line on your page at the thickness you specify. Note that Horizontal Rules go across the entire page regardless of where in the line you are when you create the Rule.

FIG. 8.14

Use Horizontal Rules to break up the content on your pages.

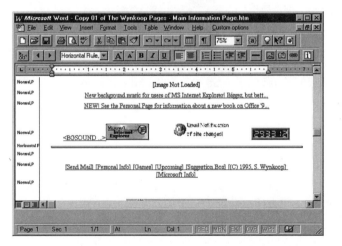

- Marquee—Marquees were introduced by Microsoft with the Windows 95 version of Internet Explorer 2.0. Marquees can be made to scroll across the screen, move from side to side on the user's display and optionally slide into a fixed position on the user's display. Figure 8.15 shows the Marquee setup dialog box.

   Note that in Internet Explorer 3.0, there is a new marquee, called from VBScript, that provides additional functionality.

Marquees are a great way to catch users' eyes as they work with your pages. Marquees can be implemented to indicate new features, or they can indicate other important bits of information.

> **CAUTION**
>
> Don't overdo it with the Marquee capabilities. You should avoid having more than two Marquees on a given Web page. More than two Marquees may initially look interesting; but, over time, people viewing your site will thank you for keeping Marquees to a minimum because they quickly become distracting.

FIG. 8.15

You can specify all of the different supported Marquee options to be applied to the finished page.

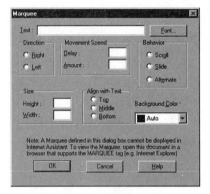

- HTML Markup—This option allows you to put manual HTML tags into the source for the page. This allows you to implement new features, unsupported capabilities, and other things that may be beyond the scope of the Assistant.

Format Menu Options The format menu understandably provides a number of options that control the look and feel of your pages. As you can see in Figure 8.16, the entire set of options is specific to the Web environment, though many are implemented in parallel with Word options.

FIG. 8.16

The Format menu offers selections to control many of the overall aspects associated with the form, ranging from background images and sound to how levels and numbering are handled.

Table 8.1 summarizes the options and how they are used in general. For more information you should look up the tags associated with the options and how they are implemented in HTML.

Table 8.1   Format Menu Options

Menu Option	Description	BASE HTML Tag
Background and Links	Sets up background image and colors used for hyperlinks on the page	<BODY>
Background Sound	Background music or sound that plays when the page is loaded	<BODY>, <BGSOUND SRC=...
Font	Allows you to select the font you want to display on the page*	<FONT>
Increase Font Size, Decrease Font Size	Affects the text you have selected.	N/A
Style	Applied as standard Word Style capabilities	N/A
Center Align, Left Align	Set the alignment for the selected text.	<ALIGN=...>

Microsoft provides support for True Type Fonts on Web pages. To enable these fonts, use a special format of the <FONT> tag. The new extensions to this tag allow you to indicate a True Type font face to use in the display of your page, such as <FONT FACE="Comic Sans MS">. Since these are new extensions, you'll need to code them using the HTML Markup menu option described in the previous section.

The balance of the options allow you to work with the indenting levels for the pages and are implemented the same as they are in a typical Word document editing environment. Remember, the key is to create the content as you normally would; then allow the Assistant to convert it to HTML for you.

Tools Menu Options   The Tools menu hosts a single custom option, Proxy Server. If you are using a gateway product, you'll need to specify the name of the gateway in the dialog shown in Figure 8.17.

FIG. 8.17
Proxy Servers can be set up to provide a good level of protection between your users and the Internet. Proxy servers control how your system is accessed both for incoming and outgoing requests.

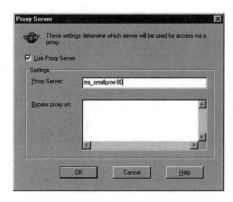

▶ For additional information about firewall security, see Chapter 9, "Firewalls and Proxy Servers."

Table Menu Options   The table menu is much the same as the standard Word options, except that it presents the different options and items you can control about tables as top level menu choices. In other words, all of the different attributes you can control about HTML tables are represented on the menu. See Figure 8.18 for the options that are presented.

FIG. 8.18

You can control many of the different aspects for how the table will look, ranging from heading rows to style of lines between the cells.

 Tables are the core of sites as they become more organized and adept at displaying the information presented. If you consider some alternative uses for tables, you'll quickly see why.

If you have a series of graphics that you need to line up, for example, you can use tables and cells in the tables to contain the graphics, thus ensuring that all of your information will be exactly in line.

Tables also provide great ways of placing content on the user's display proportionally to the display size. Because tables can dynamically size, your content displayed in the table can size as well, but still stay in the confines of the appropriate cell.

You can also use tables to create a newspaper-like look and feel on your pages. Simply write a "column" of information (column 1) in the first cell. For the second and subsequent columns, simply add a new column to the table and insert your text as needed. The table will resize to the user's desktop, and you will have the effect you want of having snaking columns or simply side-by-side stories.

N O T E   Tables, frames, and other user interface control items are among the fastest-changing elements in the content wars between the different major players in the browser market. To provide for many of the features that users are coming to expect, many different extensions are being created as the HTML specification is expanded.

Since the specification is growing so quickly, and from so many different fronts, be sure to check on the latest capabilities of your target browser. In the cases specifically relating to this book and the systems that are set up with it, the Microsoft Internet Explorer is the browser targeted for the majority of the clients that are expected. When you review specification extensions, keep in mind your target audience and always be sure to check to see what the impact is on other browsers.

In some cases, features you implement that are specific to one browser will prevent another browser from seeing your content at all, which is probably not a good way to go about having a popular site! This might be the case with the use of Frames or other leading-edge features for a given browser. ▪

Microsoft Excel Internet Assistant

One of the more challenging things that you will work with in terms of complexity in HTML is probably the use of tables. Tables get their difficulty from the fact that they include cells, borders, and many other attributes that define the look of the table and how it is used by the user. Add to that the many different uses for a table and you'll quickly find out that, while they look great when finished, they're very difficult to completely hand-code in many cases.

As mentioned in the previous sections, the Word Assistant can be a significant help in preparing tables because it will convert your word processing tables into HTML tables. What can you do if you have workbooks full of information and need to be able to create HTML to correlate with it? You have probably guessed by now that you could use the Excel Internet Assistant.

The Excel Internet Assistant takes the range of cells you indicate and creates the HTML for you. It will take care of formatting, fonts, coloring, and so on. It will create the HTML in a format that you can use in a stand-alone fashion, or it will create only the series of HTML statements that are required to create the table you indicate. In the latter case, you can then paste this HTML into another page for display among other information.

The Excel Internet Assistant is easy to install and use, but it doesn't offer the same Web-browsing capabilities of the Word Assistant. With that in mind, it's an excellent quick-and-dirty tool for table creation from existing spreadsheet-type information.

ON THE WEB

As with all of the tools covered in this book, you should always check the Internet to see if a more recent version is available. The Excel Internet Assistant, and information about updates, is available at <**http://www.microsoft.com/msexcel**>.

Installing the Excel Assistant

The installation of the Excel Assistant consists only of copying the Assistant's Add-In utility file to a location on your system where you'll know where to find it. The file, HTML.XLA, simply needs to be somewhere you can access it on your system. You may want to place this in your \MSOFFICE\EXCEL subdirectory to be able to find it quickly later.

Included on the CD with this book are all of the Internet Assistants, including the Excel Assistant.

N O T E If you will be using the Internet Assistant for Excel often, you should consider placing the
XLA file in your XLSTART subdirectory. This will allow Excel to load the Add-In automatically
each time it starts. If you do this, you will not need to follow the steps below to register the Add-In for
Excel. ■

Once you have placed the file on your system, you can open the XLA file directly and a new
option will be placed on your menus, as shown in Figure 8.19.

FIG. 8.19

A new option, Internet
Assistant Wizard, lets
you start the Assistant
from within Excel.

Understanding How the Excel Assistant Works

Since you're already likely to be familiar with Excel, you are already familiar with the different
formatting options. These include everything from number formatting to text formatting, colors to fonts, and more. None of these options changes and you can, for the most part, convert
standard workbooks to HTML.

Once you have created your sample text, highlight the range you want to convert. In the following steps, you'll convert the worksheet range shown in Figure 8.20.

FIG. 8.20

The sample range
includes fonts, shading,
colors, and other
formatting that will help
show off the translation
capabilities of the
Assistant.

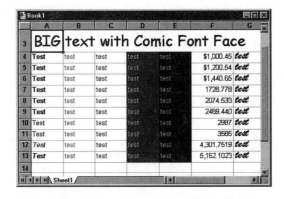

Select the range to convert and select Tools, Internet Assistant Wizard from the menu system.
This will start the Assistant; and, as shown in Figure 8.21, you will be prompted to confirm the
range you want to convert.

FIG. 8.21

To begin the conversion, you can either highlight the range to convert, or you can manually type it into the Wizard.

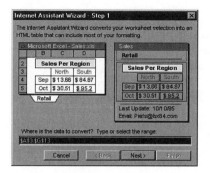

N O T E You can also highlight the range by moving the dialog box out of the way on your display and highlighting the cells you want to use for the HTML conversion. ▪

Once the range is correctly displayed, select the Next button. The dialog box shown for Step 2, shown in Figure 8.22, is where you tell the Wizard which type of HTML output you would like to receive.

FIG. 8.22

The Wizard can create an entirely new page or insert your new table into an existing page.

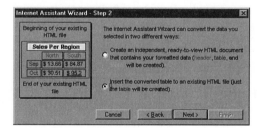

The difference between the two options amounts to opening and closing HTML statements that will or will not be created based on your decision. In addition, if you select the Existing Table option, the Wizard expects you to have an already existing HTML page. For more information, see the next two sections.

Creating a New HTML Page

If you choose the "Create an independent..." option, you'll be able to indicate some additional items for the page. These items will make the page more complete and allow you to set up headings, text, and a footer for the page. See Figure 8.23 for an example of the Step 3 dialog box.

N O T E The items shown in Figure 8.23 are the items that are not included in the option to insert your new table into an existing page. ▪

FIG. 8.23

You should always specify an e-mail address for your page. This allows someone to write you a quick note if they can contribute to the information on the page.

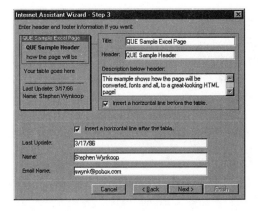

Since you have so many different formatting options available to you with Excel, the Wizard offers you the option of ignoring your formatting and creating a simple table to display the information you have selected. In some cases, this can be preferable to allowing the Wizard to attempt to convert the formatting. This could be the case when you have a heading, such as the one used in the sample, that spans the top of the columns. As you can see in Figure 8.18, the heading spans multiple columns and influences the appearance of other columns on the output. More information will be provided about working with this type of situation at the end of this section on the Excel Wizard.

Figure 8.24 shows the dialog box that allows you to indicate whether you want to convert the formatting, font, and other attributes of the range you specified. If you indicate that you do not want the information formatted, the table will be created to show only the information in text mode.

FIG. 8.24

It's probably a good idea to allow the Wizard to convert formatting, at least initially because you can re-run it later without the formatting.

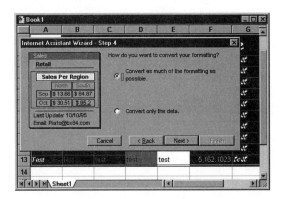

The final bit of information you provide to the Wizard is the name of the file you want to create. You need to specify where you want the file placed on your system. You should probably put this file into a working area where you can test it prior to rolling it over into a site mirror that you may have on your system. Select Finish to save the HTML to the file you indicated (see Figure 8.25).

FIG. 8.25

You will need to specify a fully qualified path to the location that you want to use to save the HTML that will be created.

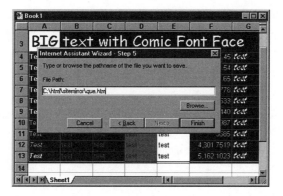

You now have a new page created for you based on the information you provided and the information in the underlying worksheet. Figure 8.26 shows the results of the conversion.

FIG. 8.26

You can see that some formatting is changed in the output. In particular, the heading in the table is different from the original in the worksheet.

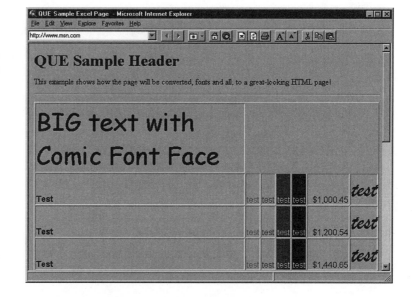

You may have to make some fine adjustments to the results to make them look exactly as you would like, but you'll find that the Wizard creates a great starting point.

In the next section you find out how you can create a table and insert it into an existing page, saving the time needed to integrate the two pages.

Inserting the Table Into an Existing Page

If you have an existing page into which you would like to place your table, you can indicate so as shown in Figure 8.20. When you do, you'll need to have the receiving page already set up with a special tag included in it. You must have a tag, included as a comment, to indicate where in the document you would like to include the table. Specify the following tag in your document:

```
<!--##Table##-->
```

> **N O T E** If you use the Internet Assistant for Word to create the page, you cannot just type the text into your document. Instead, you must use the Insert, HTML Markup option from the menus. Type the preceding "Table" code at the prompt to save it to your page in the correct format.
>
> Also, be sure to save and exit the document in the Word Assistant prior to trying to insert the table. If you still have the file open in Word, you may receive a sharing violation or file in use error message when the Excel Wizard attempts to save the table to the file. ■

You will next be prompted to indicate whether you want to save the formatting you applied to the region. As is the case when creating an entire page, it's probably a good idea to allow the Wizard to apply the formatting at least the first time around.

Lastly, you will be prompted for the name of the file that will be the resulting HTML source. The Wizard will take the original file with the insert tag, merge the table code into the HTML, and save the results to the file you indicate. In the example here, Listing 8.2 shows an excerpt from the code that's created.

Listing 8.2   HTML21_1.HTM—Portion of the HTML Created by the Wizard

```
<HTML>
<HEAD>
<META NAME="GENERATOR" CONTENT="Internet Assistant for
➥Microsoft Word 2.0z">
<TITLE>Untitled</TITLE>
</HEAD>
<BODY>
<P>
Que Sample Page
<P>
This page was created first, and then the table was inserted into
it.
<HR>
<P>
<!-- The following table has been generated by the Internet
➥Assistant Wizard for Microsoft Excel. You can find this add-in
➥on "http://www.microsoft.com/msoffice/freestuf/msexcel/
➥index.htm" -->
<!-- ----------------------- -->
<!-- START OF CONVERTED OUTPUT -->
<!-- ----------------------- -->
<Table border>
<TR VALIGN="bottom">
<TD ALIGN="left"><FONT FACE="Comic Sans MS" SIZE=+6>
BIG text with Comic Font Face</FONT></TD>
<TD ALIGN="right"><FONT FACE="Arial">
```

```
</FONT></TD>
<TD ALIGN="right"><FONT FACE="Arial">
</FONT></TD>
<TD ALIGN="right"><FONT FACE="Arial">
</FONT></TD>
<TD ALIGN="right"><FONT FACE="Arial">
</FONT></TD>
...


...
</TR>
</Table>
<!-- ----------------------- -->
<!-- END OF CONVERTED OUTPUT -->
<!-- ----------------------- -->
<HR>
<P>
You can just blah blah blah blah ...
</BODY>
</HTML>
```

You can see that the comment line tagging where you would like to place the table was re-moved and the table code was inserted.

Microsoft PowerPoint Internet Assistant

The PowerPoint Internet Assistant is an interesting tool to add to your content creation toolbox. One of the difficult things about creating Web content is creating good graphics, good layout, and the presentation of those pages once created. Worse yet, if your presentation is entirely graphical in nature, such as might be the case with technical drawings, online presen-tations, and so on, creating the navigational hooks between pages can be a tedious task. This is where the PowerPoint Internet Assistant can help you.

The PowerPoint Assistant gives you the capability to translate an entire PowerPoint presenta-tion into a series of pages that represent your presentation in both text and graphical presenta-tion. Your users will be able to see the graphics just as you designed them; and they'll be able to choose to see the text on the slides, or they may want to simply move between the slides directly.

ON THE WEB

As with all of the tools covered in this book, you should always check the Internet to see if a more recent version is available. The PowerPoint Internet Assistant and information about updates is available at <**http://www.microsoft.com/msoffice**>.

In the coming sections, you will see how to install the PowerPoint Internet Assistant and what you can expect as you save your files in the new manner.

Installing the PowerPoint Internet Assistant

The installation of the PowerPoint Internet Assistant is started by running the file IA4PPT95.EXE. This file is a self-extracting ZIP file that will install all of the necessary files on your system to run the PowerPoint Internet Assistant.

Included on the CD with this book are all of the Internet Assistants, including the PowerPoint Internet Assistant.

When you start the installation, you will be asked to confirm that you want to install the Assistant. Only a few files are copied to your system to enable the process, so the installation procedure is very quick. Once installed, the setup program will display a message box indicating the success of the installation.

Understanding How the PowerPoint Assistant Works

The PowerPoint Assistant works by adding a new option to the menus, Export as HTML, as shown in Figure 8.27.

FIG. 8.27

The PowerPoint Assistant is implemented as a new Export process option on the File menu.

The PowerPoint Assistant works differently from the other Assistants that have been covered thus far. In the other environments, you ran a process that would create the needed HTML. With PowerPoint, there are no changes to the operation of the system whatsoever. Instead, when you are ready to create the pages, you choose the new option to Export as HTML from the File menu. This causes the process of creating the pages to start.

When you start, you will first be asked where you want to save the pages and in what format the graphics should be saved. This is shown in Figure 8.28. In most cases, you should select GIF for the graphical format. GIF files tend to be a bit smaller and can "fade in" on the user's system, potentially making the pages readable more quickly than with JPEG images.

> **N O T E**   If you are creating new pages for an existing series of pages, you should first delete all files that you are replacing, or move them to a backup subdirectory. This is because if you have fewer files on the new series than were there before, you will end up with "remnant" files on the system that are not necessary for your site. Cleaning out the directory before placing the files there ensures that only those files that are created with a given use of the Assistant will be used. ■

FIG. 8.28
You must indicate where you want to save the new files and in what format the image should be saved.

For each slide in your PowerPoint presentation, the Assistant will create two forms for your Web site. There will be one form that is the Text representation of the slide, and one that is the graphical representation. Your users will have the ability to choose how they want to see the slides as they work with your site.

N O T E Each slide may require as much as 30K in disk space. If your presentation is large, you may need to direct your new pages to a disk drive with more free space. ■

CAUTION

With the Internet Information Server, the opening page for your site directories is DEFAULT.HTM by default. The Assistant will create pages with a starting page of INDEX.HTM, the default on some other systems. You have three different options when you create these automated pages.

1. You can change the page name on the first page from INDEX.HTM to DEFAULT.HTM.

2. You can change the default startup page in the Internet Information Server to be INDEX.HTM. See Chapter 5, "Setting Up and Configuring a Web Server," for more information on setting up the server software and establishing the various default settings.

3. You can specify the full URL when referencing the new site. For example, if your site is located at **<http://www.mysite.com/slideshow>**, you can specify **<http://www.mysite.com/slideshow/index.htm>**.

The slides are created based on two templates located in your powerpnt subdirectory. The files, IMAGE.TPL and TEXT.TPL, set up the format for the Assistant as it saves the slides for your site. Listings 8.3 and 8.4 show the default layouts for these files.

Listing 8.3   IMAGE.TPL—The Template Used to Create the Graphical Image Pages

```
<HTML>
<HEAD>
<**TITLE** <TITLE>%s</TITLE> **TITLE**>
</HEAD>
<BODY>
<CENTER>
```

continues

Listing 8.3 Continued

```
<**HEAD***<H1>%s</H1> **HEAD***>
<P>
<**IMAGE** <TABLE BORDER=5> <TD><IMG SRC="%s"></TD></TABLE>**IMAGE**>
</P>
<P>
<TABLE>
<TD HEIGHT=100 WIDTH=60>
<**PREV***
<A HREF = "%s"><IMG SRC="p2hprev.gif" ALIGN=BOTTOM ALT="Previous slide"
BORDER="0">
</A> **PREV***> </TD>
<TD HEIGHT=100 WIDTH=60>
<**NEXT***
<A HREF = "%s"><IMG SRC="p2hnext.gif" ALIGN=BOTTOM ALT="Next slide"
BORDER="0"></A>
 **NEXT***> </TD>
<TD HEIGHT=100 WIDTH=60>
<**FIRST**
<A HREF = "%s">
<IMG SRC="p2hup.gif" ALIGN=BOTTOM ALT="Back to the first slide"
BORDER="0"></A>
**FIRST**> </TD>
<TD HEIGHT=100 WIDTH=60>
<**MODE***
<A HREF = "%s">
<IMG SRC="p2htext.gif" ALIGN=BOTTOM ALT="View text version"
BORDER="0"></A>
**MODE***> </TD>
</TABLE>
</CENTER>
<BR>
</p>
<**NOTES**
<Font size=4> <STRONG> Notes:</FONT></STRONG>
<HR  SIZE=3>
<P> %s </P> **NOTES**>
<**TEXT***<!-- %s  --> **TEXT***>
</Body>
</HTML>
```

Listing 8.4 TEXT.TPL—Template for Text-Based Pages

```
<HTML>
<HEAD>
<**TITLE** <TITLE>%s</TITLE> **TITLE**>
</HEAD>
<BODY>
<**HEAD***<H1>%s</H1> **HEAD***>
<**TEXT***<P>%s</P> **TEXT***>
<P>
<TABLE>
<TD HEIGHT=100 WIDTH=100>
```

```
<**PREV***
<A HREF = "%s">Previous slide </A>**PREV***> </TD>
<TD HEIGHT=100 WIDTH=100>
<**NEXT***
<A HREF = "%s">Next slide </A> **NEXT***> </TD>
<TD HEIGHT=100 WIDTH=150>
<**FIRST**
<A HREF = "%s">Back to the first slide </A> **FIRST**> </TD>
<TD HEIGHT=100 WIDTH=150>
<**MODE***
<A HREF = "%s">View Graphic Version </A> **MODE***> </TD>
</TABLE>
<BR>
</p>
<**NOTES**
<FONT size=4><STRONG> Notes: </FONT></STRONG>
<HR SIZE=3>
<P> %s </P> **NOTES**>
</Body>
</HTML>
```

You can make changes to these files to allow for how you want your pages to look. You will probably want to add copyright notices and e-mail addresses as default information, and perhaps a link to an overall Web site as well. In any event, if you don't care for some element of style applied to these pages as a default, these are the templates you use to make changes in how the slide shows are translated.

Reality Check...

At the IntelliCenter Reality Check site, the Assistants were used to create the information pages and sample class content. The following items have been implemented at the site:

- Overview of the company—This information, already available in the company brochures, was translated using the Word Internet Assistant. This saved retyping, reformatting, and the time to format the information with a common look and feel.

- Sample class materials—Since this information was originally prepared in Word, the conversion to Web materials was accomplished using the Word Internet Assistant as well. Some reformatting, described below, is required to break apart longer pages into readable materials and to make the pages look "just right" with graphics, but content is converted easily.

- Sample course overview materials (presentations)—By using the PowerPoint Wizard, it was possible to put some sales materials and overviews of classes on the Web. These materials were converted without modifications.

The things that required additional conversion centered on graphics. When a document has a graphic on the page, it will require additional help and possible reformatting when it comes to the final presentation of the page on the Web. In the sample pages brought up, there were cases where it was necessary to resize graphics to a more appropriate size for Web page review.

It will also be necessary to take the pages created by the Wizards and review them online while you work with the HTML directly. In some cases, you can make small changes to the pages, for example, left-aligning a graphic to make text flow around it, that will make the pages more readable online. In addition, you may want to remove some formatting that does not produce the desired effect.

One item noticed with the Word Assistant is that if you have a variety of fonts implemented in the document you're converting, it may be necessary to "clean up" the resulting HTML. In conversions created for the Reality Check site, it seemed that the Assistant occasionally missed "turning off" a font or style, requiring manual updates to the HTML. The closing HTML is typically the same as the opening tag, but with a forward slash inserted. For the <BODY> tag, for example, the closing tag is </BODY>.

In general, the Wizards and Assistants provided a great way to convert existing content and create new pages. When it comes to "tweaking" the appearance, though, you will likely want to use a simple text editor, perhaps NOTEPAD or Windows Write, to make the small adjustments.

From Here...

In this chapter you have learned about some of the things you need to think through if you decide to bring up an Intranet site. The following chapters and sections provide additional information that relates to the information provided in this chapter:

- Chapter 3, "Planning an Intranet Site," goes into some additional tools that may help with the presentation of the content on your site.

- Chapter 5, "Setting Up and Configuring a Web Server," shows how you install and configure the server software you select for your site.

- Chapter 9, "Firewalls and Proxy Servers," shows how you can implement the safeguards needed to ensure that company-confidential information stays confidential.

- Chapter 12, "Search Engines," will help you implement a key tool in Intranets – the search engine for your site materials.

- Chapter 18, "Basic HTML Techniques," shows more about the HTML that is produced behind the scenes.

- Chapter 19, "Advanced HTML," will help explain more fine-tuned features and capabilities of HTML that you can add to your page.

Firewalls and Proxy Servers

Putting your server on the Internet exposes you to a number of threatening influences. The types of people on the Internet range from those interested in causing harm to your network and information contained on it to those who just want to look at your Web pages. The average users are more likely to be the latter of these, looking largely for good content on your site. These users are intent on getting all the information they can from your site, short of trying to break into areas in which they're not welcome.

You need to make a fundamental decision before you move to the Internet. Regardless of your plans for your server and the components of it, you need to decide how you'll protect your internal networks from those who have no business seeing them. To take no action at all is, quite simply, an act of ignorance. This would likely cause you problems in the future, if not immediately. Getting into information that you have no business seeing is a process that works like a magnet. Once users realize they can find some information, they'll look for more. This can be deadly to your corporate network, to its confidential and proprietary information, and to your clients. After all, their information is also likely to be stored on your network. Make no mistake, if you're going to connect a system to the Internet, you should take steps to protect it.

What is a firewall?

Find out what a firewall is and how it can help protect your Internet installation against unscrupulous users.

What are the key elements of a firewall?

There are a number of different features that a firewall can rely on to protect your site. Find out more about these so you can make an informed decision about what you need.

What is a proxy server?

Proxy servers offer a different type of protection from firewalls. Learn how they work and what they're best used for on your network.

What alternatives are there?

Learn about new alternatives coming on the market from industry leaders and see how these may influence your purchase decisions for firewalls.

N O T E This chapter focuses less on UNIX versus Windows NT implementations and more on the technology of firewalls and proxy servers. This is largely because when you select the right solution or combination of solutions for your installation, the concepts and approaches will be largely the same in their implementation. ■

This is not to say that you need to spend thousands of dollars protecting your network. There are simple steps you can take to insulate your internal network from the Internet. In this chapter, you learn how you can implement these physical steps. You also learn how they differ from vendor-supplied solutions. There are pros and cons on both sides of the security dilemma.

N O T E As of this writing, Microsoft's Proxy Server, code-named "Catapult," is in Beta. When this book goes to press, this product will probably be nearing release. You can find out more information about this product on the Que Reality Check Web site, located at **http://www.mcp.com/que/developer_expert/backokit/index.html**. You can also browse updated materials at the author's Web site, located at **http://www.pobox.com/~swynk**.

As the technologies change, you'll also find other updates here, along with notices of any upcoming revisions of this and other books. ■

True firewalls entail software or hardware solutions, or both, developed specifically for providing the firewall functionality. These packages range greatly in price, depending on the features you want to implement. This is one purchase you should fully understand before buying. You need to shop extensively to make sure to get the right solution for you. This portion of the book provides information to help you understand the majority of the different options that are available from these packages and how you can implement a physical solution to protect your network. ■

Creating a Physical Wall—No Wired Access

At the most basic level, you can protect your internal network from Internet users by physically removing your network server from the internal network. Obviously, as a stand-alone server, it will be impossible for network users to access anything other than the Web or FTP server. This is, in many cases, the safest and best place to start.

In practical implementation, you might not know what features you need until you have requests from users to provide Internet access. If you bring up the server in this manner, you can get your server online and provide content to the Internet community. You can then start working with users to determine to what information they need access.

Of course, this simply doesn't mesh with the Intranet concept. What good is a server to your Intranet if it's not physically connected to the Intranet? This leads to two other alternatives. First, you can create a mirror type of server implementation. Using this concept, you create a dual server environment with one server on the Internet and one on your Intranet. This is a real chore to implement. It is even more of a chore to keep current between the two sites, even with replication. The positive side of this is that it's a physical barrier between the Internet and your Intranet.

The other approach you can take is to put your server on both networks. This is probably the best of the low-cost approaches. Be sure you are careful in how you set up the network cards though, as a wrong setting here, specifically that of forwarding packets between the cards, will remove any protection provided. Consider the drawing in Figure 9.1 for an example.

FIG. 9.1

Setting your server up on multiple networks can be the first step toward physically separating your internal network from the Internet.

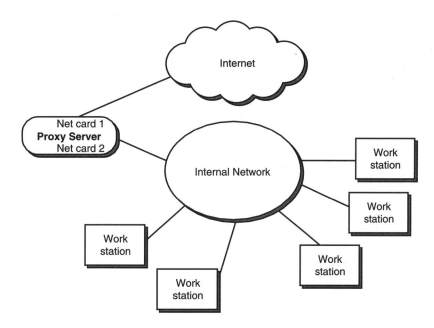

For one adapter, you'll have an IP address that is known to the Internet by way of your DNS servers. This is the IP address over which you will have Internet access. You also use this address to set up your public Web page. The other adapter will have an internal network-assigned IP address, making it available on your internal network.

You should physically wire your network so that the Internet connection is not hooked up to your internal network hubs. Keep your Intranet server separated and on its own physical network. When you have users who need direct Internet access, you can provide this by placing an additional network card in their systems. Then, you need to set up that card to access the Internet.

When you set up your network this way, make absolutely certain that you deselect the Enable IP Forwarding option on the Microsoft TCP IP Properties sheets for the TCP/IP protocol. If you leave this item selected, the server will become a bridge between the two network adapters, completely defeating the entire purpose of this approach.

For an example of the TCP/IP properties dialog box, see Figure 9.2.

FIG. 9.2
If you leave the Enable IP Forwarding option selected, packets can be routed from one network adapter to the other, opening your internal network to the Internet.

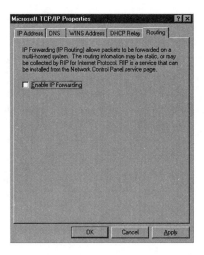

NOTE If you select this approach, you are able to create a public Web page site and a private Web site, if you're interested in doing so. The technique is identical to a Multi-home or Virtual Server installation. ▨

Once you have completed these steps, you have a server that is visible on the Internet. It is, at the same time, available on your Intranet, without having any type of bridge or gateway between the two. You are providing protection from the Internet. However, you are also preventing access for your users in their need to get out onto the Internet. This is a situation in which a true firewall and gateway scenario come into play. You will need to go a step further in your functionality when your user base begins demanding access to the Internet from desktop systems.

When this happens, it is no longer an Intranet versus Internet issue, nor is it a server-based issue. It quickly becomes an issue of providing the access needed, but also protecting the assets of your company's network. Firewalls are there for just this purpose. They validate incoming packets and also allow outgoing information allowed to travel beyond the firewall as determined by the configuration of the firewall.

Working with Firewalls

A number of different firewall approaches are employed to provide the access that suits your needs. Firewalls require an additional step on the way to and from the Internet. They require that you authenticate yourself along the way. This can range from a company-approved IP address list to user IDs and passwords to thumb prints and encrypted access code words that change on every access. The type of authentication that is employed by the systems varies depending on the approach of the package and what the needs are.

A number of different approaches are offered by firewalls. A number of different focuses also dictate what the firewall is looking for and protecting against. There are even some new terms to learn, such as *spoofing*.

Spoofing occurs when one user pretends to be another by changing the IP address and other low-level network access information. Most often this approach is employed to get around a firewall that uses packet filtering to control access. *Packet filtering* occurs when the firewall monitors the IP addresses as the gating mechanism for controlling access. You establish a range of IP addresses that are allowed in or out through the firewall. A person who spoofs the IP address will gain access to this relatively simple firewall approach by fooling the IP checking process.

There are other, more complex approaches. Other important features exist that you will want to learn about as well.

ON THE WEB

http://www.ncsa.com   At this site you can learn more information about firewalls and the rating and review system that is now being applied to them. Certain systems exist, such as the SATAN program, that will try to defeat your security and issue feedback on the success of your approach to protect your network. More information on the results of running this and other testing applications against the well-known firewalls is maintained at this site.

Application Level Filtering

This type of filtering takes place between two known quantities. One is the originating application, and the other an authorized destination. In other words, your application, known to the firewall, makes a request to access a location through the firewall. Once authenticated, the firewall acts as intermediary to transfer packets of information between the destination and the application.

By providing this bridge between the two locations, the firewall can maintain control over the destination for all incoming packets. If a packet comes in from the destination and is bound for an invalid internal address or application, it can be logged and ignored.

Application Level Security

With this type of control, the firewall establishes that you, the user, are allowed access to the resources you request. Once you establish this, usually by providing a user ID and password, you have an open band of communication between your system and the remote one. This provides the same convenience of the packet filtering, but controls the access to authorized personnel. It also gives a more dynamic access approach, as the user might be able to request access to a new resource. This can occur even if the firewall is not yet aware of the new resource, as long as the user is authorized to request the access.

Device Limits for Users and Groups

Most firewall applications enable you to define devices that can be used by certain users. On an NT-based system, you can supplement or even replace this functionality by using the NT-based security layers in which you can accomplish much of the same functionality.

Integration with the NT Security Model

Systems are now starting to appear on the market that integrate completely with the NT security model. One example is the Microsoft product code-named *Catapult* that employs user groups in NT to determine what types of access will be afforded different users on the system. You can assign read/write FTP, Web, and Usenet News access to different users independently from one another.

Invisible Intranet

At no time should someone on the Internet be able to casually see your internal systems. This is the whole point of the firewall. Be sure that your internal systems are not accessible by simply indicating their IP addresses. An unauthorized user should not be able to browse the different computers on your internal network.

Logging Capabilities

At the heart of the firewall is accountability. This doesn't include only the failed attempts in which the firewall stepped in and prevented access. In some cases, it can be good to know what sites people are requesting and what types of data are used, as well as other information. This is useful because it can help determine your own internal content that you provide from your server. It can also help optimize your users' time on the Internet, serving to curb the tendency to "surf the Web" all day long.

In a practical example of this, simply telling people that you have this capability can go a long way to controlling misuse of the Internet. In retail, many of the camera panels you see over cashier stations are simply mirrored panels. There are no cameras watching from behind the panels. However, there could be. In an experiment conducted at a retail location that was experiencing cashier pilfering, mirrored panels were installed. The cashiers were casually told that the "cameras" were installed to protect them. When the thought of being watched settled in, the pilfering stopped without the time and expense of really monitoring the cashiers to determine the problem areas. The same can be true of controlling misuse of the Internet. Yes, you will still have those who abuse the privilege; however, you will largely find that passive monitoring goes a long way toward controlling the problem.

Packet Filtering

As indicated at the beginning of this section, packet filtering is probably the most passive and vulnerable mechanism for controlling access to your network. With packet filtering, you indicate which IP addresses can get out of and into your network, to and from the Internet, respectively. This is the place in which spoofing can come into play. In this way, someone can pretend to be another by simply modifying his IP address. Then, this person can gain access to your network.

Password Management

Password management will likely be a mix at worst, or a fully integrated solution at best. When you have systems that are granted access to the Internet, you will want to tighten password management a bit and begin paying attention to valid password durations and controlling the renewal of passwords. You might recall that you can tell NT to automatically expire passwords at set intervals. For more information, see Figure 9.3.

FIG. 9.3
Consider changing passwords every 30 days to help add a layer of protection to your network.

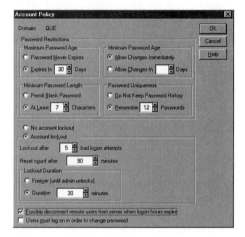

This example dialog box shows several key options within the User Manager that help in managing your user base. Consider establishing the password history monitoring system. This will prevent the user from bouncing between two different passwords, alternating from one month to another. Also, you might want to set the number of failed attempts before the account is temporarily disabled. This will prevent someone from continually attempting access with different passwords until finding the correct one.

Real-Time Monitoring and Alerts

Of primary importance in the firewall implementation is your ability to react to problems. If you have after-the-fact analysis of the system, it won't do you much good if someone does manage to get in. The only thing you will most likely do in this case is try to figure out what happened. The key is to be able to react to and take back control over a problem situation. This means that the firewall should have mechanisms in place to notify you immediately of any suspected problems.

You might want to consider a solution that supports a pager. Alternatively, you can implement a system that e-mails you about a possible problem. This system can then forward the e-mail message to your pager using a wireless gateway product.

On the CD accompanying this book is an evaluation version of two wireless products that might help in this area. The Integra Wireless Messaging Server for Microsoft Exchange lets you send wireless messages from Microsoft Exchange. You can use the Inbox Assistant to look for firewall-related messages and automatically forward them to your pager.

WinBEEP is a stand-alone product, also on the CD, that will let you send alpha-numeric messages to your pager without using Exchange. For more information, review the documentation included on the CD.

Firewalls Should Be Hassle-Free

Perhaps one of the biggest requirements for the firewall is that your users be aware of it as little as possible. If users are constantly required to alter how they normally work to accommodate the firewall, they will soon grow frustrated with it. This will pose a challenge to get them to keep using it.

System Inactivity Timeout

If a system is inactive for any period of time, the firewall should stop access to it. Of course, you should be able to control this timeframe. The reason is that you'll be one of the only people who can determine a valid timeframe. Once a system goes inactive for this time period, however, users should be required to authenticate themselves to the system once again.

This is similar to the screen saver with password option. When you step away from your computer, you put this screen saver option on. Then, whoever sits down at your computer cannot casually use it without providing a password to clear the screen saver. The same is true of the Internet connection. If you have authenticated yourself to the system, it knows that the proper user is working on it. If you step away from your system and others use it, these people should be required to log on and authenticate themselves to the system.

Time Limits for Users and Groups

As with the NT time limits, the firewall will probably be capable of limiting access times for users and groups of them. This comes in two forms, the first of which is actual time online. You might need to limit the overall amount of time a series of users is online. You can establish this time limit. Then, you can have the firewall implement it, preventing access beyond that time limit.

The second approach to this is actual logon time. You will be able to set up times during which a given user or group is allowed to log on. If users are outside this time limit, they will not be granted access to the Internet. This is to your benefit if you have variable shifts of people who might be signing on. You can limit logon times to those times when these people are on duty. This will keep them from unnecessarily using the system after hours.

Understanding Application-Level Considerations

In some cases, your application will need to be updated, configured, or modified to properly work with a firewall. This can mean indicating the computer name for the server that is acting as the firewall. Alternatively, it can mean providing password information that is used to access the firewall server. Figure 9.4 shows an example of specifying this information for WS_FTP, an FTP client application.

FIG. 9.4

If you don't set up a firewall-type connection, the application software will not be capable of accessing the external sites because the firewall will not allow it through.

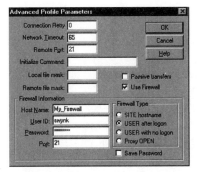

In Internet Explorer, the firewall server is referred to as a proxy server. As you can see in Figure 9.5, you need to provide the computer name for the server. You can also tell Internet Explorer about systems that should not be accessed through the proxy. In this case, the internal servers have been provided, telling Internet Explorer to go directly to those servers to connect.

FIG. 9.5

In Internet Explorer, you can click the icon by using the right mouse button. Then, you can select properties and set up the Proxy server information on the Connection tab.

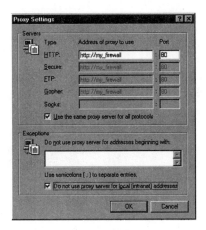

The changes you must make to your application will depend completely on how that application implements proxy or firewall servers. Consult your application documentation for information about how these applications should be configured.

Understanding Firewall Alternatives

The following information, taken from the National Computer Security Association's (NCSA) Web pages at **http://www.ncsa.com**, provides data on additional firewall products that have been tested and certified by the NCSA. Check their Web site frequently for emerging technologies, ongoing testing, and additional certifications that are currently underway.

For information, contact:

> Kevin J. Stevens
>
> Marketing/Communications
>
> (717) 258-1816 ext. 224
>
> (717) 243-8642 Fax
>
> e-mail: **kstevens@ncsa.com**

The National Computer Security Association has announced the results of the initial round of Firewall Certification Testing (Version 1.0) at NCSA Labs. The firewall developers and their products that have successfully completed the certification process include the following:

Company Name	Product Name
Atlantic Systems Group	TurnStyle™ Firewall System
Border Network Technologies, Inc.	BORDERWare™
Milkyway Networks, Inc.	Black Hole™
CheckPoint Software Technologies, Inc.	CheckPoint Firewall-1
Digital Equipment Corporation	AltaVista™ Firewall
Global Technology Associates, Inc.	GFX Internet Firewall System
Harris Computer Systems Corporation	CyberGuard™ Firewall
IBM	Secured Network Gateway
Livermore Software Labs, International	PORTUS™ Version 2
ON Technology Corporation	ON Guard™
Raptor Systems, Inc.	Eagle™
Technologic, Inc.	Interceptor™ Firewall System
Trusted Information Systems, Inc.	Gauntlet™ Internet Firewall Ver. 3.1
Radguard, Ltd.	CryptoWall™
Sun Microsystems	SunScreen™ SPF-100
NEC Technologies	PrivateNet™ 1.0.1A

Other firewall products will continue to be certified as they are submitted to NCSA Labs. The criteria of Version 2.0 for NCSA Firewall Certification will be announced at NCSA's Firewalls and Web Security Conference, September 30, 1996, in San Jose, California.

NCSA Certified Internet Firewall products are tested against a standardized and evolving suite of attacks while enabling desired business functions to be accomplished. Manufacturers with Internet firewall products meeting these standards are authorized to use the NCSA Certified logo for marketing and other promotional purposes.

NCSA Firewall Product Certification provides assurance to end users that a certified firewall product can be configured to protect an internal network against a suite of current threats tested by NCSA while enabling important business functions to operate effectively in an Intranet/Internet environment.

Part
II
Ch
9

Certification means that NCSA, acting as an independent laboratory, has verified that a firewall product meets the current published certification criteria. Information on firewall certification testing procedures, as well as products that are currently certified, is posted on the NCSA Web pages (**http://www.ncsa.com**).

"The NCSA Firewall Certification process will eliminate some confusion in the marketplace," according to Sam Glesner, the NCSA Firewall Consortium Manager. "With NCSA certification as a meaningful starting point, firewall users and potential buyers can better evaluate the right products for their specific networks."

"Certification will simplify the evaluation, purchase, and installation of firewalls," said Dr. Peter Tippett, President of NCSA. "Certification is not meant to imply perfect security, but rather that significant risk reduction will be achieved using an NCSA-Certified Firewall."

Working with Proxy Servers

Proxy servers provide several different levels of functionality for your networks. A typical proxy server is used on an Intranet to provide external Internet access to your internal users. The key to providing connectivity to the desktop is to provide the Internet as a controlled resource. As you saw in the prior sections about firewalls, providing security on the connection to the Internet is really your responsibility as Webmaster. You need to make sure that, while you provide the best level of service possible, you also provide comprehensive protection for your user base.

N O T E   Proxy servers introduce some new variables at the user level that you have a responsibility to address. These include educating your users about the "correct" use of Usenet newsgroups, letting the users know about what your company considers appropriate in terms of content reviewed on company time, and so on.

It's important that you take some time to work out a company policy statement about what you expect of the people using your network. This is as much protection for your company as it is laying down the law. You don't want to come across as a dictatorship, but it's extremely important that you have formal policies that indicate that your company retains the right to manage control over access to the Internet for business use.

continues

continued

You will find that many people consider such official policies to be "over the edge" in how they control and specify what information is considered appropriate; but if you don't call out these guidelines, you are in effect saying that anything goes. Protect your users and your company by instituting a policy now that you can mold and use to provide the guidance you need. ■

A proxy server's main goal is to provide enhanced connectivity for your users in their outbound requests. You don't use a proxy server to control access to your Web site, and you don't use a proxy server to provide firewall-type protection, though proxy servers are often used in conjunction with firewalls. You do use a proxy server to provide Internet connectivity and active caching of content for your users.

(Proxy servers are a way of providing centralized, controlled access to the Internet. A proxy server provides access to the most common protocols, FTP, HTTP, Gopher, and sometimes HTTP-S (Secure HTTP), depending on the proxy server software you use. The proxy server serves as a middle-man in the process of submitting and returning your requests to and from the Internet.

For example, when you request a page from a site, your local browser makes the request of the proxy server instead of the actual site containing the content. The proxy server receives the request and sends it off to the site you requested. See Figure 9.6 for a diagram of this process.

FIG. 9.6

An example of the typical proxy, Internet site request cycle.

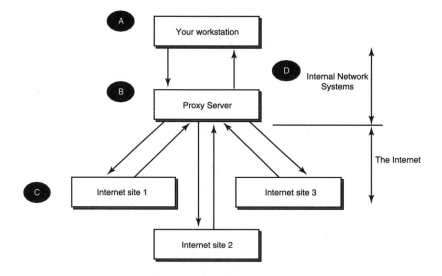

The process breaks down into four different phases:

■ From your client software, you make a request for access to a site. This request may be from your browser to access a Web page, or it may be from your FTP client to download a file from an Internet site.

■ The proxy server receives your request and prepares to work with the site to fulfill the request. In some cases, and in most newer versions of proxy servers, the proxy server will first search its local cache to see if the information you need is already on the system. If so, the request is fulfilled from cache directly, avoiding the need to access the Internet at all. If not, the request is forwarded to the requested site.

■ The server makes the request of the site you indicated and retrieves the information needed. If the server is caching the types of request you made, the content is placed in cache and prepared to be returned to your client application.

■ The information is returned to your application, just as if you were directly attached to the Internet. To your application, it was a simple matter of requesting the page or file that was needed. The balance of the work was performed by the proxy server.

Setting Up Your Client Software

Setting up the client software to use the proxy server is typically a rather simple process. With Microsoft's Internet Explorer, for example, you simply right-click the desktop icon and select Properties from the resulting menu. When you do, select the Connection tab. The key option to select is the Connect through a proxy server check box. See Figure 9.7.

Next, press the Settings button to provide the proxy server information for the different services you may be using. Figure 9.8 shows the configuration options for the Settings button.

FIG. 9.7
You need to configure your client software for access through a proxy server.

FIG. 9.8
You can indicate a different proxy server for different proxy services.

As you can see, you can provide a different server and a different port for each protocol for which you want to use the proxy server. Also, if you host or attach to an Intranet, you can save significant connect times by selecting the Do not use proxy server for local (Intranet) accesses option. This decreases access times for the local servers because the proxy will not be referenced and the computer names can go through a local name resolution, rather than an Internet name resolution effort.

N O T E   If you have left your installation at its defaults for port values, the HTTP service will generally be located on port 80. In many cases, the alternative port setting used is 8080, a somewhat standard port used for testing HTTP server installations. ■

T I P   If you use the same server for the different protocols you want to support, you can still specify port 80 on the first option for HTTP access and then select the Use the Same Proxy Server for All Protocols option. The proxy server will be able to sort out the requests coming from your client software and point them to the correct port.

Netscape Navigator 3.0 is set up in much the same way, by selecting the Options, Network Preferences, Proxies tab. Next, select from the different proxy configuration options so they match your installation correctly.

N O T E   In many installations, the proxy port will be overridden by the system administrator. If you are the administrator for the system, be sure to document the port settings for your users; and if you're one of the people accessing the system, check with your system administrator for the correct values to use for your proxy server. ■

Understanding the Key Features of Your Proxy Server

There are several key features that you use when you set up a proxy server. These include the following items:

- Cache management
- Filtering and access control
- Utilization reporting
- Performance
- Security

Each of these items, which may or may not be present in every proxy server you consider or implement, must be understood in order to more fully use your server software. The first of these, cache management, includes many different aspects of working with documents from the locally stored cache.

Cache Management   The cache works to improve performance in a couple of different ways. The first and foremost goal of the cache is to provide local access to frequently reviewed content. This content, when first retrieved at the request of a user's system, is stored on the server.

When the same page is requested by a different user, that information is retrieved from the cache, saving the time to wait for the retrieval over the Internet.

N O T E Different software vendors call caching by different terms. For example, Microsoft refers to this as URL caching, while Netscape calls it replication. Though there are some different, smaller features within each implementation, on an overall basis it all refers to the caching of information from the remote host. ■

The second thing that caching does to help performance is to lessen the traffic over the line you have installed to the Internet. As you can imagine, if you are able to retrieve pages from the cache, you'll save accesses to the connection, resulting in better throughput for the remaining users who request information not yet in the cache.

If you have a slower connection to the Internet, a proxy server that uses the caching approach can significantly help manage the traffic over your connection to the Internet.

Filtering and Access Control   When you implement desktop access to the Internet you introduce a new toy to a lot of users. This toy will certainly result in new knowledge resources for them, new research capabilities; and it should be a goal that the Internet provides a good return on investment for your company. At the same time, not all material on the Internet is relevant to workday efforts.

As you monitor your system, you will undoubtedly notice that access is being made to sites that are really not relevant to your line of business. This is lost time to your business; with a good proxy package, you can control this access.

N O T E In one example, a site administrator had found that, during normal business hours, nearly 60 percent of his site's volume was coming from a very large computer manufacturer. This would be fine if the site were not hosted by a magazine famous for its female-oriented pictorials. You can prevent this type of misuse of your system by applying a filter to a specific domain name. ■

You can generally apply these filters to the outgoing content requests. You can usually apply filters based on IP, Host, or DNS-based information. For example, if you wanted to control access to the dontgohere.com site, you could limit access based not only on the root site, but also on all pages and resources located on that site.

CAUTION

If you limit access to a site and want to ensure that the access is indeed controlled, you should limit by both the site name, as in dontgohere.com provided above, and the site's IP address. You can determine the site IP address by using the PING utility.

At the command prompt, type PING dontgohere.com and you'll receive the IP address for the site. Provide both of these bits of information to the filtering application to ensure tighter controls on the site.

Utilization Reporting   You will need to ensure that you have logging turned on for the same reasons as logging for your overall Web site. In order for you to manage your site and the services you offer, you need to know how people are using your proxy server. This is the only way to gauge the performance of your server and to make sure you're able to provide the level of service your users require.

Once you set up the logging, be looking for ways to find the exceptions in the logging information. It's a simple fact of life that if you expect to find meaningful information in the logs, it becomes more and more difficult over time. There will be just too much information to cull through. Look for ways to find the things that stick out as breaking from the normal usage. These might include usage patterns significantly higher on one system when compared with others on your network, excessive hits on a site that may be questionable, and so forth.

In short, you need to develop a way to separate the standard "noise" level on the system from the items of note that represent peaks in usage or access levels.

Security   One final note about what to expect from your proxy server, and that is a certain amount of protection from inbound requests. If you have your server on the Internet, you'll want to be protecting against intruders. This is where your firewall typically comes in, giving you the barrier between your systems and those of the potential intruder.

The proxy server can provide an added level of benefit in this area. In most server software, you have the ability to designate which IP addresses from your internal network will be published from the proxy server out to the Internet. In other words, the proxy server can provide a gatekeeper to protect your workstation IP addresses from being accessible from the Internet. To the Internet, the address would simply not exist.

This is important because you will have to allow access to certain systems through the firewall, or they would not have access to the Internet to provide the proxy services. Since, when you provide this access, you potentially provide a loophole in the firewall's protection, the ability for the proxy to support its addresses is a real necessity. You typically configure the IP addresses allowed access in a configuration settings file that is read by the proxy server. You can change this list at any time, allowing for expansion of your network when you need to add new proxy servers or other systems requiring access in this manner.

Understanding Remote WinSock Services

Microsoft has introduced an interesting twist to the more traditional proxy services. While traditional proxy services provided coverage for HTTP, FTP, and Gopher services, this left holes in the additional, newer protocols that have come into being. Of special note in this arena is the NNTP protocol. Though not new, it provides access to the Usenet news groups and is certainly an excellent source of research and support contacts for your company in many cases.

To support these types of services, Microsoft introduced Remote WinSock Services, or RWS. Included as part of their proxy server package, RWS simply replaces the WinSock DLLs on your system with those that recognize the access through the server. You have control at the proxy server to apply the same restrictions on access as you would with the more traditional proxy services. You can limit access to sites, protocols, and so on.

Because only the standardized DLLs are switched out, this solution typically works quite well where you're using a mix of third-party software for access to the Internet, including news readers, FTP client applications, RealAudio type feeds, and so on. There is usually no impact on your existing applications whatsoever, and you're immediately able to have the protection from the Internet provided by the proxy server.

Part
II

Ch
9

Reality Check

At the Integra Technology Reality Check site, we implemented a script that returns usage patterns for the proxy server. This is done by checking the hits on the `proxy.dll` file as logged by the server software. The result is a list of IP addresses and access counts per address, such as the following:

```
IP Address                                          Hits
-------------------------------------------    ----------
128.1.4.82                                          12775
128.1.4.41                                          10165
128.1.5.9                                           10041
128.1.5.98                                          9751
128.1.4.74                                          8182
128.1.5.8                                           7580
128.1.4.40                                          6575
128.1.4.7                                           6458
128.1.5.27                                          5639
128.1.4.62                                          5081
128.1.4.33                                          4234
128.1.4.83                                          3988
128.1.5.39                                          3389
128.1.4.61                                          3004
128.1.5.30                                          2907
```

The following is the excerpt from the SQL Script that produces this information:

```
Select "IP Address"=clienthost, "Hits" = count(substring(logtime,10,2))
from wwwlog
where
    (
        charindex("proxy.dll",target) > 0
    )
group by clienthost
order by "hits" desc
```

This information clearly shows that in the top five usage IP addresses alone, there is a 50 percent difference in the number of hits on the proxy server. This fact brought about some investigation into what was causing the higher number of hits. It turns out that the user at the other end of that IP address is using PointCast™, a product that repeatedly checks back with a news and advertising service at regular intervals. This accounted for the increased usage on that machine. We now keep profiles on the types of applications people are using at the desktop so we have an idea of what represents unusual usage.

From Here...

Security is a major consideration in your network when you begin allowing access to the Internet. Saying that firewalls and the other options are a good idea is a vast understatement. Related materials are found in the following areas:

- The NCSA Web site, located at **http://www.ncsa.com**, is an excellent reference for firewalls, techniques, companies with products, and more.

- Chapter 5, "Setting Up and Configuring a Web Server," details different setup options that you'll want to consider when you install your server, including logging options.

- Chapter 11, "Usage Statistics," provides more information about analyzing the patterns of use on your server.

## CHAPTER 10

Maintenance Utilities

Site maintenance is one thing that sort of creeps up on you. One moment you've got your entire site logged in your head and you know all of the different pages, their links, and so forth. The next moment, you suddenly realize your site now contains many times the number of pages you originally envisioned, and you can quickly become lost. This can be especially true if you're running a site where other people have access to posting files and information to the site. Intranets are famous for growing astronomically fast once opened to the user population.

Web management tools are, in fact, pretty sparse as of this writing, but there are a couple of alternatives available now that can help with the task of managing your site. Some key features that you're looking for in a site management tool include the following:

Learn how to use the FrontPage Explorer to manage links on your site

The FrontPage Explorer offers a graphical, link-oriented view of your site, showing you where links are broken and helping you manage the relationships between pages.

Learn how to use the FrontPage Editor to work with content on your site

The Editor provides a what-you-see-is-what-you-get, or WYSIWYG, environment for working with HTML pages. You can create an entire site without looking into the HTML code being generated for you behind the scenes.

Learn how to install the FrontPage extensions for IIS

By using the FrontPage extensions for IIS, you can enable interactive authoring on your site without the need for network shares or the use of file transfer protocol, or FTP.

Learn how to use WebBots

WebBots offer some interesting automated capabilities for your pages. From forms to site maps, the Bots can save you quite a lot of time when used on your site.

- Link management —Your site management tool should allow you to check your pages for broken links and indicate which links have a problem.

- Management of live links—The tool should allow you to change a page referenced by other pages and have those external references update to the new page. This means that if you remove a page that is referenced by other pages, those links should, at your authorization, be removed from those other pages.

- What you see is what you get, or WYSIWYG, editing—This is becoming an issue more and more as companies make the Intranet available to their users. Being able to edit exactly as you'll see your content is a big plus to these types of packages.

- A graphical web view—This is important because, just as the old saying indicates, a picture is worth a thousand words. This holds true for Web development. With a good graphical view of your web site, you can see where links are, what types of links are present and, in many cases, where links exist that you may not expect.

The challenge of managing and maintaining a site will probably lead you to look into many different tools to help in this arena, but there's a good chance that you'll find that Microsoft's FrontPage product, and America Online's AOLPress product are among the top contenders in this field. This chapter focuses on these packages with an emphasis on FrontPage, only due to space constraints. Both of these packages warrant your consideration for this type of tool.

Information on these tools is available on the Internet at:

- Frontpage: **http://www.microsoft.com/msoffice/frontpage**. You also receive FrontPage with NT Server version 4.0 or later as part of the IIS package. You can also obtain this from the sitebuilder site, located at http://www.microsoft.com/sitebuilder. As of this writing, FrontPage 97 has gone into Beta and is available on the Microsoft site.

- AOLPress: **http://www.aolpress.com**. You can download AOLPress free of charge from this location.

In this chapter, you'll see how FrontPage can be used to generate a complete site template, how you can use the WYSIWYG editor, and what it means to add intelligent components, called Bots, to your site's pages. FrontPage allows you to take great strides toward tracking page dependencies, seeing page relationships graphically, and reusing different aspects of your site's pages, like toolbars and background colors, in a site-wide fashion.

N O T E The FrontPage product is a complex authoring environment with more capabilities than can be fully explored in this chapter. This information is provided to get you familiar with FrontPage. It should also give you an idea of how the software works, what the intended audience for it is, and whether it may be interesting to you in the development and management of your Intranet and Internet sites. ■

Microsoft's FrontPage product first originated with Vermeer Technologies, the creators of FrontPage. The FrontPage product includes several key components that are covered in this chapter. They are:

- FrontPage Personal Web Server—A Web server that runs under Windows and allows you to create and test your pages without the need for an NT Server or Workstation as it runs in Windows '95.
- FrontPage Explorer site management software—Lets you work with your site on an overall basis. The familiar Windows Explorer-type interface helps you get around your site easily and maps out your site, including page dependencies.
- FrontPage Editor—Makes all others obsolete in a number of areas. First, it's WYSIWYG in that it allows you to enter and format your content right on screen without regard for the underlying HTML code. Second, it allows you to read a page, make changes, and save the page back to the server without having to know and understand the FTP protocols that are typically needed to update the pages on the host.
- FrontPage TCP/IP Test Program—Inventories your system and tests the TCP/IP and Windows protocols to make sure they are available.
- FrontPage Administrator—Allows you to manage the installation of the server extensions, assign installations to specific virtual or multi-homed servers, and more.
- FrontPage Server Extensions—Make it possible to use all the different features of FrontPage with your server. The extensions also provide added functionality to the system to support the FrontPage Explorer and its control of the site.

AOLPress takes a more integrated approach, and it presents its tools in two different products.

- AOLPress—The software that allows you to manage your web site, including web maps, link management, page creation, and so on. This tool is run on the client system and can access web pages on the Internet or on the local system.
- AOLServer—Web server software that works with AOLPress to let you interactively edit your web site.

NOTE These application environments are functionally very similar. The point of this chapter is to give you an overview of how these tools work and what you should be thinking about as you evaluate your options for site management software. To that end, this chapter will not fully explore either product, but instead will focus on FrontPage and will have comparisons of approaches between FrontPage and AOLPress called out as possible.

This chapter should be read more with a "how to start the management tool evaluation process" approach than a definitive guide to these products.

In the coming sections, you'll see how you can put the different pieces of FrontPage to work for you to help manage your site or sites.

Part II
Ch 10

Installing Microsoft FrontPage

The first thing you must do, regardless of your plans to use FrontPage on the server, is install the different components of the FrontPage client. To start the setup process, run the SETUP.EXE application that is included as part of the FrontPage software. Depending on how you received FrontPage, this is either part of an overall ZIPped archive file or it is on the distribution media on which you received FrontPage.

After you start the application, you'll be welcomed to the setup process and you'll need to confirm the starting location for the FrontPage system. You'll then be prompted to select either a Typical installation or a Custom installation. See Figure 10.1 for an example.

FIG. 10.1

Custom installations give you more control over the items to be installed and where they are located.

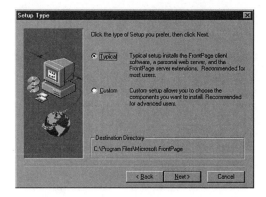

In the case of a Typical installation, the different applications are installed with all of the different default options. With the Custom installation, you can indicate which of the three major component areas you want to install. See Figure 10.2.

FIG. 10.2

If you're running short on disk space, it can be a good idea to limit the software components that will be installed.

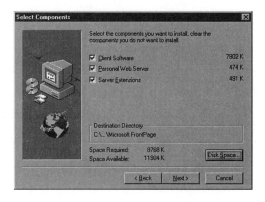

The Disk Space button allows you to select the destination drive for the files and gives you an indication of how much overall space is needed for the options you've selected. As is typical with most standardized Windows installations, you'll next be prompted for the select name for the program group or menu selection from the Start, Programs menu. This defaults to Microsoft FrontPage but you can rename the group to anything you like, which might make it easier to remember.

Once you provide the program group name, you'll be shown a preview of what the setup program is about to do. You can scroll down through the listing, like the one shown in Listing 10.1 below, to verify that the different options you've selected are acknowledged.

Listing 10.1 (NOT ON DISK): Listing on FrontPage Installation Options

```
Installing a fresh copy of FrontPage in:
    D:\Program Files\Microsoft FrontPage

The following components will be installed:
    Client Software
    Server Extensions
    Personal Web Server

Upgrading the Personal Web Server in:
    D:\fpeval\webs\Server
Content Directory for Webs:
    D:\FPEVAL\WEBS\CONTENT

Name of Program Folder:
    Microsoft FrontPage
```

Part
II

Ch
10

After you complete the installation, the final prompt offers to start up the FrontPage Explorer. If you want to begin working with FrontPage immediately, simply click on Finish with the option for the Explorer selected. If you already have a FrontPage-enabled server on your network and you have rights to that server, you'll be able to connect to it and begin working with installed Webs on that server.

The next step depends on what you are trying to do. This can be working on creating a Web site with the FrontPage Personal Web Server or working with IIS to create or manage a site. If you want to begin working on a site with the FrontPage server or if you are going to access a site that already has the FrontPage extensions installed for IIS, you can start work right away.

If, on the other hand, you still need to implement the extensions for your IIS server, skip to the section, "Installing FrontPage Server Extensions for IIS," before continuing. If you don't, some of the utilities explained next will not work because they won't be able to connect to the server correctly.

Using the FrontPage Server Administrator

The FrontPage Administrator is the application you use to control the server extensions. The administrator gives you access to the following items:

- Installation of server extensions

- Installation of upgrade server extensions when updates are issued for FrontPage

- Uninstallation of server extensions on servers or ports

- Server extension and configuration verification to confirm that extensions are installed correctly and operating as needed

- Control whether Authoring is enabled or disabled for a given server or port

- Control secured access, including limiting access for a given user to a specific port or server

Each of these items uses the servers defined in the Select port number list box. By default, Web servers operate on port 80. You may notice this when you access certain sites because they list their address as **http://www.mysite.com:80**, which indicates that port 80 should be used. This is the default port address, though, so it's not usually necessary to indicate the port unless a different port is used.

N O T E   In some systems, typically those that are UNIX-based, you'll notice that a port of 8080 is referenced. This port is a standard port used to bring up a test server or one that is not necessarily in production.

An interesting application of the port, especially on proprietary networks as in an Intranet, is to bring up the server on a port other than the norm. This prevents access altogether to parties not knowing the correct port number. In other words, you can bring up your Internet server on port 81, for example, and anyone accessing your site and not specifying port 81 on the URL will not get to the content on the site.

Since port addresses are valid from 0 to 65535, you have quite a range of addresses available to you when adding this layer of security to the site. Keep in mind, though, that there may be some lesser-known, less-capable browsers that are not able to indicate the port or that force the browser to port 80.

If this is the case, these browsers may not be able to access your site. If you decide to use a port other than the standard, you should test extensively with the software that you expect to use on your site. ■

When you work with the different features of FrontPage, you work with independent servers. A server is an instance of your software associated with a given port. If you've set up multi-homed or virtual servers, you work with each server independently. If you are working in this type of environment, you'll be indicating which server you're working with based on the IP address you're using.

Installing Server Extensions   You use the FrontPage Administrator to install the server extensions both when you first set up your server and later if you decide to add the extensions to another server. The installation process is straightforward. You simply select the Install button to begin.

You'll be prompted for the type of server you're installing. The list of software you see represents a few of the more common server extensions that can be installed. See Figure 10.3 for an example.

FIG. 10.3

Select the type of server extension you're installing. This will enable interactive Web site development with your server.

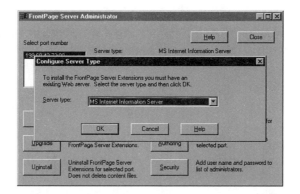

Next, you're prompted for the Server Port and Multi-Hosting address information. This request for Multi-Hosting information is presented regardless of whether you have implemented virtual servers on your system. For the port, indicate 80 or the port you are setting up for your IIS system. If you do not have a multi-home system, you can skip the Multi-Hosting text box and click the OK button.

The final step confirms that you want to install the extensions to the server and the dialog box shows you the different processes the system will use in response to your request. When you select OK, you'll be prompted for the Name and Password of the administrator for the site. These will be used later to control access to the server. You should be sure to indicate a user and password combination that has administrative privileges on the server. Be sure you write these down as you'll need them in the future when you administer the server.

N O T E If you're using FrontPage in an NT domain environment, you'll need to specify the user name a bit differently. If you're referring to a user in the current domain, you can simply provide the user's name. If you want to indicate a user from a different domain, use the format:

`<domain>\<user>`

This shows where the user is originating and where the password authentication should occur. ■

When you install the extensions, the process is substantial as several new directories are created, permissions are assigned, and default pages are created. In short, the entire Web site is created for the server you indicate.

It's a good idea to use the Check option, explained later in this chapter, to confirm the successful installation of the server extensions. If you experience problems, you can uninstall the extensions for a selected server and reinstall them.

Available Server Extensions   As of this writing, the extensions available for FrontPage are contained in the table below. This information was taken from the FrontPage site, located at **http://www.microsoft.com/frontpage/productinfo/brochure/fpquick2.htm**.

Web Server	Solaris 2.4	SunOS 4.1.3	IRIX 5.3	HP/UX 9.03	BSD/OS 2.1	Windows NT	Windows 95
Microsoft IIS	**N/A	N/A	N/A	N/A	N/A	X	N/A
Personal Web Server	N/A	N/A	N/A	N/A	N/A	X*	X*
O'Reilly WebSite	N/A	N/A	N/A	N/A	N/A	X*	X*
NCSA	X	X	X	X	X	N/A	N/A
CERN	X	X	X	X	X	N/A	N/A
Apache	X	X	X	X	X	N/A	N/A
Open Market Web Server	X	X	X	X	X	N/A	N/A
Netscape Communications Server	X	X	X	X	X	X*	N/A
Netscape Commerce*** Server	X	X	X	X	X	X*	N/A

Web Server	Solaris 2.4	SunOS 4.1.3	IRIX 5.3	HP/UX 9.03	BSD/OS 2.1	Windows NT	Windows 95
Microsoft IIS**	N/A	N/A	N/A	N/A	N/A	X	N/A
Personal Web Server	N/A	N/A	N/A	N/A	N/A	X*	X*
O'Reilly WebSite	N/A	N/A	N/A	N/A	N/A	X*	X*
NCSAX	X	X	X	X	N/A	N/A	
CERNX	X	X	X	X	N/A	N/A	
ApacheX	X	X	X	X	N/A	N/A	
Open Market Web ServerX	X	X	X	X	N/A	N/A	
Netscape Communications ServerX	X	X	X	X	X*	N/A	
Netscape Commerce*** ServerX	X	X	X	X	X*	N/A	

Denotes Web servers whose corresponding FrontPage Server Extensions ship in the FrontPage 1.1 box. For all other servers, available FrontPage Server Extensions may be downloaded from this site.

**NOTE: Important information regarding these extensions is provided in the following list:

- *You must install FrontPage and have IIS installed on your machine before installing the FrontPage Server Extensions for IIS.*

- *IIS requires Windows NT 3.51 or Windows NT 4.0.*

- *Running Windows NT 3.51 on an i386 platform, IIS requires Windows NT Service Pack 3 or higher. You can install Service Pack 3 as part of the IIS Server installation. You can download this and other updates to the IIS application at http://www.microsoft.com/windows/common/IISArchive.htm.*

- *You must be logged into Windows NT Server as an administrator during the installation and usage of the FrontPage Server Extensions for IIS.*

- *Microsoft FrontPage Server Extensions for IIS also require the FrontPage Server Administrator 1.1, which comes with FrontPage 1.1.*

- *The FrontPage Server Extensions for IIS support either the NTFS or FAT file systems.*

***NOTE: Microsoft FrontPage 1.1 supports Netscape Commerce Server but does not support SSL (Secure Sockets Layer). Thus, you must disable SSL in the Netscape Commerce Server before you can use FrontPage against it. Once you are done authoring/making changes, you can re-enable SSL for the Commerce Server. For security conscious customers who want to use FrontPage v1.1 with the Netscape Commerce Server, the best mode of operation is outlined in the following list:

- *Keep a separate copy of the web where all development is done. This copy should only be accessible to internal authors, and can be served by a copy of the Netscape Commerce server that has SSL turned off all of the time. The Personal Web Server with Windows NT Workstation is another option for the development web.*

- *Use the Netscape HTML administration interface to take the web off-line, either by restricting access to a single IP address or something similar. Then disable SSL for the server, again using the Netscape HTML administration interface.*

- *Use the FrontPage 1.1 CopyWeb command to copy the development web to the production web.*

- *Use the Netscape HTML interface to re-enable SSL for the production server, and then to open up access once again.*

Uninstalling Server Extensions   Uninstalling the server extensions is quite simple. Select the Server you want to uninstall and select Uninstall. You'll be asked to verify that you want to continue, and FrontPage will let you know that content on the server will not be disturbed and only the extensions for the server software are involved.

If you select OK, the extensions are removed from the port and the action is confirmed by a final dialog box. You need to uninstall server extensions on each server you've created as they are individually maintained.

Checking Server Extensions   The Check option is a quick way to confirm that your server extensions are working correctly. Select the server you want to test, then click on the Check button. The utility verifies that the server is responding correctly to calls to the extended FrontPage capabilities, and it confirms that all supporting operations have been completed, including directory rights and locations.

If any problems are encountered, FrontPage notifies you of what it has found. You'll need to correct each problem noted individually, and then rerun the utility because the process terminates if a problem is found. See the final note under "Installing Server Extensions" above for an example of what you may encounter when you test a new installation.

Enabling or Disabling Authoring Capabilities   Authoring in FrontPage is what makes the FrontPage Explorer and FrontPage Editor so unique and powerful. Using these tools with Authoring enabled on the server allows you to create and edit Web content on the fly in a graphical environment without regard for the HTML code behind the scenes.

When you select the Authoring button, the resulting dialog box shows the current state of the authoring flag and will allow you to change it. See Figure 10.4.

FIG. 10.4

Once you begin to put your site into production, you may want to control access to the site more carefully. By explicitly turning on Authoring, you can make sure you are aware anytime someone is making changes.

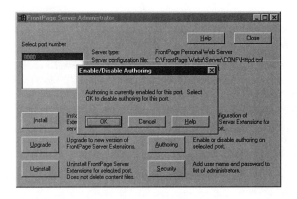

Since this is either enabled or disabled, selecting OK reverses the current state of the option. Once the option is disabled, users attempting to access the site with the FrontPage Explorer and FrontPage Editor are not able to do so. The only access method is to use a Web browser to browse content as you'd expect to do at a "normal" site.

Setting Up Security on Servers   Security, from the FrontPage administrator's viewpoint, is enforced by controlling who can administer the server and its associated extensions. You can set up administrators on a system-wide basis or you can set them up only for a given server. Select the Security button to start working with the users. See Figure 10.5.

To create new FrontPage administrators, you only need to indicate a user name and password. The user name does not have to map to a login name, although this can make it much easier for the users of your system to remember. You may also want to define a username, perhaps

"ADMINS" with a suitable password, that is used by all administrative type employees using the system. This allows you to issue a single username and password when it comes time to share the system.

FIG. 10.5
Additional administrators can be defined, allowing you to share the load of managing the site.

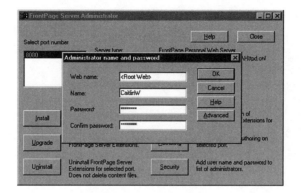

N O T E If you're using FrontPage in an NT domain environment, you'll need to specify the user name a bit differently. If you're referring to a user in the current domain, you can simply provide the user's name. If you refer to a user from a different domain, use the format:

`<domain>\<user>`

This shows where the user is originating and where the password authentication should occur. ▪

A very powerful feature of the security capabilities for FrontPage is that you can define administrators and then limit their domain of control to only those servers on which they belong. To create a system-limited administrator, first enter the name, password, and confirmed password information as usual.

Next, select the Advanced option. You'll be able to indicate the IP address of the server you want to limit the user to. This can be a great way to pass on administration capabilities to appropriate individuals so they can manage their own content and features. At the same time, you won't be forced to completely open your system to people who don't necessarily need to know about the site as a whole from an administrative standpoint (see Figure 10.6).

N O T E You can indicate the address in much the same way as the address masks you provide when setting up the IIS server. For each segment that you want to make a wildcard, one that supports any value in that segment of the IP address, you can substitute an asterisk (*) for the value.

For example, suppose all your Intranet Sports aficionados are using the server located at 198.68.42.15 and all the racing fans are referencing a server at 198.68.42.33. You can create a sports administrator who has access to the address 198.68.42.* and the same person can administer both sites. ▪

FIG. 10.6
You may want to consider creating an administrator for each major Web server you install. This significantly eases the burden of administration of the entire site.

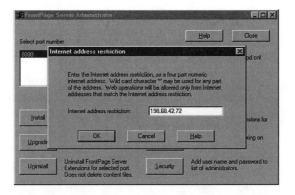

Concepts Behind the Explorer, the Editor, and the AOLPress Editing Environment

The AOLPress environment provides both web page selection and editing/creation from within the AOLPress environment.

The FrontPage Explorer and the FrontPage Editor work together to provide you with a range of capabilities that weave directly into the server and its extensions. As an overview, here are some of the many things you can do with the FrontPage and AOLPress client applications:

- Create new Webs in FrontPage, or MiniWebs in AOLPress
- Create new pages
- Edit existing pages
- Create image maps that allow people to click on pictures on your site as a means of navigating the site without worrying about creating the mapping files that are needed to allow this functionality
- Create new "sub-Webs" and insert them into an existing tree of pages
- Create forms
- With FrontPage, you can also create intelligent Web content capable of automatic generation of a table of contents for your site or able to insert common elements into your pages, making maintenance of the look and feel of your site much more straight-forward

While neither package is the end of all HTML coding, they are great tools that can help you create solid, standardized pages that provide a starting point for your site.

You can take the pages created here and add to them capabilities covered elsewhere in this book, including adding IDC capabilities. Just because you're using the FrontPage extensions, you are not precluding the use of other ISAPI extensions.

▶ For more information about Internet Database Connectivity pages and how you can work with ODBC data sources, see "Database Access and Integrity," Chapter 22.

The FrontPage Explorer is the tool you use to browse your site. As you can see in Figure 10.7, the interface is much like the Windows Explorer and File Manager with a listing of the tree structure of your site on the left-hand side of the application and the detail pages shown on the right.

FIG. 10.7

The FrontPage Explorer lets you see several different views of the same information, including a detailed listing of file names, modification dates, and relationships between the pages on your system.

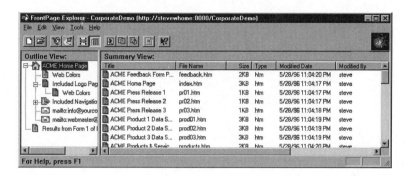

Part

II

Ch

10

There are two basic modes that you can use to work with your site. Chances are good that you'll be switching between them because they both are applicable and useful in different situations. When you're working with content and trying to keep your arms around the files that make up your site, the detail listing shown in Figure 10.7 makes a lot of sense.

There are times, however, when you need to see not only which files are on the system, but how they relate to each other, what files are referenced by other files, and more. Figure 10.8 shows the Link View, a view that shows graphically how your site is laid out relative to the page you have highlighted in the left-hand pane.

FIG. 10.8

The Link View makes understanding how pages relate straight-forward.

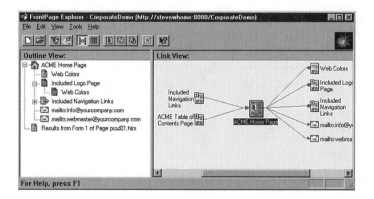

In AOLPress, this is referred to as Webizing a directory. In Figure 10.9, you can see that the graphical presentation of the pages uses the same approach to showing the links relative to a given point in your Web.

FIG. 10.9
AOLPress' "Webize'd" view of the site shows the links between pages, both internal and external to your site.

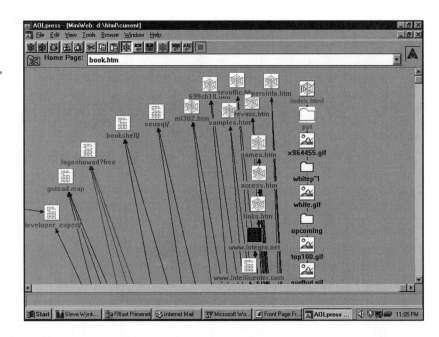

You can double-click any page in the right pane to load it in the Editor. From there, you can make modifications to the page or simply cancel editing and return to the Explorer.

The editors bring with them a nice feature: the ability to manage the links and relationships between the pages on your site, all automatically.

When you are editing pages, it can quickly become a problem navigating the different links between pages. This is especially true if your site allows people to wander around the site from one page to another regardless of whether they're really related pages. See Figure 10.10.

FIG. 10.10
The Explorer keeps track of inbound and outbound links for all pages in the current Web, making necessary changes if you change files within those links.

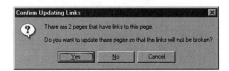

 TIP Even if you prefer to write your own original HTML code, using the Administrator to manage the site links, page references, and other relative links is a time-saving use of the tool. There are many times when a site goes through a set of revisions in which links are broken inadvertently and different pages become inaccessible.

If you code your own HTML or if you make manual changes to Explorer-driven HTML, this code is parsed and the relationships are managed while under the control of FrontPage when the pages are loaded into the FrontPage Explorer.

A good approach to site development is to follow three steps within a given revision cycle:

1. Allow FrontPage to create the initial Web, content, and formatting.
2. Make manual changes to the code to fit your needs for custom content, presentation, or other items.
3. Use FrontPage to insert new pages, remove pages, or change links to pages. This also includes making changes to file names on the server.

If you do, you'll be taking the greatest advantage of the FrontPage tools while, at the same time, ensuring that you're able to add your own flair to the site in terms of custom coding.

In the next few sections, you'll see some of the key features of FrontPage and how you can use them with your Web site and content to leverage existing materials across the pages on the site.

Using the Site Wizards to Create Webs

It's a daunting task to start a new Web site. There are many decisions regarding content, look and feel, and more that all drive your choices about the site. Of course, the first step is to bring up a skeleton site, complete with a home page, as a starting point. If you have a tool that will also help you standardize the site and make it easier to make site-wide changes later, all the better. This is where FrontPage comes in.

FrontPage provides you with several different Site Wizards to help you start a new Web site. These Wizards will help you by prompting you for some key information and then creating the site. Once created, the site includes code that activates some of the FrontPage functionality, such as server-side includes and more. The following Web Page Wizards are included with FrontPage:

- Normal Web includes a single page, the starting point for a new Web.
- Corporate Presence Web includes company home page, including logo and look and feel pages, mailto: account references, and a search results form.
- Customer Support Web includes welcome page, bug report page, and a suggestions page.
- Discussion Web includes both frame-based and standard page-based HTML to provide a discussion capability between people posting.
- Empty in which no pages are created, only the supporting directory.
- Learning is a learning site featuring a learning FrontPage starting point with references to cooking lessons, recipes, and so on.

■ Personal creates a single page with several links to areas that may be of interest from a home page.

■ Project creates a simple starting point with an opening page with information about a project.

This is quite an array of sites being offered. Chances are good, however, that your site won't fit the provided templates, entirely, straight out of the box. It's still a good idea to start with the Wizards and then follow with changes manually or through the FrontPage Editor and Explorer applications. The Wizards make use of all of the different capabilities whenever possible and your later modifications can take advantage of these. As an example, the Wizards create base pages that use included files showing the background and foreground colors, the logos, and other graphics to be included, and more.

To start the Wizard from within the FrontPage Explorer, select File, New Web. You'll be asked to indicate the type of Web you want to create. When you consider which Web to create, remember that your site will undoubtedly include attributes from more than one of the provided samples. If this is the case, you need to consider which of the Webs listed will most closely fit your environment without modification.

If you seem to have a tie between more than one topic, consider selecting one now and then coming back and creating a new Web with the other information you need. As you'll soon see, you can join these two Webs rather simply, and you'll save the hassle of writing the HTML code for the second site (see Figure 10.11).

FIG. 10.11
Select the type of Web that most closely fits what you need for the new site.

N O T E If you select the box to add the new Web to the current Web, it is placed in the Home directory you defined in the Web Server properties within IIS's administration utilities. The application will not need a new URL to access it but it is important to note that if any pages are found to duplicate the current content on that site, you'll be prompted about which page to keep.

At first this may seem fine, but keep in mind that all sites have a root page, and FrontPage commonly names these root pages INDEX.HTML. Since this file is included in both Webs and since the file is the starting point for the Web, you'll be best served in most cases to create a new Web. You do include it in the current Web, but you'll make manual links to the INDEX.HTML file created for the new Web. ■

When you create sites in this way, you'll be able to come back and simply link the sites using a single home page that provides links to the pages. Select a type of Web you'd like to create and select OK. When you do, you'll be prompted for the server you want to install the new Web to, along with the name of the Web that you need to create.

N O T E   A FrontPage *Web* is a series of directories, starting with the Home directory for the server you indicated when you started the FrontPage Explorer. The name of the Web you provide when you create the new Web becomes the directory name and is located in the Home directory for the server.

For this reason, you should use caution when naming the new Web. If you want to replace an existing Web, you can indicate the same name as the already running Web. When you do, you'll overwrite the existing system, and you'll be able to make and save the changes.

When you access one of these Webs, you need to include the project or Web name in the URL. For example, if you're naming the Web, "Jack," you can show that you want to access the Jack Web by providing **http://www.<MyServer>.com/jack/**. You can and probably should add a link to the Jack Web site from your home page. ▓

Select the server you want to install the Web onto and show the name of the Web to create. In Figure 10.12, you'll see that you can show the TCP/IP name for the server but you can also provide the IP address or other name that can be resolved on your network.

FIG. 10.12

The name you provide for your Web becomes the subdirectory name for the Web.

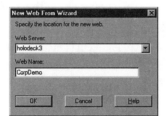

When you select OK, the Web creation process starts. The first thing that happens is that the Wizard creates the new directory structure in which the site is created. You'll be prompted for the administrator username and password for the site. You must have administrative rights to create new Webs on a server. See Figure 10.13 for an example.

FIG. 10.13

Specify an administrator who has been set up for the current Web to add a new Web to the site.

The next steps depend on the type of Web you're creating. The examples shown are what you can expect for using the Corporate Presence Web. The next step starts the Wizard and shows what you will be doing to set up the Web. When you select Next, you're presented with the first set of prompts to help you tune the kinds of information you want to have on your site.

It's a good idea to select each of these kinds of information if this is your first Web for your business. If nothing else, it provides you with a skeleton of a site map to get started. See Figure 10.14 for an example.

FIG. 10.14

There are several content options for setting up your site.

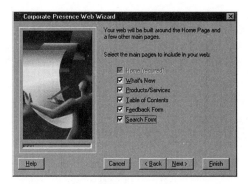

Each of these options corresponds to a page, or series of pages, that is created for you. Most will have placeholders for the information you need to provide. This is information like product overviews, service descriptions, etc.

When you select Next, you'll be prompted to indicate what sections you want to include on the home page for your site. Once again, these sections provide a good map of the kinds of information that might be helpful to include on your page. Some or all of the options may apply to *your* work, so select the topics carefully. Keep in mind that you can always remove topics later if you change your mind. Figure 10.15 shows the topic selections for the Corporate Presence Wizard.

FIG. 10.15

The topics offered are outlined on the home page for your site.

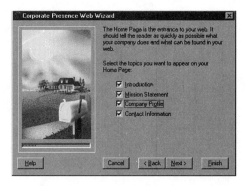

Each topic is placed on your home page with a separator bar. The format of the page is selected in later steps with the Wizard but the content outline remains the same, providing you with the starting point.

The next steps in the wizard process give you the opportunity to fine-tune the pages that will be created and the topics that appear on each of them. In Figure 10.15, you showed which pages you wanted to be created on an overall basis. In the next few steps, you'll be able to control what topical headings are shown to the user. In Figure 10.16, you can see an example of this.

FIG. 10.16
You can control what items appear on each of the pages you requested.

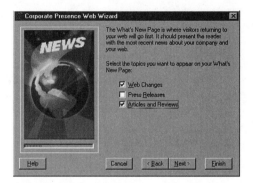

As with the topics for the home page, you can select all of them here and then remove them later. Alternatively, you can fine-tune your selections on each of the dialog boxes that follow. There is one dialog box for each original page you request and each has check boxes to show which topics you want to include. The topics offered for each page are covered next.

What's New Page   On the What's New Page, you have the option of including Web changes, press releases, articles, and reviews. It's a good idea to include a What's New Page because it shows that things are changing and growing. It also leads the people browsing the site to believe that they should check back to see what's new. This page often becomes a bookmarked page in people's browsers.

Products and Services Page   The Products and Services page is where you can specify the number of products and the number of services you'll be providing information about. This number determines the number of headings included on the page. Each product and service can have several different options. See Figure 10.17 for an example.

The Feedback Form   The Feedback Form gives you the place to prompt for the full name, job title, company affiliation, mailing address, telephone number, fax number, and e-mail address. It's highly recommended that, unless you have a specific reason not to, you should include each of these fields in your request for information from the user. In almost all cases, more information about a user and the request for help are better than less information, even non-technical, about the person submitting the question.

FIG. 10.17
For the products and services page, you need to provide feedback on what additional sections to include to describe your products and services.

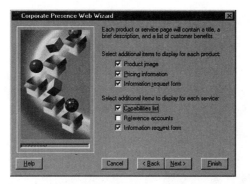

You have two options for storing form results. You can save them in <u>t</u>ab-delimited format or you can save them as HTML. If you'll be providing the results back to the Web, as may be the case with a comments section that is open to the public for discussion, use the <u>w</u>eb-page format. If you'll be using the information in other packages, such as Access, Excel, Word, and others, you'll want the results to be stored in the <u>t</u>ab-delimited format since it's much easier to work with in these circumstances.

Table of Contents Form   When you select the Table of Contents, TOC, you have access to several nice features. Option 1, <u>K</u>eep page list up-to-date automatically, makes sure the user always sees the most current listing of the pages on your site. With rare exceptions, you should select this option.

> **N O T E**   One exception relates to an emerging site, which is one with pages that are in production, and others that are under construction and not yet public. In cases like this, it may be desirable to turn off the automatic update feature. If you plan to have hidden pages, such as pages under construction, or in any other case where you would have pages that are not public, you should consider turning this option off. ▪

The <u>S</u>how pages not linked into web option relates to you manually putting pages on the Web and your option to include or exclude them from the table of contents. If you select this option and have pages on your site that are not accessible from other pages, they automatically become accessible from the table of contents as well. Leaving this option disabled is likely to be your best bet, allowing for behind the scenes work on your pages without the fear that they might automatically appear to a user browsing the site.

The final option, <u>U</u>se bullets for top-level pages, is where you can control how the Table of Contents outline-type view looks with regard to top-level pages. If you deselect this option, the pages are still shown but they are merely indented and do not include the bullet notation next to them. This is purely a personal preference.

Setting Up Common Page Attributes   The options that control each page's look and feel are next. These options control what is shown on each page. See Figure 10.18.

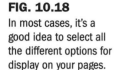

FIG. 10.18
In most cases, it's a good idea to select all the different options for display on your pages.

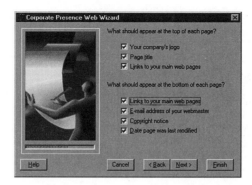

In most cases, you'll want to select all options. Some items of particular importance are the Links and Webmaster e-mail address items. These are good etiquette to include on your pages. The first, the links, gives users an easier time finding the links to other pages. If they are reading a page and get to the bottom and want to move on, they'll have access to the outbound links right there for them, and the links will be available when they enter the page.

The Webmaster e-mail address should be included on all pages you publish. If you don't tell people how to get in touch with you in case of problems, suggestions, and how they can contribute to the site you won't have their valuable feedback. The golden rule of Web content creation is to always include a way for the user to contact the author of the site.

The other item you should nearly always include is the copyright notice. Remember, it's easy to copy content from the Web. By declaring your copyright on all materials, you decrease the likelihood that materials will be "borrowed" for use elsewhere. A common practice is to have a copyright statement say something like the following:

All original content on these pages (on the Wynkoop Pages site) is (c) 1994-1997 Stephen Wynkoop. Other materials are (c) or (R) of their respective owners. All items are presented as-is without warranty or guarantee for fitness of use for your purposes.

The following pages offer options and a preview of the impact of them on your site for the kinds of graphics colors and backgrounds used. These are purely your personal preference.

The Under Construction Option   When you select Next, you're asked if you want to include the Under Construction indication on your pages. There is a heated debate among HTML developers regarding whether this information should be present on a site. In favor of the logo and text is the fact that, if you're reviewing a site and wondering "is this all there is?" the logo provides a clue. If you see an Under Construction sign, you'll know that more is coming and you should check back.

Purist Web developers on the con side of the discussion say that all Web content is, by definition, under construction. By putting this indication on pages, it's redundant and takes up bandwidth that could be better used elsewhere.

Part
II

Ch
10

It is, of course, entirely up to you. If you select this option, the Under Construction indication is included on each page that is created for you.

Completing the Process　The next two pages prompt you for your company information, including name, company, address, phone numbers, and e-mail addresses.

The final option is to show the to-do list after the site has been created. This recommended step gives you the starting point for your work and you'll be able to jump in to update the pages. It also gives you a good idea of what the Wizard left for you to do, and what it was able to do for you. When you select Finish, the Web and to-do list are created for you as shown in Figure 10.19.

FIG. 10.19

The to-do list shows all open tasks that need to be completed before you bring the site online publicly.

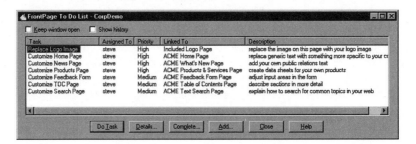

From the to-do list, you can work directly with the items to be completed. As you do, the editor is called up to let you work with the files, and you can check things off the to-do list as you complete them.

If you want to return to the to-do list later, you can do so from the FrontPage Explorer. Select Tools, Show To Do List and you can begin working with the list again. There is also an option under the Edit menu that allows you to manually add items to the list.

In the coming sections, you'll see how to work with the pages created by the Wizard. From templates to Bots, there are a number of capabilities that represent leverage for you in your site-management efforts.

Template-Based Web Site Creation

FrontPage brings some interesting extensions to bear on your site with an emphasis toward providing a more complete and standardized authoring environment. Typical Web development means writing the HTML code, uploading it to the server, and then testing it. As you've seen earlier in this chapter, the FrontPage approach is much more WYSIWYG in nature, giving you the chance to work in the environment that users experience when they visit your site.

Figure 10.20 shows what a starting page might look like for a basic corporate information site.

Something that has traditionally been missing in Web content-development environments is the ability to share a look and feel across the site. By sharing elements between pages, you are able to create a template of pages, apply the template to the site's pages, and leverage your efforts in the future should your site change. The leverage comes from the idea that you can make one change to an underlying template file, and it will be propagated throughout the site.

FIG. 10.20
An example of a basic home page for a corporate site.

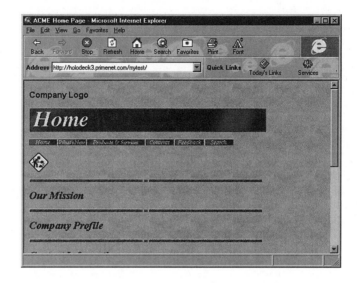

Listing 10.2 shows a sample of how FrontPage annotates the HTML for its use.

N O T E Vermeer is the name of the company that first created FrontPage. There are some tags that are still evident in the source HTML documents for the FrontPage product that refer to the Vermeer tags. These are not meant as anything more than unique features for the FrontPage system. ▪

Listing 10.2   (NO FILE): HTML Excerpt with Included Files

```
<body stylesrc="_private/style.htm">
<!--VERMEER
   BOT=Include
   TAG="BODY"
   U-Include="_private/logo.htm"
 --><p><img src="images/hhome.gif" alt="[Page Banner Image]" align=bottom
width=472 height=48> </p>

<!--VERMEER
   BOT=Include
   TAG="BODY"
   U-Include="_private/navbar.htm"
 -->
```

You can see from the listing that the FrontPage-specific features are enclosed in comments. When the FrontPage server sends the file to the browser, it parses the file and makes the

Part
II
Ch
10

changes to the outgoing HTML. The result is a page that, if not served by a FrontPage server, is still displayed on the browser, albeit not with the include files. Since the extensions are placed within the comments, they will not cause problems with other environments.

There are two files included in this excerpt, and each has a different purpose. You'll have to consider where it makes sense to include content as include files or just coded directly into the document you're working with. The determining factor becomes whether the information is used on other pages. In the example, since the logo appears on each page on the site, as it probably will on your site as well, this is a prime candidate for using the include file approach.

The LOGO.HTM file is very short and very straightforward. It provides the company logo positioned as wanted and includes any desired links associated with the logo. Listing 10.3 shows the LOGO.HTM file in its entirety.

Listing 10.3   (NO FILE): The LOGO Include File Referenced by All Pages on the Site that Will Show the Logo

```
<!DOCTYPE HTML PUBLIC "-//IETF//DTD HTML//EN">
<html>
<head>
<title>Included Logo Page</title>
<meta name="GENERATOR" content="Microsoft FrontPage 1.1">
</head>
<body stylesrc="style.htm">
<p><img src="../images/logo.gif" alt="[Company Logo Image]" align=bottom
➥width=120 height=24> <!--VERMEER
   BOT=PurpleText
   PREVIEW="-- replace with your logo image"
   S-Viewable=" "
 --></p>
</body>
</html>
```

You'll notice one thing immediately when you review the file. It contains a type of include itself. This include, referenced in the

```
<body stylesrc="style.htm">
```

line, uses the style.htm file to establish background images, colors, and text coloring. Again, by including this file, you're assured that all files will have the same background images, same colors, and same approach to presentation.

Perhaps even more important, when you decide to change the background color, you can change it in one place and the entire site changes, all at once, and all to the same new background. If you consider a medium-size site with perhaps 20k pages, the time savings on implementing a change such as this can be enormous. Use the include files whenever possible.

An excerpt from the STYLE.HTM file is shown in Listing 10.4.

Listing 10.4   (NO FILE): Partial Listing of STYLE.HTM Showing the Color and Background Settings

```
<HTML>
<HEAD>
<TITLE>Web Colors</TITLE>
</HEAD>
<BODY BACKGROUND="../images/blutxtr1.jpg" BGCOLOR="#babdd3">
<H2>Web Colors</H2>
<HR>
<P>
```

An example of putting the include files to good use is also the navigation button bar. It may seem strange at first but when you consider the capabilities it extends to your pages, it's worth the effort. Figure 10.21 shows what the navigation bar alone looks like.

Part
II
Ch
10

FIG. 10.21

The included navigation bar hosts links to the pages represented by the buttons.

In addition to providing the common graphical look and feel, the navigation bar includes the URL links that represent the buttons. Since this is included on each page, and sometimes at both the top and bottom of the page depending on the options you select, having the links be consistent and always available to other locations on your site gives the user the ability to quickly move about the site.

Listing 10.5 shows the HTML behind the graphic.

Listing 10.5   NAVBAR.HTM: The Included Navigation Buttons Also Provide Important Link Information

```
<!DOCTYPE HTML PUBLIC "-//W3O/DTD HTML//EN">

<html>
<head>
<title>Included Navigation Links</title>
<meta name="FORMATTER" content="Microsoft FrontPage 1.1">
</head>
<body background="../images/blutxtr1.jpg" bgcolor="#babdd3"><p>
<a href="../index.htm">
<img src="../images/bhome.gif" alt="[Home Icon]" border="0"
 width="56" height="14"></a>
```

continues

Listing 10.5   Continued

```
<a href="../news.htm"><img src="../images/bnews.gif"
 alt="[What's New Icon]" border="0" width="58" height="14"></a>
<a href="../products.htm">
<img src="../images/bprdsrv.gif" alt="[Products Icon]"
 border="0" width="117" height="14"></a>
<a href="../toc.htm"><img src="../images/btoc.gif"
 alt="[TOC Icon]" border="0" width="60" height="14"></a>
<a href="../feedback.htm"><img src="../images/bfeed.gif"
 alt="[Feedback Icon]" border="0" width="59" height="14"></a>
<a href="../search.htm"><img src="../images/bsrch.gif"
 alt="[Search Icon]" border="0" width="58" height="14"></a>
</p>
</body>
</html>
```

Each button is individually painted, and each is referencing a different page on the site. If you need to add a new button or even if you want to add an image or additional text, or modify the buttons here, you can make the one change, and you're set site-wide.

Saving a Page as a Template   You can create your own template pages and, when you create a new page, you can base it on the templates you create. This is much the same as the capability in Word that allows you to create a document template and then use that template to base other pages on as you create them. This allows you to "inherit" styles, common links, and other features.

To create a template, first create the page or call it up in FrontPage Explorer. When you have it created and representing the page that you want to use as a starting point template, select File, Save As and provide the name and page title when prompted. See Figure 10.22.

FIG. 10.22

Be sure to give a descriptive title to your page as it will help you select the correct page later when you create other pages based on it.

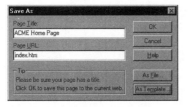

Next, select As Template. When you do, you'll be prompted for the final step, which is a description of the page. Later, when you create pages based on this one, this description is shown as a way to determine which page you're working with. Be sure to be as descriptive as possible. See Figure 10.23 for an example.

FIG. 10.23
In the description,
name the elements
included in the
template for future
reference.

Finally, for each image you've placed on the page, you'll be asked whether you want to save the image as part of the page image. Typically, you can just select Yes to All and you'll be done. When you do, the images associated with the page are saved to a private area on your Web and are available to other pages as you create them.

After the save process has been completed, you'll be ready to create pages based on your new template.

Starting a New Page Based on a Template   Once you've created template pages or if you plan to use the provided templates, the process of starting a page is easy. Select File, New, and you'll be presented with a list of the different templates available on the system. These templates include any templates you've created as well. See Figure 10.24 for an example listing of templates.

Part
II

Ch
10

FIG. 10.24
The different templates
available include those
that ship with
FrontPage and those
that you've created
since installing the
FrontPage application.

When the page is loaded into the Editor, it already contains all the different attributes it had when you created the template, including graphics, background colors, background music, headers, button bars, and so on. When you create a site, you should consider giving the site a common appearance and approach. When you do so, the users who visit your site get a familiar feeling as they enter the different pages on the site because they all carry the same theme.

To do this, consider creating a template that encompasses, at the very least, the different properties associated with the page. To set these properties, right-click on the page and select Page Properties from the fly-out menu. When you do, the result is the dialog box shown in Figure 10.25.

FIG. 10.25
Without exception, the properties associated with a page should be considered prime candidates to be used from a template.

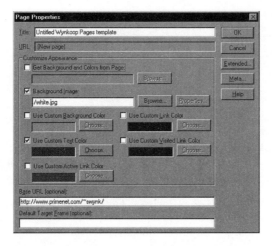

Each of these items affects your users' perception of your site. Notice that if you select the "Get background and colors from page" option, the remaining items are grayed out. This is because the editor is pulling this information from the style sheet page you indicate. This takes the template concept one step farther, allowing you to base individual templates on other foundation-type templates.

In the next section, you'll see how to use automated processes called Bots to create included files, custom markup entries, and more.

Using WebBots

WebBots, or Bots, are specially inserted commands in your HTML document. You can tell when you're working with a Bot-type of area on the page because your cursor pointer changes to a robot-type cursor:

This means that the content or item under the cursor at that location is not a standard page command. You implement a Bot by selecting Insert, Bot. See Figure 10.26 for an example of the dialog box listing the different supported WebBots.

Once inserted, the process runs at the intervals shown and modifies the content or behavior of your Web document as requested. The Bots are covered in the next few sections.

The Annotation WebBot   Annotations are like comments because they allow you to document your page. In FrontPage, these annotations have the added benefit of being visible in the Editor, but they are invisible when viewed from production Web browsers that later access your site.

FIG. 10.26
WebBots can be customized by developers. Your listed Bots may vary depending on what options you have installed.

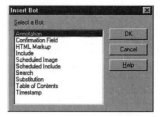

The Confirmation Field WebBot   The confirmation Bot pulls information from another form field and displays it automatically. This is helpful on a "Your submission has been received, Steve" type of page where you want to pull some bit of information, and redisplay it to the user.

The HTML Markup WebBot   It's impossible for FrontPage to anticipate all different extensions for HTML. To accommodate the changing HTML world, the HTML Markup Bot was created. This Bot provides you with an opportunity to type in any HTML you wish. FrontPage does not validate the code you enter, so you'll need to test these kinds of pages extensively.

The Include WebBot   When you select the Include option, you'll be prompted for the URL of the file to include. These includes become part of the HTML that is provided to the requesting client application.

The Scheduled Image WebBOT   The Scheduled Image Bot is an interesting way to promote your site or just to give feedback to users that something time-critical will be happening. In many cases, you'll find that you don't have time to continually review and rewrite the code on your site to take into account past events. Removing these events from the listing or changing the header graphic from "Coming Soon" to "Recent Events" can be overlooked, causing your site to look stale and outdated.

When you insert a Scheduled Image Bot, you show the date and time range it will run, along with the image to be shown. See Figure 10.27 for an example.

FIG. 10.27
Use the Scheduled Image Bot to promote certain activities on your site or to show that something will be changing soon.

You can also provide an image to be shown after the time period has elapsed. One application of this technology might be the NEW! tags that are popular on pages. When a new item comes on-line, place the NEW! graphic on the page using the Scheduled image BOT. Turn off the graphic after 14 days or whatever time that makes sense.

Using this approach, you can announce the new items on your site but at the same time avoid the problem in which a user always sees NEW! on the items on your site, even when they have been on display for more than a month.

The Scheduled Include WebBOT   The Scheduled Include Bot works in the same way as the Scheduled Image Bot. A common application for these in a combined environment might be a page that allows people to register for a contest. You can set the initial graphic and include file to display the contest graphic and the form to allow registration.

Once the registration deadline has passed, the graphic automatically changes to one showing that registration has ended. In addition, the form is not displayed but instead displays a message asking the user to forward all comments or requests to the sales department.

The Search WebBot   The Search Bot adds search capabilities to your Web, allowing people to indicate what they're looking for and a way to find it. Once users have found something of interest, they can simply click on it and be taken to the page directly.

As you can see in Figure 10.28, you can indicate the prompt for the information to search for, and you can provide the caption for the button that starts off the process. You also have control over the width of the search text, something that should be changed to approximately 40 characters to provide users with a bit more breathing space when they tell you what they need.

FIG. 10.28

Search capabilities are extremely important if you're running a commercial Web site.

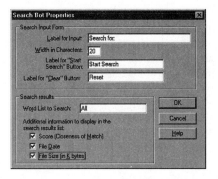

If you don't change the length of the text box, the user can indicate more than 20 characters. The text box scrolls as the user types in the search criteria.

If you're bringing up a commercial site, one that has reasonable depth and quantity when it comes to the pages available, you'll always want to provide a search mechanism somewhere on the site. Generally, you'll find it's a good idea to create a button on the button bar and allocate it to pulling up a search page for the user.

The Substitution WebBot   The Substitution WebBot is likely to be used in the footer material for your pages. This Bot can pull information about predefined variables and display it on the page. The predefined variables provided with FrontPage out of the box are as follows:

- ModifiedBy—Who made the last changes to the page.

- Description—From the Comments field of the Explorer' Properties dialog box, this is the current description for the page. Be careful not to confuse this with the title of the page.

- Page-URL—This shows the runtime URL that is being used to access the page. Of course, this changes based on whether the system is internal to your organization or not. But, in general, the Page-URL presents the URL with any relative paths resolved.

You can create additional predefined variables for other tasks, like a common copyright message, Webmaster URL, and so on. To do so, return to FrontPage Explorer and select Tools, Web Settings. On the resulting dialog box, the Parameters tab contains the variables that can be retrieved. You can add and remove existing user-defined variables here as well.

The Table of Contents WebBot Providing an overall site map is a big plus for users of your site. It's also not one of the easier things to manage. The Table of Contents Bot exists just for the purpose of automating the creation and management of a site map based on the relationships between the Web pages. In Figure 10.29, you can see the different options that are available when you define a Table of Contents Bot.

Part

II

Ch

10

FIG. 10.29
The Table of Contents Bot can be configured to automatically catch new pages as they are added to the site.

The various options are straightforward, providing you with control over what items are included and how they are displayed. Perhaps the most significant option is the final check box, Recompute table of contents.

If you select this option, you'll not have to update this page to know that it always has the latest list of pages and page hierarchies. The task of managing the pages is automated, running whenever the page is accessed. Although it is a good option, it can also be a time-consuming one. If your site is large, it can take quite awhile to create the table of contents.

If you leave this final option deselected, you can manually update the listing by opening the page in the Explorer and then saving it to the Web again.

The Timestamp WebBot The Timestamp Bot provides just that, a timestamp for your page. You have a choice of showing the time the page was last changed or you can show the time the page was last automatically generated. As you can see in Figure 10.30, you can also show the date and time formats.

FIG. 10.30

It's a good idea to always include a "last changed" date for most pages on your site.

In general, you should stamp all pages you create with a standard footer that includes the Webmaster e-mail address, the time the page was last updated, and information about any copyrights you are claiming. If you create your pages based on templates, it is a simple thing to include this information on each page on the site, just by including the footer template in the overall template for the site.

Reality Check

At the Intellicenter Reality Check site, we implemented a fully FrontPage-enabled site. This aided greatly in the shared tasks associated with bringing up the site quickly, while, at the same time, accounting for the security issues that come with the Internet.

FrontPage Explorer was used to import and include pages that had been created elsewhere, and we used the Editor to touch up pages created with some of the Assistants.

One of the problems encountered was FrontPage's handling of HTML features and tags that have been introduced since the release of FrontPage. For example, the MARQUEE and BGSOUND options were displayed as unknown with a <?> symbol on the page. The HTML is still present if you select the <?> and select Properties from the right-click menu.

We weren't able to completely preview the page as it would appear, because the Editor did not support these tags. The Editor appeared to lose carriage returns (<br>) when it encountered an unknown bit of HTML, making dual-marquee lines appear in need of an extra carriage return. Once the manual carriage returns were added, the site pages appeared correctly.

When the site was initially created, the to-do list was used to manage the pages. This provided some help in assigning which responsibilities were undertaken by the team members. In addition, the Bots, and the Wizards for new Webs were helpful in setting up a common feel throughout the site and for providing good functionality in discussion groups.

From Here...

This chapter only began to explore FrontPage's different capabilities. FrontPage is an excellent site management tool, and if you can make it available to those responsible for maintaining the content on your site, you'll be doing a big favor for those individuals.

For more information on FrontPage, be sure to reference the following:

- The Microsoft Web site's FrontPage home page. The URL is **http:// www.microsoft.com/msoffice/frontpage**.

- Watch for updates to this information, and the supporting utilities at **http:// www.pobox.com/~swynk**.

## CHAPTER 11

Usage Statistics

Getting your Web server or servers installed and configured is only the first step in operating a Web site. Now you must begin the important maintenance work to keep the site running smoothly. Because your Web site is a very public window to your information processing world, you need to project and maintain a professional image.

Ongoing maintenance activities are associated with the server or servers, and other tasks are associated with the materials being published on the servers. Usage statistics assist your analysis of the needs in these maintenance areas.

Your Web site needs to be accessible. Hardware and software performance are the key factors that determine the accessibility. Usage statistics provide important data about the demands being placed on your site.

Accessibility isn't the only consideration. The quality of the material available on your site is equally important. Usage statistics can provide insight into the public reaction to the material in your Web site.

What's in the logs

There are two sets of content formats for log files: NCSA/CERN and IIS.

Servers generate log files in different formats

The formats vary, from ASCII flat files to SQL databases. Is one preferable to the other?

How to convert IIS log files to Common Log File format

Comparison and analysis of information from IIS and other Web servers may require having the data in a common format.

How you interpret the logs

What does all this information mean? Is the activity you're experiencing a little or a lot? Does the level of activity meet your goals? Third-party analysis tools can help.

Real-life examples of logging for a site

One of the Que Reality Check Sites, **http://www.integra.net**, is using IIS and logging the activity to a Microsoft SQL Server database. They're using SQL Server scripts to analyze activity.

To evaluate this usage, you need to know:

- How often each server is being accessed
- Which pages are being accessed most often
- Which service is being accessed
- Who's accessing your Web site

All major server software provides logging options. The information content varies between the NCSA/CERN design and Microsoft Internet Information Server (IIS) design. The formats of the logs also vary from ASCII flat files to ODBC databases. All major Web servers provide log information that is useful.

Your primary concern won't be lack of data. The server logs each request for service and file transfer. Your concern will be to extract meaningful information from the mass of data. Even moderately busy servers may accumulate as much as 10M of data per month in the log files. As with mining gold, the trick is to remove all the good parts hidden in the mass of material. ■

Looking at the Logs for Content

The server logs each request for service by a client. In the process of responding to a service request, the server may transfer multiple files, such as the HTML page and any embedded graphics. After the client makes the initial service request, the server may transfer other pages in response to the selection of a hyperlink on the Web page. If the request is for a file transfer by FTP, the FTP server may come into use to transfer the file.

NCSA/CERN Log Content

CERN is the Centre Europeen pour la Recherche Nucleaire, which is the European particle physics lab where the World Wide Web originated in 1989. NCSA is the National Center for Supercomputing Applications, which is located at the University of Illinois at Champaign-Urbana. NCSA developed and distributed NCSA Mosaic, which was the first important Web browser. The first logging format was named for NCSA/CERN.

The contents of the NCSA/CERN log file are called the Common Log File format. This format is used by most Web server systems regardless of the platform/operating system, including Netscape Enterprise Server 2.0 for Windows NT. Table 11.1 explains the contents of the log file sample shown below. The entry that may occur between the two dashes after the client address is for the user name in case of a non-anonymous connection.

```
123.124.125.0 - - [20/Aug/1996:15:18:23 -0700]
➥ "GET /apage.htm HTTP/1.0" 200 2083
```

Table 11.1   Data Elements in the Log File

Item	Description
Address	IP address of the client that requested the object from the server
Username	User name, if non-anonymous access was requested, of the person gaining access to the system (this will be dashes if anonymous access was provided)
Date/Time	Date and time stamp the request was received
Transfer Method	HTTP function used (GET/PUT)
Virtual Path	Location and name of the object transferred
Protocol	Protocol and version used to fulfill the request
Status	Resulting status from the operation
Bytes Transferred	Total number of bytes transferred to fulfill the request

N O T E   At the end of the time stamp is a number in the form of -0700. This number represents the offset of the time stamp from Universal or Greenwich Mean Time (GMT). A simultaneous event occurring in New York and Los Angeles, for example, would have time stamps that vary by three hours. By observing the offset number, you can see that the events occur simultaneously. ■

Figure 11.1 shows a log created by Netscape Enterprise Server 2.0 for Windows NT.

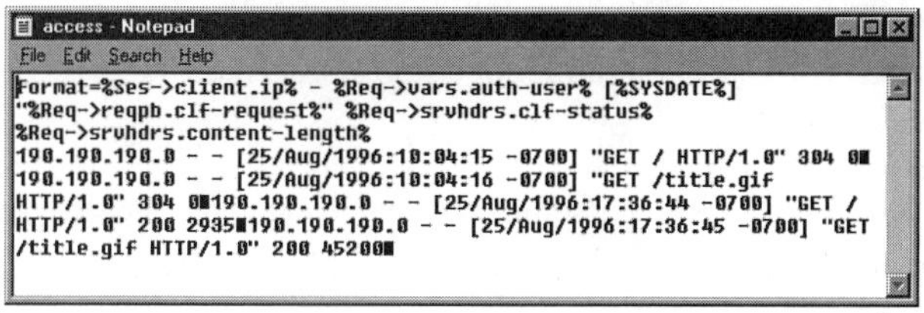

FIG. 11.1
In this Netscape log file and in Common Log File format logs, the fields aren't comma- or tab-delimited. The first line is a header line with the field names.

Microsoft Internet Information Server Log Content

There are several differences in the IIS log files and the Common Log File format logs. IIS log files contain every item of information in the Common Log File format, plus several other items.

Among the common items is one difference relating to the time-stamp offset. In the IIS logs, the offset isn't shown. The time stamp shown indicates only the time on the server when the request was received.

Another difference is that IIS provides Gopher and FTP services as part of the IIS software. The activity for these servers can be logged in the same log file, with an indication of the service fulfilling the request being noted in the log file entry.

The other significant difference in the IIS log file is that it's comma delimited. The contents of the log entries in a IIS log file in the sample below are explained in Table 11.2.

```
10.75.176.21, -, 8/21/96, 14:23:22, W3SVC, SOFTCOYOTE, 190.190.190.0,
➥ 29342, 298, 3548, 200, 0, GET, /samples/admin.htm
```

Table 11.2   Data Elements in the MS IIS Log File

Item	Description
Address	IP address of the client that requested the object from the server
Username	User name, if non-anonymous access was requested, of the person gaining access to the system (this will create a dash if anonymous access was provided)
Date	Date of the transfer
Time	Time of the transfer
Service	The name of the service that performed the transfer. W3SVC is the World Wide Web Server; the other services are FTP and Gopher
Computer Name	The computer name of the Server
IP Address	The IP Address of the Server
Processing time	The time required in milliseconds
Bytes received	The number of bytes in the request
Bytes sent	The number of bytes sent in response
Service status	The code for the service; 200 indicates success as an example
NT status	The Windows NT status at the end of the operation; 0 indicates success as an example
Transfer Method	HTTP function used (GET/PUT)
Operation target	The file that is being transferred; this entry will also include any parameters that may have been required by the operation
Target of the operation	This field also contains any parameters for the operation is required.

Figure 11.2 shows a log created by IIS 2.0 for Windows NT 4.0.

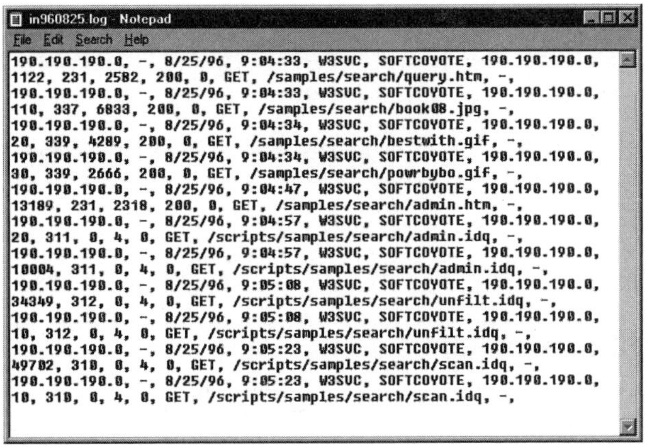

FIG. 11.2

In this log file, which is in the IIS format, the fields are comma-delimited.

```
in960825.log - Notepad
File  Edit  Search  Help
190.190.190.0, -, 8/25/96, 9:04:33, W3SVC, SOFTCOYOTE, 190.190.190.0,
1122, 231, 2582, 200, 0, GET, /samples/search/query.htm, -,
190.190.190.0, -, 8/25/96, 9:04:33, W3SVC, SOFTCOYOTE, 190.190.190.0,
110, 337, 6833, 200, 0, GET, /samples/search/book00.jpg, -,
190.190.190.0, -, 8/25/96, 9:04:34, W3SVC, SOFTCOYOTE, 190.190.190.0,
20, 339, 4289, 200, 0, GET, /samples/search/bestwith.gif, -,
190.190.190.0, -, 8/25/96, 9:04:34, W3SVC, SOFTCOYOTE, 190.190.190.0,
30, 339, 2666, 200, 0, GET, /samples/search/powrbybo.gif, -,
190.190.190.0, -, 8/25/96, 9:04:47, W3SVC, SOFTCOYOTE, 190.190.190.0,
13189, 231, 2310, 200, 0, GET, /samples/search/admin.htm, -,
190.190.190.0, -, 8/25/96, 9:04:57, W3SVC, SOFTCOYOTE, 190.190.190.0,
20, 311, 0, 4, 0, GET, /scripts/samples/search/admin.idq, -,
190.190.190.0, -, 8/25/96, 9:04:57, W3SVC, SOFTCOYOTE, 190.190.190.0,
10004, 311, 0, 4, 0, GET, /scripts/samples/search/admin.idq, -,
190.190.190.0, -, 8/25/96, 9:05:08, W3SVC, SOFTCOYOTE, 190.190.190.0,
34349, 312, 0, 4, 0, GET, /scripts/samples/search/unfilt.idq, -,
190.190.190.0, -, 8/25/96, 9:05:08, W3SVC, SOFTCOYOTE, 190.190.190.0,
10, 312, 0, 4, 0, GET, /scripts/samples/search/unfilt.idq, -,
190.190.190.0, -, 8/25/96, 9:05:23, W3SVC, SOFTCOYOTE, 190.190.190.0,
49702, 310, 0, 4, 0, GET, /scripts/samples/search/scan.idq, -,
190.190.190.0, -, 8/25/96, 9:05:23, W3SVC, SOFTCOYOTE, 190.190.190.0,
10, 310, 0, 4, 0, GET, /scripts/samples/search/scan.idq, -,
```

N O T E IIS provides a utility that you can use to convert IIS log files to Common Log File format. The utility, convlog.exe, is run from the command line.

In the time recorded in the IIS log files, there's no GMT offset. This is taken care of with a parameter that's set in the convlog syntax. The parameter is the offset from GMT. ■

Part
II

Ch
11

Looking at the Log Formats

Your Web server will produce log files in one of three formats. Two of the file formats are flat ASCII files and the other is an RDBMS database format.

ASCII Flat Files

Several statistical analysis programs work with the log files. You may choose to use these files with your own applications. If you do, the following will provide some information on the exact formatting of these files.

Common Log File Format   The key to working with any text file is to understand the format in detail. The log files are no exception. Here are some key points to the file format:

- Data fields are space (ASCII 32) delimited.
- HTTP Method, Virtual Path, and Protocol fields are enclosed in double quotes.
- Each line is terminated with a line feed (ASCII 10) but no carriage return.
- Each field is variable length.

If you're writing an application that will read these files, pay special attention to the fact that each line isn't terminated with a carriage return. This means that you'll need to do some manual parsing of the lines, looking for the line feed character, to determine the end of each line.

MS IIS ASCII Log File Format   If you're working with an IIS ASCII log file, the differences are as follows:

- The data fields are comma-delimited.
- Each row is terminated by a line feed (ASCII 10)/carriage return (ASCII 13) combination.
- Each field has a leading blank space, except the first.

In the next section, you'll see how the ODBC version of the logging is formatted.

IIS ODBC Database Format

IIS provides for logging to an ODBC data source. The advantage provided by this method is the capability to extract information from the log database using Structured Query Language (SQL). Table 11.3 lists the data fields, their data types, and field sizes.

Table 11.3   The SQL/ODBC RDBMS Table Structure

Data Field	Data Type	Field Size
ClientHost	char	50
Username	char	50
LogDate	char	12
LogTime	char	15
Service	char	20
Machine	char	20
ServerIP	char	50
Processingtime	int	
Bytesrecvd	int	
Bytessent	int	
Servicestatus	int	
Win32Status	int	
Operation	char	200
Target	char	200
Parameters	char	200

The IIS ODBC log table contains one field that isn't present in the ASCII flat file—the Parameters field. In the ASCII flat file, the parameters are included as part of the Target field.

Extracting data from the ODBC log table is performed by using SQL select statements. The documentation for the database engine you're using provides information on performing these queries.

Some database systems provide for the export of data into ASCII delimited files. This would make possible the combination of data from an ODBC log with the data from an ASCII flat file.

Converting IIS Log Files to Common Log File Format

IIS includes a log file conversion utility, `convlog.exe`, that converts the IIS ASCII flat-file log files to the Common Log File format. This utility is run from the command line.

To run `convlog`, choose Start, Programs, Command Prompt. When the command-line window opens, change to the IIS subdirectory, which is the default location for the `convlog.exe` utility. To view the syntax of `convlog`, run the utility without any parameters. You'll be presented with the help information as shown in Figure 11.3.

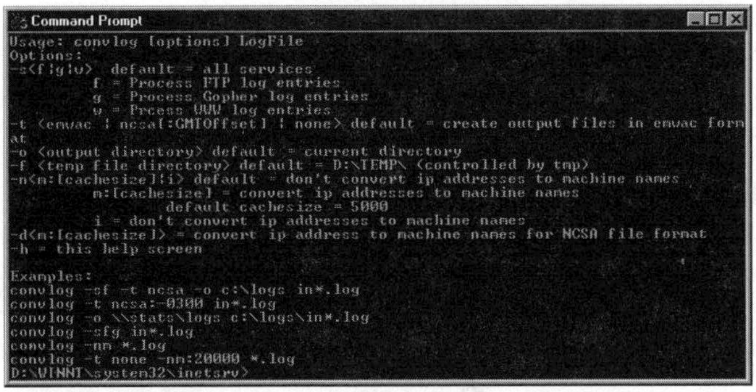

FIG. 11.3

The help may be displayed at any time by typing **convlog -h** for the help file option.

Part
II
Ch
11

The syntax of `convlog.exe` is as follows:

```
convlog -s[f|g|w] -t [emwac | ncsa[:GMTOffset] | none] -o [output directory]
➡ -f [temp file directory] -h LogFilename
```

The parameters are as follows:

- `-s[f|g|w]` specifies which service log entries to convert. `f` means FTP log entries, `g` means Gopher log entries, and `w` means Web log entries.

- `-t [emwac|ncsa[:GMTOffset]|none]` specifies the target conversion format and the GMT Offset. `ncsa` stands for NCSA Common Log File format, and `emwac` is the European Microsoft Windows NT Academic Centre log file format.

- `-o` specifies the output directory. The default is the current directory.

- `-f` specifies the temp file directory. The default is C:\Temp.

- `-n[m[cachesize]|I]` specifies whether to convert IP addresses to computer or domain names. `m` means to convert IP addresses; `I` means don't convert IP addresses.

- ▪ -h displays help information.
- ▪ LogFilename specifies the name of the log file to be converted.

Figure 11.4 shows the contents of the IIS log file that will be converted in Notepad.

FIG. 11.4

The log file may contain log entries for FTP, Gopher, and WWW activity.

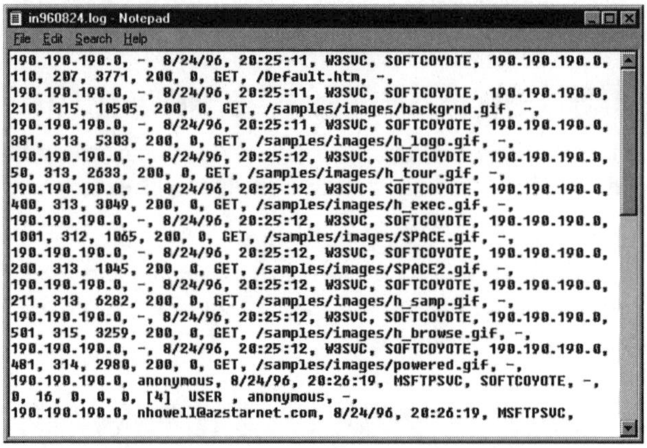

Figure 11.5 shows the command-line window with the commands entered to convert the log file.

FIG. 11.5

Both the input file and the output file will be in the current directory.

Figure 11.6 shows the command-line window after the conversion is executed.

Figure 11.7 shows the contents of the converted log file.

N O T E   convlog creates the name for the converted log file. ▪

A difference between the convlog output log file and a file created in the Common Log File format by Netscape (refer to Figure 11.1) is that the lines created by convlog are terminated with a carriage return (ASCII code 13) and line feed (ASCII code 10). The lines created by Netscape don't have the carriage return (ASCII code 13).

FIG. 11.6
convlog.exe provides some statistics on the conversion processing.

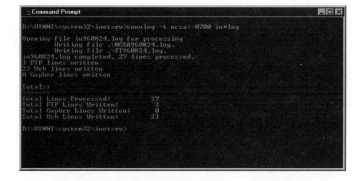

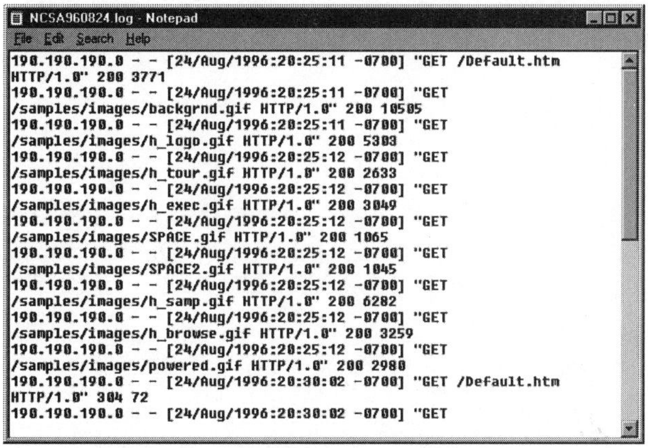

FIG. 11.7
The output log file doesn't have the header line that's shown in Figure 11.1.

Interpreting the Logs

These packages vary from freeware that produces a series of reports to very sophisticated analysis tools. The best course to follow is to check the various options and find the best fit for your budget and situation.

This discussion of these packages isn't meant to be all-encompassing for every possible package on the market. You'll need to consider these packages, as well as others, in your decision about an appropriate tool for your installation.

N O T E Each of these packages was downloaded and examined at no cost except for the download time, so consider free as well as fee-based options when you consider tools for your site(s). ■

Prime Time Stats

The version of Prime Time Stats available for evaluation was the Beta 1 release, current as of this writing. It was obtained from **http://www.dsi.org/dsi/prime_time.htm**.

Prime Time Stats is designed to run with the data from IIS's log files. The installation program is well organized and provides a backup of any replaced files. These backups are placed in a folder named Backup, which is a subdirectory of the Prime Time Stats folder Prime.

> **N O T E** The available version of Prime Time Stats didn't have help files or any other documentation. It has some "to be added" features, and occasional minor user interface bugs are to be expected in a Beta 1 product. On the whole, the product seems reasonably robust and didn't produce any bad results. ▨

Prime Time Stats keeps a set of running data that's extracted from the log data. The data includes the following:

- Client
- Machine
- Server
- Service
- Target

The log data can be extracted from either IIS ASCII flat files or an ODBC data source. If IIS is using ODBC, Prime Time Stats should work with any ODBC-compliant database engine that's used for IIS logging. However, the beta version didn't allow for testing this feature.

Figure 11.8 shows the Data Source selection dialog. Figure 11.9 shows the dialog for the ASCII flat files, and Figure 11.10 shows the dialog for the ODBC/SQL Server data source.

FIG. 11.8

In addition to selecting the data source type, the user can select which data to update.

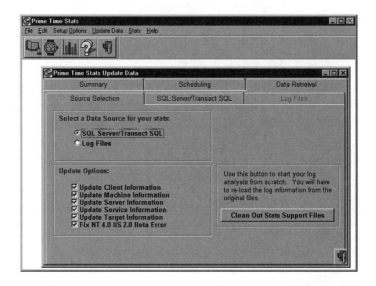

FIG. 11.9
This dialog allows the selection of files and the subsequent start of the update process.

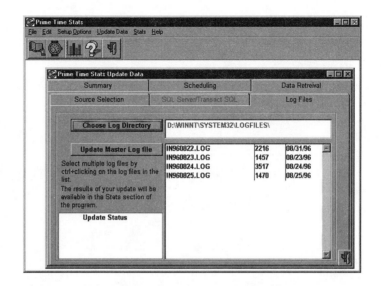

FIG. 11.10
The SQL Server dialog provides for a standard ODBC connection.

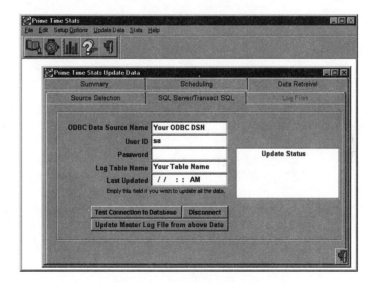

The type of data that's extracted from the log files includes the following:

- Date
- Hour of the Day
- Week of the Year
- Quarter of the Year
- Number of Hits

- Processing time in Milliseconds
- Bytes Sent
- Bytes Received

You can schedule the update as shown in Figure 11.11. You also can start it manually.

FIG. 11.11
You can schedule the update of the analysis files to run automatically.

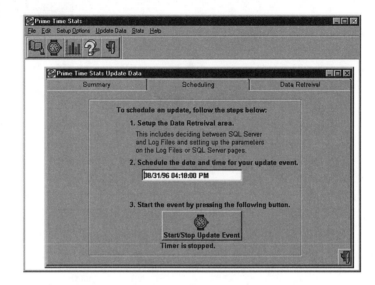

Prime Time Stats also provides graphing capability, as shown in Figure 11.12. It also will create printed reports.

FIG. 11.12
The graphing can be changed to reflect hourly, daily, monthly, and quarterly times.

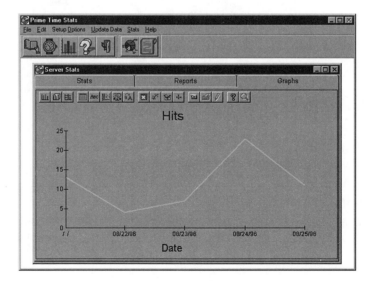

Figure 11.13 shows the Print Preview function.

FIG. 11.13

This shows an example of the print preview option for Prime Time Stats.

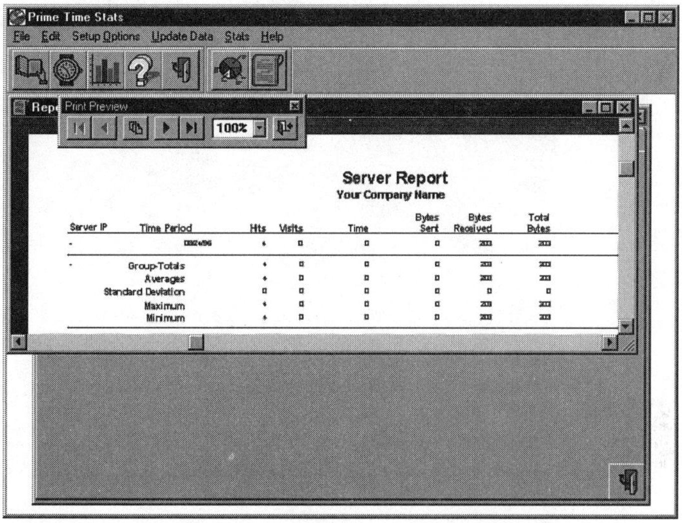

The fact that it was a Beta 1 version, and therefore incomplete, limited the evaluation of Prime Time Stats. It does appear to be worth a second look in your selection of a statistical analysis package, however.

Wusage

The version of Wusage that was available for evaluation was a 30-day evaluation copy of version 4.12, obtained from **http://www.boutell.com/wusage/download.html**.

Wusage is a released product that's designed for the analysis of Common Log File format log files. It won't work with the IIS log file format or the European Microsoft Windows NT Academic Centre (EMWAC) format.

You need to decompress the file you download, as it will be provided in a compressed file suitable for your operating system. The default directory for Wusage is Wusage4.12.

Wusage runs from the command line and produces output in HTML format. The following steps run Wusage:

1. Open a command-line window and change the directory to the directory where the Wusage program files are located (see Figure 11.14). This will be Wusage4.12 for the download version.

2. Type **makeconf** and press Enter. You're asked a series of questions, starting with the name of the configuration file. Figure 11.15 shows the name of testWusage.con being entered. After this is entered, press Enter.

FIG. 11.14

Windows NT uses the familiar DOS commands for directory navigation.

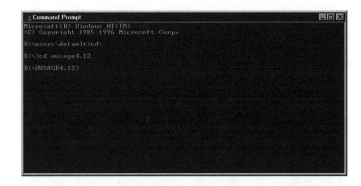

FIG. 11.15

Wusage.con is the default configuration file name and is used if you leave this blank.

3. The path and file name of the log file are requested next. In Figure 11.16, D:\Wusage4.12\sample.log is entered.

FIG. 11.16

Beginning with version 4.12, a directory can be supplied and all valid log files will be analyzed.

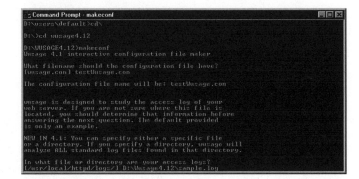

Figure 11.17 shows the header information for the reports being supplied.

4. The directory for the reports is requested next. You may want to make this an empty directory.

FIG. 11.17
If you want to change the report titles, you must delete the configuration file and re-enter the data.

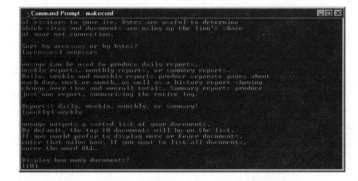

5. The next series of questions deal with the sort sequence of the report; the periods for summarization and the number of documents; sites that access your server; your domain name; and so forth. Answer these question as indicated in the instructions. Figure 11.18 shows some of these questions and the answers. After the last question is answered, the configuration file is created.

FIG. 11.18
Changing any of the parameters requires re-creating the configuration file.

6. You're now ready to run Wusage and create reports. At the prompt on the command line, enter **Wusage c- *configfilename*** (see Figure 11.19).

FIG. 11.19
The reports created by this program are in HTML format.

To view the reports created by Wusage, open the file Index.htm in the Report directory that was created in the configuration file. The reports created by Wusage are a combination of graphs and tables. As you look at some samples of the reports, you will see that there is much useful information. Figure 11.20 shows a graph that presents the total number of hits and the number of bytes transferred. This information can be useful in assessing the load on a server.

FIG. 11.20

Graphs are automatically created.

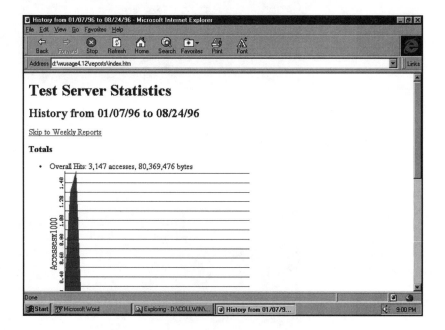

The information is also broken down by week as can be seen in Figure 11.21.

The information is also presented with the data being grouped by hour of the day. This will give indications of the time of day when peak loads occur and when the lightest activity is happening as shown in Figure 11.22. This would help plan the schedule of maintenance activities.

FIG. 11.21
Information is presented in tables as well as graphs.

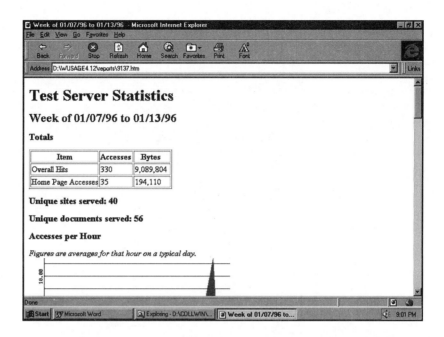

FIG. 11.22
Accesses are plotted by hour.

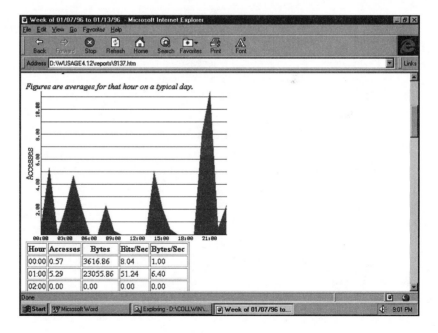

Knowing the actual number of bytes transferred and the bytes per second can help plan the proper hardware configuration. Figure 11.23 shows the average figures by hour of the day.

FIG. 11.23
This display shows the load on the server by hour.

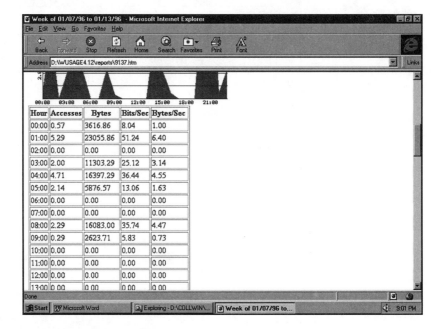

Hour	Accesses	Bytes	Bits/Sec	Bytes/Sec
00:00	0.57	3616.86	8.04	1.00
01:00	5.29	23055.86	51.24	6.40
02:00	0.00	0.00	0.00	0.00
03:00	2.00	11303.29	25.12	3.14
04:00	4.71	16397.29	36.44	4.55
05:00	2.14	5876.57	13.06	1.63
06:00	0.00	0.00	0.00	0.00
07:00	0.00	0.00	0.00	0.00
08:00	2.29	16083.00	35.74	4.47
09:00	0.29	2623.71	5.83	0.73
10:00	0.00	0.00	0.00	0.00
11:00	0.00	0.00	0.00	0.00
12:00	0.00	0.00	0.00	0.00
13:00	0.00	0.00	0.00	0.00

Knowing which documents are accessed the most can assist in the selection of these documents for review to see if there are ways of reducing the number of bytes that must be transferred on each access. Figure 11.24 lists the 10 most accessed Web pages on your site.

Analysis of the results codes of each transfer will reveal any problems. Tracking the type of data shown in Figure 11.25 will show any growing trend of errors.

Wusage also comes with a full set of documentation in HTML format. The documentation is quite thorough. If you're using a Web server that creates Common Log File Format log files, Wusage is worth evaluating.

Intersé Market Focus

The version of Intersé that was available for evaluation was a Standard Edition 30-day evaluation copy of version 2.0, obtained from **http://www.interse.com/**. Intersé is a comprehensive analysis package. It presents two modules—the Import Module and the Analysis Module.

Import Module   The Import Module is used to extract data from the log files and add the data to the Intersé database. The easy-to-use Import Module is comprehensive in the file formats that it imports (see Figure 11.26). These file formats include the following:

■ Common log file format

■ NCSA combined with servername log file format

- EMWACS log file format
- NCSA with servername log file format
- Intersé extended log file format

FIG. 11.24
Knowing which documents are accessed most is important in understanding your Web server.

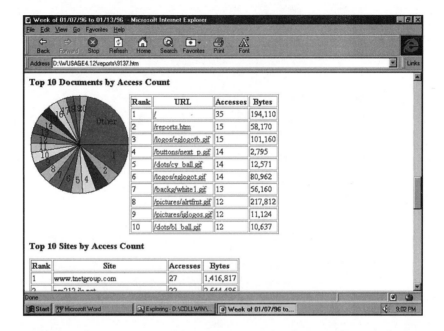

FIG. 11.25
Result code data provides insight into possible problem areas.

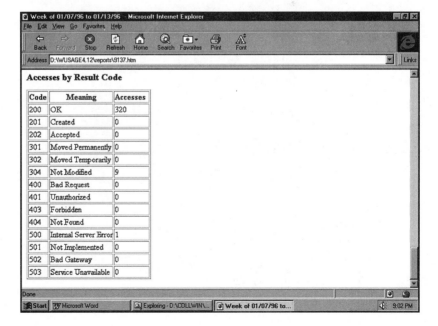

FIG. 11.26

The server and log file is selected from the Import Module.

- Open Market log file format
- Microsoft IIS standard log file format
- Spry Web Server ASCII log file format
- Microsoft IIS extended log file format
- UUNET log file format
- NCSA combined log file format
- WebStar log file format

Intersé also supports IIS ODBC logs, as well as several FTP and Gopher formats.

Analysis Module After the data is imported from the log files, you're ready to begin the analysis. The reports and analyses are predefined. The user is required to select only the analysis and report desired (see Figure 11.27). The reports are produced in HTML format for easy distribution.

FIG. 11.27

Each analysis provides multiple options for the ensuing log analysis.

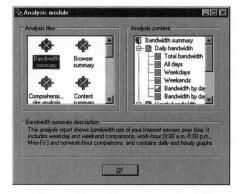

After the analysis is performed, you can view the report by opening the HTML document with a Web browser. The first section of a report is the heading information (see Figure 11.28).

The report next provides summary information, as shown in Figure 11.29. This report is opened by selecting a Hyperlink on the report shown in Figure 11.28.

FIG. 11.28

The report heading provides information about the data analyzed.

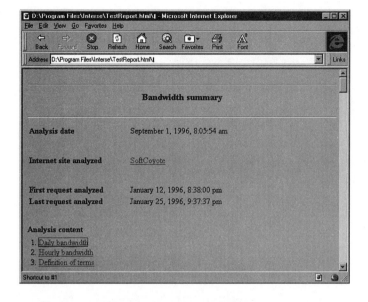

FIG. 11.29

The summary data distinguishes between weekday and weekend data.

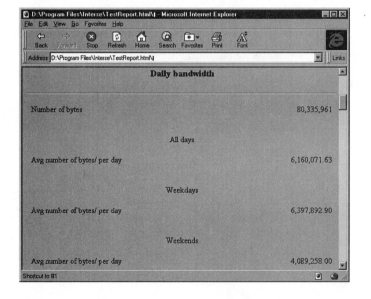

The old saying that a picture is worth a thousand words holds true for analyzing log information. By using graphs to analyze the logs, you can gain a useful view of the data and more easily understand the information. Figure 11.30 shows an example of this type of graph.

The graph data is supported by a table of the data represented in the graph (see Figure 11.31).

FIG. 11.30
The Intersé graphs provide a good way to review your log files.

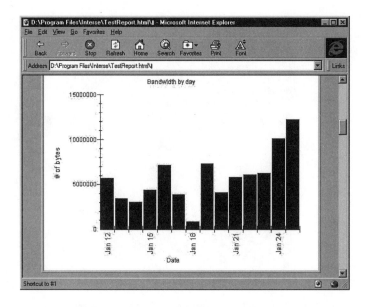

FIG. 11.31
Showing the total volume and the percentage that the volume represents helps understanding of the data.

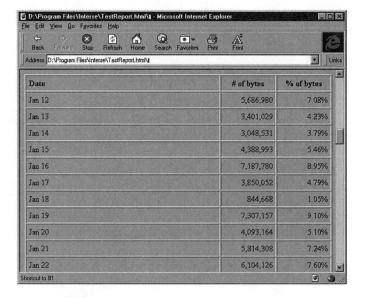

Intersé includes a definition of terms section in each report (see Figure 11.32). This useful feature helps you understand the information presented.

In addition to the Bandwidth Summary shown starting in Figure 11.28, Intersé provides for the following analyses:

- Browser Summary—Information about the Web browser used by clients.
- Comprehensive Site Analysis—Data about activity on all parts of the site.
- Content Summary—Analysis of the activity by content area.
- Executive Summary—A high level presentation of several factors.
- Geography Summary—A summary by geographic location of the accessing system.
- Organization Summary—A summary by the domain (e.g. com, gov, edu) accessing the Web site.
- Path Summary—A summary of the logical disk path of the data accessed.
- Request Summary—Analysis of the type of file requested, (e.g., .HTML, .gif, and so on)
- Request Trends—Trend projections for the type of file requested.
- Traffic Summary—Web site traffic by period of time. For example by day, hour, week or month.
- User Summary—Summary of requests by individual users.
- Visit Summary—Analysis of the repeat visits of users.
- Visit Trends—Trend projections based on the visit data.

FIG. 11.32
The definitions help explain the information provided.

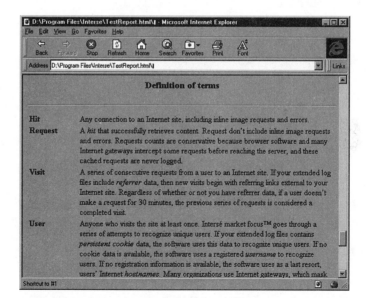

Intersé provides a database of domain names with the geographic location and other demographic data about the site. By using this data, Intersé can perform a very meaningful reverse lookup of client sites.

With the flexibility of Intersé, it's hard to envision a question that can't be answered in one of the standard analyses. If you think of such a question, the ability to customize is available. If you want serious, comprehensive analysis of your Web site, Intersé is worth consideration.

Part
II

Ch
11

MarketWave Hit List

The version of Hit List that was available for evaluation was the Professional Edition 30-day evaluation copy of version 1.0, obtained from **http://www.marketwave.com/**.

Hit List is a comprehensive Web site analysis tool that can import data in IIS ASCII flat-file format, ODBC database format, Common Log File format, and several other formats, including FTP log files. Hit List lets you design a report with a flexible set of tools that give control of all aspects of the analysis and report format.

You can base a new report on an existing report, so you can change an existing report without designing from scratch.

Hit List provides a large selection of well-thought-out predefined reports that present the information in an understandable format. The predefined analyses and reports include the following:

- Complete Analysis—A comprehensive set of analysis information that can be archived for documentation of all aspects of site activity. Figure 11.33 shows an example.
- Executive Summary—A high level extract from the Complete Analysis.
- Last Month—A 30-day summary of activity.
- Last Week—A seven-day summary of activity.
- Marketing Report—Data that reflects activity by marketing goals.
- Path Analysis—Presents data organized by the logical path of the target file.
- Request & Visit Analysis—Data regarding the types of requests (e.g., .html, .gif, and so on) and the requesting domain and site.
- Summary Report—Relevant totals regarding site activity.
- Technical Analysis—A review of the errors and transfer rates.
- Today—A snapshot report of the current activity.
- Yesterday—A snapshot report of the previous day.

The reports produced by Hit List are in HTML format and will be opened automatically after running Hit List with your default Web browser. The report file is Output.htm.

N O T E Output.htm is re-created each time you run an analysis. If you want to save a report, you need to rename and save the existing document before rerunning the analysis. ■

Figure 11.33 shows the top section of the Complete Analysis report.

Well-designed reports will include summary data, as shown in Figure 11.34.

FIG. 11.33

The opening section of the report provides a list of contents of the report.

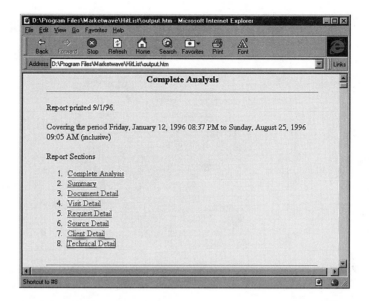

FIG. 11.34

The summary data provides an indication of the magnitude of data that has been analyzed.

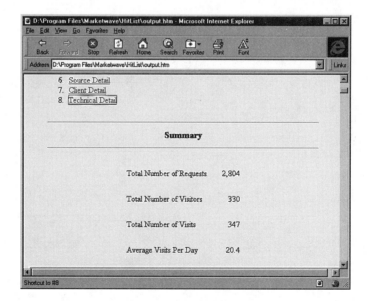

The graphing provided in Hit List is very flexible. Figure 11.35 shows the use of a 3-D bar chart.

Part

II

Ch

11

FIG. 11.35
Day-of-week data shows the busy days and could assist in planning backup and mainte-nance functions.

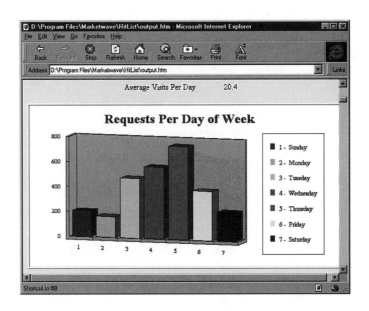

Hit List provides explanatory information at the top of the data tables explaining the contents of the table. This also includes pointers to online help information, as shown in Figure 11.36.

FIG. 11.36
The use of color in the background to set off data is effectively used in Hit List.

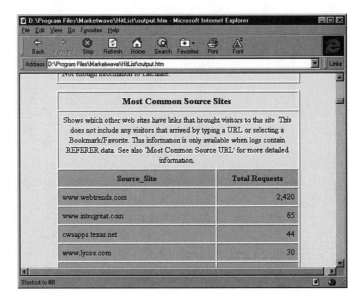

Hit List provides for reverse lookup of client IP addresses. This can be useful in generating demographic data about the users of your Web site.

Hit List also lets you publish the analysis reports through the use of e-mail with either Microsoft Exchange or POP/SMTP. Combined with the report-scheduling feature of Hit List, the reports can be set up once and then executed with no intervention.

WebTrends

The version of WebTrends that was available for evaluation was a 30-day evaluation demo copy of version 2.01. It was obtained from **http://www.webtrends.com/**.

WebTrends is designed to work with Common Log File format log files. The ability to design your own reports is provided. The standard reports are impressive in the use of graphics to present data.

Created in HTML format, each report has an assigned name. For example, the Executive Summary Report is saved as EXECTV.HTM by default. The user can set this file name parameter.

Figure 11.37 shows an example of graphing in WebTrends; Figure 11.38 shows a sample of a supporting table.

FIG. 11.37
The use of 3-D provides an effective presentation of the data.

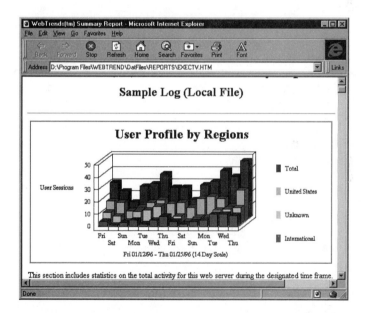

The reports are run against Common Log File format files with no alteration to the log file needed. In general, WebTrends appears worth consideration and evaluation if you're using a Web server that produces Common Log File format log files.

Other Analysis Tools

Two other analysis tools were identified but not reviewed. These are both licensed freeware and provide a budget-saving alternative.

FIG. 11.38
The supporting tables are well organized and readable.

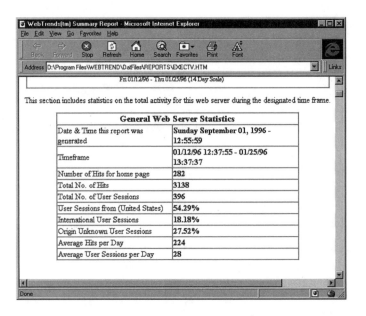

The first is Analog, now available in several versions for many platforms. It's not available for a Windows 32-bit platform; it's in the process of being ported to Windows NT/Windows 95. You can obtain this software at **http://www.statslab.com.ac.uk/~sret1/analog**. Analog is designed only for the Common Log File format log files.

The second is IISTATS, which is designed for IIS and requires Windows NT Perl 5 to run. This can be obtained at **http://www.cyber-trek.com/iistats**. Information on how to obtain NT Perl 5 is provided at the iistats site.

Choosing Your Analysis Tool

There's no shortage of analysis tools to choose from. You'll want to create a clear set of criteria for the analysis that you want to perform. You can then use this criteria as a check list as you evaluate each alternative tool. The key to choosing the correct tool is to decide what it is you want a tool to measure before evaluating and selecting the tool.

Reality Check

One advantage of selecting the option to log activity to a Microsoft SQL Server 6.5 ODBC data source in IIS is the ability to use SQL Server scripts. In a Que Reality Check Site, **www.integra.net**, IIS is the installed Web server.

The Webmaster created the SQL Server 6.5 script shown in Listing 11.1 to monitor the Web server activity level. The database is structured as detailed in the section IIS ODBC Database Format in this chapter.

Listing 11.1 SLQ Server 6.5 Script—Creating an Analysis Report of the Web Server

```
Select "Web Activity Summary Follows"

select "Hit Summary" = count(*), "Date" = substring(logtime,1,8)
from wwwlog
where
     (
          charindex("HTM",target) > 0
     )
group by substring(logtime, 1, 8)

select ""

Select "Time of day"=substring(logtime,10,2), "Hits" =
➥ count(substring(logtime,10,2)), "Outgoing Volume" = sum(bytessent)
from wwwlog
where
     (
          charindex("HTM",target) > 0
     )
group by substring(logtime,10,2)


Select "Page" = substring(target,1,50), "Hits" = count(target)
from wwwlog
group by target
Order by "hits" desc

select "Hits, by page, alpha sorted."
Select "Page" = substring(target,1,50), "Hits" = count(target),
➥ "Volume" = sum(bytessent), "Last Download" = max(logtime)
from wwwlog
where
     (
          charindex("zip",target) > 0
     )
group by target
Order by "Last Download" desc
```

The script in Listing 11.1 produces the report shown in Listing 11.2.

Listing 11.2 Web Server Activity Report—The Activity on www.integra.net

```
Web Activity Summary Follows

(1 row(s) affected)

Hit Summary Date
----------- --------
```

---

continues

Part
II

Ch
11

Listing 11.2   Continued

```
306         19960626
303         19960627
181         19960628
55          19960629
73          19960630
143         19960701
174         19960702
244         19960703
129         19960704
221         19960705
174         19960708
...


(56 row(s) affected)


-


(1 row(s) affected)

Time of day Hits        Outgoing Volume
----------- ----------- ---------------
00          73          445612
01          60          237076
02          58          236044
03          55          203931
04          60          227139
05          171         639305
06          154         645292
07          310         991525
08          672         2309256
09          823         2265204
10          707         2117344
11          443         1367933
12          512         1678696
13          751         2018385
14          537         1901520
15          529         1858042
16          476         1361353
17          329         842682
18          213         606820
19          182         752391
20          234         760017
21          180         752527
22          117         399470
23          100         444262

(25 row(s) affected)

Page                                             Hits
------------------------------------------------ -----------
/scripts/proxy/xxxxxx.dll                        133301
```

```
/global/07_31_yyyyy.jpg                          35383
/Default.htm                                      2305
/images/restwith.gif                              1592
/images/slackoff.gif                              1417
/mysite.htm                                       1329
/goodtools.htm                                    1273
/qtools.htm                                        1270
/index.htm                                         1263
/rightbutn.htm                                     1243
/images/shoe.gif                                   1186
/images/biglogo.gif                                1169
/zzzzzzzz.htm                                 1102
/images/robe.jpg                                   1025
...
.


(572 row(s) affected)


----------------------------
Hits, by page, alpha sorted.

(1 row(s) affected)

Page                                      Hits    Volume      Last Download
----------------------------------------- -----   ---------   ---------------
/ccccc/product1.zip                        30     36377718    Aug 27 1996 12:29AM
/ccccc/product2.zip                        26     93376646    Aug 27 1996 10:08AM
/uuuuuu/mmm/beta/abc_nt4.zip               24     22917266    Aug 27 1996 10:06AM
/uuuuuu/wwwwww/pppp/product3.zip            7     500574      Aug 27 1996  9:59AM
/uuuuuu/wwwwww/sssss/product4.zip         175     12410117    Aug 27 1996  9:49AM
/PPPPP/DDDDD/VVV/Product5.gif              53     31516       Aug 27 1996  8:01AM
/uuuuu/wwwww/nnnnnn/Product6.zip          120     30882074    Aug 26 1996 12:36PM
/uuuuu/wwwww/nnnnnn/Product7.zip           48     31693334    Aug 25 1996  7:41PM
/sssssss/vvvvv.zip                          2     6036        Aug 25 1996  1:43PM
/uuuuu/bbb/Product8.zip                     9     24080108    Aug 23 1996 12:30AM
/uuuu/bbb/Product9.zip                     18     37176554    Aug 23 1996  4:49AM
...

/uuuuu/bbb/Product10.zip                    8     11685617    19960715 9:56:29.000
/iiiii/ddddddd/vvv/Product11.gif      1         679          19960715 12:36:27.000

(25 row(s) affected)
```

This listing is an example of the use of the Web server log data to monitor a Web site. Graphing this data would produce an additional view of the data. Also, you can generate simple trend lines by using a spreadsheet that will perform trend line graphing.

One of the maintenance plans for such a site could be to periodically redefine the script to evolve to the showing of exception data and to define multiple scripts that could be run for historical documentation.

From Here...

Understanding the activity on your Web server is an important element in the puzzle that you'll examine regularly as you create and maintain your Web site. Successful Web sites share the characteristic of constant change and evolution.

As more information becomes available to you, you'll change those parts that don't produce the desired results and enhance those elements that work. Planning is a key to success. It's important that the plan be used as an iterative element with constant review and revision. Understanding the use of logging data available with the various servers will help you in your choice of a Web server.

Logging data will also help you in the determinations necessary for a decision to upgrade and expand your equipment and software. The following chapters will help you do your planning:

- Chapter 2, "Choosing a Web Server and Service Provider," gives information to assist in your choice of Web server software and an Internet service provider (ISP).

- Chapter 5, "Setting Up and Configuring a Web Server," describes the issues and questions that need resolution in the process of configuring your Web server.

- Chapter 6, "Setting Up an FTP Site," helps you create of an FTP site in conjunction with your Web site.

- Chapter 10, "Maintenance Utilities," helps your understanding of the maintenance utilities available and how they're used in the maintenance of your Web site.

- Chapter 14, "Marketing Your Web Site," covers methods of marketing your Web site to your target audience.

## CHAPTER 12

Search Engines

The World Wide Web is a rich environment in which the mass of material can obscure the very item of information that your user/client wishes to find. The situation is little improved on an Intranet implementation of a Web server. To deal with this problem, search engines and search services have been created. One of the key factors in enabling the users to find your Web site is getting it properly indexed in the various search services as discussed in Chapter 14, "Marketing Your Web Site."

Once a user locates your site, you can enhance the user friendliness of your site by offering a search function that will assist in the navigation of your site. Enabling the searching of your site increases the accessibility and value of the information that you have published.

In very simple terms that will be expanded in this chapter, a search engine creates an index of the contents of the documents published at your Web site. It also provides functions that identify documents that match various search criteria. The search criteria can be properties of the document, or the presence of a word in the text of the document.

How to install the search engines

Where can you get these search engines and how are they installed.

How a search engine scans the documents in the Web site

Scanning is the process of identifying documents to be indexed.

How the search engine filters the data in the documents

Filtering sorts out what, from the documents, can be searched.

How the indexes are created for your Web site

The index is the key to the power of a search engine.

How to create query forms

Your users need a way to communicate with the search engine. The query form is the vehicle.

How a query results set is formatted

When the results set is built, it requires formatting to make sense to the user.

How the query language works

What type of questions can you ask of the search engine.

N O T E This chapter is designed to present the reader with a conceptual understanding of the operation of two of the local search engines. It is not intended as a "How To" manual even though there is "How To" for the two search engines. It is the purpose of this chapter to assist you, the reader, in understanding search engines so that you can better choose a search engine for your Web site. ▧

This chapter looks at two local search engines, the Microsoft Index Server and the Excite for Web Servers search engine. The Microsoft Index Server operates in a Windows NT/Microsoft Internet Information Server environment. Excite for Web Servers is based in PERL which is a somewhat older technology. Excite for Web Servers will support most Web servers since it is not integrated into the functions of the server. ▧

Installing the Search Engines

Both of the search engines that are discussed are obtained from the World Wide Web. The Microsoft Index Server can be downloaded from **http://www.microsoft.com/ntserver/ search**. The Excite for Web Servers search engine can be downloaded from **http:// www.excite.com**. The documentation for both is included in the download.

N O T E PERL (Practical Extraction and Report Language) is an interpreted language. The syntax is very similar to C. It is free, and is widely used for the creation of CGI scripts. The current version is PERL 5. The documentation that is provided with PERL is quite good. ▧

Downloading the Search Engines

There are several options that you can select from when downloading either of these search engines.

Microsoft Index Server Options   The first option that the Microsoft Index Server requires is the selection of a platform. The platforms available are the following:

- Alpha
- I386
- MIPS
- Power PC

The second option is the language. There are nine options for language. The key to remember here is that the language that you select is not the language that is selected in the Regional Settings of the Control Panel, or even the language used by the system operators. It is the language of the documents that will be indexed. The choices are as follows:

- All—All seven languages are supported.
- Dutch
- English—International
- English—U.S.
- French
- German
- Italian
- Spanish
- Swedish

When you have made these choices, you will download the correct self-extracting, self-installing .EXE file.

Excite for Web Servers Options   Excite for Web Servers provides versions for several different operating systems. These are as follows:

- SunOS 4.1.4
- HP-UX 9.05
- Solaris 2.4
- IBM AIX 3.2
- SGI IRIX 5.3
- BSDI 2.0
- Intel Windows NT
- Dec OSF—Not yet available but planned.
- Linux—Not yet available but planned.

After you choose the correct operating system, you will download the correct self-extracting, self-installing .EXE file.

Running the Install Programs

You can run the install programs from any directory, including the directory that you saved the file in during the download.

Microsoft Index Server   The instructions for installing the Microsoft Index Server are as follows:

1. Choose Start, Run and enter the path to the downloaded file as shown in Figure 12.1.

Part
II

Ch
12

FIG. 12.1

The idxsvenu.exe install file is the U.S. English version of Microsoft Index Server.

2. Click OK to continue as shown in Figure 12.2.

FIG. 12.2

If you decide to remove Microsoft Index Server later, the documentation contains complete instructions.

3. Approve the EULA (End User License Agreement) by clicking OK as shown in Figure 12.3.

FIG. 12.3

The EULA must be approved or installation is stopped.

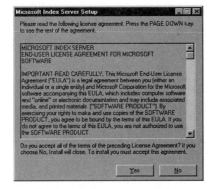

4. Click Continue to keep going as shown in Figure 12.4.

FIG. 12.4

You are provided with a second chance to stop the installation process.

5. Enter the path to the Scripts directory as shown in Figure 12.5.

FIG. 12.5
The Scripts directory is a virtual directory in the WWW Home directory. This provides logical access to the Scripts directory.

6. Enter the path of the WWW Home directory as shown in Figure 12.6.

FIG. 12.6
The WWW Home directory, or WWW virtual root directory, is the logical area that clients may visit with a Web Browser.

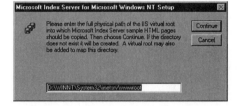

7. Enter the path for the creation of the Index directory. The default is to create a directory \Catalog.wci on the root directory of your system drive as shown in Figure 12.7.

FIG. 12.7
In the example seen here, the Index directory will be D:\Catalog.wci.

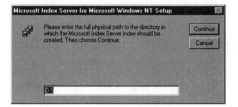

Part
II

Ch
12

8. The installation process is now finished. Note the location of the Query.htm document as shown in Figure 12.8. Opening this document with your Web browser and running any query will start the indexing process.

FIG. 12.8
When you create a link from your Default.htm file to Query.htm, you will have created the ability to search your site.

The Microsoft Index Server is now operational in the default configuration.

Excite for Web Servers The instructions for installing Excite for Web Servers are as follows:

1. Choose Start, Run and enter the path to the downloaded file as shown in Figure 12.9.

FIG. 12.9

The ews_nt(1).exe file shown here is for the Windows NT version of Excite.

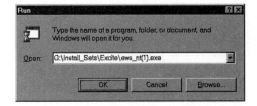

2. Click Next to continue as shown in Figure 12.10.

FIG. 12.10

The Windows Install/ Uninstall function can be used to remove Excite for Web Servers.

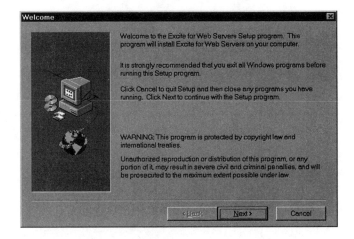

3. Choose the directory for installation as shown in Figure 12.11.

FIG. 12.11

You must specify the directory where the installation files are located.

4. Choose the directory for the CGI-BIN files to be installed as shown in Figure 12.12.

FIG. 12.12
The CGI-BIN directory is where the administration programs are located.

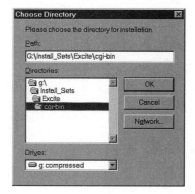

5. Choose the directory for the Excite HTML files as shown in Figure 12.13.

FIG. 12.13
The Excite HTML files include the help and documentation.

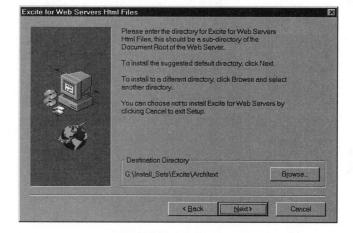

Part
II

Ch
12

6. Choose the directory for the installation of Excite for Web Servers as shown in Figure 12.14.

7. If you want the administration of Excite to be password-protected, enter a password, as shown in Figure 12.15.

8. The installation process is now finished as shown in Figure 12.16.

The Excite for Web Servers is now installed and ready to be configured and implemented.

Both the Microsoft Index Server and Excite for Web Servers can be installed on the same Web site without any apparent problems.

FIG. 12.14

You must specify an existing directory for Excite in which to install.

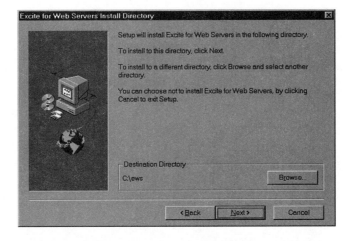

FIG. 12.15

This does not have to be the same password as any existing account.

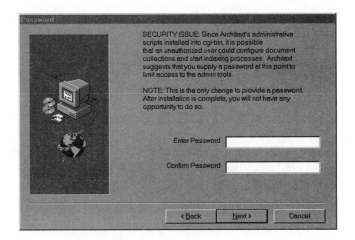

FIG. 12.16

The AT-start.exe can also be run from the command line.

Scanning the Documents

Microsoft Index Server calls the process of inventorying documents that are to be indexed *scanning*. In Excite for Web Servers, the process is accomplished by creating a *collection*.

N O T E The processes of scanning, filtering, and indexing are performed automatically by Microsoft Index Server. These processes can be set to be automatic in the Excite for Web Servers as well. ■

Microsoft Index Server

A *scan* creates a list of documents that will be *filtered* and *indexed*. Filtering and indexing are covered in the next two sections of this chapter.

The directories that are indexed are scanned. The directories that are indexed are all of the directories that are listed in the MS IIS WWW virtual root as shown in Figure 12.17. A virtual directory may even be on another server.

FIG. 12.17

Open this display by choosing Start, Programs, Microsoft Internet Server (Common), Internet Service Manager. Highlight the WWW service and the menu item Properties, Service Properties and click the Directories tab.

Part
II

Ch
12

There are two types of scan, a Full Scan and an Incremental Scan. When a scan is performed, the MS Index Server creates a list of documents included in the indexed directories.

In a Full Scan, all of the files in the indexed directories are included in the list. A full scan is performed for a directory the first time it is included as an indexed directory in an incremental scan. New documents, and documents that have changed, are included in the list. Each document in the list is going to be filtered and indexed by MS Index Server.

A Full Scan can be forced from the Administration Pages. To force a full scan, choose Start, Programs, Microsoft Index Server (Common), Index Server Administration. With the

Administration page open, click Start for Force scan virtual roots: as shown in Figure 12.18. In the next page, select the type of scan; No Scan, Incremental Scan, or Full Scan to be performed for each virtual root as shown in Figure 12.19.

FIG. 12.18

The admin.htm page provides the basic administration of the Index Server.

FIG. 12.19

All of the directories in the MS IIS WWW virtual directories are shown. These directories are indexed directories.

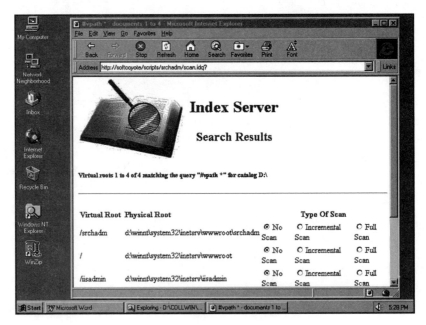

Excite for Web Servers

The creation of a Collection in Excite for Web Servers is accomplished by creating a *YourCollectionName*.conf file, in which *YourCollectionName* is a name of your choosing. You can create the *YourCollectionName*.conf by using any text editor, such as Windows NotePad. Listing 12.1 is an example of a .Conf file.

Listing 12.1   YourCollectionName.Conf File—A Sample .Conf File

```
<Collection YourCollectionName>
ArchitextRoot D:\ews
IndexExecutable D:\ews\architextIndex
SearchExecutable D:\ews\architextSearch
StemTable D:\ews\stem.tbl
StopTable D:\ews\stop.tbl
CollectionContents d:\winnt\system32\inetsrv\wwwroot
CollectionIndex D:\ews\collections\index
CollectionInfo D:\ews\collections\index.cf
PerlRoot D:\ews\perl
HtmlRoot d:\winnt\system32\inetsrv\wwwroot
CgiBin d:\winnt\system32\inetsrv\CGI-BIN
ArchitextURL /Architext/
ConfigRoot d:\winnt\system32\inetsrv\wwwroot\Architext
Password
OSType WindowsNT
</Collection>
```

This .conf file becomes input to the architextIndex.exe program which actually produces the index for the collection. The line CollectionContents specifies the files to be included in the collection. The files that can be indexed are HTML and Text files. The use and syntax of architextIndex.exe is described in the section "Indexing the Web Site," later in this chapter.

Part
II

Ch
12

Filtering the Documents

Filtering is the process of deciding what will be included in the index. One of the issues is noise words. These are the words such as in, of, the, etc. Another issue is file type. File type refers to whether the file is ASCII test or a binary.

Microsoft Index Server

The Microsoft Index Server extracts text and properties from files that it understands. The filter DLLs are capable of reading HTML, text, Microsoft Word, and Microsoft Excel documents. For these file types, a full text filtering is performed. The properties of the document are also filtered. These properties include size, date last altered, name, and author.

The Microsoft Index Server cannot do a full text scan on binaries such as bitmaps and compressed files. It can, however, filter the properties such as size, name, and date last altered.

The filtering is accomplished by a filter DLL. There is multiple-language support available. A document that has a paragraph in English and a paragraph in French will be filtered first by the English support DLLs, and then by the French support DLLs.

After the filter DLLs finish, the word-breaker DLLs are invoked. The word-breaker DLLs parse the text into words. These words are then placed in Word Lists, which are the raw material of the indexing process.

Excite for Web Servers

Excite does not have a separate function that performs the filtering process. This process is included in the indexing function. Similar issues are dealt with in Excite. The Excite indexing function, which is discussed in more detail in the next section "Indexing the Web Site," deals with the noise words. In Excite they are called *stop words*.

Excite can deal only with HTML and text documents and does not capture the properties of the documents.

Indexing the Web Site

The process of indexing is the creation of the actual indexes that are used during a search operation.

Microsoft Index Server

Microsoft Index Server uses three types of indexes:

- Word Lists —Words and properties extracted from a document first appear here. These are small in memory indexes. These will be merged into a Shadow Index when the system has available system time, or the Word List reaches a certain size.
- Shadow Index—Unlike a Word List, the Shadow Index is a persistent index. This means that it is stored on disk. When there is system time available, the Shadow Index will be merged into the Master Index.
- Master Index—This index is optimized for the best performance. The MS Index Server will provide the fastest performance when all of the Word Lists and Shadows Indexes have been merged into the Master Index.

The indexes are created automatically by the Microsoft Index Server. The merges are performed automatically based on parameters set in the System Registry. There are three types of merges:

- Shadow merge—The combining of one or more Word Lists and one or more Shadow Indexes into a single Shadow Index.

- Master merge—The combining of all Shadow Indexes with the Master Index into a single Master Index.

- Annealing merge—A special type of Shadow merge that is performed based on a number of factors including system idle time and settings in the System Registry.

All of the merges and all of the index maintenance are taken care of automatically. This includes recovery of the indexes in the event of a dirty shutdown.

Excite for Web Servers

The creation of an index in Excite is performed by a command line program named architextIndex.exe. Listing 12.2 shows a sample command line execution with the flag settings.

Listing 12.2   architextIndex.exe—An Example Command Line with Flag Settings

```
D:\ews>architextIndex.exe -c "architext.conf" -stem "stem.tbl" -stop "stop.tbl"
-R "TestCase"
```

The settings for architextIndex.exe are as follows:

- -c "architext.conf"—This is the collection configuration file.

- -stem "stem.tbl"—This is the stem table. Stems are word forms such as *run, running, ran* and so on.

- -stop "stop.tbl"—This is the noise words table. Noise or stop words are such things as *the, a, and, an*, and so on . These types of words are ignored for indexing.

- -R "TextCase"—This is the name with which all of the index files will be created. For example TestCase.IDX.

After architextIndex runs the first time for a collection, it can be set to run for updates based on a timed parameter.

Creating Query Forms

In order for a user to search your Web site, you must provide a query form. The query form serves the purpose of passing parameters for the search to the search engine.

Figure 12.20 shows a sample query page created by using NotePad for Microsoft Index Server. Listing 12.3 is the HyperText Markup Language version of the query page.

Part
II

Ch
12

FIG. 12.20

This form accepts the search argument and submits it to the Microsoft Index Server search engine.

Listing 12.3   My Query Form—An Example of the HTML for a Simple Query Form

```
<!DOCTYPE HTML PUBLIC "-//IETF//DTD HTML 3.0//EN" "html.dtd">
<HTML>
<META NAME="DESCRIPTION" CONTENT="Sample query form for MS Index Server">
<HEAD>
    <TITLE>My Query Form</TITLE>
</HEAD>
<BODY BGCOLOR="#FFFFFF" TEXT="#000000" LINK="#000066" VLINK="#808080" ALINK="#FF0000"
TOPMARGIN=0><TABLE>
    <TR>
        <TD VALIGN=MIDDLE><H1>My Query</h1><BR><H2>Simple Content Query</H2></TD></TR>
    </TR>
</TABLE>
<HR WIDTH=75% ALIGN=center SIZE=3>
<p>
<FORM ACTION="/scripts/samples/search/query.idq" METHOD="GET">
    Enter your query below:
    <TABLE>
        <TR>
            <TD><INPUT TYPE="TEXT" NAME="CiRestriction" SIZE="60" MAXLENGTH="100"
VALUE=""></TD>
            <TD><INPUT TYPE="SUBMIT" VALUE="Execute Query"></TD>
            <TD><INPUT TYPE="RESET" VALUE="Clear"></TD>
        </TR>
        <INPUT TYPE="HIDDEN" NAME="CiMaxRecordsPerPage" VALUE="10">
        <INPUT TYPE="HIDDEN" NAME="CiScope" VALUE="/">
        <INPUT TYPE="HIDDEN" NAME="TemplateName" VALUE="query">
```

```
            <INPUT TYPE="HIDDEN" NAME="CiSort" VALUE="rank[d]">
            <INPUT TYPE="HIDDEN" NAME="HTMLQueryForm" VALUE="/samples/search/ query.htm">
        </TABLE>
    </FORM>
    </BODY>
    </HTML>
```

Line 17 of Listing 12.3 mentions the Query.idq file with the GET method. This is the file that actually submits the search argument variable, CIRestriction, to the search engine. Listing 12.4 shows the contents of the Query.Idq file.

Listing 12.4   Query.IDQ File—An Example of the IDQ File that Executes the Query

```
# This is the query file for the MyQuery.htm query form.
[Query]
HKEY_LOCAL_MACHINE\System\CurrentControlSet\Control\ContentIndex\
↪IsapiDefaultCatalogDirectory
# These are the columns that are referenced in the .htx files
# when formatting output for each hit.
CiColumns=filename,size,rank,characterization,vpath,DocTitle,write
# Do a recursive search (ie all directories under CiScope).
CiFlags=DEEP
CiRestriction=%CiRestriction%
CiMaxRecordsInResultSet=300
CiMaxRecordsPerPage=%CiMaxRecordsPerPage%
CiScope=%CiScope%
# This is the .htx file to use for formatting the results of the query.
CiTemplate=/scripts/samples/search/%TemplateName%.htx
CiSort=%CiSort%
CiForceUseCi=true
```

The rank column, referred to in Listing 12.4, is the rank developed by the search engine based on the degree of match to the search argument.

N O T E   The process in Excite for Web Servers is logically very similar to the process in MS Index Server. Excite uses PERL CGI scripts instead of the IDQ files. ▪

Looking at the Query Results Set

Once the query has been submitted to Microsoft Index Server search engine, the results set is returned using a .HTX file as the template, in this case, Query.HTX. Listing 12.5 is the HTML of Query.HTX.

Part
II

Ch
12

Listing 12.5   Query.HTX File—An Example of the HTX File that Formats the Result Set

```
<HTML>

<!--
    <%CiTemplate%>

    This is the formatting page for query results.  This file defines
    how the result page header, rows, and footer will appear.
-->

<HEAD>
    <!-- The title lists the # of documents -->

    <%if CiMatchedRecordCount eq 0%>
        <TITLE><%CiRestriction%> - no documents matched.</TITLE>
    <%else%>
        <TITLE><%CiRestriction%> - documents <%CiFirstRecordNumber%> to
<%CiLastRecordNumber%></TITLE>
    <%endif%>
</HEAD>

<BODY BGCOLOR="#FFFFFF" TEXT="#000000" LINK="#000066" VLINK="#808080" ALINK="#FF0000"
TOPMARGIN=0>

<TABLE>
    <TR>

        <TD VALIGN=MIDDLE><H1>My Query</H1><br><center><h2>Search
Results</h2></center></TD>
    </TR>
</TABLE>

<!-- Print a header that lists the query and the number of hits -->

<H5>
    <%if CiMatchedRecordCount eq 0%>
        No documents matched the query "<%CiRestriction%>".
    <%else%>
        Documents <%CiFirstRecordNumber%> to <%CiLastRecordNumber%> of
        <%if CiMatchedRecordCount eq CiMaxRecordsInResultSet%>
            the best
        <%endif%>
        <%CiMatchedRecordCount%> matching the query
        "<%CiRestriction%>".
    <%endif%>
</H5>

<!--
    This table has a link to a new query page, a previous button, and
    a next page button.  The buttons are only displayed when appropriate.
-->

<TABLE WIDTH=80%>
```

```
<!--
    Query.htm set HTMLQueryForm as the name of the page to return to
    for a new query.
-->

<TD> <A HREF="<%HTMLQueryForm%>">New query</A> </TD>

<!-- Define a "previous" button if this isn't the first page -->

<%if CiContainsFirstRecord eq 0%>
    <TD ALIGN=LEFT>
        <FORM ACTION="/scripts/samples/search/query.idq" METHOD="GET">
            <INPUT TYPE="HIDDEN"
                NAME="CiBookMark" VALUE="<%CiBookMark%>" >
            <INPUT TYPE="HIDDEN"
                NAME="CiBookmarkSkipCount" VALUE="-<%CiMaxRecordsPerPage%>" >
            <INPUT TYPE="HIDDEN"
                NAME="CiMaxRecordsInResultSet" VALUE="<%CiMaxRecordsInResultSet%>" >
            <INPUT TYPE="HIDDEN"
                NAME="CiRestriction" VALUE="<%CiRestriction%>" >
            <INPUT TYPE="HIDDEN"
                NAME="CiMaxRecordsPerPage" VALUE="<%CiMaxRecordsPerPage%>" >
            <INPUT TYPE="HIDDEN"
                NAME="CiScope" VALUE="<%CiScope%>" >
            <INPUT TYPE="HIDDEN"
                NAME="TemplateName" VALUE="<%TemplateName%>" >
            <INPUT TYPE="HIDDEN"
                NAME="CiSort" VALUE="<%CiSort%>" >
            <INPUT TYPE="HIDDEN"
                NAME="HTMLQueryForm" VALUE="<%HTMLQueryForm%>" >
            <INPUT TYPE="SUBMIT"
                VALUE="Previous <%CiMaxRecordsPerPage%> documents">
        </FORM>
    </TD>
<%endif%>

<!-- Define a "next" button if this isn't the last page -->

<%if CiContainsLastRecord eq 0%>
    <TD ALIGN=RIGHT>
        <FORM ACTION="/scripts/samples/search/query.idq" METHOD="GET">
            <INPUT TYPE="HIDDEN"
                NAME="CiBookMark" VALUE="<%CiBookMark%>" >
            <INPUT TYPE="HIDDEN"
                NAME="CiBookmarkSkipCount" VALUE="<%CiMaxRecordsPerPage%>" >
            <INPUT TYPE="HIDDEN"
                NAME="CiMaxRecordsInResultSet" VALUE="<%CiMaxRecordsInResultSet%>" >
            <INPUT TYPE="HIDDEN"
                NAME="CiRestriction" VALUE="<%CiRestriction%>" >
            <INPUT TYPE="HIDDEN"
                NAME="CiMaxRecordsPerPage" VALUE="<%CiMaxRecordsPerPage%>" >
            <INPUT TYPE="HIDDEN"
                NAME="CiScope" VALUE="<%CiScope%>" >
            <INPUT TYPE="HIDDEN"
```

Part

II

Ch

12

continues

Listing 12.5   Continued

```
                    NAME="TemplateName" VALUE="<%TemplateName%>" >
             <INPUT TYPE="HIDDEN"
                    NAME="CiSort" VALUE="<%CiSort%>" >
             <INPUT TYPE="HIDDEN"
                    NAME="HTMLQueryForm" VALUE="<%HTMLQueryForm%>" >
             <INPUT TYPE="SUBMIT"
                    VALUE="Next <%CiRecordsNextPage%> documents">
          </FORM>
       </TD>
    <%endif%>
</TABLE>

<HR>

<!--
    The begindetail/enddetail section describes how each row of output
    is be formatted.  The sample below prints:

       - record number
       - document title (if one exists) or virtual path of the file
       - the abstract for the file
       - the url for the file
       - the file's size and last write time
-->

<dl>

<%begindetail%>

    <p>
    <dt>
        <%CiCurrentRecordNumber%>.
        <%if DocTitle isempty%>
            <b><a href="<%EscapeURL vpath%>"><%filename%></a></b>
        <%else%>
            <b><a href="<%EscapeURL vpath%>"><%DocTitle%></a></b>
        <%endif%>
    <dd>
        <b><i>Abstract:   </i></b><%characterization%>
        <br>
        <cite>
            <a href="<%EscapeURL vpath%>">http://<%server_name%><%vpath%></a>
            <font size=-1> - <%if size eq ""%>(size and time unknown)<%else%>size
<%size%> bytes - <%write%> GMT<%endif%></font>
        </cite>

<%enddetail%>

    </dl>
    <P>
```

```
<!-- Only display a line if there were any hits that matched the query -->

<%if CiMatchedRecordCount ne 0%>
    <HR>
<%endif%>

<TABLE WIDTH=80%>

    <!--
        Query.htm set HTMLQueryForm as the name of the page to return to
        for a new query.
    -->

    <TD> <A HREF="<%HTMLQueryForm%>">New query</A> </TD>

    <!-- Define a "previous" button if this isn't the first page -->

    <%if CiContainsFirstRecord eq 0%>
        <TD ALIGN=LEFT>
            <FORM ACTION="/scripts/samples/search/query.idq" METHOD="GET">
                <INPUT TYPE="HIDDEN"
                    NAME="CiBookMark" VALUE="<%CiBookMark%>" >
                <INPUT TYPE="HIDDEN"
                    NAME="CiBookmarkSkipCount" VALUE="-<%CiMaxRecordsPerPage%>" >
                <INPUT TYPE="HIDDEN"
                    NAME="CiMaxRecordsInResultSet" VALUE="<%CiMaxRecordsInResultSet%>" >
                <INPUT TYPE="HIDDEN"
                    NAME="CiRestriction" VALUE="<%CiRestriction%>" >
                <INPUT TYPE="HIDDEN"
                    NAME="CiMaxRecordsPerPage" VALUE="<%CiMaxRecordsPerPage%>" >
                <INPUT TYPE="HIDDEN"
                    NAME="CiScope" VALUE="<%CiScope%>" >
                <INPUT TYPE="HIDDEN"
                    NAME="TemplateName" VALUE="<%TemplateName%>" >
                <INPUT TYPE="HIDDEN"
                    NAME="CiSort" VALUE="<%CiSort%>" >
                <INPUT TYPE="HIDDEN"
                    NAME="HTMLQueryForm" VALUE="<%HTMLQueryForm%>" >
                <INPUT TYPE="SUBMIT"
                    VALUE="Previous <%CiMaxRecordsPerPage%> documents">
            </FORM>
        </TD>
    <%endif%>

    <!-- Define a "next" button if this isn't the last page -->

    <%if CiContainsLastRecord eq 0%>
        <TD ALIGN=RIGHT>
            <FORM ACTION="/scripts/samples/search/query.idq" METHOD="GET">
                <INPUT TYPE="HIDDEN"
                    NAME="CiBookMark" VALUE="<%CiBookMark%>" >
                <INPUT TYPE="HIDDEN"
```

Part

II

Ch

12

continues

Listing 12.5   Continued

```
                       NAME="CiBookmarkSkipCount" VALUE="<%CiMaxRecordsPerPage%>" >
               <INPUT TYPE="HIDDEN"
                       NAME="CiMaxRecordsInResultSet" VALUE="<%CiMaxRecordsInResultSet%>" >
               <INPUT TYPE="HIDDEN"
                       NAME="CiRestriction" VALUE="<%CiRestriction%>" >
               <INPUT TYPE="HIDDEN"
                       NAME="CiMaxRecordsPerPage" VALUE="<%CiMaxRecordsPerPage%>" >
               <INPUT TYPE="HIDDEN"
                       NAME="CiScope" VALUE="<%CiScope%>" >
               <INPUT TYPE="HIDDEN"
                       NAME="TemplateName" VALUE="<%TemplateName%>" >
               <INPUT TYPE="HIDDEN"
                       NAME="CiSort" VALUE="<%CiSort%>" >
               <INPUT TYPE="HIDDEN"
                       NAME="HTMLQueryForm" VALUE="<%HTMLQueryForm%>" >
               <INPUT TYPE="SUBMIT"
                       VALUE="Next <%CiRecordsNextPage%> documents">
           </FORM>
       </TD>
   <%endif%>
</TABLE>

<P><BR>

<!--
    If the index is out of date (for example, if it's still being created
    or updated after changes to files in an indexed directory) let the
    user know.
-->

<%if CiOutOfDate ne 0%>
    <P>
    <I><B>The index is out of date.</B></I><BR>
<%endif%>

<!--
    If the query was not executed because it needed to enumerate to
    resolve the query instead of using the index, but CiForceUseCi
    was TRUE, let the user know
-->

<%if CiQueryIncomplete ne 0%>
    <P>
    <I><B>The query is too expensive to complete.</B></I><BR>
<%endif%>

<!--
    If the query took too long to execute (for example, if too much work
    was required to resolve the query), let the user know
-->

<%if CiQueryTimedOut ne 0%>
    <P>
```

```
    <I><B>The query took too long to complete.</B></I><BR>
<%endif%>


<!-- Output a page number and count of pages -->

<%if CiTotalNumberPages gt 0%>
    <P>
    Page <%CiCurrentPageNumber%> of <%CiTotalNumberPages%>
    <P>
<%endif%>

</HTML>
```

Figure 12.21 shows the output formatted with the Query.HTX file.

FIG. 12.21
The format calls for 10 items per page.

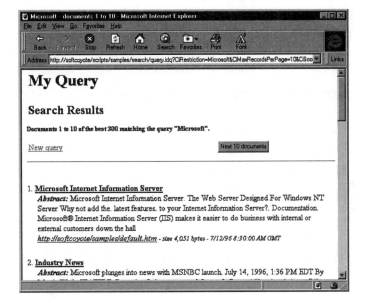

Understanding the Query Language

The power and utility of a search engine are determined by two factors. The first is the speed with which a query is answered. The second, and arguably the more important, is how flexible and thorough the query language is. If a query language were to only do exact matches, as an example, its usefulness would be very limited.

Microsoft Index Server

There are two basic types of query for the Microsoft Index Server search engine, text and property.

Text Searches   In text searches, both single words and phrases can be searched. All of the noise words are stripped out of the search argument before it is formulated. There are several operators that can be used in text searches:

- AND—Chicago and Springfield will produce pages with both Chicago and Springfield in them. If you want the phrase "Chicago and Springfield", using quotes will treat the and as part of a phrase and not an operator.

- OR—Chicago or Springfield will produce pages that have either in them.

- NEAR—Works much like AND. Chicago NEAR Springfield will return a page if both are on the same page.

- AND NOT—Chicago AND NOT Springfield will return pages with Chicago, only if Springfield is not present.

- Single asterisk—comput* will return pages with words that have the prefix comput such as computer, computing or computed.

- Double asterisk—fly** will return pages with words from the same stem such as fly, flew, flown, flying.

- Free-Text—Prefaces with $contents. As an example, "$contents how do I paginate in Microsoft Word?" would return pages that mention pagination and Microsoft Word.

Queries can also be made on the properties of a document. Some of the properties that can be queried are:

- size—File size in bytes.
- write— Last date the file was altered.
- docauthor—Author of the document.
- name—Name of the file.

Various logical operators can be used in these queries such as equal (=_),greater than (>), less than (<), and equal to or greater than (=>). An example of a property query would be @size > 1000000. A file returns if its size is greater than 1 million bytes.

Text queries can be combined with property queries. As an example, Chicago and @size > 10000 returns a page that contains Chicago in the text and is larger than 10,000 bytes.

N O T E   The query language for Excite for Web Servers is similar to the Microsoft Index Server. The principal differences are that properties cannot be queried with Excite. ■

From Here...

Providing a Web search engine will enhance the accessibility of the information to the users of your site. This chapter has explored two alternatives. One is supported only on the Windows NT Microsoft Internet Information Server environment. The other, Excite for Web Servers, is supported on many platforms and is independent of the Web server used. It can be employed with any Web server that supports PERL CGI scripting. For related information to the topics in this chapter, see the following resources:

- Chapter 2, "Choosing a Web Server and Service Provider," provides additional items to be considered for choosing the server software.
- Chapter 13, "Forms and Surveys," gives insight into the use of forms for the search engine.
- Chapter 14, "Marketing Your Web Site," where you will investigate the part of search engines in your marketing program.
- Chapter 17, "Browsers and Your Web Server," that explores considerations required to deal with the various browsers.
- Chapter 18, "Basic HTML Techniques," provides information on creating the pages for your search.

Part
II

Ch
12

## CHAPTER 13

Forms and Surveys

The draw of the Web is that of anonymity in the sense that you can browse around Web sites, visiting sites all around the world without really identifying yourself or your interests in the information presented. This is a benefit to the user, but it makes it extremely difficult to create a Web site and then gauge the effectiveness of the site and the people visiting the site.

Forms offer a good way of interacting with users. Although information about users' computing environment is exchanged with your server when they access your site, this does little to identify the users, their position at their company, or other bits of information that are helpful in understanding your Web-based audience. This is where forms come in on your site.

One of the most versatile and exciting capabilities of the World Wide Web is to send information from Web clients back to the Web servers by using fill-in forms. This method is how Web users can enter search words and phrases, comments and suggestions, and, in the growing world of electronic commerce, even credit card numbers and addresses for purchases made over the Internet.

At the heart of the Web's interactive capability is support for forms and scripts. On the client side, users enter information in fill-in forms containing familiar windows controls such as text input fields, check boxes, and push buttons. The browser then sends the form data to the server for processing.

How to create HTML forms

Forms take your Web site to the next step, offering a way to gather information from the visitors to your site. Find out how to make the best use of the technology.

Learn how form data is retrieved from the user

Web protocols use the GET and POST methods to send information from the client to the server systems. See how these are represented and interpreted during the communications loop.

How to use the "mailto" command to send form data as e-mail

E-mail is one way to send information from forms to a specific destination and can be provided in formatted or unformatted fashion.

▶ Additional information about databases and interaction with forms is provided in Chapter 22, "Database Access and Integrity."

There are several commonly used methods to exchange form information between the client and server software. Among these are Common Gateway Interface (CGI) scripts that can be written in languages such as C/C++, Perl, ADA, and Visual Basic. These languages produce highly customized, robust, rapidly executing code, which translates into good performance for the end users of the applications. ■

Introducing Forms and Scripts

When a user submits a form from a browser, the browser gathers up the different fields and their values as they are represented on the form. These values are sent to the server in the form of the requested URL, provided by the browser as the next request of the server.

When the server receives the request, it passes the form data to a processing script, and then passes control to the script. The script reads and processes the form data as needed, returning the results to the client application.

Forms are just the user-interface and don't provide any inherent limitations on what can be done by the server with the information once it's submitted. A significant factor in the process is the fact that processes not necessarily native to the server software can be run as scripts. This might mean that you create an application that queries a database, one that sends a mail message without the user intervention, or it may mean that the information passed from the client software is added to a log file.

In the next sections, you'll learn how to create the form and how it interacts with the server software.

▶ This chapter won't spend a lot of time investigating or explaining HTML language elements. For more information about standard HTML, review Chapter 18, "Basic HTML Techniques," and Chapter 19, "Advanced HTML."

Creating Forms

The work of creating forms doesn't require any additional software; standard editors and HTML creation utilities typically include support for form controls on a Web page. The important thing is to ensure that the editor you select has support for form fields like text boxes, radio buttons, and other user-interaction controls.

That said, there are several standard elements that will need to be created when you build forms-based solutions. These include header information, how to process the form when it is submitted, and so forth. In the next sections, you'll see how these portions of the Web page are populated and how they affect the use of forms on the site.

Setting Up the Form Header

When a user submits a form, the browser sends the form data to the server by embedding the information in the URL. The *form header* tells the browser how to construct the URL to send to the server. It specifies the location of the processing script on the server and the HTTP method to be used to send the data. The following is a sample header instruction:

```
<FORM ACTION="URL"  METHOD={GET¦POST}>
    Form text and elements
</FORM>
```

The form METHOD, the manner in which the information on the form is processed, is either "GET" or "POST." In a typical form, POST is chosen because it causes form data to be sent by itself in a separate transaction.

By contrast, the GET method causes form data to be appended to the request of the server in the form of additional items in the requested address. If the address has too many ASCII characters, it may not be correctly processed by the server due to constraints on how the conversation between the server software and client software interact.

The ACTION element specifies the URL and can also be used to specify parameters. Use the closing </FORM> tag to show where the form ends. Every named field with a value between the FORM tags will be sent to the server when the ACTION is executed.

Although the FORM tag can be omitted if there is only one form section used, you must include it in multiple-form documents and, to comply with HTML coding standards, you should include it whenever you start a form definition.

Creating Input Fields

The Web-page form consists of the standard graphical controls such as text boxes, check boxes, and menus that you've become accustomed to in your use of Windows and Windows-based applications.

As you create the form elements, you give each a name that eventually becomes a variable name that the processing script on the server uses. You can use several types of controls to gather information in forms. These controls are listed in Table 13.1.

Table 13.1   Example Controls Used in Forms and Their Associated Tag Containers

Type of Control	Tag
Check box	<INPUT TYPE= "CHECKBOX" NAME=. . .>
Hidden field	<INPUT TYPE="hidden" NAME=. . .>
Menu	<SELECT>. . .<OPTION>. . .</SELECT>

continues

Table 13.1 Continued

Type of Control	Tag
Password box	<INPUT TYPE="PASSWORD" NAME=...>
Push button	<INPUT TYPE="{SUBMIT|RESET}" NAME=...
Radio button	<INPUT TYPE="RADIO" NAME=...>
Text box	<INPUT TYPE="Text" NAME=...>
Text window	<TEXT AREA>...</TEXT AREA>

Each of these controls also has a NAME= parameter, which allows you to indicate what the data value will be associated with. For example, if you create a Text Box control, you would want to be sure to assign a name to the control, as that would be referenced by the server-side script when it interprets and acts on the value contained in the control.

 T I P For the Radio Button control, you'll use the same name for each control in the set of options you're presenting to the user. The value returned for the variable is the value you indicate in the VALUE parameter to the HTML tag for the radio button.

Using Text and Password Boxes

Text and *password* boxes are simple data entry fields, nearly identical in function. The difference between the two comes in how information is displayed by each of the controls. Standard text boxes show text as the user types it in, fully readable. When you use the password version of the text box, all text will show up as asterisks, much like most Windows applications on the market today. This is helpful to prevent someone spying on your typing and learning your passwords as you enter them. The general form for a text or password field in HTML is the following:

```
<INPUT TYPE="{TEXT¦PASSWORD}"  NAME="name" [VALUE="default text"]
    [SIZE="width, height"]  MAXLENGTH="length">
```

Use the SIZE attribute to specify the display size of text and password boxes. The format is [SIZE="*width, height*"]. The default width is 20; the default height is 1. This value represents the height and width of the control based on the given number of letters and the associated rows.

N O T E In some browsers, the SIZE option will not correctly wrap text in a field. The text box will be shown correctly with the appropriate number of rows, but when you type in the text box, the text will not wrap as you'd expect. If you experience this problem, or if you'd like to maintain the largest compatibility with browsers, be sure to refer to the TEXT AREA tag. This tag is covered in the next section. ■

You can specify the maximum number of characters that will be allowed to be entered by using the MAXLENGTH attribute. A simple sign-on form, which accepts a user's name and password, would look like the one shown in Figure 13.1.

FIG. 13.1
A sample form that requests user name and password information from the user.

 With password-type fields, you are also prevented from copying the field. With a standard field, you can highlight the contents of the field and then select Edit, Copy, or Cut so you can place the text elsewhere. With a password field, your browser will not have the cut or copy options available.

An example of the HTML code behind the scenes for the form is provided in Listing 13.1. Notice that there is an opening <FORM> statement, followed by the form submission information; in this case, the form is processed by a script, /isapi/ie/ie_reg1.idc.

Listing 13.1 Example Form HTML Source

```
<HTML>
<HEAD>
<TITLE>Sample Text and Password Controls</TITLE>
</HEAD>
<BODY>
<FORM METHOD=POST ACTION="/scripts/que/forms/pwtext.idc">
Enter your name:          <INPUT TYPE="TEXT"  NAME="UserName" SIZE="40,1"
MAXLENGTH="80"><br>
Enter your password: <INPUT TYPE="Password"  NAME="UserPassword" SIZE="15,1"
MAXLENGTH="15"><br>
<hr>
<INPUT TYPE="SUBMIT" VALUE="Logon">
<INPUT TYPE="RESET" VALUE="Clear">
</form>
</BODY>
</HTML>
```

Part
II

Ch
13

The submit button shown on the form is an action button. Action buttons are discussed under "Submit and Reset Buttons" in the following section, but, in short, they cause the form information to be sent to the server system's script, outlined in the opening POST statement.

Multiline Text Windows   The <TEXT AREA> tag is an expanded version of <INPUT TYPE="TEXT">. A *text area* is a multiline text window complete with scroll bars. The format for a text area is as follows:

```
<TEXT AREA  NAME=Aname" [ROWS=rows] [COLS=columns]>
    Default_text
</TEXTAREA>
```

Use the ROWS and COLS attributes to specify the number of rows and columns in the text area. You can place the default text between the opening and closing <TEXTAREA> tags.

The Text Area is a text box in which you place your cursor and begin entering text, with the added benefit of word wrap and scroll bars if applicable.

Check Boxes and Radio Buttons   It's often the case where you need to present more than one choice to users and allow them to select one or more options. As with typical Windows-based applications, this is where you use check box and radio button controls.

The difference between check boxes and radio buttons is that with radio buttons, only a single choice can be made from the related radio button selections. Once a selection is made, if a second selection is made, the first is deselected and the last selection is made current. In a survey, this relates to a "Select only one from the list below."

With check boxes, the user can select as many different related items as needed. In a survey, this is equivalent to saying "Select one or more of the following."

The syntax of the HTML tag is as follows:

```
<INPUT TYPE="{CHECKBOX¦RADIO}"  NAME="Name"  VALUE="Value" [CHECKED]>
```

When you create a series of radio buttons, you name them all the same. This way, the browser knows what radio buttons should be mutually exclusive, preventing a multiple selection. Note that this also allows you to have more than one grouping of radio buttons on a given page. If you have two or more distinctly named groups, only the radio buttons within each respective group will be exclusive.

When you have a series of check boxes, you'll name each check box uniquely. This is how the information is submitted to the server with a unique name. Once a check box is selected, the VALUE of that selection is what is returned to the server when the form is submitted.

In the form shown in Figure 13.2 are two groups of radio buttons and one group of check boxes.

The HTML behind this form is shown in Listing 13.2. You can see from both the form and the listing that there are two sets of radio buttons and one set of check boxes.

TIP If you plan to have radio button groupings, make sure you make it visually obvious to the user what buttons are grouped together. Putting frames or lines between the groups helps the user understand the group of selections that are available for a given option.

FIG. 13.2

Sample form with radio buttons and check boxes.

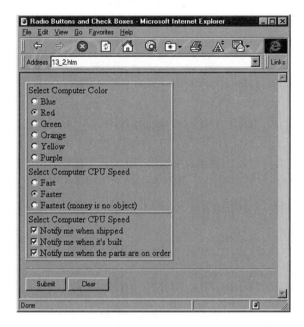

Listing 13.2   Source Code for 13FIG_02.HTM

```
<HTML>
<HEAD>
<TITLE>Radio Buttons and Check Boxes</TITLE>
</HEAD>
<BODY>
<FORM METHOD=POST ACTION="/scripts/que/forms/select.idc">
<table border=1>
   <tr>
      <b>Select Computer Color</b><br>
      <INPUT TYPE="RADIO"   NAME="Color"   VALUE="Blue" >Blue<br>
      <INPUT TYPE="RADIO"   NAME="Color"   VALUE="Red" >Red<br>
      <INPUT TYPE="RADIO"   NAME="Color"   VALUE="Green" >Green<br>
      <INPUT TYPE="RADIO"   NAME="Color"   VALUE="Orange" >Orange<br>
      <INPUT TYPE="RADIO"   NAME="Color"   VALUE="Yellow" >Yellow<br>
      <INPUT TYPE="RADIO"   NAME="Color"   VALUE="Purple" >Purple<br>
   </tr>
   <tr>
      <b>Select Computer CPU Speed</b><br>
      <INPUT TYPE="RADIO"   NAME="CPU"   VALUE="Fast" >Fast<br>
      <INPUT TYPE="RADIO"   NAME="CPU"   VALUE="Faster" >Faster<br>
      <INPUT TYPE="RADIO"   NAME="CPU"   VALUE="Fastest" >Fastest (money is no
➥object)<br>
   </tr>
   <tr>
      <b>Select Computer CPU Speed</b><br>
      <INPUT TYPE="CHECKBOX"   NAME="Shipped"   VALUE="Shipped" >Notify me when
shipped<br>
```

continues

Listing 13.2   Continued

```
     <INPUT TYPE="CHECKBOX"  NAME="Built"  VALUE="Built" >Notify me when it's
➡built<br>
     <INPUT TYPE="CHECKBOX"  NAME="Ordered"  VALUE="Ordered" >Notify me when
the parts
➡ are on order<br>
   <tr>
</table>
<hr>
<INPUT TYPE="SUBMIT" VALUE="Submit">
<INPUT TYPE="RESET" VALUE="Clear">
</form>
</BODY>
</HTML>
```

Setting Up Your Submit and Reset Buttons   Once you've created your form, you need to have a way the users can send in the form and activate the script that will accept the information on the form. Good programming also dictates that you should give the users a way out, a way to correct any mistakes they may have made in entering information on your form.

HTML supports two buttons that allow exactly this procedure. The SUBMIT and RESET buttons are there so you can present the users with a button that responds just as it would as a standard Windows button control. When you use these buttons, they are predefined to respond in a very fixed fashion. The SUBMIT button sends the data to the host, and the RESET button clears all information on the form and returns all controls to their default values.

From the example in the previous section, shown in Listing 13.2, you can see the general syntax of the button is as follows:

```
<INPUT TYPE="SUBMIT" VALUE="Caption">
<INPUT TYPE="RESET" VALUE="Caption">
```

You indicate the caption for the button in the VALUE parameter. This is a good way to customize the button so it makes more sense to the users in the context of the form. You might want to change this to "Place Order" on an order form, or "Send Bug Report" for a bug report form.

You need to place a submit button on all forms as it's the only way you have of submitting the information on the form and initiating action on the server. The only exception is the case where your form has only one field. In this case, if the user simply presses Enter, the form is submitted based on the value in the opening <FORM> tag.

You can also use multiple submit buttons on your form. For an example, see Figure 13.3.

You do this by having more than one set of FORM container tags on your page. The page shown, taken from the Primenet Services for the Internet pages, has several such sections, shown in the page excerpt in Listing 13.3.

FIG. 13.3

Forms can contain more than one Submit button.

Listing 13.3 Example HTML for Multiple Submit Buttons

```
<FORM METHOD="post" ACTION="http://www.primenet.com/cgi-bin/finger?
➥ newsadm@primenet.com">
    <P>
    <CENTER>
    <INPUT TYPE="SUBMIT" VALUE="Click this button for the latest Server
➥ Status">
    </CENTER>
</FORM>
<HR>
<H2>User Account Information</H2>
<BLOCKQUOTE>
Enter your username and password below and click &quot;Submit&quot;
➥to receive complete account information.
</BLOCKQUOTE>
<FORM method=post action="http://pinnacle.primenet.com/cgi-bin/
➥ user_change?acct">
    <UL>
        <LI>Username: <INPUT NAME="username" VALUE="" >
        <LI>Password: <INPUT TYPE="password" NAME="password" VALUE="" >
    </UL>
    <P>
    <INPUT type="submit"><INPUT TYPE="RESET">
</FORM>
```

Part

II

Ch

13

As you might gather from the listing, any given submit button relates to the ACTION defined for the form container tags in which it resides. Using this approach, you can support many different form submissions from a page, allowing the users to select the best or most appropriate action based on what they want to do.

Establishing Hidden Fields   When you create forms, there may be times when you want to store information to be submitted with the form, but don't necessarily need to display certain fields to the users. These fields can be set up as HIDDEN and won't be shown to the user, but will still be transmitted when the form is submitted.

You create a hidden field by using a TYPE attribute, indicating that the field is not visible:

```
<INPUT TYPE="HIDDEN"  NAME="Name"  VALUE="Value">
```

You typically use hidden fields to convey fixed information that is required for a process to complete, but not provided by the user. For example, if you have an order entry form, and you want to pass in a version field that indicates what version of the page submitted the form, you could do so with the following field definition:

```
<INPUT TYPE="HIDDEN"  NAME="Version"  VALUE="102096.004">
```

This can be helpful, but probably the most used feature of hidden forms is a multiple-form process that must carry forward information from one form to another. An example of this might be a series of forms that sign up a user for a magazine subscription. You may want to set up address information, type of business information, and payment information on three different pages. When the last form is submitted, you want to send all of the information from all three pages. Using hidden fields, you can store information from page to page and then submit the entire package at the appropriate time.

Formatting Forms by Using Tables

One approach to form layout is to use non-breaking spaces, " " wherever needed to manually line up the fields and columns on your form. See Listing 13.4.

Listing 13.4   Source Code for FIG13_4.HTM

```
<HTML>
<title> "Magnificent Multi-Column Form"</title>
<H3><center>ORDER FORM</center></H3>
<form>
<table>
<tr><td>
First Name:      <INPUT TYPE=text
➥NAME="firstname" SIZE=15>
</td>
<td>
Last Name:
        <INPUT TYPE=text  NAME="lastname" SIZE=20>
</td>
```

```
<tr><td>
Street Address: <INPUT TYPE=text  NAME="Address1" SIZE=15>
</td>
<td><P>
ST   ZIP:       <INPUT TYPE=text
➥NAME="Address2" SIZE=20>
</td>
<tr><td>
Work Phone:    <INPUT TYPE=text  NAME="phone1" SIZE=15>
</td>
<td><P>
Home Phone: <INPUT TYPE=text  NAME="phone2" SIZE=20>
</td>
<tr><td> <BR>
<B> How will you pay for your purchase?</B><BR>
<INPUT TYPE="RADIO"  NAME="Payment"   VALUE="MC">MasterCard<BR>
<INPUT TYPE="RADIO"  NAME="Payment"   VALUE="Visa">Visa<BR>
<INPUT TYPE="RADIO"  NAME="Payment"   VALUE="AmEx">American Express<P>
<td>
  <BR><B>         Check
➥all that apply.</B> <BR>
        <INPUT TYPE="CHECKBOX"
➥NAME="Overnight" VALUE="Yes">Ship Overnight<BR>
        <INPUT TYPE="CHECKBOX"
➥NAME="SameAddress" VALUE="Yes">Ship to Above
 Address<BR>
        <INPUT TYPE="CHECKBOX"
➥NAME="CallFirst" VALUE="Yes">Call Before
 Shipping           
</td>
<tr><td>
 <INPUT TYPE="SUBMIT"  VALUE="Submit" ><BR>
 <INPUT TYPE="RESET"  VALUE="Reset " >
</tr>
</form>
</table></html>
```

As you can see in Figure 13.4, the results are typically close, but not quite perfect, when it comes to lining up columns of information in this manner.

You'll probably find that, frequently, a more concise, easier to implement option is in order when it comes to laying out the form and making sure it makes the most possible sense to users. In many cases, this entails multiple columns and multiple rows of information that must be laid out to support several different browsers. This can be quite a task if you plan to use non-breaking spaces.

Perhaps the best approach in the HTML world is to use tables on your forms to accomplish these types of tasks. Tables can be used to create two or more column forms that can display a large number of text input boxes on a single 24-line Web page. With multi-column forms, the end user does not need to scroll down to finish a form or to reach the SUBMIT or RESET buttons.

FIG. 13.4

Lining up information on forms by using non-breaking spaces can be tricky at best.

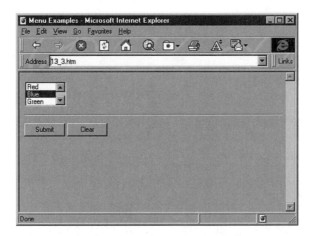

Another advantage of using tables is that the tables are able to scale properly to the user's browser working area. If you use percentage sizes on your table definition, the percentages will be used relative to the overall display size currently in effect when the page is loaded, preserving the layout of your form.

When using the <td> tag, columns can be spaced on the page by using the following method, (where a full-sized page equals 100 percent).

```
<tr>
    <td width=45%> . . . <td>
    <td width=35%> . . . <td>
    <td width=20%> . . . <td>
<tr>
```

Notice that the sum of the three widths is 100 percent. By using <td> percentages, it is much easier to horizontally position columns containing graphics on the Web page.

Tables may also be nested in tables to precisely position multiple column lists on a particular part of a Web page.

▶ For more information on tables, refer to Chapter 19, "Advanced HTML."

Understanding How Browsers Send Form Data

Now that you have seen what goes into creating the form, it's important to understand what happens when the user finally submits the form, whether it be by clicking a submit button or pressing Enter on a single-field form.

You may recall that forms use one of two different approaches to submit information—either a GET or a POST action as called out in the opening FORM tag.

```
<FORM METHOD=POST ACTION="/scripts/que/forms/select.idc">
```

The opening tag calls out the method of transmission and it indicates what the receiving process will be in the Action attribute. All of this takes place over the standard browser protocol, HTTP. The way the information is transferred to the server will depend on which way the form is set up to send in the information.

You'll recall from other discussions throughout this book that URLs are exchanged between the client system and the server, with the requested page being called out in the URL. This indicates to the server software which page should be returned. Whether you're using the GET or POST approach, both start out by using the Action parameter as the base URL. In the preceding example, it would be the equivalent of manually entering the following for the URL you want to open:

```
http://scripts/que/forms/select.idc
```

Of course, this doesn't transfer any field information to the server. That's where the GET and POST methods come in.

Using the GET Approach   If you use the GET approach to submit information, the information from your form is simply appended to the URL. The data is separated from the base URL by a question mark and the information is then added to the address.

```
http://scripts/que/forms/select.idc?Username=Steve+Wynkoop&UserPass=Password
```

You'll recognize the Username and UserPass parameters as the named fields from an earlier example. These are the control names you establish when you name the text and password fields on your form. The text entered by the user is placed after an equal sign and multiple fields are separated by an ampersand "&" sign.

Relative to how the form information is received by the server, the user-supplied information is provided in the same format. You may recall, however, that if you use the GET approach, since all information is appended to the URL, you can run into problems if the resulting URL request string is too long for the server to handle. Long strings often are approximately 256 characters, though it varies from server to server.

Using the POST Method   The POST method is the preferred method of sending information to the server because it alleviates the problem of too much information being passed as part of the URL. The POST method sends the form information as a type of upload to the server, allowing the browser to send the form contents in a transaction started when the URL is received by the server. You'll notice that with the GET option, you can see the modified URL with the data appended when you access a site after pressing submit.

With the POST method, you'll not have the modified URL, only the original URL with the question mark added to the end, indicating that there is form data to follow. The data is sent in the same manner as with the GET option where a pair of information is created, matching the name of the field with the contents of the field as entered by the user.

In some browsers on the market today, you have the ability to use the POST method to send more than just fields. With Netscape Navigator, for example, you can send entire files using this approach. You can drag a file to Navigator and drop it on the workspace. If the server supports the operation, the file will be uploaded by using the POST method.

Though sending files is not a mainstream application of this protocol yet, it's a sure bet it will be in the very near future as more users gain broader access to the storage systems on the Internet.

Using the Mailto Command

By using the mailto command, form data can be processed and sent as e-mail to specified URLs. Instead of using a long CGI script path in the form header, type in the word **mailto** followed by the e-mail address (see Listing 13.5.)

Listing 13.5   Code Fragment

```
<H3>This is an  Example of the use of mailto-forms:</H3>
<FORM METHOD=POST ACTION="mailto:anyuser"anyaddress.com"><P>
<PRE>Input your name:<INPUT TYPE="TEXT" NAME="NAME" SIZE=30,1 MAXLENGTH=30><P>
Select one option and SEND:<P>
<SELECT SIZE=3 NAME="Selection"><OPTION SELECTED>VISA<OPTION>MASTERCARD<OPTION>
➥AMERICAN EXPRESS</SELECT>
<INPUT TYPE="SUBMIT" VALUE="SEND">
<INPUT TYPE="RESET" VALUE="CLEAR">
</PRE><P>
</FORM>
```

In order to have e-mail that is formatted, additional programming is needed. Either CGI script written in C/C++, Perl, (UNIX), Aida, or Visual Basic can be used on commercially available software. One example of currently available software is Allaire's Cold Fusion—which can be used by applications developers to rapidly create applications. Because Cold Fusion uses English-like commands, code maintenance is not especially difficult (see Listings 13.6 and 13.7).

Listing 13.6   HTML Document Form Input

```
<HTML>
<TITLE>Quick Order Form</TITLE>
<H1>Order Form</H1>
Please enter Your shipping address:<P>
<FORM ACTION="/cgi-bin/dbml.exe?template=c:\cfusion\template\cfpro\mailer.dbm"
➥METHOD=POST>
Your name:<INPUT TYPE="TEXT"  NAME=Full_Name"
÷SIZE="30" MAXLENGTH="30"> <P>
Street Address: <INPUT TYPE="Text"  NAME="Address1"   SIZE="30"><P>
```

```
City,   ST ZIP:<INPUT TYPE="Text"  NAME="Address2"   SIZE="30"><P>
<H2> How will you pay for your purchase?</H2>
<INPUT TYPE="RADIO"  NAME="Payment"   VALUE="MC">MasterCard<P>
<INPUT TYPE="RADIO"  NAME="Payment"   VALUE="Visa">Visa<P>
<INPUT TYPE="RADIO"  NAME="Payment"   VALUE="AmEx">American Express<P>
<INPUT TYPE="SUBMIT"  VALUE="Submit" ><P>
</FORM>
</HTML>
```

N O T E The form header contains path information that invokes Cold Fusion on the Web Server, as well as starting up a template, which is a short file containing tags that send the e-mail. ■

Listing 13.7 mailer.dbm

```
<HTML>
<HEAD><TITLE> EasyMail Program </TITLE></HEAD>
<BODY>
<CFOUTPUT>
<!---The next line goes back to the sender--->
<H3> Your E-mail has been sent.</h3>
</dboutput>
<HR>
</BODY>
</HTML>

  <CFMAIL
    FROM="Form.EmailAddress#
    TO="yourname"yourcorp.com"
    SUBJECT="E-mail sent to you!">

This is the new location of #Form.firstname#  #Form.lastname# :

Extension: #Form.Extension#
Email: #Form.Email#
Building: #Form.location#

This is a SAMPLE message
that is very nicely formatted.

</CFMAIL>
</BODY>
</CFMAIL>


< --- OUTPUT -

From: anyname.anycorp.com
To: yourname"yourcorp.com
Subject: E-Mail sent to you!
```

continues

Part

II

Ch

13

Listing 13.7   Continued

```
This is the new location of Jonathan Smith:

Extension: 8756
E-Mail: anyname"anycorp.com
Building: Bldg2

This is a SAMPLE message
which is nicely formatted.

....................................
```

N O T E   The CFMAIL tags begin the e-mail output section. This template, which uses Allaire's Cold
Fusion software on the Web server, can be modified to include additional fields or message
content. ▨

From Here...

The following chapters provide additional information that you may find helpful in creating
your forms for use on the Internet.

- Chapter 16, "Conducting Transactions on the Internet," will provide in-depth information
  on how to enable sales-type transactions on your Web pages.
- Chapter 18, "Basic HTML Techniques," will show you how to get started with the HTML
  on which you'll base your forms pages.
- Chapter 19, "Advanced HTML," provides additional information on HTML and the use of
  tables and other techniques to keep your pages looking the best they can.
- Chapter 20, "ActiveX and the Internet," shows how you can implement ActiveX controls
  on your pages, adding new capabilities for offering choices and feedback to the users of
  your pages.

Enhancing Your Web Site

## CHAPTER 14

Marketing Your Web Site

Many people take the "if you build it, they will come" approach to marketing their Web sites. But creating a perfect Web site doesn't guarantee that your target audience will visit it. The Internet has over 50 million Web pages at over 230,000 Web sites. You must help your audience find you, or you'll be lost in the crowd.

This chapter shows you how to increase the number of visits to your Web site and how to market to your target audience. ■

How to target specific audiences

Your marketing efforts should focus on the people who need your products or services, so you'll get better results with less effort.

How to make your marketing strategies work together

The Internet isn't the only way to market your products and services. By coordinating all of your marketing efforts, your results will improve.

How to make search tools find your Web site

Many people find information on the Web by using search engines and directories. You need to be sure that these tools provide links to your Web pages.

How to advertise your Web site

You can get other Web sites to link to yours by exchanging links or advertising. Both strategies can be used to focus on your target audience.

How to use the rest of the Internet

The Web isn't the only way to promote your business or organization on the Internet. You can also use e-mail, newsgroups, and mailing lists. But, use them carefully!

Targeting Your Audience

For most Web sites, your marketing efforts shouldn't just focus on maximizing the number of visits, or *hits*. Instead you should attract the right people to your site—those who will buy your products or services.

Before you begin marketing your Web site, decide who you want to attract. Think about the age, gender, geographical location, income, education, and occupation of your target audience.

Web users are a valuable audience because they typically have above-average income and educational levels. Every six months since January 1994, researchers at Georgia Tech in Atlanta have surveyed thousands of Internet users. According to their most recent survey, the average household income for an Internet user is $59,000 and 56 percent of Internet users have college degrees.

The survey of more than 11,000 Internet users also found that the percentage of females using the Web is over 30 percent and is increasing, as is the number of people in countries other than the United States. As Figure 14.1 shows, Internet users have a wide range of occupations, but people who work in education, computers, management, and other professionals are most likely to use the Web. For detailed survey results see **http://www.cc.gatech.edu/gvu/user_surveys/**.

Once you have a general picture of your audience, think about its related interests. If you sell camping gear, your audience may also be interested in travel, sporting equipment, and the environment. If the members of your target audience are corporate decision-makers, they might also be interested in using the Web for stock research and financial news. Considering your audience's related interests will give you ideas about other places on the Web where you can market or advertise your site.

You may find that different sections of your Web site attract different audiences. For example, if you make cutting-edge scientific equipment, you might want potential customers to read detailed product and sales information, existing customers to read customer support information, and students to read educational information.

Considering Your Target Audience When Designing Your Web Site

When you design your Web site, you should also think about your target audience. Chapter 19, "Advanced HTML," talks more about this, but here are a few hints:

- Does your audience access the Web primarily from slower home connections or from faster connections at work or school? If a large portion of your audience has a slow connection to the Web, you should minimize your file sizes and be sure that your Web site makes sense to those who browse without loading images. The Georgia Tech Research Corporation survey found that nearly two-thirds of Internet users access the Web with 28.8K or 14.4K modems.

  Be aware that faster technologies, such as cable modems, are just around the corner. Soon your audience will expect to see more animation, sound, and video. You'll also need to make sure your server can keep up with growing bandwidth as you market your Web site and your traffic increases.

- Is your audience attracted by a bold, modern look? Or, would it be more comfortable visiting a Web site with a more traditional look? For example, compare the design of the HotWired Web site at **http://www.hotwired.com/frontdoor/** to the Janus Funds site at **http://networth.galt.com/www/home/mutual/janus/**.

- Is your audience likely to use the latest software and Web browser plug-ins? Or, is it uncomfortable with downloading and installing viewers for new types of media?

- Once you've attracted your audience, be sure it keeps coming back by providing useful information. Also, add fresh content to your Web site on a regular basis.

Knowing If You Reach Your Target Audience

You'll want to get feedback about whether your marketing efforts are working—and about which strategies are most effective. The following list shows how you can get this information.

- Provide feedback forms, a guestbook, or some other way for visitors to register at your Web site. A form such as the one shown in Figure 14.1 gives you a chance to find out how visitors found your site. Keep track of this information so that you can continue to market and advertise in the places that give you the best results.

FIG. 14.1
This feedback form asks how the reader found the site.

- Access log files can include information about which Web pages contain the links that your visitors followed to find your Web site. See Chapter 11, "Usage Statistics," for detailed information about reading access logs.

- You can survey customers formally or informally to find out how many of them are aware that you have a Web site and how many of them have visited it. For example, you can have your telephone support staff briefly ask callers about their Web use.

Part
III
Ch
14

If you find you aren't reaching your target audience, keep reading to learn how to market and advertise your Web site.

Coordinating Your Marketing Strategy

Marketing your Web site should not be separate from your other marketing efforts. By combining them and by using some additional low-cost strategies, you'll increase your results.

N O T E   According to a recent survey of Internet users by the Georgia Tech Research Corporation, people learn about Web sites from the following sources, so your Web site marketing efforts should target several of them. (Survey respondents could choose multiple information sources.)

Links from other pages	90.7%
Search engines	83.1%
Magazines	64.7%
Word of mouth/friends	58.5%
Usenet newsgroups	44.4%
Newspapers	39.3%
Television	34.6%
E-mail signatures	32.5%
Books	26.9%

The following list shows some ways to combine your marketing efforts.

- If your company or organization produces printed marketing or other advertising materials, be sure your URL is included. If you are the Webmaster for your company, this is your chance to increase your visibility within the company by coordinating your efforts with other departments.

- Include your URL on business cards, letterhead, invoices, packing lists, catalogs, newsletters, and other corporate identity materials. If you have a business location open to the public, you might want to install a computer so that customers can visit your Web site.

- Encourage employees to include your organization's URL in their e-mail signature as shown in Figure 14.2.

- You may also want to educate your employees about Netiquette. Although blatant advertising is frowned upon in many newsgroups and e-mail lists, providing information about products or services your company provides and your Web address for more information is generally accepted. See the "Direct E-Mail" section for detailed information about e-mail and newsgroup advertising Netiquette.

- If your Web site provides customer support information, be sure your product directs customers to your site. In this way you can save a lot of money on phone calls and postage.

FIG. 14.2

This e-mail signature includes the company's URL.

Mutual fund brokers are required to provide customers with a fund prospectus before their purchases. Before the Web, brokers had to mail the prospectus. Now many companies encourage their customers to read the information on the Web. This strategy enables people to invest faster and it cuts brokers' postage and printing costs.

 If possible, make your URL short and easy to remember or to guess. Which URL would you remember better if you saw it on a television commercial?

`www.companyname.com`

or

`http://division.somename.com/product/index.html`

Many marketers now omit the *http://* prefix from the URL they advertise. Recent versions of popular browsers, such as Netscape Navigator and Internet Explorer, automatically add this prefix when it is omitted from the URL. Experienced Web users will add http:// if their browsers require it, but newer users often find http:// confusing because they don't understand what it means.

Making Search Engines Find Your Web Site

The recent Georgia Tech Research Corporation survey found that 83.1 percent of Web users find information by using search engines, such as WebCrawler and Infoseek. How does all that information get into the search engine?

Search engines have *robot* programs that travel around the Web by following links, and they index the text in the Web pages that they find. You can submit your URL to these search engines so that their robots will visit your Web site.

Many people also use category-based directories, such as Yahoo! and Magellan. Items are added to the categories by hand, so it usually takes longer to get your Web site listed in a directory.

There are a number of ways to make search engines find your pages and to increase the chances that your pages will be listed near the beginning of the search results. The methods are discussed in the following sections.

URL Submission Services

There are *lots* of search engines and directories on the Web. Most have a page with a form that you can use to submit your Web site for inclusion. Look for links that say "Add URL" or "Add Site."

Part

III

Ch

14

Submitting your Web site to each search tool individually takes a long time however. Luckily, there are services that will submit your site to multiple search tools. You can type information about your site once and send it to several search tools. Most of the submission services are free for 10 to 20 popular search tools. To submit your site to their full list, often more than 300 search tools, the charge varies from $60 to $500.

After you submit your Web site, it could take up to a month for the search engines to list it. Although the robot that indexes your site will probably visit within a few days, the information it finds usually is added to the database every two to four weeks. Listings in selective directories might take even longer because their employees must visit your site to decide whether to include it.

If you think your Web site is especially cool, go ahead and submit it for awards like "Cool Site of the Day." For a list of the hundreds of awards Web sites can win, go to **http://www.yahoo.com/Computers_and_Internet/Internet/World_Wide_Web/Best_of_the_Web/**.

N O T E What follows is a list of some of the search engines and directories that are currently popular. You can check the ones to which you've submitted your Web site.

Of course, new search tools are added to the Web all the time. Today's most popular search tool might be eclipsed by a new one tomorrow. The best strategy is to list your Web site in as many free locations as possible.

Popular search engines include the following:

AltaVista: **http://www.altavista.digital.com/**
Excite: **http://www.excite.com/**
HotBot: **http://www.hotbot.com/**
Infoseek: **http://www.infoseek.com/**
Lycos: **http://www.lycos.com/**
Open Text: **http://www.opentext.net/**
WebCrawler: **http://www.webcrawler.com/**

Popular subject directories include the following:

Yahoo!: **http://www.yahoo.com/**
Galaxy: **http://www.einet.net/galaxy.html**
Magellan: **http://www.mckinley.com/**

Other kinds of sites to which you can submit your URLs include the following:

Business and industry-specific directories
Internet Malls
Regional directories
"Site of the Day" directories
Site review directories
"Yellow Page" directories
"What's New" directories

Submit It!   The most well-known submission service is Submit It!, at **http:// www.submit-it.com/**. Submit It! is shown in Figure 14.3. It currently enables you to add your Web site address to 16 popular search tools for free. For about $60, you can submit pages to their growing list of search tools, which currently numbers more than 200. Educational and nonprofit groups can get this service for only $30. Submit It! saves the information you provide, and your $60 subscription enables you to make changes and to submit your site to the new search tools they add during your one year subscription. You can also print reports of the search tools to which you've submitted your Web site.

FIG. 14.3
Submit It! helps you submit your URL to many search engines and directories.

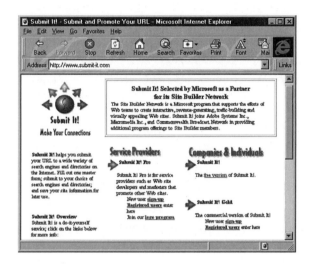

1. Go to **http://www.submit-it.com/**.
2. Click on the links in the Submit It! overview to get more information to help you decide whether you want to use the free version of Submit It! or if you want to pay to use Submit It! Gold or Submit It! Pro.
3. To use the free service, follow the link and fill out the form that asks for information about the page you want to submit.
4. To use Submit It! Gold or Submit It! Pro, follow the link to sign up. You need to fill out a form to indicate how you'll pay for the service. When Submit It! receives your payment, they'll send you an account number by e-mail. Then you can use the account number to access a more powerful submission system. An online manual explains how to use this submission system.

Other Submission Services   If you use a submission service, be sure to keep a list of the locations to which it submits your URL. Note that a number of the popular search engines in the checklist are not included in the free group, such as Magellan, Excite, HotBot, Lycos, and Open Text.

To submit your URL to even more locations, you can either use the Add URL page for the individual search tools you find, or you can use any of the following services:

Part

III

Ch

14

■ !Register-It!, at **http://www.register-it.com/**, is similar to Submit It! It will submit your URL to 16 search tools, and most of them are different than the ones Submit It! provides for free. Their free list includes Excite, Lycos, and Open Text. The !Register-It! Professional service submits to more than 300 search locations for about $500.

■ Use the following pages, which provide several links to the "Add URL" page of many Web search tools:

  ● Go Net-Wide, at **http://www.shout.net/~whitney/html/gopublic.html**, provides an alphabetized list of search tools with the most popular ones in bold type.

  ● The Internet Promotions Megalist, at **http://www.2020tech.com/submit.html**, contains a long list of search tools that includes a number of regional directories and industry-specific categories.

  ● OnLine's Web Promote, at **http://www.online-biz.com/promote/**, provides links to the "Add URL" page of more than 600 search tools.

  ● WebStep Top 100, at **http://www.mmgco.com/top100.html**, contains links to the top 100 places to list your Web site for free.

Remember to keep track of the search tools to which you submit your Web site. A list is useful if your site's address changes or if the contents of your site change substantially.

Moving Your Web Site Up in the Search Results

Being indexed by a search engine doesn't automatically make your page easy to find. The text and HTML tags in your page determine which search keywords will match your page and whether your page will be near the top of the list or near the bottom.

Different search engines index pages differently. Some index all of the text and others index only the first few paragraphs. Some give weighted scores, with higher scores given to words found in the <TITLE> tag and in any <H1> or other heading tags.

The following are some strategies that cause search engines to list your pages closer to the top.

■ In the <HEAD> section of your page, include a <META> tag like the following:

```
<META NAME="KEYWORD" CONTENT="keyword list">
```

The keyword list should include all of the words you can think of that a person might use to find the information you provide. Remember to include various forms of words, such as singular and plural nouns and multiple verb forms. For example, you might include "dive, dives, diving" in the keyword list.

If your Web site provides information about scuba diving in California, the <HEAD> section for your main page might look like the following example:

```
<HEAD>
<TITLE>Kelp Dive Tours</TITLE>
<META NAME="KEYWORD" CONTENT="scuba, scuba dive, scuba diving,
```

```
                        dive, dives, diving, ocean, underwater, kelp, sea lions,
tank,
                  marine, California, Catalina, Channel Islands, Monterey,
Pacific">
</HEAD>
```

Of the major search engines, AltaVista, Infoseek, HotBot, and Open Text currently use the <META> tag keywords.

- You can also include a description of a page in the <HEAD> section. Some search engines will use this description in the list of search matches. If you don't include a description here, most search engines use the first part of the first paragraph of text in your page. Include the description in the <HEAD> section as follows:

```
<HEAD>
<TITLE>Kelp Dive Tours</TITLE>
              <META NAME="DESCRIPTION" CONTENT="Dive the beautiful kelp
forests
of the California coast with Kelp Dive Tours. Our Web site has
              real-time visibility and temperature data for 10 dive
sites.">
</HEAD>
```

The <META> tag is particularly useful if your page uses images to display words or to communicate your message, and if the first paragraph of actual text doesn't make sense without the images.

Of the major search engines, AltaVista, Infoseek, and HotBot currently use a description provided with a <META> tag.

- You should also include important keywords in the page <TITLE> and in the <H1>, <H2>, and <H3> tags. Some search engines do not look at the <META> tags, but almost all look at the title. Many search engines give higher scores to text in the page title and in headings. Both HotBot and Lycos give high priority to words in the <TITLE>. Excite gives high priority to words in the first punctuated sentence in the page.

- Some search engines sort results with equal scores alphabetically, like Yahoo!. If it makes sense, give your page a <TITLE> beginning with the letter "A" or a number. Be sure your title is still descriptive. Don't just use a list of keywords preceded by "1." People should know what you have to offer from the title listed by the search tool.

Technically, the sort order uses the ASCII values of the characters. This means that the sequence of the characters before the uppercase letters is:

```
! " # $ % & ' ( ) * + , - . / 0 1 2 3 4 5 6 7 8 9 : ; < = ? ? @
```

However, Yahoo! and other search tools can't search for some of these characters because they have special meanings to programs that run on the Web. For example, Yahoo! ignores ! in a search string, so it's best to avoid using a company or product name that includes characters that search tools can't find.

- If you aren't sure which category best fits your Web site, choose the one that comes first in the alphabet. For example, when you search Yahoo!, matches are sorted alphabetically according to their categories.

Part
III

Ch
14

■ Some search engines give higher scores to repeated words. Others may penalize you for repeated words. For example, Infoseek doesn't count keywords that your page repeats more than seven times. Lycos also does not count words that occur many times.

■ Be sure the keyword density in the page is high. Many search engines compare the number of times the search term occurs to the total number of words in the page. By minimizing the number of non-keywords in the page and maximizing the number of keywords, you can move your page higher in the list of results.

■ If your page uses frames, use the <META> tags and be sure that the <NOFRAMES> section of the page contains a descriptive paragraph with your search keywords. You don't want the page description shown by a search tool to say, "Use Netscape to view this page." Most search engines don't automatically index files referenced in the <FRAME> tags. Be sure that the text in the <NOFRAMES> section links to important pages on your Web site so that the search engines can follow links and index these other pages.

■ The preceding suggestion is also useful if your page is created on-the-fly with JavaScript or any other language run by the browser. Search engines won't run these scripts, so be sure any search keywords you use are included as <META> tags or as text in the page. Also, be sure to put JavaScript statement inside comments (like this: <!- - comment - ->) or as attributes inside other tags to prevent search engines from indexing your script statements.

■ If your pages contain graphics instead of text, be sure the text is also included, even if it is lower on the page. For example, if you use an image for your company logo, be sure that your company name appears somewhere in the text. This will also help people who browse with images turned off.

■ Use the alt attribute for the <IMG> tag to specify alternate text for images. Some search engines will index this alternate text.

■ Some search engines sort matching pages according to their popularity, which is based on the number of other Web pages they find that link a page. Excite, Lycos, Magellan, and WebCrawler currently use such popularity rankings. You can submit the pages of other Web sites that have links to your pages to the search engines to help move your page up in the search results.

Blocking Access by Robots

Search engines use robots to crawl around the Web looking for pages to index. When you submit the address of a Web page to a search engine, the robot will be scheduled to index that page. Most robots index the address you submit and the pages to which it links. Robots index from one to three levels of linked pages at each site.

You can hide pages from robots for any of the following reasons:

- If you have temporary pages or pages with content that changes frequently, you might not want a search engine to index them because they may not exist later or the content may be completely different.

- You may want to hide detailed pages and pages with duplicate information so the search engine lists your home page instead of the less important pages.

- You may have links to CGI scripts that you don't want robots to use, such as links for voting on issues.

- Robots are used for things other than creating indexes for search engines. In fact, almost any programmer can create a robot to travel the Web. Some of the robots ask for files repeatedly and can really slow a server on a slow computer or a computer with a slow Internet connection. If you are getting a lot of traffic from robots, you may want to limit the pages they look at or to exclude some robots altogether.

To hide pages from robots, create a file called robots.txt in your page root directory. For example, if your server's URL is **http://www.mycompany.com**, the URL for the file should be **http://www.mycompany.com/robots.txt**. You can't create separate files in each directory because robots only look at the file in the page root directory.

The file enables you to specify which directories and files you don't want robots to visit. You can do this for all robots or for specific robots. Polite robots check this file and follow the rules you set. Listing 14.1 shows an example of a robots.txt file.

Listing 14.1   A Sample ROBOTS.TXT File# /robots.txt File for http://www.mycompany.com/

```
# Lets our own robot index all our pages.
User-agent: internal_robot
Disallow:

# Tells two unwanted robots they shouldn't look at any files.
User-agent: unwanted_robot_1
User-agent: unwanted_robot_2
Disallow: /

# Tells all other robots they can look at any files except the
# ones in the "tmp" directory and the /sales/hidden.html file.
User-agent: *
Disallow: /tmp/
Disallow: /sales/hidden.html
```

You can include comments that begin with #, and you can use multiple User-agent or Disallow lines in a group.

Part

III

Ch

14

The User-agent lines should match the User-agent HTTP header used by the robot. You can usually find this information in your server's access logs. See Chapter 11 for details about reading access logs. Use * as the User-agent for a set of rules you want to apply to any robots you don't mention elsewhere in the file.

The Disallow lines indicate the path to directories and files the robot should not access. The path you specify should be relative to the page root directory because URLs on your Web site that begin with this path are disallowed. For example:

■ Disallow: /

Disallows robot access to all files on your server.

■ Disallow: /prices

Disallows robot access to all files in the /prices directory and any file in the pageroot directory that begins with "prices."

■ Disallow: /prices/

Disallows robot access to all files in the /prices directory.

■ Disallow: /prices/old/

Disallows robot access to all files in the /prices/old directory.

■ Disallow: /prices/hidden.html

Disallows robot access to the /prices/hidden.html file.

You can't use paths like /product/*_old.html. The path must be an URL or partial URL, so you can't use wildcards or other expressions to match files as you do on a UNIX or DOS command line.

If you don't have permission to create or change the robots.txt file in the page root directory, some robots also check for the following <META> tags in HTML files:

■ <META NAME="ROBOTS" CONTENT="NOINDEX">

Tells search engine robots they shouldn't index this page. They can follow links from this page to other pages, however.

■ <META NAME="ROBOTS" CONTENT="NOFOLLOW">

Tells search engine robots they can index this page, but they shouldn't follow links to other pages.

■ <META NAME="ROBOTS" CONTENT="NONE"

Tells search engine robots they shouldn't index this page or follow its links.

TIP Although polite robots follow the rules you provide, robot programmers aren't forced to make their robots follow the rules. Robots can access any file that someone browsing the Web can access, unless you require a username and password. If your Web site is being swamped by a robot that doesn't look at the /robots.txt file or the <META NAME="ROBOTS"> tag, see **http://info.webcrawler.com/mak/ projects/robots** for information about contacting the robot's owner.

Getting Additional Links to Your Site

Following links from other pages is the most common method used to find Web sites. There are several ways to get other sites to link to yours:

- Reciprocal links from related sites
- Internet Link Exchange
- Paid advertising

The following sections describe how to get these types of links.

Reciprocal Links

How do you get other Web sites to link to yours? The best way is to simply ask.

Links from sites related to your business are especially valuable because there is likely to be some overlap between their audiences and your target audience. Think about related companies and make a list that includes the following categories. Remember to talk with people in other departments to get a more complete list.

- Corporate partners
- Sponsors
- Customers or clients
- Suppliers and vendors
- Distributors and other sales channels
- Employees
- Industry groups in which your company participates
- Nonprofit groups to which your company donates
- Any other organizations that might be willing to link to your Web site

Find out which of the organizations and people on your list have Web sites. Send e-mail to the Webmasters for the sites, invite them to visit your Web site, and tell them that you want to trade links.

On your Web site, you can make links wherever you mention organizations that have agreed to trade links. Alternately, you can create a separate page with links to all of the organizations that have links to your site.

Some commercial Web sites have a policy against linking to other sites. Their goal is to keep people at their site for as long as possible, and they view links to other sites as "Exit doors." However, a list of links to related businesses can be a handy information resource that your audience can save as a bookmark in order to return again and again. Be sure your link page entices repeat visitors to look at the rest of your site by updating it with fresh messages about the latest additions.

Part
III

Ch
14

TIP Make it as easy as possible for others to create links to your Web site. Provide your logo in a variety of sizes so they can display it and link it to your Web site. Write a short summary of your products or services for them. You can even e-mail the HTML code you want them to use.

Free Links from the Internet Link Exchange

A more formal way of getting free links to your Web site is to participate in the Internet Link Exchange. This exchange program displays over a million advertisements per day on over 40,000 Web pages that have agreed to trade banner advertising links with other Web sites.

Each time the banner ad on your site is displayed, you get half of an advertising "point." For each full point, your own ad is displayed once. The other half of the ads are for the Internet Link Exchange program itself and for the companies that sponsor this free service.

Figure 14.4 shows a sample banner that might appear on your site if you participate in the Internet Link Exchange:

FIG. 14.4
Internet Link Exchange banners look similar to this one.

Commercial and noncommercial sites can join the Internet Link Exchange, and you can choose to display ads for commercial sites, noncommercial sites, or both. Sites that are pornographic, racist, or otherwise inappropriate can't join. There is also a rating system you can use to prevent your site from displaying ads for other potentially offensive sites, like those that promote alcohol, contain partial nudity, or use strong language.

To join the Internet Link Exchange, do the following:

1. Visit **http://www.linkexchange.com/** to learn more about the program. It also has a newsgroup for members.
2. Fill out the form provided to join the service.
3. You'll receive an e-mail message that gives you a HTML code to add to your page. The code displays a linked advertising banner. After you add the code to your page, each time someone views the banner, half a point will be added to your account.
4. Create an advertising banner for your site and submit it so that other sites will begin to display it. See the section on "Creating Better Banner Graphics" for hints about how to design better banners.

 TIP A number of the Internet Link Exchange members have volunteered to design banner ads for free. Many are skilled graphic artists who want to show off their work, and the Internet Link Exchange site provides links to their Web sites. However because they are willing to work for free, there is usually a long waiting list. Browse through the winners of the Internet Link Exchange banner design contest to find other banner design experts.

Paid Advertising Banners

The amount of paid advertising on the Web has grown dramatically in the last year. Estimates of the total market for Web advertising in the year 2000 are as high as one billion to five billion dollars. Most of the advertising is in the form of banners.

You've probably seen ads on the Web like the ones in Figure 14.5. Often, the ads are for big companies like Microsoft, Netscape, AT&T, and IBM. They have huge Web advertising budgets. Does that mean your company can't afford to advertise on the Web? Not at all. If you focus on a narrower audience, you may be able to afford to place your ads on the same sites as the big companies.

FIG. 14.5

These are some examples of advertising banners.

Purchasing Advertising   You don't need to go through an advertising broker to purchase Web advertising. Most search engines that accept advertising have a link to advertising information. If you don't see it on the main page, try links that say things like "Info," "Help," or "About this search engine." Typically, you can send e-mail to request an advertising rate card. You'll also get information about the sizes of banner images and the types of image files they accept. Most search tools accept only GIFs with maximum file sizes of about 7K. Some search tools accept animated GIFs.

 TIP Details about advertising on individual Web sites change frequently. The following are URLs and e-mail addresses for advertising information from several of the major search engines:

Deja News: **http://www.dejanews.com/ratecard.html**

Excite: **http://www.excite.com/Info/advertising.html**

HotBot: **rick@hotwired.com**

Infoseek: **sponsors@infoseek.com**

Lycos: **http://www.lycos.com/lycosinc/advertising.html**

Open Text: **http://index.opentext.net/advertising/advertise_here.html**

WebCrawler: **http://www.gnn.com/ads/index.html**

Yahoo!: **http://www.yahoo.com/docs/pr/adop.html**

Most of the major search tools have a minimum advertising charge of $500 to $1,000 per month. Each time someone views your banner it usually costs from two to six cents. Often they will quote their rates by giving you a CPM figure, which is the cost for 1,000 displays. So you can limit the number of times your ads are shown to the number you can afford.

In fact, some rates for advertising on the Web may go down. So many Web sites offer advertising that the supply may be greater than the demand. More than 60 percent of Web ads appear on the top 10 advertising sites, including Infoseek, Lycos, and Yahoo!. Sites that accept advertising but aren't in the top 10 are under pressure to lower their rates. Advertising on a smaller Web site related to your industry may be cost effective. To find lower-cost sites, search the Web for advertising rates and a keyword related to your industry.

The major search tools enable you to display your ads only in specific categories or when people use specific search keywords. In fact, Lycos plans to enable you to target people browsing from an e-mail domain in a particular country or company.

Target a specific audience for your product. If you sell mountain climbing equipment, advertising to people who don't climb mountains won't do you much good. So you should choose "climbing" and "mountain" as the search keywords for your advertising.

Some search engines enable you to purchase a particular position in the search results for a particular keyword. On Open Text you can buy a "Preferred Listing" that lists your Web site at any slot from 1 to 10 when a search keyword you selected is used.

Other Web sites that accept advertising include many that provide current news, sports, or stock quotes. Think about the types of sites your target audience might visit, then, see if any of them accept advertising. In particular, look for sites that enable you to target topics related to your business.

Creating Better Banner Graphics   Banner advertising usually has two goals: to create name recognition and to draw attention to your Web site.

The first goal is to create name recognition or branding. At the very least you want people who hear your company name to think, "Yes, I've heard of them." Almost anyone can create a Web site, so name recognition is an important part of convincing people that you're a real company.

The second goal is to draw people into your Web site. To do this, you must get people to click your ad. The ratio of the number of people who see the ad to the number of people who click the ad is called the *click-through ratio*.

Click-through ratios will vary substantially depending on the ad you use and how well you target your audience. Typical click-through ratios can range from 250:1 (0.4%) to 10:1 (10%). Lycos reports an average click-through ratio of 25:1, but there is no guarantee when you purchase advertising.

To improve the click-through ratio for your banner ads, follow these rules:

- Be sure your image looks professional. Pay a freelance graphic designer to create it if you don't have one on staff.
- Use striking colors that attract attention. Because of the way our eyes work, colors like red and yellow seem closer and attract more attention. Colors like blue and purple seem farther away.

■ Create interest by using an entertaining, funny, or controversial headline. A little mystery is good, but don't turn people off with references to political or religious viewpoints with which they may disagree strongly.

■ Use the word "Free" if possible, even if you have to find something free to offer. For example, provide free information if it's valuable to your audience. "Win" is another good word to use. Provide games, contests, coupons, and information to attract your target audience. Try to make people really want what you have to offer.

■ Include a call to action. Usually this means putting the words "Click here" in your image. It seems a bit silly as most people know that Web ads are linked to the advertiser's Web site, but including them almost always improves the click-through ratio.

■ Don't use too many words. Keep the message simple.

■ Include your name or URL so that you at least get some name recognition from people who don't click the image.

■ Include some alternate text for your image if the advertising site supports it. Many people won't wait to see your banner displayed, and the alternate text for the image will be all they see.

■ Be sure you know the size requirements, in pixels, for the site that will display the ad. Most want a non-transparent GIF file smaller than 7K in size.

■ Use animated GIFs if the site permits them. However, be sure that the still image shown by browsers that don't support animated GIFs conveys your message.

■ Test a variety of banners and keep track of which ones produce the best click-through ratio. If you advertise in a variety of places, keep track of which ones give the best click-through ratio.

■ Remember to coordinate your print and online advertising strategies. The image you present to your audience online shouldn't conflict with the image you present in print.

For more advertising banner design tips, see **http://www.photolabels.com/ betterbanners.shtml**.

Online Shopping Malls

The number of people shopping on the Web is increasing. If your store sells products on the Web, you might want to advertise through one or more online shopping malls.

There are lots of online shopping malls. Yahoo! lists over 700. Just as you should carefully choose the location of a physical store, you should avoid spending money to put your online store in a shopping mall that gets little traffic. Visit **http://www.100hot.com/shopping/** for a list of the online shopping malls that are currently attracting the most visitors.

Some online malls enable you to list your store for free and charge a fee for various levels of increased visibility. These malls generally contain more stores and attract more traffic than malls with fewer stores. The Internet Mall at **http://www.internet-mall.com/** and shown in Figure 14.6 is an example of this type of mall. Most of the services described in the section on

Part
III

Ch
14

"URL Submission Services" submit your store for free listings at some popular online shopping malls.

FIG. 14.6
The Internet Mall is one of the largest online malls.

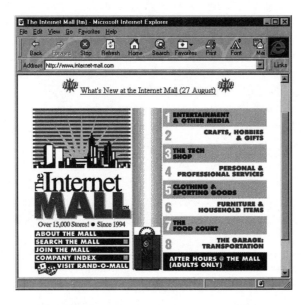

Other malls charge for all listings. Some are only open to merchants whose Web pages are located on their Web server. Because there are so many malls, it pays to ask several questions about a mall before sending any money. Ask the following questions:

- How much traffic do they get? You don't want to spend a lot of money advertising at a mall that gets very little traffic.

- Is the traffic figure a count of hits or a true count of the number of visitors? Hits are often inflated by counting every file that gets downloaded, including all the graphics. Larger malls have a separate company audit their number of visitors.

- What are the costs? Use the costs and the amount of traffic you expect to determine how much you're paying for each visitor. Compare these costs to the amount you would pay for targeted banner advertising.

- How is the mall marketed and advertised? Malls that advertise effectively will have a growing amount of traffic.

- How are stores within the mall advertised? Look at the mall interface to see how difficult it will be for visitors to find your store.

- What kind of results do the existing stores get? Talk to the existing stores to learn whether or not they are satisfied.

■ If you have an existing store, can the mall simply link to that store? Some malls require your store's Web pages to be housed on their server.

■ If you want your Web site stored on the mall's server, ask about the software they provide for designing stores. Most enable customers to browse and to add items to their "shopping carts." Ask about what methods they use to be sure credit card transactions are secure.

■ On what type of server does the mall run and how fast is the server's Internet connection? You want stable and fast access to your store.

Selling Advertising with the Commonwealth Network

In addition to advertising your Web site, you can sell advertising space on your site. However, unless you get a lot of traffic, it probably won't be cost effective to hire people to sell advertising. Remember, more than 60 percent of Web advertising is on the top 10 advertising sites.

The solution is to work with other sites to solicit advertising. You can do this through several advertising networks, including the Commonwealth Network which is located at **http:// commonwealth.riddler.com/**.

The Commonwealth Network is similar to the Internet Link Exchange. It displays banner ads for other sites. But instead of getting ads for your site in exchange, you are paid 3/4 of a cent for each ad your site displays.

Be aware that you are paid once for all of the accesses to your Web site from a particular host during one day. So all of the accesses from anyone@aol.com in one day count as one person.

Using the Rest of the Internet

Using the Web to market and advertise your site isn't the only way to use the Internet to promote it. The rest of the Internet also offers great promotion methods. However, you should be careful. Although commercialism is accepted on the Web, many other parts of the Internet frown upon sales and marketing activities. You will need to present your marketing messages as information, not as a sales pitch.

URL-Minder Service

Suppose you want to notify the people who have visited your Web site when you update it. The easiest way is to add a form for the URL-minder service to your page, so that your visitors can sign up to be notified when your page changes.

The URL-minder is a free service. You can use it yourself to receive e-mail whenever any page on the Web changes. For details, see **http://www.netmind.com/URL-minder/** as shown in Figure 14.7.

Part
III

Ch
14

FIG. 14.7
The URL-minder checks
Web pages for changes.

To make it easy for your visitors to register one of your pages with the URL-minder, add a form
with HTML like the following to one of your pages:

```
<FORM METHOD="GET" action="http://www.netmind.com/cgi-bin/uncgi/url-mind">
<p>Your e-mail address:
<INPUT TYPE=TEXT NAME="required-email" SIZE=40>
<INPUT TYPE=HIDDEN NAME=url VALUE="Full_URL_of_page_to_register">
<INPUT TYPE=SUBMIT
    VALUE="Register to receive e-mail when we update this page.">
</FORM>
```

You might want to add this form to your "What's New" page so that visitors are notified when
you change the page. Use the full URL of your "What's New" page instead of
"Full_URL_of_page_to_register." For example:

```
<INPUT TYPE=HIDDEN VALUE="http://www.mycompany.com/whatsnew.html"
NAME=url>
```

The form you add should look similar to one in Figure 14.8:

FIG. 14.8
Your URL-minder form
might look like this one.

When visitors type an e-mail address and click the submit button, they'll see a page that
prompts them to confirm their e-mail message and to click the button again. Then they'll be
registered for messages about changes to your page.

The URL-minder Web site also contains information about how to do the following:

- Customize the confirmation page.
- Limit which parts of the page the URL-minder compares to find changes.
- Enable visitors to select the page they want to register.

With the URL-minder, you can't get a list of people who have registered to get e-mail when you update your page. Also, you can't customize the e-mail message you send to those who have registered to receive updates about your page. Your visitors may like having this privacy.

If you want to contact people directly, you can encourage them to give you their e-mail addresses.

Direct E-Mail

One of the challenges of advertising on the Web is that it's a pull medium, which means that your customers have to go to Web pages. Web pages don't come to them. This means that you depend on the target audience's desire for your product or services. In contrast, e-mail is a push medium. You can send e-mail on any schedule you choose.

E-mail also has advantages over regular direct mail. Because there are no printing or postage costs, it's almost free. In addition, many people are more likely to read an e-mail message than a direct mail flyer.

> **CAUTION**
>
> It is *very* important to avoid using e-mail to send unsolicited advertising. It's called *spamming* and is seriously frowned upon by the Internet community. Spamming may ruin your business reputation on the Internet. The Web includes blacklists of companies that have distributed spam. In addition, you'll probably get so much hate e-mail, called *flames*, in response to a spam that your system's e-mail capacity will be overloaded.

Following are some rules of Netiquette for sending e-mail to potential customers without risking retribution or your reputation:

- Send e-mail messages only to those who have registered for this information. Don't send unsolicited e-mail advertising. Your Web site should include a feedback form or guestbook for visitors to fill out. Include a field for their e-mail address and a check box similar to the ones in Figure 14.9:

FIG. 14.9
A feedback form should notify people if you plan to send them e-mail.

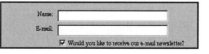

- Your e-mail message should always tell people *why they are getting the message* and *how they can remove their e-mail addresses* from your mailing list. For example:

```
Hello Jane Johnson,

You signed our guestbook back in August 1996 and asked us to send you
information about our future product releases. Well, XYZ Corp just
released KitchenSink V3.2. This product includes the following new features:
```

```
o Digital temperature selection
o Built-in soap dispenser
o Improved no-stain surface

See our Web site at http://www.xyzcorp.com/ for details, or call 800-555-4567.

If you don't want to receive any more messages from XYZ Corp, please send
e-mail that says "unsubscribe" to emaillist@xyzcorp.com.
```

- Be sure your message is informative. Don't make it sound like a sales pitch. Instead of saying, "You'll lose your job unless you buy our product," say "We think this information may be useful."

- You may want to include industry-related information that is not specific to your products. If you have enough material, you can create an e-mail newsletter that will position you as the expert in your field. To do this, you'll want to read about creating e-mail mailing lists in the next section.

- Keep your messages fairly short. If you need to send a long message, be sure the information about why you are sending the message and about how to be removed from your list is near the beginning.

- Be sure the addresses of people on your list are not visible when you send an e-mail message. This protects their privacy and prevents them from accidentally replying to everyone on your list. If you send e-mail directly, you can hide the addresses by putting all of the e-mail addresses in the BCC: field. BCC stands for blind carbon copy. This field sends your message to everyone on the list although the distribution list remains hidden. Another way to hide the e-mail addresses is to create an e-mail mailing list as described in the next section.

- Provide an informative subject line such as, "New version of KitchenSink released."

- Limit your line lengths to 80 characters at the most. In fact, line lengths of about 50 characters are even better because they are easier to read.

- Don't use all capital letters. On the Internet, THIS IS CONSIDERED SHOUTING.

- Proofread your message. If your e-mail program has a spellchecker, use it! If it doesn't have a spellchecker, you can cut and paste your message into a word processor and spell check it there.

 Your existing customers are a great source for future sales. You can use e-mail to try to make them repeat customers or to generate word-of-mouth advertising. Be sure you provide ways for existing customers to easily add their e-mail addresses to your list.

- Provide a space for an e-mail address on the mail-in postcards used to register products.

- Tell your customer support staff to ask for e-mail addresses.

- If you receive e-mail from potential customers asking for information, add them to your list.

- Be sure your suppliers, distributors, and employees also receive copies of important e-mail marketing messages.

Newsgroups and Mailing Lists

Usenet newsgroups and e-mail lists focus on particular topics. You should gather a list of newsgroups and e-mail lists devoted to your industry.

To search for a newsgroup or e-mail list, go to **http://www.liszt.com/**, which can search a database of descriptions with over 15,000 newsgroups and over 48,000 mailing lists as shown in Figure 14.10.

FIG. 14.10

Liszt enables you to search a database of mailing list and newsgroup topics.

To search the contents of past postings to newsgroups, go to Deja News at **http://www.dejanews.com/**. You can search for newsgroups that discuss your industry. As you can see in Figure 14.11, if you sell plumbing supplies, you might find that the **alt.aquaria.marketplace** and **cbd.procurements** newsgroups often discuss plumbing.

FIG. 14.11

Deja News enables you to search newsgroup postings for topics related to your industry.

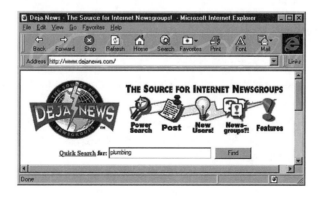

Part

III

Ch

14

If newsgroups and e-mail lists related to your business or organization already exist, you should be sure that at least one knowledgeable employee reads the postings and participates in the discussions.

If there is no newsgroup or e-mail list, it's a great idea to start one. In fact, even if an e-mail list already covers your industry, it's a great idea to create e-mail lists that you can use to send announcements to your existing customers. See Appendix B to learn how to use the software included on the CD-ROM to start and manage an e-mail list.

What follows are some additional Netiquette rules to remember when working with newsgroups and e-mail lists. Remember, your reputation is very important on the Internet.

- Avoid posting blatant advertising. It is frowned upon in many newsgroups and e-mail lists. However when someone has a problem you can solve, post information about how your company can solve it and give the appropriate contact information. It's okay to say, "I'm biased because I work for XYZ, but I think we have the best solution."

- It's usually okay to announce new products in a newsgroup or e-mail list devoted to your industry. Consider how others make such announcements and whether anyone complains about them. Keep your message brief and provide the facts. Avoid making it sound like an advertisement.

- If there is no e-mail list for your category of products or services, start one. Your organization can be seen as "the expert" by providing the service. If you start an e-mail list, decide whether you want to create an unmoderated or moderated list.

  - An unmoderated list is not edited at all. The list software simply sends copies of all the messages the list receives to all the members of the list.

  - A moderated list is one that is edited by someone at your company. You can shorten postings that are too long. You can remove postings that don't belong, like ones that ask how to subscribe or to be removed from the list. Be careful about editing postings with which you don't agree. Members of a company's moderated list might become upset if they think you are restricting their freedom of speech. Moderating a mailing list may also make you legally responsible for the content. Consult a lawyer if you have questions.

  - You can also create an announcement list to which only your company can post. The people who receive the list can't use it to send messages to other list subscribers.

- Encourage employees who use e-mail to include your organization's URL in their e-mail signature. Educate your employees about Netiquette to prevent them from giving your company a bad reputation on the Internet.

- If someone posts negative messages about your products or services, try to contact them directly to solve any problems. You probably don't want to argue in front of all the people who read the newsgroup or e-mail list. If you turn them into happy customers, they might be willing to post a retraction.

If you create a public mailing list, add it to **http://www.liszt.com/**. Also, don't forget to add instructions on your Web site for subscribing to your mailing list.

Follow the same rules if you participate in forums or chat groups on America Online or other online services. Don't send advertising to all the members of the group. If someone has a problem your company can solve, send an informative message to that person directly.

Reality Check

Digital Instruments (DI) sells scanning probe microscopes, a class of instruments that enables people to look at surfaces on much smaller scales than ordinary optical microscopes. As Figure 14.12 shows, the microscopes can show individual atoms on some samples.

FIG. 14.12
DI's "NanoTheater" includes microscope images of individual atoms.

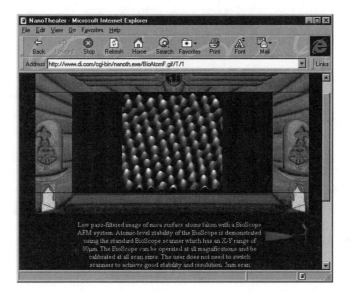

I regularly consult with a group of DI employees to develop their Web site at **http://www.di.com/**. As a result of the marketing efforts described here, DI's Web site gets about 100 visitors per day, which is pretty good considering its fairly small target audience.

DI's Target Audiences

DI identified a number of different audiences. Likewise, you may find that you have several different audiences.

- Potential customers—For people who might want to purchase one of their microscopes, the Web site includes technical details about all of the microscopes and examples of ways to use them. It also includes contact information for the regional sales representatives.

- Existing customers—A number of "Support Notes" provide information about solving specific technical problems. In addition, the "Application Notes" show new ways to use the microscopes. DI adds to these sections regularly. "The Web site helps us keep communication flowing to our customers, who are our most important asset," according to Terry Mehr, the Marketing Communication Manager at DI.

Part
III

Ch

14

■ General public interested in science—For this audience, DI's goal is to increase the percentage of the general public that has heard of atomic force microscopes. To help do this, we created the "NanoTheater," which is a fun place that displays pictures taken with these special microscopes. Responses to the NanoTheater have been very positive.

The commercially important audiences of potential and existing customers generally access the Web from a faster connection at a university, a research lab, or a large corporation. Because the audience has faster connections, the site can contain fairly large graphics.

The first two audiences are also comfortable with an academic look. They aren't looking for postmodern colors, but they do want to see cool pictures taken with the microscopes. They are willing to read a fair amount of text online or to print it for reading later. They are accustomed to the academic format with its introduction, background, methods, results, conclusion, and footnotes. This format shows them that DI does real science, something they respect.

DI's Coordinated Marketing Strategy

"Our Web site is an important part of our overall marketing strategy," Terry Mehr says. "We print our Web address on everything from our letterhead, to our newsletter, to our print advertising. It's very important on an international level. People can contact us directly, despite different time zones."

Digital Instruments' sales staff knows what information is available on the Web site, and directs potential customers to read it to get technical details.

DI's Web site has a feedback form for visitors that enables them to request printed literature and to sign up to receive the company's newsletter. Mehr says DI receives about five requests per day from people who use the feedback form.

Moving the DI Site Up in Search Results

We noticed that DI's home page was not listed near the top of the search results when the search keywords were "atomic force microscope" or "scanning probe microscope," which were the most likely search terms for these products.

The reason was that the home page had a lot of graphics but not much text. We made the following changes to the home page:

■ Added the following <META> tags to the page:

```
<META NAME="KEYWORD" CONTENT="atomic force microscopes, atomic force micros-
copy,
atomic force, atomic, scanning probe microscopes, scanning probe microscopy,
microscope, microscopy, AFM, SPM, Digital Instruments, scanning tunneling,
STM,
NanoScope, NanoProbe, AutoTune, AutoWafer, BioScope, LiftMode, MultiMode,
NanoTheater, Nanovations, TappingMode, BioScope, magnetic force microscopy,
MFM,
scanning capacitance microscopy, chemical, lateral, friction, electric,
imaging,
lithography, semiconductors, nanotechnology, biotechnology, electrochemis-
```

```
try,
surfaces, materials science">

<META NAME="DESCRIPTION" CONTENT="Digital Instruments is the leading manu-
facturer
of scanning probe microscopes, including atomic force microscopes. Since our
founding we have been the market leader in performance, innovation, quality,
and service, as well as sales volume.">
```

- Changed the home page title to "Digital Instruments—Atomic Force and Scanning Probe Microscopes."

We also wanted to add a text description near the top of the page for search engines that don't use the <META> tags. However, management did not want to change the look of the page. This restriction gave us a chance to test the effects of keywords in the <TITLE> and <META> tags separately.

After making these changes, we resubmitted DI's home page to the search engines listed below. As a result, when the major search engines searched for "atomic force microscopes," DI's position changed as follows:

Search Engine	Before*	After	When Effects Seen
AltaVista	12th	no change	>6 weeks
Excite	41st	9th	3 weeks
HotBot	50th	1st	2 weeks
Infoseek	9th	no change	>6 weeks
Lycos	67th	no change	>6 weeks
Open Text	70th	1st	6 weeks

The before rankings are for any page on DI's Web site. Prior to the changes, a detailed technical page was always listed long before the home page. The after rankings are for DI's home page.

AltaVista, HotBot, and Infoseek claim to support <META> tags, so we expected the ranking to change for all three. Open Text does not make any claims about supporting the <META> tags, but from the results, they probably do. It also appears that AltaVista and Infoseek update their databases less often than HotBot.

Additional Links to the DI Site

Digital Instruments exchanges links with a number of customers, vendors, and related research groups.

- Many of DI's customers have Web sites where they display the results of their research. DI encourages these customers to add links to the Digital Instruments Web site.
- DI encourages customers to submit images for use in its annual calendar and in the "User's Showcase" of the NanoTheater. In addition, it often publishes research papers as Application Notes. Customers whose images and papers are published online are encouraged to provide links to the DI Web site.

Part
III

Ch
14

- DI lists a number of reciprocal links on its "Related Web Sites" page at **http://www.di.com/Biblio/RelWebs.html**. The list includes links to university and industrial laboratories, print and online publications, professional and trade organizations, and suppliers.

DI currently doesn't believe it needs to advertise on the Web because its print ads in scientific and trade journals reach its audience effectively.

An unexpected free link appeared when DI's Web site won the Top 5 percent of the Web award from Point, at **http://www.pointcom.com/**.

Promoting DI on the Rest of the Internet

DI learned that there weren't many messages about the kinds of microscopes it makes on the **sci.techniques.microscopy newsgroup**. So DI decided to start two e-mail lists.

- It uses an announcement list to send messages to existing customers. For example, DI uses it to announce new products and seminars.

- To encourage general discussion of products and techniques, DI started a separate e-mail list. It is for its customers and for people who use machines made by other companies. Sponsoring the list supports DI's image as the technology leader in the field. Postings include such topics as imaging techniques, calibration, specialized probes, and sample preparation.

From Here...

In this chapter, you've learned how to target audiences, how to coordinate your marketing efforts, how to increase you site's visibility to search engines, how to advertise on the Web, and how to use the rest of the Internet. Other chapters in this book provide related information:

- One way to learn which of your marketing efforts have been successful is to analyze your access logs. Chapter 11, "Usage Statistics," explains how to examine these logs.

- Another way to evaluate your marketing efforts is to encourage feedback from your visitors using forms. Read Chapter 13, "Forms and Surveys," to learn how to create and use forms.

- In addition to marketing your Web site, you may want customers to purchase your products from your Web site. Chapter 16, "Conducting Transactions on the Internet," explains how to make secure transactions over the Web.

- This chapter explained the importance of focusing on your target audience. Chapter 19, "Advanced HTML," also discusses how to design Web pages for your audience.

## CHAPTER 15

Data Encryption and Digital Signatures

The Web is, by definition, still an electronic wild frontier in how it works with all of the different types of systems that are operating. This means that, on the whole, your server needs to work at the lowest common denominator when dealing with requests from browsers. This also means that it's difficult to establish a secure transaction environment. The reason is that you don't know what type of interaction you can have with the receiving end of the conversation.

How to create a secure server environment

You will find out what adding the capability for a secure server can mean to your environment. You'll see what it brings to your server, and how you can use it to better control information flow on your Web site.

How to apply for, and receive, a signed certificate for your server

You learn how to work with a registration authority to obtain the *digital certificate* for your server, enabling the secured transactions capabilities of your system.

How to implement on your system the certificate, and what it means to your users

Putting the protection of a registered certificate into place on your server is the key to protecting information on your system. You learn how to create the key, and how you implement it on your server.

How to digitally sign the software you provide for download, and why you can do this

Using some tools publicly available, you can apply a *digital signature* to your software. This enables you to certify its source and content.

ON THE WEB

An excellent source of information exists on how these digital IDs and signatures integrate into different browsers, server software, and e-mail packages. This source is the VeriSign site, located at **http://www.VeriSign.com/site_idx.html#faqs**. A number of documents there address the different facets of integrating the security into your environment.

N O T E If you're looking for a version of the Apache software that will support SSL (Secure Sockets Layer) , you can download it from the Internet at **http://apachessl.c2.org/**. This version is for use only in the United States. ■

This open environment means that, under normal circumstances, the information you send to a remote system is available to people on the network, if they want to tap into conversation. This can include form-based data, clear text passwords, and much more. Much of the active research on the Internet concerns how to make the Web a better place in which to conduct business. This issue is also applicable if you're implementing an Intranet, as you'll likely be dealing with many of the same issues that relate to privacy of information. When you begin making more personal types of information available, such as personnel files and pay rates, you establish the need for secure communications at different locations on your server.

Digital certificates, a way of vouching for the program code you post on your site, are based on the same technology as Pretty Good Privacy, or PGP security. You have a *digital signature*, which appears to be a random block of letters, numbers, and symbols. The following block of text shows what the start of a signature block might resemble:

```
MIIBrTCCARYCAQAwcDELMAkGA1UEBhMCVVMxEzARBgNVBAgTCldBU0hJTkdUO4x
EDAOBgNVBAcTB1JFRE1PTkQxEDAOBgNVBAoTB0VYQU1QTEUxDTALBgNVBAsTBFRP
VVIxGTAXBgNVBAMUEHd3dy5teWNvbXBhbnkuY28wgZ4wDQYJKoZIhvcNAQEBBQAD
gYwAMIGIAoGBDBku5DMBNnYZQI+cpitWsLGxMwf/mHl9t1flG05NoFrLJQcJKZbh
B9jAAWDCau7kD+usYd0C0tyTyhMkhg76/5Mqr8itZEhSF61OCb5+719abTy0sX7x
...
```

You learn different ways to enable this security, and what this means to your organization, in this chapter. You'll also see how to create a server environment that gives you this added security measure. This helps you provide sensitive data to your legitimate users without fear of access by a third party. ■

Knowing When to Use Secure Transactions

When you send information related to your Web service over an Internet or Intranet, the information travels in ASCII format. This means that anyone who knows how to spy on transactions on the network is able to easily see the information that is being exchanged. By implementing a security layer on particular directories on your system, you control the transmission of information. You can also encrypt it to prevent other people from seeing discernible text.

It's likely that you'll be providing secure or confidential information on your Intranet. Therefore, you're going to want to apply the security layer to the server. You need to understand some of the following key concepts about secure transactions:

- The people accessing your network must be using a browser that supports SSL. This means that some of the lesser-known browsers won't be able to work with your site's protected directories. These browsers will still, however, be able to work with public access information.

N O T E There are even FTP, Telnet, and other clients now coming on the market that will enable you to use SSL encryption for their sessions. Though many of these are not mainstream as of this writing, you can expect SSL encryption to become a fairly common approach to data access on the Internet: People are becoming more security conscious. ■

- Implementing your secure server requires several steps. One of these steps, obtaining the certificate from the certificate authority, is completely outside your control. You need to plan on a minimum of two weeks for the Central Authority to fulfill your request, and return a key to be installed at your site.
- You can typically apply SSL control only to the Web server-based content.
- Remember that SSL is a complement to, not a replacement for, operating system level security on your system. These technologies represent two different approaches to security. With SSL, you're controlling how the information is sent over the network. With the operating system directives, you're controlling access to the information. The operating system dictates whether or not the user can access the pages at all.
- With most server software, you can protect directories on a case-by-case basis. You don't have to protect the entire site, although you can do so, if necessary. Protection of a directory safeguards its hierarchy when access is attempted from that virtual directory. This directory is not protected, however, when accessed from another directory. This seems a bit odd at first. Consider, however, the following scenario:
  - You create a virtual directory to MyDirectory, the name of which is Virtual1. You have set up this virtual directory to be secure. MyDirectory has two different subdirectories, sub1 and sub2.
  - You create a second virtual directory, also pointed to MyDirectory, with the name of Virtual2. This access point is not secure.
  - When you access Virtual1, information exchanged is secure, as it is if you're accessing the subdirectories under Virtual1 by way of Virtual1. In other words, the *URL* **https://holodeck3/virtual1/sub1** is secure. The reason is that it is accessed through the Virtual1 access point.
  - By contrast, when you access Virtual2, information is not securely transmitted. Also, if you're accessing **http://holodeck3/virtual2/sub1**, the nonsecure aspect of the link remains.

This last item is extremely important, with respect to both implementation and caution. You need to be careful, as you can inadvertently provide unsecured access to content that you intend to be protected, undoing all of your hard work to provide the secure channel to the information. For this reason, Microsoft recommends that you maintain two distinct trees of information on your site. One tree should be for public, non-SSL information. The other should be for SSL-encrypted information.

Of course, there is an upside to this as well. To make your site more available to different types of browsers, you can offer both secure and non-secure access to information. Many sites offer the user a choice when accessing their pages. The user can employ the SSL connection, or use a non-protected access method. To do this, you can have two different links on your pages that take the user into the protected areas: one that uses the SSL path, and one that doesn't.

Understanding Secure Channels

The process of creating and using the secure channel of communications requires a few items that are behind the scenes. As you'll soon see, the server has a key that identifies it. This key indicates to the browser that this is the server for which the browser is searching. The server and the client software exchange this key. This exchange enables the client to use the key to decrypt information sent to it from the server.

Two processes open and maintain the secure channel. In the first, key information is exchanged. In the second, the protocol to front-end the HTTP service is established. In this way, the information coming in from the client system is decrypted before it gets to the server applications. This makes the SSL completely transparent to the services that use it—a very important factor if it is to coexist without regard for the applications that it is protecting.

The request passes to the HTTP layer. This layer then uses and responds to the information, giving the response back to the SSL layer. SSL encrypts the information, and submits it to the TCP/IP layer for communication back to the client software (see Figure 15.1).

After the secure channel is open and running between the server and the client, SSL's only function is to encrypt and decrypt the information flowing between the two. It makes the use of the secure channel completely transparent to the server.

On the client side, the SSL component is responsible for nearly the same process—that of encrypting and decrypting the information. The difference, of course, is that the SSL engine uses the key provided by the server to do this work, not a key that it maintains separately.

This is somewhat similar to giving people a copy of your house key so that they can watch your house while you're away. They have a key when they need it. When their job is finished, however, they no longer need the key. They discard it, or return it to you.

FIG. 15.1
The SSL layer encrypts and protects the information flow between the server and the client system.

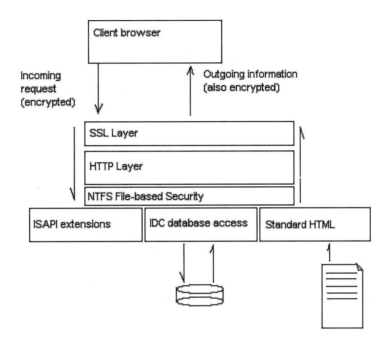

Creating and Working with Digital Certificates

The process of creating the keys that your server uses involves several steps, as mentioned earlier. *Certificate Authorities* are in the business of authenticating you, the user of the keys. In essence, they are vouching for your good nature. When a Central Authority issues a key, it's not so much that the authority is certifying your character. The authority is more or less indicating that the key you are using correctly identifies you to the client system on a completely unique and accurate basis.

Keeping this in mind, you'll quickly understand the small bit of red tape that accompanies setting up your server to be secure with the SSL techniques. The authority must ensure that the right party is receiving the certificate. In addition, your key must absolutely, uniquely identify you. The issuing agency, therefore, must make very sure that it has the information needed to generate your key.

Generating Keys

First, you need to generate the request for the key. This is typically done over e-mail. The process requires that you create a certificate request using a special utility provided with your server software. The process varies among servers, and the examples here are using *IIS*. Keep in mind that the same concepts and logical steps will need to be followed for your server, regardless of what software you're using. For this reason, it is important to understand the key steps involved in this process.

> **N O T E** If you'll be using SSL-based pages on your site, be sure to include this as a criterion when you select your web server software. Not all web servers provide this capability yet. You'll want to be sure to have the capability prior to bringing up your system.
>
> Also, if you live outside the United States, you might have additional considerations in obtaining a system that supports SSL. This is due to export restrictions on the technology. These restrictions are imposed by the US government in an effort to protect vital encryption secrets from those who are not allies. Again, check with the supplier of the server software to make sure that it has a version that supports SSL encryption. ■

The IIS utility, the Key Manager, is located on the Microsoft Internet Server menu. Figure 15.2 shows how this utility initially appears when you start the process of generating keys.

FIG. 15.2
The initial display for the Key Manager lists on the current network the different servers that are known.

You might first have to make your server visible to the Key Manager utility. If you don't see the appropriate server listed in the dialog box, you'll need to add it. To do this, select Servers. Then, choose Connect to Server. You are prompted for the name of the server to add to the list. You can indicate the server by computer name, or by IP address. For an example of this dialog box, see Figure 15.3.

When you want to add a server, you first give its computer name to the utility. Then, the utility attempts to contact the server to ensure it is accessible. When the server has been added to the list successfully, you'll see it appear in the list of servers. If you receive a message that reads, Unable to administer remote machine, double-check the computer name spelling. Alternatively, you can try specifying the IP address directly.

For any active systems on your network, you can see the details regarding the installed certificate on the pane to the right of the dialog box. If the server you have highlighted does not have a certificate installed, the pane to the right appears grayed out.

FIG. 15.3

You can manage any number of servers from a single management workstation. This enables you to balance both the time spent and the hassle of implementing certificates with the need to work directly on the desired server.

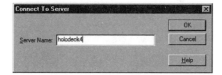

To create a new key, click the server you want to work with using the right mouse button. Then, select Create Key Request. Alternatively, you can select Key. Then, choose Create New Key. When you do, you see a dialog box that enables you to create the keyfile. You can then send this file to the certificate authority you're going to use. Figure 15.4 shows this dialog box containing some example information.

FIG. 15.4

Fill in all information about your organization as needed. Remember that the more information you provide, the more unique the key request will be.

N O T E The information that you provide to create the keys is the same regardless of the platform you are using. UNIX, Windows NT, DOS-based systems and all others will require the same pieces of information to generate the key that will be used on your system. ■

You will need a number of properties to specify that will help you create the key request. Table 15.1 shows the different parameters, and what each of them means in the context of the certificate request.

Table 15.1   Key Manager Parameters

Key Name	This is the friendly name of the key. It is used to generate the default file name for the key, shown at the bottom of the dialog box in the Request File text box. In previous utilities, this was referred to as the private_key parameter.
On the CD	On the CD accompanying this book, there is a file containing a grid on which you write down the options you use to create the key. You can print the file, KEYGEN.DOC, and use it for each key you request. You should carefully write down each option and parameter you use. It is imperative that, if you later need to recreate the request for some reason, you are able to do so.
Password	This is the password with which you're creating the key. This password is critical to the process of creating the key: Be sure to write it down.
Bits	You can create a key of three distinct sizes, each of which indicates a different level of security. As the size of the key gets larger, the security of the channel increases, as well. The options are 512, 768, or 1024—each representing measurements in bits. The default is a 1024-bit key.
Request	This represents the name and location of the file that will contain the certificate request. You will send this file to the certificate authority. An extension of REQ is automatically added to the resulting file.
Distinguishing Information	The next items are combined to create the distinguished name for your server, and subsequently, the certificate.
Organization	This represents the name of the company that will be running the server.
Organizational Unit	This is department that will be running the server. This helps distinguish the server from others that might be running within a large corporation.
Common Name	The name that users will employ to access the system. For your Intranet-only server, this can be the computer name, such as **HOLODECK3**. For an Internet server, this should include both the system and domain names, such as **www.intellicenter.com** or **www.integra.net**, rather than just intellicenter or even **integra.net**. In prior versions of the software, this was referred to as the CN parameter, indicating the net address of the system.
Country	This is the name of the country in which the server will be based.
State/Province	This is the state or province in which the server will reside.

| Locality | This is the locality or town in which the server will reside. |
| Request File | This represents the name of the file in which you'll be storing the key information. This is very important to note, as you'll be sending this file to the certificate authority as part of this process. |

> **CAUTION**
>
> Be sure you spell city and state names fully. This is a requirement from the Certifying Authority (CA) in most cases. It serves to more fully qualify the certificate request. If you don't, your request might be bounced from the CA, adding unnecessary time to the process of obtaining your certificate.

NOTE The parameters you pass as the distinguished site name are all provided as a single string, enclosed in quotes. ▓

> **CAUTION**
>
> Don't embed commas in the information you provide to create the distinguished name. For example, Custom Solutions, Inc. would not be valid. The reason is that the comma is used to indicate the break between the different characteristics of the distinguished name. By placing a comma in the string, you're indicating that the field is completed, and the parsing routine should move to the next field.

Clicking OK prompts you to confirm the password you entered. Be sure to enter a password that exactly matches the original you provided. If you don't, Key Manager indicates that the passwords don't match. The system then returns you to the Key Manager dialog box to confirm or change the password. Keep in mind that the password is case sensitive.

After you have successfully generated the key request, you'll receive a message indicating that you need to send the file to the certificate authority. The file you indicated for the Request File is created with the certificate request. The following is an example of a certificate request:

```
----BEGIN NEW CERTIFICATE REQUEST----
MIIBrTCCARYCAQAwcDELMAkGA1UEBhMCVVMxEzARBgNVBAgTCldBU0hJTkdUT04x
EDAOBgNVBAcTB1JFRE1PTkQxEDAOBgNVBAoTB0VYQU1QTEUxDTALBgNVBAsTBFRP
VVIxGTAXBgNVBAMUEHd3dy5teWNvbXBhbnkuY28wgZ4wDQYJKoZIhvcNAQEBBQAD
gYwAMIGIAoGAeAku5DMBNnYZQI+cpitWsLGxMwf/mH19t1flG05NoFrLJQcJKZbh
B9jAAWDCau7kD+usYd0C0tyTyhMkhg76/5Mqr8itZEhSF61OCb5+719abTy0sX7x
iuJuDhkeQl6eW3+r7al4XSp2roF6xhu2VwgPNJjpfTpjHztGo55hwRsCAwEAATAN
BgkqhkiG9w0BAQQFAAOBgQBbaQuqjvYYZ1hWG+giDKz9DrpAsu+PJpihAFeTjw/+
wGYVu4HUvIOdKJpGPs9VOxRzEZesk1uMkz+qmCixLsSkrnt2T8O7nnClrYKGcJdl
d/nz1rol7HlXNS+kl6YezoHEquoWyi7qFW+El4UEksiElKpscSdWxgKgHuwqsKBp
kg==
----END NEW CERTIFICATE REQUEST-----
```

If you look at the certificate request file listing, MyKEY file, you'll quickly see that it appears to be just a jumble of characters. The file contains an encrypted form of the request information that you provided in the dialog box. Once you have requested the certificate, it appears in the Key Manager with the pending status indicated in the pane to the right. For an example of how this dialog box now appears, see Figure 15.5.

FIG. 15.5

You can quickly see the status of all servers and their keys in the Key Manager.

You send this information to the certificate authority for signing. The authority uses it as the basis for the key that is issued to you. These examples use VeriSign. Others, however, are under consideration by the various Web server vendors, and will be in production reasonably soon.

N O T E   Under a UNIX system, such as the Apache SSL server, the key file is created with your hostname as the primary portion of the file name. The extension KEY is added to the file name to indicate that it's a private key file. With respect to a certificate, it is also stored in a file named after your domain. For example, if your domain name is www.intellicenter.com, the following key and certificate files will be used by default:

www.intellicenter.com.key

www.intellicenter.com.cert

These files are created by default in the /usr/local/ssl directory on your system. ■

Next, you send your request to the certificate authority for both validation and signing. *Signing* is the process of producing the complementary key to the certificate request that you submit.

Sending in Your Certificate Request

When the certificate authority receives your request, this authority asks you to take certain actions. First, you need to e-mail your certificate request file to the certificate authority. This is the starting point for what the authority will create for you.

With VeriSign, and others reviewed, you must fax and mail a letter, on company letterhead, to the certificate authority. This letter takes responsibility for the key, and indicates who the responsible Webmaster people are for the site. The letter also indicates the name you'll be using for the site.

On the CD

The following letter is available on the CD included with this book. Use the file named VERISIGN.DOC as a starting template for the letter you need to send. Note that the letter, and possibly even the requirement to send it in the first place, can vary from one authority to another. If you're using a service other than VeriSign, be sure to check the specific requirements for submissions.

VeriSign, Inc.
Attn: Digital ID Services
2593 Coast Avenue
Mountain View, CA 94043
USA

VeriSign's Server Name (also referred to as Common Name) is <your server name>.

I, <person signing this letter>, hereby attest that the following individuals are employees of <company>. I further attest that they are authorized to operate the software referred to as the Microsoft Internet Information Server.

<name>	<address>	<email ID>
<name>	<address>	<email ID>
<name>	<address>	<email ID>
<name>	<address>	<email ID>

I understand that use of the Digital ID requested by this letter is subject to the terms of the Secure Server Legal Agreement. That document can be found at **http:// www.VeriSign.com/microsoft/legal.html**. The secure Server Legal Agreement is also available upon request from VeriSign at 2593 Coast Avenue, Mountain View, CA 94043.

<company> hereby certifies to VeriSign, Inc. that it has the right to use the name presented in the Organization field within the Server Name. The proof of right to use the name is based on registering the respective organization name with the state, country, or city in which the Server will be operated.

<Name>

<Title>

N O T E When you send in your request, you should include the older version command line equivalent for the certificate request. As of this writing, this was a requirement. The reason is that VeriSign uses it to validate the key request that you send in. To do this, include the following information with your key request message:

KEY REQUEST COMMAND LINE:

```
keygen [password] Key Request "C=US, O=Joe's Barber Shop,
 S=Washington, L=Redmond, CN=barber.com"
```

You can determine the information for this command line from the Key Manager display, and from using the information presented in Table 15.1. These two lines provide any additional information needed to complete your key request. ■

CAUTION

Be sure to remove your password from the command line when you submit it to the authority. You can substitute [password] or some other place holder in the command line to protect the privacy of your key.

Once you've submitted the information, you must wait for the signed certificate to be e-mailed back to you. When you receive it, save the key to a text file on your system. Listing 15.1 shows a sample certificate.

Listing 15.1   Partial Certificate Listing

```
----BEGIN CERTIFICATE----
MIICWjCCAccCBQJ6AAjLMA0GCSqGSIb3DQEBAgUAMF8xCzAJBgNVBAYTAlVTMSAw
HgYDVQQKExdSU0EgRGF0YSBTZWN1cml0eSwgSW5jLjEuMCwGA1UECxMlU2VjdXJl
...
...
fKhP4wfgwI4w59ubZ3xuDnzvULxk7H4wu/A/36GtC6B4weyNqmhCUB29xbWVP29w
178esPfem//YpkBy1jLly+ynA82iGN0gu2UCAwEAATANBgkqhkiG9w0BAQIFAAN+
ADhQaghTBWWOkc4IzYEoOriKmJGXRsDcTHfGwAZ52nelXhaVVtQQxQhQqXjSmcSE
4sfuesfZTsZTlbhEscG27cVH2ktY7CRcO3C7BMFBvNqEdLPPCXyZdiqZBCprsROU
xAfjPTSXXMYa1/2ccBRbPS58n75nlEAugbOfHFAn
----END CERTIFICATE----
```

When you receive and save the certificate information, be sure you save it with the BEGIN CER-TIFICATE and END CERTIFICATE monikers in place. This indicates to the Key Manager in which place the certificate starts and stops. At this point, you're ready to install the certificate, and begin applying it to your system's directories.

Installing Digital Certificates on Your Server

The certificate you receive will appear similar to the one that the preceding section shows. Once again, the text block has no obvious meaning, and appears to be a set of jumbled characters. Rest assured, however, that this certificate information provides quite a lot of information about your site, indicating everything from your distinguished name to the expiration date of the certificate.

N O T E   Certificates generally expire one year after their issue. The cost for renewing a certificate is typically much less than the cost of registering a new name, often less than half of the fee required to initially set up your system's address on the Internet. In addition, the application process should be reduced, often not requiring much more than simply paying the renewal fee. ■

Next, use the Key Manager utility, also located on the Internet Server menu option from your Start menu, to register the certificate. There are a number of different ways to apply a certificate to your site. Your approach will vary according to what type of security you're trying to provide on the site.

The Key Manager application has a number of capabilities. Only one of these has the capability to set up certificates for your server that apply to the server as a whole. Other capabilities include setting up the certificate for use on multihomed or Virtual Servers.

Installing the Certificate on Your System   Once you receive your certificate, you need to install and validate it for your system. The Key Manager lists any *open* or yet-to-be-validated keys when you start the application. These keys appear with a red line through the key name. For an example of open keys, see Figure 15.6.

FIG. 15.6

Keys that have been requested, but not yet validated for use on your server, are shown with the "No Key" icon.

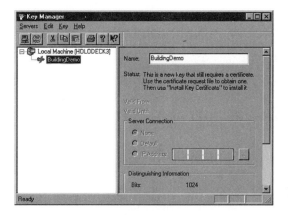

To install the certificate, use the right mouse button to click the key request that you used to create the request for the certificate. From the menu, select Install Certificate. You'll need to select the file into which you saved the validated certificate so that you can apply it to the site. After you do, the system prompts you for the password that you used to create the original key request (see Figure 15.7).

FIG. 15.7

You must provide the same password that you used to request the certificate when you started the process of certifying your server.

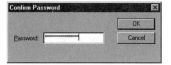

After you provide the password, the system reminds you that until you apply the certificate to a specific server, the certificate is valid but not in use. As you can see in Figure 15.8, the default application of the certificate when you initially install it is None. This indicates that it is installed, but not applied to any content or directories.

FIG. 15.8

You must apply a certificate to a server to activate it on your site.

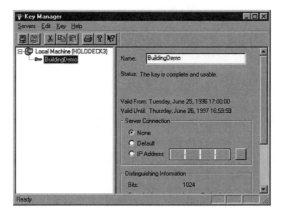

When you apply your certificate, you'll need to first determine your goals for its use on the site. If you are planning to provide the certificate against all transactions for this server, you'll be able to use the Default option. This applies the certificate system-wide against your site.

N O T E   The installation process under UNIX only requires running the certificate installation application provided with the software. Though it varies by server software, with the Apache Server, you run an application named getca, passing in the hostname to be certified. Check your server documentation for the specifics of installing the certificate for your server software. ■

Some cases might exist in which you have a separate certificate for different IP addresses serviced by this server. In those cases, you'll need to take a slightly different approach. The next sections show how you can apply the certificate in these scenarios to get the most out of your site.

Installing the Certificate on a Single Server System   If you will be using the same certificate for all requests on a given server, you can make the same certificate available to all directory configurations. You do this by selecting the Default option in the Server Connection frame in the Key Manager dialog box. This option simply indicates that if there are multiple virtual or multihomed servers installed on this system, they are all going to be using the same certificate. Figure 15.9 shows that you can also tell, referring to the Key Manager server display, that the key is the default key for all activity designated as secure for that server.

This sets up the certificate in such a manner that when you create an SSL-protected directory, it automatically uses this certificate. Keep in mind that just because you relate a certificate with a server, you don't have to protect every directory provided by that server. It simply means that the SSL capabilities are available when you need them.

FIG. 15.9

The Key Manager indicates whether an installed certificate is for a specific Virtual Server or a general application for the server.

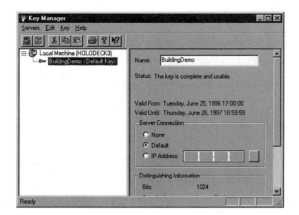

Part

III

Ch

15

Installing the Certificate on a Multihome or Virtual Server System   If you have a Virtual Server environment, you might want to install separate certificates for each Virtual Server you are hosting. You can associate a given certificate with a specific IP address. Alternatively, you can use a certificate for all Virtual Servers supported by the server.

N O T E   There are restrictions on how you can use the certificate, and to which types of multiserver support you can apply it. You should carefully read your Certificate Authority's Use and Guidelines documents for more information about whether you can use a common certificate in a multihomed server environment.

If you're setting up Virtual Servers to serve the same content, as might be the case when you've established an Intranet and Internet presence on a single machine, you can probably use the certificate for both server sessions.

On the other hand, you might have a Virtual Server set up, and each virtual server represents a different company name, URL, or common name, for example, **www.integra.net**. In these cases, you should apply for separate and distinct certificates. Also, if your server is otherwise related to a different line of business, you should apply for a separate certificate. There are usually discounts for single businesses purchasing multiple certificate licenses. This should, therefore, save some of the upfront costs associated with these scenarios. ■

To select a specific Virtual Server, choose the IP Address option in the Server Connection frame. Then, provide the IP address for the server against which you want to apply the certificate. Once you provide the address, the Key Manager updates the pane to the left to show the IP address associated with the certificate. For an example of this, please see Figure 15.10.

Once installed, the certificate will be activated. It is, however, available only for the server you called out. You must get a separate certificate for the balance of your site if there are other Virtual Servers, and if the need arises.

FIG. 15.10
When you assign a specific IP address to a given certificate, the Key Manager shows the IP next to the certificate under the server heading.

N O T E If you later change your mind and decide that you want to provide the certificate capabilities on a more site-wide basis, you can uninstall the certificate. Then, you can reinstall it with the Default option selected. You can also select the certificate and change its association with the Server Connection by simply selecting a different radio button from the dialog box.

If you do perform a reassignment of this type, you'll need to set up your protected directories again, verifying that SSL remains enabled. ■

Removing Installed Certificates You might want to uninstall a certificate for a number of reasons. You might want to remove the certificate if you've had it on the system and have determined that you no longer need to provide the secure content.

A certain amount of overhead is associated with providing a secure connection. As you might imagine, encrypting and decrypting information on both ends of the link to your site can have a noticeable impact on performance.

If you have content that does not need to be under SSL protection, you should consider removing the SSL encryption.

To remove an installed certificate, click the certificate entry under the server heading you need using the right mouse button. Select D̲elete from the menu. When you do, the system asks you to verify that you want to remove the certificate (see Figure 15.11).

N O T E Changes that you make to the keys and certificates on your system are not actually applied until you commit the changes to your system. You commit changes by selecting Servers. Then, you select Commit Changes Now. Alternatively, you can exit the Key Manager and indicate that you want the changes saved when prompted. ■

FIG. 15.11
When you remove a certificate, you also erase the protection from the SSL-enabled directories. The system prompts you to confirm that you want to remove the SSL certificate from your system.

When you have confirmed the removal of the certificate, its reference disappears from the dialog box. You can reinstall the certificate, if needed. However, you'll need to give the same information you used to generate the original, including the password and other items that are required to create the distinguished name for your system. If you don't, the certificate installation fails.

Applying the Certificate to Your Directories

When you install the certificate using the Key Manager, it is applied only to the server. It's not applied to any content or directories on your system. If you have directories that contain content that must remain secure, you need to specify them.

> **CAUTION**
>
> There's an important distinction between providing a secure transaction, such as the preceding, and securing your Web site. SSL and the certification process provides a private channel between a Web browser-type environment and your site. This ensures that no unauthorized person can steal information from the connection.
>
> SSL does not provide protection against unwanted intruders. You'll notice that, as you use SSL-protected directories, you're not authenticated at all. The reason is that the server sets up a secure session between the browser and your server. The server does not care who the user is. It only ensures that the information sent to the user arrives intact, and that no other people are able to intercept and understand the packets of information being transferred.

Next, you apply the certificate to your Web site. To do so, start the Internet Service Manager. Then, select the WWW service. From the property sheets, select the Directories tab. You apply a certificate on a directory-by-directory basis, enabling you to provide both secure and nonsecure content to your users.

When you assign secure status to a directory, be sure that no parent directory is unsecured. In other words, you might have a directory structure in which SUBDIR1 is inside MAIN. Don't provide an unsecured access point to MAIN, and then secure SUBDIR1. Someone coming in from the MAIN directory has full, unsecured access to the SUBDIR1 area. The reason is that SUBDIR1 is not an accessed directory through a virtual directory that provides the SSL encryption.

N O T E   When you install a certificate against a given server, you should stop and restart the WWW service. The reason is to make sure the service sees the newly installed certificate. If you don't, the SSL option might not be available when you try to associate it with a directory. ▪

Figure 15.12 shows an example of the dialog box that enables you to indicate the SSL flag on a directory.

FIG. 15.12
When you edit an existing virtual directory, or when you create a new virtual directory, you can specify that it should be used with the SSL encryption.

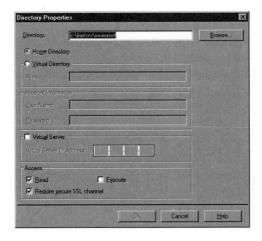

Once you set the SSL flag, all accesses that employ that directory require the use of SSL.

When you set up a site, consider whether you want to force people to use SSL, or only provide it as an option. If you want to give it as an option, you can provide one virtual directory to the secure content, and another one that isn't. Then, based on users' selections when they are browsing your server, you can take them to either the secure or nonsecure pages. The physical files remain the same. The reason is that you can create two virtual directories to reference the same physical location on your system. The links that you provide your users make the distinction between protected and unprotected content merely by selecting an appropriate hyperlink from your site.

Establishing a Secure Session

Now that you've installed the certificate, you can modify your installation to provide secure content. The largest difference you'll see as system administrator is the use of a slightly different URL to access pages that are secure.

You might recall that there are several different types of URLs, ranging from HTTP: to NEWS:. This is the way the browser knows what type of protocol to use to access the site. In the case of an SSL site, you'll use yet another variation the URL. When you see a reference to a site with an HTTPS: URL, you know that it's using data encryption, and so does your browser. When a user visits the site, the secure connection is automatically set up.

In the previous section, you learned how you can provide both secure and unsecured links to the same content on disk. For an example of this, consider the following scenario:

- You have set up two directories, s_content for secure content, and content for unsecured content.
- Both virtual directories point to the same directory on your hard disk.
- The content you're providing is an order form.
- Some of your users are concerned about secure transactions, and others aren't.

You can offer links on your pages, as follows:

```
...
<a href="http://www.mysite.com/s_content/default">Secure
 transaction pages...</a>
<a href="https://www.mysite.com/content/default">Unsecure
 transaction pages...</a>
...
```

You've pointed both URLs to the same content. The user, therefore, can decide how to access the content on your site. This is a good way to provide access to order forms and other information in which it might be desirable to have secured access, but it should not be required. In cases in which you want to strictly enforce the use of the secure channel, you can simply not provide the non-HTTPS: URL.

When a user accesses the content on an HTTPS: URL, the balance of the conversation between the Web site and the browser remains secure, until the user accesses a different, non-HTTPS URL.

Signing Your Software with Digital Signatures

When you distribute software from your site, you take responsibility for that software. You need to provide some assurances to the users downloading it that it does not contain anything you didn't mean it to hold. This requires, in essence, a signature vouching for the software. Of course it's not possible for you to actually sign the software. You can, however, digitally sign it, providing your company's digital signature that vouches for the software's authenticity.

When you decide to sign your code, you'll need to first get the certificates that will be applied to the code. As you do with the SSL certificates, you'll need to go through a Certificate Authority. One example of such a company is VeriSign, located at **http://www.VeriSign.com**. You can sign up for either a personal or a corporate certificate for software, depending of course on what type of software you're certifying.

The costs vary substantially for the two. A personal software certificate is currently costing approximately $20 from VeriSign. A corporate certificate runs about $400. One nice feature is that you can obtain some certificates on-line directly from their Web site. You can start the process of obtaining an ID at **http://digitalid.VeriSign.com/codesign.htm**.

Once you've obtained your certificate, you need to apply it against the software that you want to certify. You do this with an application, `signcode.exe`, that is provided as part of the Microsoft ActiveX SDK. You can download the SDK from the Microsoft Web site at **http://www.microsoft.com/msdownload**. A properly signed application or other file will display a certificate when accessed by a compliant browser.

When you receive your certificate, you'll get two different files. The first, with an extension of SPC, contains your software publishing credentials. These are provided as part of the sign up process, and include the following for a personal certificate:

- Your name
- Your street address, that is not disclosed to third parties, if you indicate as such
- Your e-mail address
- Your date of birth
- Your Social Security number
- Your previous address, if you have moved in the past two years

If you are applying for a corporate certificate, the following information will become part of it. This information is required during the sign-up process:

- Your organization name
- Your organization address
- Your company's DUNS number, if available
- Technical contact name
- Technical contact address
- Technical contact e-mail address
- Technical contact phone number
- Technical contact fax number
- An organizational contact

Of course, in either case, you'll also be prompted for billing information.

The other file that will be provided as part of this process is the private key file. It provides the other half of the equation when compared with the publishing credentials. The extension on the private key file is PVK. You will need both the PVK and SPC files to sign your code.

Once you have these, you can use the `signcode.exe` application, provided as part of the ActiveX SDK in the `BIN\I386` folder, to sign your applications.

N O T E Even though the folder naming convention suggests that this will run only in Windows NT, you'll find that you can still run it in Windows 95. ▨

Signcode can be run in one of two modes. The first is from the command line; the second is to use the Wizard. The command line enables you to indicate the various parameters as part of the command you use to start the application. The syntax of the command is as follows:

```
signcode
-prog filename.EXE
-name displayname
-info additionalinfo
-spc publishingcredentials.SPC
-pvk privatekey.PVK
```

Table 15.2 explains the parameters of the command for the application.

Table 15.2 These Signcode Parameters Help You with the Command to Start the Application

Parameter	Description
-prog *filename*	This provides the name of the executable to sign.
-name *displayname*	This friendly name displays as the descriptive name of the signed application.
-info *additionalinfo*	This is a location, usually a site on the Web, that provides more information about the software.
-spc *credentials*	This is your software publishing credentials file, with the file extension SPC.
-pvk *privatekey*	This is your private key file, with the file extension PVK.

 You can also run the Signcode application with no command line parameters. If you do, a Wizard will be started that will walk you through the process of signing your code. It is a process that is very easy to follow, and takes only a couple of minutes to complete.

After you've completed the command, the code will be signed and updated on your system. You can check to make sure the signing was successful by running the chktrust.exe application, also provided with the SDK. Chktrust's only parameter is the name of the file that you want to verify.

Chktrust will display the certificate for your software so you can confirm that it was correctly signed. You'll also be able to see what other people will view when they access your signed code. It's always a good idea to test the code signature prior to posting it for the public.

N O T E   Always work with a copy of your file, not the original. The code signing physically changes the file, adding information about your credentials. While unexpected, if anything happens during the signing process, you don't want to ruin the only copy of the code that you have. ■

As a final test, open the file by choosing the standard File. Then, choose Open and select your recently signed file. When prompted, indicate that you want to open it. After the file is transferred, you should be prompted with the certificate showing the information you provided. If you are not prompted with this information, verify the code signing again using `chktrust`. Then, reapply the signature, if needed.

As a rule, you should sign *all* code provided by your site, whether it be for internal or external use. It really is your responsibility as webmaster to ensure that the software provided your users is as safe as possible. It also means that more users will be apt to trust it and download it if it is signed by a reputable company. This means more potential customer downloads.

Reality Check

At the Reality Check sites, the SSL capabilities are very important. At the Integra site, the SSL approach secures transactions to enable the real-time purchase and download of software from the site. By using SSL, you can retrieve credit card and other payment information without worrying about giving that information to people who have no business with it.

The Integra site features download options for retail builds of software, downloads of evaluation copies, and more. The SSL enables you to provide these items directly to the user without requiring any other correspondence or calls to the user to get payment information before the download.

At the IntelliCenter Reality Check site, SSL not only receives orders and payments for classes, but also protects transcripts for students. The transcripts give students information on what classes they've attended to date. It is important, therefore, that the information be transferred correctly. IntelliCenter also uses the SSL encryption for transferring company-sensitive information when accessing company databases for maintenance, reporting, and other purposes. This enables users to retrieve critical company information, such as data on marketing and finance, and other items. This can all be transmitted over the Internet, without worrying about having the information either become corrupted or fall into the wrong hands.

One lesson learned is that the length of time required to get a certificate can vary enormously, requiring anywhere from two to eight weeks. Be sure to keep this in mind when you apply for your certificate, as it can severely impact your ability to provide for electronic commerce on your site.

From Here...

SSL can bring a good level of protection to your site. This level of protection enables you to confidently allow even financial transactions on your site. You should consider the following additional sources of information for related topics:

■ Chapter 2, "Choosing a Web Server and Service Provider," gives you insight into the workings of the NT Server security subsystem. This chapter also helps you to control access to your server, with respect to this subsystem.

■ Chapter 9, "Firewalls and Proxy Servers," covers providing Firewall access to and from your Intranet to the Internet. While SSL encrypts information, it does not provide access controls to the information you are hosting.

■ Que's *Special Edition Using Windows NT Server* by Roger Jennings goes into great detail on the inner workings of the NT security system, and how you can use it to control access to your server from an Intranet perspective.

Conducting Transactions on the Internet

You've set up your Web server, started advertising, and are beginning to experience some activity on your site. Now, you are hungering for more ambitious mountains to climb, and have dreams of becoming a huge success on the Web. Assuming that you already have your product ready to sell, all you need to do is assemble a few pages of HyperText Markup Language (HTML) to entice customers, add a form to capture buyer's credit card numbers, and you're in business! Can this be so simple?

Unfortunately, setting up shop on the Web isn't quite so easy. Most users are wary of sending their credit card numbers over the Internet without some sort of assurances that they won't be trusting the wrong person. If a hacker finds your credit card number on the Internet, how will you know to cancel the card? Do you use only cards that are close to their credit limits, thereby denying the hacker the ability to charge much? What happens with the card number once it has been received by your Web server? Will some other hacker with ill intent be able to lift the number from your server hard drive?

Find out about security technologies on the Web

You'll see how you can apply some of the emerging standards to your Web site in an effort to secure the information coming into and going out of your site.

See how you implement a secure certificate on a Netscape server

Find out what steps are necessary to implement a secure certificate on your server, making it possible to support the Secure Sockets Layer protocol.

Learn about the different transaction funding options that are available

Several different options are available to help you conduct secure transactions, these different types of electronic funds are outlined and explained so you'll know exactly how they work and what to expect from the different options available.

Fortunately, the attractiveness of conducting business transactions over the Internet has spurred numerous companies to develop solutions to all these problems. Today, the more challenging question is deciding which of the Internet transaction technologies to use. This chapter examines the following subjects:

■ This chapter examines the individual issues involved in conducting financial transactions over the Internet, in particular over the World Wide Web.

■ This chapter discusses what is involved in configuring your Web server to use Secure Sockets Layer (SSL) to encrypt all information that is passed between your Web server and the buyer's Web browser.

■ This chapter helps you to understand the emerging Secure Electronic Transactions (SET) standard which is emerging from a collaboration among Microsoft, Netscape, VISA, and MasterCard.

■ This chapter helps you examine the currently available alternatives while waiting for SET to become widely available. ■

Examining Issues Surrounding Transactions on the Internet

Before reviewing the details of conducting transactions over the Web, take a quick look at some of the issues that have to be taken into account. By now, just about everyone has read stories about rouge hackers cruising the Internet, looking for credit card numbers to steal. This is the root of several issues with which you have to be concerned, as shown in the following list.

■ Credit card numbers need to be encrypted before transmission over the Internet.

■ Vendors need to make sure that the credit card number received belongs to the person making the purchase.

■ Vendors need to make sure that customers' credit card numbers cannot be stolen from the vendor's server.

■ Vendors need to have a secure connection for receiving credit authorization approval from the issuing bank.

Encrypting Credit Card Numbers

Sending your credit card number over the Internet unencrypted is similar to picking up your telephone, dialing a number at random, and giving your credit card number to the person on the other end of the line. There's a good chance that the person at the other end will be honest and not abuse your good credit. There's also a chance, however, that the person will turn around and call the Home Shopping Network and order everything available using your card number.

Dishonest hackers are not going to be looking for credit card numbers floating across the Internet at random. These people will more likely be targeting traffic going into and out of a vendor's Web site. The hacker's job will become much more difficult if the traffic going into and out of the vendor's Web site is encrypted.

> **N O T E** Current U.S. export law prohibits the exporting of strong encryption technology to other countries. While that means that the version of Secure Sockets Layer (SSL) that is built into most Web browsers can be broken, it takes a large amount of computing power to accomplish this. The likelihood of a hacker having the computing power available to decrypt an encrypted credit card number is very low. Hackers proficient at what they do will know of many targets that are easier to hit and will provide good financial return. They would rather spend their time decrypting these targets' SSL communications, hoping to find a credit card number.
>
> While the current browser encryption technology is very good, some companies feel that it is not enough. For this reason, both Microsoft and Netscape have released a version of their browsers, offering a much more complex "unbreakable" type of encryption, available only within the U.S. Other countries are beginning to develop their encryption technologies outside U.S. borders. In this way, these countries are avoiding the export laws. This is an area of such importance that it will continue to improve, despite the efforts of the U.S. government. ■

Verifying Buyer Identity

As a vendor selling a product, you want to make sure that the person making a purchase is the one who has authorization to use the credit card number you receive. Next time you purchase something using a credit card over the phone, pay attention to how much information is requested. It's more than just the card number. The information requested involves the expiration date and name on the card, and often includes the billing address. This all ensures that the vendor can be certain that the person making the purchase has authorization to use the card in question. If the vendor only checks for available credit on the card, the buyer can purchase a large amount of merchandise before the vendor actually charges the account. The vendor might find that in the time between checking for available credit and placing the charge on the card, the account has been canceled. This leaves the vendor holding a bad credit card number. The buyer then gets away with the merchandise.

Security of Credit Card Numbers on the Vendor's Server

Once you have customers placing orders and sending you their credit card numbers to pay for your merchandise, you owe it to your customers to protect their credit card numbers from being stolen from your server by a hacker.

> **CAUTION**
>
> The threat of credit card numbers being stolen from a vendor server cannot be underestimated. The well-publicized Kevin Mitnik case a couple of years ago is a good example. The case was triggered by finding a file containing credit card numbers of customers of a popular Internet Service Provider (ISP) on a server of another ISP.

Several options are available for keeping credit card numbers secure from hackers. These options include the following:

- Keep all credit card numbers in a strongly encrypted form.
- Keep all credit card numbers on a different server, behind a strong firewall, that cannot be accessed from the Internet.
- Use one of the alternatives to credit cards discussed later in this chapter.

Obtaining Bank Approvals

Once your customers have placed their orders and given you their credit card numbers, you need some way of getting an approval on the charge. If the merchandise you are selling has to be shipped, you can use a regular telephone to obtain the credit approval before you ship the order. If, on the other hand, you are selling some form of electronic goods that your customers can have immediately, you need to have some sort of automated method of getting credit approvals. You can have a dial-up connection into the various credit card approval systems, using a modem connected to your server. Keep in mind that this can be a potential bottleneck if you have multiple customers making purchases all at once, depending on how your approval software is written. Another option is to have a network connection, within your firewall, to one of the credit card approval networks. This would enable multiple credit approvals to be processed at the same time, and produce faster response to the customer.

Implementing Secure Sockets Layer (SSL)

No matter which payment method and technology you choose to use in your Web store, you should provide your customers with the feeling that no anyone can see their credit card, or Ecash (electronic cash) number that is transmitted across the Internet, unencrypted. This means implementing Netscape's Secure Sockets Layer (SSL) in your Web server. There are other encryption methods available. SSL, however, has become the standard for Web-based technologies, for servers and browsers from the majority of manufacturers, including Microsoft and Quarterdeck.

Implementing Secure Sockets Layer on a Web server is a five-step process, as follows. Figure 16.1 also explains these steps.

1. Generate a Key Pair File and a Request File using utility provided with the Web server software.
2. Send Key Pair and Request Files to a Certificate Authority, such as Verisign, found at **http://www.verisign.com/**. This action requests a certificate.
3. Receive the certificate that the Certificate Authority generates.
4. Install the resulting certificate on your server.
5. Activate SSL security on your Web server.

N O T E Verisign, at **http://www.verisign.com/**, asks that you initiate the process of requesting the SSL certificate with them before generating the key pair and request files on your server (see Figure 16.1). Part of the initial certificate request involves initiating a relationship with Verisign. In this way, Verisign verifies that you are authorized to request an SSL certificate for your company, and that your company does own the rights to the server DNS entry. ■

N O T E The turn around time in generating the RSA certificate is listed as three to five days. The process can, however, take as much as two to three weeks, if demand is high. Depending on which Certificate Authority you choose, you might have to renew your certificate on an annual or semi-annual basis. ■

FIG. 16.1

These steps help you activate Secure Sockets Layer on a Web server.

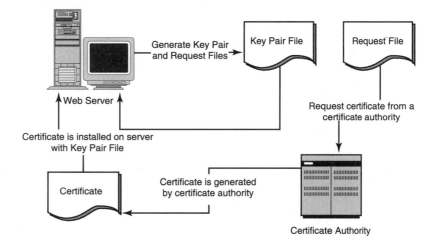

 The steps taken in generating a certificate request and configuring a Web server for Secure Sockets Layer is different for each server. These steps also can change with each new upgrade. Be sure to read the instructions that came with your server so that you know the steps you need to take.

CAUTION

The certificate generated by the Certificate Authority is a RSA Public and Private Key combination that uses the password employed in generating the Key Pair and Request files to encrypt the keys. This RSA encryption key contains the server name and location, as specified in the key generation. Once a certificate has been requested for a particular Web server, do not change the name of the server. If you do, your customers will receive a rather nasty message stating that the RSA keys were not issued to the server on which they are being used. This is not the type of message that makes customers feel confident that the information they provide will be kept secure.

Generating a Key Pair for Netscape Server

The Netscape utility that generates the request file is referred to as *SEC-KEY*. With the Netscape utility, there are more steps that have to be taken to complete the request generation beyond just running the generation utility. These steps are as follows:

1. At the DOS (or UNIX) prompt, change to the /bin/httpd/admin/bin directory underneath the Netscape server root directory.

2. Type **SEC-KEY** to run the key generation program.

3. When prompted, type the location for the new key pair file. Usually, this is in the **httpd-<servername>/config** directory with the name **ServerKey.db**.

4. At this point, you see a progress meter on-screen. If you are running on a Windows platform, move the mouse at random. If you are on a UNIX terminal, press keys at random intervals. The SEC-KEY utility is employing the time intervals between these actions to generate random numbers for use in generating your key pair.

5. When prompted, enter a password for use in administering your server security. The password must be at least eight characters long, and must contain at least one nonalphabetical character, perhaps a number or punctuation mark, somewhere in the middle.

6. Retype the password for verification.

7. For now, you are finished with the SEC-KEY utility. Go into the Server Manager. Then, choose Encryption|Generate Key.

8. In the Key Pair form, fill in the path for the place in which the key pair file should be created. You should make sure that only the Netscape server has read and write access to this directory.

9. Click *OK*. The server will create the new key pair file.

Generating a Certificate Request for Netscape Server

Generating a certificate request is a separate procedure on Netscape servers. This is performed through the Server Manager. You follow these steps:

1. In the Server Manager, choose Encryption|Request Certificate.

2. In the Certificate Authority field, enter the e-mail address for the Certificate Authority that you have chosen.

3. Specify whether this is a new certificate or a renewal.

4. Enter the location and password for your key file. This information is not sent to the Certificate Authority.

5. Enter your identification information. This is the Distinguished Name information that you entered in the last argument of the IIS KEYGEN utility. Please see Table 16.1.

6. Enter your phone number. This will be used by the Certificate Authority personnel if they need to discuss your certificate.

7. Click *OK*. The server automatically generates the request e-mail. Then, the server sends it to the Certificate Authority specified in the Certificate Authority field.

Installing a Certificate on Netscape Server

Once you have received your RSA certificate from your Certificate Authority, you install it using the Server Manager. You follow these steps:

1. In the Server Manager, choose Encryption|Install Certificate.
2. Click This Server.
3. Name the certificate.
4. If you saved the e-mail containing the certificate as a file, you can add to it the full path and file name. Alternatively, you can paste in the text from the e-mail in the space provided.
5. In the Certificate Database field, specify the certificate database into which to copy this certificate. The default is named ServerCert.
6. Click *OK*. The server decrypts the message, extracts the certificate, and saves it to the database specified.

N O T E Netscape servers maintain a list of certificates from Certificate Authorities. If the Certificate Authority you are using isn't already included in this list, you will need to request a certificate for the Certificate Authority. This enables the Netscape server to trust the RSA certificate received from the Certificate Authority. ▓

Once the certificate has been installed, you can turn SSL on from the Server Manager by choosing **Encryption|On/Off**.

Understanding Secure Electronic Transactions Standards

The Secure Electronic Transaction (SET) protocol began as two competing standards efforts. The first effort was a joint one led by VISA and Microsoft. The second effort was also a joint effort led by MasterCard and Netscape. Eventually, all parties decided to pool their efforts and develop one consolidated effort. Joining this effort were organizations such as GTE, IBM, SAIC, Terisa, and Verisign. As of this writing, the effort is still under way, and has not been completed. By the time this book reaches the bookstore shelves, however, there is a good chance that the SET protocol will have been finalized. Initial versions of SET software might be appearing on the market from companies such as Microsoft and Netscape.

The SET protocol is being created for several reasons, some of which include the following:

■ As the Internet began going through phenomenal growth in the consumer market, everyone started to realize the potential for Web-based commerce. The financial powerhouses of VISA and MasterCard realized that if they did not step into the fray and provide their own secure payment technologies, they risked losing their preeminent position in the world of transactions that are not based on cash.

■ Most established financial institutions were looking for a single unified secure transaction technology that would not drastically alter their current existing systems. VISA and MasterCard were in a position to provide this. The reason is that the banks were already tied into the MasterCard and VISA networks.

■ As you see later, there already are several electronic transaction technologies available on the market. Each of the existing technologies, however, has very stringent limitations on where consumers can make purchases. To be able to make the purchase, consumers would also have to subscribe to the same payment technology as the Web vendor with whom they want to do business.

■ Most existing transaction technologies dealt with one or more of the issues surrounding electronic transactions. None, however, dealt with all the issues previously outlined.

An Overview of the SET Protocal Used in Financial Transactions

The SET protocol is an involved one using a combination of existing encryption, certificates, and payment processing technologies to achieve its goals. SET is designed to work not only with current credit cards, but also with debit cards, electronic cash, and checks. The SET protocol follows these steps:

1. The customer makes a purchase with merchant. The customer sends the merchant an encrypted SET charge slip containing the authorized payment amount, credit card account number, and identification certificate.

2. The merchant decrypts the order, shipping address, and payment amount information. The merchant does not have the ability to decrypt the credit card account number, or any other sensitive identification information.

3. The merchant adds to the SET charge slip the identification certificate. Then, the merchant forwards the encrypted charge slip to the merchant's bank or charge processing agent.

4. The bank decrypts the credit card account number and identification certificates. Credit authorization and settlement is processed through current credit processing channels and networks.

5. The bank sends an authorization back to the merchant to approve, or reject, the purchase.

6. The merchant sends the customer a receipt, showing the items purchased and the amount paid.

7. The charge is settled between the credit issuing bank and the customer through the normal billing process.

Figure 16.2 outlines these steps.

FIG. 16.2
These are the steps for
the basic SET
transaction protocol.

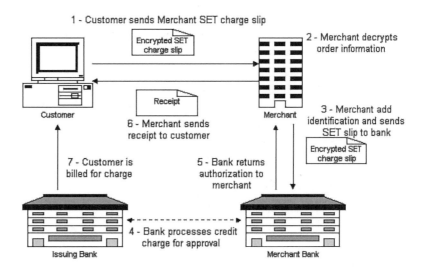

N O T E   The entire SET protocol specification can be obtained from VISA corporation at **http://
www.visa.com/cgi-bin/vee/sf/set/intro.html**. ▪

Two Different Forms of Encryption for the SET Protocol

The SET protocol uses two different forms of cryptography to achieve the level of encryption
necessary to provide the separate levels of decryption required in a transaction. These are
Secret-Key encryption, and *Public-Key* encryption.

Secret-Key Encryption   Secret-Key encryption, also known as symmetric cryptography, uses
the same key to encrypt and decrypt the message. The same key is used to encrypt and decrypt the message. Therefore, both the sender and receiver of the message have to have the
same encryption key. This makes Secret-Key encryption impractical for the millions of users
on the Internet. The reason is that the key would have to be transmitted unencrypted, thus
making it easily stolen. This would defeat the purpose of using encryption in the first place.

Secret-Key encryption is however already used heavily within the banking industry. The reason is that a limited number of institutions need to know each other's encryption keys. Also,
this encryption form is commonly used to encrypt PIN numbers on banking cards.

Public-Key Encryption   Public-Key encryption, also known as Public/Private Key or asymmet-
ric encryption, uses two closely related keys to encrypt and decrypt messages. Either key can
be used to encrypt a message. The other key, however, has to be used to decrypt the message.
This makes Public-Key encryption ideal for use over the Internet.

By transmitting a public key to another user, messages can be passed back and forth between
the two users in an encrypted form. The first user can encrypt the messages with the private
key. The second user can decrypt the messages with the first user's public key. Likewise, the

second user can encrypt messages using the first user's public key. Then, the first user can decrypt the messages using the private key. As long as the private key is kept private, the messages can be safely sent in an encrypted form.

If both users are passing messages using a single Public/Private key pair, the public key could be intercepted. In this way, message passed from the key owner to the other user could be decrypted. Because of this danger, both users normally transmit their public keys to each other. Each participant encrypts his or her messages to the other using the other user's public key. This ensures that the messages can only be decrypted using the key owner's private key. This is what makes Public-Key encryption a very secure form of communication.

Combining Secret and Public Key Encryption   In the SET protocol, both of these encryption methods are used to provide an additional layer of security. There are several steps to this process, outlined in the following list:

1. First, the message sender generates a new secret encryption key, and uses it to encrypt the message to be sent.

2. Next, the secret encryption key is encrypted using the public key of the message recipient. This provides a "digital envelope" around the message.

3. Upon receiving the encrypted messages, the recipient uses his private key to decrypt the secret encryption key.

4. The secret encryption key is now used to decrypt the original message.

Certifying Messages by Using Digital Signatures   Finally, the origin of messages is certified by using digital signatures. A digital signature is generated through an algorithm that creates a 160-bit unique message checksum. This checksum is then encrypted using the sender's private key. The digital signature has to be decrypted using the sender's public key. This verifies that the message was sent by the key owner. The message checksum algorithm is such that changing one bit in the message will significantly alter the checksum result. This makes it obvious whether or not the message was tampered with en route.

N O T E   The SET specification requires the message sender to use two separate Public/Private Key combinations. The purpose of the first key combination is to exchange keys. This enables the other participant to send you messages. The second key pair is used exclusively for creating digital signatures to verify the authenticity of your messages. Remember that the messages you send are encrypted using the public key of the other user's message key combination. ▨

Passing Messages Using Encryption Methods Requires SET Certificates

Before any message passing begins, you want to be sure that the public keys you are using for exchanging messages belong to the person or corporation with whom you want to be exchanging messages. The ideal way to do this would be to exchange public keys over a closed network.

Unfortunately, the Internet is anything but a closed network. The alternative chosen for the SET protocol is to exchange public keys encrypted within a digital signature of a third party person or organization whom you both trust. This means that both parties must have the public key of the third party organization already on their system. Then, the key is available to decrypt the digital certificate containing the other party's public key.

This means that each participant needs to have acquired an identification certificate for both the message and signature public keys from a Certificate Authority before participating in SET-based transactions.

 TIP The latest versions of browsers from Netscape and Microsoft, among others, ship with several certificates already installed for various Certificate Authorities.

NOTE To acquire a personal certificate from a Certificate Authority, you will need to prove to the CA that you are who you claim to be. Just as you had to provide proof that you have authority to acquire digital certificates for your company to enable SSL on your Web server, you will need to furnish notarized proof of your identity to the Certificate Authority. ■

Discovering Microsoft and Netscape Transaction Alternatives

The SET protocol specification has not been finalized. Microsoft and Netscape, therefore, have software available for enabling merchants to provide credit card processing on the Web. Although neither is totally SET compliant, both take similar approaches to solving the credit processing situation. The primary limitation to both the Microsoft and Netscape interim solutions is that each works with a small number of banks for credit authorization processing. Both corporations have announced that they will be providing SET compliant transaction technologies shortly after the SET specification is finalized.

Examining Transaction Alternatives

Prior to the SET protocol initiative, there have been several companies who have produced various technologies for providing the Web with electronic transaction technology. All of the following companies are still in business, and provide a very good product to their customers. Once the SET protocol is finalized, however, and SET server software becomes available, just how many of the following corporations that provide financial services will stay in business remains to be seen.

CommerceNet

CommerceNet is an industry association that brings together providers of the various pieces of technology needed to enable Internet commerce. CommerceNet also is a Certificate Authority, and issues SSL and Digital Signature certificates. CommerceNet was originally organized to enable and influence the direction that transaction technology takes. It has established several working groups and pilot projects that have been a great influence on the direction that transaction technology has taken. CommerceNet can be found at **http://www.commerce.net/.** Figure 16.3 shows its home page. CommerceNet does not provide financial transaction processing; it does not, therefore, compete with the SET initiative.

FIG. 16.3

This is the home page for CommerceNet.

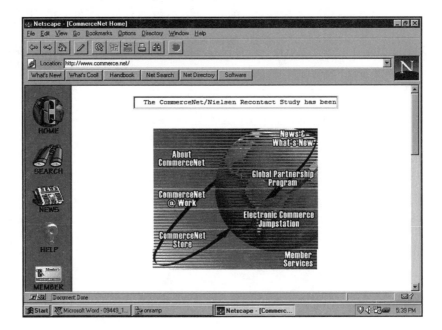

CyberCash

CyberCash provides a proprietary technology for enabling credit card transactions over the Internet. With the CyberCash technology, only the merchant has to have a relationship with the CyberCash Corporation. The merchant has to place a CyberCash Pay button on their Web page.

Once customers have selected the desired goods and services, they press the Pay button. The CyberCash client software is downloaded and activated on the customer's computer. The customer decides how much information the merchant is allowed to see. Once the customer has entered all the appropriate information, the credit card information is sent to the CyberCash processing server.

The server performs the credit authorization. Once the authorization has been received by the merchant, the transaction is completed. CyberCash uses the customer's regular credit cards, and the customers do not need to subscribe in any way to the CyberCash system. There is, therefore, a good chance the CyberCash will survive the debut of SET.

CyberCash can be contacted at **http://www.cybercash.com/**. Figure 16.4 shows its Web page.

FIG. 16.4

This is the Web page for CyberCash Corporation.

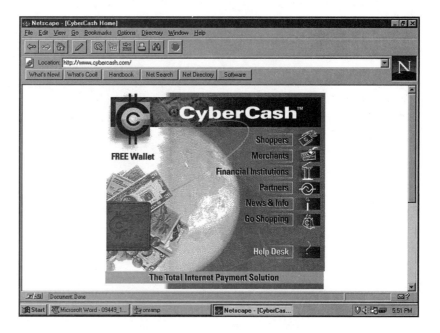

DigiCash

DigiCash provides Ecash technology that is used in electronic wallets and smart cards. In early 1995, DigiCash began an experiment using the Ecash technology over the Internet. DigiCash's primary focus is not Web-based transaction technology, but portable systems for conducting transactions that are not based on cash.

DigiCash has teamed up with both MasterCard and VISA to look into the potential of embedding DigiCash's smart card technology into credit and debit cards. Considering the company's focus on forms of electronic transactions that are not based on the Web, DigiCash is likely to be around for quite some time.

DigiCash can be found at **http://www.digicash.com/**. Figure 16.5 shows the company's Web page.

The First Virtual Internet Payment System

The First Virtual Internet Payment system takes the approach of keeping the financial portion of the transaction completely off the Internet. In the First Virtual system, customers have to open an account with First Virtual Holdings, Inc. using a MasterCard or VISA credit card. Customers decided how much credit to themselves.

FIG. 16.5

This is the main Web page for DigiCash Corporation.

In return, First Virtual gives customers a personal VirtualPIN number to be used in conducting transactions with First Virtual merchants. Once customers have placed an order with a merchant, they give the merchant their VirtualPIN number. Then, First Virtual confirms the transaction with the customer before transferring the appropriate funds to the merchant.

The First Virtual system requires that both the merchant and customer be subscribers to the system. Because of the requirement that both seller and buyer subscribe to the system, and the incompatibility with the SET protocol, along with the fact that the company will be in direct competition with SET, First Virtual might end up closing its doors sometime after the SET protocol is finalized.

In the meantime, First Virtual can be found at **http://www.fv.com/**. Figure 16.6 shows First Virtual's Web page.

Open Market

Open Market provides end-to-end software and hardware for businesses to quickly set up a storefront on the Internet. The Open Market system requires that the merchant already have a relationship with a credit processing and approval organization.

Open Market provides a system that is ready for plugging in your products—hooking up to your bank or clearing house on one end, and the Internet on the other. Considering the nature of Open Market's technologies, there is a good chance that it will be offering SET compliant systems shortly after the SET specification is finalized, competing with Microsoft and Netscape.

FIG. 16.6

This is the main Web page for First Virtual Holdings, Inc.

Open Market can be found at **http://www.openmarket.com/**. Figure 16.7 shows its Web page.

FIG. 16.7

This is the main Web page for the Open Market Corporation.

Reality Check

In an industry in which standards are the basis for every application, the standard for transaction technology is not available yet. It will be soon. In the meantime, what is available includes a number of proprietary technologies for conducting financial transactions.

The SET standard should be finalized sometime during the Fall of 1996, with SET systems appearing on the market by early 1997. At that time, there will be a standard protocol available for conducting financial transactions on the Web, with server software becoming available from Microsoft, Netscape, Open Market, and many others.

In the meantime, you might find merchants selling merchandise over the Internet, taking credit card numbers. If any merchants you come across are not using SSL, don't even think of giving them your credit card number. If the merchant is using SSL, you can be confident that your credit card number will be kept safe and secure, or you can take your business elsewhere.

You might be planning on setting up a storefront on the Internet. You can wait until SET compliant systems become available. Alternatively, you can buy a current system from a vendor, such as Open Market, Netscape, or Microsoft, who will likely upgrade your system to comply with SET once the standard is finalized.

From Here...

This chapter has taken a look at the current state of electronic transaction technology for use in setting up a storefront on the Internet. You examined the issues surrounding transactions, including encryption, certification, and security. You also looked at the process of installing Secure Sockets Layer on both Microsoft and Netscape Web servers. Then, you took a close look at the emerging Secure Electronic Transaction specification, and how that will provide a standard for building transaction technologies for Web-based commerce. Finally, you took a brief look at some of the other transaction technologies currently available on the Internet.

From here, you might want to read more to better understand Internet security and data encryption to learn how to protect your systems and any data you might be transmitting over the Internet. You also might want to take a look at HTML forms and CGI programming to gain an understanding of how you can get information from surfers on the Web. You might want to check out the following chapters:

- To gain an in depth understanding of firewalls and network security, see Chapter 9, "Firewalls and Proxy Servers."
- To learn how to set up HTML forms to enable your customers to provide your Web site with information, read Chapter 13, "Forms and Surveys."
- To understand encryption, digital signatures and certificates, read Chapter 15, "Data Encryption and Digital Signatures."
- To learn how to connect your Web site to a database to provide an extensive inventory of merchandise to sell, see Chapter 22, "Database Access and Integrity."

## PART IV

Understanding the Content Possibilities for Your Site

## CHAPTER 17

Browsers and Your Web Server

Web browsers are central to your network implementation. Today's browsers are the desktops of tomorrow, offering ready access not only to the information on your local system, but also to the local network and to the Internet. Browsers promise to be just that: information browsers for content in general.

Today, browsers enable you to point and click your way around the network, whether it's either the local or the worldwide network. When you view a page, expect to see several different items. Figure 17.1 shows a typical page layout containing both "hot spots" on the graphics image, and hyperlinks as text links.

Find out how browsers work with sites on the Internet and Intranet

Browsers use several protocols to work with content on the Internet. Find out what the URLs mean, and how you can use them.

Compare the browsers, and learn how they differ

In the world of Internet browsers, there is much competition among the companies that are actively developing browsers.

See what types of information are exchanged between the server and your system

Your system maintains a wealth of information about the server with which it is working at any given time. This is also true with respect to what the server can determine about your system.

FIG. 17.1

When you view an unfamiliar page, move your cursor around to locate "hot spots" on graphics, or to determine what items represent links.

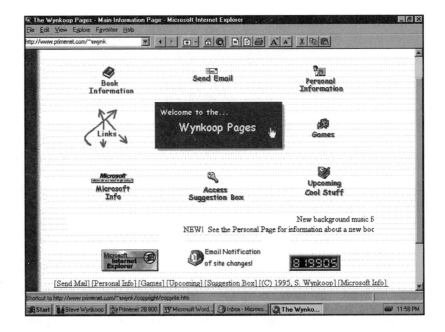

Browsers retrieve information from a site as text and graphics. The text that is received is in Hypertext Markup Language or HTML. HTML provides directives on the location and formatting of text, pictures, and hyperlinks. It's beyond the scope of this book to provide you with a complete reference for HTML. There are, however, many examples of how to use HTML to format pages. Other examples deal with many topics that concern your users, including how to provide additional content functionality.

Browsers set up a conversation of sorts with the Web server. This conversation enables the server to direct packets of information to your system. Graphics are encoded and sent to your system if it requests them. In most browsers, you have the option of not sending graphics as a default. This saves time in loading the image. Newer versions of mainstream browsers are now caching images on your local system, making the load time for images on pages you frequent significantly less.

N O T E On an Intranet, it is unlikely that you experience the same kinds of challenges that deal with speed and throughput that you encounter with the Internet. The network is largely local. For this reason, you enjoy the throughput afforded by a full-speed connection to the Web server at the speed of your local area network. In these types of environments, loading graphics is not typically an issue that warrants turning off the images. ∎

HTML is the base language for all Web page-based content. The HTML pages you access have many different components, including URLs, and hyperlinks to those URLs. Graphics can be called out as "hot" images. These images enable the user to click them to move to a new page. Alternatively, the link can be text that is underlined and appears in a different color on the user's monitor.

Web browsing is the client/server environment at its best. Your client software, the Web browser, requests a page from the server, and the server complies. The server returns only the requested page. Then, the server effectively disconnects from your browser, moving on to other requests. Using this specific request-specific response approach, a Web server serves a very significant number of users without bandwidth, performance, or other resource contention.

 TIP One of the hottest topics on the Web today is how to optimize, extend, and develop applications for use across the Internet and corporate Intranets. To that end, several emerging and developing technologies support this effort. JAVA, VRML, HTML 3, VB Script, ActiveX, and others surface in the marketplace at a dizzying pace. For more information on these exciting technologies, review Chapter 20, "ActiveX and the Internet," and Chapter 21, "Java Applets and the Internet."

N O T E In some cases, you keep a persistent connection to the Server. In most cases, however, the connection establishes when requesting a page. Then, the connection is dropped. ■

Most of the information retrieved from a Web site is contained in pages. In most cases, pages take a bit of time to digest at the user location. This means the server has some time before an additional request comes from the user. In fact, the user might follow a link on the page to a different server somewhere else on the Intranet or Internet.

 TIP It might surprise you that you can insert hyperlinks into standard documents. From within Word, if you've installed the Word Assistant, select Insert, HyperLink. A dialog box appears that enables you to specify any URL to insert into your document.

If you distribute the document, and users read it with Word or the Word viewer, they can click the link. Then, it is followed. The type of link determines whether the user's current browser, Word or Word Viewer in this case, is used to view the object. The link also determines whether a more appropriate viewer is called up.

When browsers communicate with a server, they exchange a fair amount of information about your environment. For example, consider Listing 17.1. It shows a sample set of headers exchanged between a browser and a server.

Listing 17.1 Sample Headers Exchanged When Working with Web Content

```
GATEWAY_INTERFACE = 'CGI/1.1'
HTTP_ACCEPT = 'image/gif, image/x-xbitmap, image/jpeg, image/pjpeg, */*'
HTTP_ACCEPT_LANGUAGE = 'en'
HTTP_CONNECTION = 'Keep-Alive'
HTTP_HOST = 'www-1.openmarket.com'
HTTP_REFERER = 'http://www-1.openmarket.com/browsertest/'
HTTP_UA_COLOR = 'color8'
HTTP_UA_CPU = 'x86'
HTTP_UA_OS = 'Windows 95'
HTTP_UA_PIXELS = '800x600'
```

continues

Listing 17.1   Continued

```
HTTP_USER_AGENT = 'Mozilla/2.0 (compatible; MSIE 3.0B; Win32)'
PATH = '/sbin:/usr/sbin:/bin:/usr/bin:/usr/local/bin:/usr/contrib/bin'
QUERY_STRING = ''
REMOTE_ADDR = '198.68.42.72'
REMOTE_HOST = 'swynk.tus.primenet.com'
REQUEST_METHOD = 'GET'
SCRIPT_NAME = '/browsertest/form/nph-dumpid.cgi'
SERVER_NAME = 'www-1.openmarket.com'
SERVER_PORT = '80'
SERVER_PROTOCOL = 'HTTP/1.0'
```

As you can see, there is a lot of information here, including those tidbits that the client application knows about the server. Some of this information might concern, for example, the protocol and port that is used. ■

Understanding the Differences Among Browsers

Philosophical differences exist among the top most quickly progressing browsers from Netscape and Microsoft. These differences might impact your decision about which browser, if any, to standardize for your company. Two core issues represent differences in each company's approach to working on the Internet. These issues are as follows:

■ Handling add-in functionality

■ Supplemental language support

Add-in functionality refers to the nonbrowser components that are needed to support the extended content on the Internet. These types of utility functions include items such as support for RealAudio™, ActiveX controls, and other custom modules.

These items are typically referred to as add-ins or plug-ins, and are made to work with the browser. They provide access to the content on the pages that you view. With Netscape, plug-ins are provided, after the fact, from different vendors that support the Netscape browser. The majority of Netscape plug-ins are provided by these outside vendors. Netscape has recently released support for ActiveX controls with the use of a plug-in to facilitate the technology.

Microsoft supports the plug-in model. The company, however, prefers to provide the added functionality with the ActiveX control approach. Microsoft provides many different ActiveX controls, and several are built into the browser. In this way, you won't have to further download them to make the controls available.

Browsers made by both Netscape and Microsoft support Java natively, though the implementation has been in place for a longer period of time in the Netscape browser. As of this writing, ActiveX scripting, or VBScript, is supported only in the Microsoft browser.

One key factor between the two rival browsers is that Internet Explorer from Microsoft is free. Netscape's browser is not, although with the Gold version of the Netscape browser, an HTML editing environment is included.

Other browsers, and there are many of them in widespread use, typically support the more traditional Web-browsing capabilities, providing for navigation, graphics viewing, and HTML 2.x functionality. In many cases, these browsers will not support the latest features, including style sheets, frames, or scripting languages, though there are exceptions.

Deciding on the Best Browser

Selecting the best browser is a tough decision—if you'll be making the decision, one that is absolute. "Absolute" means that if you're looking for a single browser that is the best in all fields, there really isn't one available, regardless of whether it's provided free of charge, or for a fee.

If you're looking for a browser to standardize on for an Intranet situation, it would probably be best to select the browser that the people who created your server software provide. The reason is that you'll know whom to go to if any problems arise that appear to be related to compatibility between your browser and the server.

If you're simply looking for the most common and widely accepted browser, the numbers to support that decision are up in the air at this moment. Consider Table 17.1, extracted from a site on the Internet that monitors its incoming traffic.

Table 17.1   This Table Concerns Site Access by the Browser

Top Agents	Number of Files	Percent
Mozilla/2.02 (Win16; I)	184	5.75
Duppies/1	1174	5.44
Mozilla/2.0 (compatible; MSIE 3.0; Windows 95)	130	4.06
Mozilla/3.0b6Gold (Win16; I)	129	4.03
Mozilla/2.0 (Win16; I)	127	3.97
Mozilla/3.0 (Win95; I)	117	3.66
WebCrawler/2.0 libwww/3.0	107	3.34
Mozilla/2.01 (Win16; I)	101	3.16
Mozilla/3.0 (Macintosh; I; PPC)	92	2.88
Mozilla/1.22 (Windows; I; 16bit)	86	2.69

This information represents accesses against the surveying site, and shows the number of files and overall percentage relative to number of total accesses on the site for each browser type.

These top 10 browsers represent only 40 percent of the browsers in use. You might see a browser type on the list that you do not recognize, possibly even a user-built browser. All of this adds to the confusion of selecting the right browser for a given task.

General consensus is that the Microsoft browser is somewhat faster loading graphics, but requires substantially more disk space than the Netscape browser. The debate regarding the scripting languages and technologies is ongoing, and is expected to continue, with a steady merge toward common support for these development environments.

Netscape provides more cleanly integrated tools. They include the company's mail client and Web page development features. These tools run within the Netscape environment. They can make it easier for your users to find these applets and have less trouble running them.

Understanding URLs

This chapter presents several different services to offer your users, ranging from full-blown World Wide Web HTML pages to Gopher services. You might have noticed the lack of information on user-oriented tools to gain access to this information. Helpful advances in browser technology offer this information to your users more seamlessly. These advances do not require user understanding of either the genesis of the information or the specific services providing the information.

Remember, your specified URL starts with a prefix, often *http*: in the cases discussed previously. The http: in these cases indicates a Web server connection, directing the browser how to communicate to the server processes.

N O T E With your Intranet setting, you can specify only the server name. The browser generally resolves the server name to an IP address. Then, the browser attempts to attach to that server's Web service. The Web service is generally considered the default protocol in these cases.

You can accomplish the same connection, using the examples in this chapter, by requesting either of the following URLs:

> **http://holodeck3**
>
> **holodeck3** ▓

The URL prefixes that Table 17.2 shows are generally supported by mainstream browsers.

Table 17.2   The URLs Begin with these Common Prefixes

Prefix	How the Prefix Operates
File:	Opens a network drive file for browsing. Note: You do not require a connection to a Web, FTP, or Gopher server for this protocol. Example: `File:///c:\mydir\myfile.htm`
Http:	Opens an HTML document for viewing. Example: `http://holodeck3/` or `http://www.microsoft.com/ie/ie.htm`
Https:	Opens a secure HTML document for viewing. This requires the establishment of a Secure Socket Layer conversation with the server. Example: `https://holodeck3`
Gopher:	Opens a Gopher session. Example: `gopher://holodeck3`

Prefix	How the Prefix Operates
FTP:	Opens a file transfer protocol, or FTP session. Example: `ftp://www.intellicenter.com/myfile.zip`
NEWS:	Opens a news server. Example: `news://msnews.microsoft.com`

You might encounter other prefixes. The ones in the preceding table, however, will more likely appear on the Internet. `telnet:`, for example, establishes a telnet session to the address you indicate, and "news:" attempts to attach to a UseNet news service. Many of these protocols that are less commonly implemented can actually execute utilities dedicated to support them.

From Here...

In this chapter, you've learned more about some of the behind-the-scenes aspects of the Web browser. You'll be working with several considerations when you decide to standardize on a browser. In most cases, you'll find it best to standardize on more than one. This is probably the best choice, whatever your needs, for compatibility and flexibility. For more information about the technologies that you'll want to consider supporting, see the following chapters:

- Chapter 21, "Java Applets and the Internet," goes into more detail about working with Java-based applications on Web sites.

- Chapter 23, "Network/Video Conferencing, Internet Phone, and Real Audio," shows what some of the different add-ins and plug-ins are that you might want to consider supporting in your browser.

Part
IV
Ch
17

## CHAPTER 18

Basic HTML Techniques

As you've seen throughout this book, the Internet is made up of a huge array of documents. The Internet gives you nearly unlimited access to documents, software, and other types of information located around the world. HTML is used to format these Internet documents. It turns what would otherwise be monotonous text files into visually pleasing, hyperlinked documents. HTML is the foundation for your Web site, and connects it to the vast arena of information known as the Internet. ■

Learn the basic elements that make up a hypertext document, or Web page

A hypertext document is a document formatted, or coded, with Hypertext Markup Language, or HTML, tags for use on the Internet.

Learn the fundamentals of creating a Web page

As with any programming, there are basic rules to follow. This chapter explains the basic requirements of a properly formatted hypertext document for use on your Web site.

Become familiar with the tools that are available to assist you in creating these Web pages

HTML editors can be your best friend or your worst nightmare. They range from simple text editors to What You See Is What You Get" (WYSIWYG) word processor-like applications.

Learn how and when to use images in your Web page

Not everyone has a speedy connection to the Internet. You will need to understand the difference between a document that has effective graphics and something that would be considered a waste of bandwidth.

A Brief History of HTML

The original HTML specification, in use since 1990, supported only the basic connection of documents using a hyperlink as well as structure characteristics such as level headings and basic font characteristics, including bold and italics. With the increase of the Internet's popularity came HTML 1.0. This specification, or version, included a wider range of text styles as well as in-line images. The specification for HTML 2.0 incorporated the use of tables and the now increasingly popular <FONT> tag for even greater formatting enhancements. HTML 3.2, the most recently published HTML draft, incorporates frames for multitiered Web sites, Cascading Style Sheets, JAVA, and support for other technological advancements.

HTML 3.0

HTML 3.0 was originally named HTML+, and was intended as a simple addition to HTML 2.0 to support table and figure elements. So many additions were suggested that it was decided to rename it as a major revision, HTML 3.0. The problem with HTML 3.0 was the great leap it took from HTML 2.0. The deployment and implementation of HTML 3.0 was considered impractical, and this version was never published as a specification.

HTML 3.2

HTML 3.2 is currently considered a Request For Comments draft. This version, however, will probably be considered final by the release of this book. It is also the version referenced in the next few chapters of this book. HTML 3.2 is a major version update from HTML 2.0. This latest version, however, is not as boundless as HTML 3.0 was, and gives more consideration to enhancing the current elements instead of creating new ones. The HTML 3.2 specification also allows for full control over the manipulation of text through Cascading Style Sheets. Cascading Style sheets, or Style Sheets, give you control over text that had only been possible before with images. The boundaries of text formatting played a major role in the browser-wide support for in-line images. In-line images created a spark in the eye of the Internet community, and graphics showed up in Web pages everywhere. Large graphics were added to sites with no consideration for the speed of a typical user's connection to the Internet. Abuses of this sort lessened the bandwidth on many sites, and caused heavily loaded servers to slow the transfer of the files.

Creating a Web Page

To learn how to put all these elements together properly, you must first understand the basic structure of a hypertext document, and what needs to be included in the source, or source code. It might seem somewhat cryptic at first. Soon, however, you'll see how to use these features to create a compelling and useful Web site.

Using what would be considered basic elements by today's standards, you can create a Web site that is easy to manage. Figure 18.1 shows the World Wide Web Consortium's public home page for HTML.

FIG. 18.1
The most basic HTML
elements come
together.

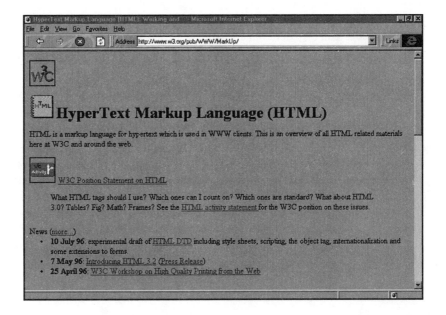

If you have ever browsed the Internet, you have already seen many of the elements of a Web page. Some of these elements are the header, body, and footer of the page. Table 18.1 shows the fundamental HTML tags of every Web page.

Table 18.1   The Basic HTML Document Elements Show the Beginning of Documents and Some of Their Characteristics

Elements	What These Elements Show
`<HTML>...</HTML>`	This is the main document container. It specifies the beginning of a hypertext document.
`<HEAD>...</HEAD>`	This specifies information pertinent to the document characteristics, and sometimes the formatting.
`<BODY>...</BODY>`	This specifies when the browser should start displaying the document.

Table 18.1 includes the basic elements that every Web page must have to be viewed with a Web browser. The `<HTML>` tag specifies the beginning of a Web page. This element must be used in order to be viewed with a Web browser. The `<HEAD>` tag specifies the page header. Anything contained in this tag will not be displayed as content on the Web page. Finally, the `<BODY>` tag specifies the place in which the content is to be displayed in the browser.

Part
IV

Ch
18

In addition, you might find it easier to look at pages in a logical manner, breaking them up into sections that help determine what information appears in which locations on the page. Table 18.2 provides an example of what these sections might be.

Table 18.2 You Might Break Web Pages into Some of These Logical Sections

Page Sections	Content of These Sections
The Header	This usually contains the company logo or home page title.
The Body	This incorporates text, hyperlinks, images, and other graphical enhancements to the page. This section is considered the "meat" of the page. The body of the page is also the place in which you'll find enhancements, such as JAVA applets and ActiveX scripting and controls.
The Footer	The footer often contains hyperlinks to copyright information and other pertinent data about the creation and maintenance of the Web page.

N O T E Don't let the mention of Java applets and ActiveX controls confuse you. Although this type of content is beyond the scope of this chapter, it is mentioned in an effort to break down what is currently used as content on the Internet. Chapter 20, "ActiveX and the Internet," and Chapter 21, "Java Applets and the Internet," both offer explanations of these technologies. ■

Understanding the Header

As previously mentioned, the Header is the place in which you will most likely place a company logo and other pertinent information. If your site doesn't catch the interest of the people browsing it, they will likely move on. Keep this in mind as you design your page. You can include large graphics of your company's logo that will download rather quickly with a direct connection to your Web site. The person viewing your site with a 9,600-baud connection, however, might find the download time too long. Another section later in this chapter discusses tips on adding these images.

Understanding the Body

The body of a Web page is basically the same as the body of any other document. This is the place in which your content and graphics go. You might have basic text explaining your company mission and goals, and hyperlinks to other Web pages, as well as other HTML enhancements. A section later in the chapter discusses these enhancements.

The graphics you insert here should be carefully thought out. Assume the typical user has a 14.4-kilobaud modem, and limit your Web pages to 45 kilobytes in overall size, with the addition of graphics. When considering the overall size, do not include images displayed on previous pages that might already be cached. This is a good rule of thumb when it comes to Web page design. This rule will be followed throughout the next few chapters.

Figure 18.2 is an example of these logical sections at work. At the top is the logo and the navigational toolbar. The body holds the directory for the site, and the footer contains the logos of products supported by the site.

FIG. 18.2
The header usually contains a logo.

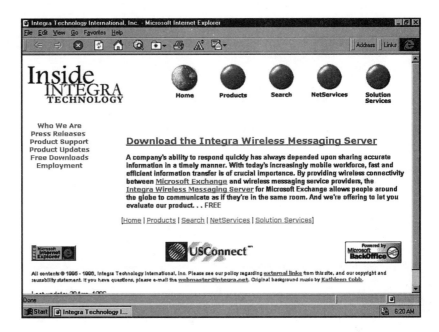

Fundamentals of HTML

As the name implies, HTML is a markup language. It is based on another markup language known as Standard Generalized Markup Language (SGML), a machine-level markup language used for defining text attributes and formatting other markup languages. It is also similar to BASIC, in which the browser is doing the interpreting. However, it is not interpreted in the same manner. With HTML, you insert element tags, also referred to as tags, around and between standard ASCII text. Next, you save it with an HTM or HTML extension. You then view it with a browser. In this case, the browser does the interpreting. See Chapter 17, "Browsers and Your Web Server," to learn more about how browsers work.

▶ You can find more information on the structure of HTML in *Special Edition Using HTML, Second Edition.*

Using HTML Tags

Tags are used to format HTML documents. They are inserted at various locations in and around the text so that it can be formatted to your liking. There are two major groups of tags: the *container element* and the *marker element*. A container element is exactly as it sounds.

It uses two tags—an open tag and a close tag. These specify that the text contained in the tags should be formatted a particular way. On the other hand, the marker element specifies a place on the document where a specific element should be displayed. The marker elements do not need a close element.

All tags are contained in corner brackets. The close tag of a container is represented with a forward slash. Table 18.3 provides a few examples of container tags.

Table 18.3 HTML Container Tags Can Hold Formatting Specifications

```
<HTML>...</HTML>
<H1>...</H1>
```

In contrast, a marker element is only one tag. There is no beginning or end. You can think of it as planting a flag in your Web page. Table 18.4 shows some examples of marker tags.

Table 18.4 These Are Commonly Used HTML Marker Elements

```
<BR><HR>
<IMG>
```

T I P An issue that is generally debated is whether the <P> tag is a container or marker tag. It is used to specify a new paragraph. For our purposes, though, it will be used as a container.

Adding Element Attributes

HTML elements alone are somewhat restrictive to the design of a Web page, and don't offer much control. By adding attributes to HTML elements, you can specify a font face and color for a particular sentence or paragraph. You can also specify the dimensions of an image that will appear on a Web page. Not only do these attributes give you more control over your Web pages, they also offer a wider variety of styles from which to choose.

For example, from within the <BODY> tag, you can specify the background color or image of the page, the text color, and the color of a viewed link. You can also choose the color of both a newly presented link and one that is being clicked. Figure 18.3 shows body tag attributes for specifying these colors.

FIG. 18.3
Attributes are added to tags to provide greater control over the appearance of a page.

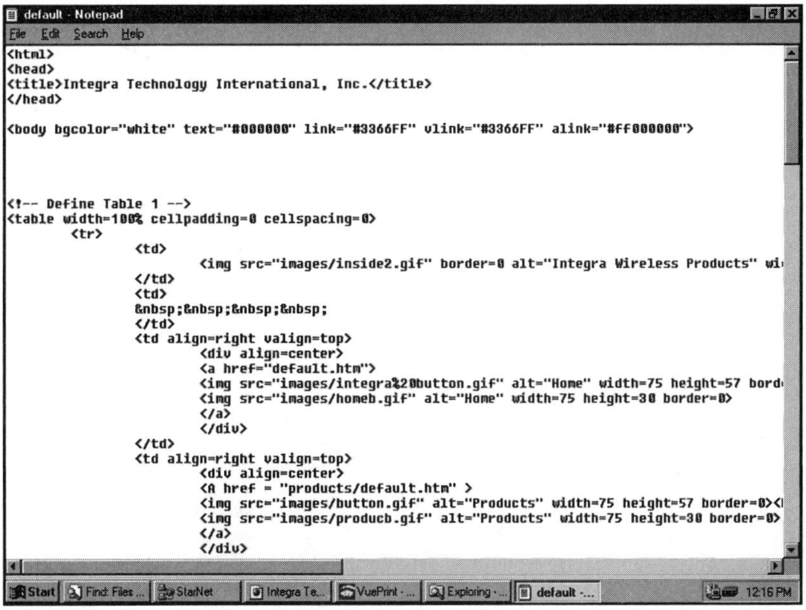

Formatting Rules

There are some basic formatting rules that remain true for all browsers. These basic formatting rules are what you should always keep in mind when creating your Web site. The following list discusses these:

- Blank space is ignored.
- Tags are not case-sensitive.
- Exact alignment is browser-dependent.

Blank Space Is Ignored

With browsers, users can control many aspects of how a Web page is displayed. Users can resize the browser window, and specify font sizes and colors. In browsers, text is automatically wrapped when it gets too close to the right margin. The place in which you insert a carriage return or line feed is not necessarily where a browser will display either one of these. This is not limited to carriage returns, either; only one space between characters is recognized. Anything more than that must be defined with the appropriate tag. For this reason, you must define every blank space that you want to appear in your Web page. The following listing and figure are an example of the browser ignoring undefined white space (see Figure 18.4).

```
<html>
<head>
<title>Blank Space is Ignored</title>
<body>
<h1>Blank Space is Ignored</h1>
<p>
This first line ends <i>here</i>
in the source, even though it is
not displayed as such.

Also, the additional carriage
return is ignored.
</p>
<b> The    three    spaces   between
   each   word   is   ignored   as
   well.</b>
</body>
</html>
```

FIG. 18.4

When viewed with a browser, this text is displayed differently.

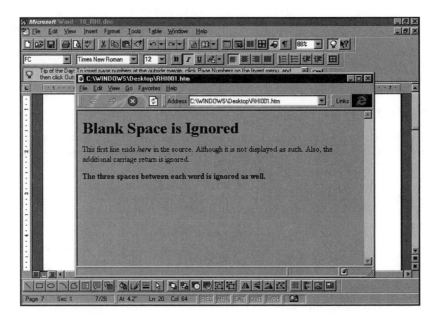

Tags Are Not Case-Sensitive

As you might have noticed from previous code samples, the tags have been written in lower-case. You can choose to use upper- or lowercase, or case that is mixed. It really doesn't make any difference in the displayed document. To make the editing and updating process of your Web pages easier, though, you might decide to use all uppercase tags.

Exact Alignment Is Browser-Dependent

You can use certain tag attributes to define specific text placement in the browser. While these tags often generate the same overall results from one browser to another, their exact placement varies. The reason is the way that browsers are programmed. In Microsoft Internet Explorer, there may be a margin of five pixels each on the left and the right. In Netscape Navigator, this margin may be seven pixels. While these numbers seem minute, this affects how and when the words wrap around the edge. You need to be careful where you insert line breaks and paragraphs.

Understanding the Basic Components of a Web Page

The basic HTML elements you will need to format the text for your Web pages can be broken down into eight sections. The following list outlines these sections:

- Header elements
- Headings
- Text styles
- Paragraphs and line breaks
- Lists
- Special Characters
- Hyperlinks
- Images

Part
IV

Ch
18

Header Elements

The only required header element for a Web page is the HTML open and close tag. Everything contained in those tags will be displayed as the Web page. There are, however, other header elements that you can use for both manipulating the output of the page and containing information pertinent to the document, such as copyrights. Table 18.5 lists and explains these header elements.

Table 18.5   Header Elements Help You Manipulate Information in Your Document

Element Name	Element Tag	Element Attributes
Document Title	`<title>...</title>`	No attributes
Document Location	`<base="URL">`	No attributes
Meta-information	`<meta>`	HTTP-EQUIV, CONTENT, URL

Using Tags for a Document Title   You use Title tags when you want to give a title to the document. The title is generally not included in the body of the Web page, unless you are using a Lynx browser. In this case, it is included at the top of the displayed page. In Internet Explorer, Netscape Navigator, and most other Windows platform browsers, the title is displayed in the title bar of the window. Older versions of Mosaic, though, display the document title in its own separate section of the browser window.

The document title is useful in many ways. If you include a title in the document, and someone bookmarks your page, the title becomes the default name of the bookmark. This makes it easily identifiable to users who often visit your Web site, and have bookmarked a specific page. It is also beneficial when indexing your site with a search engine. With search engines, the document title is often used as a way to index the site. It is also what the search engine uses as the link to the page. If you do not provide a document title, the first few characters in the document will be used. In most cases, though, it would be considered prudent to include one.

Using the Base Tag to Indicate Document Location   The Base tag is a marker used to specify the document's location on your server. This tag is used when providing links with relative paths instead of exact path names. With the exception of a few, most browsers save local copies of Web pages. If you were to view one of these cached documents, all relative paths specified in the anchor and image tags would be considered local. This would be the case if you did not use the Base tag. Although this tag is not required, using it assures that the links will always be pointed in the right direction, whether your page is being displayed on someone's local machine or on your Web server.

Adding Meta-Information About Your Document   Current HTML specification enables you to include other meta-information about your document through the use of Meta tags. Meta-information is data about your document that goes beyond what has already been specified in other header tags. The information is embedded in the document header. It is not visible on the page, with one exception.

The Meta tag cannot be used alone. You need to define it using attributes. Table 18.6 lists these attributes with their respective functions.

Table 18.6   You Can Add Meta Tags to Your Document and Define Them Using Appropriate Attributes

Attribute	Attribute Definition
HTTP-EQUIV	This binds the META elements to an HTTP response header.
NAME	This names properties of the document, such as keywords and author names. This is used instead of HTTP-EQUIV.
CONTENT	This defines a value for the two previous attributes.
URL	This specifies another document to bind to the HTTP response header, Refresh. It is used only with the CONTENT attribute.

NOTE The values of the Meta tag's attributes are not HTML-specific. Therefore, anything you use should be accepted by the browser with no problem. Oftentimes, though, other organizations define the Meta attribute values that they recognize.

A good example of this is the Infoseek search engine. You might want to index your site under specific keywords. You can use HTTP-EQUIV=KEYWORDS to define the keywords with which your site should be indexed. ■

By using these attributes, you can specify the author's name, the expiration date of the document, and implement what is known as a *client pull*. A client pull is where the browser automatically refreshes the page with no interaction of the user. To specify the author of the document, you would use the following:

```
<META NAME="Author" CONTENT="Author's name">
```

You use the Name attribute instead of an HTTP response header to specify the author. The reason is that no HTTP response header for an author's name is available. However, to specify the author's contact information, you would use the following HTTP response header:

```
<META HTTP-EQUIV="Reply-to" CONTENT="author@host.com">
```

Many browsers implement their own HTTP response headers, and other types of Meta information. To find out more about these, refer to the documentation on your browser.

Supporting Level of Headings

The current HTML specification, along with all previous specifications, supports six levels of headings that are used to make text stand out at various degrees. The first is <H1>. It is a container. Therefore, it needs to be closed with </H1>. The last is <H6>. This element was intended for outlines, although it can be implemented as a vague specification of font size. It is vague because the actual size of the text varies among browsers. The browsers only have to recognize <H1> as the most important, and <H6> as the least. The following listing shows how to use Level Headings and Figure 18.5 is an example of how these are interpreted by the browser.

> **CAUTION**
> Although you can use level headings for the specification of a font size, it is not a recommended practice. Some browsers might be confused when a level heading is used out of context. If one of the goals of your Web site is to be cross-platform-compatible, do not use this technique.

```
<html>
<head>
<title>Level Headings</title>
<body>
<h1>Level 1 Heading</h1>
<h2>Level 2 Heading</h2>
<h3>Level 3 Heading</h3>
```

```
<h4>Level 4 Heading</h4>
<h5>Level 5 Heading</h5>
<h6>Level 6 Heading</h6>
</body>
</html>
```

FIG. 18.5
Internet Explorer
interprets six levels of
headings.

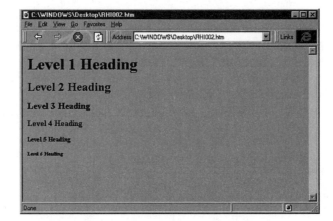

Level headings currently support only two attributes. These are ALIGN and CLASS. The align attribute is used to align the text either to the left, center, or right of the page. Figure 18.6 shows the six levels of headings when the align attribute is implemented. The following is the code for using the align attribute:

```
<html>
<head>
<title>Aligned Level Headings</title>
<body>
<h1 align=left>Level 1 Heading</h1>
<h2 align=left>Level 2 Heading</h2>
<h3 align=center>Level 3 Heading</h3>
<h4 align=center>Level 4 Heading</h4>
<h5 align=right>Level 5 Heading</h5>
<h6 align=right>Level 6 Heading</h6>
</body>
</html>
```

The class attribute is used in conjunction with Cascading Style sheets. Chapter 19, "Advanced HTML," discusses these.

FIG. 18.6
These are aligned level headings.

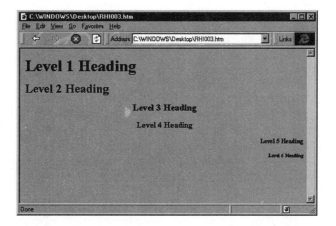

Supporting Text Styles

Text styles can be broken into two categories, physical and logical. Physical styles are font attributes, such as italics, bold, strikethrough, and underline. These generally have only one interpretation. They usually cannot be modified by a user's preferences set in the browser. Logical styles can be overridden by browser preferences, and can have multiple interpretations, depending on the attributes used.

Physical Text Styles A few physical styles are supported in HTML. Table 18.7 lists these styles.

Part
IV

Ch
18

Table 18.7 HTML Supports Certain Physical Text Styles	
Element Name	**Element Tag**
Italics	`<I>...</I>`
Bold	`<b>...</b>`
Underline	`<u>...</u>`
Strikethrough	`<strike>...</strike>`
Font	`<font>...</font>`

These tags for physical text styles are self-explanatory. Text enclosed in the italics element will be rendered as such. The same is true for bold, underline, and strikethrough. The following listing and Figure 18.7 provide an example of how these elements are usually rendered.

```
<html>
<head>
<title>Physical Text Styles</title>
<body>
<h1>Physical Text Styles</h1>
This renders in <i>italics</i>. This text will appear in <b>bold</b>;
this is <u>underlined</u> and this is <strike>strikethrough</strike>.
Of course this is a <tt>fixed-width font</tt>.
</body>
</html>
```

FIG. 18.7
You use these text styles for specifying text to be rendered in italics, bold, underline, strikethrough, and fixed-width font.

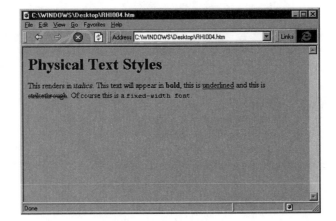

 Although most of these styles cannot be taken a step further with attributes, because they have no attributes, they can be embedded. This is a process formally referred to as nesting within the physical text element, or font. With the font element, you can specify the font size and color.

The Font Element The font element was originally introduced by Netscape to specify a relative font size, and was not included in the HTML 2.0 specification. Microsoft has since expanded it by adding the color and face attribute. Since then, the font element has been added to the HTML 3.2 specification and it also recognizes the color and face attributes.

With the size attribute, you can specify a relative value for modifying the font size. The other attributes are beyond the focus of this chapter. Chapter 19, "Advanced HTML," discusses these.

Logical Text Styles Unlike the physical text elements, logical text elements are defined by the user. That is, users can select from their browser's Preferences menu which font to use for both proportional font and fixed-width font elements. Some of these elements, though, depend entirely upon the browser manufacturer. The reason is that there is no specification pertaining to how they should appear. Table 18.8 lists these elements along with their typical renderings.

Table 18.8   Users Can Choose Logical Text Styles to Fit Their Needs

Element Name	Element Tag	Description
Subscript	`<sub>...</sub>`	Subscript style
Superscript	`<sup>...</sup>`	Superscript style
Strong	`<strong>...</strong>`	Bold
Emphasis	`<em>...</em>`	Italics
Citation	`<cite>...</cite>`	Italics
Address	`<address>...</address>`	Italics
Definition	`<dfn>...</dfn>`	Italics
Teletype	`<tt>...</tt>`	Fixed-width
Keyboard	`<kbd>...</kbd>`	Bold
Code	`<code>...</code>`	Fixed-width
Blockquote	`<blockquote>...</blockquote>`	Left and right indent

Many of these tags are redundant, and can easily be replaced in the code with the corresponding physical style. Logical styles at the programming level, however, can prove useful because of their literal meanings. The following listing and Figure 18.8 shows an example of these tags:

```
<html>
<head>
<title>logical text styles</title>
</head>
<body>
<h1>Logical Text Styles</h1>
<p>
Logical text styles make it easier on the person coding the Web page. For
➥example,
<sub>Subscript</sub> and <sup>Superscript</sup> are much easier to insert than
➥the
font tag.  You can also use the <strong>strong</strong> element to make your
➥point
clear but you can <em>emphasise</em> it just as easily.
</p>
<p>
Italics can be replaced with a <cite>citation</cite> or a <dfn>definition</dfn>
➥while
<kbd>keyboard</kbd> renders in bold. Fixed-width fonts like <tt>teletype</tt> and
<code>code</code> also come in handy.
</p>
<p>
Finally, <blockquote>blockquote</blockquote> indents on the left and right and
requires its own line.  So does <address>address</address>
</body>
</html>
```

FIG. 18.8
Logical text styles at the
programming level can
prove more useful than
physical styles.

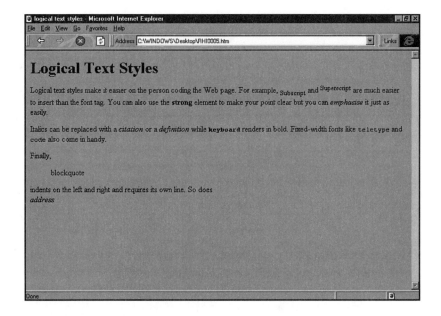

Lines, Paragraphs, and Line Breaks

Only one line style is available in the current HTML specification—a *horizontal rule* (<HR>).
A horizontal rule is a marker element. Therefore, it does not need a closing element. It appears
on the page as a carved horizontal line that by default spans the width of the page. With the
HEIGHT and WIDTH attributes, however, it can be set to span various lengths.

Usually, a horizontal rule is displayed with the current document's background color. HTML 3.2 does
not have the capability for colored horizontal rules. If you are optimizing your site for Internet Explorer
2.x and later or Navigator 3.0, however, you can use a table to produce a colored horizontal line. The
following sample will produce a red horizontal line across the page.

```
<table border=0 bgcolor=#ff0000>
<tr>
<br>
</tr>
</table>
```

Paragraphs are specified with the <P> tag. Using this tag adds two carriage returns to the document—one immediately following the text that precedes it, and one more to add a blank line. It
can be used as a marker or container element. For our purposes, however, it has been used as
a container. It also supports the ALIGN and CLASS attributes. The line break, specified with
the <BR> tag , is a marker element. It adds only one carriage return to the document, and supports no attributes. The following listing and Figure 18.9 provide an example of this idea.

```
<HTML>
<HEAD>
<TITLE>Lines, Paragraphs and Line Breaks</TITLE>
```

```
</HEAD>
<BODY>
<h1>Lines, Paragraphs and Line Breaks</h1>
<p>White space is ignored The user must, therefore, use the paragraph element to
➥create white
space in your Web page.
</p>
A line break can be used to end a line when you do not want it to wrap around
the edge.<br>
<hr>
</BODY>
</HTML>
```

FIG. 18.9
White space in the code is ignored. The user must, therefore, employ lines, paragraphs, and line breaks.

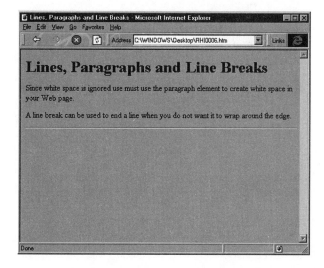

Using Lists to Manipulate Presentation of Information

Level headings are not the only way to create an outline in HTML. There are multiple types of lists supported in HTML that you can use for manipulating the way information is presented. Table 18.9 shows some of these. They are unique from most other HTML elements. The reason is that they require both container and marker elements. The container element is used to enclose the list itself, while marker elements are used for the data.

Table 18.9 Formatted Lists Help You Present Information

Element Name	List Container	List Item
Unordered	`<ul>...</ul>`	`<li>`
Ordered	`<ol>...</ol>`	`<li>`
Directory	`<dir>...</dir>`	`<li>`
Menu	`<menu>...</menu>`	`<li>`
Definition List	`<dl>...</dl>`	`<dd>,<dt>`

Although these lists differ slightly, some of the formatting is universal. List items are indented slightly from the left. There is usually a line break between each item. The differences between these lists, though, are few. In an unordered list, the list items are distinguished with bullets. The ordered list items, in contrast, use numbers or other predefined characters. Menus and directories often use the same formatting styles and attributes as the unordered list. Definition lists, however, display text marked with the <DD> tag with no indent, and text marked with the <DT> tag indented slightly to the left. Figure 18.10 shows the many types of lists available.

FIG. 18.10
Formatted lists provide another way of outlining text in Web pages.

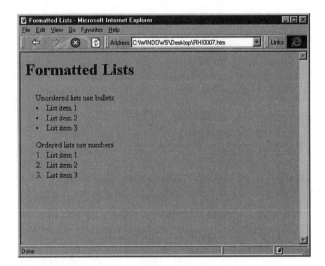

 You can nest text styles in formatted lists. Now, you can try nesting level headings to refine your outline.

CAUTION
Menu and directory lists are quite new to HTML. Many browsers, therefore, still do not support them. Once again, if your goal is cross-platform compatibility, you should not use either of these types of lists.

Special Characters

So far, HTML coding isn't that complicated. However, what happens when you need to use quotes, greater than or less than signs, or ampersands? That's the purpose of these special characters. There are many characters with reserved meanings in HTML. Therefore, a list of escape sequences has been specified, and continues to be updated as HTML progresses.

Reserved Characters   The reserved characters in HTML are the less than and greater than signs (<..>), for obvious reasons. Quotation marks (") are also included. The reason is that these are used for specifying strings and paths. Ampersands are also included. The reason is that they are used by these escape sequences. Table 18.10 lists these escape sequences along with their meanings.

TIP Most browsers are required to recognize these escape sequences. Unfortunately, there is nothing there to keep these escape sequences from blending in with other text and causing a jumbled mess. To prevent this, add a semi-colon (;) to the end of each.

Table 18.10   Escape Sequences Are for Characters with Reserved Meanings

Element		Displayed As
&lt	<	Less than
&gt	>	Greater than
&quot	"	Double quotation mark
&amp	&	Ampersand

HTML Comments   You can also add text to your HTML source that will not be displayed in the browser. This process is formally referred to as *commenting*. To add comments to your document source, use the following example code:

```
<!-- Add your comment here -- >
```

CAUTION

At design time, comments can prove to be useful for removing a particular element or style without deleting it. When the document is ready to be published on your Web site, though, delete the tags that you commented out. The reason for doing this is that some browsers are confused by elements within comments. If you do not do this, you risk having a Web page that displays as garbage.

NOTE   As you will see in later chapters, comments are also used with the various scripting languages. This is to avoid displaying the script on the page. ■

Foreign Language Characters   As you might already know, HTML is based on the ISO-Latin1 character set. The ISO-Latin1 character set includes characters for all Latin-based languages. These are also available within HTML. Similar to the previous escape sequence, these characters are defined with an ampersand at the beginning, and ended with a semicolon. The difference is the character itself is defined by the corresponding ASCII character number. This also works for most any ASCII character: Use the ampersand to start, and a semicolon to end it. Table 18.11 lists the extended Latin characters.

Table 18.11 These Are the ASCII Escape Sequences for Latin Characters

Character	Description	Latin Character Produced
&#192;	Capital A,	grave accent
&#193;	Capital A,	acute accent
&#194;	Capital A,	circumflex accent
&#195;	Capital A,	tilde
&#196;	Capital A,	dieresis or umlaut mark
&#197;	Capital A,	ring
&#198;	Capital AE,	diphthong
&#199;	Capital C,	cedilla
&#200;	Capital E,	grave accent
&#201;	Capital E,	acute accent
&#202;	Capital E,	circumflex accent
&#203;	Capital E,	dieresis or umlaut mark
&#204;	Capital I,	grave accent
&#205;	Capital I,	acute accent
&#206;	Capital I,	circumflex accent
&#207;	Capital I,	dieresis or umlaut mark
&#208;	Capital Eth,	Icelandic
&#209;	Capital N,	tilde
&#210;	Capital O,	grave accent
&#211;	Capital O,	acute accent
&#212;	Capital O,	circumflex accent
&#213;	Capital O,	tilde
&#214;	Capital O,	dieresis or umlaut mark
&#216;	Capital O,	slash
&#217;	Capital U,	grave accent
&#218;	Capital U,	acute accent
&#219;	Capital U,	circumflex accent
&#220;	Capital U,	dieresis or umlaut mark
&#221;	Capital Y,	acute accent

Character	Description	Latin Character Produced
Þ	Capital Thorn,	Icelandic
ß	Small sharp s,	German
à	Small a,	grave accent
á	Small a,	acute accent
â	Small a,	circumflex accent
ã	Small a,	tilde
ä	Small a,	dieresis or umlaut mark
å	Small a,	ring
æ	Small ae,	diphthong
ç	Small c,	cedilla
è	Small e,	grave accent
é	Small e,	acute accent
ê	Small e,	circumflex accent
ë	Small e,	dieresis or umlaut mark
ì	Small i,	grave accent
í	Small i,	acute accent
î	Small i,	circumflex accent
ï	Small i,	dieresis or umlaut mark
ð	Small eth,	Icelandic
ñ	Small n,	tilde
ò	Small o,	grave accent
ó	Small o,	acute accent
ô	Small o,	circumflex accent
õ	Small o,	tilde
ö	Small o,	dieresis or umlaut mark
ø	Small o,	slash
ù	Small u,	grave accent
ú	Small u,	acute accent
û	Small u,	circumflex accent
ü	Small u,	dieresis or umlaut mark

Part

IV

Ch

18

continues

Table 18.11	Continued	
Character	**Description**	**Latin Character Produced**
&#253;	Small y,	acute accent
&#254;	Small thorn,	Icelandic
&#255;	Small y,	dieresis or umlaut mark

Links to Other Pages

Hyperlinks are what Web pages are all about. Of course, you can have one document that is so long that you have to scroll for a while to get to the bottom of it. Alternatively, you can section the document, and provide links to the pieces. Also, hyperlinks enable you to go from one location to the next. This reduces the need to type in a document address, or URL, every time a user wants to view another document.

Hyperlinks consist of only two parts: the document anchor and the document address (URL). The anchor is what links the text or image to another page. The address is to what place it is linked. The format of the tag is `<A HREF="URL">...</A>`. A means Anchor, and HREF means hyperreference. It needs only a `</a>` to close.

Anchoring Text and Graphics   You can anchor both text and graphics. Text anchors commonly appear as underlined text that is bright blue on graphical browsers and in bold for nongraphical browsers, such as Lynx. Graphics anchors appear in the same way that the regular image would, except they have a border around them. This distinguishes them from other nonlinked images.

Creating Links   You can use any text or graphics you choose to make a link. The only requirement is that it is contained within the anchor tag. Otherwise, it wouldn't work, obviously. To do this, insert the anchor tag around the text or image that you want to be linked.

```
The following text is linked to a document named
<A HREF="nowhere.htm">Nowhere.htm</A>
```

The URL you specify can either be a full path statement, such as **http://www.mcp.com/que**, or it can be a relative path statement. You should use a relative path statement if you are linking to a document stored on your server, for example, **subdirectory/anything.html**.

N O T E   To link an image to a page, replace the text within the anchor container with the image tag. The next section, "Inserting Images in Web Pages," discusses using the image tag in greater detail. ■

T I P   If you have ever browsed the Internet, you might have seen pages that use statements such as `Click Here` for their links. Do not design your page in this way! Be more creative and seamlessly integrate the link with the flow of the text. This adds a professional look to your site, as well as doing away with extraneous text that a user might overlook.

Inserting Images in Web Pages

As mentioned previously, graphics are most likely the reason behind the Internet's popularity. Without them, the only option you have to display and convey information is through static text. The current HTML specification supports only one graphics type—the Compuserve GIF 87 format, or Graphics Interchange Format, developed in 1987. This means that a graphical browser such as Internet Explorer will automatically download and display GIFs that have been embedded in Web pages. Many browsers also support the JPEG format, or Joint Photographic Experts Group, and the GIF 89a format, or transparent and animated GIFs. However, the support for these images is not a part of the current HTML specification. No browser, therefore, is required to support it.

Image Tags

Images are not HTML elements themselves. You cannot, therefore, put an image directly into a Web page. It must be maintained as a separate file. The most widely used element for inserting images is the <IMG> tag. The image is not an element itself. Therefore, you must include a *source statement* (SRC) to tell the browser from what place to get it. The resulting tag should resemble this:

```
<IMG SRC="URL">
```

Images follow the same rules as text; they are read from left to right. This means the default location of an image in the browser would be aligned on the left side of the document. Unfortunately, HTML 3.2 does not enable you to use a horizontal alignment tag. It does, however, support vertical alignment, along with the other attributes listed in Table 18.12.

Part

IV

Ch

18

Table 18.12   IMG Tag Attributes Help You to Insert Images

Attribute (Function)	Description
ALIGN (TOP¦MIDDLE¦BOTTOM)	This helps you with vertical alignment in relation to the text.
ALT	This helps you with alternative text for nongraphical browsers.
ISMAP, USEMAP	You use these for specifying CERN and NCSA image maps, and client-side image maps, respectively.

Figure 18.11 shows the default alignment of an image in relation to the surrounding text.

```
<HTML>
<HEAD>
<TITLE>Images</TITLE>
</HEAD>
<BODY>
<img src="warning.gif">The image has been aligned to the left by
default.
</BODY>
</HTML>
```

FIG. 18.11
Images are aligned to the left by default.

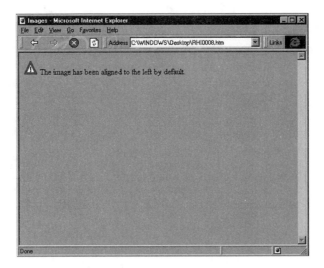

By adding the tag, you can align the top of the image with the surrounding text (see Figure 18.12).

```
<img src="warning.gif" align=top>Now the text is aligned with the top of the
image.
```

FIG. 18.12
By adding the ALIGN attribute, you can gain some control over the placement of an image.

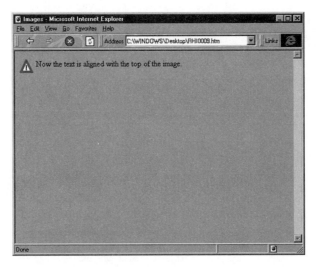

Using Image Maps to Define an Image

Occasionally, a simple hyperlinked image, or series of hyperlinked images, is not adequate with which to navigate your site. The solution is an image map. Image maps simply define the coordinates of an image as "hot spots" that, when clicked, will jump to another page. There are two parts to the most image maps: the image itself and the map definition file. This method is a much more feasible solution in most cases (see Figure 18.13). The reason is that there are too many variables to consider when laying out separate images in a specific pattern.

FIG. 18.13

Image maps provide an alternative method of navigating around your site.

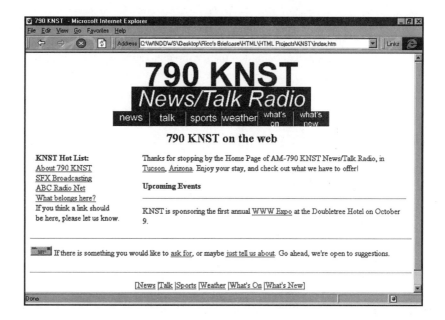

There are three types of image maps: CERN, NCSA, and client-side image maps. The first two require a CGI (common gateway interface) program to build and define the relation between the map definition file and the image. A *client-side* image map requires only a map definition and the image itself. The following few sections discuss these three types of image maps.

CERN Image Maps   All image maps require a line-by-line definition of the image map's "hot spots." CERN (Conseil Européen pour la Recherche Nucléaire) image maps use the following format:

Table 18.13   CERN Image Map Parameters Help to Define an Image

Shape	Shape Definition	Jump Location
rect	(x1,y1) (x2,y2)	URL
rectangle	(x1,y1) (x2,y2)	URL
circ	(cx,cy) r	URL
circle	(cy,cy) r	URL
poly	(x1,y1) (x2,y2) (x3, y3)…	URL
polygon	(x1,y1) (x2,y2) (x3, y3)…	URL

The first part defines the shape of the hot spot. You can use both the long and short shape definitions in CERN image maps. The second defines the coordinates of the hot spot on an X,Y axis. The third (URL) defines the URL to which to jump when that specific region is clicked.

With rectangles, you use the x1,y1 x2,y2 coordinates to define upper left and lower right points of the rectangle. The coordinates of circle, cx, cy, define the center of the circle itself, and the r defines its radius. The polygon coordinates define the vertices of the polygon. Figure 18.14 shows a CERN map definition file for the navigational toolbar in Figure 18.14.

FIG. 18.14

A CERN image is applied to a navigational toolbar.

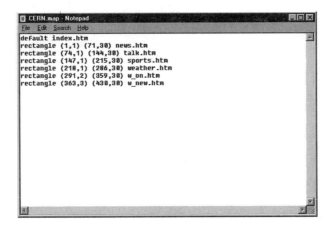

NCSA Image Maps   NCSA (National Center for Supercomputer Applications) image maps are quite similar to CERN image maps. The only differences are the shape names and format of coordinate definitions.

Table 18.14   NSCA Image Map Parameters Differ from CERN Image Maps in Shape Names and Format of Coordinate Definitions

Shape	Jump Location	Coordinates
rect	URL	x1,y1 x2,y2
circle	URL	cx,cy x1,y1
poly	URL	x1,y1 x2,y2 x3,y3 ...

As you can see, NCSA image maps use only the short shape names. Also, the URL to which to jump is specified before the coordinate definitions. The coordinates are placed in parentheses. The coordinates themselves, though, are defined in the same manner. Figure 18.15 shows the NCSA map definition file for the toolbar in Figure 18.13.

FIG. 18.15

NCSA image maps vary only slightly from CERN image maps.

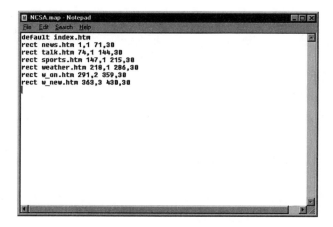

Client-Side Image Maps   Client-side image maps, CSIMs for short (pronounced see-sim), are by far the most sensible option, if you plan on including image maps. They are exactly as the name sounds, client-side. This means there are no third-party applications necessary, such as a CGI program. They require no server processes, and you do not need a separate file for the map definition. The drawback to a CSIM is that it requires a browser that supports HTML 3.2. Otherwise, it will not work.

CSIMSs are HTML elements themselves, and are quite easy to work with. The basic syntax of the element is as follows:

```
<MAP NAME="mapname">
<AREA SHAPE="shape" COORDS="x1,y1 x2,y2..." HREF="jump location">
</MAP>
```

CSIMs also use the same shape and coordinate definitions as NCSA image maps. Once you have defined the image map, you simply add the elements to the Web page that will use the image map. Figure 18.16 shows a CSIM map definition element for the toolbar in Figure 18.11.

FIG. 18.16

Client-side image maps are actually HTML elements.

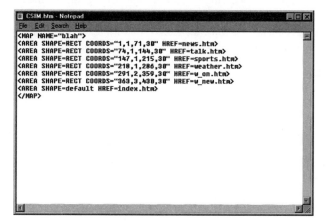

Linking to Image Maps

Now that you have your image and your map definition, you need to establish a relationship between the two. This is done by linking the image to the map definition file, and adding an attribute to the image tag.

To link to a CERN or NCSA image map, use the following example:

```
<a href="URL">
<img src="URL" ISMAP>
</a>
```

Notice that the syntax of the hyperlink is no different than a hyperlink to another Web page, with one exception. The URL is the path to the map definition file, and the ISMAP attribute has been added to the image tag. ISMAP simply tells the browser that the image is an image map.

Linking to a CSIM is similar to linking to a CERN or NCSA image map. The difference is in the image tag. For a CSIM, you would use the attribute USEMAP="#mapname." The syntax is as follows:

```
<img src="URL" USEMAP="#mapname">
```

Use the octothorp (#) to tell the browser the map definition is found on the same page as the image.

N O T E The next section discusses the use of HTML editors to help you create your Web pages. There are also image map editors available to help you create your image maps. One of these, Map Edit, can be found on the Internet at **http://www.boutell.com/mapedit/**. An image map editor is also included on the CD named Map This. Both of these editors have proven to be quite useful for many Web developers, saving countless hours of work. ■

Examining HTML Editors

Coding HTML documents is simple. Insert a few HTML tags in and around text to produce a Web page. Think about this: A minimal Web site will involve about seven pages, at the very least. Constantly having to update all those files with text editor can prove to be tedious and time-consuming. Also, keeping up with the rapid expansion of HTML is almost impossible.

HTML editors can range from a simple Notepad type of program that has menus and toolbars for inserting HTML tags to a What You See Is What You Get word processor-like application. These can be useful tools for managing a fast-paced, ever-changing Web site.

Reasons for Using Editors

If you are new to HTML, you should consider using an editor. It has preprogrammed tags that you can insert with the click of a button. Some don't even require seeing the code. These display the page as it would appear through a browser in real time. A drawback to this is most don't include the most recent HTML additions. The reason is that it takes time to program and test some of these applications; they never seem to keep up with the latest standard. They do try to include most of the tags. They always miss a few, however.

To make up for this, many HTML editors enable you to add custom tags as well as check the HTML syntax of the document. Some even have features, such as a multifile, find-and-replace function that enables you to make quick changes to your documents. This is useful if you plan to constantly change the look of your Web site to keep people coming back.

Types of Editors Available

Three types of HTML editors are available: simple text-based editors, What You See Is What You Get (WYSIWYG) applications, and add-ons to existing applications, such as macros. The following few sections discuss each type.

Text-Based Editors   You can use any ASCII text editor, such as Emacs or Windows Notepad, to create an HTML document. This still requires being familiar with tags, and how they can work for and against each other. Some programs take ASCII text editors a step further by adding menus full of tags. They also aren't limited to a 32-kilobyte file size, such as Windows Notepad.

Hot Dog   Hot Dog is considered by many people to be the best text-based editor on the market. It comes in two versions, Pro and Standard.

Both versions, Hot Dog Standard and Hot Dog Pro, include extensive menus and toolbars full of tags. They even have escape sequences—an excellent idea as many people haven't memorized an ASCII chart. They also have an autosave feature as well as an automatic backup feature that provides protection against power outages and system crashes. They also include their own implementation of a file manager for managing projects.The Standard version is best for small Web sites because it lacks many of the features that the Pro version has.

Only the Pro version enables you to add custom tags to the toolbars. It also incorporates a real-time output viewer that displays the Web page as you add to it. This gives you a WYSIWYG feel. However, this version provides tag-level control.

Both versions are available as 32-bit and 16-bit applications, and can be downloaded for 30-day evaluations. To download a 30-day evaluation copy of Hot Dog Standard or Pro, go to **http:// www.sausage.com**.

CMed   CMed is a probably the most useful text-based editor—it is as simple as Windows Notepad, and complex enough to include most of the more recent HTML tags, as well as Microsoft and Netscape extended tags. It is very useful for quickly editing your Web pages. It does not, however, include any project-oriented or Web site-oriented features. To download a 30-day evaluation copy of CMed, point your Web browser to **http://www.iap.net.au/ ~cmathes**.

HTML Assistant   HTML Assistant is also an excellent editor. It has many features for managing your Web pages and Web site. It is not as easily customized as Hot Dog or Pro. However, it has a browser preview feature that enables you to preview your document in your browser of choice with the click of a button. It can also import Rich Text Formatted documents, and convert them to HTML. Unfortunately, this doesn't always produce the desired results because of the differences between HTML and RTF. To download a 30-day evaluation version of HTML Assistant, go to **http://www.brooknorth.com/welcome4.html**.

WYSIWYG Editors   WYSIWYG editors are designed to speed up the production and maintenance of a Web site. They almost completely shelter you from the code. The major drawback to WYSIWYG HTML editors is the programmers must know how the tag will be rendered in a browser. With text-based editors, the only requirement is knowing the tag syntax. However, the need to know how these tags will be displayed causes many WYSIWYG editors to lag far behind the HTML standard. WYSIWYG editors are more useful in an Intranet situation in which the styles aren't as important as the content.

Front Page   Front Page is Microsoft's WYSIWYG solution, and is limited to the 32-bit Windows platform. There are countless wizards to hold your hand through the creation process. Those familiar with Microsoft Word will feel at home with this editor. As you can see in Figure 18.17, the toolbars are almost identical, and enable you to easily customize. Another feature is the capability to insert custom tags, although you will not be able to view these custom tags through Front Page.

FIG. 18.17
Microsoft Front Page is not only an editor, but a site management tool, as well.

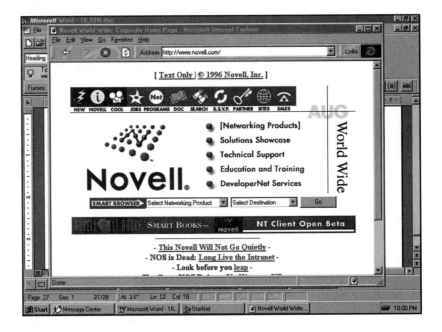

Front Page's major drawback is the redundancy of the tags it uses. For example, to define a section of text as being the color blue, and using Arial as the font, you would simply use the following tag:

```
<font face="arial" color="blue">. . .</font>
```

Front Page treats every attribute as a separate tag. It would, therefore, use the following instead:

```
<font face="arial"><font color="blue">. . . </font></font>
```

The more styles you use, the larger the file is going to be. And large files of any sort can slow down your servers, as well as take longer for the page to display. As mentioned previously, WYSIWYG editors are more suited for Intranets in which the bandwidth is nearly unlimited.

Netscape Navigator Gold   Not only is Navigator a browser, but it comes as a WYSIWYG HTML editor, too—Navigator Gold. Although the browser itself is lacking in many areas, the editor is by far the best WYSIWYG editor available. The reason is not so much the features. The most recent version of Navigator Gold ships with the latest version of the Navigator browser, so this editor always contains most of the latest tags. Anyone familiar with the browser and a word processor should have no trouble using it. Figure 18.18 provides an example of the Navigator Gold interface.

FIG. 18.18

Navigator Gold's interface is a cross between the Netscape browser and a word processor.

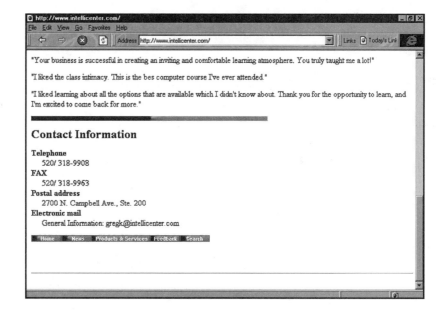

Navigator Gold includes an online template, available from the Netscape site, for basic HTML documents. This editor also provides the functionality to create your own templates. You can browse your Web site with the editor and update links and styles as you're testing everything else. Unfortunately, it also uses redundant tags, leaving it more useful in an Intranet environment.

One feature on which most other WYSIWYG editors fall short is platform availability. Navigator Gold is available on the same sixteen platforms as the browser.

Application-Based Editors   Application-based editors are somewhat WYSIWYG. They are usually macros that you simply use to convert your existing document into HTML. Others are mini-applications or applets that plug in to word processors to convert your documents. There are also `Perl` scripts available for UNIX that convert TeX and LaTeX documents into Web pages.

Internet Assistants from Microsoft   Microsoft Offers an entire family of Internet Assistants for its Office 95 suite. One is Internet Assistant for Microsoft Word. Internet Assistant for Word is available as a plug-in for Word 6.0 and 7.0, and is as simple as saving your Word document with an HTML or HTM extension. When you do this, Internet Assistant for Word automatically formats your document with the appropriate tags, and your Web page is created. There are no tags to remember and the only change to the Microsoft Word interface is an addition to the formatting toolbar, which is illustrated in Figure 18.19. Unfortunately, Internet Assistant suffers from the same tag redundancy as WYSIWYG editors.

FIG. 18.19
The only thing different about the Word interface is an addition to the formatting toolbar.

Microsoft also offers Schedule +, Access 7.0, Excel 7.0, and PowerPoint assistants that plug in to their respective applications. These, similar to WYSIWYG editors, are geared to an Intranet environment. The Internet Assistants can be downloaded for free at **http://www.microsoft.com/msdownload/**.

Working with Graphics for Web Sites

Working with graphics for Web sites can be complicated. Graphics on your Web site are intended to enhance the user's experience. Unfortunately, the technology available limits how much you can enhance it. Graphics can take your Web site to the next level in a user's experience. These images, however, can also work against you. Many people don't take into consideration what a typical user's configuration is. They put enormously large graphics on their pages, slowing the download time. This makes the user wait longer for your page. The wait can eventually lead a user to completely lose interest in your site.

Small Graphics

Obviously, the smaller the graphics, the better. This doesn't mean smaller dimensions, just smaller file size. One way to limit the file size on your graphics is to confine them to 16 colors. The reason is that the more colors you use, the larger the file is: More colors have to be mapped. Using 16 colors also assures cross-platform compatibility. If you cannot keep within the confines of 16 colors, try to make the upper limit 256 colors.

Load-Time Considerations

Always assume the typical user has a 14.4-kilobaud modem. Although 28.8-kilobaud modems are popular, there are still 14.4 users out there, and even 9,600 users. As a rule, you should limit the total size of a page to 45 kilobytes. That includes the HTML file itself, and all graphics included on the page. Do not add in images that will have been previously viewed.

For example, you might include the file `widget.gif` on your index page. Then, you might insert it again on a subsequent page. You would not add the file size to any of the other pages. The reason is that once it has been downloaded, it will most likely be cached and not have to be downloaded again.

From Here...

As you have seen, HTML is nothing more than an ASCII text file with special formatting elements added to help you manipulate the output of the page. There are also a wide assortment of tools available that you can use to make the HTML coding process easier and more efficient.

The following chapters and resources can provide you with more information on HTML and its related areas:

- Chapter 19, "Advanced HTML," will take you further inside HTML and its capabilities.
- Both Chapter 20, "ActiveX and the Internet," and Chapter 21, "Java Applets and the Internet," discuss the potential of your Web site.
- The official Request for Comments draft of HTML 3.2 can be found on the Internet at **http://www.w3.org/pub/WWW/TR/WD-html32.html**.

Part
IV

Ch
18

Advanced HTML

Once you have learned the concepts of HTML, you can begin to understand its exact limitations. You may already know that older HTML elements do not allow much control over the layout of your document. Fortunately, HTML has progressed enough over the past six years that past complaints of design restrictions have been taken into consideration.

HTML 3.2, the most recent draft, allows formatting, such as tables, that can be used not only for laying out data in spreadsheet fashion, but also for controlling the alignment of your text and images. It also allows for multi-level Web sites through the frame elements. But the biggest complaint that Web designers have had, though, is downward compatibility. HTML is progressing so rapidly that not everyone can keep up. This means you must take into consideration browsers that support only text, graphical browsers that are behind on the HTML standard, and graphical browsers that are on the leading edge of HTML. This can be done with the recent addition of Cascading Style Sheets.

Learn how tables can provide you with greater control over the layout of a page

Not only are tables good for displaying information in a cell-by-cell format, but you can also gain control over your page by laying out information in a table format.

See how to create a multi-level Web site with frames

Use frames to display your Web site in a more "user-friendly" fashion. As with other HTML elements, they can also be misused and can disrupt the dynamic exchange of information.

Learn what Style Sheets are and how to apply them to your Web site

Some browsers cannot keep up with the ever-changing world of HTML. Because of this, you will need to understand what options are available to keep your Web site compelling and downward compatible.

Understand the goals of good Web page design

Follow some basic guidelines to keep your Web site marketable to the entire spectrum of Internet surfers.

N O T E Although HTML is a relatively simple markup language, this chapter assumes knowledge of the basic use of HTML elements. If you are new to HTML or have little knowledge of it, read Chapter 18, "Basic HTML Techniques," before reading this chapter. ■

Working with Tables

Table definitions are similar to formatted list definitions in that they consist of a hierarchical structure of multiple HTML elements. Tables, unlike formatted lists, consist entirely of container elements. They are defined row by row, then each cell is defined either as a table header or as table data. Both rows and cells must be defined with their appropriate containers.

The containers used are rather easy to understand. A table row uses the <TR> tag, a table header uses <TH>, and table data uses <TD>. Note that these are all closed with the original tag with a "/" added to the beginning of the tag.

Table Elements

Listing 19.1 shows the HTML used for a basic table layout; likewise, Figure 19.1 shows how they would be displayed in the browser. All of the elements used are supported by most major graphical browsers.

Listing 19.1   RHI0001.HTM—The Basic Table Elements

```
<html>
<head>
<title>A Basic Table Definition</title>
</head>
<body>
<TABLE border=1>
<TR>
<TH>Header 1</TH><TH>Header 2</TH><TH>Header 3</TH>
</TR>
<TR>
<TD>row 2,cell 1</TD><TD>row 2, cell 2</TD><TD>row 2, cell 3</TD>
</TR>
<TR>
<TD>row 3, cell 1</TD><TD>row 3, cell 2</TD><TD>row 3, cell 3</TD>
</TR>
</TABLE>
</body>
</html>
```

FIG. 19.1

The basic table elements at work.

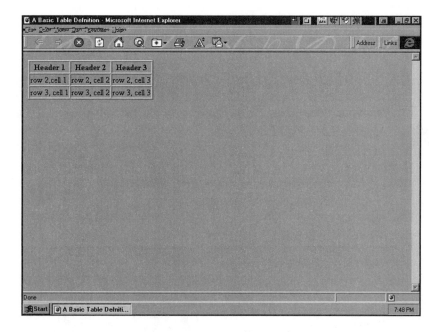

The basic table elements are shown in Table 19.1:

Table 19.1   The Five Table Elements

<table>...</table>	The table container itself
<tr>...</tr>	To define a table row, use these
<th>...</th>	A table header consists of these tags
<td>...</td>	Use these for regular table cells
<caption>...</caption>	A table caption is possible with these tags

Part

IV

Ch

19

When using these elements you must also take into consideration browser defaults. Browsers are programmed to display elements in specific ways unless told otherwise; these are known as the browser's default settings. You may have noticed the use of the BORDER attribute in the opening table tag; this is because some browsers, by default, display tables without a border unless otherwise told.

The same is true for the table header element. You may have noticed that it is displayed in bold; this is because Internet Explorer (like many others), by default, displays table headers in a bold-weight font. The header is usually centered within the cell as well. The table caption is usually displayed directly on top or directly below the table itself—it is not considered part of the data and will not appear within the table border. And the contents of the table data tag are usually aligned to the left by default.

> **CAUTION**
>
> The table header (<TH>) is usually rendered in a bold font. To work around this, you can use text styles from within the cell, but keep in mind that not all browsers will support this. The best work-around for this problem is the use of a Style Sheet. Style Sheets are explained later in Cascading Style Sheets.

Also note that table cells are not required to contain any data. They can be made to appear blank by providing the cell with no data (such as <td></td>). You can also make them appear blank by using the nonbreaking space escape sequence ( ) as the cell data. Although these two techniques are essentially based on the same idea, they are displayed very differently. Figure 19.2 illustrates the different uses of empty table cells.

FIG. 19.2
Empty table cells are based on the same idea, but the two techniques produce very different results.

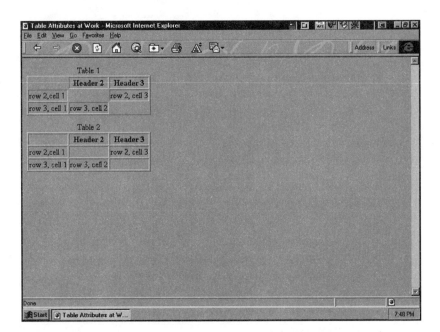

> **CAUTION**
>
> When using tables for controlling the page layout, the first empty-cell technique (<td></td>) can really cause a mess on your page. Some browsers do not always recognize empty table cells if they are not aligned with other cells horizontally. This is because the browser has nothing to compare it to and, therefore, cannot instinctively tell the difference between an empty cell and a cell that contains data.

Unless your style restrictions do not permit this, always use the method of applying a nonbreaking space. This is because the cell is not really empty; the nonbreaking space is its data.

Table Element Attributes

The table elements are pretty straight forward and easy to remember. What isn't so easy is remembering which attributes go with which tags. Table 19.2 lists each element attribute with its appropriate element.

Table 19.2 Table Element Attributes

Attribute	Argument(s)	Applies to
Border	numeric (0-10)	<table>
Cellpadding	numeric (0-10)	<table>
Cellspacing	numeric (0-10)	<table>
Width	numeric(relative or exact)	<table>
Colspan	numeric	<td>, <th>
Rowspan	numeric	<td>, <th>
Valign	top, middle, bottom	<td>, <th>
Align	left, center, right	<td>, <th>
Align	top, bottom	<caption>

Part
IV

Ch
19

The Table Element's Attributes   As you can see, the table element itself supports four attributes. The border attribute defines a border for the table. The cellpadding and cellspacing attributes give you control over precious white space in your table. And the width attribute allows you to define the width of the table.

The Border Attribute   The border attribute in newer browsers defaults to zero. This means if you need to have a border around your table you must first specify one. This is done by adding the border attribute to the table tag.

```
<table BORDER=1>
```

The Cellpadding Attribute   The cellpadding attribute, although used in the table element, controls the table cells. When used with the table tag, it defines the amount of blank space between the actual table data and the table boundaries. Keep in mind that if you do not use a table border, the results of this attribute will not be as visible. The following is an example of how to use it within the table element.

```
<table CELLPADDING=5>
```

Like the border attribute, you can specify any number between zero and ten (most browsers default to three).

The Cellspacing Attribute   The cellspacing attribute is quite similar to the cellpadding attribute. It is defined in the table element because it affects the entire table. The difference is the cellspacing attribute defines the amount of blank space between each cell, and the cellpadding attribute defines the spacing within each individual cell.

```
<table CELLSPACING=5>
```

Once again, any number between zero and ten is acceptable and most browsers default to three.

The Width Attribute   As you may have noticed in Figure 19.1, the table width was determined by the width of the first row of data. Unfortunately, the current HTML draft does not officially define how a browser should determine the width of the table. This means it is left up to the software developers programming the browser to decide how wide the table should be in certain instances. Because of this, a table will often look different from one browser to another.

To work around this problem, you can add the width attribute to the table element. You can define it either with an exact measurement in pixels or in a relative measurement with percentages. Since there is no limit to the physical length of a document, there is no limit to how many pixels wide it can be. Inserting the width attribute is the same as inserting other attributes.

```
<table WIDTH=100>
```

Listing 19.2 provides an example of the HTML used to produce the tables shown in Figure 19.3. Table 1 has a border of five pixels, the cellpadding and cellspacing are both five pixels, and the width is 100 pixels. Table 2 has no border, no cellpadding, no cellspacing, and the width is not defined.

Listing 19.2   Two Contrasting Table Definitions

```
<HTML>
<HEAD>
<TITLE>Table Attributes at Work</TITLE>
</HEAD>
<BODY>
<table BORDER=5 CELLPADDING=5 CELLSPACING=5>
<caption>Table 1</caption>
<tr>
<th>Header 1</th><th>Header 2</th><th>Header 3</th>
</tr>
<tr>
<td>row 2,cell 1</td><td>row 2, cell 2</td><td>row 2, cell 3</td>
</tr>
<tr>
<td>row 3, cell 1</td><td>row 3, cell 2</td><td>row 3, cell 3</td>
</tr>
</table>
<br>
<table BORDER=0 CELLPADDING=0 CELLSPACING=0>
<caption>Table 2</caption>
```

```
<tr>
<th>Header 1</th><th>Header 2</th><th>Header 3</th>
</tr>
<tr>
<td>row 2,cell 1</td><td>row 2, cell 2</td><td>row 2, cell 3</td>
</tr>
<tr>
<td>row 3, cell 1</td><td>row 3, cell 2</td><td>row 3, cell 3</td>
</tr>
</table>
</BODY>
</HTML>
```

FIG. 19.3

Table element attributes allow for much greater control over the display of your Web page.

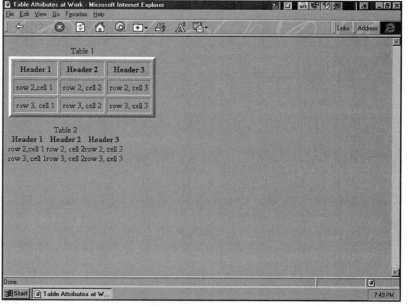

Cell Element Attributes   The table headers and table data elements can be generalized as one group, cell elements. This is because the only difference between the two is the default formatting. This means that the element attributes they share will produce the same results in either tag.

The Align and Valign Attributes   The more you work with HTML, the more you will appreciate being able to have some control over the alignment of text. This idea holds true for tables. Though it is not always useful when using tables in a spreadsheet fashion, it can be useful when using a table to format your Web page or site.

The align attribute is used for the horizontal alignment of cell data and the valign attribute is used for the vertical alignment of data. In Table 19.1, the valid arguments for the align attribute are left, center, and right. Using these arguments, you can horizontally align the cell data to the

Part
IV

Ch
19

left or right edge of the table cell as well as center it within the table cell. Valid arguments for the valign attribute are top, middle, and bottom. Like the align tag, you can use these to vertically align the cell data to either the top or bottom edge of the table cell, or you can vertically align it to the middle of the cell.

Aligning text is not as easy as it seems. The alignment is not defined on an exact scale, it is relative. Therefore, if there is only one line of data in your cell, the browser has nothing to judge it against and is in turn relative to nothing so it does not align it as you chose.

Listing 19.3 and Figure 19.4 illustrate this idea. In the first table, there is only one row so the cell data is relative to nothing and the browser has no way of aligning it. The second table, on the other hand, consists of two rows—the first is the actual cell data. The second row is just a placeholder used to demonstrate this concept.

Listing 19.3   The Source of Figure 19.4

```
<HTML>
<HEAD>
<TITLE>Aligned Cell Data</TITLE>
</HEAD>
<BODY>
<table border=1 cellpadding=10 cellspacing=5>
<caption align=top>Table 1</caption>
<tr>
<td>Cell 1</td><td ALIGN=center>Cell 2</td><td ALIGN=right>Cell 3</td>
</tr>
</table>
<table border=1 cellpadding=10 cellspacing=5>
<caption align=top>Table 2</caption>
<tr>
<td>Cell 1</td><td ALIGN=center>Cell 2</td><td ALIGN=right>Cell 3</td>/tr>
<tr>
        <td colspan=3>The quick brown fox jumped over the lazy dog.</td>
</tr>
</table>
```

The Colspan and Rowspan Attributes   Fortunately, tables are not limited to being an exact grid. It is possible to make a cell element span multiple columns and rows. This is done by inserting the colspan and rowspan attributes within the cell element. Listing 19.4 and Figure 19.5 illustrate this idea.

Listing 19.4   The Source of Figure 19.5

```
<HTML>
<HEAD>
<TITLE>Column and Row Spanning</TITLE>
</HEAD>
<BODY>
<table border=1 cellpadding=10 cellspacing=5>
<tr>
```

```
<th COLSPAN=3>This header cell spans all three columns</th> .
</tr>
<tr>
<td ROWSPAN=2>This data cell spans two rows</td><td>Cell data 1</td><td>
➥Cell data 2</td>
</tr>
<tr>
<td>Cell data 3</td><td>Cell data 4</td>
</tr>
</table>
</BODY>
</HTML>
```

FIG. 19.4
The first cell is aligned
to the left (by default),
the second is centered,
and the third is aligned
to the right.

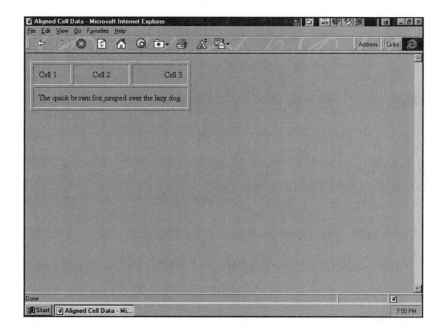

The attribute arguments for colspan and rowspan are a little different than the other attribute arguments. Yes, they are numeric, but you can only span as many columns and rows as the table has.

 The default vertical alignment for cell data that spans multiple rows is "middle." To change this, simply add the valign attribute with its appropriate argument to align it to the top or bottom of the cell.

Part
IV

Ch

19

FIG. 19.5
Using the colspan and rowspan attributes opens the door to many more formatting and style options.

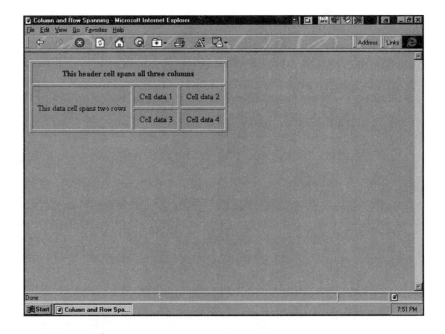

T I P Since not all browsers support tables, you may want to consider using preformatted, tab-delimited, ASCII text. To do this, simply lay out your table with a text editor, then add the following to the source of your document where you want the table to appear.

```
<PRE>
insert your tab delimited text here
</PRE>
```

The <PRE> tag means preformatted text. Anything contained in this tag should not be altered in any way by a browser.

Working with Frames

The introduction of frames has opened the door to a new level of Web site access and user experience. Frames add control to your Web site by creating independently changeable and scrollable windows within the main browser window. This feature enables you to include static portions of your Web pages for items such as frequently used toolbars and menus, as well as information that you feel needs to be permanently visible, such as copyright information.

If you understand how to create formatted lists and how to lay out table cells, you should have no problem with frames. The frame elements are implemented in the same manner as a formatted list—one container element with separate marker elements to define each item or section. However, the layout is similar to that of table cells where you have the option to define rows and columns. What makes them unique is that each separate frame requires its own source page which is simply a predesigned page that will fill the frame.

FIG. 19.6
Netscape Communication Corporation's home page is one example of what you can do with frames. The frames on the bottom of the page give a "Windows Explorer" feel to the site.

Frame Elements

The frame elements are quite easy to remember because there are only three widely recognized elements. These are <frameset>, <frame>, and <no frames>. The first, <frameset>, is a container that's used for identifying the elements within it as frames. The <frame> tag is a marker similar to the image tag; it is not a standalone element and must have a source defined. The <no frames> tag is used for browsers that do not support frames so they can view your Web site as well.

- **<frameset>**—This is the container of the frame defining elements.
- **<frame>**—This is the marker that defines the frame.
- **<no frames>**—Use this to provide content for browsers that do not support frames.

Part
IV

Ch
19

Using the Frameset Element The frameset container is very much like the <UL> tag that defines an unordered list. It can only be used to define the layout of what is contained within it. It also replaces the body tag in your HTML source because it is being used to define where the content of the page begins. A simple frameset is shown in Listing 19.5.

Listing 19.5   RHIO006.HTM—A Simple Frameset

```
<HTML>
<HEAD>
<TITLE>A Sample Frameset</TITLE>
</HEAD>
<frameset rows="15%, *">
      <frame src="RHI0006src1.htm" >
      <frame src="RHI0006src2.htm">
</frameset>
<BODY>
</BODY>
</HTML>
```

In a browser, it would be displayed as shown in Figure 19.7.

FIG. 19.7

A simple frameset.

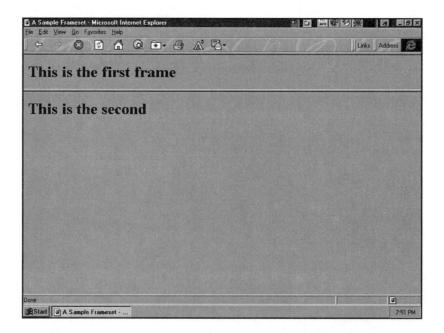

Unlike most other HTML elements, most of the frame elements cannot exist without attributes being defined. The frameset element has only two widely used attributes, ROWS and COLS (columns). These attributes' arguments are also slightly different from most other elements.

To define them you must use a value list that defines the size of each column and row. The following code excerpt is from Listing 19.2 and gives an example of the syntax.

```
<frameset rows="15%, *">
```

NOTE A value list is simply a list of frame size definitions. They are separated by commas and can be either relative or exact values. Note that you can also use the asterisk (*) as a wildcard, which means use whatever is left over. ■

Notice that the first row was defined as 15 percent of the page while the second used a wildcard that basically means use whatever is left over. You will also notice that there is no column value list. This is because if you do not include one, the browser assumes it is only one column that spans 100 percent of the page. Likewise, you can omit the row value list if you are only breaking the page into columns, but you must include at least one. Otherwise, only the first frame definition will be used, thereby completely defeating the purpose of the frame elements.

The frameset element can also be nested within itself and often times must be nested. This is because when you are defining your column and row value lists, the browser associates the first value in each row value list with the first value defined in the column value list. For example, by looking at the following source you might assume that it would produce three frames. The first frame definition appears as though it would be one row, not divided by any columns. And the second seems as though it would be defined as one row separated by two columns (see Listing 19.6).

Listing 19.6   Defining Frames in this Manner Does Not Always Produce the Desired Results

```
<HTML>
<HEAD>
<TITLE>A Frames Don't</TITLE>
</HEAD>
<frameset rows="15%, *" cols="20%, *">
<frame src="rhi0006src1.htm">
<frame src="rhi0006src2.htm">
<frame src="rhi0006src3.htm">
</frameset>

</HTML>
```

Part
IV

Ch
19

As you can see in Figure 19.8, this method did not produce the desired result. Instead of displaying three frames, it displayed four. This is because it assumed one frame for each definition in the value lists.

FIG. 19.8
Four frames show
instead of three.

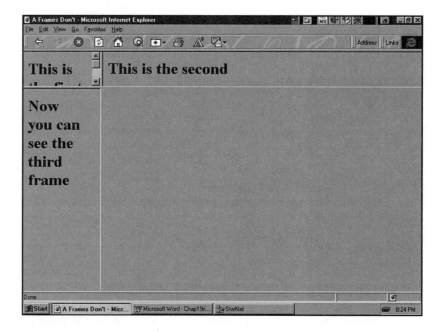

To produce the desired result, use the method in Listing 19.7:

Listing 19.7   This Method Gives You Control over the Frames

```
<HTML>
<HEAD>
<TITLE>A Frames Do</TITLE>
</HEAD>
<frameset rows="15%, *">
<frame src="rhi0006src1.htm">
<frameset cols="20%, *">
<frame src="rhi0006src2.htm">
<frame src="rhi0006src3.htm">
</frameset>
</HTML>
```

Notice that in Figure 19.9, the second frameset needed to be nested after the first frame definition because the second row was to be divided into columns. Like tables and formatted lists, all the frame elements follow a hierarchical structure.

Using the Frame Element   Using the frame element is very much like using the image element. You must define a source because it is not a standalone element. The frame element is not a container and does not need a closing tag. The frame definition takes place on one line. Also, it must be contained within the frameset element, otherwise the browser will not recognize it. The syntax is this:

```
<frameset cols="50, *">
<FRAME src="URL"> <FRAME src="URL">
</frameset>
```

FIG. 19.9
Finally, only three
frames.

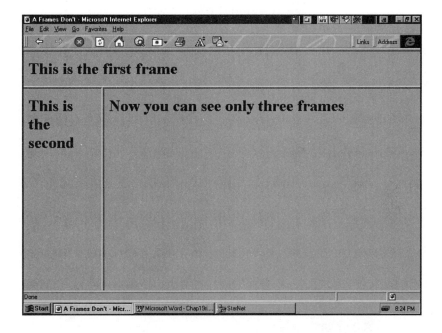

Notice that the source of the frame was defined in the same way you would an image, with the
SRC attribute. To define the source file of the frame, add the SRC attribute to the frame tag
then tell it where the file is in the form of a URL. Also notice that there must be as many frame
tags as there are defined frame rows and columns. This means if you define three rows in the
row value list (such as 15%, 25%, *), then you must have three frame tags that give the source of
each frame; otherwise, you will be left with a blank frame.

The frame element also supports three attributes; they are NORESIZE, SCROLLING, and
NAME. The NORESIZE attribute is an exclamation, so it does not have any valid arguments.
On the other hand, the SCROLLING attribute does have two valid arguments, yes and no.

NORESIZE does exactly as its name implies; it does not allow the frame to be resized. Keep in
mind, though, if you want to optimize the user's experience at your site, adding this attribute
will not allow the user to make the Web page fit to their screen. If you do choose to use this
attribute, you should define your frames in a relative measurement (value%) instead of exact.

The SCROLLING attribute is as simple to understand as the NORESIZE. Simply insert the
attribute with its appropriate argument and you will be able to either scroll through a page or
not scroll through the page. Understanding why to use it is slightly more difficult and cannot
be illustrated with screen captures, so you will have to try this on your own. Occasionally you
will have a source file that does not take up enough screen space to require scrolling, but you
will still see the scrollbar (active or otherwise). This is because a certain amount of white space

Part
IV

Ch

19

is assigned to every edge of the browser as a margin. If your page seems as though it should fit but a scrollbar still appears, you can assume it is the margin causing the problem and you will need to use the SCROLLING attribute to get rid of it.

The NAME attribute is used to name your frames; simply insert the NAME attribute in each frame element and give your frames separate, distinguishable names. So why do you want to name your frames? Well, not only do frames extend the HTML draft by adding elements, they also extend the Anchor element with the TARGET attribute.

The TARGET attribute's valid arguments depend entirely upon the name of your frames. Once you have named your frames, you can specify a particular frame as a destination for a hyperlink using TARGET. This can be extremely useful when using frames for static toolbars or other forms of navigation.

Using the NOFRAMES Element   Now that you have your frames laid out, you need to know how to make it possible for the lower end browsers to see your site. That is, since the frameset element is only an extension to HTML, other browsers that do not support the frames' extensions cannot see a document that is formatted as such.

This is done with the NOFRAMES element. Since the <frameset></frameset> container replaces your body tag, all you need to do is insert your alternate viewing material with this container. Listing 19.8 and Figure 19.10 illustrate how to use this container and how it works.

Listing 19.8   Use the NOFRAMES Tags So Older Browsers Can See Your Web Site

```
<html>
<head>
<title>Another Frames Example</title>
</head>
<frameset rows="50, *">
<frame src="cool.htm">
<frame src="wow.htm">
</frameset>
<NOFRAMES>
Here is where your alternate material goes.
</NOFRAMES>
</html>
```

FIG. 19.10
When viewed with Lynx, the frames do not show up.

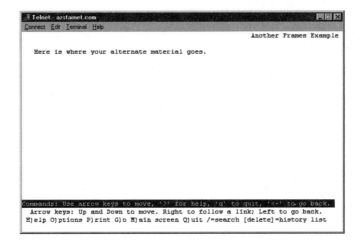

Working with Style Sheets

By now, you hopefully understand what's basically involved in creating these Web pages for your site. Unfortunately, you still need to understand what makes your site look "good." If you have ever browsed the Internet, you have seen sites that go beyond the browser's default color scheme and implement their own colors for text and hyperlinks. You may have also seen sites that implement "graphics-only" navigation, but it doesn't take hours to load. So how did they do it?

Before you implement colors and images you must know what colors and images you want or need. So first you must decide on a style sheet for your site. Used loosely, a style sheet is simply a common style, or look, for your site. You first decide on the style (and probably document it), then you insert the necessary tags into the HTML code. You should already have an idea of what you want it to look like. Now it is time to review the options and make some decisions.

Style Sheets in General

Style sheets, used generically, are quite an arbitrary concept. Most of it is just a thought or decision on your part, although documenting what you decide would be a good idea. The overall appearance of your site, how you will present your information, and just how much information you will present is what you need to include in your style sheet. I'm sure by now you want to dive in and start coding the content for this Web site, but wait.

What you will need to take into consideration is listed and discussed below.

- **Color Scheme**—The color scheme of your Web site is very important to attracting visitors.

- **Navigation**—A site that is not easy to navigate will quickly turn away visitors.

Part
IV

Ch
19

N O T E The generic term style sheet should not be confused with the recently suggested addition to HTML, Cascading Style Sheets. The two are indeed closely related, but two different concepts. Cascading Style Sheets are discussed in the section that follows. ■

Deciding on a Color Scheme   The color scheme for your Web site includes the background color, the text color, links that haven't yet been followed, links that have been followed, and active links (links that are being clicked). All of these have default values that you can override with certain HTML tags, but before you can override them you must decide what colors you want them to be.

Of course you do not have to define colors for all of these. After all, the default text color in most browsers is black, and it seems to get the message across fine. On the other hand, the default background color in many browsers is gray, which you may find to be rather ugly and decide that you want your own color for your site. The default link colors are an "iffy" situation; most browsers' defaults are blue for a link that hasn't been visited and purple for links that have been visited. These may or may not go with your chosen background color. It's up to you.

Background Colors   When deciding on your background color you must keep something in mind: the signal to noise ratio, where the signal is the text and the noise is your background. You've probably seen sites where the designer did not take this into consideration so the text blends with the background too much to the point where you cannot read it—stay far away from this.

A good idea for a background color is white. Though it may come off at first as boring and plain, it makes almost no noise against any text color you decide, aside from white of course. It also saves a lot of time in this process, giving you more time to decide on your basic text and hyperlink colors. Still, you may decide white is too plain and go with another color, but always remember the signal to noise ratio.

Text Colors   The base text color (what most of your text will appear as) is probably best left as black, unless it tips the scales on the signal to noise ratio. This is because it has no reason to stand out from anything else; it is simply text provided to the user to read.

What may require a different color are the headers (not level headings) you use. Whether it is a simple paragraph title or a section title, you may want to make these different colors so they stand out from the rest of your text.

Link Colors   Defining link colors are something you may or may not want to do. If you make any of your text blue that isn't a link, the user may get confused by the identical colors. When defining link colors, you should choose a color that will both stand out from the text and maintain the flow of the text. It should stand out because it is a link, and a link is something the user needs to know about. But they should also maintain the flow of the text so the user does not get distracted from what they are reading.

Navigation   Navigation around your site is very important. The user needs to know how to find something on your site. If this does not come easy to them, the user will probably end up going to another site to find what they need. If you're planning a small site, simple links (or hyperlinked images) at the top of each page will suffice as a navigational toolbar. If you are planning a large site, such as putting your entire company on the Internet, you will want to include more than one navigational toolbar for your site.

For example, the home page of Integra Technology provides two different methods of navigation. At the top there is a toolbar that breaks down each division of the company/Web site. Then, towards the top of the page but in the content area, there is another directory of what can be found in that particular section. This is illustrated in Figure 19.11.

FIG. 19.11
Navigation for a large scale Web site needs to give the user quick access to anything and everything they need to know.

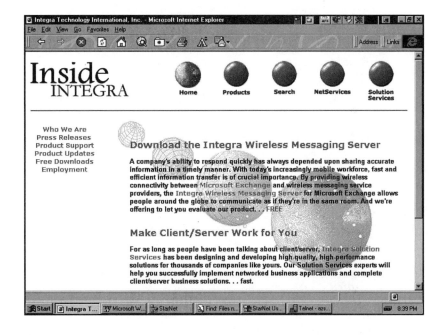

When using frames, this task is simplified. You can simply create one frame that never changes, which contains your navigational toolbar.

Colorization

Now that you have decided on what colors you are going to use, you now need to know how to make them a reality with HTML. This is easily done with a few attribute additions to the tags you are already using, and a scientific calculator that supports hexadecimal.

Color is implemented in HTML in two ways, either the literal color name or in hexadecimal format RRGGBB (where R is red, G is Green, and B is blue). The literal color name only works if it is one of 16 named colors; they are as follows:

- aqua
- black
- blue

- fuchsia
- gray
- green
- lime
- maroon
- navy
- olive
- purple
- red
- silver
- teal
- white
- yellow

These colors may be all you need, but in some instances you will need different shades of these colors. To do this you will first need the red, green, and blue decimal values for the color; for instance, the decimal values for a shade of blue are 0, 49, 156. Now you will need to translate those decimal values into hexadecimal values. The previous example would translate to 00, 31, 9C. Then insert a pound sign (#) in front of it and you're ready to insert the color into your page.

There are only two HTML elements that officially support color attributes; they are <BODY> and <FONT>. The attributes they support are quite different.

- **BGCOLOR**—Use this in the body tag to change your page's background color.
- **TEXT**—This changes the color of the text as a whole; use it in the body tag.
- **LINK**—This attribute is used to change the color of links that have not yet been followed.
- **VLINK**—Again, use this in the body tag. It changes the color of links that have been followed.
- **ALINK**—The last of the body attributes, this changes the color of an active link (while a user is clicking it).
- **COLOR**—This changes the color of the text contained in the font tag.

N O T E The previous method is what's defined in the HTML 3.2 draft—what is meant by "officially supported." Microsoft, though, has taken the colorization idea to another level. It originally implemented these ideas into Internet Explorer 2.0, and they are now supported by Internet Explorer 3.0 and Netscape Navigator 3.0. But since it is not a part of the official draft, don't weight your site on these techniques.

Using the BGCOLOR attribute, you can change the background of entire tables by inserting it in the table tag, or you can change the background of a single table cell by inserting it in either the <TH> or <TD> tag. It's that simple. ▓

Cascading Style Sheets

Cascading Style Sheets are one of the newest and most popular additions to HTML, but unless you're using Internet Explorer 3.0 you probably don't know it. Cascading Style Sheets provide a method of predefining all the styles you plan on incorporating in your Web site in one file, instead of having to use the same style tags over and over.

Cascading means there is a hierarchical order to each style. If you implement a style for two tags and use those tags together, the cascading order means it chooses the style that appeared first (such as the first tag you used) instead of making some sort of arbitrary decision that the developers of the browser implemented. And you can easily guess (if you don't already know) where the Style Sheets portion of the name comes from.

N O T E The Cascading Style Sheet draft (CSS1) is still in draft format, so most browsers do not support this. But because of the nature of Cascading Style Sheets, this is not a problem. If you do not have a browser that supports Cascading Style Sheets you will not be able to see the fancy formatting that the Style Sheet defines, but the structure of the document is still in place.

Unfortunately, the only commercial browser that supports Cascading Style Sheets is Internet Explorer 3.0; so if you care more about how good your document looks as opposed to how structurally sound it is, do not implement Style Sheets only. Use redundant tags, the same tags you would to format it for Navigator or Mosaic, along with the added style tags to make it look that much better for Internet Explorer users. ▓

How Do Cascading Style Sheets Work? First, to understand Cascading Style Sheets, you must have a good handle on HTML and what it can and can't do. You already know that HTML limits you to what fonts you can use, where you can place text, and how you can manipulate text. So you resort to using images. Which is fine for the occasional callout or logo, maybe even a section header or two, but it all adds up to more download time for the user.

Also, if you decide to change the style of your Web site, you will find changing each and every color on each and every page to be tedious. Moreover, if you miss a seemingly minute detail such as a forgotten quotation mark, your pages will become un-viewable in most browsers. Cascading Style Sheets is the solution to these problems.

Cascading Style Sheets are a way of manipulating the output of certain elements in one place at one time. For example, if you had three headings on one page and you wanted the first two to be displayed in blue and the last in green, it would require three separate font tags. However, with Cascading Style Sheets, it would only require an attribute to be added to the existing tag (see Listing 19.9). The following listings illustrate this idea.

Part

IV

Ch

19

Listing 19.9 This Is How You Would Define Font Colors Without a Style Sheet

```
<html>
<head>
</head>
<body>
<h1><FONT COLOR="blue">Level 1 Heading</font></h1>
<h2><FONT COLOR="blue">Level 2 Heading</font></h2>
<h3><FONT COLOR="green">Level 3 Heading</font></h3>
</body>
</html>
```

With Cascading Style Sheets, all you need is to do is define the style once, and then add an attribute to each heading tag (see Listing 19.10).

Listing 19.10 This Example Uses a Style Sheet

```
<html>
<head>
<STYLE TEXT="text/css">
<!--
.headings
        {color: blue;}
.lastheading
        {color: green;}
-->
</STYLE>
</head>
<body>
<h1 class=headings>Level 1 Heading</h1>
<h2 class=headings>Level 2 Heading</h2>
<h3 class=lastheading>Level 3 Heading</h3>
</body>
</html>
```

Both of these examples produce the same results. However, if you were to forget one of the closing font tags in the first example, all the headings would probably turn out blue (probably because some browsers are smarter than others and know where to insert missing tags). With the Cascading Style Sheets example, there is no end tag to forget so there is nothing to worry about.

Cascading Style Sheets Syntax   As you may have noticed in the previous example, the style sheet syntax is not like normal HTML syntax, though it is similar. In Cascading Style Sheets you have element-classes and pseudo-classes. An element-class means you define a style for an existing HTML element, the paragraph (<P>) tag for example. A pseudo-class is a made-up class that you insert into an existing HTML element, like the example from the previous section. The pseudo-class is defined in the style sheet with a period before the class name then is implemented in an existing element using the CLASS attribute.

Once you know what type of class you want, you can define the style. Like HTML elements, classes have attributes and attribute arguments. First you open the definition with a curly brace ({), then you insert your attributes and arguments; note that each attribute is separated by a semicolon (;). Once you have defined your class's attributes, you close it with another curly brace (}). The following example is a style defined using an element class for the paragraph element:

```
[element]
{font-family: "Arial";
font-size: 10pt;
color: "blue";}
```

The attributes and arguments supported by Cascading Style Sheets are shown in Table 19.3.

Table 19.3   Cascading Style Sheets Attributes and Arguments

Attribute	Argument
color	any RGB hexadecimal value or any of the sixteen named colors
background	any RGB hexadecimal value or any of the sixteen named colors
font-family	serif; sans-serif; roman, or any font name (e.g. Arial)
font-size	any numerical value defined in either pixels or points
margin-left	any numerical value defined in pixels
margin-top	any numerical value defined in pixels
text-align	left, center, right
text-decoration	underline, none
text-style	italic

Implementing Style Sheets   There are three methods of implementing Style Sheets; each is listed and discussed below:

- Linked styles—Linked styles give you the capability to control the style of your Web site with one file.
- Embedded styles—Embedded styles can be used to vary the style of your site from page-to-page.
- Inline Styles—Inline styles are useful when you need to override the settings in a linked or embedded style sheet.

The linking method gives you the greatest control over your Web site because you only need to define the Style Sheet once, then link all the other pages to it. To link to a Style Sheet you must first define it and save it with a CSS extension. Then insert the following tag between the <head>...</head> container:

Part
IV

Ch
19

```
<link rel=stylesheet text="text/css" href="URL">
```

Embedded styles are exactly what they sound like—a Style Sheet embedded in the page. To embed the Style Sheet you would use the <style>...</style> container and insert your style definitions within it. Though there is no requirement as to where to insert this container, the best location to add it is usually between the <head>...</head> container.

The inline style method changes the Style Sheet syntax somewhat, but the attributes and arguments are the same. When you have an element in which you want to insert an inline style, simply add the STYLE attribute in the element and define the style on the spot. I would not recommend using this method because it comes very close to defeating the purpose of Cascading Style Sheets, at least as far as the document structure is concerned.

Optimizing Your Pages

As you can see, there are many options to consider when designing your Web pages. You must first understand how to create and format the pages, as well as understand how to make them look good. It is very easy to get caught up in all this and forget about making your pages *act* good. That means the way your page is displayed from one browser to another and how fast it loads in any given browser. Also, you must take into consideration those that are not able to view your page in anything better than a text-based browser or those that cannot view your page at all because of a physical impairment. Speech browsers are already in the works, so you should start planning now before you get so deep into the design of your site that a quicker route to downwards compatibility would be to create an entirely redesigned site.

Images versus Text-Based Formatting

If you have done any HTML coding, you are familiar with the confines of it. You cannot overlap text with images, nor can you overlap text with text. One long-term solution for this drawback is the Cascading Style Sheet draft, because with it you can define the X and Y coordinates of the text (in the form of margin-top and margin-left). For now though, at least until Cascading Style Sheets are widely supported, you are left with images as a solution.

This is not to say you should use images everywhere in place of text; by all means, do not do that. But there are situations where an image would be more appropriate than text. For example, you may want to add a drop-shadow to the text to give it a three-dimensional look. Since most browsers do not support Cascading Style Sheets, you cannot overlap text with text (or anything for that matter); the workaround would be to create an image with a drop-shadow and insert it in your page.

Image Size Goals

Simply put, your number one image size goal is to keep them as small as possible. Realistically, though, you are probably going to be using many images in your Web pages so it is a good idea to limit the size of each. A good size goal for any Web page on your site is 45 kilobytes. This includes the size of the document itself plus each image. A document this size will take less than one minute to load during peak access hours over a 14.4 kilobaud connection. Anything longer than a minute will probably turn away many users, especially impatient ones.

This number is not as restricting as it sounds, though. Do not include images that will have been previously downloaded in the equation. This is because most browsers save images from Web pages as they download them, instead of just deleting them. So if you include a toolbar on your home page, also referred to as the indexing page, you will not need to add that to the total of any subsequent pages that use it.

 T I P One way to keep your image size down is to stay within a 16-color palette because each color you use adds to the total size of the image. Staying within this palette may seem a bit restricting, but you must take your users into consideration when designing your site.

Text-Only Versions of Your Pages

To keep your Web site open to every type of browser, a text-only version of your site would probably be more than a good idea. This is because level headings and other text-level elements do not matter to text-only browsers in the sense that the browser will simply ignore it. However, table elements can cause confusion in these browsers because they do not take any of the elements into consideration. Think about this: when you define tables in the HTML source, you define them vertically even if the output is horizontal. A text-only browser does not care about the elements and ignores them so it displays each table cell as it appears in the source (vertically). It may seem tedious to reformat the content you spent hours and hours formatting to look great, but there are two things you can do to keep the time spent on these pages low and keep them looking good.

The first is the cut-and-paste method. When you finish designing the graphical version of your Web site, simply select the text displayed in your browser and paste it into a separate HTML file that will be the text-only version of your page. Then all you need to do from there is insert the appropriate Anchor tags for defining your links.

The second is slightly more time-consuming, but it ensures that your pages will be displayed somewhat as you intend for the graphical version of your site. This is done with the <PRE>… </PRE> container, which means pre-formatted text. Anything within these tags will not be altered by the browser, it will be displayed exactly as it appears in the source. Now insert tab-delimited text into the HTML source and you can produce a similar result as if the browser were displaying the graphical version of your site.

 T I P The Integra Technology Web site (http://www.integra.net) has been formatted with a number of tables. This made the site easier to design and maintain because of the control tables give you over the layout of a page. Updating the page is simply a matter of cutting and pasting new content into the source.

Cascading Style Sheets have also been implemented at the site. The entire site uses only two style sheets that control the look of the all the pages.

Part
IV
Ch
19

From Here...

In this chapter you have learned how to insert tables into your Web pages to give you more control over the format. You have also seen how you can create a "framed" Web site that will allow greater flexibility when designing your Web site. Keep in mind, though, there are still undiscovered ways to tweak HTML to make it display as you want. The best way to find these tricks is to try something that breaks the rules of HTML. After all, the HTML draft up to this point has been very loose in exactly how elements should be displayed.

■ More information on Cascading Style Sheets can be found in the CSS1 draft, available at **http://www.w3.org/style/**.

■ The explanation of HTML in this book has been brief because it is not the focus of the book. An excellent HTML resource can be obtained through Que's *Special Edition Using HTML, Second Edition*.

## CHAPTER 20

Active X and the Internet

In Chapter 21, you will learn what is involved in working with scripting languages that you can embed in your pages. By implementing the different properties, objects, and methods, you can add some very nice content and presentation to your pages. You've seen how to code these changes to your pages, and what it takes to provide the ActiveX objects to the users that are browsing your pages.

In this chapter, you'll learn how the ActiveX Control Pad can help in the development of your pages. You'll also get additional details on the ActiveX controls you may consider using on your pages. ■

Find out about the ActiveX Control Pad

See how this tool can make creating ActiveX-enabled page development easier.

See the different properties for some of the more common controls

If you'll be using some of the different common ActiveX controls on your pages, this chapter will give you more information on working with the different properties and methods on those objects.

Learn about the concerns that you'll be faced with for down-level browsers

See what steps you can take to make your site accessible by the different non-ActiveX browsers that are on the Internet.

Active X Scripting

Scripting is introduced into your pages using the <OBJECT> container tags in HTML. Since browsers will skip unrecognizable HTML tags, the <OBJECT> tag is ignored when it's encountered by an incompatible browser. You can see an example of this in the following code excerpt.

```
<OBJECT ID="Marquee1" WIDTH=70% HEIGHT=60 TYPE="application/x-oleobject"
        CLASSID="CLSID:1A4DA620-6217-11CF-BE62-0080C72EDD2D">
        <PARAM NAME="szURL" VALUE="book.htm">
        <PARAM NAME="ScrollPixelsX" VALUE="0">
        <PARAM NAME="ScrollPixelsY" VALUE="-3">
        <PARAM NAME="ScrollDelay" VALUE="200">
</OBJECT>
```

The same is true if you're adding scripting to your page. Because you enclose the scripting in <SCRIPT> container tags, the scripting is ignored if it's not recognized by the browser loading the page.

```
<SCRIPT LANGUAGE="vbscript">
<!--
        Sub Marquee1_OnLMouseClick()
                Window.location.href = "http://www.mcp.com/que/developer_expert/"
        end sub
-->
</SCRIPT>
```

Notice that the code portion of the listing, containing the functional statements for the browser to load and execute, is actually presented as a comment. This will let a browser that does not recognize the VBScript attribute ignore the statements. In the next sections, you'll find out how to ensure other browsers don't end up looking at blank content on your site when they visit. Also, you'll find out about tools you can use to ease the process of putting ActiveX scripting on your page, regardless of whether it's for VBScript or JavaScript.

Maintaining Backward-Compatibility

Only the Internet Explorer 3.0 supports the object tag through its Microsoft HTML extension. No other browser offers this advantage. Browsers that do not support this tag will leave an empty space in the page where you intended an ActiveX control to be displayed. Fortunately, there is a way you can create pages to work around this problem.

Since the <object>...</object> container element will not be recognized by browsers that do not support it, you can embed other tags within the container. However, this does not interfere with the way the control is displayed in Internet Explorer 3.0 because it will not recognize any tag within the <object>...</object> container except <PARAM>. The following example is an example of a downward-compatible object tag.

```
<OBJECT ID="IEPOP1" WIDTH=0 HEIGHT=0
 CLASSID="CLSID:7823A620-9DD9-11CF-A662-00AA00C066D2">
     <PARAM name="MenuItem[0]" value="Item 1">
     <PARAM name="MenuItem[1]" value="Item 2">
     <PARAM name="MenuItem[2]" value="Item 3">
<h1>You really should upgrade to Internet Explorer 3.0</h1>
</OBJECT>
```

Using the ActiveX Control Pad

Microsoft introduced the ActiveX Control Pad because it was obvious that there are some significant hurdles to clear before ActiveX controls will be commonplace on HTML pages. In particular is the use of the OLE ClassID that represents the ActiveX object on the user's system. This ID, represented by a long string of numbers and letters, presents a situation where you'd have to memorize each string that represents the different controls you want to use. The following line shows an example of one of these ClassID strings.

```
CLASSID="CLSID:1A4DA620-6217-11CF-BE62-0080C72EDD2D"
```

You may recognize this as the key in your system's Registry. The ActiveX Control Pad takes care of four different key areas that will help you incorporate these technologies in your Web pages:

- ClassID management
- Appropriate container object scripting
- Access to properties and methods associated with ActiveX controls
- Ability to add Javascript or VBScript to your pages with the same tool

Each of these is covered in one of the next four sections.

ClassID Management

To add a new ActiveX object, right-click the left side of the edit screen. This presents a menu of options. Select Insert ActiveX Control from the menu to be presented with a listing of the different ActiveX controls currently installed on your system. See Figure 20.1 for an example.

When you select the item you want on your page, you'll be shown an editing dialog specific to the control you've selected, and a listing of the common properties for the object. You can edit these different properties and make changes to the look of the object in a fashion similar to the Visual Basic forms painting environment.

N O T E There are properties in addition to those shown in the Properties dialog box for other objects. Though most common properties are listed in the dialog box, you'll still need to be familiar with the documentation provided with the ActiveX control to fully manipulate it in many cases. ■

FIG. 20.1

You can select from the menu of items available on your system.

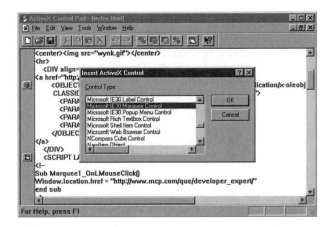

In Figure 20.2, you can see an example of these types of dialog boxes. The ActiveX control is the standard label control. The editing box reflects changes to the font, bold and size properties, as well as changing the text to italic.

FIG. 20.2

You can make changes to the visual aspects of the control that will be automatically updated in the code on your page.

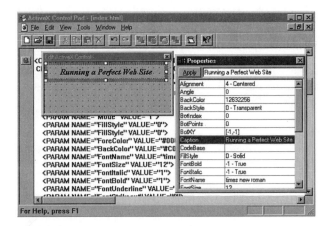

When you exit the dialog boxes, you'll notice the code to support the object is automatically placed in the code on your page. See Figure 20.3 for an example.

Appropriate Container Object Scripting

In the following HTML listing, the code is enclosed in the appropriate HTML container tags that will prevent it from causing problems with browsers that don't support the different aspects of ActiveX. These tags and the syntax for presenting the object are a nice benefit of using the Control Pad.

FIG. 20.3

The code to support the object, including any changes you make to properties, is automatically included in the HTML for your page.

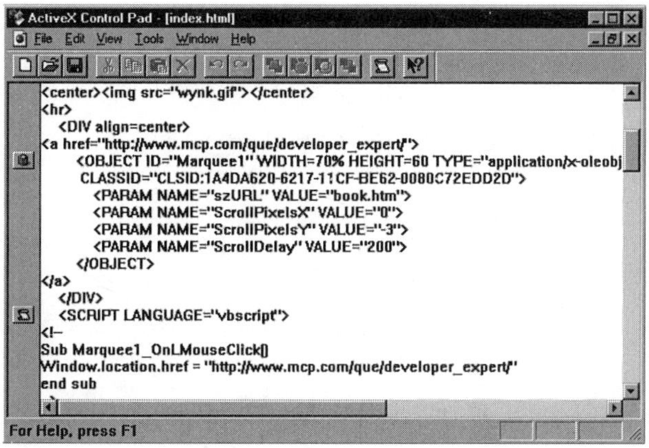

```
<OBJECT ID="Marquee1" WIDTH=70% HEIGHT=60 TYPE="application/x-oleobject"
    CLASSID="CLSID:1A4DA620-6217-11CF-BE62-0080C72EDD2D">
    <PARAM NAME="szURL" VALUE="book.htm">
    <PARAM NAME="ScrollPixelsX" VALUE="0">
    <PARAM NAME="ScrollPixelsY" VALUE="-3">
    <PARAM NAME="ScrollDelay" VALUE="200">
</OBJECT>

<SCRIPT LANGUAGE="vbscript">
<!--
    Sub Marquee1_OnLMouseClick()
    Window.location.href = "http://www.mcp.com/que/developer_expert/"
    end sub
-->
</SCRIPT>
```

If you initially use the Control Pad to edit your pages, you're assured of the proper tags within your file.

N O T E The indenting you see is not provided by the Control Pad. These are added after the fact for readability. While the Control Pad will indent and break parameters across lines for easier reading, you'll still want to hand-edit the resulting HTML to fit your coding style. ■

Access to Properties and Methods

When you click the script scroll on the left margin of a page, you're taken to the Script Wizard— a dialog box that helps you set up the scripting for your page. This dialog box, shown in Figure 20.4, lets you work with the objects on the page, the properties and methods associated with them, and the code that will be working with them.

Part
IV

Ch
20

FIG. 20.4

The Script Wizard will help work through the different code options on your page.

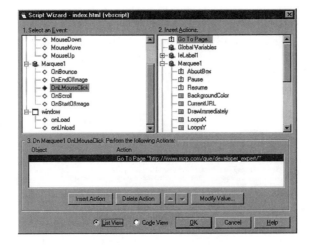

Select from among the different events of the left pane, then select what you want to do as a result of the event on the right pane. The details of the procedure are provided in the lower pane. You can switch between the more user-friendly List View and the developer-centric Code View by selecting the appropriate radio button on the bottom of the dialog box. See Figure 20.5 for an example of the code view for the procedure shown in Figure 20.4.

FIG. 20.5

Code view may be a more comfortable way for traditional developers to work with a page's settings.

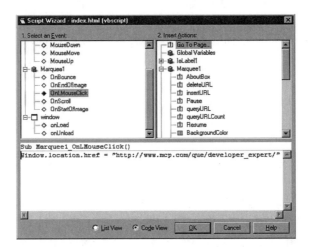

In either mode, you browse the different objects and can interactively walk through their associated properties. Objects listed with the square and exclamation point are methods, whereas objects with the box and lines in it are properties on the associated parent object. When you select either, you'll be prompted to provide any parameters needed for the item.

The Option to Use VBScript or JavaScript

Under the Tools menu of the Control Pad, you can select Script Wizard to set up which language— JavaScript or VBScript—you want to have the script generated for. When using the Script Wizard, the type of language is shown in the title bar of the dialog box. See the previous figures for examples of VBScript, and Figure 20.6 shows an example of a JavaScript editing session.

FIG. 20.6

The ability to provide for both JavaScript and VBScript is a feature that helps ease transition between the two approaches.

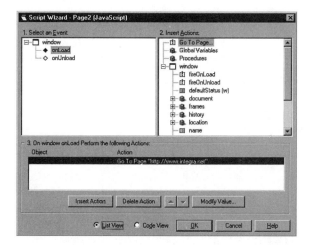

N O T E You'll notice slightly different methods and properties in some cases when switching between the languages. This is attributed to the languages and their use of the objects. You can still make most functions happen in both languages, but it may be addressed differently. ■

In the remaining sections, you'll receive details on working with some of the most common ActiveX controls. The ActiveX controls you will work with are similar to those. Properties and methods, at least by name, are becoming somewhat standardized. Learning these standards can save you time and energy later when you're working with different controls.

Examples of ActiveX Controls

Before you can understand how ActiveX controls work in your document, you must first understand how to insert them in your document. This is done with the `<OBJECT>...</OBJECT>` container element. This is similar to Java's `<APPLET>...</APPLET>` container element, but, as you can see, ActiveX controls use `OBJECT` as their identifier. The `<OBJECT>` tag itself requires a few attributes, or you have no control. The following attributes are generally available for most controls.

- ■ `classid` Defines what control you are using.
- ■ `codebase` Defines the path to the ActiveX control on the Internet in case the user does not have the control on his or her system.

- height   Defines the height of the control in pixels.
- ID   Provides the tag a name so you can reference it in your scripting.
- width   Defines the width of the control in pixels.
- type   Defines the MIME type of the control, which is always application/x-oleobject

The properties of the ActiveX control are defined with the <PARAM> element. These elements are inserted within the <OBJECT>...</OBJECT> container element. Within each <PARAM> tag are two required attributes, NAME and VALUE. The NAME attribute is used for the property name and VALUE is the property definition. An ActiveX control definition would look similar to this:

```
<CONTROL ID="IeLabel1" WIDTH=0 HEIGHT=0
 CLASSID="CLSID:99B42120-6EC7-11CF-A6C7-00AA00A47DD2">
    <PARAM NAME="Caption" VALUE="Default">
    <PARAM NAME="Alignment" VALUE="4">
    <PARAM NAME="Mode" VALUE="1">
    <PARAM NAME="ForeColor" VALUE="#000000">
    <PARAM NAME="BackColor" VALUE="#A0B8C8">
    <PARAM NAME="FontName" VALUE="Arial">
    <PARAM NAME="FontSize" VALUE="12">
</CONTROL>
```

Many of the properties of an ActiveX control have default values so there's no need to define every property of the control. Despite these default values, it would be a good idea to define each property so you can maintain full control over the control.

Once you understand how to insert these controls, you can begin to understand what controls are available.

Animated Button Control   The animated button control is similar to a command button in Visual Basic, but instead of an icon, it uses an Audio-Video Interleaved (AVI) animation. It cycles through specific frames of the animation depending on the state of the control.

The animated button control supports the following properties:

- URL   Defines the path on your server to the AVI animation.
- DefaultFrStart   Defines the starting frame of the control when in its Default state.
- DefaultFrEnd   Defines the end frame of the control when in its Default state.
- DownFrStart   Defines the start frame when in the Down state.
- DownFrEnd   Defines the end frame when in the Down state.
- FocusFrStart   Defines the start frame of the control in the Focus state.
- FocusFrEnd   Defines the end frame when in the Focus state.
- MouseoverFrStart   Defines the starting frame when in the Mouseover state.
- MouseoverFrEnd   Defines the end frame when in the Mouseover state.

You may have noticed from the previous list, the animated button control supports four states.

- Default
- Down
- Focus
- Mouseover

The animated button control is in its Default state when no other events are occurring on the page. It is in the Down state when the button is being pressed. The Focus state occurs when the animated button has the focus of the page. The Mouseover state occurs when the mouse pointer is moved over the button.

The capability to change the control's properties depends on the following events:

- `ButtonEvent_Click`   This event is fired when the animated button is clicked.
- `ButtonEvent_DblClick`   Similar to the previous event, but it is fired when the button is double-clicked.
- `ButtonEvent_Enter`   This event is fired when the mouse enters the defined button area.
- `ButtonEvent_Focus`   This event is fired when the button has the focus of the page.
- `ButtonEvent_Leave`   This event is fired when the mouse exits the defined button area.

Chart Control   The Chart Control is used to add charts and graphs to your document. It supports seven types of charts.

- Area Chart
- Bar Chart
- Column Chart
- Line Chart
- Pie Chart
- Point Chart
- Stocks Chart

Each of these types of charts supports the following properties:

- `BackStyle`   Defines whether the background of the chart is transparent(0) or opaque(1).
- `ChartType`   Defines the exact chart type. See Table 20.1 for its acceptable values.

Part

IV

Ch

20

Table 20.1   ChartType Values

Accepted Value	Description
0	A pie chart
1	A pie chart with a wedge taken out
2	A point chart
3	A stacked point chart
4	A full point chart
5	A line chart
6	A stacked line chart
7	A full line chart
8	An area chart
9	A stacked area chart
10	A full area chart
11	A column chart
12	A stacked column chart
13	A full column chart
14	A simple bar chart
15	A stacked bar chart
16	A full bar chart
17	An HLC stock chart
18	An HLC stock chart in Wall Street Journal format
19	An OHLC stock chart
20	An OHLC stock chart in Wall Street Journal format

- **ColorScheme** — Defines the color scheme of the chart and is derived from a predefined set of colors (0-4).
- **Columns** — Defines the number of columns in the chart.
- **ColumnIndex** — Defines the column index. Note that it is used in conjunction with the DataItem property.
- **ColumnNames** — Use in conjunction with the ColumnIndex property to label of each column.
- **DataItem** — Used with the corresponding RowIndex and ColumnIndex grid mapping. For example, if you wanted a data item to appear in column 5, row 2 you can refer to the location as `<param name="DataItem[2][5]" value="value">`.

■ DisplayLegend   Used to display the chart's legend. To show the legend, use one (1), and zero (0) will hide the legend.

■ GridPlacement   This defines how the grids are drawn on the chart, based on the value. A zero (0) will display it in the background and a one (1) will display it in the foreground of the chart.

■ hgridStyle   Defines whether or not to display a horizontal grid on the chart. The accepted values are zero (0) for no grid, one (1) for a solid grid, two (2) for a bold grid, three (3) for a dotted grid, and four (4) for a bold, dotted grid.

■ Rows   Defines the number of rows in the chart.

■ RowNames   Used in conjunction with the RowIndex property to name each row.

■ Scale   Can be used to scale the chart's measurements.

■ URL   If you do not want to specify the chart data within the control itself, you can specify the path to an ASCII format data file that contains the chart data.

The chart control definition does not necessarily have to contain the chart data. Using the URL property allows you to specify a data source, an ASCII text file, that contains the information for the chart. The following describes the proper format of the text file.

Chart_type (equivalent to the ChartType property)

row_count (equivalent to the Rows property)

column_count(same as Columns)	TAB	Column_name1	TAB	Column_name2
row_name1(same as RowNames)	TAB	row1_data1	TAB	row1_data2
row_name2	TAB	row2_data1	TAB	row2_data2

Gradient Control   The gradient control can be used for filling specified areas on the page with color transitions. It uses only a few properties to define the control, but the limited number of properties does not limit the use of the control. Table 20.2 lists the gradient control properties.

Table 20.2   Gradient Control Properties

Property	Value	Description
Direction	0- transition is horizontal 1- transition is vertical 2- transition is toward the center 3- transition is toward the corner 4- transition is diagonal up 5- transition is diagonal down 6- transition is around the StartPoint coordinate	Defines the direction of the color transition

continues

Table 20.2 Continued

Property	Value	Description
	7- transition is across the line from `StartPoint` to `EndPoint`	
`EndColor`	Hexadecimal value (#rrggbb)	Defines the color of the object after the transition
`EndPoint`	x,y	Coordinates of the ending point of the gradient
`StartColor`	Hexadecimal value (#rrggbb)	Defines the color before the transition
`StartPoint`	x,y	Coordinates of the starting point of the gradient

CAUTION

Be careful when defining the size of the gradient. If you make it too large, you may encounter a bug in Internet Explorer that stops response. In addition, you may have to reboot your system before being able to continue working in Internet Explorer.

It appears that there is a problem in how IE works with values that are too large.

Label Control   With the label control, you can create effects with text that are not possible with standard HTML. You can manipulate the angle the text is displayed as well as the font style and color of the text.

The Label control supports the properties shown in Table 20.3.

Table 20.3 Label Control Properties

Property	Value	Description
`Angle`	numerical in degrees(CCW)	This defines the rotation of the caption.
`Caption`	Text string	This is what defines the text string you want to be displayed on the page.
`Alignment`	0- left, top 1- center, top 2- right, top 3- left, center 4- center, center 5- right, center 6- left, bottom	This will align the text on the page.

Property	Value	Description
	7- center, bottom 8- right, bottom	
BackStyle	0- Transparent 1- Opaque	This defines whether a background will be displayed.
FontName	TrueType font name	Use this to change the font of the text string.
FontSize	Numeric (points)	This defines the size of the font.
FontItalic	0- False 1- True	Defines whether or not the font will be displayed in italics.
FontBold	0- False 1- True	Defines whether or not to weight the font in bold.
FontUnderline	0- False 1- True	Defines whether or not to underline the font.
FontStrikeout	0- False 1- True	Renders the font in strikeout style.
Mode	0- Normal 1- Normal, with rotation 2- include user input without text-rotation 3- include user input with text-rotation	Defines how to render the text.

At runtime, you can change the properties with any of the following events:

- **Click** This event fires when the label is clicked.
- **DblClick** Similar to the Click event, but it fires on a double-click.
- **Change** This event fires when the label caption changes.
- **MouseDown** This event fires when the mouse button is pressed when the pointer is over the control.
- **MouseUp** This event fires when the mouse button is released.
- **MouseMove** This event fires when the mouse is moved over the label.

Pop-Up Menu Control   Pop-up menus, similar to the menus that appear when you right-click something in Windows 95, can be added to Web pages for alternative methods of navigation. These can be quite useful when space on the page is limited.

Part

IV

Ch

20

The Pop-up Menu supports only two properties, `ItemCount` and `MenuItem[x]`. `ItemCount` cannot be modified at runtime and MenuItem[x] is used to define each item listed on the menu. Note that the number of menu items must correspond to the number defined in the `ItemCount` property. The Pop-up menu supports only the `Click()` event. The `click` event is fired when you click one of the menu items. The object definition for a Pop-up Menu would look similar to this:

```
<OBJECT ID="IEPOP1" WIDTH=0 HEIGHT=0
 CLASSID="CLSID:7823A620-9DD9-11CF-A662-00AA00C066D2">
     <PARAM name="ItemCount" value="3">
     <PARAM name="MenuItem[0]" value="Item 1">
     <PARAM name="MenuItem[1]" value="Item 2">
     <PARAM name="MenuItem[2]" value="Item 3">

</OBJECT>
```

Preloader Control   The Preloader control is a performance-enhancing feature of ActiveX. It downloads files from a specific URL and caches them to be used later. This can be very useful to decrease download times for any given object or file. Be careful when using multiple controls at once, it will speed up the loading of subsequent pages and slow down the loading of the page it's implemented on.

The Preloader control supports the following properties.

- ■ `Enable`   This is used to enable (1) or disable (0) the control.
- ■ `URL`   Use this to specify the path to file that is to be downloaded.

The events supported by this control are `Complete` and `Error`. `Complete` is fired when the download is complete, and `Error` is fired if the download cannot be completed.

Stock Ticker Control   The need for constantly updated information on the Internet has given birth to the Stock Ticker control. It downloads information at specified intervals and immediately displays it on the Web page without having to reload the entire page. The downloaded information is displayed scrolling from right to left in the control, and the user will not notice the update.

The Stock Ticker control supports the properties described in Table 20.4.

Table 20.4   Stock Ticker Control Properties

Property	Value	Description
BackColor	Hexadecimal (#rrggbb)	This defines the background color of the Stock Ticker.
DataObjectActive	0- inactive 1- active	This defines whether or not the Stock Ticker is "on."

Property	Value	Description
DataObjectName	URL	This defines the path to the data file that contains the displayed information.
ForeColor	Hexadecimal (#rrggbb)	This defines the color of the text in the Stock Ticker.
OffsetValues	numeric (pixels)	This defines how much the separate row will be staggered.
ReloadInterval	numeric (seconds)	This defines how often the information will be downloaded from the URL specified.
ScrollSpeed	numeric	This defines how fast the information will scroll.
ScrollWidth	numeric	This defines how wide the scrolling data will be. Note that this cannot be wider than the width of the object but it can be smaller.

Like the Chart control, the Stock Ticker requires a specially formatted ASCII text file. This file is XRT format. A description of XRT format follows:

```
RT
DataName1 <TAB> DataValue1 <TAB> DataValue2
DataName2 <TAB> DataValue1 <TAB> DataValue2
```

Each line ends with a carriage return and the file must be saved with either a .DAT or .XRT extension.

Timer Control   The Timer control inserts an invisible timer in your page. It can be called with VBScript to animate the label control, change properties on controls, or fire any other event at a regular interval. It supports only two properties and one event, Timer. The properties are listed in Table 20.5.

Table 20.5   Timer Control Properties

Property	Value	Description
Enabled	true,false	This property is used to enable or disable the timer.
Interval	numeric (milliseconds)	This can be used to set the timer update intervals.

Part
IV

Ch
20

Reality Check

You need to be very careful to consider your audience with these technologies. Make sure you are able to address your target audience with the pages you develop. If you implement a lot of ActiveX controls, they'll likely be compatible with a significant portion of the browsers coming to your site; however, be certain to provide for those browsers not capable of using the controls.

At the Integra International site, we put counters on the home page to determine how many browsers coming to the site were unable to see the new controls, unable to see frames, or, in general, not seeing the site as we'd intended. These counters helped us determine where to make changes and where our site was working appropriately.

We were, and continue to be, surprised by the number of older browsers coming to the site. Current tests indicate that about 10 percent of the people coming to the site are unable to see frames or ActiveX controls. If your sales are depending on the Internet to get your message out, this is a significant number. This became a very strong planning point on the development of this and other sites.

From Here...

This chapter shows some of the finer points in working with ActiveX controls. These controls provide for the next step in Web page design, but certainly add a level of programming to your pages. For more information on scripting and the technologies behind it, see the following resources:

- Chapter 15, "Data Encryption and Digital Signatures," shows how you can provide digitally signed ActiveX controls on your site. These protect the user from uncertain downloads as they browse Web pages.

- Que's *Special Edition Using ActiveX Scripting* is now available and provides a comprehensive reference to the ActiveX development capabilities.

- The Microsoft and Netscape sites, **http://www.microsoft.com** and **http://www.netscape.com**, respectively, and the Sun Microsystems site located at **http://www.sun.com**, all provide comprehensive resources for researching Java, ActiveX, JavaScript, and VBScript technologies.

## CHAPTER 21

Java Applets and the Internet

- What Java is, where it came from, and where it is going
- What features and functionality are available in Java applets
- The different types of applications that can be built by using Java
- How the Java runtime environment built into Web browsers protects your computer from errant or virus-infected Java applets
- Gain an understanding of the different areas of functionality built into the Java language
- Take a look at some of the Java development tools and utilities available to make the task of building Java-based Web applets easier

The last couple of chapters have looked at some of the newest technologies to allow you to build dynamic Web pages. The only problem is, all of these technologies have increased your work two or three times over. If you want your Web pages to be available for everyone, regardless of which browser they might be using, or what platform that browser is running on, you've got to duplicate your work. If you include any scripting, do you create one version using JavaScript, and another using VBScript? What is the difference between the two, and which is more likely to be supported by the Web surfers who visit your Web site, assuming that your visitors have a newer browser that does support one of the two? Then when you get into ActiveX controls, you have to have one control for those viewers running Windows 95, another for Macintosh users, and any number of others for viewers running the various flavors of UNIX.

Fortunately, there is an alternative available to you. Most of the major browser vendors have either added support for Java into their latest browsers, or have announced that Java will be included soon. Once Java support is included in the majority of Web browsers, it will provide you with the capability to develop an applet once, include it in your Web page, and not have to worry about what browser or platform the viewers of your page happen to be running.

Java provides Web developers with a platform- and browser-independent way of creating dynamic Web pages.

This chapter introduces you to Java, what it can and can't do, and how it fits in with other Web technologies. What is not covered in this chapter is how to build and program Java applets. Java is a full-feature programming language, and there are numerous books available on the subject (and to do it justice would require an entire book). ■

Understanding Java

Given the propensity toward caffeinated drinks that computer programmers exhibit, it probably comes as no surprise that, given enough time, someone would eventually name a programming language after one of the most popular of these drinks, namely Java. Taking a look at the most obvious of Java-enhanced Web sites, Java has had a similarly caffeinating effect on Web development. Now, instead of seeing the standard variation on the "Under Construction" sign on various Web sites, you might see Duke (the official Java mascot) drilling away with his noisy jackhammer (see Figure 21.1).

FIG. 21.1
Duke, the official Java mascot of Sun Microsystems, drilling away with his jackhammer.

Web page animations are the most visible sign of Java's fast acceptance and usage within the World Wide Web community. With such widespread usage, it's hard to remember that Java is a young programming language. Because of Java's youth, there are few tools available (yet) for programming in it. What tools are available are mostly adapted from other tool sets (mostly C++ development environments and tools), although this situation is rapidly changing.

Java's Origins

Java wasn't always destined to become an Internet fixture. Instead, Sun originally designed Java as a programming language for use in small appliances, such as TV set-top boxes and cellular phones. This design constraint forced Sun to keep Java small enough to fit in the limited storage and memory of these small devices, and portable so that it could be easily moved from one manufacturer's equipment to another. The Java language had other constraints such as the need for it to build bug-free code, as most devices into which it would be going wouldn't be capable of easily downloading the latest bug-fix.

> **CAUTION**
>
> Java was originally adapted from the C++ programming language. Because of this origin, you will see aspects of Java described by using a lot of terms that are part of the standard C++ vocabulary. Most of these terms will need no explanation or definition to anyone who knows the C or C++ programming languages. If you don't know the C++ language, you might not want to try to read the next paragraph or two in detail, but instead just lightly skim over them. If you need a more in-depth explanation of how Java works and how to build applets by using Java, pick up a copy of **Java Unleashed** from Sams.net.

Sun approached this task by taking C++ and redesigning it. First, they eliminated the need for the language features that cause the most problems and bugs; Java has no pointers, and arrays are implemented as collections to prevent programmers from overrunning the end of the array into memory allocated to other variables. Next, they built in strong data types to make it easier to use. Java has an actual string data type, it does not use arrays of characters to handle textual strings. To keep Java applications small, the designers built a set of core libraries to be provided as part of the runtime environment. These libraries contain most of the various types of base functionality that would be needed by Java applications, including network communications and Graphical User Interface (GUI) objects and routines. Last, to make the language portable, the designers decided not to make the Java compiler produce machine executable code, but to produce bytecode, which is converted to native machine executable code at runtime by the Java interpreter.

N O T E   One of the biggest contributors to fatal application bugs are pointers. Programmers who have spent any amount of time using C or C++ can tell you that most, if not all, of their fatal bugs turned out to be problems with pointers. Pointers are also a key feature necessary for creating most computer viruses. Take both of these factors into consideration, and you might find yourself agreeing with the designers of Java that it would be better off without pointers. In fact, Java has no facilities for programmable memory management. Instead, Java has good object creation methods, and automatic background garbage collection, freeing the programmer from the necessity of dynamic memory management. ▪

The Ultimate Remote Control   After Sun engineers built an early version of Java, they needed an application to show off its capabilities. The first attempt at this was to build a hand-held remote control designed to control home entertainment by allowing the user to select a movie and drag it across the user interface to the television, providing a highly sophisticated and user-friendly movies-on-demand remote control. With this remote control, you could select CNN, NBC, HBO or any of the other television and cable networks, without learning what channel on which each is to be found. The Java developers at Sun first demonstrated this remote control to Sun executives in August of 1992.

Part
IV

Ch
21

Unfortunately, Sun's drive to use Java as an embedded-system programming language never took off. In March of 1993, Sun lost a bid to create TV set-top boxes for Time Warner to their UNIX rival, Silicon Graphics. A few months later, Sun again lost a deal to create devices for 3DO. After the letdown of not getting any of the contracts that were being handed out to design and build set-top boxes for providing movie-on-demand services, the folks at Sun began looking around to see what else they could do with this new language they had created.

N O T E   Embedded Systems are computers built into other things such as cars, dishwashers, microwaves, and so on. Because the primary purpose of these things is not to be used as a computer, but for some other purpose, the built-in computer that controls it is called an "embedded system." ■

HotJava   It was about this time that the World Wide Web began taking off in popularity with the advent of the NCSA Mosaic Web browser. Some of the developers in the Java division of Sun looked at this early version of the graphical Web, with its static text and images, and realized that they had the opportunity to make it better. They immediately sat down to build their own Web browser with Java. This new Web browser had all of the capabilities of all other browsers with one major exception—it could run Java applets (small programs created using the Java programming language) that were placed within Web pages. With Java applets embedded, Web pages had the capability to come alive with animation, and interact with the user in numerous other ways. Web pages were no longer static text and images, but living, moving, and interacting applications. The programmers at Sun decided to name their new browser HotJava.

Once Sun built their HotJava Web browser, they knew they had to get it into the hands of as many users as possible to educate the Internet community on what was possible. Sun looked at the phenomenal growth of Netscape, and decided to follow Netscape's lead by giving away not only the HotJava browser, but also the Java compiler and development tools as well. Java caught the eyes of several influential members of the Internet community, and soon Netscape was leading the pack to license this new language from Sun. Soon, every major browser vendor was making announcements that they, too, would be licensing Java from Sun and building it into their Web browsers. The final plank for Java becoming an Internet standard was in early December of 1995 when Microsoft announced that it would license Java from Sun for adding to its Internet Explorer browser (this was followed several months later with the announcement that Java would be built into the next version of the Windows operating system, providing full application support on all Microsoft platforms).

N O T E   This chapter is only an overview of the current state of Java technologies. For more information, and the latest news on Java and Java related technologies, see **http://www.gamelan.com/**. ■

Java Future

With Java becoming integrated into the operating system of the primary desktop operating system throughout the world, along with the advent of the Network Computer (NC, a low-cost desktop computer with no floppy disk or hard drive), there is a strong feeling within the computer industry that, over the next few years, C and C++ are going to be relegated to systems programming (such as operating systems, device drivers, and so on), while most applications programming will be done by using Java. Several new technologies enable this to happen:

■ Preemptive multitasking operating systems becoming standard on most desktops. Java needs a preemptive multitasking operating system underneath it to allow Java applications to run as multithreaded applications. With the arrival of Windows 95, the last major non-preemptive operating system (MS-DOS) was on its way out.

■ The development of Just-In-Time compilers from Borland, Symantec, Microsoft, and other companies. These Just-In-Time compilers convert the Java bytecode into native executable machine code before running the Java applet. This enables Java applications to achieve execution speeds comparable to applications written in C and C++.

■ The explosive growth of networked computers. The majority of computers are connected to a network in some capacity. Whether it is a handful of computers in a small office, a home computer connected to the Internet through a dial-up connection, or a large corporate Intranet (a private network running Internet technologies), most computers are hooked up to some sort of network. This enables a new model for software usage and distribution. Computer users will soon be able to select just the software componets they need from a cental storage area, and rent these components for only as long as they are needed. This model lends itself to the portable, platform-independent nature of Java more than the other platform-dependent programming languages.

■ The continuing expansion of the capabilities of the Java language, including the Java Database Connector (JDBC) and the integration of Java with the Common Object Request Broker Architecture (CORBA), allowing it to work with other rsources in a distributed computing environment.

■ The arrival of Rapid Application Development (RAD) tools designed for building Java applications and applets. These tools provide programmers with an extended collection of classes, with numerous application and window controls with substantial low-level code already written, freeing the programmer to focus on the user interface and high-level application logic in a Visual Basic-like development environment.

■ The arrival of JavaBeans (by the time this book reaches the bookstore shelves), enabling Java applets and components to coexist and communicate with existing legacy systems. JavaBeans is a Java component architecture that enables Java to be compatible with ActiveX and OpenDoc, as well as any other technology that runs on any platform capable of running Java applications.

N O T E More than any other factors, the last of the previous new Java technologies (JDBC, CORBA integration, RAD tools, and JavaBeans) will be deciding factors in Java becoming a major programming language for corporate application development. The corporate computing environment is the arena where the platform-independence of Java is likely to have the most impact, and the upcoming Java technologies will serve the needs of the corporate computing environment to be able to quickly build applications that integrate with existing and disparate systems. ■

Java Is Object-Oriented

Java was designed from the ground-up as an object-oriented programming language. It was originally designed from the C++ language, with some extensions from Objective C thrown in, and came out looking a lot like the Smalltalk object model. Java does have inheritance, but not multiple inheritance. Java has method overloading, but not operator overloading. Java does not have structures for grouping sets of variables, you have to build an object class around the variables, complete with methods for setting and retrieving variable contents. There is no cheating on the object model like that available in C++ (C++ has often been used as a "better" C); instead, Java follows the Smalltalk model and forces the programmer to follow a strict object-oriented model.

N O T E   An object-oriented programming language is one that allows the programmer to build self-contained "objects." The programmer can assemble these objects into a larger, more complex application by defining the interactions between the parts, much like a car engine is assembled by using a lot of small parts or "objects." ■

Java Is Dynamic

Java employs a very flexible interface model for resolving methods. This model gives Java the rare capability of allowing programmers to alter and enhance ancestor object classes without having to recompile any of the descendent object classes.

This capability allows a programmer to replace a fundamental piece of an application without having to rebuild the entire application. This is the equivalent of an auto mechanic replacing a faulty brake pad on your car without having to take the tires off. This ability is a tremendous aid when new functionality has to be added or corrected in applications in use on the Internet (or any other network).

Java Is Secure

The designers of Java took special pains to make sure that Java applets could not cause any harm to the computer on which they were running. Every Java-enabled browser has a security manager built-in that limits certain capabilities of the Java applets. Among other functions, the security manager examines and validates the Java bytecode to make sure that it has not been altered or corrupted. The security manager also limits the Java applets access to the hard drive of the computer to specific directories, if it allows access at all.

N O T E   The HotJava browser allows the user to configure a set of directories to which the Java applets are restricted. The Netscape browser does not allow Java applets to access the user's hard drive at all. Most other Web browsers that have Java support take one of these two approaches. ■

An additional function that the security manager performs is limiting other computers to which a Java applet can connect. Java applets running within a Web browser are limited to connecting only with the server from which the applet was downloaded. This is to prevent an unsuspecting Web browser from loading a Web page that contains a Java applet, only to find that the Java applet connects to another, previously unknown computer, and allows that other computer an avenue of access to your computer or network.

N O T E There have been several news reports about weaknesses in the Java security manager implementation. Most of these weaknesses have been identified by well-equipped research facilities working under open conditions. Both Netscape and Sun have been very encouraging to these efforts, and very proactive in searching out and fixing any security weaknesses that may exist within their security manager implementations. As a result, the Java security manager in the most current release of the Netscape Navigator is very robust with no known security weaknesses. ▪

Java Is Portable

One of the features of Java's portability is that Java applications look like they are native to the operating system on which they are running. If you run a Java application on a computer running Windows 95, for instance, the Java application looks and feel like a native Windows 95 application. If you take the same Java application and run it on a Macintosh, the application looks and feels just like a native Macintosh application. Likewise if you run it on a Sun workstation, the Java application looks and feels like a native Solaris application. This is different from most other portable programming languages, most of which require significant modifications to look and feel like the applications built with them are native to each different operating system.

Java Is Multithreaded

Java is a *multithreaded* programming language. This means that it can perform several different tasks all at the same time. With any multithreading programming language comes the need to be able to synchronize the multiple threads of execution, and coordinate access to shared variables. Most programming languages offer a complicated set of mutexes, semaphores, or other facilities to limit simultaneous access to key shared memory and variables. Java has greatly simplified thread synchronization and shared variable access coordination with a simple synchronization class of thread functionality.

N O T E For programmers who have never programmed in multithreaded environments, learning how the various thread synchronization mechanisms work can be intimidating. The simplicity of the Java thread synchronization methods removes a large amount of complexity from this difficult-to-understand topic (see Figure 21.2). This area of functionality could make Java one of the best programming languages available for teaching programmers the concepts of multithreaded programming and thread synchronization. ▪

Part
IV

Ch
21

FIG. 21.2
A Java application with
four threads running
simultaneously.

Understanding the Differences Between Applications and Applets

There is an impression within the community of casual Web users that Java is primarily used for spicing up Web pages. Because of this limited domain of applicability, they don't see what all the excitement is behind Java, and why there is such a large number of programmers (and other technical types) claiming that it is the direction that all network application programming will be going in the near future. In reality, enhancing Web pages is just one of the many types of applications for which Java can be used. Three basic types of applications that can be created by using Java are as follows:

- Console (character-based) applications
- Stand-alone (windowed) applications
- Applets

Console (Character-Based) Applications

Java is capable of building extensive character-based applications, complete with screen, file and network I/O (Input/Output) functionality. This is an excellent Java application type to use for creating process-intensive applications that have little interaction with the user. Screen I/O is mostly limited to what a C++ program would be able to produce using the standard streams, or printf() and scanf() functions, as can be seen in Figure 21.3.

FIG. 21.3

A console Java application listing information about a file specified by the user.

Stand-Alone (Windowed) Applications

Java can be used to build full-featured windowed applications, complete with pull-down menus, dialog windows, and other features common to graphical-user interfaces. The types of application you can create range from simple single window utilities (see Figure 21.4), to full-blown, business applications with hundreds of windows.

FIG. 21.4

A Java calculator application.

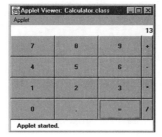

Applets

Java applets are the type of Java application that most users are familiar with, as seen in Figure 21.5. A *Java applet* is a small application that is embedded within a Web page. An applet is limited in functionality, partly by the browser security manager, but also by the context in which it is running. Applets rarely open any additional windows, and if they do, the Web browser usually displays a message to the user about the window being untrusted. This is an alert to the user that the Java applet is going beyond the functionality to which the browser Java Security Manager would like the applet to be limited.

Part
IV

Ch
21

FIG. 21.5

A Java applet included in a Web page, demonstrating a little bit of the off-the-wall humor to be found on the World Wide Web.

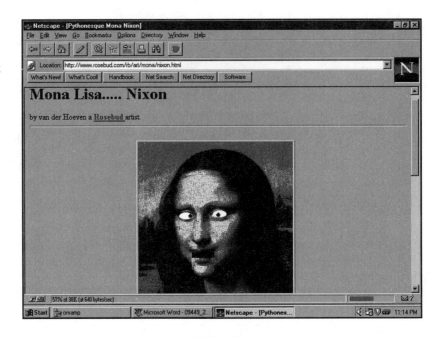

Examining Security Issues and Concerns

Because of the way Java applets run, security is a concern for many users and site administrators. When you are browsing the Web and you visit a page that has a Java applet on it, the Java applet is downloaded to your computer and begins running before you know what it is, and what it will do. How do you know that the Java applet on that Web page doesn't have some sort of virus built into it? How do you know that it is not going to search your hard drive until it finds your electronic banking records, transfer it to some malicious hacker who will use the information to drain every last cent from your account by the next morning? If you think for very long about all the ways in which an applet could potentially cause harm to you or your computer, you can easily understand why the latest feature that all of the firewall manufacturers are boasting is the capability to prevent Java applets from coming through the firewall. To protect unsuspecting Web surfers from the evil Java hacker, current browsers contain a Java Security Manager that tries to limit Java applets in the following ways:

- Limiting access to the browser computer
- Limiting access to other computers
- Limiting access to other Java classes
- Limiting access to environment information
- Verifying the Java bytecode
- Allowing the user to turn off all Java support

N O T E You can get more information on Java security issues from Netscape's site at **http://home.netscape.com/**, as well as Microsoft at **http://www.microsoft.com/**. However, the largest amount of information can be found through Gamelan's Java Resource Directory at **http://www.gamelan.com/**. ■

Limiting Access to the Browser Computer

While certain steps have been taken to eliminate the programming features most used in creating memory viruses (Java has no pointers, making it difficult to snoop around in memory not specifically allocated to the Java applet), Java could easily be used to create certain types of viruses. One of the key ways that Java could infect a computer is by writing infections into other programs already on your computer, or by consuming your entire hard drive.

To prevent this type of infection by Java applets, the Java security manager built into Java-enabled Web browsers limits the amount and type of access that Java applets have to the computer hard drive. In some browsers, the security manager allows the user to determine how much, and to what areas on the hard drive, the Java applets have access. Others (such as Netscape) don't allow any access to the computer hard drive. If the Java applets can't touch the hard drive, they can't do any damage.

Limiting Access to Other Computers

Any time another computer is able to establish a connection to your computer, that other computer has the potential to gain access to any portion of your computer. Once that outside computer has access to your computer, it can snoop around and gain access to your entire network. Because of this, to completely protect your computer and network, Java could be prevented from connecting to any other computer. Unfortunately, this greatly limits the usefulness of most Java applets.

Most Java applets have a legitimate need to connect to another computer, whether to access images to be loaded, or to communicate with a database. Because of this, the designers of the Java security manager decided to limit Java applets to connecting with the computer from which it was loaded. This means that any database with which the Java applet needs to communicate, and any images that it needs to load, must all be located on the same computer from which the Java applet was loaded.

Limiting Access to Other Java Classes

If a Java class is only able to connect to the computer from which it was loaded, but it can access a Java class that was loaded from a different computer, the first Java class has an avenue by which it could establish a connection to another computer. This would, in essence, circumvent all of the effort that had gone into limiting which computer to which a Java class could connect. To prevent this situation, the Java security manager prevents Java classes that were not loaded from the same computer from accessing each other. The only Java classes that a Java applet can access are those that are loaded from the same computer or those on the browser computer hard drive (in the Java class path, designated by the CLASSPATH environment variable).

Part
IV
Ch
21

Limiting Access to Environment Information

There is a lot of information about you, your computer, and your corporate network available in the browser environment in which you might be running Java applets. Some of this information might be crucial for the Java applet to know (such as browser vendor, Java interpreter version, and so on), while there is other information that you don't want the Java applet, or the creator of the Java applet to know (such as your e-mail address, the TCP/IP address of your network server, and other secure information). To prevent abuse of information that is available in environment variables, the Java security manager limits which environment variables Java applets are able to access.

> **CAUTION**
>
> Just because Java applets are limited in which environment variable they are able to access, does not mean you are safe from Web programmers from being able to access that information. There have been numerous news reports documenting how certain vendors have been able to access e-mail addresses and TCP/IP addresses in order to build a profile of the user visiting specific Web sites. This is usually done through a combination of JavaScript (usually not Java) and client-side cookies. Just because Java is not able to grab the information, doesn't mean it can't be grabbed by a creative and inventive programmer.

Verifying the Java Bytecode

When a Java applet is loaded into your Web browser, it usually hasn't traveled directly from the serving computer to your computer. Instead, it has traveled through several computers on the way. This means that there were several opportunities for the Java bytecode to have been corrupted or infected. Because of this likelihood, the Java interpreter has a bytecode verifier built in. As the Java runtime interpreter is loading the Java applet (and the Java Just-In-Time compiler in the newest browsers), it double-checks the Java bytecode, to make sure that it is all legal and valid Java code, and that it hasn't been corrupted or infected on it's way to your computer. This is basically a last-minute check to make sure that the Java applet can be safely run on your computer, without causing any harm to your system (or other applications).

Choosing Not to Run Java Applets

Finally, if even with all of these precautions, you (or your corporate network security administrator) feel Java applets still cannot be trusted, you have the option of turning all access to them off. As you can see in Figure 21.6, you have some flexibility in what you turn off—Java applets, JavaScript, or both. Of course, these options vary depending on which Web browser you are using.

N O T E JavaScript is a scripting language derived from Java. It can be placed in an HTML document and is interpreted and executed by the browser. JavaScript is discussed in detail in Chapter 24, "JavaScript." ■

FIG. 21.6
Netscape Navigator security control dialog box, where Java applets can be turned off, to prevent any potential problems.

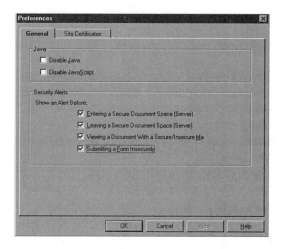

Examining the Basic Java Language

In the Java language, everything is built as an object, which in Java is called a *class*. Attributes and methods of a class can be accessed via the class itself, using the dot notation standard in C++, Delphi, PowerBuilder, SmallTalk, and Visual Basic (e.g., to check the status of a check box or radio button would use something like "if (rbThisOption.checked) ..."). Also like C++, the curly braces ({}) are used to define scope, which are the equivalent of "begin" and "end" in languages such as Pascal, Basic, and several 4GL (fourth generation languages) such as PowerBuilder and Delphi. To get familiar with the structure of a Java application, see Listing 21.1, which is the well-known "Hello World!" application.

N O T E Attributes are the settings used to control the appearance and behavior of an object. For instance, a button on an application window has attributes that control where the button is located on the window, what text appears on the button, how big the button is, and so forth. ■

N O T E Methods are the actions taken within the application. For instance, when you click the mouse button, the button's method is run. The method is what performs the actions that result from the click. If the button closes the current window, the button's method is what closed the window. ■

Listing 21.1 The Ubiquitous "Hello World" Java Programming Example

```
class HelloWorld {
   public static void main (String args[]) {
      System.out.println("Hello, World!");
   }
}
```

Part
IV

Ch
21

N O T E You can find the preceding, and many other example Java applications, accompanied by a tutorial on the language at **http://java.sun.com/doc/**. You can also find many Java enthusiasts on the Web who make the source code to their Java applets freely available from their Web sites. ▓

T I P Java is a case-sensitive language. Many programmers coming to Java from case-insensitive languages like Visual Basic, Delphi, and PowerBuilder have trouble with this, and get frustrated when the compiler tells them their functions have not been defined. The other thing to be aware of is the Java naming convention, which is to name functions by using whole words without underlines ("_") between words. The first word in the function name is all lowercase, while the first letter in all subsequent words is uppercase. This makes a function to set text on a control to be named *setText*, not *SetText* or *settext*.

Java Class Packages

Similar to C++, the Java base classes are organized into *packages*. Each package contains several Java classes that are descendants of common ancestor classes, or have similar functionality. Each Java class has to specify which classes and packages it needs to know about and use. This is done using the import directive before any Java code, as in Listing 21.2.

N O T E The packaging of like functionality into a common file is used in most programming languages. In Java, these groupings are called *packages*, while in most other programming languages these groupings are called *libraries*. The difference in names is purely semantic. ▓

Listing 21.2   The Import Section in a Typical Java Applet

```
import java.awt.*;
import java.applet.*;
import java.io.IOException;
import java.lang.Math;
import java.util.Date;
```

N O T E The standard Java packages follow a simple naming convention. The class names are composed of three sections, separated by periods. The first section specifies that the class to be imported is a Java class. The second section specifies the package in which the class is to be found. The third section specifies the class name. An asterisk (*) can be substituted for the class name, and is understood to mean that the entire package should be imported. Using this naming convention, the import section in Listing 21.2 includes the entire AWT (Abstract Windowing Toolkit) and Applet packages, the IOException class from the I/O package, the Math class from the Language package, and the Date class from the Utility package. ▓

The Language Package   The language package, known as *java.lang*, contains the core classes that make up the Java language. These are the Java classes without which you would not be able to write even the simplest Java application. Among the classes included in the language package are the following:

- The *Object* class, from which all other classes are descendants (all other Java classes are built on top of this class).
- The data type wrapper classes (such as *Integer, Boolean,* and *Character*). These are classes built around the basic data types.
- *String* classes, containing the basic text-handling functionality for the Java language.
- The *Math* class, which contains all of the basic mathematical functions for the Java language.
- *System* and *Runtime* classes, which allow applets to access system and environment information.
- Thread classes, which enable Java applications to be doing two (or more) things at the same time.
- Exception handling classes, which provide Java applications the ability to recover from errors, whether programmer or otherwise.
- *Class* and *Process* classes (these are the classes that load and run other classes).

The Utilities Package   The Utilities package, known as java.util, has a lot of classes that perform various utility functions. These include classes for working with dates, generating random numbers, and working with data structures. Among the classes included in the utility package are as follows:

- The *Date* class provides calendar date and time functionality to Java applications
- Data Structure classes provide various data structures used for storing data (such as BitSet, Dictionary, Hashtable, and so on.)
- The *Random* class provides a random number generator
- The *StringTokenizer* Class (for parsing strings into individual characters and substrings)
- The *Observer* interface provides an interface for use by objects that observe other objects. The observer objects wait for changes in the object that is being watched, and then take the appropriate action for the change that occurred
- The *Enumeration* interface provides an interface for defining a set of values (such as the set of colors; black, white, red, blue, green, and so on.)

N O T E   Notice in the Utilities package that there are not only classes, but also items referred to as *interfaces*. An interface is not a class, but is a prototype for a class (or abstract class). In essence, it is a class that contains no code, only functions and methods. Interfaces allow the programmer to implement any number of descendant classes, each with its own unique functionality, but all with a common set of functions and methods. Descendants of an interface must implement the functionality for all of the methods defined in the ancestor, since there is no functionality in the ancestor. ■

The I/O Package   The I/O package, known as java.io, contains classes for reading from and writing to various input and output sources, including files (just because applets are limited in their file access doesn't mean that the language doesn't support file I/O). There are numerous input and output stream classes to handle just about any type of input or output you might need, whether it is a file, user, or other device with which your application is exchanging data. Among the classes in the I/O package are as follows:

- Input stream classes (including InputStream, BufferedInputStream, and ByteArrayInputStream) are used for reading data from an input source. The input source could be the keyboard, a file, memory, or anything else that can contain data.

- Output stream classes (including OutputStream, BufferedOutputStream, and ByteArrayOutputStream) are used for writing data to an output source, including the computer monitor, a file, memory, or anything else that can contain data.

- File classes (File and RandomAccessFile) provide access to, and information about files.

- The *StreamTokenizer* class, which is used for parsing strings of text.

The Windowing Package   It is with the Abstract Window Toolkit (AWT), known as java.awt, where Java applet programming begins to look like a GUI programming language. The AWT package contains a complete windowing library, complete with most of the GUI widgets that users have come to expect in a windowing application. Most of the classes in the AWT package are descendants from one common ancestor class, Component. Among the classes included in this package are the following:

- The *Component* class, is the foundation upon which every user-interface element is derived. This holds the basic screen-oriented information (such as position on screen, size, color, and so on).

- The *Button* class is used for all clickable buttons that trigger actions.

- The *Canvas* class provides an area on which you can place other user-interface components.

- The *Checkbox* class, used for both check boxes and radio buttons.

- The *Panel, Frame,* and *Window* classes, within which can be placed all other components in this package.

- The *Label* class is used to display unmodifiable text on the screen.

- The *List* class, used for multi-select lists and drop-down list boxes.

- The Scrollbar class allows the user to scroll through text and list areas that cannot be fit onto the screen.

- The Text area classes provide areas into which the user can type textual information.

- The Menu classes, for providing the user with pull-down menus (because Java applets are generally run within Web browsers, menus cannot be used within an applet, only within a stand-alone Java application).

- The *Graphics* class, used to draw images on the screen.

Because of the complexity of programming GUI applications, it is easy to see that the classes in the AWT package are among the most difficult aspects of Java applet programming. However, that is beginning to change. As shown in the section "Reviewing Java Development Tools," Java development environments are beginning to arrive in the marketplace that have drag-and-drop screen painters, making Java GUI programming much easier. One of the biggest differences that you see between these Java screen painters and Visual Basic or Delphi is in the level of complexity. You find that there is a lot fewer details to take care of with Java because it is a more straightforward approach to GUI implementation.

N O T E The details that programmers have to pay attention to when writing GUI applications are far fewer in number than is normal when creating applications for Windows or Macintosh. The primary reason for this simplicity is the portability of Java. Because a Java applet runs on Windows, Macintosh, and UNIX, looking like a native application on each, most GUI controls are mostly limited to common sets of functionality. This means you are giving up access to some details of each particular GUI platform for the capability to have the same applet run on all GUI platforms. ■

The Applet Package The Applet package, known as `java.applet`, contains the Applet class and a few applet-related interfaces. Most of the interfaces included in this package have to do with applets, providing hooks into the runtime environment. One interface included, the AudioClip interface, is a non-applet interface. The AudioClip interface is used to load and play sound files.

N O T E In its current implementation, Java is very limited in what it can do with audio files. All that a Java applet can do with an audio clip is play it in an endless loop. The audio capabilities of Java will probably be expanded on in future versions of the language. ■

One thing that helps keep Java applets small and light is that it has virtually no audio or graphic displaying capabilities. Instead, it takes advantage of the built-in graphics and audio handling functionality in the Web browser. Other special functionality that is built into the applet class is functionality to pause and run the applet as the user leaves and re-enters a Web page.

The Networking Package The Networking package, known as `java.net`, contains a complete networking implementation. The classes in the networking package fall into two general functional areas:

1. Web interface and extension classes, which deal with Web-oriented aspects of Internet communications (such as URLs, URL Encoding, Handling Content, and so on).
2. Basic network interface classes (socket programming classes), which provide basic connection and communications functionality over a network.

> **N O T E**   Java applets rely on the Web browser to perform certain functions that the applet can count on being available. When the Java applet needs to display a GIF or JPEG image, it lets the browser do all of the work. This provides the Java applets the flexibility to provide support for all file types that are supported by the Web browser, or any associated plug-ins and ActiveX controls. ■

By building these two areas of network functionality into the Java language, Java became an excellent language for building network, Internet, and Web-oriented applications. Among the classes included in the Networking package are the following:

- The URL and URLConnection classes provide the Java applet access to resources in the Internet through the HTTP protocol.
- The URLEncoder class is used to encode text in the form of a URL, so it can be passed to a CGI script.
- The URLStreamHandler class is used to open connections by using non-HTTP communications over the Internet.
- The Socket class is used to provide basic TCP/IP network connections and communications. This class is the basis for the ServerSocket and DatagramSocket classes.
- The ServerSocket class is used to add server functionality to a Java application.
- The DatagramSocket class is used to send broadcast TCP/IP communications over a network.
- The DatagramPacket class is used for the packets of information that are sent over a network in a broadcast message.
- The InetAddress class is used to represent a computer name and it's TCP/IP address.
- The ContentHandler class (for handling MIME objects) is used to handle various MIME content types and file types.
- The SocketImpl class is used to provide the raw networking functionality to the Socket classes.

Placing a Java Applet into a HTML Page

Placing a Java applet into a Web page is a simple matter of placing the <APPLET> tag in the desired location within the BODY section of the HTML page. The APPLET HTML tag has three key attributes that should always be used (as shown in Listing 21.3), and several more that are optional.

Listing 21.3   A Simple Java Applet Tag, with the Display Width and Height Specified

```
<APPLET CODE="Example.class" WIDTH=283 HEIGHT=190>
</APPLET>
```

If the applet takes one or more parameters, you include <PARAM> tags between the <APPLET> and </APPLET> tags to specify these. A more complex example of an applet tag using a single parameter can be found in Listing 21.4.

Listing 21.4   A More Complex Applet HTML Tag with a Single Parameter

```
<APPLET CODEBASE="http://java.sun.com/JDK-prebeta1/applets/NervousText"
CODE="NervousText.class" width=400 height=75 align=center >
<PARAM NAME="text" VALUE="This is the Applet Viewer.">
</APPLET>
```

In this listing, the CODEBASE attribute provides the URL where the Java class can be found, and the CODE attribute provides the Java class to be loaded and run. A complete listing of Java applet attributes is provided in Table 21.1.

Table 21.1   Java Applet HTML Tag Attributes

CODEBASE	This attribute provides the base URL where the applet can be found. This is the directory in which the applet is located, not the applet itself. If this attribute is not provided, then the URL of the HTML document is used.
CODE	This attribute gives the name of the applet class. This is a required attribute. This attribute must be relative from the base URL provided in the CODEBASE attribute.
ALT	This attribute gives text to be displayed if the browser understands the APPLET tag but cannot run the Java applet.
NAME	This attribute give the applet instance a name that can be used by other applets running within the same HTML page to find and communicate with each other.
WIDTH/HEIGHT	These attributes are required and provide the initial width and height (in pixels) to be used for the applet display area. These attributes do not include the display area for any dialogs and windows that are opened by the applet.
ALIGN	This attribute specifies the alignment of the applet. Values are the same as for the <IMG> tag.
VSPACE/HSPACE	These attributes specify the number of pixels above and below, or on each side of the applet. These are used in the same way as the corresponding attributes for the <IMG> tag.

Part
IV

Ch
21

The PARAM tag has only two attributes, both of which are required. These are provided in Table 21.2.

Table 21.2   The PARAM HTML Tag Attributes

NAME	This is the parameter name. The Java applet uses this parameter name to retrieve the parameter value; it's important to make sure this attribute matches what the applet expects.
VALUE	This is the parameter value the Java applet receives.

N O T E   Each parameter needed by a Java applet must have a PARAM tag within the APPLET tags. If you have a Java applet that takes four parameters, for example, then you must have four <PARAM> tags between the <APPLET> and </APPLET> tags. ■

T I P   You can place HTML tags between the <APPLET> and </APPLET> tags. These instructions are executed in browsers that don't understand the APPLET tags, while browsers that do understand the APPLET tags ignore the HTML tags. This enables you to place some text in a HTML page where a Java applet should be seen, telling users that in order to experience the full effect of your HTML page, they should upgrade to a browser that supports Java.

Reviewing Java Development Tools

About a year ago, if you wanted to work with Java, you were limited to downloading the SDK (Software Development Kit) from Sun, and using the command-line tools. You had to spend the time to learn about the various configuration elements, how to set them up and maintain them, and provide your own editor. That is no longer the case. There are several Java IDEs (Integrated Development Environment) available now, with more on the way. These come with an editor that is tuned for Java, providing syntax color-coding, and pull-down menu compiling, running, and debugging. Some of the more advanced tools are already providing drag-and-drop window layout capabilities, and some are providing their own compilers that perform much faster than the original Sun compiler.

N O T E   The Java tools market is moving fast. New tools are being announced almost daily. The list of tools provided here may be outdated by the time you read this. The best place to look for new information on Java tools and utilities is Gamelan's Java Resource Directory at **http:// www.gamelan.com/**. ■

Commercial Java Development Environments

With Java becoming as popular as it has, as quickly as it has, it should surprise no one that the major development tool vendors are coming out with Java IDEs. Just about all of the commercial Java IDEs are derived from existing development environments from each of the vendors, maintaining the look and feel of the tools from which they were derived (e.g, Microsoft's Visual

J++ uses the same development environment as Microsoft's Visual C++, Borland's initial Java tool set uses their Borland C++ development environment, and so on).

Symantec Cafe and Visual Cafe   Symantec's Cafe is the first commercial Java IDE to arrive on the Microsoft Windows platform, and as of when this is being written, is the only commercial IDE to be available on both the Windows and Macintosh platforms. Cafe comes with its own compiler, which is faster than the JDK compiler (which is also included), and a Just-In-Time compiler. Cafe is a complete Java development environment, complete with a debugger and resource editor for creating windows for use in Java applications. Symantec also made a reduced functionality version called "Cafe Lite" available for downloading from their Cafe Web site at **http://cafe.symantec.com/**.

Symantec did an impressive job by getting Cafe (see Figure 21.7) on the market as quickly as it did, but the immaturity of the tool shows in several unpolished features and functions. Symantec is committed to providing frequent updates to Cafe through its Web site at **http://cafe.symantec.com/** and each update has shown significant improvement over the previous versions. Among the updates has been support for the Netscape Internet Foundation Classes, a set of Java classes that are bundled with the latest versions of the Netscape browsers (version 3.0 and higher), and a RAD (Rapid Application Development) version named Visual Cafe.

FIG. 21.7
Symantec's Cafe Java development environment.

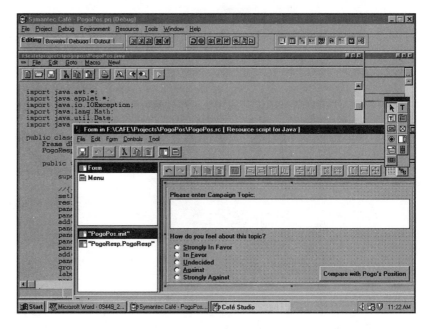

N O T E   There are a few distinguishing characteristics of a RAD development tool that set it apart from a normal IDE development tool. The most visible difference is that the primary user interface is not the code editor, but the screen painter. With this comes an extensive class library and application framework, allowing the programmer to focus primarily on the application specific logic, not the underlying functionality. ■

Metrowerks CodeWarrior   Metrowerks CodeWarrior is a Macintosh-based IDE for developing applications in Java, C/C++, and Object Pascal. It uses plug-in compilers, enabling you to add compilers for other languages and platforms quickly and easily. It includes most of the bells-and-whistles that you expect from a full-feature IDE, including class browser, integrated debugger, and applet viewer. For information on the various versions of CodeWarrior and their capabilities, visit the Metrowerks Web site at **http://www.metrowerks.com/**.

RougeWave JFactory   JFactory (see Figure 21.8) is based on RougeWave's popular zApp application framework. Like zApp, JFactory supplies the class libraries, screen painter, code editor, and project manager. It does not provide a Java compiler, debugger, or applet viewer, but works with the JDK from Sun. RougeWave has also released several special-function Java libraries, JTools, JMoney, and JWidgets. For information on JFactory or other RougeWave Java libraries, visit RougeWave's Web site at **http://www.rougewave.com/**.

FIG. 21.8
RougeWave's JFactory
Java development
environment.

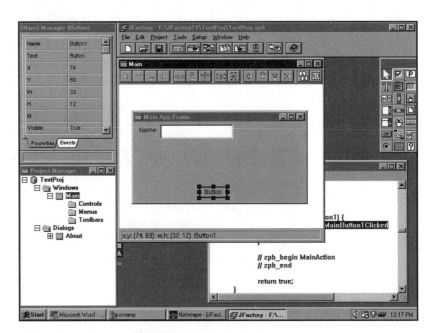

Borland Latte   Borland has shown signs of new life lately with the announcement and introduction of several Internet and Java tools. The first product they released was a Java plug-in for their C++ development environment. This Java plug-in included an excellent Java debugger and Just-In-Time compiler (Borland later licensed its JIT compiler to Netscape for inclusion in Navigator 3.0).

By the time this book is published, Borland should have released its Java RAD development tool, code named Latte (the name may have changed by the time it is released) (see Figure 21.9). Latte is based on Borland's award winning Delphi development tool, and the first release of Latte will be built by using Delphi (Borland plans to develop later releases of Latte using Java, so that it will be completely portable to all platforms on which Java will run). Latte includes Borland's Baja Java library and framework, which has been accepted by SunSoft as part of the JavaBeans standard. Borland has decided that Internet development tools is the direction that their company needs to be taking, and it shows in the products that they are coming out with. Information on Borland's Internet tools can be found at **http://www.borland.com/**.

FIG. 21.9
Borland's Latte Java development environment.

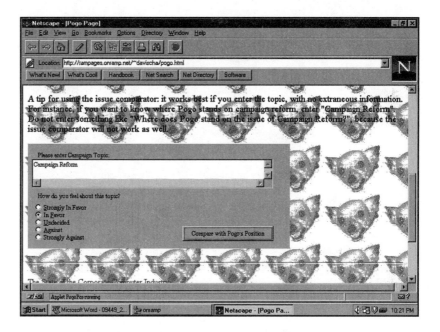

Natural Intelligence Roaster   Natural Intelligence's Roaster is another Macintosh-based Java development environment. It is not as complete as other Java development environments, and like JFactory, depends on the tools bundled with the JDK from SunSoft. Information on Roaster can be found at **http://www.roaster.com/**.

Microsoft Visual J++   Visual J++ is Microsoft's entry in the Java development tools arena. Visual J++ (see Figure 21.10) uses Microsoft's Developer Studio as the development environment, so if you are already familiar with their Visual C++ tool (version 4.0), you should be in comfortable surroundings. Visual J++ does have a few elements that sets it apart from the other Java tools. First, it is tightly integrated with Microsoft's Internet Explorer (IE) Web browser, and uses IE as the applet viewer and debugger. Visual J++ also has the capability to take Visual C++ resource files (.RC) and convert them into Java windows and menus. Visual

Part
IV

Ch
21

J++ is tightly tied to Microsoft's ActiveX technology, making it easy to build interaction between the two. For more information on Visual J++, see Microsoft's Web page at **http://www.microsoft.com/**.

FIG. 21.10

Microsoft's Visual J++ development tool.

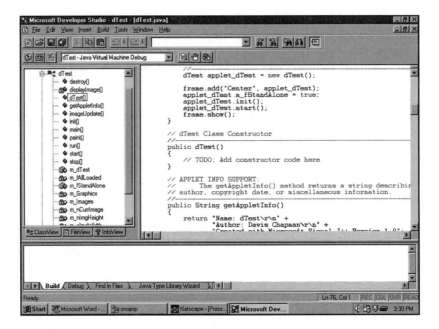

Shareware Java Development Environments

Along with the commercial Java development tools, there is a number of shareware and freeware Java development tools available over the Internet. Although the freeware tools may not have all of the features of their commercial equivalents, most of the shareware ones often go beyond their commercial counterparts. The success of the shareware market in Internet and Java tools has influenced the commercial vendors to follow the lead of the shareware vendors, providing free, limited functionality/time, evaluation versions of their tools. Most of these work for 30 days, after which they hope to have you convinced that you need to fork over the money to buy the full-blown version.

N O T E Shareware is software that is freely available for potential users to use and try before buying. Shareware is still commercial software, and you are required to pay for it; you just get to use it before you decide to buy it. There are many different approaches to Shareware, from building in a time limit over which it can be used, after which it will not work, or leaving some functionality disabled until a full license has been bought. There are many resources available from which shareware Java tools can be found; one of the most popular is Tucows (The Ultimate Collection Of Winsock Shareware) at **http://www.tucows.com/**, or any of their mirror sites, or Gamelan at **http://www.gamelan.com/**. ■

Diva   Diva is a freeware IDE for building Java applets. Diva falls on the low-tech end of the IDEs for Java, providing little more than a Java editor and project control. All other tools (such as compiler, applet viewer, and debugger) are expected to be provided via the Java JDK from SunSoft. Information about Diva can be found at **http://www.qoi.com/javaside.html**.

Java Workshop   The Java Workshop is the Java IDE from SunSoft. This is a very good IDE with tight integration with the JDK tools. There are a lot of people who think that this is the best Java IDE available. Information on the Java Workshop can be found at **http://java.sun.com/**.

Mojo   Penumbra Software's Mojo is one of the first RAD Java development environments to be available for Java development. Mojo has a drag-and-drop window painter with several extended widgets, and automatically builds the Java application code around the window layout. Mojo is one of the first tools to really allow visual Java application development. Like most shareware Java tools, Mojo can be downloaded for a 30 day evaluation, after which Penumbra hopes that you buy a full license. More information on Mojo can be found at **http://www.penumbrasoftware.com/**.

Java Tools and Utilities

Along with the Java development environments, there has also been a growth in Java add-ons and utilities. Some of these enable you to add on additional functionality into your Java applications, and some are prebuilt Java applets into which you can feed your image files, or other configuration information, and have a ready-made Java applet for inclusion in your Web pages. Some of these are commercial; some are shareware.

Kinetix Hyperwire   Kinetix's Hyperwire is a tool for creating interactive applets without programming. It works with VRML (Virtual Reality Markup Language) to enable users to create 3-D applets and titles. For information on Hyperwire, see Kinetix's Web site at **http://www.ktx.com/**.

BulletProof Jagg   BulletProof Jagg is a set of Java libraries that enable Java applets and applications to talk to a database. Jagg is limited to working with an ODBC database running on a Windows NT server. BulletProof can be found at **http://www.bulletproof.com/**.

Aimtech Jamba   Aimtech's Jamba is a visual authoring tool for interactively building Java applets without knowing the Java programming language. Using Jamba for building Java applets is very much like using Microsoft FrontPage for building HTML pages; it removes you from having to know the ins and outs of Java coding, but at the same time it takes away a certain level of control. Information on Jamba can be found at **http://www.aimtech.com/**.

Part
IV

Ch
21

Sausage Software Utilities (BookWorm, Clikette, Egor, and Swami)   No discussion of Java tools and utilities would be complete without discussing the rapidly growing collection of tools and Java applets pouring out of Sausage Software. This is the same company that created the popular Hot Dog HTML editor. They have created a collection of prebuilt Java applets that can be added to any HTML page, and instantly add various sets of creative new functionality. All of their applets are available on 30-day trial basis, after which most of them disable themselves. Among the prebuilt applets that are available from Sausage Software are described in Table 21.3.

Table 21.3 Sausage Software Prebuilt Java Applets	
Egor	Claimed by Sausage Software as the first commercial Java applet, Egor enables you to place a Java animation on an HTML page by simply configuring the Egor applet with the appropriate image files. It will also play an audio file with the animation.
Flash	Flash is a tool to allow you to display text in the status line at the bottom of a browser.
Clikette	Clikette is a tool for creating 3-D image buttons that can be placed in HTML pages that will take users to another URL.
Bookworm	Bookworm is a Java applet that will take multiple URLs, and place them in a scrolling list box. This provides a space conservative way of placing a large number of links into a drop-down style listbox. By the user selecting a URL from the list, Bookworm will take the user to the selected site.
Swami	Swami is a simple text animator. It allows the user to select the text and one of several animation styles, and provides the animated text on the user's Web page.

At the rate that Sausage Software is churning out new applets, they are bound to have at least a half-dozen more Java applets by the time this book reaches the bookstore shelves. To get the latest information on applets available from Sausage Software, see their Web page at **http://www.sausage.com/**.

Reality Check

Java is a young but rapidly growing language. There is a large amount of interest in the language, and what it can be used for. Up until this point in time, most of what Java can be used for is just speculation. Java has mostly been used for entertainment purposes, providing animated buttons and areas of the Web. Using Java applets for anything more substantial is just beginning to be seen.

Part of the reason for the current state of Java usage has to be the primitive state of Java development tools. As better tools become available, the integration and usefulness of Java applets on Web pages is beginning to become more substantial. There are some Web sites using real-time database access with Java applets to provide up-to-the-minute information such as stock market prices or breaking news headlines.

> **CAUTION**
>
> If you choose to develop Java applets using only the free JDK tool set, be prepared to spend a substantial amount of time and effort getting your environment configured correctly. Some users have spent weeks working with Sun, trying to get their Java environment working correctly. If you plan on doing server-side Java, be prepared to spend even more time on the configuration.

For the next year or two, there will be an ongoing battle for dominance of the Web between the Java and Microsoft ActiveX camps. Both technologies will be around for quite a while, and they may end up living a peaceful coexistence. In the meantime, they will be competing for Web space, and as a result, you will continue to see the "This site best viewed using..." on a large percentage of Web sites. Both technologies are very immature, and have a long way to go before they can be considered "mature."

From Here...

In this chapter, you learned about the history of Java and saw a little of the direction in which it is heading. You looked at the features and functionality that make Java such an attractive programming language for use over the Internet. And, finally, you took a brief look at the available tools for working with and creating Java applets.

Java is a very complete and complex language, and cannot be covered in any depth in a single chapter. Fortunately, there are several good books available on Java. If you want to use an integrated development environment, spend some time checking out the free 30-day trial versions of the various tools. This allows you to get a tool with which you feel most comfortable. From here, you might want to check out the following chapters:

- To gain an understanding of the ActiveX technology, read Chapter 20, "ActiveX and the Internet."
- To understand non-Java based means of accessing server-side databases, see Chapter 22, "Database Access and Integrity."

Part
IV

Ch
21

## CHAPTER 22

Database Access and Integrity

Corporate database systems are built on making information widely available to qualified users. The information in these situations comes from many sources, ranging from discussion groups to proprietary systems. Probably the biggest repository of mass information is the database. If you've ever just browsed a database, without specifying meaningful criteria, you know what *mass* information means: There is often so much information represented that it makes the information less useful.

By making databases available on your Web server, you can help users make sense of this information and, at the same time, you'll be able to control access and presentation without the need for any special software to begin using the database effectively. In short, you have a new avenue to provide this access to the information that is probably already stored on your network.

Learn about database access from your Internet server

See how to add database access to your site and create dynamic pages that can use SQL-formatted queries to update or retrieve database information.

Learn about the Internet Database Connector

Microsoft's IDC is a powerful tool to use in adding the new capabilities to your system and at the same time, provide a secure environment in which your pages can be run.

See how you can use an ODBC data source for logging server accesses

Creating logs that can be queried to spot trends is important to the continuing management of your site. You'll see how you can use an ODBC data source to store this information, making it easier to create custom reports and retrieve the information you'll need.

N O T E   This chapter focuses largely on the capabilities included with Microsoft's Internet Information Server, included on the CD that accompanies this book.

The focus on the Microsoft product is due to the fact that you can access any ODBC database for which you have a 32-bit ODBC driver, making the interface one of the most open on the market today. You can access everything from an Access database to a remote SQL Server from your Web pages. ■

Database access with the Microsoft Internet Information Server is provided by giving you ODBC connectivity to the HTML pages that execute on the server when the user makes a request of the system. In this chapter, you'll see how to set up pages, what types of information you can provide, and how you can enhance the presentation of the information to make it the most meaningful to the people that request it. ■

CAUTION

Be aware that the database connector files are likely to contain and convey sensitive, and sometimes very confidential, information. For example, they may contain query information that calls out column names, table names, and database sources that map to your ODBC configurations on the server.

In addition, when users click a link to a database connector file, they'll be able to see where you're keeping your scripts and other programs, as this information will show up in the URL that is displayed to them.

It is extremely important that your programs, scripts, and supporting files reside in the scripts subdirectory structure and that you provide Execute-only privileges on that directory. Be sure you do not provide Read privileges. This opens your system to unneeded possibilities for trouble as people can browse and review the applications that are the core of your system.

For more information, refer to Chapter 5, "Setting Up and Configuring a Web Server."

Introducing the Internet Database Connector

The Internet Information Server (IIS) provides access to the ODBC layer with the use of the Internet Database Connector (IDC). The IDC acts as a go-between for your system, providing the interaction between what is seen in the browser in terms of HTML, and how the information is queried at the database level. The overall access layer map is shown in Figure 22.1.

When users specify the IDC file in the URL from the browser, they are instructing the IIS system to use the IDC file and its statements to query the database and return the results. The IDC is specified in the URL, but the HTX file, or HTML Extension file, is what is actually returned to the user. The HTX file, still a standard HTML file, indicates how the resulting data is displayed, what lines constitute the detail lines of information, and more.

From Figure 22.1, you can see that the engine doing the database work with ODBC is HTTPODBC.DLL. This DLL, included when you install the IIS system, is an Internet Server API (ISAPI) application that runs as an extension to the server software. This extension is database-aware and is able to use the two source files required to give the information back to the user.

FIG. 22.1
The IDC provides for access to any ODBC data source.

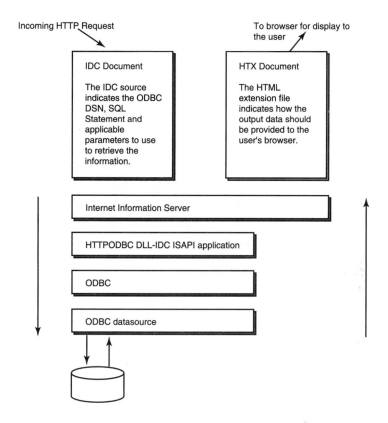

Incoming HTTP Request

To browser for display to the user

IDC Document

The IDC source indicates the ODBC DSN, SQL Statement and applicable parameters to use to retrieve the information.

HTX Document

The HTML extension file indicates how the output data should be provided to the user's browser.

Internet Information Server

HTTPODBC DLL-IDC ISAPI application

ODBC

ODBC datasource

 T I P If you did not install the ODBC component of IIS, you'll need to do so to use the IDC. This not only installs the ODBC portions of the environment, but it also configures the server to be aware of the IDC files you'll be using. If you do not install the ODBC components, when users click the IDC link on their Web page, they'll see a prompt to download the IDC file, rather than view the results of the query. See Figure 22.2 for an example of this prompt.

FIG. 22.2
If the server does not recognize the database connector, it will try to download the IDC page to the requesting user, rather than processing it and returning the results.

When you install IIS, the ODBC option must be selected. Although it may not indicate disk space requirements if you have already installed ODBC from other applications, it is still necessary to install ODBC to activate the IDC capabilities (see Figure 22.3).

continues

continued

FIG. 22.3

It's a good rule of thumb to select ODBC for all installations.

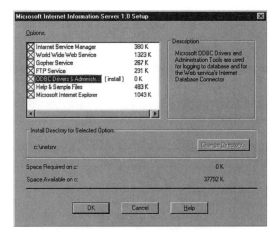

Listing 22.1 shows a sample IDC file, taken from the samples included with the server. The sample installs into the \SCRIPTS\SAMPLES folder on your system in the IIS directory structure.

Listing 22.1   A Simple IDC Source File

```
Data source: web sql
Username: sa
Template: sample.htx
SQLStatement:
+SELECT au_lname, ytd_sales from pubs.dbo.titleview
➥where ytd_sales>5000
```

When this file is loaded by IIS, IIS examines the extension and determines what application should be used for the source file. For certain items, including the IDC extension, the server come preinstalled, knowing what to do with the source when it's requested. One of the powerful capabilities and features of IIS is that it is able to use the same Windows-based extension resolution to determine what to do with a given request. Files with a GIF extension, for example, are known to be graphic images, and files with an IDC extension are database connector applets. You set up custom keys in the Registry. Associations are set up in the following subkey:

```
HKEY_LOCAL_MACHINE
SYSTEM
CurrentControlSet
Services
W3SVC
Parameters
ScriptMap
```

If you add a new entry, make it of the type REG_SZ and indicate the extension to associate with it. You need to include the period before the extension, such as **.idc**, to correctly map the association. For the value, indicate the path and file name that executes when the specified extension is loaded. Remember: Provide the path from the root and start the path with a backslash as this ensures, regardless of the current working directory, that IIS can locate the application.

If you are indicating parameters to the call, you can use a %s on the key value where you indicate the application to run. For example, suppose you have a DLL that you want to run anytime a request is received to open a file with a .FUN extension. Your entry would be as follows:

```
.fun = c:\inetsrv\scripts\test\fundll.dll %s %s
```

When you use this option, the first time you use the %s, you receive the application to run that is passed to the URL. For example, if the FUNDLL is an application that processes a text file and searches it for a given value, you would expect the user to be passing in the name of the text file and the value to search for within it. When you provide the URL at the browser level, you first indicate the location of the file you want to run. A question mark is added by the browser, followed by any applicable parameters to the call.

For the examples here, the URL that is used is similar to the following:

```
http://holodeck3/scripts/search.fun?text+to+find
```

The resulting command line is the following:

```
c:\inetsrv\scripts\test\fundll.dll search.fun text+to+find
```

In the preceding line, each of the two items specified (the source file and search text) are passed as parameters.

> **N O T E** Since parameters are passed as a single string to your application, as in the preceding example with the text+to+find string, your application must be able to parse out the plus signs and rebuild the string, most likely in a buffer that can be used by your application to search the database or text file, as needed.

The results-formatting file, or HTX file, is where things can get a little tricky. As you'll see throughout this chapter, the real power and capability of your system is exposed with the HTX file. Until the information is provided to the template, it's of no use to the requester as he will have not yet seen the information. You can have one of the best, most comprehensive databases around, but, if the presentation of the data is not what your audience needs, the information might as well be under lock and key.

Listing 22.2 shows a simple HTX template, provided in the samples with the IIS product, which displays the results of a query.

> **Listing 22.2 HTX Source Files Provide Template Information for the Display of Results from Database Queries**

```
<HTML>
<HEAD><TITLE>Authors and YTD Sales</TITLE></HEAD>
<BODY BACKGROUND="/samples/images/backgrnd.gif">
<BODY BGCOLOR="FFFFFF">
<TABLE>
<TR>
<TD><IMG SRC="/samples/images/SPACE.gif" ALIGN="top" ALT=" "></TD>
<TD><A HREF="/samples/IMAGES/db_mh.map"><IMG SRC=
➥ "/SAMPLES/images/db_mh.gif" ismap BORDER=0 ALIGN="top" ALT=" ">
</A></TD>
</TR>
<tr>
<TD></TD>
<TD>
<hr>
<font size=2>
<CENTER>
<%if idc.sales eq ""%>
<H2>Authors with sales greater than <I>5000</I></H2>
<%else%>
<H2>Authors with sales greater than <I><%idc.sales%></I></H2>
<%endif%>
<P>
<TABLE BORDER>
<%begindetail%>
<%if CurrentRecord EQ 0 %>
<caption>Query results:</caption>
<TR>
<TH><B>Author</B></TH><TH><B>YTD Sales<BR>(in dollars)</B></TH>
</TR>
<%endif%>
<TR><TD><%au_lname%></TD><TD align="right">$<%ytd_sales%></TD></TR>
<%enddetail%>
<P>
</TABLE>
</center>
<P>
<%if CurrentRecord EQ 0 %>
<I><B>Sorry, no authors had YTD sales greater than </I>
➥ <%idc.sales%>.</B>
<P>
<%else%>
<HR>
<I>
The Web page you see here was created by merging the results
of the SQL query with the template file SAMPLE.HTX.
<P>
The merge was done by the Microsoft Internet Database Connector and
➥ the results were returned to this web browser by the Microsoft
```

```
➥ Internet Information Server.
</I>
<%endif%>
</font>
</td>
</tr>
</table>
</BODY>
</HTML>
```

Right away, you will probably notice several different things with this file. First, it's a standard HTML document. There is no strange formatting, and many of the tags will be familiar if you have developed HTML before. Some of the real fun begins with the new capabilities offered by the HTX file. These new functions, above and beyond standard HTML, allow you to have the resulting Web page change depending on the information that is, or is not, returned from the query. For example, in the following section, you see the introduction of conditional testing examining for an empty set:

```
<%if idc.sales eq ""%>
     <H2>Authors with sales greater than <I>5000</I></H2>
<%else%>
     <H2>Authors with sales greater than <I><%idc.sales%></I></H2>
<%endif%>
```

There are several operators that are available when you design your pages. Throughout this chapter, you will learn more about how to use these new database-oriented features.

As mentioned earlier, the IDC source file indicates the ODBC data source that is used to access the database on your system. From the IDC file listing, you notice the "Data source" item. This item indicates that the "web sql" data source will be used. Before this sample will work on your system, you must have installed and configured the data source for that name.

In the next couple of sections, you'll see how to set up the ODBC data sources for both SQL Server and Microsoft Access. You can use any 32-bit ODBC data source with your IIS application. Changes between setting up other data sources should be minimal, so you'll find that the IDC can work with nearly any database installation you may need to use.

Building ODBC Data Sources for SQL Server Databases

One common problem with the database connector is improper setup of the ODBC data source. This problem is not unique to the SQL Server; the problem exists across database sources. Therefore, it is very important to understand how to set up the driver for access by IIS.

You may recall that IIS is running as a service. This means that, while it's running, it's not logged in as you, the administrator. It is instead running in the background and logging in when needed. When it does, it is as either the anonymous user you've set up, or as the validated user that's been authenticated by the NT security subsystem. Since you want to give this service access to a database, and since you don't know who the service will be logging in as, you need to set up the database source a bit differently than you may be accustomed to.

In recent releases of ODBC, Microsoft added a new option to the ODBC configurations. The System DSN (Data Source Name) is a way to set up a globally available data source. Since users that log on may be set up to have different access to your system and resources, you need to use the System DSN to make sure they have access to the right databases, regardless of where they log on, or who they log on as. Figure 22.4 shows the ODBC setup dialog box, started from the Control Panel.

 If you receive errors while trying to access an ODBC data source from your Web pages, one of the first things you should check is that the data source you are referencing is set up as a system data source. If, when you start the ODBC manager utility, the data source is listed in the initial dialog box, it's defined as a user-based data source, not a system DSN. Remove the user-based DSN and redefine it as a System DSN and you'll be able to see the database.

Remember, the only data sources that the Database Connector can use are the System-level data sources.

FIG. 22.4
ODBC setup for IIS requires that you select the System DSN to configure the driver.

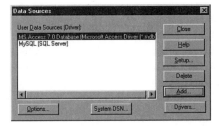

Once you select System DSN, you can use essentially the same options to set up the drivers. Note, too, that you can have more than one driver set up at the system level. This allows you to set up drivers for the different applications that you'll be running on the Web. Figure 22.5 shows the System Data Sources dialog box.

The Data Source Name you provide is what you'll be using in the IDC file as the data source, so be sure to make note of the database configuration names you set up.

FIG. 22.5

You'll need to indicate the driver, database, and other information required to connect to your database engine.

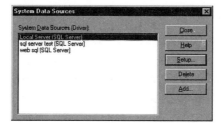

N O T E In most cases, you'll want the configuration to be as specific as possible. If it's possible to indicate a default database or table (or both), be sure to do so. It takes some of the variables out of the Web page design that you create. By specifying as much information as possible, you help make sure that the information is accessible. Of course, this serves the dual role of providing some basic controls over what the end-users see when they visit your pages. Users are less likely to be wandering around your databases if they navigate to a default database, rather than the driver or IDC file indicating the table name. ■

Building ODBC Database Sources for Microsoft Access Databases

Microsoft Access database data sources are established the same way as they are for SQL Server. You must set up each data source as a System DSN, making it available to the IDC as it logs into NT's security subsystem.

Of course, there are likely to be changes in the SQL Statement options you indicate in the IDC file. These differences relate to how Access interprets the SQL language elements. By and large, however, the statements should be nearly identical, especially in those cases where you issue SQL statements that are basically SELECT statements, rather than calling stored procedures, which are not supported by Access.

When you create the DSN, you are prompted to select the database with which ODBC should connect. Be sure to provide this information because, even though you can indicate it in code, you can make the connection to the database far more bulletproof with this option turned on. The system won't have to guess where to go to get the information.

User Rights and Security Concerns

Using the IDC for database access is a wide open door to your database system. You should avoid allowing users system administrator level access to your databases because this provides a means for anyone to have administrative access to your system. Instead, consider using either of the following two options.

The first option, if you allow anonymous connections to your site, is to be sure the user you indicate as the anonymous user (usually IUS_<machine name>) has appropriate rights to the databases he or she needs.

The login process works by first validating the user who is using the anonymous login, if it is enabled. If enabled, and the user indicated as the anonymous user does not have sufficient rights, an error message is received by the user, indicating he or she may not have rights to the object(s) requested. If anonymous login is disabled, the IDC uses the current user's name and password to logon to the database. If this fails to gain access, the request is denied and the user is prevented from accessing the database requested.

In short, if you want anonymous users gaining access to your system, you need to create the user account that you want to access the information. Next, assign the user to the database and objects, allowing access to the systems needed.

The second option is to use NT's integrated security with SQL Server. Using this method, the currently logged-in user will be logged on to SQL Server and the same rights will be in force.

Building Dynamic Web Pages

Once you have the database connection set up, you're ready to populate the database. One of the most popular ways of doing this is to create dynamic Web pages. Those that build themselves on-the-fly to provide up-to-date information are going to quickly become the mainstay of Intranets and the Internet. This will occur because, with a dynamic Web page, you can always count on getting the latest and greatest information. With the IDC, you can create these dynamic Web pages and have them work against a database to retrieve the information you want to permit the user to review.

There are three components to this type of page:

- Initial source HTML document often containing form fields or other options
- The IDC file for making and carrying out the database commands and data acquisition
- The HTX file for presenting the information returned

N O T E   While it's not the intent of this book to teach all aspects of HTML, it's important to remember that the examples provided are just that—samples. You'll need to take these samples and adapt them to your organization's way of doing business on its Intranet. In short, the HTML that may be required are the field, listbox, and checkbox options provided by HTML. Using these options, and the ODBC connectivity, you can allow the user to search the possibilities for making a meaningful interface for the user. ▪

▶ You can find out more about specific HTML elements in Chapter 18, "Basic HTML Techniques," and Chapter 19, "Advanced HTML."

When you create a form to prompt the user for information, you create fields and other controls much like you do when creating an application. You name the fields, and then pass the name and its value to the IDC to be used in your database query, if you desire. In the next sections, you will learn how to create these files and learn what makes them drive the output pages with the information from the database.

Building Initial Forms to Prompt for Values

Generally speaking, you start the process of working with a database by presenting the users with a form that allows them to select the information they need. As is often the case, you have the ability to create forms that allow input that can be used to form the SQL Statements to be passed to the data source. In the cases where you're creating a form, there are two basic HTML tags that you use. These are the INPUT and FORM tags that allow you to designate actions to take and information to accept on behalf of the user. Listing 22.3 shows a simple form that prompts for an author name to be searched for in the author's table.

Listing 22.3   Simple HTML Form to Initiate a Database Query–(queform.htm)

```
<HTML>
<HEAD>
<TITLE>
Que Publishing's Very Simple Demonstration Form
</TITLE>
</HEAD>
<h1>Sample Form for Database Access</h1>
<FORM METHOD="POST" ACTION="/scripts/que/QueForm1.idc">
Enter Name to Find in the Pubs Database: <INPUT NAME="au_lname">
<p>
<INPUT TYPE="SUBMIT" VALUE="Run Query">
</FORM>
</BODY>
</HTML>
```

The key elements are the "POST" instructions and the text box presented to the user. The FORM tag indicates what should happen when the form is executed. In this case, the form sends information to the server, hence the POST method. The program or procedure that is run on the server, to work with the information sent in, is called out by the ACTION tag. In the example, the QUEFORM1.IDC is called and passed the parameters.

N O T E   The letter case is not significant when you specify HTML tags. "INPUT" is the same as indicating "input" and does not cause any different results when it's processed by IIS. ▪

It's not immediately apparent what the form parameters might be, but if you examine the one or more INPUT fields, you can see that they are named. The following syntax is the basic element required if you need to pass information back to the host in a forms-based environment:

```
<INPUT NAME="<variable name>">
```

The *<variable name>* is the name used to reference the value provided by the user. Much as a variable is defined in Visual Basic by Dimensioning it, you must define and declare the different variables and other controls that are used by your HTML. There are other tags that can be used with the INPUT NAME tag, including VALUE, which allows you to set the initial value of the item you're declaring. For example, the following line declares a new variable, MyName, and assigns an initial value of "Wynkoop" to it:

```
<INPUT NAME="MyName" VALUE="Wynkoop">
```

For the preceding example, the intention is to create a simple form that allows the user to type in a name, or portion of the name, that can be used to search the Authors table in the Pubs database. When the HTML is loaded, as shown above, the result is that shown in Figure 22.6.

FIG. 22.6
Allowing the user to indicate values to pass to the database engine adds polished, functional benefits to your application.

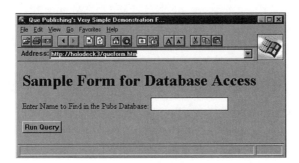

As you can see, the text box size is automatically determined for you as a default. There are Maxlength and Size tags that you can place in the INPUT NAME directive if you need to increase the size of the text box. Also notice that if you press Enter while using this form, the form is automatically submitted to the server, just as if you press the Submit button. Because there is only a single button on this form, the browser interprets this as a type of "there is only one thing for me to do, so I'll just do it automatically" situation.

The result of Listing 22.3 is that the browser opens a new URL on the server with the specification:

```
http://holodeck3/scripts/que/QueForm1.idc?au_lname=<name>
```

N O T E You'll notice that the URL shown indicates a single computer name rather than an Internet domain name. This reflects the fact that it's running in an Intranet environment. If you are running on the Internet for this access, the HOLODECK3 entry is replaced with the server you're accessing. ■

N O T E If you watch your Web browser, it may only indicate that it's loading the URL that is included up to the "?" in these examples. The protocol is still passing the parameters to the host; they are simply not shown during the transfer by some browsers. ■

The <name> is the name you indicate in the text box before pressing Enter, or clicking the submit button. The next step is to run the query against the database engine and see what results are returned.

Building Server Query Source Files

The query source files reside in files in your SCRIPTS area and have a file name extension of IDC by convention. When the URL is accessed, the server will run the indicated IDC file. As mentioned earlier in this chapter, the IDC file contains the SQL statements and directives necessary to carry out the commands, as needed. For this example, Listing 22.4 shows the source for querying the database.

CAUTION

To reiterate the previous Note about security, be sure you place your IDC files in directories that have been set up with Execute, but not Read, privileges. This is important because users can see column names, table names, SQL login names and passwords, and so on, if they can review your source files. This is all information that you want to ensure remains private.

Listing 22.4   The IDC File that Is Called by QUEForm.HTM–(queform1.idc)

```
Datasource: web sql
Username: sa
Template: queform1.htx
SQLStatement:
+SELECT au_lname, phone, address, city, state, zip
+ from authors
+ where au_lname like '%au_lname%%'
```

The output from this specific file is really nothing. The user never sees this file or output from it directly. This seems a bit strange, but the entire intent of the IDC is to define and perform the query against the data source indicated. Once the information is retrieved, the IDC calls the Template indicated and passes in the results to be returned as a Web page.

N O T E   In the example in Listing 22.4, notice that the where clause specifies like and that there is an extra percent sign in the comparison field. This is standard SQL syntax that allows you to search for wildcarded strings. You specify the part you know and the IDC appends an extra % character at the end. Because the percent sign is the wildcard for SQL Server, you can return all items that start with "B," for example.

Though your understanding of SQL need not be extensive, you will find it easier to work with the database if you have access to backup reference materials on SQL. You may want to consider Que's *Special Edition Using SQL Server* as a comprehensive guide to SQL and the management of a SQL Server. ■

Some basics about this source file are important to understand prior to working through it, to explain how it works. First, to reference a variable, you place it between percent signs, as is the case with '%au_lname%' in the preceding listing. Note that the single quotes are required as the field is a text-based type.

You can reference variables anywhere in the script. This means, even for the items that are seemingly hard-coded, you can allow the user to specify them and then call them dynamically from the IDC file.

Second, in cases where your line length is shorter than your actual line, you can call out the item you want to work on, begin specifying the values, and continue indicating the expanding values as long as you place the + in the first column of the file. (The plus sign acts as a line-continuation character for these source files.)

The Data source indicated in the IDC relates to the ODBC data source you establish with the ODBC manager in Control Panel. Remember, the data source you use with the IDC must be a system DSN. If it's not, the call to the database will fail.

The Username, and optionally the Password, override any settings you may have established in ODBC, and they override the current user name, as well, as it relates to the execution of the query. Other parameters that may be of interest or use in your integration of the IDC file into your installation are shown in Table 22.1.

Table 22.1   IDC Optional Parameters

Expires	If you submit a query over and over again, you may find that you're retrieving a cached copy of the information, rather than an updated database query. This can be especially problematic when developing applications, as you'll be continually testing the system, resubmitting queries, and so on. By setting the Expires tag, established in seconds, to a value that represents a timeframe that should pass before the query is retried, you avoid this problem. In other words, how long will it be before the information should be considered "stale" or in need of being re-freshed for viewing?
MaxRecords	If you are connected over a slower-speed connection, there are few things more frustrating than receiving a huge data file, then realizing that you need only certain bits of its information. For example, you may have a need to return only the first 100 rows of a table, as they will provide the most current, meaningful data to your sales effort. By limiting the MaxRecords, you can indicate this in the IDC file, limiting traffic and database interaction with the new option.

You can call SQL Server's stored procedures from an IDC file if you want to specify it in the SQL Statement portion of the file. To do so, use the following syntax:

```
EXEC MySP_Name Param1[, Param2...]
```

Include the name of your stored procedure in place of MySP_Name.

In the stored procedure, be sure you're returning results sets, even if they represent only a status value indicating success or failure on the operation. Remember, as with other ODBC data sources, the stored procedure is passed to the server and the client awaits the response. If your stored procedure does not return a value to the calling routine, you may give the user the impression that you caused the browser to become frozen.

From here, once you retrieve the values you want to display, you can move on to the Results-set source files. These files do the work of formatting and displaying information to the user, which will be explained next.

Building Results Source Files

The Results files are where the fun begins when working with the data that comes back from the query. The HTML extension files, with file name extensions of HTX, are referenced in the Template entry in the IDC. These files dictate how the information is presented, what the user sees, whether items that are returned actually represent links to other items, and so on.

Listing 22.5 shows the sample HTX file for the example you've been reviewing throughout this chapter. You can see that it has a few extra, not-yet-standard items that make the display of information from the database possible.

Listing 22.5 A Sample HTX File–(QueForm1.htx)

```
<! Section 1>
<HTML>
<HEAD>
<TITLE>Authors Details</TITLE>
</HEAD>
<TABLE>
<tr>
<TD>
<hr>
<P>
<TABLE BORDER>
 <caption>Query results:</caption>
 <TR>
 <TH><B>Author</B></TH>
 <TH><B>Phone</B></TH>
 <TH><B>Address</B></TH>
 <TH><B>City</B></TH>
 <TH><B>State</B></TH>
 <TH><B>Zip</B></TH>
 </TR>

<! Section 2>
<%begindetail%>
 <TR>
 <TH><B><%au_lname%></B></TH>
 <TH><B><%phone%></B></TH>
 <TH><B><%address%></B></TH>
 <TH><B><%city%></B></TH>
 <TH><B><%state%></B></TH>
```

continues

Listing 22.5   Continued

```
 <TH><B><%zip%></B></TH>
 </TR>
<%enddetail%>

<! Section 3>
<P>
</TABLE>
<%if CurrentRecord EQ 0%>
  <H2>Sorry, no authors match your search criteria (<%idc.au_lname%>).</H2>
<%else%>
  <H2>Authors with names like "<I><%idc.au_lname%></I>"</H2>
<%endif%>
</center>
</td>
</tr>
</table>
</BODY>
</HTML>
```

When the URL is accessed, the server runs the indicated IDC file. As mentioned earlier in the "Building Server Query Source Files" section, the IDC file contains the SQL statements and directives necessary to carry out the commands as needed. For this example, Listing 22.4 shows the source for querying the database.

N O T E   The lines starting with <! are comments and are not interpreted by the HTML client. ∎

In the sample HTML in Listing 22.5, notice the three sections called out. These sections are inserted only to make reading and explaining the HTML a bit easier. They aren't necessary for the functioning of the document.

In Section 1, the entire purpose is to set up the page. You need to establish fonts, set up background images, do any initial formatting, and so on. You also need to start any tables that you want to use. Because you initiate a table, add the rows to it, then turn off the table, tables represent an excellent way to present data that include an unknown number of rows. For example, as in Figure 22.7, though two rows are shown, there could just as easily have been 20. The other advantage of using tables to display your database information is that the table automatically resizes to the user's visible browser area. You don't need to worry about column widths and other formatting issues.

Section 2 is where you work with the detail lines that are returned as part of the data set. Notice this section is bracketed with a <%begindetail%> and <%enddetail%> tags. Everything between these two tags repeats once for every row returned in the data set. In the preceding example, section 2 consists largely of building the table that displays the information that is returned. The following code excerpt provides an example of this loop:

FIG. 22.7
If you use tables to display data to the user, you'll be in keeping with an already familiar metaphor for the presentation.

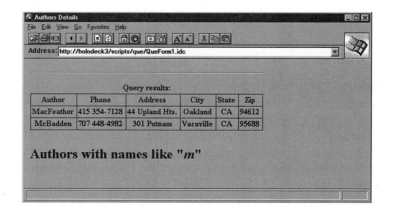

```
<! Section 2>
<%begindetail%>
 <TR>
 <TH><B><%au_lname%></B></TH>
 <TH><B><%phone%></B></TH>
 <TH><B><%address%></B></TH>
 <TH><B><%city%></B></TH>
 <TH><B><%state%></B></TH>
 <TH><B><%zip%></B></TH>
 </TR>
<%enddetail%>
```

When you indicate the data to be included, you refer directly to the column names that are in the table or view that is referenced by the IDC file. Place a <% before, and %> after each column name. In English, the preceding code snippet is reserving a row to put new data into using the <TR> tag, placing the information into the row using the <TH> </TH> tags, and ending the row using the closing </TR> tag.

You can do comparisons in your file as well. For example, if you want to check to make sure that the state was returned as AZ, you could do so in one of two ways. Obviously, the preferred method is to change your Where clause in the IDC to reflect the fact that you want to filter out non-Arizona states.

Alternatively, you could indicate here that you want to test certain values. Consider the following code sample:

```
<! Section 2>
<%begindetail%>
<%if <%state%> eq "AZ"%>
 <TR>
 <TH><B><%au_lname%></B></TH>
 <TH><B><%phone%></B></TH>
 <TH><B><%address%></B></TH>
 <TH><B><%city%></B></TH>
```

```
 <TH><B><%state%></B></TH>
 <TH><B><%zip%></B></TH>
 </TR>
<%endif%>
<%enddetail%>
```

By using the `if` construct, you can test values and conditions in the data set. You can reference variables that come from the IDC file as well. To reference these, simply prepend `idc` to the variable name from the IDC file. So, if you want to reference the incoming variable from the original HTML form, you can do so by a statement similar to the following:

```
<%if <%idc.au_lname%> eq "Wynkoop">
    <TH><B>Building series...</B></TH>
<%endif%>
```

In this case, the query returns to the IDC and pulls the value for the `au_lname` variable, makes the comparison and either executes or ignores the statements in the loop following the test. There are three different tests that you can perform. Each is described in Table 22.2.

N O T E You can also use `<%else%>` in your `If...else...endif` loop. ▪

Table 22.2	Comparison Operators for Use in HTX Files
EQ	Indicates an equivalent test, such as "Is item A equal to item B?"
GT	Tests for a condition in which one item is greater than the other.
LT	Tests for the condition in which one item is less than the other.

In addition, there are two different data set-related variables. `CurrentRecord` allows you to reference the number of times the Detail section executes. If, after the detail loop runs, you want to determine whether there are records in the data set, you can test this variable to see if it's 0. If it is, no information was returned, and you should display a meaningful message to that effect. The following code excerpt shows how an example of testing this value.

```
<%if CurrentRecord EQ 0>
  <H2>Sorry, no authors match your search crit...
<%else%>
  <H2>Authors with names like "<I><%idc.au_lname%>...
<%endif%>
```

The other tag that corresponds directly to database-oriented actions is the `MaxRecords` option. `MaxRecords` relates to the `MaxRecords IDC` variable. Using this value, you can determine the total number of records that the IDC file allows. You use both `CurrentRecord` and `MaxRecords` in conjunction with `<%if%>` statements. They are implemented as controlling variables that help in your structuring of the logical flow of the HTX file. Just keep in mind that, after the processing of the detail section completes, if `CurrentRecord EQ 0`, there are no results returned from the call.

The final section of the HTX file is used largely to close different HTML tags that were used to set up the display of information on the resulting page. Remember, HTML expects most tags in pairs, so it's a good idea to close each item properly, as in the following:

```
<! Section 3>
<P>
</TABLE>
<%if CurrentRecord EQ 0%>
  <H2>Sorry, no authors match your search criteria (<%idc.au_lname%>).</H2>
<%else%>
  <H2>Authors with names like "<I><%idc.au_lname%></I>"</H2>
<%endif%>
</center>
</td>
</tr>
</table>
</BODY>
</HTML>
```

Notice, too, that the `CurrentRecord` variable is used to determine the message that is displayed to the user. There will be either a message indicating no matches, or one explaining that what was searched for is shown. You can also see, by referencing the `<%idc.au_lname%>` variable, that you can pull the user-specified value from the form.

The results of a successful search are shown in Figure 22.8.

FIG. 22.8

A successful match will show the hits on the PUBS database table, and will then show the message indicating what was searched for.

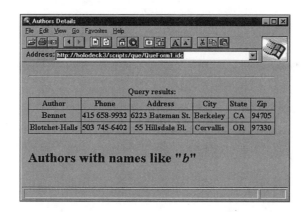

If the search of the database tables is not fruitful, the HTX displays a different message, indicating the failure of the process. Figure 22.9 shows this dialog box.

FIG. 22.9

If matches for information are not found, you should code a branch of logic to indicate the problem to the user.

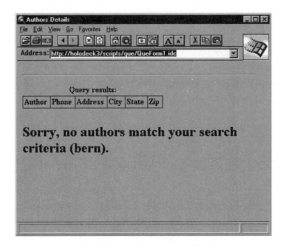

Internet Database Connector: A Summary and Example

To recap how the IDC works overall, first, you code a form or other HTML document that calls the IDC file on the server. The IDC file is located in the protected /SCRIPTS directory and contains the information necessary to open the ODBC connection and submit a query to the database engine. As the results are returned, they are merged into another document, the HTX or HTML extension document. This HTX file includes the information needed to work with both the detail records and the header/footer information for the page.

The result to the user is the display of the requested information in an HTML document style. Of course, the resulting document, based on the HTX file, can include further links to queries or drill-down information, if needed. This technique allows a user to select high-level values and then narrow the scope, but increase the detail level provided, for the information as the user is able to narrow the parameters for the operation.

An excellent example of the drill-down technique is provided in Microsoft's samples located in the guestbook application. As you query the guestbook, you are returned high-level detail about the names found. The following is a look at the HTX file's Detail section to see what exactly is done to display the information from the database.

```
<%begindetail%>
Name: <a href="/scripts/samples/details.idc?FName=<%FirstName%>
➥ & LName=<%LastName%>"><b><%FirstName%> <%LastName%></b></a>
<p>
<%enddetail%>
```

So, for each name returned by the original query, the result shows the first and last names. This HTML sets up the names as links to their own details. The code indicates the A HREF tag and references the IDC that retrieves the detail information, DETAILS.IDC. As a result, when the users click this in their browser, they immediately execute the IDC file and retrieve the next level of detail. Figure 22.10 shows what this initial screen of details looks like when the items are first retrieved.

FIG. 22.10
The initial display of the Guestbook Contents allows the user to select a name and drill down into the details for that name.

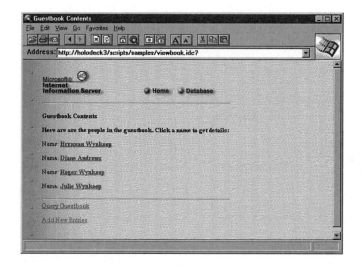

When you click a name to get the details, the IDC is called that retrieves the details from the Guests table on your system. If you take a look at the IDC, you see that it's quite simple, returning only a few columns of information based on the name selected from the previous query.

```
Datasource: Web SQL
Username: sa
Template: details.htx
SQLStatement:
+SELECT FirstName, LastName, Email, Homepage, Comment, WebUse
+FROM Guests
+WHERE FirstName = '%FName%' and LastName = '%LName%'
```

The final step is to show the information to the requester. The DETAILS.HTX template is called out in the IDC file, and it shows the detail information for the user, as requested. The detail section simply displays the user information that is provided. The HTX file makes heavy use of the <%if%> operator, and the comparison of the contents of a given field, to ensure that the only information provided to the user are those fields that are non-blank.

Listing 22.6   The Detail Section from the DETAILS.HTX File

```
<%begindetail%>
<h2>Here are details for <%FirstName%> <%LastName%>:</h2>
<p>
<b><%FirstName%> <%LastName%></b><br>
<p>

<%if Email EQ " "%>
<%else%>
Email Address: <%Email%> <br>
<%endif%>
<%if Homepage EQ " "%>
<%else%>
Homepage: <%Homepage%>
<%endif%>
<p>
Primary Web Role: <%WebUse%>
<p>
<%if Comment EQ " "%>
<%else%>
Comments: <%Comment%>
<%endif%>
<p>
<%enddetail%>
```

Providing this type of increasing detail, based on a user's selection, is good for all parties concerned. It's good for your system because it can provide only the information needed to determine the direction to go to for the next level of detail. In addition, it's good for the users because it can mean less content to shuffle through to get to the information they really need. Since they will be determining what information is delved into, they'll be able to control how deep they want to go into a given item.

This technique is useful for supplying company information. You can provide overview type items at the highest level, on everything from marketing materials to personnel manuals. Letting people select their research path also alleviates you from the responsibility of second-guessing exactly what the user is expecting of the system.

Using SQL Server's Web Page Wizard

As you're sure to have noticed, the race to bring content to your Intranet, and make all different types of information available to the user base, has been fast and furious. One of the recent advances is the capability to have the database engine automatically generate Web pages for you based on content in the database.

With SQL Server 6.5, you have the capability to schedule a task in the system to automatically create these HTML documents at time intervals, ranging from a one-time run to many times per day. You can use this capability for a number of things, including the reporting on your server's activity levels to you, as an administrator.

In this section, you see how to set up these automatically generating pages and their results. It's not possible to go into great detail on how to use the SQL Server, forming good database table design, and other administrative issues regarding SQL Server, as they warrant a much more comprehensive discussion than a single group of sections here.

▶ For more information on SQL Server 6.5, including administration and other topics, see *Special Edition Using SQL Server 6.5* from Que Publishing.

Prerequisites for SQL Server

Before you can successfully use the Web Page Wizard and the processes it creates, you must set up your server to allow for this type of access. Specifically, the Web Page Wizard relies on the task manager and the SQLExecutive service. You must have the SQLExecutive service set up to automatically start on startup of your server.

To confirm that the service is set to automatically start, select Services from the Control Panel. Scroll down the list of services that are installed until you see the SQLExecutive service (see Figure 22.11).

FIG. 22.11

Make sure the SQLExecutive service is listed with a Status of "Started" and that Startup is listed as Automatic.

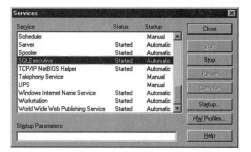

If the service is not already started, click the service and select Startup. You can set the options that govern when the service is active and, most importantly, when it starts by the operating system. Make sure you indicate a valid user account that is used to log into SQL Server. This account must exist in both SQL Server and the User database for your domain, if you are not using Integrated security, and the user name and password must be the same in both the SQL Server and the domain.

If you use integrated security, selecting a user from the domain user's list also provides the name to be logged into the SQL Server.

N O T E It's a requirement that the information you provide, as it relates to the user and password, is valid in SQL server. You also need to ensure that the account you indicate has access to the database you're reporting against, and the MSDB database (see Figure 22.12).

If you do not set up the SQLExecutive to automatically start, the services required to generate the Web content you are setting up will not be available, and the page will not be generated.

If this is the first time you set these options, and the SQLExecutive was not previously started, when you select OK to save the user ID and startup option changes, you'll need to reselect the SQLExecutive service and then select Start. ▨

FIG. 22.12

The account you indicate for logon for the service must have access to the different objects in your database(s).

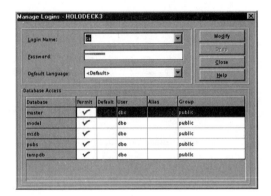

Using the Wizard

The SQL Web Page Wizard is located in the SQL Server program group on your system. You can run the Wizard from a workstation or the server. In either case, it generates the pages for you in a directory you specify later in the process.

Figure 22.13 shows the initial SQL Server login dialog box that displays after you start the Wizard. From this dialog box, you need to provide an appropriate login that will allow you access to all tables and databases that you want to use in providing content for your page.

The option to use Windows NT Security to log on assumes you're using integrated security. If you are, selecting this item means that you don't have to provide separate login account and password information, prompted for earlier in the dialog box.

Selecting the Content for the Page When you select Next >, you'll have three initial options. The first option, Build a query from a database hierarchy, allows you to use the point-and-click interface and indicate the tables and other items you want to include in your query, which will be used to generate the page. Figure 22.14 shows an example of what the tree-based architecture will look like if you select this option.

FIG. 22.13

The first step to using the Wizard is to log on to SQL Server.

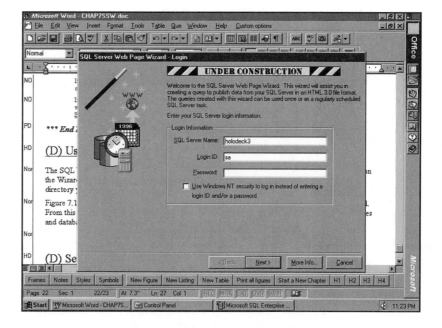

FIG. 22.14

The easiest interface is the Database Hierarchy option as it allows you to select from the listing of objects on your server when deciding which items to provide for a report.

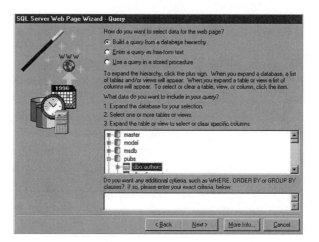

If you select the Free Form query option, you'll be able to create any SQL statement you need to fulfill the requirements for your software. Be sure to select the database you need to work against from the Which database do you want to query? list box, or you may end up querying the wrong table and you'll need to come back and rewrite the queries.

Using this option also means that you're taking all responsibility for the formation of SQL server-specific calls. The query you enter will be passed along and executed by the server. Figure 22.15 shows an example of how the dialog options work when working with the Wizard in this scenario.

Part IV
Ch 22

FIG. 22.15

If you're not sure of the syntax, be sure to use the more automated features of the Wizard for a few instances of information you want to publish.

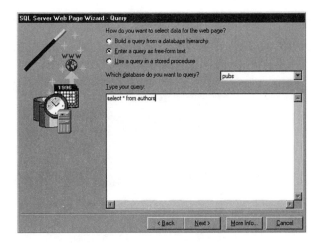

The final option you have in setting up the source of information for your page is to call a stored procedure. When you select the Use a query in a stored procedure button, you'll be able to provide information on the database and stored procedure you want to use. You'll also notice that the text of the stored procedure is shown in the dialog box. You can use this information to verify that you have selected the correct stored procedure (see Figure 22.16).

FIG. 22.16

Calling a stored procedure can be a good way to share coding you've done for an application and put it to use on your Intranet.

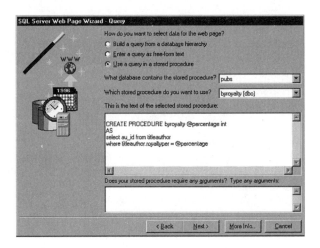

Stored procedures are a powerful mechanism for optimizing your server and providing good database query tuning. You can also take advantage of the fact that if you have another system based on SQL Server, and you're using a stored procedure to produce the results for a printed report, you may be able to reference the same stored procedure here and create the report in HTML, making it available at any time.

Setting the Update Interval   The next dialog box will prompt you for the frequency at which you'd like to have the page rebuilt. Since the database is the source of information for the page, this item may take some work. The reason is that you'll need to talk with all of the users of the application that creates the data in the database and determine how frequently it is changed.

A frequency set to be too small will cause additional overhead on the server as it handles the request. The impact on performance should be minimal, but if there are many, many requests for data pages such as this (see Figure 22.17), it may begin to show on the access times to the server.

Your time frame options, and their associated parameters, are:

- Now: no parameters
- Later: specify date and time that the page should be created (once only)
- When Data Changes: select data tables and indicate anticipated changes that should be monitored as a trigger to update the HTML code
- On Certain Days of the Week: indicate day of week and time of day
- On a Regular Basis: specify number of hours, days, or weeks that should pass before the item is regenerated

FIG. 22.17
Setting a too frequent time interval will force the server to rebuild the page without reason.

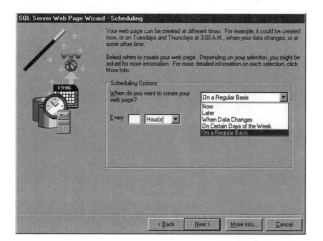

Setting Page Options   There are two different dialog boxes with information about final formatting. Formatting options include headings for the page, column names on the resulting document, or changing the title or output location of the resulting HTML code. These are the steps you'll be using to create the database-related HTML you set up. See Figures 22.18 and 22.19 for examples.

FIG. 22.18

Review the formatting options carefully. These are the items that will be used to manage the content, appearance, and other facets of your HTML's presentation.

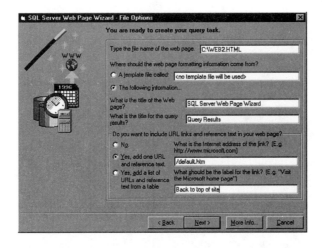

FIG. 22.19

If you are relying on the engine to do formatting for your tables If data, be sure to select the "Include column or view column names with the query results" when you set up the Wizard's Web page.

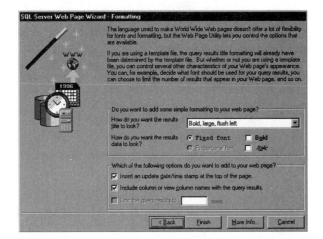

One thing that you'll want to consider including on every page you generate, is a link to another page on your site. For example, you may want to always include a link with the following attributes:

Description: Return to Home Page

URL: **http://www.*your site*.com/default.htm**

It's a good idea to come up with a set of links that you include on each page on your site. These may be back to the home page, back to a search page, and to a copyright page, for example. Consistency across your site will make it much easier for users to navigate and understand it.

Once you've made any changes you need, you can select Finish to generate the code that will be used to execute the different operations that manage the Wizard and its pages. Now, whenever the page is referenced by a browser, the HTML generated by the Wizard will be the results. The user will be able to see the new view you've constructed and will be assured of up-to-date information.

Seeing the Results in SQL Server

It's helpful to review your SQL Server installation to understand what's happening when you implement a Wizard-generated Web page. The following are a couple of things that happen when you create a page in this manner:

- A master stored procedure is inserted into your database
- A page-specific stored procedure is inserted into your database
- A new task is created to be run by the SQL Executive at the intervals you request

The master stored procedure, sp_makewebpage, is created in the database you set up. This is used by the Wizard to create the code necessary to generate the page. You won't be making changes to this, or the other stored procedures, and, if you ever want to re-create it, you can run the Wizard again and create another page in the same database. This creates the stored procedure for you.

The page-specific stored procedure is created with a name that begins with Web_ and includes a unique numeric name that includes the date it was created. In the example shown in Figure 22.20, the stored procedures created to support the demonstration pages are named Web_96042622390211 and Web_96042700554612. If you review the stored procedures, you'll see that they are encrypted, so you won't be able to make any changes to them directly. Of course, the easiest way to make any changes you need is to remove the stored procedures and their associated tasks from the SQL Server and then re-create them using the Web Page Wizard.

FIG. 22.20
Be sure not to remove the stored procedures from the database unless you also remove the corresponding task entries from the task scheduler.

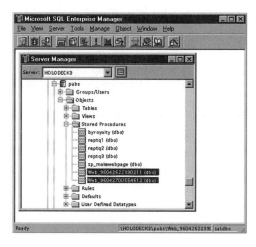

By selecting Server, Tasks... from the menus, you can review the tasks that have been created to run the page at the intervals you set up. Figure 22.21 shows what you'll see. You can quickly determine that the Web pages are queued up and ready to go.

FIG. 22.21

If there is ever a question about whether a SQL database-oriented item ran, check the Task Manager and see if there are error messages indicating a problem with the configuration.

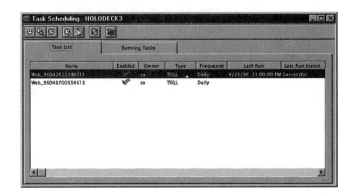

You can also check to make sure a Web page generation process is occurring as you'd expect by clicking the History button from the Task Scheduling dialog box. When you do, you'll see the dialog box shown in Figure 22.22, which indicates the times the procedure has run, and whether it was successful. It's a good idea to start with the history review process in any diagnostics you need to run in the future, should you encounter problems. In most cases, you can quickly determine exactly what's wrong by just doing some quick investigation with the Task Scheduler.

FIG. 22.22

You can verify that the pages are being generated successfully by reviewing the History logs.

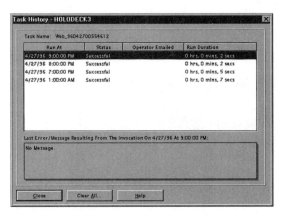

Keep in mind that you can also change the frequency at which your page is generated by modifying the task scheduling options. If you double-click the page you want to modify, you can set all of the different options that control how often the page is generated. This might be helpful if you find that, after installing several pages and your site traffic picks up, you need to lessen server load a bit to provide better throughput at peak times. Simply change the times at which the pages are generated and you'll be set.

Seeing the Results on Your Web Site

Implementing the page(s) you create on your site is a simple matter. You need to create a link to the pages, or publish the URL to your user base. Once the page is created by the SQL engine, it appears just as any other HTML document. Listing 22.7 shows the sample page created by the Web Page Wizard.

Listing 22.7   A Sample Page Created by the Wizard (Web.html)

```
<HTML>
<HEAD>
<TITLE>SQL Server Web Page Wizard</TITLE>
<BODY>
<A HREF = /default.htm>Back to top of site</A>.<P>
<HR>
<H1>Query Results</H1>
<HR>
<PRE><TT>Last updated: Apr 26 1996 10:43PM</TT></PRE>
<P>
<P><TABLE BORDER>
<TR><TH ALIGN=LEFT>au_id</TH><TH ALIGN=LEFT>au_lname</TH><TH ALIGN=LEFT>
➥ au_fname</TH><TH ALIGN=LEFT>phone</TH><TH ALIGN=LEFT>address</TH>
➥ <TH ALIGN=LEFT>city</TH><TH ALIGN=LEFT>state</TH><TH ALIGN=LEFT>zip</TH>
➥ <TH ALIGN=LEFT>contract</TH></TR>
<TR><TD NOWRAP>172-32-1176</TD><TD NOWRAP>White</TD><TD NOWRAP>Johnson</TD>
➥ <TD NOWRAP>408 496-7223</TD><TD NOWRAP>10932 Bigge Rd.</TD>
➥ <TD NOWRAP>Menlo Park</TD><TD NOWRAP>CA</TD><TD NOWRAP>94025</TD>
➥ <TD NOWRAP>1</TD></TR>
<TR><TD NOWRAP>213-46-8915</TD><TD NOWRAP>Green</TD><TD NOWRAP>Marjorie</TD>
➥ <TD NOWRAP>415 986-7020</TD><TD NOWRAP>309 63rd St. #411</TD>
➥ <TD NOWRAP>Oakland</TD><TD NOWRAP>CA</TD><TD NOWRAP>94618</TD><TD NOWRAP>1</
TD>
➥ </TR>

...
<Edited for brevity see disk file for full listing>
...

<TR><TD NOWRAP>899-46-2035</TD><TD NOWRAP>Ringer</TD><TD NOWRAP>Anne</TD>
➥ <TD NOWRAP>801 826-0752</TD><TD NOWRAP>67 Seventh Av.</TD>
➥ <TD NOWRAP>Salt Lake City</TD><TD NOWRAP>UT</TD><TD NOWRAP>84152</TD>
➥ <TD NOWRAP>1</TD></TR>
<TR><TD NOWRAP>998-72-3567</TD><TD NOWRAP>Ringer</TD><TD NOWRAP>Albert</TD>
➥ <TD NOWRAP>801 826-0752</TD><TD NOWRAP>67 Seventh Av.</TD>
➥ <TD NOWRAP>Salt Lake City</TD><TD NOWRAP>UT</TD><TD NOWRAP>84152</TD>
➥ <TD NOWRAP>1</TD></TR>
</TABLE>
</BODY>
</HTML>
```

Part
IV

Ch
22

When you view the page, all of your SQL table data will be placed into an HTML table. The links you specified will be shown at the top of the page, prior to the data from the site. Figure 22.23 shows what the top portion of this example page looks like when presented in the browser.

FIG. 22.23

The sample Web page includes information from the Pubs database and a link back to the site home page.

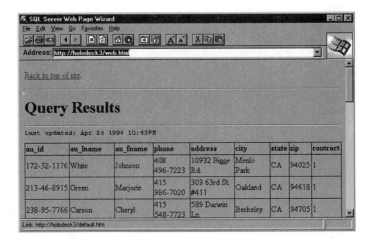

A great use of the Web Page Creation is to query the IIS logs that can be placed into SQL Server. For more information, see the next section, which will show how this can be used to remotely monitor your site.

Logging IIS Accesses to ODBC Databases

Perhaps one of the biggest improvements you can make to your system administration abilities is to log your IIS access active to an ODBC database. This way, you can start amassing excellent information about your site, including what information people are retrieving, how frequently they're visiting your site, and more.

As mentioned earlier in this chapter, to allow IIS to access your database, you'll need to set up a System DSN. Once you've completed this, you can create the database, table, and user that you need to establish the Internet Service Manager for the Web, FTP, and Gopher services you're using.

▶ More information about setting up the System DSN is found earlier in this chapter under "Building ODBC Data Sources for SQL Server Databases" and "Building ODBC Database Sources for Microsoft Access Databases."

To change logging to use your ODBC database, first double-click the service that you want to set up. In the example shown in Figure 22.24, you can see the logging options for the Web Services. Note that all of the different services use the same logging tab, so once you've set one up, you'll understand how to establish the remaining services.

Before you can point the services to the ODBC database, you need to create the database and corresponding table. Table 22.3 shows the column information for the table that will be used for the logging.

Table 22.3 Table Structure for Logging Table

Column	SQL Data Type	Access Data Type	Size
ClientHost	Char	Text	50
UserName	Char	Text	50
LogDate	Char	Text	12
LogTime	Char	Text	21
Service	Char	Text	20
Machine	Char	Text	20
ServerIP	Char	Text	50
ProcessingTime	int	Number	Integer
BytesRecvd	Int	Number	Integer
BytesSent	Int	Number	Integer
ServiceStatus	Int	Number	Integer
Win32Status	Int	Number	Integer
Operation	Int	Number	Integer
Target	Char	Text	200
Parameters	Char	Text	200

N O T E Nulls are allowed for all columns in the case of SQL Server.

You may recognize this information from the discussions about installing and setting up the server components, as the table structure maps directly to the different components of the standard log file when logged to ASCII files. Be sure to read the information about reading and interpreting the log information, presented in Chapter 3.

You set up the log table to be used by all of the different services you're logging for. You'll notice the Service column shows exactly what was being done by the user, and what operation was being performed by the server. Listing 22.8 shows the SQL Server script for creating the table.

**Listing 22.8 The SQL Server Script to Create the Logging Database
(makelog.sql)**

```
/****** Object:  Table dbo.LogTable      Script Date:
➥ 10/18/96 12:14:06 AM ******/
if exists (select * from sysobjects where id =
➥ object_id('dbo.LogTable') and sysstat & 0xf = 3)
     drop table dbo.LogTable
GO

CREATE TABLE LogTable (
     ClientHost char (50) NULL ,
     UserName char (50) NULL ,
     LogDate char (12) NULL ,
     LogTime char (21) NULL ,
     Service char (20) NULL ,
     Machine char (20) NULL ,
     ServerIP char (50) NULL ,
     ProcessingTime int NULL ,
     BytesRecvd int NULL ,
     BytesSent int NULL ,
     ServiceStatus int NULL ,
     Win32Status int NULL ,
     Operation char (200) NULL ,
     Target char (200) NULL ,
     Parameters char (200) NULL
)
GO
```

Now that the table exists for logging information, you can indicate where to log information for
each of the services. From the Internet Service Manager, double-click the service you want to
update (see Figure 22.24). Select the Logging tab to work with the different logging options.

FIG. 22.24

The next step to begin
using ODBC for logging
is to select the ODBC
option and indicate the
login and database
information.

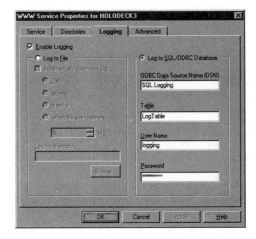

Once you've selected the Log to SQL/ODBC Database radio button, you'll be able to access the different setup fields for the logging. It's a good idea to set up a different database to manage the logging. If you do, you'll be able to more easily manage the logging information separately from the other information on your system.

In the example, a specific database, table, and user have been created to use for the logging. If you create a user, be sure you set the rights to at least Insert when you establish them on the table. Once you apply the changes, stop and restart the service—you'll be logging all server accesses to the database.

N O T E If a user is accessing your server by using the FILE: protocol, as might be the case with an Intranet, the accesses will not be logged. These types of URLs are accessed by the client and handled by the client. Although the server will be providing the file to fulfill the request, it will not show up in the database. This is one detriment to using the FILE: type URL. If you want to be able to log accesses, consider making all links standard HTTP: type URLs, rather than providing direct links to the files. ▓

When the logging is established, you can begin querying the database real time to determine the activity on your server. In the next sections, you'll see some ways to provide this information in an easy-to-use and meaningful manner.

Creating Sample Queries to Use in Reviewing Logs

The log data can quickly become overwhelming, unless you wrap it in some meaningful queries. Some good information to know about your site includes information about the following, just as a start:

- What pages are most popular?
- What time of day are people accessing the server?
- Who is accessing the server (by IP address)?

In the sample query in Listing 22.9, you can see that the database is examined to find out this information, providing summary information for hits against the server.

N O T E For the following scripts, you need to change the database table referenced to correctly identify your system configuration. Replace wwwlog and ftplog with the logging database that you use for your system logging. ▓

Listing 22.9   A Sample Script to Use for Server Reporting Web Access (www.sql)

```
SELECT "Total hits" = count(*),"Last Access" = max(logtime)
FROM wwwlog
SELECT ""

SELECT "Hit summary" = count(*), "Date" = substring(logtime,1,8)
FROM wwwlog
GROUP BY substring(logtime,1,8)

SELECT ""

SELECT "Time of day"=substring(logtime,10,2), "Hits" =
➥ count(substring(logtime,10,2))
FROM wwwlog
group by substring(logtime,10,2)

SELECT ""

SELECT "Page" = substring(target,1,40), "Hits" = count(target)
FROM wwwlog
WHERE
     (
      charINDEX("HTM",target)>0
     )
GROUP BY target
ORDER BY "hits" desc
```

In Listing 22.10, a similar script provides good feedback on FTP accesses, showing what files users are accessing on your system. Again, it's important to understand what types of things people are finding the most, and the least, helpful on your site.

Listing 22.10   A Sample Script to Use for Server Reporting FTP Access (ftp.sql)

```
select "Summary of volume by day"

select substring(logtime,1,8), sum(bytessent), sum(bytesrecvd)
from ftplog
where  bytessent > 1000
group by substring(logtime,1,8)

select ""

SELECT "Time of day"=substring(logtime,10,2), "Hits" =
➥ count(substring(logtime,10,2))
FROM ftplog
group by substring(logtime,10,2)

select ""
```

```
select "Target" = substring(target,1,40),
       sum(bytessent),
       sum(bytesrecvd),
       count(substring(target,1,40))
from ftplog
where bytessent> 1000
group by Target
order by sum(bytessent) desc
```

Keep an eye on your site and always be looking for things that can be removed or demoted to a less prominent presence. At the same time, be looking to provide room for more, new content that people are looking for and will keep them coming back in the future.

Reviewing System Logs Online

A great use of the IDC is to combine all of these different activities: logging, the IDC, the Web Page Wizard, and dynamic Web Page creation, to provide excellent feedback information online. Setting up the page is easy enough. You can simply use the Web Page Wizard to query the logging database and present a page showing the results. With this type of access, it's easier to review as it will be set up as a Web page and kept current.

Using this technique, you can create a Web page, similar to the one shown in Figure 22.25, which will let you review your site activity all while online.

FIG. 22.25

Keeping the site activity just a hyperlink click away is a good way to put the database query capabilities to use at your site.

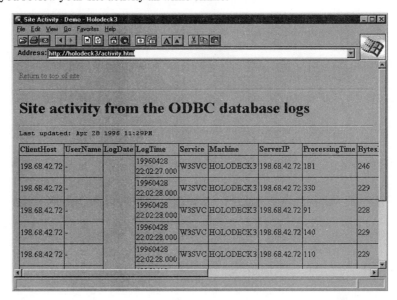

From here, it's a matter of pruning your select statement to deliver more selective information. One idea is to change the listing to return hits against the server only by minute, for example. Then, by using an IDC link, you can offer the user the ability to drill down into a given time slice to gain more detail about an activity.

Another approach is to provide summary information by user, with links to detailed log information for that user. The initial HTML page will show all users. The viewer can select the user to review, and click the name. The next HTML page shows the user's access times individually. By clicking a specific access time, the reviewing party can see the details about what was accessed by that user during that session.

Integrating the IDC and drill-down information research can really bring great leverage to you as an administrator. Remember, too, that you can place these pages into a protected subdirectory, making them available only to authorized users of your system.

Understanding Alternative Methods of Database Access

Of course, there are other ways to access databases from your site. In some cases, they involve proprietary databases, and in others, simply different language approaches. The database and the access method you select will depend largely on the type of server you're using, and will vary depending on the operating system platform you select.

You can use PERL scripts, Active Server scripting, the Internet Server API, and the Netscape Server API to access different database objects. There are even custom database engines that have been developed to support Web access.

Database access, if you've determined it is a requirement of your site, simply *must* become a determining factor in how you'll select the server software. If you're in a PC-based environment, it's hard to beat the connectivity of a server engine that supports ODBC. ODBC is a solid, established standard and the open approach of the specification gives you the leverage to create test sites, production sites, temporary databases, and more. You'll be able to work with the databases quickly and with established tools.

If you won't be using a PC-based solution, you'll need to do some significant research into the types of databases you're interested in, the impact they'll have on your system, and the requirements for integration with the Web user's environment. If you move to a system that requires Perl scripts, for example, you'll need to take the time required to learn Perl as a cost of using that environment, just as you would if you decided to use the IIS solution.

Reality Check

At the Integra Web site, the IDC is used for three different things. First, it's used to log the user's name and address information as they request download access to evaluation software. The user is prompted for the different contact elements, including name, address, and e-mail information. This information is saved to a SQL Server where the marketing team can pick it up, also over the Web, and review new sales leads.

Second, it's used to log purchases. Users are able to access the Web site, provide financial information (like credit card numbers and other information), and then purchase products directly from the Web site. Once completed, the transaction is saved to SQL Server to be passed along to the accounting department for billing purposes.

Last, database access is used to provide "Did you know" type of information on the site. The random banner that shows information about the company is generated by a mix of stored procedures and database-based information. The IDC file calls a stored procedure, which determines the next tidbit to show. Even the IDC file is automated in determining the HTX file to call when completed. By using parameters in the IDC file, a single IDC can be used to host the tidbits on any page created.

The IntelliCenter Reality Check site puts into play nearly all of the different techniques listed here, as they relate to the Microsoft Internet Information Server, including the ODBC logging. The review of the logs is a very frequent operation and is used to help drive course and online materials content from a marketing stance as well.

By putting content online, and announcing its availability both to internal student users and the customer community at large, IntelliCenter is able to see what types of materials interest people, and what other classes and activities might be of interest to customers.

In addition, as class students are assigned accounts on the IntelliCenter system, the usage statistics help drive the online research content. By looking after the content that is most requested on their system, it's possible to increase the online research materials to meet demand.

Database access is used, along with the IDC interface, to provide transcripts of the classes taken by a student, or a company's students, with access to the information guided by the individual that is signing in. A corporate leader from the company, as designated by the company, can review the different classes that have been taken by the company's employees. At the same time, an employee can review their own records, and can gain access to online materials that relate to the classes taken to date.

From Here...

As you can see, the IDC is a very powerful extension to the IIS environment. Chances are good that, after your initial installation of IIS to provide access to static HTML content, you'll quickly find that database-driven information is even more popular with the users you are serving.

This chapter touches on a number of different things. More information is provided about these topics in the following areas:

- See Chapter 9, "Firewalls and Proxy Servers," for more information about providing secure access to specific portions of your site. This is especially true if you're providing IIS logging in the way of HTML pages. This information should be kept secure in nearly all cases.

■ See Chapter 11, "Usage Statistics," for more information about the installation options regarding the logging of server accesses and how to interpret those logs.

■ See Que Publishing's *Special Edition Using Microsoft SQL Server 6.5* for more information about using SQL server, creating queries and stored procedures against the server, and more.

## CHAPTER 23

Network/Video Conferencing, Internet Phone, and RealAudio

How the Internet and Intranets are related

An Intranet makes use of Internet capabilities for better accessibility of information.

Internet and Intranet solutions

Many corporations are leading the way in implementing Intranets.

Internet Phone

Internet Phone by Vocaltec is a leader in voice and network conferencing.

RealAudio

RealAudio has now come out with Intranet solution packages.

Current network and video conferencing technologies

Check out the latest in conferencing technologies, like WebBoard and Microsoft's ActiveMovie technology.

The Internet and the Intranet are all about sharing information and communication. Every improvement made throughout an enterprise network relates to increasing speed, improving capabilities, or aiding communication in other ways. In recent months, the popularity of corporate Intranets and the Net is clear. Technological commerce is binding these two electronic environments. People still need to communicate and share information, often, especially in this modern technological world. So it should come as no surprise that the Internet and Intranets are now being increasingly used for conferencing technology.

It is interesting that it has taken so long for the Internet to employ the oldest form of human communication: face-to-face contact. Many new applications now apply the data transfer power of the Internet to allow people to actually see, hear, and speak to each other—and share documents—all in real-time. It's a far cry from e-mail, which seems comparatively outdated. ∎

Understanding Internet and Intranet Conferencing Technology

What exactly is an Intranet and how is it different from the Internet? An Intranet is an enterprise network within an organization that uses Internet technology to better communicate and share company data. Businesses are now realizing the benefits they can achieve by applying Internet technology across their own company network.

An Intranet is different from the Internet in only two ways. One difference is that an Intranet is a computer network that operates solely within a company. It is not worldwide like the Internet. The other difference is that an Intranet has access to the Internet, but non-company Internet users do not have access to the company's Intranet.

Client browsers, like Netscape Navigator 3.0 and Microsoft Internet Explorer, which adhere to a one-Window interface standard, allow easy integration with other applications. These applications—such as video conferencing, Internet phone, electronic mail, electronic faxes, and calendars—offer a variety of information that is very efficient and easy to use across the Internet.

An Intranet server supplies users with easy access to company information, while doing away with the need to replicate databases. One WWW server platform can provide support for both internal and external applications, which enables employees to share company information internally, and perform external company marketing over the Internet.

Internet and Intranet Implementations

The Internet, in conjunction with Intranets, are now being seen among the business community as very powerful tools for improving communication capabilities. With the immense amount of information that gets processed and disbursed daily within a company, an internal Website (Intranet) offers a way to streamline communication, with a central place to distribute and update company information.

Searching capabilities, along with information indexing, improve overall efficiency and accuracy by allowing employees to quickly locate and navigate through information, such as company training manuals and sales handbooks.

By storing company information electronically, production costs can be reduced by eliminating the costs associated with the daily copying and distributing of company materials.

With an Intranet, you can implement Web-based applications that enable company employees to access information, such as customer records, which allows for multiple data handling and record sharing. This interactive sharing allows employees to collaborate and share real-time resources, which facilitates the interchange of data between employees.

N O T E   An *Intranet* is simply a type of client/server system. You can also define an Intranet solution as being an overset of client-server systems. ▪

Here are a few companies that are leading the way in internal use of Intranet applications:

- HBO

  Employees have access to online market research and sales information, while high level managers have access to essential company finance information.

- MCI

  Software developers and professionals have access to MCI software programs through an online store.

- VISA

  This company's Intranet helped eliminate over a million paper documents by conducting transactions online.

If Speed Is an Issue

An Intranet receives data faster than data is received over the Internet. If the network is totally contained within a LAN, then you do get LAN speeds; for example, if the Web server is connected via LAN to the client's PCs. If you are connecting remote locations, then your speed is dependent on the Internet. If performance is really an issue, you can run your Intranet through private lines, such as frame relay. This way, you can actually contract with the phone company for actual performance levels of speed—such as 56K, 256K, and so on. The Intranet operates at approximately 100mb internally and 28.8k for remote access. After working for hours on the Intranet, the Internet is painfully slow at 28.8k, or 14.4k from home. You will be surprised at the difference client machine speed makes on Intranet LAN-based access.

Understanding Network and Video Conferencing Technology

We have all heard the phrase "a picture is worth a thousand words." I believe most people are visually oriented. By this I mean that most people assimilate concepts more easily when those concepts are introduced visually. Video conferencing takes this idea further by adding a visual reach across current audio/data communication technology.

Reviewing Microsoft's ActiveMovie Technology

The ActiveMovie API (Application Programming Interface) technology enables software developers to produce multimedia applications across multiple platforms, which combine audio and video technology.

You can create television quality applications that can be stored on the Internet in computer formats like AVI , QuickTime, or WAV files. This technology also integrates new multimedia capabilities like special effects—all in real time.

Adobe Systems, Intel, and Macromedia, along with many other developers, have decided to support ActiveMovie technology. Microsoft believes many software application titles that utilize ActiveMovie technology will soon be released.

ActiveMovie Streaming Format (ASF) is an expansive solution for sending synchronized illustrated audio over low bandwidth, in real time, over networks like the Internet and corporate Intranets. The Active Movie Player allows you to play illustrated audio files right from your Web browser, without having to download them first. In addition to the Active Movie Player, the ActiveMovie Stream Editor (which has to be downloaded separately from the Active Movie Player) allows you to create your own illustrated audio presentations in ASF. Sample Active Movie streaming formats can be found at **http://www.microsoft.com/advtech/ActiveMovie/AMStream.htm** (see Figures 23.1–23.4).

FIG. 23.1–FIG. 23.4

Sample Active Movie Streaming Format—Volcano.

Fig. 23.1

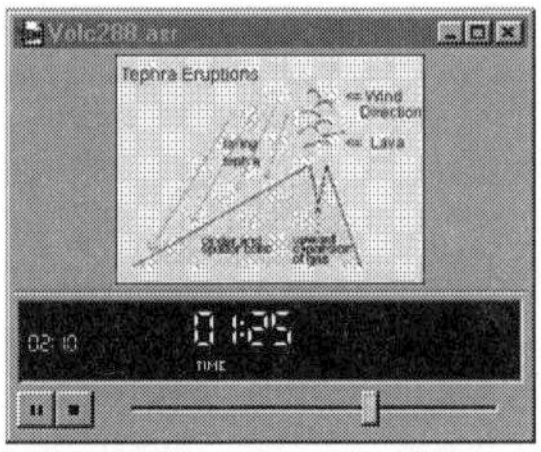

Fig. 23.2

Fig. 23.3

Fig. 23.4

ActiveMovie Player and Stream Editor can be downloaded from **http://microsoft.com/advtech/ActiveMovie/download.htm**. For more information on ActiveMovie, send e-mail to **mmdinfo@microsoft.com**.

Reviewing O'Reilly's WebBoard

WebBoard, from O'Reilly Associates, can transform your company Intranet into a conferencing community. Employees can share information, thoughts, and concepts. WebBoard enables you to design an electronic site that is ready to distribute material quickly and easily, directly to your employees.

WebBoard constructs features that are intrinsic to the Internet. WebBoard has a graphical interface, which enables employees to freely and directly conference and exchange ideas. Menu links and threaded topics allow employees to readily progress among conferences and subject matter. HTML elements and links can also be included to access other data links and images (see Figure 23.5).

FIG. 23.5
WebBoard Browser
Welcome screen.

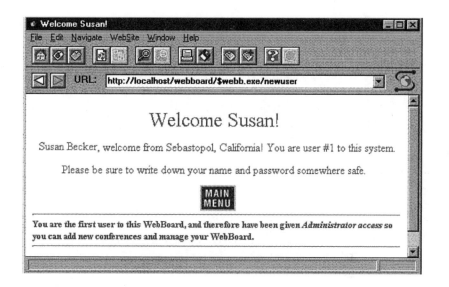

NOTE WebBoard is a full 32-bit application that is compatible with Windows 95 and Windows NT 3.51 or higher. WebBoard's open database technology uses Microsoft Access 95. WebBoard works only with Web servers that are compatible with CGI specification 1.2. ■

WebBoard incorporates the following four applications:

OLE automation servers:

■ WebBoard server.

A 32-bit multitasking conference server that is the main WebBoard application.

■ Activity Log.

This message center provides the status and happenings of the conferencing system.

OLE clients:

■ WebBoard CGI.

A windows-based CGI applet launched by the WebBoard server.

■ WebBoard Utility applet.

A command-line utility that automates common tasks.

When you start WebBoard, the WebBoard server operates in the background. The Activity Log opens and is displayed on your screen, recording each request to the WebBoard server. Users reach your WebBoard by entering the URL for the WebBoard CGI in a Web browser. Most likely, that URL is a link from elsewhere on your site or someone else's site. The WebBoard CGI interacts with the WebBoard server and responds to the user's request to display or post messages, search for text, review user information, or send e-mail. WebBoard's Utility applet provides a way to automate many WebBoard administration tasks.

Part
IV

Ch
23

WebBoard provides four different types of conferences:

- Public conferences.

  All employees can read and post messages to the conference.

- Private conferences.

  Only certain employees can read and post messages to the conference.

- Read-only conferences.

  Any employee can post messages but only the administrator or conference moderator can post messages to the conference.

- Moderated conferences.

  Any employees can read and post messages, but only the conference moderator can approve messages before they are available to employees.

WebBoard uses a large amount of system resources for its database and OLE (Object Linking and Embedding) applications. Before you can use WebBoard, you must meet certain requirements, as listed in Table 23.1.

Table 23.1   Hardware Requirements

Minimum	Recommended
486/66 DX	Pentium
16MB RAM	32MB RAM
5MB Hard Disk Space	10MB–20MB Hard Disk Space
Windows 95 or Windows NT 3.51 or 4.0	

For more information on O'Reilly & Associates WebBoard, point your browser to **http://webboard.ora.com/**. To download a 60-day demo version of WebBoard (the full version is available for $149), you can go directly to **http://software.ora.com/download/frame.html**.

Using Internet Phone

The Internet Phone (I-Phone)) by VocalTec was one of the first large-scale marketed software packages to use the Internet. With the right hardware, the I-phone allows full-duplex voice conversations. Full duplex allows communication signals to be sent and received at the same time.

The Internet Phone is shareware. Although it does not expire after a trial period, you are limited to just 60 seconds of chatting before you get unceremoniously kicked out of a conversation. However, one minute is enough to see just how useful this product is. The $30 registration fee isn't much for what it does.

Installing and Configuring Internet Phone

Anyone with FTP or Web access can download the Internet Phone from a wide variety of Internet sites, including VocalTec's home page at **http://www.vocaltec.com/**.

To install **Internet Phone**, follow these steps:

1. Double-click Iphone40.exe to extract the program files. Three subdirectories are created under the /Setup directory: Disk1, Disk2, and Disk3 (see Figure 23.6).
2. Setup.exe (which can be found in /Setup/Disk1 subdirectory) is automatically launched. The Internet Phone is installed on your system, and a program group is created for it.

Part
IV

Ch
23

FIG. 23.6
WinZip Self-Extractor–
IPHONE40.EXE.

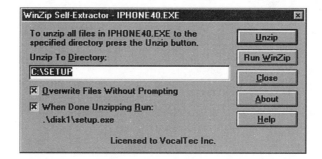

After the I-phone is installed on your system, you can be online in seconds.

If you're not connected to the Internet via a dial-up TCP/IP connection, the first thing you need to do is establish a SLIP or PPP TCP/IP dial-up connection. Once online, you can fire up the Internet Phone program.

At this point, establishing a conversation is easy (see Figure 23.7). I-phone automatically connects to an IRC (Internet Relay Chat) server and lets you start chatting.

FIG. 23.7
The layout of the Internet Phone has all the controls the user needs accessed from one screen.

Before you make your first call, take a few minutes to configure the I-phone first to get optimum results.

Configuration involves the following few steps:

1. Under View menu, choose Options. Click Global Online Directory. A list is displayed of phone servers shown in Figure 23.8.

2. Choose an IRC server. The default IRC servers are checked, or you can uncheck any IRC servers from the list.

FIG. 23.8

The Internet Phone lets you set up many IRC servers as your default phone connections.

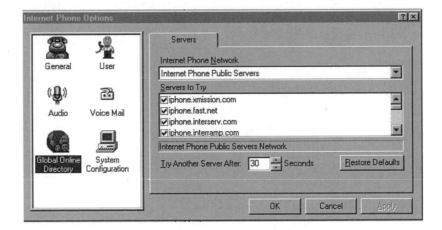

3. Under Options, choose Audio (see Figures 23.9 and 23.10). Confirm that the audio settings are what you want.

FIG. 23.9

The Audio/Sounds dialog box lets you configure sound options.

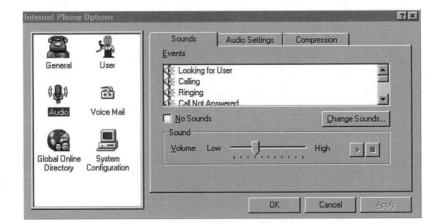

FIG. 23.10
The Audio/Audio Settings dialog box lets you configure audio options.

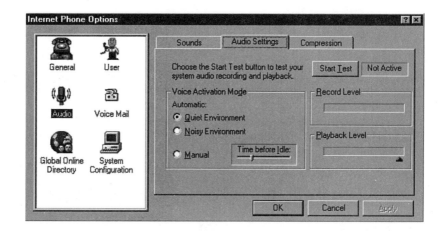

4. Choosing Set Voice Activation (VOX) Level from the Audio Settings tab allows you to set the threshold where your microphone kicks on and off as you speak (refer to Figure 23.10). (This is also done via the little button to the left of your readout—bottom right of the main I-phone box.)

5. Choose Start Test from the same Audio Settings dialog box to make sure everything is working together properly.

6. Choose User from the Options menu. Fill out your personal information. Of course, you don't have to enter any information that you feel is too personal, like your telephone number (see Figure 23.11).

FIG. 23.11
From the View Options menu, User, you can enter a little information that you would like other Internet Phone users to see.

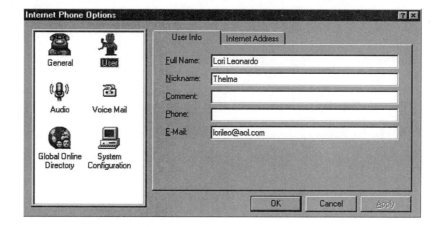

Making a Call with Internet Phone

Now you are ready to talk to someone online. Connecting is very easy. When you start the application, the main program window is displayed. The I-phone automatically connects to the

IRC servers you checked in step 2 of the configuration procedure, listed in the previous section.

Finding someone to chat with is very easy, too. By clicking the Call icon (the telephone in the upper-left corner of the I-phone window), you see a list of people and topics, called Global OnLine Directory, that is just like a list of IRC (Internet Relay Chat) channels (see Figure 23.12). You can join several topics at once. General is the best topic to join; it's also the default topic. To get a list of topics, click the Public Chat Rooms button. Be prepared for some wild topic names out there. Below, a list of users will be displayed with a little bit of information about themselves.

FIG. 23.12

The Call dialog box (Global OnLine Directory) shows people and groups you can chat with.

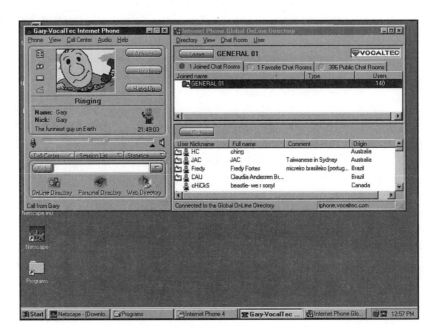

To initiate a call, double-click the person you are interested in chatting with. You hear a tone signifying that an attempt to connect is being made. If the target of your conversation is already talking to someone, you get a traditional busy signal along with a message that tells you they are busy.

When you find someone to talk to, you'll find that the voice quality is quite similar to a speaker phone. The only lag that you really notice is from long distance. Just as a transatlantic phone call experiences a bit of lag, the same lag exists with the Internet. After all, it's the same cable (or satellite link).

T I P When speaking to people from different countries, remember to avoid odd slang or excessive contractions. Also, remember to speak slowly and very clearly—accents are magnified when you can't see the person speaking.

N O T E The I-phone has some nice extras that you may find useful. You can choose the View Statistics option under the Options menu to display some useful information. The statistics sheet shows incoming and outgoing packets. On this sheet, the lost packet indicators and the average round-trip delay display are handy (see Figure 23.13). The higher the percentage gets on the lost packet indicator, the worse the quality. The round-trip delay number is in milliseconds, so if the statistic window shows a delay of 684, the round trip is .684 seconds. That may seem like a long time for computers, but it is subjectively very fast.

FIG. 23.13
When speaking with someone using the Internet Phone, you can pull up a display on the remote user you are speaking to and information on the quality of the connection.

If you wish to send Voice Mail to a friend, click the Send Voice Mail icon in the upper-left corner of the main VocalTec Internet Phone screen. A dialog box (similar to an e-mail message) will be displayed (see Figure 23.14). The recipient receives the voice mail message in the same way that he or she would receive an e-mail message.

Not every communication has to be audio. You can communicate through text by choosing the TextChat Session button on the upper-left corner of the main Internet Phone screen, under the Send Voice Mail button (see Figure 23.15).

FIG. 23.14

If a user is not available to speak to when using Internet Phone, you can pull up a Voice Mail dialog box and send a voice message.

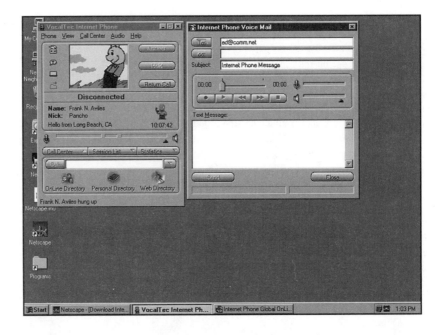

FIG. 23.15

You can have a chat session (text) by choosing the TextChat Session button on the main Internet Phone screen.

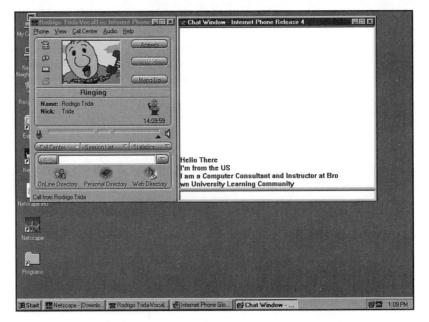

You can also view and work on projects with fellow associates in real time by choosing the Whiteboard Session button from the main Internet Phone screen, which is located under the TextChat Session button (see Figure 23.16).

FIG. 23.16
View and work on projects with fellow associates in real time by choosing the Whiteboard Session button from the main Internet Phone screen.

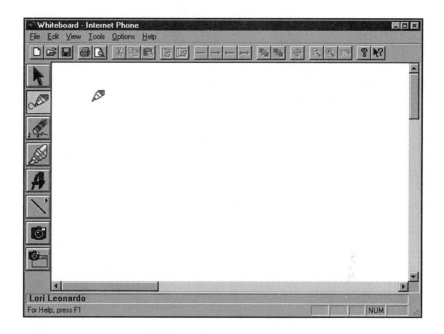

For troubleshooting and technical support, select Support Wizard from the Help menu. I-phone brings up its own browser with troubleshooting and technical support information (see Figure 23.17).

FIG. 23.17
Internet Phone Technical Support screen.

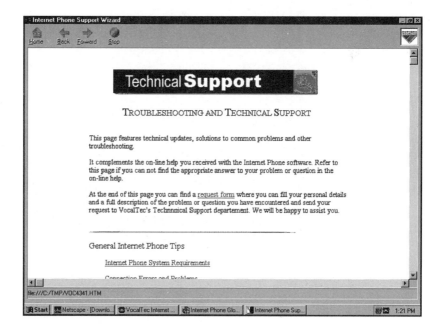

Part
IV

Ch
23

Using RealAudio

What if you have no desire to talk to someone else on the Web? What if all you want to do is listen—in real time? Real time audio is an emerging technology on the Internet, but there are a few relatively new programs that will get you involved and show you what the excitement is all about. The top contender right now is Progressive Networks' RealAudio.

RealAudio is designed to provide real-time, one-way sound transfer on the Net. RealAudio is currently freeware; you can view and download it from the RealAudio home page at **http://www.realaudio.com**.

RealAudio plays RealAudio format sound files, which have the filename extension .RAM. RealAudio can be installed as a Web browser plug-in, or Internet Explorer 3.0 users my already have the player installed with their browser. In this case, the browser can load RealAudio files directly from disk or from a World Wide Web URL address. After launching, RealAudio sets up a buffer of several seconds, which it uses to keep a few seconds of reserve time in case something disrupts the audio stream.

The buffer technique makes mass broadcasting of audio files possible. You can connect to one of many live Internet broadcasting sites. It is still very early in RealAudio's history, but even now, many radio stations are moving to set up live feeds. From talk radio, to sports, to music, RealAudio is being noticed as a way to send audio information on the Web. The ABC Information Network broadcasts news, sports, and commentaries from Peter Jennings. It is a favorite of many people is the National Public Radio site, where you can listen to your favorite PBS radio shows. Links to these and other sites can be found on the RealAudio home page listed earlier.

While RealAudio is playing, you can multitask fairly well. Using Netscape is even possible while an audio feed is transferring. Real Audio is proving to be a very stable audio Internet utility.

Currently, it is necessary to obtain a user name and password to access many of the RealAudio pages. The service is free, so the only inconvenience is obtaining these items the first time you use the service. An e-mail with your user name and password confirmation arrives very soon after applying for access.

From the RealAudio home page, you can also download utilities to create your own RealAudio .RAM files.

 T I P   Netscape Corporation apparently has a high opinion of RealAudio—Netscape has included RealAudio in the Netscape Power Pack ($54.95), a CD-ROM collection of five Netscape support utilities. The Real Audio Player is in good company; the other applications on the Power Pack CD-ROM are Netscape Chat, Smartmarks, Adobe's Acrobat Reader, and Apple's QuickTime movie viewer. With Netscape support, Real Audio is bound to have a bright future on the Web.

Installing RealAudio

A plug-in version of the RealAudio software is already built into some ealier releases of Internet Explorer 2.0, but is not currently included with later versions of 2.0 or version 3.0 at all.

1. Download the file ra32_201.exe, found on the Real Audio home page at **http://www.realaudio.com/** into a temporary folder on your hard drive.

2. Execute ra32_201.exe, which is a self-extracting compressed file, in Windows or DOS. For example, from the Windows 95 Explorer, double-click the ra32_201.exe filename in the temporary folder. After extracting its files, the RealAudio setup program automatically executes.

3. It is safe to accept the default selections for the RealAudio questions. RealAudio configures itself as a plug-in application for Netscape Navigator 3.0. For other browsers, you may need to manually set it up as a helper application. In your browser, choose Options, General, and select the Helpers tab. Add a helper application for MIME types text/sgml and text/x-sgml using the following information, which is the same for both except for the MIME subtype:

```
MIME type: audio
MIME Subtype: x-pn-realaudio for the other
Suffixes (or extensions): .ra, .ram
Program: xxx/raplayer.exe (where xxx is the path to the folder where you
installed RealAudio)
```

That's it. You're ready to go.

Using RealAudio

A list of RealAudio locations is kept at URL **http://www.prognet.com/contentp/hotcoolnew.html** (see Figure 23.18).

FIG. 23.18
You can access an extensive list of RealAudio sites at this URL.

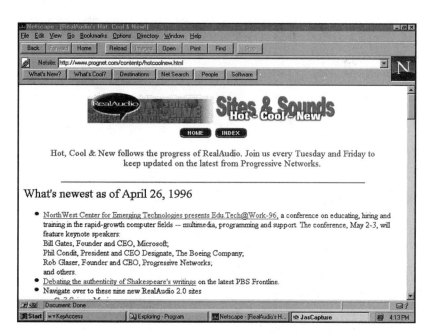

You can jump to a virtual radio station, directly located at **http://www.theflash.com/**, and choose from a playlist of selections as shown in Figures 23.19 and 23.20.

FIG. 23.19

http://
www.theflash.com/

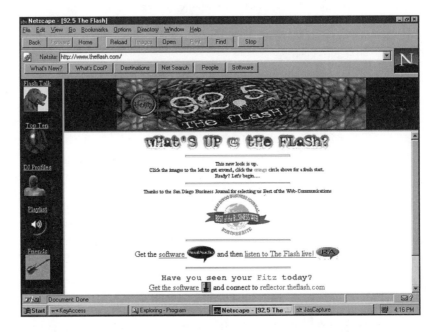

FIG. 23.20

The Playlist at http://
www.theflash.com/

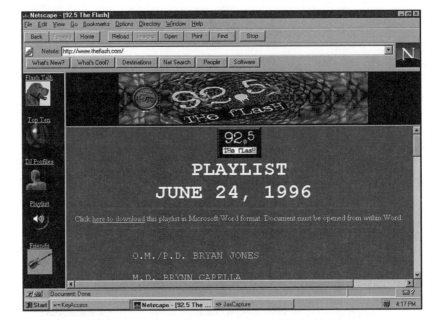

T I P A good place to find .RAM files is the Internet Radio Network at **http://town.hall.org/radio/**. They have over 200 hours of files online, and regularly broadcast the proceedings of Congress over the Web in real time. (The files are available in .WAV format, too.)

RealAudio Intranet Solutions

Progressive Networks' Intranet packages allow corporations to effectively convey audio over their own company network. Companies like Hewlett Packard, Lucent Technologies (formerly AT&T Network Wireless), and NASA use RealAudio Intranet solutions to communicate with, and train, their employees. Brown University was one of the first to use RealAudio for online lectures.

The RealAudio Intranet System 100 Kit includes the RealAudio Intranet Server, 100 RealAudio licenses for Windows, Macintosh, or UNIX, the WebShow Publishing Kit for Web slide shows, and one year of technical support, all for $3,995. If more than a 100 licenses are necessary, you can obtain the RealAudio Intranet System 500 (up to 500 licenses) for $14,995. For more information on RealAudio's Intranet solutions, check out its site, located at **http://www.RealAudio.com/Intranet/success.html**, or call 1-800-230-5975.

You also can use RealAudio if your company has a firewall installed. Companies like MCA and BellSouth Communications have structured a secure RealAudio Intranet through their corporate firewalls. RealAudio offers a free Firewall Proxy Kit that can be downloaded at **http://www.RealAudio.com/intranet/firewall.html**. This kit contains source code and specifications for building a transparent or application-level firewall proxy; or, you can choose a TCP option that enables companies to receive RealAudio without making any changes to their existing firewall.

RealAudio is an application to watch; it is changing nearly as fast as the Internet itself. After all, if major radio stations and television networks notice RealAudio, you should too.

Examining the Future of Network and Video Conferencing

Network/video conferencing over the Internet is still in its early stages, and, therefore, has a tremendous amount of potential in such technology. Just as the telephone revolutionized conversation early in this century, Internet/Intranet conferencing software could initiate another revolution in the way users communicate and share information.

In the near future, fiber optic data lines may be common in every home. One fiber optic cable running into your house could handle phone, live video feeds, cable TV, and Internet WAN (Wide Area Network) connections—and still be able to accommodate a lot more data. Until widespread fiber optic data distribution is a reality, however, there is still much more that can be done with existing technology. Refinements are being made to the electronic hardware we are all using now. In conjunction with the hardware improvements, programmers are always making better software.

The future of audio on the Internet includes the following possibilities:

- Conference calling in full duplex
- The Internet answering machine ("Sorry, I'm not online now")
- Talk forwarding to other terminals
- Sending files to each other as you talk about something
- Remote talking, so you don't have to be sitting in front of your computer

What will happen in the future with this technology is still just speculation. The many different voice utility applications will probably settle into one standard (or a very few).

Voice communication on the Internet has the potential of becoming as popular as the World Wide Web. It is a very possible that on business cards, people will someday have Internet voice contact information right under their e-mail address.

N O T E For more information regarding voice communications on the Internet, check out the Internet Phone FAQ (Frequently Asked Questions) file on UseNet. This file is posted on the 5th and 19th of each month to the UseNet newsgroups **alt.internet.services**, **alt.bbs.internet**, **alt.culture.internet**, **alt.winsock.voice**, **alt.winsock.ivc**, **comp.sys.mac.comm**, **comp.os. mswindows.apps.comm**, **alt.answers**, **comp.answers**, and **news.answers**. The latest version of the FAQ file is also available on the World Wide Web at **http://www.northcoast.com/~savetz/voice-faq.html** and **http://rpcp.mit.edu/~sears/voice-faq.html**. ■

From Here...

The Internet continues to grow exponentially. Where at one time, only large computer facilities—universities, the government, and Fortune 500 corporations—were interconnected, today, any individual with a personal computer can hook onto the Internet and any company, large or small, can benefit from an Intranet. With the introduction of Windows 95 and Windows NT, a computer owner simply has to subscribe to the Microsoft Network, or any other commercial online service, and another member is added to the Internet community. With this growth, however, risks to security and privacy arise that were only of concern to larger facilities a few years back.

## CHAPTER 24

JavaScript

With the release of Internet Explorer 3, Microsoft has added full support for the JavaScript language. In JavaScript, you can write programs that Internet Explorer 3 executes when users load or browse your pages. The JavaScript language, which was first introduced by Netscape in its Web browser, Netscape Navigator 2, gives Web authors another way to add interactivity and intelligence to their Web pages. And, unlike Java, JavaScript code is included as part of the HTML document and doesn't require any additional compilation or development tools other than a compatible Web browser. In this chapter, you learn what JavaScript can do. ■

What is JavaScript and what can it do?

In this chapter, learn about Internet Explorer's support for Netscape's JavaScript Web browser programming language.

How do you program your Web pages by using JavaScript?

Learn how to use JavaScript to interact with Web page elements and users.

What does JavaScript consist of?

Find out about the different JavaScript language elements, and how to use them to add functionality to your Web pages.

What do JavaScript programs look like?

Examine sample JavaScript Web browser applications to see JavaScript's capabilities.

Introduction to JavaScript

JavaScript allows you to embed commands in an HTML page. When an Internet Explorer 3 user downloads the page, your JavaScript commands are loaded by the Web browser as a part of the HTML document. These commands can be triggered when the user clicks on page items, manipulates gadgets and fields in an HTML form, or moves through the page history list.

Some computer languages are *compiled*; you run your program through a compiler, which performs a one-time translation of the human-readable program into a binary that the computer can execute. JavaScript is an *interpreted* language; the computer must evaluate the program every time it's run. You embed your JavaScript commands within an HTML page, and any browser that supports JavaScript can interpret the commands and act on them.

Don't let all these programming terms frighten you—JavaScript is powerful and simple. If you've ever programmed in dBASE or Visual Basic, you'll find JavaScript easy to pick up. If not, don't worry; this chapter will have you working with JavaScript in no time.

N O T E Java offers a number of C++-like capabilities that were purposefully omitted from JavaScript. For example, you can access only the limited set of objects defined by the browser and its Java applets, and you can't extend those objects yourself. ■

Why Use a Scripting Language?

HTML provides a good deal of flexibility to page authors, but HTML by itself is static; once written, HTML documents can't interact with the user other than by presenting hyperlinks. Creative use of CGI scripts (which run on Web servers) has made it possible to create more interesting and effective interactive sites, but some applications really demand programs or scripts that are executed by the client.

JavaScript was developed to provide page authors a way to write small scripts that would execute on the users' browsers instead of on the server. For example, an application that collects data from a form then posts it to the server can validate the data for completeness and correctness before sending it to the server. This capability can greatly improve the performance of the browsing session, since users don't have to send data to the server until it's been verified as correct. The following are some other potential applications for JavaScript:

- JavaScripts can verify forms for completeness, like a mailing list registration form that checks to make sure the user has entered a name and e-mail address before the form is posted.
- Pages can display content derived from information stored on the user's computer—without sending that data to the server. For example, a bank can embed JavaScript commands in its pages that look up account data from a Quicken file and display it as part of the bank's pages.

■ Because JavaScripts can modify settings for applets written in Java, page authors can control the size, appearance, and behavior of Java applets being run by Internet Explorer. A page that contains an embedded Java animation might use a JavaScript to set the Java window size and position before triggering the animation.

CAUTION

If you read this chapter and the next (Chapter 25, "Visual Basic Script"), you will see that they are two very similar languages, with similar syntax and capabilities. Because of this, some of the material presented in this chapter is repeated in the next.

However, JavaScript and Visual Basic (VB) Script are different languages, and you should be careful not to mix them up when you are programming.

▶ See Chapter 25, "VB Script or JavaScript" for a discussion of the advantages and disadvantages of the two Web browser scripting languages.

What Can JavaScript Do?

JavaScript provides a rich set of built-in functions and commands. Your JavaScripts can display HTML in the browser, do math calculations (like figuring the sales tax or shipping for an order form), play sounds, open new URLs, and even click buttons in forms.

 A *function* is a small program that performs an action; a *method* is a function that belongs to an object.

Code to perform these actions can be embedded in a page and executed when the page is loaded; you can also write *methods* that contain code that's triggered by events you specify. For example, you can write a JavaScript method that is called when the user clicks the Submit button of a form, or one that is activated when the user clicks a hyperlink on the active page.

JavaScript can also set the attributes, or *properties*, of Java applets running in the browser. This makes it easy for you to change the behavior of plug-ins or other objects without having to delve into their innards. For example, your JavaScript code could automatically start playing an embedded QuickTime or .AVI file when the user clicks a button.

What Does JavaScript Look Like?

JavaScript commands are embedded in your HTML documents, either directly or via a URL that tells the browser which scripts to load. Embedding JavaScript in your pages requires only one new HTML element: <SCRIPT> and </SCRIPT>.

The <SCRIPT> element takes two attributes: LANGUAGE, which specifies the scripting language to use when evaluating the script, and SRC, which specifies a URL from which the script can be

Part
IV
Ch
24

loaded. The LANGUAGE attribute is always required, unless the SRC attribute's URL specifies a language. LANGUAGE and SRC can both be used, too. Here are some examples:

```
<SCRIPT LANGUAGE="JavaScript">...</SCRIPT>
<SCRIPT SRC="http://www.fairgate.com/scripts/common.JavaScript">...</SCRIPT>
<SCRIPT LANGUAGE="JavaScript"
   SRC="http://www.fairgate.com/scripts/common">...</SCRIPT>
```

JavaScript itself resembles many other computer languages; if you're familiar with C, C++, Pascal, HyperTalk, Visual Basic, or dBASE, you'll recognize the similarities. If not, don't worry; the following are some simple rules that will help!xou understand how the language is structured:

- JavaScript is case-insensitive, so document.write and DOCUMENT.WRITE are the same.

- JavaScript is pretty flexible about statements. A single statement can cover multiple lines, and you can put multiple short statements on a single line—just make sure to add a semicolon (;) at the end of each statement.

- Curly braces (the { and } characters) group statements into blocks; a *block* may be the body of a function or a section of code that gets executed in a loop or as part of a conditional test.

JavaScript Programming Conventions

Even though JavaScript is a simple language, it's quite expressive. In this section, you learn a small number of simple rules and conventions that will ease your learning process and speed your use of JavaScript.

Hiding Your Scripts   You'll probably be designing pages that may be seen by browsers that don't support JavaScript. To keep those browsers from interpreting your JavaScript commands as HTML—and displaying them—wrap your scripts as follows:

```
<SCRIPT LANGUAGE="JavaScript">
<!-- This line opens an HTML comment
document.write("You can see this script's output, but not its source.")
<!-- This line opens and closes a comment -->
</SCRIPT>
```

The opening <!-- comment causes Web browsers that do not support JavaScript to disregard all text they encounter until they find a matching -->, so they don't display your script. You do have to be careful with the <SCRIPT> tag, though; if you put your <SCRIPT> and </SCRIPT> block inside the comments, Internet Explorer 3 ignores it.

Comments   Including comments in your programs to explain what they do is usually good practice; JavaScript is no exception. The JavaScript interpreter ignores any text marked as comments, so don't be shy about including them. You can use two types of comments: single-line and multiple-line.

Single-line comments start with two slashes (//), and they're limited to one line. Multiple-line comments must start with /* on the first line and end with */ on the last line. Here are a few examples:

```
// this is a legal comment
/ illegal -- comments start with two slashes
/*      Multiple-line comments can
        be spread across more than one line, as long as they end. */
/* illegal -- this comment doesn't have an end!
/// this comment's OK, because extra slashes are ignored //
```

> **CAUTION**
>
> Be careful when using multiple-line comments—remember that these comments don't nest. For instance, if you commented out a section of code in the following way, you would get an error message:
>
> ```
> /* Comment out the following code
>  * document.writeln(DumpURL()) /* write out URL list */
>  * document.writeln("End of list.")
>  */
> ```
>
> The preferred way to create single-line comments to avoid this would be as follows:
>
> ```
> /* Comment out the following code
>  * document.writeln(DumpURL()) // write out URL list
>  * document.writeln("End of list.")
>  */
> ```

Part

IV

Ch

24

The JavaScript Language

JavaScript was designed to resemble Java, which in turn looks a lot like C and C++. The difference is that Java was built as a general-purpose object language, while JavaScript is intended to provide a quicker and simpler language for enhancing Web pages and servers. In this section, you learn the building blocks of JavaScript and how to combine them into legal JavaScript programs.

N O T E JavaScript was developed by the Netscape Corporation, who maintains a great set of examples and documentation for it at **http://search.netscape.com/comprod/products/ navigator/version_2.0/script/script_info/**. ■

Using Identifiers

An *identifier* is just a unique name that JavaScript uses to identify a variable, method, or object in your program. As with other programming languages, JavaScript imposes some rules on what names you can use. All JavaScript names must start with a letter or the underscore character (_), and they can contain both upper- and lowercase letters and the digits 0 through 9.

N O T E JavaScript does not distinguish between cases, so UserName, username, USERNAME, and any other combination of lower- and uppercase letters spelling out "username" will all refer to the same thing in a JavaScript program. ■

JavaScript supports two different ways for you to represent values in your scripts: literals and variables. As their names imply, *literals* are fixed values that don't change while the script is executing, and *variables* hold data that can change at any time.

Literals and variables have several different types; the type is determined by the kind of data that the literal or variable contains. The following is a list of the types supported in JavaScript:

- **Integers**—Integer literals are made up of a sequence of digits only; integer variables can contain any whole-number value.

- **Floating-point numbers**—The number 10 is an integer, but 10.5 is a floating-point number. Floating-point literals can be positive or negative, and they can contain either positive or negative exponents (which are indicated by an *e* in the number). For example, 3.14159265 is a floating-point literal, as is 6.023e23 ($6.023 10^{23}$, or Avogadro's number).

- **Strings**—Strings can represent words, phrases, or data, and they're set off by either double (") or single (') quotation marks. If you start a string with one type of quotation mark, you must close it with the same type.

- **Booleans**—Boolean literals can have values of either `true` or `false`; other statements in the JavaScript language can return Boolean values.

Using Functions, Objects, and Properties

Before we go any further, let's talk about functions, objects, and properties. A *function* is a piece of code that plays a sound, calculates an equation, or sends a piece of e-mail, and so on. An *object* is a collection of data and functions that have been grouped together. The object's functions are called *methods*, and its data are called its *properties*. The JavaScript programs you write will have properties and methods, and they'll interact with objects provided by Internet Explorer 3 and its plug-ins (as well as any other Java applets you supply to your users).

 TIP Here's a simple guideline: an object's properties are the information it knows; its methods are how it can act on that information.

Using Built-In Objects and Functions   Individual JavaScript elements are *objects*; for example, string literals are string objects, and they have methods that you can use to change their case, and so on. JavaScript also provides a set of useful objects to represent the Internet Explorer 3 browser, the currently displayed page, and other elements of the browsing session.

You access objects by specifying their name. For example, the active document object is named `document`. To use `document`'s properties or methods, you add a period and the name of the method or property you want. For example, `document.title` is the title property of the `document` object, and `"Explorer".length` calls the length member of the string object named `"Explorer."` Remember, literals are objects, too.

Using Properties   Every object has properties—even literals. To access a property, just use the object name followed by a period and the property name. To get the length of a string object named `address`, you can write the following:

```
address.length
```

You get back an integer that equals the number of characters in the string. If the object you're using has properties that can be modified, you can change them in the same way. To set the color property of a house object, just use the following line:

```
house.color = "blue"
```

You can also create new properties for an object just by naming them. For example, say you define a class called `customer` for one of your pages. You can add new properties to the customer object as follows:

```
customer.name = "Joe Smith"
customer.address = "123 Elm Street"
customer.zip = "90210"
```

Finally, knowing that an object's methods are just properties is important. You can easily add new properties to an object by writing your own function and creating a new object property using your own function name. If you want to add a `Bill` method to your `customer` object, you can do so by writing a function named `BillCustomer` and setting the object's property as follows:

```
customer.Bill = BillCustomer;
```

To call the new method, you use the following:

```
customer.Bill()
```

Array and Object Properties   JavaScript objects store their properties in an internal table that you can access in two ways. You've already seen the first way—just use the properties' names. The second way, *arrays*, allows you to access all of an object's properties in sequence. The following function prints out all the properties of the specified object:

```
function DumpProperties(obj, obj_name) {
    result = ""          // set the result string to blank
    for (i in obj)
        result += obj_name + "." + i + " = " + obj[i] + "\n"
    return result
}
```

You see this code again in the "Sample JavaScript Code" section, and we explain in detail what it does. For now, knowing that you can use two different but related ways to access an object's properties is enough.

HTML Elements Have Properties, Too   Internet Explorer 3 provides properties for HTML forms and some types of form fields. JavaScript is especially valuable for writing scripts that check or change data in forms. Internet Explorer's properties allow you to get and set the form elements' data, as well as specify actions to be taken when something happens to the form element (as when the user clicks in a text field or moves to another field). For more details on using HTML object properties, see the section "HTML Objects and Events."

JavaScript and Internet Explorer 3

Now that you have some idea of how JavaScript works, you're ready to learn about how Internet Explorer 3 supports JavaScript.

When Scripts Get Executed

When you put JavaScript code in a page, Internet Explorer 3 evaluates the code as soon as it's encountered. As Internet Explorer 3 evaluates the code, it converts the code into a more efficient internal format so that the code can be executed later. When you think about this process, it is similar to how HTML is processed—browsers parse and display HTML as they encounter it in the page, not all at once.

Functions don't get executed when they're evaluated, however; they just get stored for later use. You still have to call functions explicitly to make them work. Some functions are attached to objects, like buttons or text fields on forms, and they are called when some event happens on the button or field. You might also have functions that you want to execute during page evaluation; you can do so by putting a call to the function at the appropriate place in the page, as follows:

```
<SCRIPT language="JavaScript">
<!--
myFunction()
<!-- -->
</SCRIPT>
```

Where to Put Your Scripts

You can put scripts anywhere within your HTML page, as long as they're surrounded with the <SCRIPT> and </SCRIPT> tag. Many JavaScript programmers choose to put functions that will be executed more than once into the <HEAD> element of their pages; this element provides a convenient storage place. Since the <HEAD> element is at the beginning of the file, functions and JavaScript code that you put there will be evaluated before the rest of the document is loaded.

Sometimes, though, you have code that shouldn't be evaluated or executed until after all the page's HTML has been parsed and displayed. An example is the DumpURL() function described in the "Sample JavaScript Code" section later in the chapter; it prints out all the URLs referenced in the page. If this function is evaluated before all the HTML on the page has been loaded, it misses some URLs, so the call to the function should come at the page's end.

Internet Explorer 3 Objects and Events

In addition to recognizing JavaScript when it's embedded inside a `<SCRIPT>` tag, Internet Explorer 3 also exposes some objects (and their methods and properties) that you can use in your JavaScript programs. Also, Internet Explorer can trigger methods you define when the user takes certain actions in the browser.

Browser Objects and Events

Many events that happen in an Internet Explorer browsing session aren't related to items on the page, like buttons or HTML text. Instead, they're related to what's happening in the browser itself, like what page the user is viewing.

The *location* Object   Internet Explorer 3 exposes an object called `location`, which holds the current URL, including the hostname, path, CGI script arguments, and even the protocol. Table 24.1 shows the properties and methods of the `location` object.

Table 24.1   Internet Explorer's location Object Containing Information on the Currently Displayed URL

Property	Type	What It Does
href	String	Contains the entire URL, including all the subparts; for example, **http://www.msn.com/products/msprod.htm**
protocol	String	Contains the protocol field of the URL, including the first colon; for example, `http:`
host	String	Contains the hostname and port number; for example, `www.msn.com:80`
hostname	String	Contains only the hostname; for example, `www.msn.com`
port	String	Contains the port, if specified; otherwise, it's blank
path	String	Contains the path to the actual document; for example, `products/msprod.htm`
hash	String	Contains any CGI arguments after the first # in the URL
search	String	Contains any CGI arguments after the first ? in the URL
toString()	Method	Returns `location.href`; you can use this function to easily get the entire URL
assign(x)	Method	Sets `location.href` to the value you specify

The *document* Object   Internet Explorer also exposes an object called `document`; as you might expect, this object exposes useful properties and methods of the active document. The `location` object refers only to the URL of the active document, but `document` refers to the document itself. Table 24.2 shows `document`'s properties and methods.

Part
IV

Ch
24

Table 24.2 Internet Explorer's document Object Containing Information on the Currently Loaded and Displayed HTML Page

Property	Type	What It Does
title	String	Contains title of the current page, or Untitled if there's no title
URL or Location	String	Contain the document's address (from its Location history stack entry); these two are synonyms
lastModified	String	Contains the page's last-modified date
forms[]	Array	Contains all the FORMs in the current page
forms[].length	Integer	Contains the number of FORMs in the current page
links[]	Array	Contains all HREF anchors in the current page
links[].length	Integer	Contains the number of HREF anchors in the current page
write(x)	Method	Writes HTML to the current document, in the order in which the script occurs on the page

The *history* Object   Internet Explorer maintains a list of pages you've visited since running the program; this list is called the *history list*, and can be accessed through the Internet Explorer 3 *history* object. Your JavaScript programs can move through pages in the list using the properties and functions shown in Table 24.3.

Table 24.3 Internet Explorer's history Object Containing Information on the Browser's History List

Property	Type	What It Does
previous or back	String	Contains the URL of the previous history stack entry (that is, the one before the active page). These properties are synonyms.
next or forward	String	Contains the URL of the next history stack entry (that is, the one after the active page). These properties are synonyms.
go(x)	Method	Goes forward x entries in the history stack if $x > 0$; else, goes backward x entries. x must be a number.
go(x)	Method	Goes to the newest history entry whose title or URL contains x as a substring; the string case doesn't matter. x must be a string.

The *window* Object   Internet Explorer 3 creates a window object for every document. Think of the window object as an actual window, and the document object as the content that appears in the window. Internet Explorer 3 provides the following two methods for working in the window:

- alert(*string*) puts up an alert dialog box and displays the message specified in string. Users must dismiss the dialog box by clicking the OK button before Internet Explorer 3 lets them continue.

- confirm(*string*) puts up a confirmation dialog box with two buttons (OK and Cancel) and displays the message specified in string. Users can dismiss the dialog box by clicking Cancel or OK; the confirm function returns true when users click OK and false if they click Cancel.

HTML Objects and Events

Internet Explorer 3 represents some individual HTML elements as objects, and these objects have properties and methods attached to them just like every other. You can use these objects to customize your pages' behavior by attaching JavaScript code to the appropriate methods.

Part

IV

Ch

24

Properties for Generic HTML Objects   The methods and properties in this section apply to several HTML tags; note that there are other methods and properties, discussed after the following table, for anchors and form elements. Table 24.4 shows the features that these generic HTML objects provide.

Table 24.4   Properties and Methods that Allow You to Control the Contents and Behavior of HTML Elements

Property	Type	What It Does
onFocus	Function	Called when the user moves the input focus to the field, either via the Tab key or a mouse click
onBlur	Function	Called when the user moves the input focus out of this field
onSelect	Function	Called when the user selects text in the field
onChange	Function	Called only when the field loses focus and the user has modified its text; use this function to validate data in a field
onSubmit	Function	Called when the user submits the form (if the form has a Submit button)
onClick	Function	Called when the button is clicked
focus()	Function	Call to move the input focus to the specified object

continues

Table 24.4	Continued		
blur()	Function	Call to move the input focus away from the specified object	
select()	Function	Call to select the specified object	
click()	Function	Call to click the specified object, which must be a button	
enable()	Function	Call to enable (un-gray) the specified object	
disable()	Function	Call to disable (gray out) the specified object	

Note that the focus(), blur(), select(), click(), enable(), and disable() functions are methods of objects; to call them, use the name of the object you want to affect. For example, to turn off the button named Search, you type **form.search.disable()**.

Properties for Anchor Objects   Hypertext anchors don't have all the properties listed in Table 24.4; they have only the onFocus(), onBlur(), and onClick() methods. You modify and set these methods just like others. Remember that no matter what code you attach, Internet Explorer 3 is still going to follow the clicked link—it executes your code first, though.

Properties for Form Objects   Table 24.5 lists the properties exposed for HTML FORM elements; the section "HTML Objects and Events" also presents several methods that you can override to call JavaScript routines when something happens to an object on the page.

Table 24.5	HTML Forms with Special Properties that You Can Use in Your JavaScript Code	
Property	**Type**	**What It Does**
name	String	Contains the value of the form's NAME attribute
method	Integer	Contains the value of the form's METHOD attribute: 0 for GET or 1 for POST
action	String	Contains the value of the form's ACTION attribute
target	Window	Window targeted after submit for form response
onSubmit()	Method	Called when the form is submitted; can't stop the submission, though
submit()	Method	Any form element can force the form to be submitted by calling the form's submit() method

Properties for Objects in a Form   One of the best places to use JavaScript is in forms, because you can write scripts that process, check, and perform calculations with the data the user enters. JavaScript provides a useful set of properties and methods for text INPUT elements and buttons.

You use INPUT elements in a form to let the user enter text data; JavaScript provides properties to get string objects that hold the element's contents, as well as methods for doing something when the user moves into or out of a field. Table 24.6 shows the properties and methods that are defined for text INPUT elements.

Table 24.6   Properties and Methods that Allow You to Control the Contents and Behavior of HTML INPUT Elements

Property	Type	What It Does
name	String	Contains the value of the element's NAME attribute
value	String	Contains the field's contents
defaultValue	String	The initial contents of the field; returns " " if blank
onFocus	Method	Called when the user moves the input focus to the field, either via the Tab key or a mouse click
onBlur	Method	Called when the user moves the input focus out of this field
onSelect	Method	Called when the user selects text in the field
onChange	Method	Called only when the field loses focus and the user has modified its text; use this function to validate data in a field

Individual buttons and check boxes have properties, too; JavaScript provides properties to get string objects containing the buttons' data, as well as methods for doing something when the user selects or deselects a particular button. Table 24.7 shows the properties and methods that are defined for button elements.

Table 24.7   Properties and Methods that Allow You to Control the Contents and Behavior of HTML Button Elements

Property	Type	What It Does
name	String	Contains the value of the button's NAME attribute
value	String	Contains the VALUE attribute
onClick	Method	Called when the button is pressed
click()	Method	Clicks a button and triggers whatever actions are attached to it

Radio buttons are grouped so that only one button in a group can be selected at a time. Because all radio buttons in a group have the same name, JavaScript has a special property, index, for use in distinguishing radio buttons. Querying the index property returns a number, starting with 0 for the first button, indicating which button in the group was triggered.

For example, you might want to put the user's cursor automatically into the first text field in a form, instead of making the user manually click the field. If your first text field is named UserName, you can add the following in your document's script to get the behavior you want:

```
form.UserName.focus()
```

Programming with JavaScript

As you've learned in the preceding sections, JavaScript has a lot to offer page authors. It's not as flexible as C or C++, but it's quick and simple. Most importantly, it's easily embedded in your WWW pages, so you can maximize their impact with a little JavaScript seasoning. This section covers the gritty details of JavaScript programming, including a detailed explanation of the language's features.

Expressions

An *expression* is anything that can be evaluated to get a single value. Expressions can contain string or numeric literals, variables, operators, and other expressions, and they can range from simple to quite complex. For example, the following is an expression that uses the assignment operator (more on operators in the next section) to assign the result 7 to the variable x:

```
x = 7;
```

By contrast, the following is a more complex expression whose final value depends on the values of the quitFlag and formComplete variables:

```
(quitFlag == TRUE) & (formComplete == FALSE)
```

Operators

Operators do just what their name suggests: they operate on variables or literals. The items that an operator acts on are called its *operands*. Operators come in the two following types:

- **Unary operators**—These operators require only one operand, and the operator can come before or after the operand. The -- operator, which subtracts one from the operand, is a good example. Both --count and count--subtract one from the variable count.

- **Binary operators**—These operators need two operands. The four math operators (+ for addition, - for subtraction, * for multiplication, and / for division) are all binary operators, as is the = assignment operator you saw earlier.

Assignment Operators   *Assignment operators* take the result of an expression and assign it to a variable. JavaScript doesn't allow you to assign the result of an expression to a literal. One feature that JavaScript has that most other programming languages don't is that you can change a variable's type on-the-fly. Consider the following:

```
function TypeDemo()
{
    var pi = 3.14159265
    document.write("Pi is ", pi, "\n")
    pi = FALSE
    document.write("Pi is ", pi, "\n")
}
```

This short function first prints the (correct) value of *pi*. In most other languages, though, trying to set a floating-point variable to a Boolean value would either generate a compiler error or a runtime error. JavaScript and Java happily accept the change and print *pi*'s new value: `false`.

The most common assignment operator, =, simply assigns the value of an expression's right side to its left side. In the previous example, the variable x got the integer value 7 after the expression was evaluated. For convenience, JavaScript also defines some other operators that combine common math operations with assignment; they're shown in Table 24.8.

Table 24.8   Assignment Operators that Provide Shortcuts to Doing Assignments and Math Operations at the Same Time

Operator	What It Does	Two Equivalent Expressions
+=	Adds two values Adds two strings	x+=y and x=x+y `string = string + "HTML"` and `string += "HTML"`
-=	Subtracts two values	x-=y and x=x-y
*=	Multiplies two values	a*=b and a=a*b
/=	Divides two values	e/=b and e=e/b

Math Operators   The preceding sections gave you a sneak preview of the math operators that JavaScript furnishes. You can either combine math operations with assignments, as shown in Table 24.8, or use them individually. As you would expect, the standard four math functions (addition, subtraction, multiplication, and division) work just as they do on an ordinary calculator.

The negation operator, -, is a unary operator that negates the sign of its operand. To use the negation operator, you must put the operator before the operand.

JavaScript also adds two useful binary operators: -- and ++, called, respectively, the *decrement* and *increment* operators. These two operators modify the value of their operand, and they return the new value. They also share a unique property: They can be used either before or after their operand. If you put the operator after the operand, JavaScript returns the operand's value and then modifies it. If you take the opposite route and put the operator before the operand, JavaScript modifies it and returns the modified value. The following short example might help clarify this seemingly odd behavior:

```
x = 7;    // set x to 7
a = --x;  // set x to x-1, and return the new x; a = 6
b = a++;  // set b to a, so b = 6, then add 1 to a; a = 7
x++;      // add one to x; ignore the returned value
```

Comparison Operators   Comparing the value of two expressions to see whether one is larger, smaller, or equal to another is often necessary. JavaScript supplies several comparison operators that take two operands and return `true` if the comparison is true, and `false` if it's not. (Remember, you can use literals, variables, or expressions with operators that require expressions.) Table 24.9 shows the JavaScript comparison operators.

Table 24.9   Comparison Operators that Allow Two JavaScript Operands to Be Compared in a Variety of Ways

Operator	Read It As	Returns *true* When:
==	Equals	The two operands are equal
!=	Does not equal	The two operands are unequal
<	Less than	The left operand is less than the right operand
<=	Less than or equal to	The left operand is less than or equal to the right operand
>	Greater than	The left operand is greater than the right operand
>=	Greater than or equal to	The left operand is greater than or equal to the right operand

TIP   The comparison operators can be used on strings, too; the results depend on standard lexicographic ordering, but comparisons aren't case sensitive.

Thinking of the comparison operators as questions may be helpful; when you write the following:

`(x >= 10)`

you're really saying, "Is the value of variable x greater than or equal to 10?" The return value answers the question, `true` or `false`.

Logical Operators   Comparison operators compare quantity or content for numeric and string expressions, but sometimes you need to test a logical value—like whether a comparison operator returns `true` or `false`. JavaScript's logical operators allow you to compare expressions that return logical values. The following are JavaScript's logical operators:

■   &&, read as "and." The && operator returns `true` if both its input expressions are true. If the first operand evaluates to `false`, && returns `false` immediately, without evaluating the second operand. Here's an example:

```
x = TRUE && TRUE;        // x is TRUE
x = FALSE && FALSE;      // x is FALSE
x = FALSE && TRUE;       // x is FALSE
```

- ■ ||, read as "or." This operator returns `true` if either of its operands is true. If the first operand is true, || returns `true` without evaluating the second operand. Here's an example:

```
x = TRUE || TRUE;        // x is TRUE
x = FALSE || TRUE;       // x is TRUE
x = FALSE || FALSE;      // x is FALSE
```

- ■ !, read as "not." This operator takes only one expression, and it returns the opposite of that expression, so `!true` returns `false`, and `!false` returns `true`.

Note that the "and" and "or" operators don't evaluate the second operand if the first operand provides enough information for the operator to return a value. This process, called *short-circuit evaluation*, can be significant when the second operand is a function call. For example,

```
keepGoing = (userCanceled == FALSE) && (theForm.Submit())
```

If `userCanceled` is `true`, the second operand—which submits the active form—isn't called.

Part
IV
Ch
24

Controlling Your JavaScripts

Some scripts you write will be simple; they'll execute the same way every time, once per page. For example, if you add a JavaScript to play a sound when users visit your home page, it doesn't need to evaluate any conditions or do anything more than once. More sophisticated scripts might require that you take different actions under different circumstances; you might also want to repeat the execution of a block of code—perhaps by a set number of times, or as long as some condition is true. JavaScript provides constructs for controlling the execution flow of your script based on conditions, as well as repeating a sequence of operations.

Testing Conditions   JavaScript provides a single type of control statement for making decisions: the `if...else` statement. To make a decision, you supply an expression that evaluates to `true` or `false`; which code is executed depends on what your expression evaluates to.

The simplest form of `if...else` uses only the `if` part. If the specified condition is true, the code following the condition is executed; if not, it's skipped. For example, in the following code fragment, the message appears only if the condition (that the document's Last Modified field says it was modified before 1995) is true:

```
if (document.lastModified.year < 1995)
    document.write("Danger! This is a mighty old document.")
```

You can use any expression as the condition; since expressions can be nested and combined with the logical operators, your tests can be pretty sophisticated. For example:

```
if ((document.lastModified.year >= 1995) && (document.lastModified.month >= 10))
    document.write("This document is reasonably current.")
```

The `else` clause allows you to specify a set of statements to execute when the condition is `false`.

Repeating Actions   If you want to repeat an action more than once, you're in luck. JavaScript provides two different loop constructs that you can use to repeat a set of operations.

The first, called a `for` loop, executes a set of statements some number of times. You specify three expressions: an *initial* expression that sets the values of any variables you need to use, a *condition* that tells the loop how to see when it's done, and an *increment* expression that modifies any variables that need it. Here's a simple example:

```
for (count=0; count < 100; count++)
    document.write("Count is ", count);
```

This loop executes 100 times and prints out a number each time. The initial expression sets the counter, `count`, to zero; the condition tests to see whether `count` is less than 100, and the increment expression increments `count`.

You can use several statements for any of these expressions, as follows:

```
for (count=0, numFound = 0; (count < 100) && (numFound < 3); count++)
    if (someObject.found()) numFound++;
```

This loop either loops 100 times or as many times as it takes to "find" three items—the loop condition terminates when `count >= 100` or when `numFound >= 3`.

The second form of loop is the `while` loop. It executes statements as long as its condition is true. For example, you can rewrite the first `for` loop in the preceding example as follows:

```
count = 0
while (count < 100) {
    if (someObject.found()) numFound++;
    document.write("Count is ", count)
}
```

Which form you use depends on what you're doing; `for` loops are useful when you want to perform an action a set number of times, and `while` loops are best when you want to keep doing something as long as a particular condition remains true. Notice that by using curly braces, you can include more than one command to be executed by the `while` loop (this is also true of `for` loops and `if...else` constructs).

JavaScript Reserved Words

JavaScript reserves some keywords for its own use. You cannot define your own methods or properties with the same name as any of these keywords; if you do, the JavaScript interpreter complains.

 TIP   Some of these keywords are reserved for future use. JavaScript might allow you to use them, but your scripts may break in the future if you do.

The following are the reserved keywords:

abstract	double	instanceof	super
boolean	else	int	switch

break	extends	interface	synchronized
byte	false	long	this
byvalue	final	native	threadsafe
case	finally	new	throw
catch	float	null	transient
char	for	package	true
class	function	private	try
const	goto	protected	var
continue	if	public	void
default	implements	return	while
delete	import	short	with
do	in	static	

N O T E Because JavaScript is still being developed and refined by Netscape, the list of reserved keywords might change and/or grow over time. Whenever a new version of JavaScript is released, it might be a good idea to look over its new capabilities with an eye toward conflicts with your JavaScript programs. ■

Command Reference

This section provides a quick reference to the JavaScript commands that are implemented in Internet Explorer 3. The commands are listed in alphabetical order; many have examples. Before you dive in, though, here's what the formatting of these entries mean:

- ■ All JavaScript keywords are in monospaced font.
- ■ Words in *italics* represent user-defined names or statements.
- ■ Any portions enclosed in square brackets ([and]) are optional.
- ■ {*statements*} indicates a block of statements, which can consist of a single statement or multiple statements enclosed by curly braces.

The *break* Statement   The break statement terminates the current while or for loop and transfers program control to the statement following the terminated loop.

Syntax:

```
break
```

Example:

The following function scans the list of URLs in the current document and stops when it has seen all URLs or when it finds a URL that matches the input parameter searchName:

```
function findURL(searchName) {
    var i = 0;
    for (I=0; i < document.links.length; i++) {
```

```
        if (document.links[i] == searchName)
        {
            document.write(document.links[i])
            break;
        }
    }
```

The *continue* Statement   The `continue` statement stops executing the statements in a `while` or `for` loop, and skips to the next iteration of the loop. It doesn't stop the loop altogether like the `break` statement; instead, in a `while` loop, it jumps back to the condition, and in a `for` loop, it jumps to the update expression.

Syntax:

```
continue
```

Example:

The following function prints the odd numbers between 1 and x; it has a `continue` statement that goes to the next iteration when `i` is even:

```
function printOddNumbers(x) {
    var i = 0
    while (i < x)
    {
        i++;
        if ((i % 2) == 0)     // the % operator divides & returns the remainder
            continue
        else
            document.write(i, "\n")
    }
}
```

The *for* Loop   A `for` loop consists of three optional expressions, enclosed in parentheses and separated by semicolons, followed by a block of statements executed in the loop. These parts do the following:

- The starting expression, `initial_expr`, is evaluated before the loop starts. It is most often used to initialize loop counter variables, and you're free to use the `var` keyword here to declare new variables.

- A `condition` is evaluated on each pass through the loop. If the condition evaluates to `true`, the statements in the loop body are executed. You can leave the condition out, and it always evaluates to `true`. If you do so, make sure to use `break` in your loop when it's time to exit.

- An update expression, `update_expr`, is usually used to update or increase the counter variable or other variables incrementally used in the condition. This expression is optional; you can update variables as needed within the body of the loop if you prefer.

- A block of statements are executed as long as the condition is `true`. This block can have one or multiple statements in it.

Syntax:

```
for ([initial_expr;] [condition;] [update_expr])
{
    statements
}
```

Example:

This simple `for` statement prints out the numbers from 0 to 9. It starts by declaring a loop counter variable, `i`, and initializing it to zero. As long as `i` is less than 9, the update expression increments `i`, and the statements in the loop body are executed.

```
for (var i = 0; i <= 9; i++)
{
    document.write(i);
}
```

The *for...in* Loop   The `for...in` loop is a special form of the `for` loop that iterates the variable `variable-name` over all the properties of the object named `object-name`. For each distinct property, it executes the statements in the loop body.

Syntax:

```
for (var in obj)
{
    statements
}
```

Example:

The following function takes as its arguments an object and the object's name. It then uses the `for...in` loop to iterate through all the object's properties. When done, it returns a string that lists the property names and their values.

```
function dump_props(obj, obj_name) {
    var result = ""
    for (i in obj)
        result += obj_name + "." + i + " = " + obj[i] + "\n"
    return result;
    }
```

The *function* Statement   The `function` statement declares a JavaScript function; the function may optionally accept one or more parameters. To return a value, the function must have a return statement that specifies the value to return. All parameters are passed to functions *by value*—the function gets the value of the parameter but cannot change the original value in the caller.

Syntax:

```
function name([param] [, param] [..., param])
{
    statements
}
```

Part

IV

Ch

24

Example:

```
function PageNameMatches(theString)
{
    return (document.title == theString)
}
```

The *if...else* Statement   The if...else statement is a conditional statement that executes the statements in block1 if condition is true. In the optional else clause, it executes the statements in block2 if condition is false. The blocks of statements can contain any JavaScript statements, including further nested if statements.

Syntax:

```
if (condition) {
    statements
} [else {
    statements}]
```

Example:

```
if (Message.IsEncrypted()) {
    Message.Decrypt(SecretKey); }
else {
    Message.Display();
}
```

The *return* Statement   The return statement specifies the value to be returned by a function.

Syntax:

```
return expression;
```

Example:

The following simple function returns the square of its argument, x, where x is any number.

```
function square( x ) {
    return x * x;
}
```

The *this* Statement   You use this to access methods or properties of an object within the object's methods. The this statement always refers to the current object.

Syntax:

```
this.property
```

Example:

If setSize is a method of the document object, then this refers to the specific object whose setSize method is called:

```
function setSize (x, y) {
        this.horizSize = x;
        this.vertSize = y;
}
```

This method sets the size for an object when called as follows:

```
document.setSize (640, 480);
```

The *var* Statement   The var statement declares a variable *varname*, optionally initializing it to have *value*. The variable name *varname* can be any JavaScript identifier, and *value* can be any legal expression (including literals).

Syntax:

```
var varname [= value] [, var varname [= value] ] [..., var varname [= value] ]
```

Example:

```
var num_hits = 0, var cust_no = 0;
```

The *while* Statement   The while statement contains a condition and a block of statements. The while statement evaluates the condition; if *condition* is true, it executes the statements in the loop body. It then reevaluates *condition* and continues to execute the statement block as long as *condition* is true. When *condition* evaluates to false, execution continues with the next statement following the block.

Syntax:

```
while (condition)
{
    statements
}
```

Example:

The following simple while loop iterates until it finds a form in the current document object whose name is "OrderForm," or until it runs out of forms in the document:

```
x = 0;
while ((x < document.forms[].length) && (document.forms[x].name != "OrderForm"))
{ x++; }
```

The *with* Statement   The with statement establishes *object* as the default object for the statements in block. Any property references without an object are then assumed to be for *object*.

Syntax:

```
with object
{
    statements
}
```

Example:

```
with document {
    write "Inside a with block, you don't need to specify the object.";
    bgColor = gray;
}
```

Part
IV

Ch
24

Sample JavaScript Code

Picking up a new programming language from scratch can be difficult—even for experienced programmers. To make mastering JavaScript easier for you, this section presents some examples of JavaScript code and functions that you can use in your own pages. Each example demonstrates a practical concept.

Dumping an Object's Properties

In the section "Array and Object Properties," you saw a small function, DumpProperties(), that gets all the property names and their values. Look at that function again now to see it in light of what you've learned:

```
function DumpProperties (obj, obj_name) {
    var result = ""      // set the result string to blank
    for (i in obj)
        result += obj_name + "." + i + " = " + obj[i] + "\n"
    return result
}
```

As all JavaScript functions should, this one starts by defining its variables using the var keyword; it supplies an initial value, too, which is a good habit to start. The meat of the function is the for...in loop, which iterates over all the properties of the specified object. For each property, the loop body collects the object name, the property name (provided by the loop counter in the for...in loop), and the property's value. You access the properties as an indexed array instead of by name, so you can get them all.

Note that the function itself doesn't print anything out. If you want to see its output, put it in a page (remember to surround it with <SCRIPT> and </SCRIPT>). Then, at the page's bottom, use the following where *obj* is the object of interest and *objName* is its name:

```
document.writeln(DumpProperties(obj, objName))
```

Building a Link Table

You might want to have a way to generate a list of all the links in a page automatically, perhaps to display them in a separate section at the end of the page, as shown in figure 24.1. DumpURL(), shown in Listing 24.1, does just that; it prints out a nicely formatted numbered list showing the hostname of each link in the page, when called with document.writeln(DumpURL()).

On the CD

Listing 24.1   37LST01.HTM   Using DumpURL() to Display a Numbered List of All the URLs on a Page

```
function DumpURL()
{
    // declare the variables we'll use
    var linkCount = document.links.length
    var result = ""

    // build our summary line
```

```
result = "<hr>\nLink summary: this page has links to <b>" +
    linkCount  + "</b> hosts<br>\n"
result += "<ol>\n"

// for each link in the document, print a list item with its hostname
for (i=0; i < linkCount ; i++)
    result += "<li> " + document.links[i].hostname + "\n"

// add the closing HTML for our list
result += "</ol><hr>\n"
return result
}
```

FIG. 24.1

The DumpURL ( )
function creates a list
of all the links in a
page.

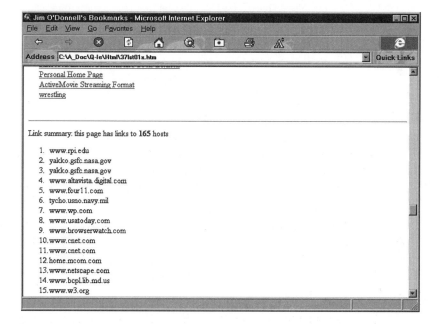

In Listing 24.1, this function starts by declaring the variables used in it. JavaScript requires that you declare most variables before using them, and good programming practice dictates doing so even when JavaScript doesn't require it. Next, you build the summary line for your table by assigning a string literal full of HTML to the result variable. You use a for loop to iterate through all the links in the current document and add a list item for each to the result variable. When you finish, you add the closing HTML for your list to result and return it.

Updating Data in Form Fields

Several times, we have mentioned the benefits of using JavaScript to check and modify data in HTML forms. Now look at an example that dynamically updates the value of a text field based on the user's selection from one of several buttons.

To make this example work, you need two pieces: the first is a simple bit of JavaScript that updates the value property of an object to whatever you pass in. Here's what it looks like:

```
function change(input, newValue)
{
    input.value = newValue
}
```

Then you need to change the onClick method for each button you want to include so that it calls your change() function. Here's a sample button definition:

```
<input type="button" value="Mac"
    onClick="change(this.form.display, 'Macintosh')">
```

When the button is clicked, JavaScript calls the onClick method, which happens to point to your function. The this.form.display object points to a text field named display; this refers to the active document, form refers to the form in the active document, and display refers to the form field named display.

Of course, this requires that you have a form INPUT gadget named display.

Validating Data in Form Fields

Often when you create a form to get data from the user, you need to check that data to see if it's correct and complete before sending mail, or making a database entry, or whatever you collected the data for. Without JavaScript, you have to post the data and let a CGI script on the server decide if all the fields were correctly filled out. You can do better, though, by writing JavaScript functions that check the data in your form *on the client*; by the time the data gets posted, you know it's correct.

For this example, require that the user fill out two fields on the form: ZIP code and area code. Also, present some other fields that are optional. First, you need a function that returns true if something appears in a field and false if it's empty:

```
function isFilled(input)
{
    return (input.value.length != 0)
}
```

That's simple enough. For each field you want to make the user complete, you override its onBlur() method. The onBlur() method is triggered when the user moves the focus out of the specified field. Here's what your buttons look like:

```
<input name="ZIP" value=""
    onBlur="if (!isFilled(form.ZIP)) {
                alert('You must put your ZIP code in this field.');
                form.ZIP.focus() }">
```

When the user tries to move the focus out of the ZIP code button, the code attached to the onBlur() event is called. That code, in turn, checks to see whether the field is complete; if not, it nags the user and puts the focus back into the ZIP field.

Of course, you could also implement a more gentle validation scheme by attaching a JavaScript to the form's Submit button, as follows:

```
<script language="JavaScript">
function areYouSure()
{
    return confirm("Are you sure you want to submit these answers?")
}
</script>
<input type=button name="doIt" value="Submit form"
    onClick="if (areYouSure()) this.form.submit();">
```

Figure 24.2 shows the Web site at **http://www.resortguide.com/javascript/ FormVerification.html**, which is a great demo of form field validation using JavaScript. You can use Internet Explorer to load this Web site, and select View, Source to see how it works.

FIG. 24.2

Unless you have entered values in each field, including a valid e-mail address and phone number, JavaScript will not let you submit this form.

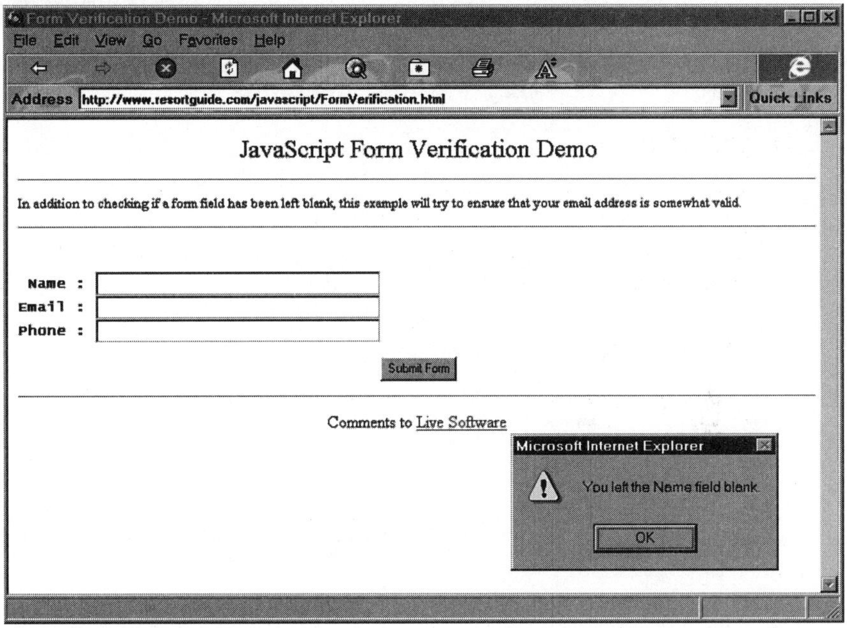

An RPN Calculator

If you ask any engineer under a certain age what kind of calculator he or she used in college, the answer is likely to be "a Hewlett Packard." HP calculators are somewhat different from other calculators; you use *reverse Polish notation*, or RPN, to do calculations.

With a regular calculator, you put the operator in between operands. To add 3 and 7, you push 3, then the + key, then 7, and then = to print the answer. With an RPN calculator, you put the operator *after* both operands. To add 3 and 7, you push 3, then Enter (which puts the first operand on the internal stack), then 7, and then +, at which time you see the correct answer. This oddity takes a bit of getting used to, but it makes complex calculations go much faster, since intermediate results get saved on the stack.

Here's a simple RPN example. To compute $((1024 * 768) / 3.14159)^2$, you enter the following:

```
1024, Enter, 768, *, 3.14159, /, x²
```

The correct answer is 6.266475×10^{10}, or about 6.3 billion.

When Netscape introduced JavaScript, they provided an RPN calculator as an example of JavaScript's expressive power—it is still a good example today. Take a detailed look now at how it works. Figure 24.3 shows the calculator as it's displayed in Internet Explorer 3. Listings 24.2 and 24.3 show the HTML document. The HTML code is shown in Listing 24.2, and the JavaScript functions are shown in Listing 24.3. (Note that they are really in the same file; we've just split them for convenience.)

FIG. 24.3

Internet Explorer 3 displays the RPN calculator as a table of buttons, with the accumulator and the stack at the top.

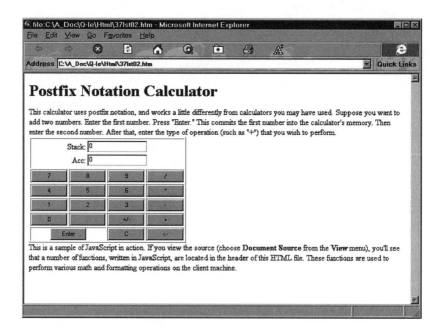

The HTML Page   Listing 24.2 shows the HTML for the calculator's page. For precise alignment, all the buttons are grouped into a table; the *accumulator* (where the answer's displayed) and the *stack* (where operands can be stored) are at the top.

Listing 24.2   37LST02.HTM   The HTML Definition for the RPN Calculator Example

On the CD

```
<h1>Postfix Notation Calculator</h1>

This calculator uses postfix notation, and works a little differently
from calculators you may have used. Suppose you want to add two
numbers. Enter the first number. Press "Enter." This commits the first
number into the calculator's memory. Then enter the second number.
```

After that, enter the type of operation (such as "+") that you wish to perform.

```html
<form method="post">

<table border="1" align=center>
<tr align="center">
<td colspan = 4>

<table border="0">
<tr>
<td align=right>Stack:</td><td><input name="stack" value="0"></td>
</tr>
<tr>
<td align=right>Acc:</td><td><input name="display" value="0"></td>
</tr>
</table>

</td>
</tr>

<tr align=center>
<td>
<input type="button" value=" 7 "
  onClick="addChar(this.form.display, '7')">
</td>
<td>
<input type="button" value=" 8 "
  onClick="addChar(this.form.display, '8')">
</td>
<td>
<input type="button" value=" 9 "
  onClick="addChar(this.form.display, '9')">
</td>
<td>
<input type="button" value=" / "
  onClick="divide(this.form)">
</td>
</tr>

<tr align=center>
<td>
<input type="button" value=" 4 "
  onClick="addChar(this.form.display, '4')">
</td>
<td>
<input type="button" value=" 5 "
  onClick="addChar(this.form.display, '5')">
</td>
<td>
<input type="button" value=" 6 "
  onClick="addChar(this.form.display, '6')">
</td>
<td>
```

continues

Listing 24.2 Continued

```
<input type="button" value=" * "
  onClick="multiply(this.form)">
</td>
</tr>

<tr align=center>
<td>
<input type="button" value=" 1 "
  onClick="addChar(this.form.display, '1')">
</td>
<td>
<input type="button" value=" 2 "
  onClick="addChar(this.form.display, '2')">
</td>
<td>
<input type="button" value=" 3 "
  onClick="addChar(this.form.display, '3')">
</td>
<td>
<input type="button" value=" - "
  onClick="subtract(this.form)">
</td>
</tr>

<tr align=center>
<td>
<input type="button" value=" 0 "
  onClick="addChar(this.form.display, '0')">
</td>
<td>
<input type="button" value=" . "
  onClick="addChar(this.form.display, '.')">
</td>
<td>
<input type="button" value="+/-"
  onClick="changeSign(this.form.display)">
</td>
<td>
<input type="button" value=" + "
  onClick="add(this.form)">
</td>
</tr>

<tr align=center>
<td colspan="2">
<input type="button" value=" Enter " name="enter"
  onClick="pushStack(this.form)">
</td>
<td>
<input type="button" value=" C "
  onClick="this.form.display.value = 0 ">
</td>
<td>
```

```
<input type="button" value=" <- "
  onClick="deleteChar(this.form.display)">
</td>
</tr>

</table>
</form>

This is a sample of JavaScript in action. If you view the source
(choose <B>Document Source</B> from the <B>View</B> menu), you'll
see that a number of functions, written in JavaScript, are located
in the header of this HTML file. These functions are used to
perform various math and formatting operations on the client
machine.
```

Part IV
Ch 24

Notice that each button has an onClick() definition associated with it. The digits 0 through 9 all call the addChar() JavaScript function; the editing keys, C for clear and <- for backspace, call functions that change the value of the accumulator. The Enter key stores the current value on the stack, and the +/- button changes the accumulator's sign.

Of course, the operators themselves call JavaScript functions, too; for example, the * button's definition calls the Multiply() function. The definitions aren't functions themselves; they include function calls (as for the digits) or individual statements (as in the "clear" key).

The JavaScript   Of course, all these onClick() triggers need to have JavaScript routines to call. Listing 24.3 shows the JavaScript functions that implement the actual calculator.

On the CD

Listing 24.3   37LST03.HTM   The JavaScript Code that Makes the RPN Calculator Functional

```
<script language="JavaScript">

<!-- hide this script tag's contents from old browsers

// keep track of whether we just computed display.value
var computed = false

function pushStack(form)
{
    form.stack.value = form.display.value
    form.display.value = 0
}

//
// Define a function to add a new character to the display
//
function addChar(input, character)
{
    // auto-push the stack if the last value was computed
```

continues

Listing 24.3   Continued

```
        if(computed) {
         pushStack(input.form)
         computed = false
        }

        // make sure input.value is a string
        if(input.value == null || input.value == "0")
            input.value = character
        else
            input.value += character
}

function deleteChar(input)
{
    input.value = input.value.substring(0, input.value.length - 1)
}

function add(form)
{
    form.display.value = parseFloat(form.stack.value)
                       + parseFloat(form.display.value)
    computed = true
}

function subtract(form)
{
    form.display.value = form.stack.value - form.display.value
    computed = true
}

function multiply(form)
{
    form.display.value = form.stack.value * form.display.value
    computed = true
}

function divide(form)
{
    var divisor = parseFloat(form.display.value)
    if(divisor == 0) {
     alert("Don't divide by zero, pal...");
     return
    }
    form.display.value = form.stack.value / divisor
    computed = true
}

function changeSign(input)
{
    // could use input.value = 0 - input.value, but let's show off substring
    if(input.value.substring(0, 1) == "-")
     input.value = input.value.substring(1, input.value.length)
```

```
      else
        input.value = "-" + input.value
  }
  <!-- done hiding from old browsers -->
  </script>
```

As you saw in the HTML shown in Listing 24.2, every button here is connected to some function. The `addChar()` and `deleteChar()` functions directly modify the contents of the form field named `display`—which is the accumulator—as do the operators (`add()`, `subtract()`, `multiply()`, and `divide()`).

Listing 24.3 shows off some subtle but cool benefits of JavaScript that would be difficult or impossible to do with CGI scripts. First, notice that the `divide()` function checks for division by zero and presents a warning dialog box to the user.

More important, in this example, all the processing is done on the client—imagine an application like an interactive tax form, where all the calculations are done on the browser and only the completed, verified data gets posted to the server. ●

Part

IV

Ch

24

## CHAPTER 25

Visual Basic Script

In addition to support for Netscape's JavaScript language, Microsoft has given Internet Explorer 3 its own scripting language, Visual Basic Script (VB Script), which is based on the Visual Basic and Visual Basic for Applications languages. Just as those two languages made it much easier to create applications for Windows and within the Microsoft Office suite, respectively, VB Script was designed as a language for easily adding interactivity and dynamic content to Web pages. VB Script gives Web authors the ability to allow Internet Explorer, and other compatible Web browsers and applications, to execute scripts to perform a wide variety of uses, such as verifying and acting on user input, customizing Java applets, and interacting with and customizing ActiveX Controls and other OLE-compatible applications. ■

What is Visual Basic (VB) Script?

In this chapter, you'll find out about Visual Basic Script, Microsoft's own scripting language for adding interactivity to Internet Explorer and other applications.

How is VB Script related to Visual Basic for Applications and Visual Basic?

Find out how VB Script is related to the Microsoft's Visual Basic for Applications and Visual Basic programming environments.

How does VB Script interact with Internet Explorer?

Learn how to use VB Script to interact with Internet Explorer through the Internet Explorer object model.

What are the VB Script language components?

Learn about the different components of the VB Script programming language.

What Is Visual Basic Script?

Like the JavaScript language, first introduced by Netscape and fully supported by Microsoft in Internet Explorer 3, the VB Script scripting language allows you to embed commands into an HTML document. When an Internet Explorer user downloads the page, your VB Script commands are loaded by the Web browser along with the rest of the document and is run in response to any of a series of events. Again, like JavaScript, VB Script is an *interpreted* language; Internet Explorer interprets the VB Script commands when they are loaded and run. They do not first need to be *compiled* into executable form by the Web author who uses them.

VB Script is a fast and flexible subset of Microsoft's Visual Basic and Visual Basic for Applications languages, designed to be easy to program in and for quickly adding active content to HTML documents. The language elements are mainly ones that will be familiar to anyone who has programmed in just about any language, such as `If...Then...Else` blocks and `Do`, `While`, and `For...Next` loops, and a typical assortment of operators and built-in functions. This chapter attempts to give you an overview of the VB Script language and show you examples of how to use it to add greater interaction to your Web pages.

> **N O T E** If you are familiar with JavaScript, or have read the previous chapter that discusses it, you will find parts of this chapter to be very similar. That is because JavaScript and VB Script are similar languages, with similar syntax, that can perform many of the same functions.
>
> So, if you know JavaScript, you can probably skip ahead to the "Programming with VB Script" and "Sample VB Script Code" sections later in this chapter, and should probably check out the "VB Script or JavaScript" discussion in the last section. Even if you know JavaScript, unless you have read the previous chapter on JavaScript, you will want to read the "VB Script and Internet Explorer 3" section for information on manipulating elements of the Web browser by using VB Script. ■

Why Use a Scripting Language?

HTML provides a good deal of flexibility to page authors, but HTML by itself is static; once written, HTML documents can't interact with the user other than by presenting hyperlinks. Creative use of CGI scripts (which run on Web servers) has made it possible to create more interesting and effective interactive sites, but some applications really demand programs or scripts that are executed by the client.

One of the reasons VB Script was developed was to provide Web authors a way to write small scripts that would execute on the users' browsers instead of on the server. For example, an application that collects data from a form and then posts it to the server can validate the data for completeness and correctness before sending it to the server. This capability can greatly improve the performance of the browsing session, because users don't have to send data to the server until it's been verified as correct. The following are some other potential applications for VB Script:

■ VB scripts can verify forms for completeness, like a mailing list registration form that checks to make sure the user has entered a name and e-mail address before the form is posted.

■ Pages can display content derived from information stored on the user's computer—without sending that data to the server. For example, a bank can embed VB Script commands in its pages that look up account data from a Quicken file and display it as part of the bank's page.

■ Because VB Script can modify settings for OLE objects and for applets written in Java, page authors can control the size, appearance, and behavior of OLE controls and Java applets being run by Internet Explorer. A page that contains an embedded Java animation might use a VB script to set the Java window size and position before triggering the animation. VB Script can be used to set properties for Internet Explorer 3 itself, since it supports OLE automation.

What Can VB Script Do?

VB Script provides a fairly complete set of built-in functions and commands, allowing you to perform math calculations, play sounds, open up new windows and new URLs, and access and verify user input to your Web forms.

Code to perform these actions can be embedded in a page and executed when the page is loaded; you can also write functions that contain code that's triggered by events you specify. For example, you can write a VB Script method that is called when the user clicks the Submit button of a form, or one that is activated when the user clicks a hyperlink on the active page.

VB Script can also set the attributes, or *properties*, of OLE controls or Java applets running in the browser. This way, you can easily change the behavior of plug-ins or other objects without having to delve into their innards. For example, your VB Script code could automatically start playing an embedded .AVI file when the user clicks a button.

How Does VB Script Look in an HTML Document?

VB Script commands are embedded in your HTML documents, either directly or via a URL that tells the browser which scripts to load, just as with JavaScript (and other scripting languages). Embedded VB Scripts are enclosed in the HTML container tag <SCRIPT> and </SCRIPT>.

The <SCRIPT> element takes two attributes: LANGUAGE, which specifies the scripting language to use when evaluating the script, and SRC, which specifies a URL from which the script can be loaded. The LANGUAGE attribute is always required, unless the SRC attribute's URL specifies a language. LANGUAGE and SRC can both be used, too. For VB Script, the scripting language is defined as LANGUAGE="VBS". Some examples of valid SCRIPT tags are as follows:

```
<SCRIPT LANGUAGE="VBS">...</SCRIPT>
<SCRIPT SRC="http://www.rpi.edu/~odonnj/scripts/common.VBS">...</SCRIPT>
<SCRIPT LANGUAGE="VBS" SRC="http://www.rpi.edu/~odonnj/scripts/common">...
</SCRIPT>
```

VB Script resembles JavaScript and many other computer languages you may be familiar with. It bears the closest resemblance, as you might imagine, to Visual Basic and Visual Basic for

Applications because it is a subset of these two languages. The following are some of the simple rules you need to follow for structuring VB scripts:

■ VB Script is case-insensitive, so `function`, `Function`, and `FUNCTION` are all the same. Microsoft has released coding conventions that include a recommended naming and formatting scheme for constants, variables, and other aspects of VB scripts. They are discussed in the "Recommended VB Script Coding Conventions" section in this chapter.

■ VB Script is flexible about statements. A single statement can cover multiple lines, if a continuation character, a single underscore (_), is placed at the end of each line to be continued. Also, you can put multiple short statements on a single line by separating each from the next with a colon (:).

VB Script Programming Hints

You should keep in mind a few points when programming with VB Script. These hints will ease your learning process and make your HTML documents that include VB scripts more compatible with a wider range of Web browsers.

Hiding Your Scripts   Because VB Script is a new product and is currently supported only by Internet Explorer 3—though Oracle, Spyglass, NetManage, and other companies plan to license the technology for future versions of their Web browsers—you'll probably be designing pages that will be viewed by Web browsers that don't support it. To keep those browsers from misinterpreting your VB script, wrap your scripts as follows:

```
<SCRIPT LANGUAGE="VBS">
<!-- This line opens an HTML comment
VB Script commands...
<!-- This line closes an HTML comment -->
</SCRIPT>
```

The opening `<!--` comment causes Web browsers that do not support VB Script to disregard all text they encounter until they find a matching `-->`, so they don't display your script. Make sure that your `<SCRIPT>` and `</SCRIPT>` container elements are outside the comments, though; otherwise, Internet Explorer 3 ignores the whole script.

Comments   Including comments in your programs to explain what they do is usually good practice; VB Script is no exception. The VB Script interpreter ignores any text marked as a comment, so don't be shy about including them. Comments in VB Script are set off by using the REM statement (short for remark) or by using a single quotation mark (') character. Any text following the REM or single quotation mark, until the end of the line, is ignored. To include a comment on the same line as another VB Script statement, you can use either REM or a single quotation mark. However, if you use REM, you must separate the statement from the REM with a colon (the VB Script multiple-command-per-line separator).

Recommended VB Script Coding Conventions   Microsoft has released a whole set of suggestions on how to format and code VB Script programs. The purpose of these suggestions is to standardize the format, structure, and appearance of VB Script programs to make them more readable, understandable, and easier to debug. The full document is available through the Microsoft VB Script home page at **http://www.microsoft.com/vbscript/**.

Some of the major points are summarized as follows:

- **Variable and Literal Naming**—Because variables and literals are interchangeable and have no fixed data types, distinguish between them by establishing a consistent naming convention.

  Literals should be named in all uppercase, with words separated by underscores; for example, MAX_SIZE or END_TIME.

  Variables should have descriptive names and be given a prefix indicating the data type they are being used for. Some examples of these prefixes are shown in Table 25.1.

Table 25.1 Recommended Variable Name Prefixes by Data Type

Type	Prefix	Example
Boolean	bln	blnFlag
Single	sng	sngPi
Double	dbl	dblPi
Long	lng	lngPi
Integer	int	intCount
Date (Time)	dtm	dtmToday
String	str	strFilename
Byte	byt	bytCounter
Error	err	errReturn
Object	obj	objForm

Part
IV
Ch
25

- **Variable Scoping**—VB Script variables may either be scoped at the script level, in which they are accessible by all procedures in the script, or procedure level, in which case they are local to the procedure. It is recommended that variables be given the narrowest scope possible—that is, procedure level—to reduce potential conflicts with variables in other procedures.
- **Object Naming**—Again, to make code more easily understandable, you should prefix object names to indicate the type of object. Table 25.2 gives a few examples.

■ **Comments**—Procedures should be commented with a brief description of what they do, though not how they do it, since this information may change over time. Comments within the procedure should explain how the procedure functions. Arguments should be described, if the use isn't obvious.

■ **Formatting**—As procedures, conditional statements, and loop structures are used, they should be indented to make the structure of the program more easily understood. The recommended amount of each level of indent is four spaces.

TIP You may find the suggested naming conventions discussed previously to be cumbersome, and be tempted to not follow them. If so, you should probably develop a naming convention of your own, comment it, and follow it.

Table 25.2   Recommended Object Name Prefixes by Type

Type	Prefix	Example
3D Panel	pnl	pnlGroup
Check box	chk	chkReadOnly
Command button	cmd	cmdExitCommon
Dialog	dlg	dlgFileOpen
Frame	fra	fraLanguage
List Box	lst	lstPolicyCodes
Text Box	txt	txtName
Slider	sld	sldScale

N O T E   We make an effort to follow most of these coding conventions in the examples presented in this chapter. However, like all programmers, we are not perfect. ■

VB Script, Visual Basic, and Visual Basic for Applications

As mentioned previously, VB Script is a subset of the Visual Basic and Visual Basic for Applications languages. If you are familiar with either of these two languages, you will find programming in VB Script very easy. Just as Visual Basic was meant to make the creation of Windows programs easier and more accessible, and Visual Basic for Applications was meant to do the same for Microsoft Office applications, VB Script is meant to give an easy-to-learn yet powerful means for adding interactivity and increased functionality to Web pages.

The VB Script Language

VB Script was designed as a subset of Visual Basic and Visual Basic for Applications. As a subset, it doesn't have as much functionality but was intended to provide a quicker and simpler language for enhancing Web pages and servers. This section discusses some of the building blocks of VB Script and how they are combined into VB Script programs.

Using Identifiers

An *identifier* is just a unique name that VB Script uses to identify a variable, method, or object in your program. As with other programming languages, VB Script imposes some rules on what names you can use. All VB Script names must start with an alphabetic character and can contain both uppercase and lowercase letters and the digits 0 through 9. Names also can be as long as 255 characters, though you probably don't want to go much over 32 or so.

Unlike JavaScript, which supports two different ways for you to represent values in your scripts, literals and variables, VB Script really has only variables. The difference in VB Script, then, is one of usage. You can include literals—constant values—in your VB Script programs by setting a variable equal to a value and not changing it. We will continue to refer to literals and variables as distinct entities, though they are interchangeable.

Literals and variables in VB Script are all of type *variant*, which means that they can contain any type of data that VB Script supports. It is usually a good idea to use a given variable for one type and explicitly convert its value to another type as necessary. The following are some of the types of data that VB Script supports:

- **Integers**—These types can be one, two, or four bytes in length, depending on how big they are.
- **Floating Point**—VB Script supports single- and double-precision floating point numbers.
- **Strings**—Strings can represent words, phrases, or data, and they're set off by double quotation marks.
- **Booleans**—Booleans have a value of either true or false.

Objects, Properties, Methods, and Events

Before you proceed further, you should take some time to review some terminology that may or may not be familiar to you. VB Script follows much the same object model followed by JavaScript, and uses many of the same terms. In VB Script, just as in JavaScript—and in any object-oriented language for that matter—an *object* is a collection of data and functions that have been grouped together. An object's data is known as its *properties*, and its functions are known as its *methods*. An *event* is a condition to which an object can respond, such as a mouse click or other user input. The VB Script programs that you write make use of properties and methods of objects, both those that you create and objects provided by Internet Explorer 3, its plug-ins, Java applets, and the like.

 TIP Here's a simple guideline: an object's properties are the information it knows, its methods are how it can act on that information, and events are what it responds to.

Using Built-In Objects and Functions   Individual VB Script elements are objects; for example, literals and variables are objects of type variant, which can be used to hold data of many different types. These objects also have associated methods, ways of acting on the different data types. VB Script also allows you to access a set of useful objects that represent the Internet Explorer browser, the currently displayed page, and other elements of the browsing session.

You access objects by specifying their names. For example, the active document object is named document. To use document's properties or methods, you add a period and the name of the method or property you want. For example, document.title is the title property of the document object.

Using Properties   Every object has properties—even literals. To access a property, just use the object name followed by a period and the property name. To get the length of a string object named address, you can write the following:

```
address.length
```

You get back an integer that equals the number of characters in the string. If the object you're using has properties that can be modified, you can change them in the same way. To set the color property of a house object, just write the following:

```
house.color = "blue"
```

You can also create new properties for an object just by naming them. For example, say you define a class called customer for one of your pages. You can add new properties to the customer object as follows:

```
customer.name = "Joe Smith"
customer.address = "123 Elm Street"
customer.zip = "90210"
```

Finally, knowing that an object's methods are just properties is important, so you can easily add new properties to an object by writing your own function and creating a new object property using your own function name. If you want to add a Bill method to your customer object, you can write a function named BillCustomer and set the object's property as follows:

```
customer.Bill = BillCustomer;
```

To call the new method, you just write the following:

```
customer.Bill()
```

HTML Elements Have Properties, Too   Internet Explorer provides properties for HTML forms and some types of form fields. VB Script is especially valuable for writing scripts that check or change data in forms. Internet Explorer's properties allow you to get and set the form elements' data, as well as specify actions to be taken when something happens to the form element (as when the user clicks in a text field or moves to another field). For more details on using HTML object properties, see the section "HTML Objects and Events" later in this chapter.

VB Script and Internet Explorer 3

Now that you have some idea of how VB Script works, you're ready to take a look at how Internet Explorer 3 supports it.

When Scripts Get Executed

When you put VB Script code in a page, Internet Explorer evaluates the code as soon as it's encountered. As Internet Explorer evaluates the code, it converts the code into a more efficient internal format so that the code can be executed later. When you think about this process, it is similar to how HTML is processed; browsers parse and display HTML as they encounter it in the page, not all at once.

Functions, however, don't get executed when they're evaluated; they just get stored for later use. You still have to call functions explicitly to make them work. Some functions are attached to objects, like buttons or text fields on forms, and they are called when some event happens on the button or field. You might also have functions that you want to execute during page evaluation; you can do so by putting a call to the function at the appropriate place in the page, as follows:

```
<SCRIPT language="VBS">
<!--
myFunction()
<!-- -->
</SCRIPT>
```

N O T E VB Script code to modify the actual HTML contents of a document (as opposed to merely changing the text in a form text input field, for instance) must be executed during page evaluation. ■

Where to Put Your Scripts

You can put scripts anywhere within your HTML page, as long as they're surrounded with the <SCRIPT> and </SCRIPT> tags. One good system is to put functions that will be executed more than once into the <HEAD> element of their pages; this element provides a convenient storage place. Since the <HEAD> element is at the beginning of the file, functions and VB Script code that you put there will be evaluated before the rest of the document is loaded.

Sometimes, though, you have code that shouldn't be evaluated or executed until after all the page's HTML has been parsed and displayed. An example would be a function to print out all the URLs referenced in the page. If this function is evaluated before all the HTML on the page has been loaded, it misses some URLs, so the call to the function should come at the page's end. The function itself can be defined anywhere in the HTML document; it is the function call that should be at the end of the page.

Part
IV

Ch
25

Internet Explorer 3 Objects and Events

In addition to recognizing VB Script when it's embedded inside a `<SCRIPT>` and `</SCRIPT>` tag, Internet Explorer 3 also exposes some objects (and their methods and properties) that you can use in your programs. Internet Explorer 3 can also trigger methods you define when the user takes certain actions in the browser.

Browser Objects and Events

Many events that happen in an Internet Explorer browsing session aren't related to items on the page, like buttons or HTML text. Instead, they're related to what's happening in the browser itself, like what page the user is viewing.

> **CAUTION**
>
> Remember that VB Script is a new language, and support for it under Internet Explorer 3 is also very new. As a result, the specifications of the language, as well as the objects, properties, methods, and events supplied by Internet Explorer, may change. Up-to-date information is always available through Microsoft's Internet Explorer Web pages at **http://www.microsoft.com/ie/**.

The *Location* Object   Internet Explorer exposes an object called `Location`, which holds the current URL, including the hostname, path, CGI script arguments, and even the protocol. Table 25.3 shows the properties of the `Location` object.

Table 25.3   Internet Explorer's Location Object Containing Information on the Currently Displayed URL

Property	What It Contains
href	The entire URL, including all the subparts; for example, **http://www.msn.com/products/msprod.htm**
protocol	The protocol field of the URL, including the first colon; for example, **http:**
host	The hostname and port number; for example, **www.msn.com:80**
hostname	The hostname; for example, **www.msn.com**
port	The port, if specified; otherwise, it's blank
pathname	The path to the actual document; for example, **products/msprod.htm**
hash	Any CGI arguments after the first **#** in the URL
search	Any CGI arguments after the first **?** in the URL

N O T E Internet Explorer object names are not case-sensitive, so references to the following are all equivalent:

```
Location.HREF
location.href
location.Href
LoCaTiOn.HrEf ▪
```

The *Document* Object   Internet Explorer also exposes an object called Document; as you might expect, this object exposes useful properties and methods of the active document. Location refers only to the URL of the active document, but Document refers to the document itself. Table 25.4 shows Document's properties and methods.

Table 25.4   Internet Explorer's Document Object Containing Information on the Currently Loaded and Displayed HTML Page

Property	What It Contains
title	Title of the current page, or Untitled if no title exists
location	The document's address (read-only)
lastModified	The page's last-modified date
forms	Array of all the FORMs in the current page
links	Array of all the HREF anchors in the current page
anchors	Array of all the anchors in the current page
linkColor	Link color
alinkColor	Link color
vlinkColor	Visited link color
bgColor	Background color
fgColor	Foreground color

Method	What It Does
write	Writes HTML to the current page
writeln	Writes HTML to the current page, followed by a \<BR\>

Part
IV

Ch
25

The *Window* Object   Internet Explorer creates a Window object for every document. Think of the Window object as an actual window and the Document object as the content that appears in the window. Internet Explorer provides the properties and methods for working in the window shown in Table 25.5.

Table 25.5   Internet Explorer's Window Object Containing Information on the Web Browser Window

Property	What It Contains
name	Current window name (currently set to return "Microsoft Internet Explorer")
parent	Window object's parent
self	Current window
top	The topmost window
location	The location object
status	The text in the lower left of the status bar

Method	What It Does
alert(*string*)	Puts up an alert dialog box and displays the message given in *string*
confirm(*string*)	Puts up a confirmation dialog box with OK and Cancel buttons, and displays the message given in *string*; this function returns `true` when users click OK and `false` otherwise
navigate(*URL*)	Takes the user to the specified *URL* in the current window

CAUTION

If you have programmed in JavaScript for Netscape Navigator, you will notice that the object model used by Netscape is very similar to the one used by Microsoft Internet Explorer. Be very careful when converting a program from one Web browser to the other and one scripting language to the other, however, to make sure that there aren't any subtle differences that might come back to haunt you.

HTML Objects and Events

Internet Explorer represents some individual HTML elements as objects, and these objects have properties and methods attached to them just like every other. You can use these objects to customize your pages' behavior by attaching VB Script code to the appropriate methods.

Properties for Generic HTML Objects   The methods and properties in this section apply to several HTML tags; note that there are other methods and properties, discussed after the following table, for anchors and form elements. Table 25.6 shows the features that these generic HTML objects provide.

Table 25.6   Methods and Events that Allow You to Control the Contents and Behavior of HTML Elements

Method	What It Does
focus()	Calls to move the input focus to the specified object
blur()	Calls to move the input focus away from the specified object
select()	Calls to select the specified object
click()	Calls to click the specified object, which must be a button

Event	When It Occurs
onFocus	When the user moves the input focus to the field, either via the Tab key or a mouse click
onBlur	When the user moves the input focus out of this field
onSelect	When the user selects text in the field
onChange	Only when the field loses focus and the user has modified its text; use this function to validate data in a field
onSubmit	When the user submits the form (if the form has a Submit button)
onClick	When the button is clicked

Part
IV

Ch

25

Note that focus(), blur(), select(), and click() are methods of objects; to call them, you use the name of the object you want to affect. For example, to turn off the button named Search, you type **form.search.disable()**.

Properties for *Link* Objects   The Link object is referenced as a read-only property array, consisting of an object for each link that appears in the HTML document. The properties of each of these objects are the same as those for Location objects. The events are onMouseMove, which fires whenever the mouse moves over a link, and onClick, which fires when a link is clicked. You can modify and set these methods just like others. Remember that no matter what code you attach, Internet Explorer 3 is still going to follow the clicked link—it executes your code first, though.

Properties for *Form* Objects   Table 25.7 lists the properties exposed for HTML Form elements.

Table 25.7   HTML Form Special Properties that You Can Use in Your VB Script Code

Property	What It Contains
name	The value of the form's NAME attribute
method	The value of the form's METHOD attribute

continues

Table 25.7   Continued

Property	What It Contains
action	The value of the form's ACTION attribute
elements	The elements' array of the form
encoding	The value of the form's ENCODING attribute
target	Window targeted after submit for form response

Method	What It Does
submit()	Any form element can force the form to be submitted by calling the form's submit() method

Event	When It Occurs
onSubmit()	When the form is submitted; this method can't stop the submission, though

Properties for Objects in a Form   A good place to use VB Script is in forms, since you can write scripts that process, check, and perform calculations with the data the user enters. VB Script provides a useful set of properties and methods for text INPUT elements and buttons.

You use INPUT elements in a form to let the user enter text data; VB Script provides properties to get the objects that hold the element's contents, as well as methods for doing something when the user moves into or out of a field. Table 25.8 shows the properties and methods that are defined for text INPUT elements.

Table 25.8   Properties and Methods that Allow You to Control the Contents and Behavior of HTML INPUT Elements

Property	What It Contains
name	The value of the element's NAME attribute
value	The field's contents
defaultValue	The initial contents of the field; returns " " if blank

Method	What It Does
onFocus	Called when the user moves the input focus to the field, either via the Tab key or a mouse click
onBlur	Called when the user moves the input focus out of this field
onSelect	Called when the user selects text in the field
onChange	Called only when the field loses focus and the user has modified its text; use this action to validate data in a field

Individual buttons and checkboxes have properties, too; VB Script provides properties to get objects containing the buttons' data, as well as methods for doing something when the user selects or deselects a particular button. Table 25.9 shows some of the properties and methods that are defined for button elements.

Table 25.9 Properties and Methods that Allow You to Control the Contents and Behavior of HTML Button and Check Box Elements

Property	What It Contains
name	The value of the button's NAME attribute
value	The VALUE attribute
checked	The state of a check Box
defaultChecked	The initial state of a check Box

Method	What It Does
click()	Clicks a button and triggers whatever actions are attached to it

Event	When It Occurs
onClick	Called when the button is pressed

As an example of what you can do with VB Script and the objects, properties, and methods outlined, you might want to put the user's cursor into the first text field in a form automatically, instead of making the user manually click the field. If your first text field is named UserName, you can put the following in your document's script to get the behavior you want:

```
form.UserName.focus()
```

Programming with VB Script

As you've learned in the preceding sections, VB Script has a lot to offer Web page authors. It's not as flexible as C or C++, but it's quick and simple. But, since it is easily embedded in your Web pages, adding interactivity with a little VB Script is easy. This section covers more details about VB Script programming, including a detailed explanation of the language's features.

Variables and Literals

VB Script variables are all of the type *variant*, which means that they can be used for any of the supported data types. Constants in VB Script, called *literals*, are similar to variables and can also be of any type. In fact, VB Script doesn't really have any "constants" in the usual sense of the word, since VB Script treats literals the same as variables. The difference lies in how the programmer uses them. Because of the fact that no differences really exist between literals and variables, and because variables can contain any kind of data, using a naming convention similar to the one described in the section "Recommended VB Script Coding Conventions" to keep track of what is what is a good idea.

The types of data that VB Script variables and literals can hold are summarized in Table 25.10.

Type	Description
Table 25.10 The Different Data Types that VB Script Variables and Literals Can Contain	
Empty	Uninitialized and is treated as 0 or the empty string, depending on the context
Null	Intentionally contains no valid data
Boolean	`true` or `false`
Byte	Integer in the range –128 to 127
Integer	Integer in the range –32,768 to 32,767
Long	Integer in the range 2,147,483,648 to 2,147,483,647
Single	Single-precision floating point number in the range 3.402823E38 to –1.401298E-45 for negative values and 1.401298E-45 to 3.402823E38 for positive values
Double	Double-precision floating point number in the range –1.79769313486232E308 to –4.94065645841247E-324 for negative values; 4.94065645841247E-324 to 1.79769313486232E308 for positive values
Date	Number that represents a date between January 1, 100 to December 31, 9999
String	Variable-length string up to approximately 2 billion characters in length
Object	OLE Automation object
Error	Error number

Expressions

An *expression* is anything that can be evaluated to get a single value. Expressions can contain string or numeric literals, variables, operators, and other expressions, and they can range from simple to quite complex. For example, the following is an expression that uses the assignment operator (more on operators in the next section) to assign the result 3.14159 to the variable x:

```
sngPi = 3.14159
```

By contrast, the following is a more complex expression whose final value depends on the values of the two Boolean variables blnQuit and blnComplete:

```
(blnQuit = TRUE) And (blnComplete = FALSE)
```

Operators

Operators do just what their name suggests: they operate on variables or literals. The items that an operator acts on are called its *operands*. Operators come in the two following types:

- **Unary**—These operators require only one operand, and the operator can come before or after the operand. The Not operator, which performs the logical negation of an expression, is a good example.

- **Binary**—These operators need two operands. The four math operators (+ for addition, – for subtraction, × for multiplication, and / for division) are all binary operators, as is the = assignment operator you saw earlier.

Assignment Operators   *Assignment operators* take the result of an expression and assign it to a variable. One feature that VB Script has that most other programming languages don't is that you can change a variable's type on-the-fly. Consider this example:

```
Sub TypeDemo
    Dim sngPi
    sngPi = 3.14159
    document.write "Pi is " & CStr(sngPi) & "<BR>"
    sngPi = FALSE
    document.write "Pi is " & CStr(sngPi) & "<BR>"
End Sub
```

This short function first prints the (correct) value of *pi*. In most other languages, though, trying to set a floating point variable to a Boolean value either generates a compiler error or a runtime error. Because VB Script variables can be any type, it happily accepts the change and prints Pi's new value: false.

The assignment operator, =, simply assigns the value of an expression's right side to its left side. In the preceding example, the variable sngPi gets the floating point value 3.14159 or the Boolean value false after the expression is evaluated.

Math Operators   The previous sections gave you a sneak preview of the math operators that VB Script furnishes. As you might expect, the standard four math functions (addition, subtraction, multiplication, and division) work just as they do on an ordinary calculator, and use the symbols +,–, ×, and /. The symbol for subtraction (–) also doubles as the negation operator. It is a unary operator that negates the sign of its operand. To use the negation operator, you must put the operator before the operand.

VB Script supplies three other math operators:

- \—The backslash operator divides its first operand by its second, after first rounding floating point operands to the nearest integer, and returns an integer result. For example, 19 \ 6.7 returns 2 (6.7 rounds to 7, which divides evenly into 19 twice).

- Mod—This operator is similar to \ in that it divides the first operand by its second, after again rounding floating point operands to the nearest integer, and returns the integer remainder. So, 19 Mod 6.7 returns 5.

Part

IV

Ch

25

■ ^—This exponent operator returns the first operand raised to the power of the second. The first operand can be negative only if the second, the exponent, is an integer.

Comparison Operators Comparing the value of two expressions to see whether one is larger, smaller, or equal to another is often necessary. VB Script supplies several comparison operators that take two operands and return `true` if the comparison is true and `false` if it's not. (Remember, you can use literals, variables, or expressions with operators that require expressions.) Table 25.11 shows the VB Script comparison operators.

Table 25.11 Comparison Operators that Allow Two VB Script Operands to Be Compared

Operator	Read It As	Returns true When
=	Equals	The two operands are equal
<>	Does not equal	The two operands are unequal
<	Less than	The left operand is less than the right operand
<=	Less than or equal to	The left operand is less than or equal to the right operand
>	Greater than	The left operand is greater than the right operand
>=	Greater than or equal to	The left operand is greater than or equal to the right operand

TIP The comparison operators can be used on strings, too; the results depend on standard lexicographic ordering.

Thinking of the comparison operators as questions may be helpful. When you write

`(x >= 10)`

you're really saying, "Is the value of variable `x` greater than or equal to `10`?" The return value answers the question, `true` or `false`.

Logical Operators Comparison operators compare quantity or content for numeric and string expressions, but sometimes you need to test a logical value—like whether a comparison operator returns `true` or `false`. VB Script's logical operators allow you to compare expressions that return logical values. The following are VB Script's logical operators:

■ And—The And operator returns `true` if both its input expressions are true. If the first operand evaluates to `false`, And returns `false` immediately, without evaluating the second operand. Here's an example:

```
blnX = TRUE And TRUE     ' blnX is TRUE
blnX = TRUE And FALSE    ' blnX is FALSE
blnX = FALSE And TRUE    ' blnX is FALSE
blnX = FALSE And FALSE   ' blnX is FALSE
```

■ Or—This operator returns `true` if either of its operands is true. If the first operand is true, ¦¦ returns `true` without evaluating the second operand. Here's an example:

```
blnX = TRUE Or TRUE     ' blnX is TRUE
blnX = TRUE Or FALSE    ' blnX is TRUE
blnX = FALSE Or TRUE    ' blnX is TRUE
blnX = FALSE Or FALSE   ' blnX is FALSE
```

■ Not—This operator takes only one expression, and it returns the opposite of that expression, so Not `true` returns `false`, and Not `false` returns `true`.

■ Xor—This operator, which stands for "exclusive or," returns `true` if either but not both of its input expressions are true, as in the following:

```
blnX = TRUE Xor TRUE     ' blnX is FALSE
blnX = TRUE Xor FALSE    ' blnX is TRUE
blnX = FALSE Xor TRUE    ' blnX is TRUE
blnX = FALSE Xor FALSE   ' blnX is FALSE
```

■ Eqv—This operator, which stands for "equivalent," returns `true` if its two input expressions are the same—either both `true` or both `false`. The statement blnX Eqv blnY is equivalent to Not (blnX Xor blnY).

■ Imp—This operator, which stands for "implication," returns `true` according to the following:

```
blnX = TRUE Imp TRUE     ' blnX is TRUE
blnX = FALSE Imp TRUE    ' blnX is TRUE
blnX = TRUE Imp FALSE    ' blnX is FALSE
blnX = FALSE Imp FALSE   ' blnX is TRUE
```

N O T E Note that the logical implication operator, Imp, is the only logical operator for which the order of the operands is important. ■

Note that the And and Or operators don't evaluate the second operand if the first operand provides enough information for the operator to return a value. This process, called *short-circuit evaluation*, can be significant when the second operand is a function call.

N O T E Note that all six of the logical operators can also operate on non-Boolean expressions. In this case, the logical operations described previously are performed bitwise, on each bit of the two operands. For instance, for the two integers 19 (00010011 in binary) and 6 (00000110):

```
19 And 6 =   2 (00000010 in binary)
19 Or 6  =  23 (00010111 in binary)
Not 19   = -20 (11101100 in binary)
```
■

Part
IV

Ch
25

String Concatenation   The final VB Script operator is the string concatenation operator, &. While the addition operator, +, can also be used to concatenate strings, using & is better because it is less ambiguous.

Controlling Your VB Scripts

Sometimes the scripts that you write are very simple and execute the same way each time they are loaded—a script to display a graphic animation, for instance. However, in order to write a script that will perform different functions depending on different user inputs or other conditions, you will eventually need to add a little more sophistication. VB Script provides statements and loops for controlling the execution of your programs based on a variety of inputs.

Testing Conditions   VB Script provides one control structure for making decisions—the If...Then...Else structure. To make a decision, you supply one or more expressions that evaluate to true or false; which code is executed depends on what your expressions evaluate to.

The simplest form of If...Then...Else uses only the If...Then part. If the specified condition is true, the code following the condition is executed; if not, that code is skipped. For example, in the following code fragment, the message appears only if the variable sngX is less than sngPi:

```
if (sngX < sngPi) then document.write("X is less that Pi")
```

You can use any expression as the condition; since expressions can be nested and combined with the logical operators, your tests can be pretty sophisticated. Also, using the multiple statement character, you can execute multiple commands, as in the following:

```
if ((blnTest = TRUE) And (sngX > sngMax)) then sngMax = sngX : blnTest = FALSE
```

The else clause allows you to specify a set of statements to execute when the condition is false. In the same single line form as shown in the preceding line, your new line appears as follows:

```
if (sngX > sngPi) then blnTest = TRUE else blnTest = FALSE
```

A more versatile use of the If...Then...Else allows multiple lines and multiple actions for each case. It looks something like the following:

```
if (sngX> sngPi) then
    blnTest = TRUE
    intCount = intCount + 1
else
    blnTest = FALSE
    intCount = 0
end if
```

Note that, with this syntax, additional test clauses using the elseif statement are permitted.

Repeating Actions   If you want to repeat an action more than once, VB Script provides a variety of constructs for doing so. The first, called a For...Next loop, executes a set of statements some number of times. You specify three expressions: an *initial* expression, which sets the values of any variables you need to use; a *condition*, which tells the loop how to see when it's done; and an *increment* expression, which modifies any variables that need it. Here's a simple example:

```
for intCount = 1 to 100
    document.write "Count is " & CStr(intCount) & "<BR>"
next
```

This loop executes 100 times and prints out a number each time.

Related to the For...Next loop is the For Each...Next loop. You use this construct as follows:

```
Dim intA(3)
intA(0) = 256
intA(1) = 324
intA(2) = 100
for each intI in intA
    document.write "intA element: " & CStr(intI) & "<BR>"
next
```

This For Each...Next loop executes the loop once for each element in the array intA, each time assigning intI to that value.

The third form of loop is the While...Wend loop. It executes statements as long as its condition is true. For example, you can rewrite the first For...Next loop as follows:

```
intCount = 1
while (intCount <= 100)
    document.write "Count is " & CStr(intCount) & "<BR>"
    intCount = intCount + 1
wend
```

The last type of loop is the Do...Loop, which has several forms, either testing the condition at the beginning or the end. When used as Do While, the test is at the beginning, and the loop executes as long as the test condition is true, similar to the While...Wend loop. Here's an example:

```
intCount = 1
do while (intCount <= 100)
    document.write "Count is " & CStr(intCount) & "<BR>"
    intCount = intCount + 1
loop
```

An example of having the test at the end, as a Do...Until, can also yield equivalent results. In that case, the loop looks like the following:

```
intCount = 1
do
    document.write "Count is " & CStr(intCount) & "<BR>"
    intCount = intCount + 1
until (intCount = 101)
```

One other difference between these two forms is that when the test is at the end of the loop, as in the second case, the commands in the loop are executed at least once. If the test is at the beginning, that is not the case.

Which form you prefer depends on what you're doing; `For...Next` and `For Each...Next` loops are useful when you want to perform an action a set number of times, and `While...Wend` and `Do...Loop` loops are best when you want to keep doing something as long as a particular condition remains true.

N O T E Additional options to the `For...Next`, `For Each...Next`, and `Do...Loop` loops are discussed in the the following section. ■

Command Reference

This section provides a quick reference to many of the VB Script statements. The statements use the following formatting:

- All VB Script keywords are in monospaced font.
- Words in *italics* represent user-defined names or statements.
- Any portions enclosed in square brackets ([and]) are optional.
- Portions enclosed in braces ({ and }) and separated by a vertical bar (¦) represent an option, of which one must be selected.
- The word `statements...` indicates a block of one or more statements.

The *Call* Statement   The `Call` statement calls a VB Script `Sub` or `Function` procedure.

Syntax:

`Call MyProc([arglist])`

or

`MyProc [arglist]`

Note that `arglist` is a comma-delimited list of zero or more arguments to be passed to the procedure. When the second form is used, omitting the `Call` statement, the parentheses around the argument list, if any, must also be omitted.

The *Dim* Statement   The `Dim` statement is used to declare variables and also allocate the storage necessary for them. If you specify subscripts, you can also create arrays.

Syntax:

`Dim varname[([subscripts])][,varname[([subscripts])],...]`

The *Do...Loop* Construct   The `Do...Loop` is a flexible structure for building loops for repeated statement execution. It can test the loop condition either at the beginning or the end of the loop, executing either while the condition is true or until it is true.

Syntax:

```
Do [{While¦Until} condition]
    statements...
[Exit Do]
    statements...
Loop
```

or

```
Do
    statements...
[Exit Do]
    statements...
Loop [{While¦Until} condition]
```

Note that if the optional condition is left out that the loop will execute indefinitely, unless the Exit Do statement is used. This statement, probably used in conjunction with an If...Then...Else construct, allows execution of the loop to be terminated from within the loop.

The *For...Next* Loop   The For...Next loop allows a block of statements to be executed a fixed number of times.

Syntax:

```
For counter = start To end [Step step]
    statements...
[Exit For]
    statements...
Next
```

As with the Do...Loop, Exit For in conjunction with an If...Then...Else condition, allows the loop to be executed before the counter has run all the way to the end.

The *For Each...Next* Loop   The For Each...Next loop is a variant of the For...Next that iterates through the values of an array or a collection of objects. For each element in the array, for instance, the loop is executed.

Syntax:

```
For Each element In group
    statements...
[Exit For]
    statements...
Next
```

The *Function* and *Sub* Statements   The Function and Sub statements declare VB Script procedures. The difference is that a Function procedure returns a value, and a Sub procedure does not. All parameters are passed to functions *by value*—the function gets the value of the parameter but cannot change the original value in the caller.

Syntax:

```
[Static] Function funcname([arglist])
    statements...
    funcname = returnvalue
End
```

and

```
[Static] Sub subname([arglist])
    statements...
End
```

Part

IV

Ch

25

Variables can be declared with the `Dim` statement within a `Function` or `Sub` procedure. In this case, those variables are local to that procedure and can only be referenced within it. If the `Static` keyword is used when the procedure is declared, then all local variables retain their value from one procedure call to the next.

The *If...Then...Else* Statement   The `If...Then...Else` statement is a conditional statement that executes statements based on test conditions being true. You can use it in a single- or multiple-line form.

Syntax:

```
If (condition) Then statements... [Else statements...]
```

or

```
If (condition) Then
    statements...
[Elseif (condition) Then
    statements...]...
[Else
    statements...]
End If
```

In the single-line form, multiple statements in either the `If...Then` or the `Else` clause must be separated by colons.

The *LSet, Mid,* and *RSet* Statements   The `LSet`, `Mid`, and `RSet` statements are used to manipulate strings. `LSet` and `RSet` are used to copy one string into another, left and right aligning it, respectively. If the receiving string is longer, the remainder is padded with spaces; if shorter, the string being copied is truncated. The `Mid` statement places one string into a specified position within another.

Syntax:

```
LSet string1 = string2
```

or

```
RSet string1 = string2
```

or

```
Mid(string1,start[,length]) = string2
```

The *On Error* Statement   The `On Error` statement is used to enable error handling.

Syntax:

```
On Error Resume Next
```

`On Error Resume Next` enables execution to continue immediately after the statement that provokes the runtime error. Or, if the error occurs in a procedure call after the last executed `On Error` statement, execution commences immediately after that procedure call. This way, execution can continue despite a runtime error, allowing you to build an error-handling routine inline within the procedure. The most recent `On Error Resume Next` statement is the one that is active, so you should execute one in each procedure in which you want to have inline error handling.

The *While...Wend* Statement The `While...Wend` statement is another looping statement, equivalent to one of the ways in which the `Do...Loop` can be used. Because the `Do...Loop` is much more versatile, it is recommended that you use that construct.

Syntax:

```
While (condition)
    statements...
Wend
```

Sample VB Script Code

Usually the quickest way to pick up a new programming language is to jump right in and try it—not spend hours studying the reference manual. And the easiest way to get started doing that is to take a look at some examples. In this section, you examine a few examples we found through the Microsoft VB Script Home page at **http://www.microsoft.com/vbscript/**. These examples give you a flavor of what VB Script can add to your Web pages.

The Classic "Hello, World!" Example

The classic first program in any new programming language is one that prints out the familiar "Hello, world!". An HTML document and VB Script for printing this message are shown in Listing 25.1.

On the CD

Listing 25.1 38LST01.HTM—The HTML Document for the Classic "Hello, World!" Program Using VB Script

```
<HTML>
<TITLE>Hello World</TITLE>
<CENTER>
    <B><I><FONT FACE="Comic Sans MS" SIZE=5 COLOR=navy>My first "Active
document"</B></I><BR><BR>
    <INPUT TYPE=BUTTON VALUE="Click me" NAME="BtnHello">
</CENTER>
<SCRIPT LANGUAGE=VBS>
    Sub BtnHello_OnClick
        MsgBox "Hello, world!", 0, "My first active document"
    End Sub
</SCRIPT>
</HTML>
```

When you view this HTML document using Internet Explorer, you should see the Web page shown in Figure 25.1. Clicking the Click me button opens the message box shown in Figure 25.2 with this favorite message.

FIG. 25.1

Clicking the Click me button runs a VB Script.

FIG. 25.2

VB Script responds to the button click event and displays the "Hello, world!" alert box.

Enhancing Client-Side Imagemaps

With Internet Explorer 3, Microsoft has added support for client-side imagemaps. This example shows how, using a VB Script, you can enhance a page with an imagemap. In this example, as the mouse cursor is moved over different areas of the map, the contents of a text field are changed to give some descriptive information about the corresponding link. This script isn't particularly amazing, but you can imagine the possibilities of being able to take certain actions depending on the position of the user's mouse cursor, without requiring a mouse click.

Figures 25.3 and 25.4 illustrate how the text field changes depending on the position of the mouse cursor. Listings 25.2 and 25.3 show the two parts of the HTML document for this example; Listing 25.2 shows the HTML code, indicating where the VB Script code should be inserted in the <HEAD> section, and Listing 25.3 shows the VB Script code.

FIG. 25.3

A simple VB script can read the position of the mouse cursor and update information in the page accordingly.

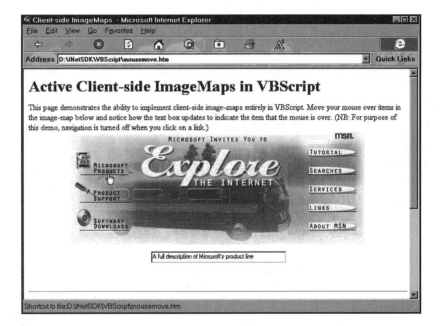

Part
IV

Ch
25

Listing 25.2   38LST02.HTM—The HTML Section: The Text in the Input Field Is Updated Depending on Where the Mouse Is

```
<html>
<head>
<script language="vbs">
<!-- insert 38lst03.htm -->
</script>
</head>
```

continues

Listing 25.2   Continued

```
<body>
<title> Client-side ImageMaps </title>

<H1> Active Client-side ImageMaps in VBScript </em> </H1>
```

This page demonstrates the ability to implement client-side image-maps entirely in VBScript. Move your mouse over items in the image-map below and notice how the text box updates to indicate the item that the mouse is over. (NB: For purpose of this demo, navigation is turned off when you click on a link.)

```
<center>
    <A id="link1" href="">
    <IMG SRC="msn-home.bmp" ALT="Clickable Map Image" WIDTH=590 HEIGHT=224
        BORDER=0>
    </A>
    <br> <br>
    <input type="text" name="text2" size=50>
</center>

<br> <br> <br>

<HR>

<H2> How it's done </H2>
```

The document contains an anchor named <tt> link1 </tt>. We define a VB procedure hooked up to the mousemove and test to see what part of the image the pointer is in, taking actions as appropriate.

```
<pre>
Sub link1_MouseMove(s,b,x,y)
last_x = x
last_y = y

if (InRect(x, y,  5, 30, 120, 85)=true) then
    DescribeLink "A full description of Microsoft's product line"

Else ...
</pre>
```

We remember the last x and y coordinate clicked on so that in the click event handler (which doesn't take x and y arguments) we can decide where the user wants to go.

"View Source" on this document for full details on how it's done.
```
</body>
</html>
```

FIG. 25.4

As the mouse moves over different parts of the clickable imagemap, the text field changes to describe the corresponding link.

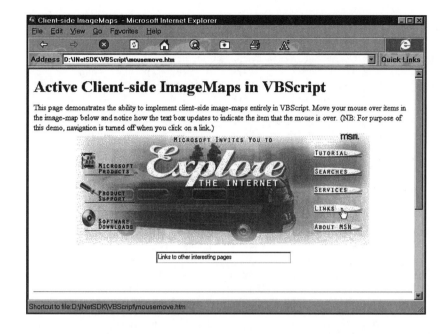

On the CD

Listing 25.3 38LST03.HTM—The VB Script Commands for Implementing the Enhanced Client-Side Imagemap

```
<SCRIPT for="link1" event="OnClick" language="VBS">
alert "hello world"
</script>

<SCRIPT language="VBS">
' Remember the last location clicked on
DIM last_x
DIM last_y
last_x = 0
last_y = 0

Sub link1_MouseMove(s,b,x,y)
last_x = x
last_y = y
if (InRect(x, y,  5, 30, 120, 85)=true) then
    DescribeLink "A full description of Microsoft's product line"
Elseif (InRect(x, y,  5, 95, 120, 135)=true) then
    DescribeLink "Microsoft's product support options"
Elseif (InRect(x, y,  5, 150, 120, 190)=true) then
    DescribeLink "Download Free Microsoft Software"
```

continues

Part
IV

Ch
25

Listing 25.3 Continued

```vbscript
Elseif (InRect(x, y,  470, 30, 570, 47)=true) then
    DescribeLink "A Tutorial on how to use MSN"
Elseif (InRect(x, y,  470, 70, 570, 87)=true) then
    DescribeLink "Search the Internet"
Elseif (InRect(x, y,  470, 105, 570, 122)=true) then
    DescribeLink "WWW Services"
Elseif (InRect(x, y,  470, 140, 570, 157)=true) then
    DescribeLink "Links to other interesting pages"
Elseif (InRect(x, y,  470, 175, 570, 192)=true) then
    DescribeLink "About the Microsoft Network"
Else
    DescribeLink ""
End If
End Sub


Sub link1_OnClick
if (InRect(last_x, last_y,  5, 30, 120, 85)=true) then
    Alert "Going to products"
    location.href = "http://www.msn.com/products/msprod.htm"
Elseif (InRect(last_x, last_y,  5, 95, 120, 135)=true) then
    Alert "Going to support options"
    location.href = "http://www.microsoft.com/support/"
Elseif (InRect(last_x, last_y,  5, 150, 120, 190)=true) then
    Alert "Going to Download Free Microsoft Software"
    location.href = "http://www.msn.com/products/intprod.htm"
Elseif (InRect(last_x, last_y,  470, 30, 570, 47)=true) then
    Alert "Going to A Tutorial on how to use MSN"
    location.href = "http://www.msn.com/tutorial/default.html"
Elseif (InRect(last_x, last_y,  470, 70, 570, 87)=true) then
    Alert "Going to Search the Internet"
    location.href = "http://www.msn.com/access/allinone.hv1"
Elseif (InRect(last_x, last_y,  470, 105, 570, 122)=true) then
    Alert "Going to WWW Services"
    location.href = "http://www.msn.com/access/ref.hv1"
Elseif (InRect(last_x, last_y,  470, 140, 570, 157)=true) then
    Alert "Going to Links to other interesting pages"
    location.href = "http://www.msn.com/access/links/other.htm"
Elseif (InRect(last_x, last_y,  470, 175, 570, 192)=true) then
    Alert "About the Microsoft Network"
    location.href = "http://www.msn.com/about/msn.htm"
End If
End Sub

Function InRect(x, y, rx1, ry1, rx2, ry2)
    InRect =  x>=rx1 AND x<=rx2 AND y>=ry1 AND y<=ry2
End Function

Sub DescribeLink(text)
    text2.value = text
End Sub

</script>
```

Interacting with Form Data

This next example shows a classic use of a client-side scripting language, one that is used to interact with the user when entering data into a form. In this case, the VB Script reads in the current state of a set of radio buttons indicating a choice of pizza, and it sets other elements in the form accordingly.

Figures 25.5 and 25.6 show this example with the pizza type selected, the check boxes showing the toppings, the text field description, and the cost.

FIG. 25.5
VB scripts can be used to assist in the filling of forms, depending on user selections of some form elements.

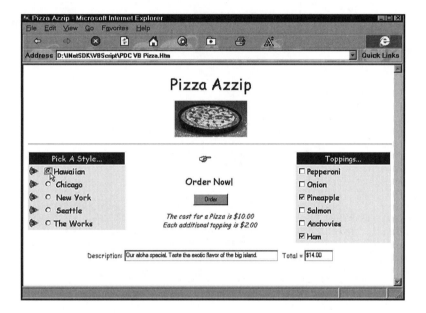

Figure 25.7 shows another function of the VB Script and its use with forms. When the user clicks the Submit button, the script verifies the user's input (including making sure that the user hasn't changed the cost field to get a cheaper pizza) before performing the appropriate action, in this case displaying the message box shown. Performing this verification locally ensures that only valid data is sent back through the Web, decreasing the amount of work that needs to be done by the Web server.

FIG. 25.6

If you use VB Script in this manner, the user is given the choice of a preset selection (for example, a "Hawaiian") or a custom selection of his or her own.

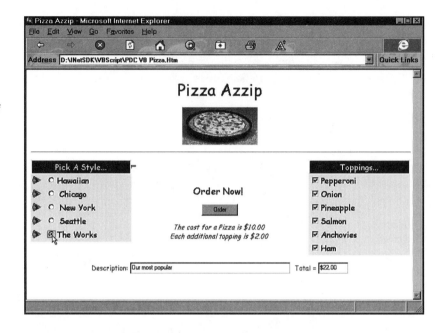

FIG. 25.7

When the user submits his or her order, the VB Script verifies the information and displays this message box.

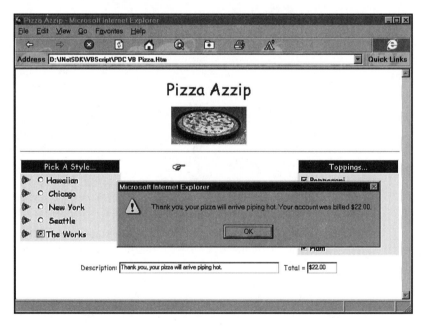

Listings 25.4 and 25.5 show the two parts of the HTML document for this example; Listing 25.4 shows the HTML code, indicating where the VB Script code should be inserted in the <HEAD> section, and Listing 25.5 shows the VB Script code.

Listing 25.4   38LST04.HTM—The HTML Section: The Toppings Check Boxes, Text in the Input Field, and Cost Are Updated Depending on Pizza Selection

```html
<HTML>
<HEAD>
<SCRIPT LANGUAGE="VBS">
<!-- Insert 38LST05.HTM -->
</SCRIPT>
<TITLE>Pizza Azzip</TITLE></HEAD>

<BODY bgproperties=fixed>

<FONT FACE="Comic Sans MS" SIZE=2>
<FONT COLOR=NAVY>

<CENTER>
   <FONT SIZE=6>Pizza Azzip<P>
   <IMG SRC="THEPIZZA.GIF" ALIGN=MIDDLE width=150 height=75>
</CENTER>

<HR>

<FONT FACE="Comic Sans MS" SIZE=2>
<FONT COLOR=NAVY>

<FORM Name="OrderForm">
<TABLE XBORDER=1 BGCOLOR="#FFFFCC" WIDTH=200 ALIGN=LEFT>
   <TR><TD BGCOLOR=NAVY ALIGN=CENTER><FONT COLOR=FFFFCC>Pick A Style...
        </TD></TR>
   <TR><TD><IMG SRC="SLICE.GIF" ALT="*" ALIGN=CENTER> 
        <INPUT TYPE=RADIO NAME=RadioGroup onClick="DoHawaiian">Hawaiian
        </TD></TR>
   <TR><TD><IMG SRC="SLICE.GIF" ALT="*" ALIGN=CENTER> 
        <INPUT TYPE=RADIO NAME=RadioGroup onClick="DoChicago">Chicago
        </TD></TR>
   <TR><TD><IMG SRC="SLICE.GIF" ALT="*" ALIGN=CENTER> 
        <INPUT TYPE=RADIO NAME=RadioGroup onClick="DoNewYork">New York
        </TD></TR>
   <TR><TD><IMG SRC="SLICE.GIF" ALT="*" ALIGN=CENTER> 
        <INPUT TYPE=RADIO NAME=RadioGroup onClick="DoSeattle">Seattle
        </TD></TR>
   <TR><TD><IMG SRC="SLICE.GIF" ALT="*" ALIGN=CENTER> 
        <INPUT TYPE=RADIO NAME=RadioGroup onClick="DoTheWorks">The Works
        </TD></TR>
</TABLE>

<TABLE XBORDER=1 BGCOLOR="#FFFFCC" WIDTH=200 ALIGN=RIGHT>
   <TR><TD BGCOLOR=NAVY ALIGN=CENTER><FONT COLOR=FFFFCC>Toppings...
        </TD></TR>
   <TR><TD><INPUT TYPE=CHECKBOX NAME=Pepperoni onClick="SetTotalCost">
            Pepperoni </TD></TR>
```

Part IV

Ch 25

continues

Listing 25.4 Continued

```
<TR><TD><INPUT TYPE=CHECKBOX NAME=Onion       onClick="SetTotalCost">
        Onion       </TD></TR>
   <TR><TD><INPUT TYPE=CHECKBOX NAME=Pineapple onClick="SetTotalCost">
        Pineapple </TD></TR>
   <TR><TD><INPUT TYPE=CHECKBOX NAME=Salmon    onClick="SetTotalCost">
        Salmon    </TD></TR>
   <TR><TD><INPUT TYPE=CHECKBOX NAME=Anchovies onClick="SetTotalCost">
        Anchovies </TD></TR>
   <TR><TD><INPUT TYPE=CHECKBOX NAME=Ham       onClick="SetTotalCost">
        Ham       </TD></TR>
</TABLE>

<FONT FACE="WINGDINGS" SIZE=6>
   <MARQUEE XWIDTH=100 DIRECTION=RIGHT ALIGN=MIDDLE BGCOLOR=WHITE>F
   </MARQUEE>
</FONT>

<BR>
<CENTER>
   <CENTER>
      <BR><FONT SIZE=4>Order Now!
      <BR><BR>
      <INPUT TYPE=BUTTON VALUE="Order" NAME="Order" onClick="DoOrder">
      <BR><BR>
      <FONT SIZE=2>
      <I> The cost for a Pizza is $10.00 </I> <BR>
      <I> Each additional topping is $2.00 </I>
   </CENTER>

   <BR CLEAR=LEFT>
   <BR CLEAR=RIGHT>
   <BR>
   Description: <INPUT NAME=Text1 SIZE=60>
   Total = <INPUT NAME=Sum VALUE="$0.00" SIZE=8><BR>
</CENTER>
<BR>
</FORM>
</BODY>
</HTML>
```

Listing 25.5 38LST05.HTM—The VB Script Commands for Interacting with Form Data; Form Data Is Automatically Updated Depending on User Input

```
<SCRIPT LANGUAGE="VBS">
'-----------------------------------------------
'-- SetTotalCost
'--
'-- This method will set the total cost of the
'-- pizza.
'--
'-----------------------------------------------
```

```
SUB SetTotalCost
Dim Form
    Set Form = document.OrderForm
    '----------
    '-- Get total number of toppings.
    '----------
    total = Form.Pepperoni.checked + _
            Form.Onion.checked      + _
            Form.Pineapple.checked  + _
            Form.Salmon.checked     + _
            Form.Anchovies.checked  + _
            Form.Ham.checked
    '----------
    '-- The price of a pizza is $10... then add the number of
    '-- toppings.
    '----------
    Form.sum.value = "$" + CStr(10 + (total * 2)) + ".00"
END SUB


'-------------------------------------------------
'-- SetDescriptionText
'--
'-- This method will set the description of the pizza.
'--
'-------------------------------------------------
SUB SetDescriptionText(strToSet)
  document.OrderForm.Text1.value = strToSet
END SUB


'-------------------------------------------------
'-- When the user clicks the order button,
'-- submit the order and alert the user that their
'-- order will be arriving soon...
'-------------------------------------------------
SUB DoOrder
    '----------
    '-- Make sure the total cost is set and
    '-- give the user a nice message.
    '----------

    SetTotalCost
    SetDescriptionText "Thank you, your pizza will arrive piping hot."

    '-- Alert is a method on the window object
    Alert "Thank you, your pizza will arrive piping hot. Your account " + _
          "was billed " + document.OrderForm.sum.value + "."
END SUB


'-------------------------------------------------
'-- SetIngredients
'--
'--    Checks/unchecks the appropriate checkboxes on the page.
'--    Recomputes cost of the pizza.
'-------------------------------------------------
```

Part

IV

Ch

25

continues

Listing 25.5 Continued

```
SUB SetIngredients(bPepperoni, bOnion, bPineapple, bSalmon, bAnchovies, bHam)
Dim Form
    Set Form = document.OrderForm

    Form.Pepperoni.checked   = bPepperoni
    Form.Onion.checked       = bOnion
    form.Pineapple.checked   = bPineapple
    Form.Salmon.checked      = bSalmon
    Form.Anchovies.checked   = bAnchovies
    Form.Ham.checked         = bHam


    SetTotalCost
END SUB



'-------------------------------------------------
'-- HAWAIIAN PIZZA
'--
'--    A Hawaiian pizza contains Pineapple and Ham.
'-------------------------------------------------
SUB DoHawaiian
    SetIngredients False, False, True, False, False, True
    SetDescriptionText "Our aloha special. Taste the exotic flavor of the
                        big island."
END SUB


'-------------------------------------------------
'-- CHICAGO PIZZA
'--
'--    A Chicago pizza contains Onion and Pepperoni.
'-------------------------------------------------
SUB DoChicago
    SetIngredients True, True, False, False, False, False
    SetDescriptionText "Capone's favorite."
END SUB


'-------------------------------------------------
'-- Seattle PIZZA
'--
'--    A Seattle pizza contains Rain... However,
'--    Rain is not a valid choice so the user can
'--    only select Salmon.
'-------------------------------------------------
SUB DoSeattle
    SetIngredients False, False, False, True, False, False
    SetDescriptionText "Our best rainy day pizza. For the fish lover in you."
END SUB


'-------------------------------------------------
'-- NEWYORK PIZZA
'--
'--    A New York pizza contains Pepperoni.
'-------------------------------------------------
```

```
Sub DoNewYork
    SetIngredients True, False, False, False, False, False
    SetDescriptionText "For a taste of the Big Apple"
END SUB

'--------------------------------------------------
'-- THEWORKS PIZZA
'--
'--    A pizza with the works contains everything.
'--------------------------------------------------
SUB DoTheWorks
    SetIngredients True, True, True, True, True, True
    SetDescriptionText "Our most popular"
END SUB

</SCRIPT>
```

Interacting with Objects

This last example shows an example of using VB Script to manipulate another Web browser object, the ActiveX Label Control. The Label Control allows the Web author to place text on the Web page, selecting the text, font, size, and an arbitrary angle of rotation. One of the exciting things about the Label Control is that it can be manipulated in real-time, producing a variety of automated or user-controlled effects.

In the following example, text is placed on the Web page using the Label Control, and form input is used to allow the user to change the text used and the angle at which it is displayed. Figure 25.8 shows the default configuration of the label, and Figure 25.9 shows it after the text and the rotation angle has been changed.

Part
IV

Ch
25

FIG. 25.8

The ActiveX Label Control allows arbitrary text to be displayed by the Web author in the size, font, position, and orientation desired.

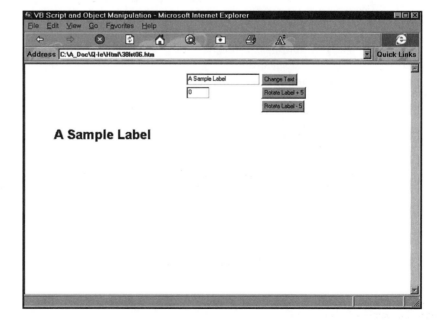

FIG. 25.9

VB Script's ability to manipulate Web browser objects allows the label parameters to be changed dynamically.

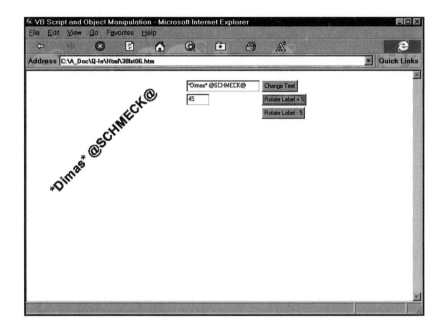

Listing 25.6 shows the code used to produce this example. Some things to note about the example are the following:

- The <OBJECT> and </OBJECT> container tag is where the ActiveX Label Control is included, and its default parameters assigned. The classid attribute must be included exactly as shown. The id attribute is the object name used by VB Script to reference the label control object. The other attributes define the size and placement of the control.

- The <PARAM> tags within the <OBJECT> and </OBJECT> container allow the Web author to define attributes of the ActiveX Label Control. The NAME, VALUE pairs are unique to each ActiveX Control, and should be documented by the ActiveX Control author. For the Label Control, they define various aspects of the appearance of the label. The NAME is also used to manipulate the value with VB Script.

- An HTML form is used to accept input and print output for information about the label control. The first text area is used to set the label text, while the second text area is used to output the current label text angle. The buttons call the appropriate VB Script routine to change the label text or angle.

- One final note about the placement of the VB scripts in this HTML document: The functions are defined in the <HEAD> section—this is not necessary, but it is common practice, so that they will be defined before used. The last <SCRIPT> and </SCRIPT> section, though, which initializes the value of the form text area showing the current angle, is placed at the end of the HTML document to ensure that the object is defined and value set before it is called.

Listing 25.6 38LST06.HTM—VB Script Can Interact with Objects

```
<HTML>
<HEAD>
<OBJECT
      classid="clsid:{99B42120-6EC7-11CF-A6C7-00AA00A47DD2}"
      id=lblActiveLbl
      width=250
      height=250
      align=left
      hspace=20
      vspace=0
>
<PARAM NAME="_extentX" VALUE="150">
<PARAM NAME="_extentY" VALUE="700">
<PARAM NAME="Angle" VALUE="90">
<PARAM NAME="Alignment" VALUE="2">
<PARAM NAME="BackStyle" VALUE="0">
<PARAM NAME="Caption" VALUE="A Simple Desultory Label">
<PARAM NAME="FontName" VALUE="Arial">
<PARAM NAME="FontSize" VALUE="20">
<PARAM NAME="FontBold" VALUE="1">
<PARAM NAME="FrColor" VALUE="0">
</OBJECT>

<SCRIPT LANGUAGE="VBS">
<!--
Sub cmdChangeIt_onClick
      Dim TheForm
      Set TheForm = Document.LabelControls
      lblActiveLbl.Caption = TheForm.txtNewText.Value
End Sub
Sub cmdRotateP_onClick
      Dim TheForm
      Set TheForm = Document.LabelControls
      lblActiveLbl.Angle = lblActiveLbl.Angle + 5
      Document.LabelControls.sngAngle.Value = lblActiveLbl.Angle
End Sub
Sub cmdRotateM_onClick
      Dim TheForm
      Set TheForm = Document.LabelControls
      lblActiveLbl.Angle = lblActiveLbl.Angle - 5
      Document.LabelControls.sngAngle.Value = lblActiveLbl.Angle
End Sub
-->
</SCRIPT>

<TITLE>VB Script and Object Manipulation</TITLE>
</HEAD>
<BODY>

<FORM NAME="LabelControls">
<TABLE>
```

continues

Listing 25.6 Continued

```
<TR><TD><INPUT TYPE="TEXT" NAME="txtNewText" SIZE=25></TD>
    <TD><INPUT TYPE="BUTTON" NAME="cmdChangeIt" VALUE="Change Text">
    </TD></TR>
<TR><TD><INPUT TYPE="TEXT" NAME="sngAngle" SIZE=5></TD>
    <TD><INPUT TYPE="BUTTON" NAME="cmdRotateP" VALUE="Rotate Label + 5">
    </TD></TR>
<TR><TD></TD>
    <TD><INPUT TYPE="BUTTON" NAME="cmdRotateM" VALUE="Rotate Label - 5">
    </TD></TR>
</TABLE>
</FORM>

<SCRIPT LANGUAGE="VBS">
<!--
Document.LabelControls.sngAngle.Value = lblActiveLbl.Angle
-->
</SCRIPT>

</BODY>
</HTML>
```

VB Script or JavaScript?

With a choice of scripting languages supported by Internet Explorer 3, the question of which to use quickly arises. The two languages are similar and have similar capabilities. Also, since they are both relatively new, you don't have a lot of history to rely on for making a choice. The following are a few points to consider:

- What language are you more comfortable with? JavaScript is based on the Java and C++ languages; VB Script, on Visual Basic and Visual Basic for Applications. If you are proficient at one of these parent languages, using the scripting language that is based on it might be a good idea.

- What are you trying to do? Both languages are object oriented and can interact with Internet Explorer 3 and other objects that it may have loaded, such as Java applets or OLE Controls. But if you will be primarily working with Internet Explorer 3 using a feature of Microsoft's ActiveX technologies, using VB Script would probably be a good idea, because it is designed with that use in mind.

- Who is your target audience? For what "general-purpose" interactivity—like processing form inputs or providing simple interactivity—who will be the audience for your Web pages? Though Microsoft has the fastest growing share of the Web browser market, Netscape's Navigator has the lion's share. Unless your Web pages are targeted at a specific audience that will definitely be using Internet Explorer, you will probably want to use JavaScript. At least in the short term, using JavaScript will ensure you maximum compatibility.

## CHAPTER 26

CGI Scripts and Server-Side Includes

Common Gateway Interface (CGI) programs allow your Web server to receive form data. They can turn your Netscape server into a dictionary, an English-to-German translator, a player of games, a search engine for any database, a poll-taker, a password checker, and much more.

Server-Side Includes (SSI) allows you to build "dynamic pages" that display different information every time a user accesses a particular URL. A simple example of an SSI is those ubiquitous "usage counters" that are so popular (and by some people considered tacky).

Most of the material presented in this chapter is platform-independent, meaning that it applies to any type of hardware or operating system. There are a few minor differences among the various platforms, which will be covered.

SSIs are very similar to CGIs in terms of how they are constructed by the system developer, though what they actually do is very different. For this reason, we will begin with a short discussion of how CGIs work, how they are put together, and later we will provide the additional information necessary to create SSIs. ■

- To configure the Netscape server to activate CGIs and SSIs
- To gather form data on the server side
- To design and install a CGI program by using various programming languages that will fully preprocess and parse the given data
- To produce a response page for the client from the CGI program
- To write simple and useful programs by using CGI, such as e-mail gateways and password checkers
- Some of the security issues involving CGI and SSI on the Web server

How Common Gateway Interface Works

The client browser initially receives an HTML document containing tags that make up a form. The form has fields, buttons, selectors, and so on, through which the user can enter data. It also contains the name of the CGI program which will be responsible for processing the data on the server side. Figure 26.1 shows the steps taken to process form data. When the form is *submitted*, the client transmits the user's data to the server (see Figure 26.1 step 1). The server then passes the form data to the CGI program (see Figure 26.1 step 2). The program then processes the data and can, as a last step, produce a "response page" that is fed to the client browser by way of the server (see Figure 26.1 step 3).

FIG. 26.1

How a CGI program works.

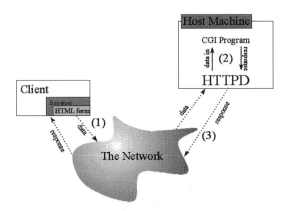

There are actually two ways by which the CGI script can produce a response page. It can:

1. Create a new page from scratch, customized according to the data entered from the client, or any number of other factors.

2. Point the client's browser to a specific URL, which the client will then request on its own.

It is important to note that a CGI program can be written by using any programming language that supports "*standard input*" and "*standard output*" (in the case of UNIX-based servers), or reads from and writes to files on disk (for Windows NT servers). This describes the majority of programming languages currently available. C, Visual Basic, FORTRAN compilers, and even the UNIX shell and Perl interpreters can serve to produce CGI programs. The only tools you need to add interactive functionality to your Netscape Web is a means by which to produce an executable program.

Choosing a CGI Programming Language

Two major considerations must be taken into account when choosing a language for CGIs. The first is that the form data is passed to the CGI program has to be *preprocessed* before it can be handled easily by the program.

N O T E Preprocessing is the operation of taking the large string handed to the CGI by the server and breaking it down into smaller strings (field values) which can be dealt with on an individual basis. More specifically, when the CGI program first receives the data, it looks something like this:

```
name1=Juan&name2=Molinari&major=Computer+Science...
```

There are some publicly available packages that make preprocessing simpler; for more details see **http://www.w3.org/hypertext/WWW/Daemon/User/CGI/cgiparse.html**. ◼

The second issue that must be taken into account when choosing a development language for CGIs is what the CGI is expected to do with the data it receives. If a CGI, for example, needs to take a list of 15 digits and return the lowest prime that contains those digits, then the programming language that is chosen to write that CGI program must be adept not only with string manipulation, but also with mathematical operations. For this reason a shell script might be a poor choice. This is, of course, a rather tame example, but it serves to illustrate the point that the easiest way to approach any task is with the right tool.

The programming language of choice for Microsoft Windows systems, as of this writing, is Visual Basic. Visual Basic (and it's C-based counterpart, Visual C++) has many constructs, libraries, and routines designed to ease the development of graphical user interface-based applications (for instance, programs that use windows, buttons, pull-down menus, and the like). Unfortunately, that is not something a CGI program needs to do. A CGI program is not meant to be interactive. It receives some data, does something with the data, and produces a response page (HTML text) that is then fed to the client. However, because of the way that the Windows NT Web server makes the data available to the CGI script, Visual Basic turns out to be more adept at receiving the data than C or Perl would be.

N O T E In this chapter we will only be presenting sample code in plain C, the UNIX shell, and in Perl. These first two were chosen deliberately because they are more generally popular and it is expected that most people reading this chapter who can program will be familiar with them. In addition, examples in Perl will be provided because it is becoming more and more popular as a CGI scripting tool. For examples on how to implement a CGI script in Visual Basic, take a look at **http://home.city.net/win-httpd/httpddoc/wincgi.htm** and **http://www.lpage.com:80/pub/src/tutorial1.html**. ◼

Writing a CGI Form Handler

As with any application in any context, the programmer must resolve certain issues before writing the first line of code.

◼ Is the server configured to execute CGI scripts?

◼ How do I write a form in HTML?

- What is the program expected to do with the data?
- Will writing to a file be involved?
- Where will the written data be placed?
- What form will the "response" to the client take?
- Will the content of the response be affected by the input data, or is the response page "fixed" and invariant?

Designing Your Forms

The HTML <FORM> tag is the beginning of the process for transmitting data from the client to the server. It contains two important options that determine:

- Which CGI program on the server will be responsible for receiving and processing the data.
- The *method* by which the data will be fed to the CGI program, either "POST" or "GET." They both have advantages and drawbacks, and both will be discussed later. For now we will say that in UNIX, POST means that the data is fed to the CGI script through standard input.

An example of a <FORM> tag using the "POST" method is the following:

```
<FORM method=POST ACTION="http:/cgi-bin/suggest.cgi">
```

Environment Variables and CGI

Environment variables contain a plethora of information useful to the CGI programmer. Access to these environment variables from a shell script is straightforward (such as $varname), and from a C program it is done by means of the getenv() function. In Windows NT, the environment variables are part of a CGI data file. It must be understood that in either case (UNIX or Windows NT) these environment variables are being made available to the CGI script by the Web server program.

All CGI scripts will receive the following environment variables:

SERVER_SOFTWARE—The name and software version of the server.

Example: SERVER_SOFTWARE=Mozilla/V1.2

SERVER_NAME—The server machine's hostname or IP number

Example: SERVER_NAME=www.lcwb.org

or

SERVER_NAME=128.21.19.79

GATEWAY_INTERFACE—The version of the CGI protocol standard being used.

Example: GATEWAY_INTERFACE=CGI/1.0

OUTPUT_FILE (Windows NT only)—This is the path and name of the file that the CGI script must write the response page to so that the server can "pass" it back to the client. UNIX CGIs don't receive this variable because they write their response pages to standard output instead of a file.

Example: OUTPUT_FILE=C:\DOS\HS063D62.ACC

The following variables are set based on the type and settings of the client.

SERVER_PROTOCOL—The protocol used by the client to transmit the request.

Example: SERVER_PROTOCOL=HTTP/1.0

SERVER_PORT—The port number through which the server received the request. This is usually 80, but it will vary if you have more than one server running on the same machine (on different ports).

Example: SERVER_PORT=80

REQUEST_METHOD—The method by which the data will be passed to the CGI script.

Example: REQUEST_METHOD=POST

HTTP_ACCEPT—This is a list of MIME types that the client accepts. This is useful for determining the content of the response page. On Windows NT Web servers, this variable will instead contain the path to a file that contains a list of acceptable types. The CGI script then has the task of reading in that file.

Example: HTTP_ACCEPT=text/plain,text,html,image/gif

PATH_TRANSLATED—This path describes the physical location on the server's hard disk of the CGI script to be executed, rather than its URL. On Windows NT Web servers, the /s will be translated to \ s.

Example: Original URL—http://www.coslabs.com/cgi-bin/mailsend

PATH_TRANSLATED="usr/httpd/docs/cgi-bin/mailsend"

SCRIPT_NAME—The relative URL path to the CGI script being executed.

Example: Original URL—http://www.coslabs.com/cgi-bin/mailsend

SCRIPT_NAME=/cgi-bin/mailsend

QUERY_STRING—If the METHOD option was set as GET, then the data will be received encapsulated in this environment variable (its format will be explained later).

Example: QUERY_STRING FIRSTNAME=Juan&LASTNAME=Molinari&ADDR=4242+16th+St.

REMOTE_HOST—This is the name of the machine running the client browser. If the name of the host cannot be found using a reverse DNS lookup, the host's IP address will be placed here and will be the same as the next entry—REMOTE_ADDR.

Example: REMOTE_HOST=ppp7.usa.net

REMOTE_ADDR—The IP address of the client will be placed here.

Example: REMOTE_ADDR=128.21.19.79

AUTH_TYPE—The authentication method used to validate the user if the document is protected.

Example: AUTH_TYPE=basic

REMOTE_USER—The name of the authenticated user if the document is protected.

Example: REMOTE_USER=katie

REMOTE_IDENT—Contains the remote user name; only if the client is running idented or another program that supports RFC 931. The content of this variable should not be used for security purposes; however, it is useful for logging server usage.

Example: REMOTE_IDENT=jenna

CONTENT_TYPE—The MIME type of data contained in a CGI form request.

Example: CONTENT_TYPE=text/plain

CONTENT_LENGTH—The number of bytes of data that makes up the form data submitted. This is a useful environment variable as it permits the allocation of sufficient memory to read in all the data before it is actually read.

Example: CONTENT_LENGTH=128

CONTENT_FILE—Pertaining only to Windows NT Web servers, this variable contains the path on disk to the temporary file created by the server program that has the data submitted by the client. The CGI must open this file and read its contents in order to receive the data.

Example: CONTENT_FILE=C:\DOS\DATABKT2.TMP

C Language CGI Examples

The following is a simple example of how one can submit data from a browser to a CGI program (the Web server), have the program parse (preprocess) the data, and produce a response page. While this example applies only to UNIX systems, it can easily be converted to other platforms by reading the particular documentation for passing data to CGI programs.

The HTML Form Page

The form shown in Figure 26.2 was created with the following HTML code:

```
<HEAD>
<TITLE>Suggestion Box</TITLE>
<base href="http://www.siligraf.net/">
</HEAD>
<BR>
<H1>Let Us Know How We Can Help You!</H1>
SilliGraf International wants to hear what you have to say about our site.
<FORM method=POST ACTION="http:/cgi-bin/suggest.cgi">
Your name: <INPUT type=text name="NAME" size=20><P>
Your Email: <INPUT type=text name="EMAIL" size=20><P>
Your comment:<TEXTAREA name="COMMENTS" cols=40 rows=4></TEXTAREA><P>
<CENTER><P><INPUT type=submit value="Submit your suggestion">
<INPUT type=reset value=Reset></P></center>
</FORM>
</BODY>
</HTML>
```

FIG. 26.2

A sample form.

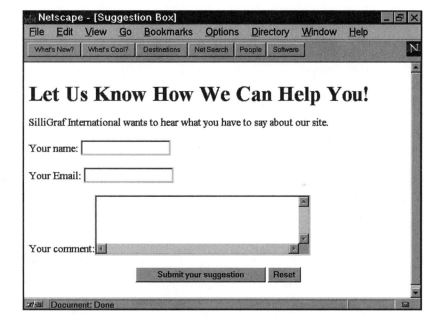

The HTML code specifies that the date entered into this form will be processed by (based on the BASE HREF) the CGI script:

```
http://www.siligraf.net/cgi-bin/suggest.cgi
```

It also defines that:

> It will use the POST method to pass the data to the CGI script (for example, through standard input).

> There are three fields in the form: NAME, EMAIL, and COMMENTS.

How Data Is Passed to the CGI Program

Once the form is set up, a CGI program must be prepared to receive the data when clients submit it. The following C program serves to illustrate how the data is actually passed to the CGI program:

```
#include <stdio.h>
main() {
  char *input = (char *) malloc(atoi(getenv("CONTENT_LENGTH")));

  setvbuf(stdout, NULL, _IONBF, 0);

  printf("Content-type: text/html\n\n");
  scanf("%s", input);
  printf("Data is:<P><BR><PRE>\n");
  puts(input);
}
```

There are some things to take note of in this program. First, the form specified that the data would be fed to the CGI program as standard input (as in METHOD=POST). For that reason, we must allocate enough memory to receive the input into a string. Since all environment variables are strings it must be converted to a number value by `atoi`. In the "Environment Variables" and CGI section we stated that the Content_Length variable specifies the number of bytes of form data submitted.

> **CAUTION**
>
> Important Note for Developers:
>
> The `setvbuf()` function is called to reduce the amount of output buffering to zero bytes. The reason this is done is to assure that the output of the program is transmitted to the client browser as it is produced. This is equivalent to including a call to `fflush(stdout)` after every printed output.

The data is read in by using `scanf`. The response page is started by printing the MIME header (Content-type: text/html). In this case, we are declaring the data type to be "text/html," which informs the client browser that the data that transmitted to it will be "an HTML document". Instead, this could have specified an image using "Content-type: image/gif." It is important to produce this MIME header in the format specified in the MIME standard. For example, please note the two trailing linefeed characters in the printed string, which generates a single "blank" line. If it is not produced according to the specification, the server will complain to the client browser (see Figure 26.3) and write an error message in the server's error log file.

If you use the previous program as the "receiving end" of a form page, the response page will contain the data submitted in the raw format as shown in Figure 26.4.

Looking at the raw data, the meaning of *preprocessing* becomes clear. There are two things that need to be done to the string of characters in order to be able to deal with the fields in an orderly manner. First, the large string needs to be broken down into individual strings, one for each field in the form and the "special characters" transmitted by the client browser to the server in the form of their ASCII value in *hexadecimal* must be converted to their original form.

FIG. 26.3
A sample error
message from an
invalid MIME.

FIG. 26.4
The "raw" format
response page.

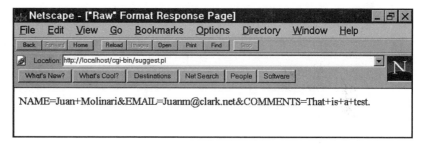

Part
IV

Ch
26

ASCII Values

The following is a complete table of ASCII values. The only ones of concern to the CGI programmer
are the "tty printable" characters, which range from 0x20 to 0x7e (and we, therefore, won't be
explaining all the non-printable codes).

```
00 nul  01 soh  02 stx  03 etx  04 eot  05 enq  06 ack  07 bel
08 bs   09 ht   0a nl   0b vt   0c np   0d cr   0e so   0f si
10 dle  11 dc1  12 dc2  13 dc3  14 dc4  15 nak  16 syn  17 etb
18 can  19 em   1a sub  1b esc  1c fs   1d gs   1e rs   1f us
20 sp   21 !    22 "    23 #    24 $    25 %    26 &    27 '
28 (    29 )    2a *    2b +    2c ,    2d -    2e .    2f /
30 0    31 1    32 2    33 3    34 4    35 5    36 6    37 7
```

continues

continued

38 8	39 9	3a :	3b ;	3c <	3d =	3e >	3f ?
40 @	41 A	42 B	43 C	44 D	45 E	46 F	47 G
48 H	49 I	4a J	4b K	4c L	4d M	4e N	4f O
50 P	51 Q	52 R	53 S	54 T	55 U	56 V	57 W
58 X	59 Y	5a Z	5b [	5c \	5d]	5e ^	5f _
60 '	61 a	62 b	63 c	64 d	65 e	66 f	67 g
68 h	69 i	6a j	6b k	6c l	6d m	6e n	6f o
70 p	71 q	72 r	73 s	74 t	75 u	76 v	77 w
78 x	79 y	7a z	7b {	7c ¦	7d }	7e ~	7f del

Preprocessing the Data

The following C program illustrates how the raw data can be divided into individual strings, each composed of one field and its value, which can then be handled individually. This general scheme can be used for any type of form submitted.

```c
#include <stdio.h>
#define MAXFIELDS 100

void makespace(char *str);
char * find_key(char *keystr, char *v[]);

main(int argc, char *argv[], char *env[])  {
  int i = 0;
  char *str;
  char *keys[MAXFIELDS]; int keycount = 0;
  char *input = (char *) malloc(atoi(getenv("CONTENT_LENGTH")));
  char outname[50];
  FILE *fd;

  setvbuf(stdout, NULL, _IONBF, 0);
  printf("Content-type: text/html\n\n");
  scanf("%s", input);

  str = (char *) strtok(input, "&");
  do  {
    keys[i] = (char *) malloc(strlen(str));
    strcpy(keys[i], str);  keycount ++;
    makespace(keys[i]);
    i ++;
    str = (char *) strtok(NULL, "&");
  } while (str != NULL);
  keys[i] = 0;  /*  cap off string vector table  */

  printf("<PRE>");
  printf("Name: %s\n", find_key("NAME", keys));
  printf("Email: %s\n", find_key("EMAIL", keys));
  printf("Comment: %s\n", find_key("COMMENT", keys));
}

/*  Looks through the given vector table for a field with name "keystr" and
    returns a pointer to its value  */
```

```c
char * find_key(char *keystr, char *v[])  {
  int i = 0;
  char *str;

  while (v[i] != 0)  {
    if ((strncmp(keystr, v[i], strlen(keystr)) == 0)  &&
      (v[i][strlen(keystr)] == '='))
      return( &v[i][strlen(keystr)+1]);

    i ++;
  }
  return (NULL);
}

/*  Takes a string and replaces all occurences of the '+' character
    with a ' '  (space), and decodes characters in hex  */
void makespace(char *str)  {
  char *new;
  char num[5];
  int i = 0; int p = 0;

  new = (char *) malloc(strlen(str));

  while (str[i] != 0)  {
    new[p] = str[i];
    if (str[i] == '+')  new[p] = ' ';
    if (str[i] == '%')  {
      num[0] = str[i+1];  num[1] = str[i+2];  num[2] = 0;
      new[p] = strtol(num, NULL, 16);
      i = i + 2;
      if (new[p] == 10) {
      new[p] = ' ';
      if (new[p-1] == ' ')  p--;
        }
    }
    i++;  p++;
  }
  new[p] = 0;
  strcpy(str, new);
 free(new);
}
```

Once fields and their values can be referenced by the values of the fields, the data could be written to a plain text temporary file, e-mailed out. For example,

```c
fd = fopen("/tmp/bucket.txt", "w");
/*  write data to file as desired  */
system("mail root@www.siligraf.net </tmp/mail.txt");
remove("/tmp/bucket.txt");
```

> **CAUTION**
>
> **Important Developer's Note:** This is not by any means a bug-free or crash-proof example; one of the reasons for this will be discussed later.

Writing Data to Disk

Writing CGI programs for the purpose of *collecting* data, such as a survey or polling form, is a different challenge when working on a random-access environment such as the Web than when dealing with a single-user interface. In the example above it is possible for two people on different client machines to submit the same form within a second of each other, thus causing two programs on the server to be executed at almost the same time. Trying to write to the same file at the same time can cause problems, such as one program writing over the other's data or a "deadly embrace," where each program is waiting (forever) for the other to complete.

The resolution of contentions such as this is very simple—don't write to the same file. The environment variable REMOTE_ADDR (which, as previously mentioned, is passed to the CGI program) contains the client machine's IP number. The following example causes uniquely-named temporary files to be created for each client that executes that CGI script:

```
char outname[100];
char command[100];
...
sprintf(outname, "%s_mail.txt", getenv("REMOTE_ADDR"));
/*  The string "outname" now looks like: "128.21.19.79_mail.txt"  */
fd = fopen(outname "w");
/* etc ...  */
```

> **N O T E**   Using the client's IP number has a double advantage. If a number of HTML forms on the server compose a multi-part questionnaire, then appending to the same temporary file as the client moves from one form to another would allow for a neat and orderly way to group all the information gathered from each client. ■

When all else fails, it is a good idea to take a look at file handles returned by the fopen() function before actually writing to the files; if, for whatever reason, a file could not be opened for writing, the program would then be able to trap the error and inform the client browser in a friendly way of the problem and who could be informed of it (as opposed to an empty screen, or partial output, which is the usual product of a crashed CGI script).

Examples in Perl

Besides C, the secondary language of choice in UNIX systems for writing CGI scripts is Perl because it is a very flexible tool for processing text strings, something that can be very involved and hard to code in C. In addition many routines have already been written in Perl which do the job of splitting the raw data into single fields which can be dealt with individually.

> **N O T E**   In the following Perl example we will use some predefined Perl routines (such as Readparse and PrintVariables) available in the file "cgi-lib.pl" that is included on the CD-ROM that comes with this book. ■

The sample form:

```
<head><title>A simple form example</title></head>
<body>
<H1>This is a simple form using cgi-lib.pl</H1>
<P>
This is a sample form which demonstrates the use of
 the <B><A HREF="cgi-lib.pl">cgi-lib.pl</A></B> library of
routines for managing form input.
</P>
<HR>
<form method="post" action="simple-form.cgi">
<H2> Pop Quiz: </H2>
What is thy name: <input name="name"><P>
What is thy quest: <input name="quest"><P>

What is your favorite color: <select name="color"> <option selected>chartreuse
 <option>azure <option>puce <option>cornflower <option>olive draub
 <option>gunmetal <option>indigo2<option>blanched almond
 <option>flesh <option>ochre <option>opal <option>amber
 <option>mustard
 </select>
<P>

What is the weight of a swallow: <input type="radio" name="swallow"
value="african" checked> African Swallow or
<input type="radio" name="swallow" value="continental"> Continental
Swallow<P>

What do you have to say for yourself <input name="text" size=60,5><P>

Press <input type="submit" value="here"> to submit your query.
</form>
<address>Steven E. Brenner / S.E.Brenner@bioc.cam.ac.uk</address>
$Date: 1994/07/13 15:01:52 $
</body>
```

The following is the script used to process the form previously listed:

```
#!/usr/local/bin/perl -- -*- C -*-

# $Header: /cys/people/brenner/http/docs/web/RCS/simple-form.cgi,v 1.2 1995/04/07
# 21:36:57 brenner Exp $
# Copyright  1994 Steven E. Brenner
# This is a small demonstration script to demonstrate the use of
# the cgi-lib.pl library

require "cgi-lib.pl";

MAIN:
{
# Read in all the variables set by the form
  &ReadParse(*input);
```

```
# Print the header
  print &PrintHeader;
  print "<html><head>\n";
  print "<title>cgi-lib.pl demo form output</title>\n";
  print "</head>\n<body>\n";

# Do some processing, and print some output
  ($text = $input{'text'}) =~ s/\n/\n<BR>/g;
                              # add <BR>'s after carriage returns
                              # to multline input, since HTML does not
                              # preserve line breaks

  print <<ENDOFTEXT;

<H1>This is the output of simple-form.cgi</H1>

You, $input{'name'}, whose favorite color is $input{'color'} are on a
quest which is $input{'quest'}, and are looking for the weight of an
$input{'swallow'} swallow.  And this is what you have to say for
yourself:<P> $text<P>

ENDOFTEXT


# If you want, print out a list of all of the variables.
  print "<HR>And here is a list of the variables you entered...<P>";
  print &PrintVariables(%input);

# Close the document cleanly.
  print "</body></html>\n";
}
```

GET versus POST

The HTML <FORM> tag has various options, one of which is the "METHOD=" option, which determines the method that data is passed to the CGI program. The two possible values for this option are "POST" and "GET." They have different effects on the CGI transaction depending on the Web server platform (UNIX or Windows NT).

As we have seen, on a UNIX system the POST option specifies that the data should be passed to the CGI program through *standard input*. The GET option specifies that the data should be passed to the program encapsulated in an *environment variable*.

N O T E   A collection of environment variables are passed to every program running in a UNIX environment. What variables are passed to a program and what their values are is controlled by the *calling process* or "parent process." In the case of a CGI script, the calling process is the Web server program. ■

On a Windows NT system, however, the meaning is slightly different. Because Microsoft Windows NT is not as robust an operating system as UNIX (in fact, it is does not provide for the passing of data directly from "parent" to "child" neither UNIX mechanism used to pass data from the server to the CGI script is possible to implement in Windows.

The Windows NT Web server creates a *data file* that contains the field names and data submitted from the client form. A CGI program running on a Windows NT server then has the added responsibility of reading in the data file. Visual Basic provides a simple way of reading in the data because the data file has the same format as Windows "INI" files. The Visual Basic function GetPrivateProfileString allows the CGI programmer to efficiently read in the form data.

There is one important difference between GET and POST that applies to all platforms because it affects functionality on the client side. When a client browser submits a form that has been declared with the GET option, the values entered into each field are encapsulated into the URL that it submits to the server as shown in Figure 26.5.

FIG. 26.5
Example of encapsulating data into an URL.

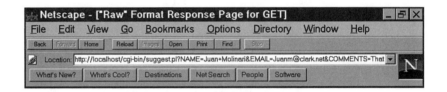

The advantage of this is that once the user submits a form, the response can be *bookmarked*. From then on, when the bookmarked is selected that same response page is produced without having to reenter the data into the form.

 TIP If the form in question pertains to some sort of search or lookup function which the user is expected to want to repeat, it may be wise to use the GET method for passing data to the CGI program.

Example of GET in UNIX Systems

The following C program attempts to produce a list of all the environment variables it receives from its calling process (the Web server). Because it does not try to read anything from standard input, you can compile this program and run it from the command line in order to test it.

```c
#include <stdio.h>

main(int argc, char *argv[], char *env[])  {
  int i = 0;
  setvbuf(stdout, NULL, _IONBF, 0);
  printf("Content-type: text/html\n\n");

  printf("<PRE>");
 while (*env != NULL)  printf("env[%d] = %s\n", I++, *env++);

  exit(0);
}
```

The output, when executed from a client browser, is something like:

```
env[0] = HTTP_REFERER=http://www.blackjack.org/c/page.html
env[1] = HTTP_ACCEPT=*/*, image/gif, image/x-xbitmap, image/jpeg
```

```
env[2]  = HTTP_USER_AGENT=Mozilla/1.22 (Windows; I; 16bit)
env[3]  = PATH=/usr/sbin:/usr/bsd:/sbin:/usr/bin:/bin:/etc:/usr/etc:/usr/bin/X11
env[4]  = TZ=MSD7MDT
env[5]  = SERVER_SOFTWARE=Netscape-Communications/1.1
env[6]  = SERVER_PORT=80
env[7]  = SERVER_NAME=www.ea.net
env[8]  = SERVER_URL=http://www.ea.net
env[9]  = REMOTE_HOST=grab.coslabs.com
env[10] = REMOTE_ADDR=128.21.19.79
env[11] = GATEWAY_INTERFACE=CGI/1.1
env[12] = SERVER_PROTOCOL=HTTP/1.0
env[13] = REQUEST_METHOD=GET
env[14] = SCRIPT_NAME=/c/compform.cgi
env[15] = QUERY_STRING=NAME=Katie+Mulligan&EMAIL=mulligan%47usa.net&
          COMMENT=this+is+my+comment
```

N O T E   This is also a good way of getting an overview of all the different environment variables that are passed to *all* CGI programs as a matter of course (REMOTE_HOST, REMOTE_ADDR, and so on). ■

As can be seen, the QUERY_STRING environment variable contains the same type and format of data as when using the POST method, except that instead of it being fed to the CGI script as *standard input*, it is passed in the form of an environment variable. The program could then make a copy of that string and process it in the exact same way as shown in previous examples.

T I P   To redirect the client browser to a different URL altogether, rather than composing a response page from scratch the CGI script has only to print one line of text (instead of the MIME header):

`Location: http:///www.sillygraf.net/otherstuff/`

The client's browser will then request that URL as if it had come from a regular hyperlink instead of being the product of a CGI script.

Writing a DOS Batch Program

It is actually possible to write a DOS batch file to act as a CGI script. As was explained before, the Windows NT Netscape server cannot pass input directly, like the UNIX version of the server, nor can it directly receive the output of the CGI program. For this reason, DOS-based CGI programs have to rely on an intermediary file which contains the form fields along with their values. The DOS-based CGI program must look at the content of the environment variable CONTENT_FILE, read it in, and write its response to the client in a file whose name is specified in the variable OUTPUT_FILE.

N O T E   This is *not* an absolute problem. The reason this applies to most situations is that the default DOS shell, COMMAND.COM, does not support standard input and output. It is possible, however, to replace the default DOS shell with another type of shell that does provide that type of support. ■

```
set out=%OUTPUT_FILE%
set in=%CONTENT_FILE%
echo Content-type: text/html                          >%out%
echo .                                              >>%out%
echo This is the data that was submitted:;           >>%out%
echo .                                              >>%out%
type %in%                                           >>%out%
```

We now have access to the data in raw form (just like a C program running on a UNIX server would) but no way to process it directly in the BATCH program. We can call a BASIC program from within the DOS batch file which can then handle the data in more intelligent ways.

Security Issues Concerning CGI Scripts

The fundamental security problem pertaining to CGI scripts stems from the fact that they are programs executed on the *server* at request of the *client*. It is possible for an improperly configured Web server to unwittingly give access to inappropriate information to a client by means of the CGI "gateway."

An absurd example of this is a CGI program that receives one line of text as its only data and then executes that text as a command entered into the shell prompt, then feeding the output back to the client. This basically gives "carte blanche" to the server from any browser. This is an unlikely example; however, there are still many dangers that must be considered when configuring a Web server to handle CGI scripts.

The administrator must ask of herself whether it is necessary to allow programs owned by any user to be executed as CGI scripts—dangers don't necessarily come from the outside. A user, taking advantage of the fact that a CGI process is owned by and executed as the *server user*, might write a CGI script in his own directory which reads sensitive files usually accessible only to the Web server such as a list of credit card numbers or passwords.

For this reason, it is usually a good idea to configure the server only to allow programs residing in a particular directory to be executed as CGI scripts. This way the Web administrator (if she is not the only user of the system) has absolute control of what programs the server does and does not execute.

Additionally, it is always a good idea to distrust any input to the Web server. Just because a form only accepts a limited subset of data values as input (such as a form composed entirely of selector gadgets, buttons, or menus) doesn't mean that those values are the only ones that could be sent to the CGI. It is entirely possible (and not particularly difficult) to "fake" the submission of a form. A user with evil intent could compose a his or her own "form" on a client, with any type of input fields, and specify the CGI script on the server in the <FORM> tag for processing.

Part
IV

Ch
26

Server-Side Includes

SSIs (also known as *Parsed-HTML and SSI*) is a means by which a Web server can produce documents that are different every time a page is accessed (dynamic content). More specifically, a Server-Side Include is a special tag that, when placed in an HTML document, causes additional HTML code to be inserted at that point. Some simple examples of how SSIs can be useful are: having a universal trailer/signature on all of your site's pages possibly, inserting the time of day into a page and reporting a hit count (how many times a page has been accessed).

Imagine that you are a mail clerk, and your job is to carry pieces of paper from one office to another. You are not required to read anything on the papers, just to deliver them. One day your supervisor says to you:

"You are doing such a great job that we're increasing your responsibilities. Every now and then you will be given a piece of paper with a big blue star at the top. That means that this special piece of paper has the name of another document on it; you are to get a copy of that document and deliver it along with the original piece of paper."

This basically describes how a Web server's functionality changes once you activate SSIs. "Out of the box" all the Netscape server does is transmit copies of files on disk over the Internet (HTML, image files, etc.) With SSIs, however, you can have special HTML files with instructions for adding more HTML code to them at the time they are being served to the client. The additional HTML code can originate from a second static file on disk, or be the output of a CGI program.

The sequence of events when processing SSIs is shown in Figure 26.6.

FIG. 26.6
How SSIs work.

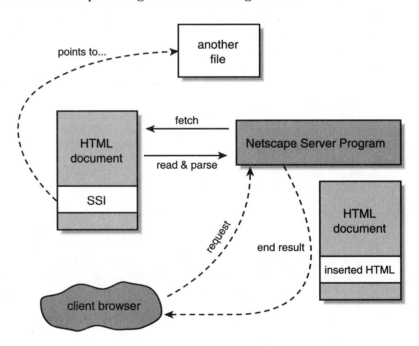

The client browser makes a request to the Web server via an URL. The server fetches the Web page that corresponds to that URL and *parses* the contents of the file looking for the special SSI tag. If it finds such a tag, it reads the file (or runs the program) which the tag points to and inserts the additional HTML code in place of the SSI tag. The resulting page is then sent back to the client browser.

Client-Side Includes

Another way of looking at SSIs is to think about *client*-side includes. You see them every day but possibly never knew it. Consider the following HTML code:

```
This is a Home Page.<P>
<IMG SRC="http://www.ea.net/images/pretty.gif"><P>
How'dya like it?
```

This HTML code is transmitted to the client browser, which then *parses* it. When it finds the <IMG SRC=""> tag it makes a second request to the server. The result of that second request is inserted at the point where the tag was located. The client has performed an "include." SSIs work in a similar way (for example, a tag is replaced by something else), except that instead of inserting an image into the page, you can insert any HTML code you want.

Configuring a Netscape Server to Activate CGI File Types and Use SSIs

As mentioned before, there are two basic types of SSIs: those which insert the contents of a file into an existing HTML document, and those that insert the output of a program. If you just want to be able to include files into your HTML documents (such as, to have a site-wide trailer on all your pages) then you can skip to step #2.

Step 1—Activate CGI as MIME Type

The first thing you need to do to use SSIs with your Netscape server is to active CGI as a MIME type, or if you choose, designate a single directory where the programs will be kept. This is the exact same step you need to take if your site is going to be receiving form data and handling by means of CGI scripts (which means that if you have already done this, you can skip to "Step 2—Allowing SSI HTML Inclusion").

CAUTION

There are two ways by which the server will acknowledge that a program is an SSI (CGI) program. The first is if it has a special file name extension (for example, *.cgi) and the server has been instructed to recognize that extension, and the second is if the program is located in a special directory that the server has been told contains CGI programs. The reason for these restrictions is related to system security and will be explained in detail further on.

Connect to the administrative port on your Netscape server by using:

```
http://www.ea.net:8080
```

You will be presented with a list of installed server(s). Select the server you want to configure. You will see the Server Configuration screen shown in Figure 26.7.

FIG. 26.7
Netscape Server
Configuration.

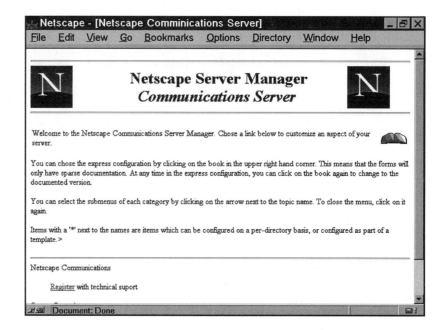

Scroll down the list of options until you see the section with the heading "CGI and Server Parsed HTML" and select it (see Figure 26.8).

FIG. 26.8
CGI and Server Parsed
HTML.

Select the link labeled "Activate CGI as a file type for part of your server" (see Figure 26.9).

FIG. 26.9

Activating the CGI file type.

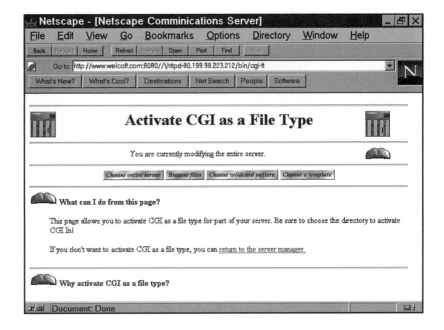

Scroll down to the bottom of the page and make sure the radio button labeled "I'd like to activate CGI as a file type" is selected. Then push "Make these changes" (see Figure 26.10).

FIG. 26.10

Making the changes.

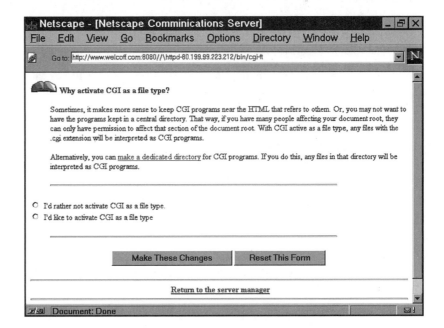

If all went well, you should see the page shown in Figure 26.11.

FIG. 26.11
Successful activation page.

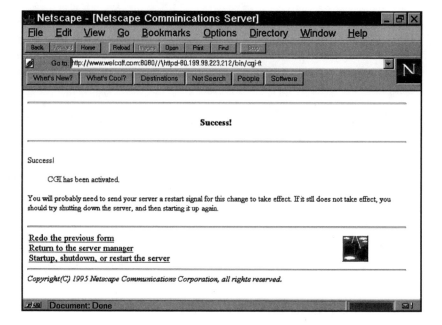

Step 2—Allowing SSI HTML Inclusion

Return to the screen that contains the menu section on "Activating CGI and Parsed HTML" (refer to Figure 26.8).

Select "Parsed HTML". Scroll down the next screen until you see a list of three different ways that your Netscape server can identify HTML files that you want to have parsed.

For now, select the option that allows you to identify these files by their extension, .Shtml.

You're done! Next you will learn how to create a Web document that contains a Server-Side Include.

Creating a Web Page Using an SSI

In this example, our HTML page informs the client browser of its IP address. The first order of business is to create the HTML file on disk which contains the SSI tag. Using your favorite text editor, create an HTML on your Web server called test.shtml and enter the following lines into it:

```
<HTML>
<BODY>

Good morning!  Your IP address is:
<P>
```

```
<!--#exec cgi="ip.cgi"-->
<P>
Have a nice day!
```

TIP If you are using a convention other than the .Shtml extension for identifying a Web page that contains SSIs, you may have to modify file name or permissions accordingly. For example, you may have specified that you want all files with the "*execute bit*" ON to be parsed by the server. In that case, after you create the file you must issue the following command from the shell prompt:

```
% chmod +x filename
```

Next, we need the script specified in the SSI tag (ip.cgi).

N O T E You may have noticed that no path was given in the "cgi=" tag, so the server program will look for it in the document home directory, which you specified when you initially configured your server. ■

In this case, the CGI is a shell script:

```
#!/bin/sh

echo Content-type: text/html
echo ""
echo "<H2>$REMOTE_ADDR</H2>"
```

The first line in the file specifies which shell program will be used to *interpret* (execute) the script. In this case, we are using the Bourne shell, which is available in every UNIX system. The second and third lines produce the *MIME header* (followed by the obligatory blank line), which must be the first thing printed out by any CGI (or SSI) program. The last line prints out the contents of the environment variable REMOTE_ADDR, as discussed earlier.

The shell script must have the "*execute bit*" On. It can be set using the command:

```
% chmod +x ip.cgi
```

Anyone accessing the URL of this HTML document should see output similar to Figure 26.12.

Part
IV

Ch
26

FIG. 26.12
Output from SSI "IP" script.

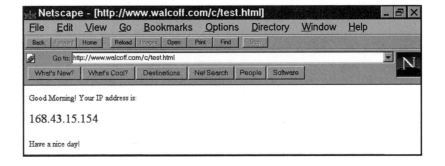

Environment Variables and SSI

SSI programs are given access to some important information in the form of environment variables just like CGIs. You can reference them using an SSI tags like:

```
<!--#echo var="REMOTE_ADDR"-->
```

Besides the standard CGI environment variables, there is an additional set that are provided especially to be included in HTML documents in the form of SSI tags. Here is a list:

DOCUMENT_NAME—The name of the HTML file being parsed by the server.

DOCUMENT_URL—The "URL path" to the same file.

DATE_LOCAL—The current date and time, in plain English.

DATE_GMT—The Greenwich Mean Time.

LAST_MODIFIED—The date and time (in the current time zone) when the HTML document was last modified (such as the date/time stamp of the HTML file on disk).

QUERY_STRING_UNESCAPED—If the HTML document that contains this SSI was actually produced by a CGI program after a form was submitted, then the query string is contained here, with any characters that are "special" to the shell escaped with a \.

We can modify the previous example to illustrate how these variables can be used with a parsed HTML document.

```
<HTML>
<BODY>
Good morning!  Your IP address is:
<P>
<!--#echo var="DOCUMENT_NAME"-->
<P><!--#echo var="DATE_LOCAL"-->
<P><!--#echo var="LAST_MODIFIED"-->
<P><!--#exec cgi="/c/ip.cgi"-->
<P>
Have a nice day!
```

The output produced by this HTML is shown in Figure 26.13.

FIG. 26.13
Using SSI specific
environment variables.

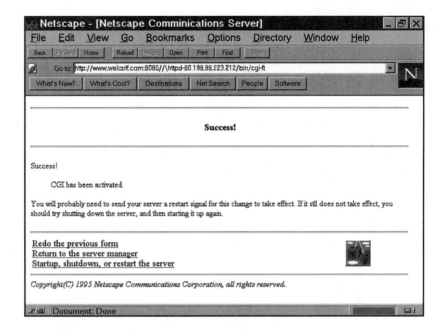

Including Simple Text Files

You don't have to write a program to have some additional HTML code inserted into your Web documents. For example, if you want to have the same "trailer" in all the documents on your site (such as a button bar, "send comments to...", and so forth), you can simply include a file from disk:

```
<!--#include virtual="/stuff/sig.html"-->
```

or, to include a file in a directory relative to the HTML page that is including it,

```
<!--#include file="../../sig.html"-->
```

```
<!--#fsize file="../../sig.html"-->
```

inserts the *size* of the file specified.

```
<!--#flastmod file="../sig.html"-->
```

inserts the date and time that the specified file was last modified.

If you want to include the output of an existing, non-CGI program into your document:

```
<!--#exec cmd="/bin/ls *.html"-->
```

Because the #exec cmd= tag causes the output of the specified program to be included directly in the current HTML, the program need not produce a MIME header.

Part
IV

Ch
26

Modifying SSI Behaviors

There are SSI tags that control the behavior of other SSI tags. If you are using the `exec cgi=` tag and your SSI program does not respond in an expected way to the server (for example, does not produce a MIME header), then the message

```
[an error occurred while processing this directive]
```

is inserted where the SSI tag was located (the rest of the HTML page code is still passed to the client). If you want to modify the error message, you can replace it by using the following:

```
<!--#config errmsg="Sorry, I goofed."-->
```

You can change the output format of the DATE_ tags by using the following:

```
<!--#config timefmt="%A %b %d %Y"-->
```

This would cause the string

```
Friday Nov 17 1995
```

to be inserted into the HTML code. The `timefmt` tag is based on the ANSI-C function `strftime()`, which serves a similar purpose. Other formatting codes (from the `strftime()` manual page) are as follows:

```
%%   same as %
%a   locale's abbreviated weekday name
%A   locale's full weekday name
%b   locale's abbreviated month name
%B   locale's full month name
%c   locale's appropriate date and time representation
%C   locale's date and time representation as produced by date(1)
%d   day of month ( 01 - 31 )
%D   date as %m/%d/%y
%e   day of month (1-31; single digits are preceded by a blank)
%h   locale's abbreviated month name.
%H   hour ( 00 - 23 )
%I   hour ( 01 - 12 )
%j   day number of year ( 001 - 366 )
%m   month number ( 01 - 12 )
%M   minute ( 00 - 59 )
%n   same as new-line
%p   locale's equivalent of either AM or PM
%        time as %I:%M:%S [AM¦PM]
%R   time as %H:%M
%S   seconds ( 00 - 61 ), allows for leap seconds
%t   same as a tab
%T   time as %H:%M:%S
%U   week number of year ( 00 - 53 ), Sunday is the first day of week 1
%w   weekday number ( 0 - 6 ), Sunday = 0
%W   week number of year ( 00 - 53 ), Monday is the first day of week 1
%x   locale's appropriate date representation
%X   locale's appropriate time representation
%y   year within century ( 00 - 99 )
%Y   year as ccyy ( e.g. 1986)
%Z   time zone name or no characters if no time zone exists
```

CAUTION

There is a bug in version 1.1 of the Netscape servers which involves the server-parsed directive:

```
<!--#config timefmt=...-->
```

It does not work properly. To work around the problem, use the following instead:

```
<!--#exec cmd="print-date"-->
```

where the file "print-date" is a shell script that contains (for example):

```
#!/bin/sh
date "+%A %b %d %Y"
```

SSI Security

Just like CGI script security, the basic security problem associated with SSIs is that they are programs executed on the *server* at the request of the *client* and these programs are executed by the "server user" (the user that owns the server programs and files). It is therefore possible for a Web server which has been improperly configured to accidentally provide access to inappropriate information through the use of SSIs.

Reading Files Without Programs

SSIs can allow access to secure/private information without the need to execute any programs at all. As shown in this chapter, SSIs can be used to include the contents of any text file into a Web document that the Web server user can read. This is still a concern for sites that have deactivated public use of CGI scripts as form-handlers, but still allows users to put SSIs in their Web pages.

CAUTION

If somebody can figure out a way to place files in your system (without even having logon access to the machine), he or she could insert a fake HTML document with an SSI that does some of the things described above. This would be a real concern on systems that have public FTP access in any way, or that routinely use NFS to provide other hosts access to its file systems.

To SSI or Not to SSI

For these reasons, the system administrator must make a serious decision about allowing a program located just anywhere in the system (as opposed to a single directory) to be executed as an SSI program (CGIs) and must pay close attention to permission flags on files, directories, and so on.

A basic security rule is to ask "What is the least number of features that must be offered (or activated) on the system to provide the type of functionality that is required?" Once you make that determination, you must think creatively about any possible ways in which somebody could use the additional functionality to gain access to sensitive information or compromise your server. ●

Part
IV

Ch
26

Appendixes

What's on the CD?

- All the sample code and applications from the book
- A collection of demonstration applications, scaled-down software and shareware
- Two electronic versions of the book—one is in HTML format, which can be read by using any World Wide Web browser on any platform. The other is in Windows Help File format, which can be easily searched and bookmarked for future reference

The CD included with this book contains the source pages and reference materials that have been referred to throughout the book. The goal of this approach is to allow you to cut and paste any applicable code examples so you can quickly reuse them.

The other, perhaps most exciting, goal of the CD is to provide new, unique, and helpful software, shareware, and evaluation software that you can use in your Internet and Intranet efforts. To that end, you'll find a huge array of software, including the add-ins, viewers, utilities, and other software packages that we've been able to arrange for you.

The CD contains several subdirectories located off the root directory. The directories you'll find on the CD will be as follows, with application, code, or chapter-specific subdirectories under each of these:

Table A.1 Directory Structure on the CD	
\HTMLVER	HTML version of the online books included on the CD
\HELPVER	The Windows Help version of the online books
\CODE	The source code from the book. Each chapter that contains sample files, source code, and so on will be contained in a subdirectory named for the chapter it references
\SOFTWARE	The software provided for your use and evaluation

Following is a brief description of the products and demos from third-party vendors that you'll find on the CD.

N O T E The products on the CD are Demos and Shareware. You may have some difficulty running them on your particular machine. If you do, feel free to contact the vendor. (They'd rather have you evaluate their product than ignore it.) ■

There are some truly innovative tools on the CD that enable you to do some fun things with your pages. Everything from ActiveX controls to Visual Basic extensions for your site, to browsers, viewers, and content creation utilities are included. Be sure to take a few minutes and browse the different toys that are available. ■

Using the Electronic Book

Running A Perfect Web Site, Second Edition, is available to you as an HTML document that can be read from any World Wide Web browser that you may have currently installed on your machine (such as Internet Explorer or Netscape Navigator). If you don't have a Web browser, Microsoft's Internet Explorer is included for you. The book can also be read on-screen as a Windows Help File.

Reading the Electronic Book as an HTML Document

To read the electronic book, you need to start your Web browser and open the document file TOC.HTML located on the \HTMLVER subdirectory of the CD. Alternatively, you can browse the CD directory by using File Manager and double-clicking TOC.HTML.

After you have opened the TOC.HTML page, you can access all of the book's contents by clicking the highlighted chapter number or topic name. The electronic book works like any other Web page; when you click a hot link, a new page is opened or the browser will take you to the new location in the document. As you read through the electronic book, you will notice other highlighted words or phrases. Clicking these cross-references will also take you to a new location within the electronic book. You can always use your browser's forward or backward buttons to return to your original location.

Installing the Internet Explorer

If you don't have a Web browser installed on your machine, you can use Microsoft's Internet Explorer 3.0 on this CD-ROM.

The Microsoft Internet Explorer can be installed from the self-extracting file in the \EXPLORER directory. Double-click MSIE20.exe or use the Control Panel's Add/Remove Programs option and follow the instructions in the setup routine. Please be aware you must have Windows 95 installed on your machine to use this version of Internet Explorer. Other versions of this software can be downloaded from Microsoft's Web site at **http://www.microsoft.com/ie**.

Reading the Electronic Book as a Windows Help File Document

To read the electronic book, simply use File Manager to browse to the \HELPVER subdirectory on the CD. Double-click RUNNING.HLP and the file will load.

Finding Sample Code

This book contains code examples that include listing headers, for example, "see Listing 10.1;" these are sample documents presented for planning purposes, and items that are indicated with the On the CD icon. For example, consider the following listing reference:

```
Listing 10.1  (10_01.HTM) -- Creating the new snarfle page...
```

This listing indicates that this particular code snippet (or example) is included electronically on the CD. To find it, browse to the \CODE subdirectory on the CD and select the file name that matches the one referenced in the listing header from the chapter indicated. In this example, you'd look in the Chapter 10 subdirectory and open the 10_01.HTM file. ●

About the Que WebReference Site

Que has set up a Web site to be used to share ideas, download software, and receive updates to certain content as new information becomes available. This information is provided to the readers of this book in an attempt to provide continuing communication between not only Que Publishing and you, the reader of these books, but also between you and your peers, those responsible for bringing online systems that are, doubtless, very similar to yours.

The site includes areas that enable you to post and review messages, see new, related information that may be helpful, and it gives you a place to post your page addresses, should you want to gain additional insight into your installation from other users who are bringing up and maintaining sites.

The URL for the site is **http://www.mcp.com/que/intranet/** and you can use the site any time you want to help support your Intranet efforts. Watch for information about available mailing lists, additional reference sites, and newsgroups that pertain to the technologies presented throughout this book.

You can also find out the addresses of other sites that are bringing up Intranets. Feel free to communicate with these sites; if they indicate that they're interested in assisting you, they can help you iron out any issues you may encounter.

This site is also the perfect location to post suggestions for upcoming titles and updates to existing titles in the Que Publishing line of books.

In addition, you can find information about Intranets at the author's site, located at **http:// www.pobox.com/~swynk**. Additional presentations, information about wireless technologies, and more are presented or linked to from the site and, of course, your feedback is always welcome. ■

Becoming a Reality Check Site

Throughout this book, you've seen references to the Que Reality Check site. The concept behind this is to provide a checkpoint of sorts on the techniques and technologies presented in a given chapter so you can see how it works where the rubber meets the road.

The Reality Check site has implemented many of the different things outlined in a given chapter and you can review them online at the site to see how they work. The other aspect of the Reality Check site is to provide additional feedback on any bumps in the road that may be encountered along the way when you implement the different techniques in a given chapter.

You can become a Reality Check site as well and display the Reality Check logo on your site, too. If you're interested, just send a quick note to **swynk@pobox.com** and indicate your site's URL if it's on the Internet. If your site is an Intranet-only implementation, state that in the message.

In addition to the address, provide information on what types of techniques you used from the book at your site. You don't need to go into the gory details, but do let us know what you've implemented. We'll take a look and issue you the logo, complete with the HTML you can use to add the logo to your pages.

- **Implement the Reality Check logo in its unaltered state on your server should you decide to show it. The logo will be unobtrusive on your pages and will simply indicate your "membership" in the program**
- **Use at least one technique from the book on your site**
- **Display the Reality Check logo on your home page**

In addition, we'll put a link from our site to yours for other people to reference. This will create a network of sites that can be used to review different approaches to the Intranet implementations.

You can combine your use of the Reality Check site approach with the WebReference materials to gain access to some great technical resources that you can use to ensure your success as the Webmaster for your site.

For examples of existing Que Reality Check sites, you can visit both **http://www.integra.net** and **http://www.intellicenter.com**. ■

Index

Complete and Return this Card for a *FREE* Computer Book Catalog

Thank you for purchasing this book! You have purchased a superior computer book written expressly for your needs. To continue to provide the kind of up-to-date, pertinent coverage you've come to expect from us, we need to hear from you. Please take a minute to complete and return this self-addressed, postage-paid form. In return, we'll send you a free catalog of all our computer books on topics ranging from word processing to programming and the internet.

Mr. ☐   Mrs. ☐   Ms. ☐   Dr. ☐

Name (first) ☐☐☐☐☐☐☐☐☐☐ (M.I.) ☐ (last) ☐☐☐☐☐☐☐☐☐☐☐☐☐☐☐

Address ☐☐☐☐☐☐☐☐☐☐☐☐☐☐☐☐☐☐☐☐☐☐☐☐☐☐☐☐☐

☐☐☐☐☐☐☐☐☐☐☐☐☐☐☐☐☐☐☐☐☐☐☐☐☐☐☐☐☐

City ☐☐☐☐☐☐☐☐☐☐☐☐☐☐☐☐☐ State ☐☐ Zip ☐☐☐☐☐ ☐☐☐☐

Phone ☐☐☐ ☐☐☐ ☐☐☐☐ Fax ☐☐☐ ☐☐☐ ☐☐☐☐

Company Name ☐☐☐☐☐☐☐☐☐☐☐☐☐☐☐☐☐☐☐☐☐☐☐☐☐☐☐☐☐

E-mail address ☐☐☐☐☐☐☐☐☐☐☐☐☐☐☐☐☐☐☐☐☐☐☐☐☐☐☐☐☐

1. Please check at least (3) influencing factors for purchasing this book.

Front or back cover information on book .... ☐
Special approach to the content .... ☐
Completeness of content .... ☐
Author's reputation .... ☐
Publisher's reputation .... ☐
Book cover design or layout .... ☐
Index or table of contents of book .... ☐
Price of book .... ☐
Special effects, graphics, illustrations .... ☐
Other (Please specify): _____ ☐

2. How did you first learn about this book?

Saw in Macmillan Computer Publishing catalog .... ☐
Recommended by store personnel .... ☐
Saw the book on bookshelf at store .... ☐
Recommended by a friend .... ☐
Received advertisement in the mail .... ☐
Saw an advertisement in: _____ ☐
Read book review in: _____ ☐
Other (Please specify): _____ ☐

3. How many computer books have you purchased in the last six months?

This book only .... ☐   3 to 5 books .... ☐
2 books .... ☐   More than 5 .... ☐

4. Where did you purchase this book?

Bookstore .... ☐
Computer Store .... ☐
Consumer Electronics Store .... ☐
Department Store .... ☐
Office Club .... ☐
Warehouse Club .... ☐
Mail Order .... ☐
Direct from Publisher .... ☐
Internet site .... ☐
Other (Please specify): _____ ☐

5. How long have you been using a computer?

☐ Less than 6 months   ☐ 6 months to a year
☐ 1 to 3 years   ☐ More than 3 years

6. What is your level of experience with personal computers and with the subject of this book?

	With PCs	With subject of book
New	☐	☐
Casual	☐	☐
Accomplished	☐	☐
Expert	☐	☐

Source Code ISBN: 0-7897-0944-9

7. Which of the following best describes your job title?

Administrative Assistant ☐
Coordinator ☐
Manager/Supervisor ☐
Director ☐
Vice President ☐
President/CEO/COO ☐
Lawyer/Doctor/Medical Professional ☐
Teacher/Educator/Trainer ☐
Engineer/Technician ☐
Consultant ☐
Not employed/Student/Retired ☐
Other (Please specify): _____ ☐

8. Which of the following best describes the area of the company your job title falls under?

Accounting ☐
Engineering ☐
Manufacturing ☐
Operations ☐
Marketing ☐
Sales ☐
Other (Please specify): _____ ☐

9. What is your age?

Under 20 ☐
21-29 ☐
30-39 ☐
40-49 ☐
50-59 ☐
60-over ☐

10. Are you:

Male ☐
Female ☐

11. Which computer publications do you read regularly? (Please list)

_____
_____
_____
_____
_____
_____
_____
_____
_____
_____

Comments: _____
_____
_____

Fold here and scotch-tape to mail.

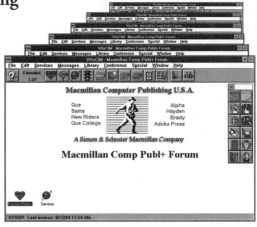